PEOPLE, MARKETS, GOODS:
ECONOMIES AND SOCIETIES IN HISTORY

Volume 6

Crises in Economic and
Social History

PEOPLE, MARKETS, GOODS: ECONOMIES AND SOCIETIES IN HISTORY

ISSN: 2051-7467

Series editors
Barry Doyle – University of Huddersfield
Nigel Goose – University of Hertfordshire
Steve Hindle – The Huntington Library
Jane Humphries – University of Oxford
Kevin O'Rourke – University of Oxford
Willem M. Jongman – University of Groningen

The interactions of economy and society, people and goods, transactions and actions are at the root of most human behaviours. Economic and social historians are participants in the same conversation about how markets have developed historically and how they have been constituted by economic actors and agencies in various social, institutional and geographical contexts. New debates now underpin much research in economic and social, cultural, demographic, urban and political history. Their themes have enduring resonance – financial stability and instability, the costs of health and welfare, the implications of poverty and riches, flows of trade and the centrality of communications. This new paperback series aims to attract historians interested in economics and economists with an interest in history by publishing high quality, cutting edge academic research in the broad field of economic and social history from the late medieval/ early modern period to the present day. It encourages the interaction of qualitative and quantitative methods through both excellent monographs and collections offering path-breaking overviews of key research concerns. Taking as its benchmark international relevance and excellence it is open to scholars and subjects of any geographical areas from the case study to the multi-nation comparison.

PREVIOUSLY PUBLISHED TITLES IN THE SERIES ARE
LISTED AT THE END OF THE VOLUME

Crises in Economic and Social History

A Comparative Perspective

Edited by

A.T. Brown, Andy Burn and Rob Doherty

THE BOYDELL PRESS

First published 2015
The Boydell Press, Woodbridge

ISBN 978-1-78327-042-2

The Boydell Press is an imprint of Boydell & Brewer Ltd
PO Box 9, Woodbridge, Suffolk IP12 3DF, UK
and of Boydell & Brewer Inc.
668 Mt Hope Avenue, Rochester, NY 14620–2731, USA
website: www.boydellandbrewer.com

A catalogue record for this book is available
from the British Library

The publisher has no responsibility for the continued existence or accuracy of URLs for
external or third-party internet websites referred to in this book, and does not guarantee
that any content on such websites is, or will remain, accurate or appropriate.

This publication is printed on acid-free paper

Typeset by BBR, Sheffield

Contents

PART I: CONCEPT AND METHODOLOGY

PART II: AGRICULTURE AND ENVIRONMENT

Figures

Tables

Contributors

Peter H. Bent is a Marie Curie Early Stage Research Fellow in the Department of Economics at the University of Oxford. He is also a PhD student in economics at the University of Massachusetts, Amherst. Before beginning his doctoral studies, he received an MSc in Economic History (Research) from the London School of Economics and an MA in Economics from the University of New Hampshire. His current research focuses on the connections between capital flows and financial crises in the global periphery during the 'first era of globalisation' from 1880 to 1913.

Catherine Casson is a lecturer at Manchester Business School, University of Manchester. She currently studies the history of entrepreneurship and the relationship between reputation and economic performance in English medieval towns. Her recent publications include a co-authored book with Mark Casson, *The Entrepreneur in History: From Medieval Merchant to Modern Business Leader* (Palgrave, 2013).

Mark Casson is Professor of Economics and Director of the Centre for institutional Performance at the University of Reading. He researches entrepreneurship, international investment, business history and transport history. Recent books include *The Entrepreneur in History*, with Catherine Casson (Palgrave, 2013), editor of *Markets and Market Institutions* (Edward Elgar, 2012), *Entrepreneurship: Theory, Networks, History* (Edward Elgar, 2010), and *The World's First Railway System* (Oxford University Press, 2009).

Samuel K. Cohn, Jr is Professor of Medieval History at the University of Glasgow, Fellow of the Royal Society of Edinburgh and Honorary Fellow at the Institute for Advanced Studies in Humanities, Edinburgh. Over the past fifteen years he has specialised in the history of popular unrest in late medieval and early modern Europe and in the history of disease and medicine. His latest books include *Cultures of Plague: Medical Thinking at the End of the Renaissance* (Oxford University Press, 2010); and *Popular Protest in Late Medieval English Towns* (Cambridge University Press, 2012). He is presently funded by a three-year Leverhulme Senior Research Fellowship on the project,

'Epidemics: Waves of Disease, Waves of Hate from the Plague of Athens to AIDS'.

Josette Duncan currently teaches in the History Department of the University of Warwick. She is a nineteenth-century social historian of medicine. Her research focuses on colonial history of medicine, history of isolation, quarantine as well as regulationism, institutionalisation, colonial public health, medical charities and migration in the British Mediterranean, with a special focus on the history of Cyprus, Malta and the Ionian Islands. She is currently working on the history of health and illness of migrants in British Mediterranean ports.

Matthew Hollow is a Research Assistant and Teaching Fellow at The York Management School. Research-wise, his work principally focuses on various aspects of nineteenth- and twentieth-century British socio-economic history. He holds a BA and an MA from the University of Sheffield and a DPhil from Oxford University, and has previously worked as a Research Associate on the Leverhulme Trust-funded 'Tipping Points' project at Durham University.

Pavla Jirková works as a researcher at the Economics Institute of the Czech Academy of Sciences (the joint workplace CERGE-EI) in Prague. She is the principal investigator of the grant project 'Restrictive plague policies and the prevention of demographic and economic crisis in the Early Modern Czech Lands' funded by the Czech Science Foundation (Registration No. GAČR 13–35304S; 2013–2017). She obtained her PhD in history at the Charles University in Prague in 2011 with a thesis entitled 'The Testamentary Practice in Jihlava in the Years 1578–1624 (Wills as Sources for the History of Family Structures, Historical Demography, and Sociotopography)'.

Alan Knight is Emeritus Professor of the history of Latin America, Oxford University, and a fellow of St Antony's College; previously, he held posts at the University of Essex and the University of Texas at Austin. He has been a Guggenheim Fellow and a Fellow of the British Academy. His publications include: *The Mexican Revolution* (2 vols, 1986); *Mexico, From the Beginning to the Spanish Conquest*, and *Mexico: The Colonial Era* (2002); *Revolución, democracia y populismo en América Latina* (2005); *La revolución cósmica* (2013); and *Repensar la revolución mexicana* (2 vols, 2013). He has also co-edited volumes on the Mexican oil industry, *caciquismo* (Mexican boss politics) and superstition in history. He is currently working on a history of Mexico in the 1930s.

John S. Lee is a Research Associate at the Centre for Medieval Studies at the University of York. He has published works on various aspects of medieval towns, markets and estates. These include *Cambridge and its Economic Region 1450–1560* (University of Hertfordshire Press, 2005); chapters in S. Rigby and M. Bailey (eds), *Town and Countryside in the Age of the Black Death* (Brepols, 2012) and B. Dodds and C.D. Liddy (eds), *Commercial Activity, Markets and Entrepreneurs in the Middle Ages* (Boydell & Brewer, 2011); and articles in *Business History Review* (2011), *The Local Historian* (2011 and 2015), and *Urban History* (2010 and 2014).

Cinzia Lorandini is Associate Professor of Economic History at the Department of Economics and Management of the University of Trento. She has published on two main strands of her research: the operation of early modern merchants, particularly those engaged in the silk trade, and twentieth-century banking history. More recently, her interests have turned to credit markets before the rise of modern banking. Her latest publications include 'Looking beyond the Buddenbrooks syndrome: the Salvadori firm of Trento, 1660–1880s', *Business History* (2015), and 'Sailing through troubled times: the Salvadori Firm of Trento during the Revolutionary and Napoleonic Wars, 1790–1815', in *Merchants in Times of Crisis (16th to Mid-19th Century)*, ed. A. Bonoldi, M. Denzel, A. Leonardi and C. Lorandini (Franz Steiner Verlag, 2015).

John Martin is Professor of Agrarian History at De Montfort University, Leicester. His main research interest is the impact of government policies on British agriculture and the countryside since the 1930s. His publications include *The Development of Modern Agriculture: British Farming since 1931* (Palgrave, 2000), co-editor of *The Encyclopaedia of Traditional British Rural Sports* (Routledge, 2005), and co-editor of *The Frontline of Freedom* (Agricultural History Review Supplement, 2007). In 2011 he was appointed Series Consultant for the *Wartime Farm* produced in eight episodes by Lion TV for BBC2 and the Open University. In 2012 he was the agricultural consultant for BBC's *Tudor Monastery Farm* series. He was the agricultural consultant for ITV's *Home Fires* series in 2015.

Ranald Michie is Emeritus Professor of History at the University of Durham. He is a recognised expert in the field of financial history, having produced numerous books and articles over a long career. Among the most notable are *The London Stock Exchange: a History* (Oxford University Press, 1999) and *The Global Securities Market: a History* (Oxford University Press, 2006). More recently he has been working on British banking history as part of the Leverhulme Trust-funded 'Tipping Points' project.

Anne L. Murphy is Reader in Early Modern History at the University of Hertfordshire. Her research interests derive from her background in finance, and concern the nature of Europe's financial markets, the behaviour of investors, and the function and relevance of financial information from the early modern period to the present day. Her publications include articles in *History*, *Financial History Review* and *Economic History Review*, and the monograph *The Origins of English Financial Markets: Investment and Speculation before the South Sea Bubble* (Cambridge University Press, 2009).

Pamela Nightingale read history at Newnham College Cambridge where she did her PhD on the history of British India in the eighteenth and later centuries and on which she published three books, and also taught for the Open University. After an invitation to write the medieval history of the London Grocers Company, she published on a book on *A Medieval Mercantile Community* (Yale University Press, 1995). She has published twenty articles, mainly on medieval economic and political history, held two senior research fellowships at the Ashmolean Museum, Oxford, and was awarded a DLitt by Oxford in 2011. Although having officially long since retired, she continues to work on an extensive study of credit in the medieval English economy between 1285 and 1530.

John Singleton is Professor of Economic and Business History at Sheffield Hallam University. He is the author of *Central Banking in the Twentieth Century* (Cambridge University Press, 2011) and the principal author of *Innovation and Independence: The Reserve Bank of New Zealand, 1973–2002* (Auckland University Press, 2006), and other books and articles on British and New Zealand economic history. He is currently working on a comparative history of disasters since 1900, which will be published by Edward Elgar.

Philip Slavin is Lecturer in Medieval History at the University of Kent. He has published widely on the late-medieval environmental, economic and social history of the British Isles, including articles in *Past and Present* and the *Economic History Review*. He is the author of *Bread and Ale for the Brethren: The Provisioning of Norwich Cathedral Priory, 1260–1536* (University of Hertfordshire Press, 2012). He is currently working on his second monograph dealing with the Great European Famine of the early fourteenth century, as experienced in the British Isles.

Paul Warde is Lecturer in Environmental History at the University of Cambridge, having previously been Professor of Environmental History at the University of East Anglia. He is Research Director at the Centre for History and Economics, Magdalene College, Cambridge, and a senior editor at History & Policy. He works on the environmental, economic and social history of early modern and modern Europe. Publications include *Economy, Ecology and State Formation in Early Modern Germany* (Cambridge University Press, 2006) and *Power to the People: Energy in Europe over the Last Five Centuries*, with Astrid Kander and Paolo Malanima (Princeton University Press, 2013).

Preface

This book began in a kitchen in Neville's Cross, in the aftermath of the global financial crisis of 2007–08. As three PhD students on ESRC scholarships, sharing a house in Durham, we enjoyed productive discussions on economic and social history over the years. There was much to disagree about, but still we remarked on the substantial common ground shared by the apparently divergent topics and time periods of our research. Crisis, as a subject of great contemporary interest, often emerged in these discussions, and we noticed some significant differences in the ways we thought of crisis as an analytical tool. This, we realised, was a conversation well worth having. It led to 'coping with crisis', a conference held at Durham University in July 2013, which had a dual function: to examine both how past societies have responded to the challenges and opportunities of crises, and also how historians have 'coped' with the concept itself. We were encouraged by the response to the call for papers, which generated over fifty papers on a diverse range of topics from medieval volcanoes to modern cooperatives. Moreover, the strong international contingent, with delegates from the UK, USA, Italy, Switzerland, the Czech Republic, Slovenia, Ukraine, Russia and Nigeria, demonstrated the relevance and importance of a comparative historical perspective on crisis.

Some of the chapters that follow emerged from papers given at the conference, but we owe a debt of gratitude to all the delegates who contributed to a stimulating and productive conversation across three days. In particular, we would like to thank Sam Cohn, Ranald Michie and Matthew Hollow for their excellent plenary talks, and the round table panel – Leigh Gardner, Alan Knight, Tony Moore, Anne Murphy and John Singleton – who helped us to define the scope of this book. A number of Durham colleagues and friends were encouraging and helpful throughout organising the conference and editing this book, especially Adrian Green, Ben Dodds, David Craig, Ranald Michie, Giles Gasper, Andy Wood and Michael Prestwich. Without the funding provided by the Economic History Society and Durham University's Department of History, Institute of Medieval and Early Modern Studies and Centre for Academic Researcher Development, this work would not have been possible. We are very grateful to the Economic History Society and the Scouloudi Foundation Publication Awards for their financial help in publishing this book. We would particularly like to thank the series editors for 'People, Markets and Goods', especially Barry Doyle whose support was invaluable, as well as Michael Middeke, editorial director of Boydell & Brewer, Megan Milan and Nick Bingham for their helpful comments and advice.

Alex Brown, Andy Burn and Rob Doherty
Durham, May 2015

The publication of this book has been made possible by a grant
from The Scouloudi Foundation
in association with the Institute of Historical Research

Introduction

Coping with Crisis: Understanding the Role of Crises in Economic and Social History

A.T. BROWN, ANDY BURN AND ROB DOHERTY

Crisis, it seems, is perpetually on the agenda. It can be a useful word, evoking urgency or emergency and hinting at the catastrophic consequences of inaction; it sells newspapers, wins votes and secures research funding. In the twenty-first century the term has been attached indiscriminately to coverage of the global financial crisis that started in 2007, as well as to warnings of the impact of climate change and unsustainable demographic growth (or conversely, ageing populations) on the economies of the future. It has been widely commented, rightly or wrongly, that orthodox economic theory is deficient in coping with crisis, and students have lobbied for widening economics syllabuses.[1] A key complaint, which echoes the comments of J.K. Galbraith and others since at least the 1980s, is that students 'finish an economics degree without any knowledge of momentous [historic] economic events'.[2] This could be changing: it seems we have rekindled our interest in the economic past. The growth in press, policy and public attention to the 'lessons of history' (searches for 'the Great Depression' were in Google's top-ten economic-related terms of 2009)[3] led Barry Eichengreen to remark in 2011 that 'this has been a good crisis for economic history'.[4]

---

1 See e.g. P. Inman, 'Economics students aim to tear up the free-market syllabus', *The Guardian* (24 October 2013); 'The demand side: teaching economics', *The Economist* (7 February 2015).
2 Post-Crash Economics Society, 'Economics, Education and Un-learning: Economics Education at the University of Manchester' Report (April 2014), at http://www.post-crasheconomics.com/economics-education-and-unlearning [accessed 11 February 2015]; J.K. Galbraith, *A History of Economics: The Past as the Present* (London, 1987).
3 http://www.google.com/intl/en-GB/press/zeitgeist2009/news.html [accessed January 2015].
4 B. Eichengreen, 'Economic History and Economic Policy', Economic History Association Presidential Address, 9 September 2011, from http://eml.berkeley.edu/~eichengr/EHA_Pres_Add_9-9-11.pdf, p. 1.

Historians have been on hand to meet demand for comparative perspectives on financial crisis, placing, for instance, 'financial folly' in the historical frame of hundreds of years.[5] This makes economic historians, according to one narrative, a rarity in the wider discipline. Guldi and Armitage's recent *History Manifesto* rejects what they see as a shrinking time horizon in professional history, a short-termism that threatens its relevance.[6] But a similar case could be made about the atomisation of history into diminutive subfields, which can be unwilling to communicate with one another. Crisis, as the chapters that follow demonstrate, is complex and multifaceted. The tendency to isolate particular *types* of crisis from the wider economy, and from social causes and impacts, limits our understanding of the term and of the economic and social past. This volume is therefore intended to open up a double-sided comparative perspective on crisis, which is both thematically and chronologically broad.

In part, this broad perspective is inspired by global visions of history that have been developed over the past few decades. Some of the most productive work has used broad comparisons to explore and explain the different trajectories of economies. This includes *The Brenner Debate*, and *Asia in the Great Divergence*, which both demonstrated the different ways societies responded to similar external impacts and how this affected their future growth.[7] Economic and social historians' use of the term 'crisis' is ripe for such a wide-ranging approach. Crises have been identified in virtually every strand of history, ranging from agrarian famines to outbreaks of disease, and from financial collapses to disasters precipitated by conflict and trade disputes. But there has been little attempt to cross the boundaries between them. A few studies have opened up complex narratives of the relationship between simultaneous crises. But in restricting their time-frame to, for instance, the fifteenth and mid seventeenth centuries, or the 1970s, they miss a further opportunity for chronological comparison.

The coverage of the chapters that follow is thematically, geographically and chronologically broad, with the intention that both the authors and readers can identify and consider the nature and meaning of historical parallels. Should we conceptualise a medieval agrarian or financial crisis completely differently from their modern equivalents? Is the late-fifteenth century a useful cut-off point, after which societies responded to crises in a more 'rational' and 'modern' fashion – as a typical political-economic metanarrative would have it? One author examines the ways in which outbreaks of disease have tended

---

5   C.M. Reinhart and K.S. Rogoff, *This Time Is Different: Eight Centuries of Financial Folly* (Princeton, 2009); G. Cooper, *The Origin of Financial Crises: Central Banks, Credit Bubbles and the Efficient Market Fallacy* (Petersfield, 2010).

6   J. Guldi and D. Armitage, *The History Manifesto* (Cambridge, 2014), pp. 1–5 and *passim*.

7   T.H. Aston and C.H.E. Philpin (eds), *The Brenner Debate: Agrarian Class Structure and Economic Development in Pre-Industrial Europe* (Cambridge, 1987); 'Asia in the Great Divergence', *Economic History Review*, 64, Special Issue 1 (2011), pp. 1–184.

to create hatred of the 'other' since the medical revolution while epidemics in antiquity more often brought societies together. Others consider how the actions of medieval merchants in the face of severe monetary contractions can reveal their understandings of crisis and the economy. How different were those from the responses of the Bank of England in the eighteenth century, or indeed governments and central banks in the twenty-first? Turning the question on its head, is 'coping' with crisis contextually specific? How do these approaches vary between different 'genres' or 'types' of crisis – whether a credit crunch, an outbreak of disease, a storm, or dearth of raw materials – as well as across time? Historical actors themselves have freely compared these different types: for instance, theories of contagion and quarantine were made in response to disease but, as we see in Chapter 12, are now widely applied in banking to emphasise the rapid and uncontrolled onset of crisis.

We make no apology for the heterodox approaches to crisis outlined in this volume: 'crisis', we believe, is a relevant and evolving term of reference that would only be artificially narrowed by a restrictive definition. But equally, it is important that historians are clear how they are using the term in each case, and how their use complements or contrasts with others. As a result, the chapters below provide divergent, considered perspectives on the historical concept of crisis, on its transformative nature, and the causes and consequences of crises. Some chapters are explicitly methodological, asking if and how crisis can be measured by historians or historical actors; how it was and is perceived; whether an *imagined* crisis can be different from a *real* crisis; and if crisis can be seen to follow a predictable pattern or course. Other contributors make deliberately wide-ranging comparisons across time. And others offer detailed and focused studies of particular crises on the ground, asking how the contemporary actors understood what was happening and how they attempted to 'cope'. The following chapters have been arranged into a thematic structure: overarching methodological chapters are followed by chapters on agriculture and the environment, then by disease, banking and finance, and finally trade and industry. Each part offers chronological breadth, generally covering what historians would call 'medieval', 'early modern' and 'modern', with connections beyond these time-frames wherever possible. This introduction examines historical and current meanings of 'crisis', placing the chapters in this book into comparative context, to consider the roles crises have played, and can play, in economic and social history.

I

The word 'crisis' did not always have the ubiquity it would enjoy in the twentieth century, nor the breadth of meaning. When it first entered English it had a principally medical definition, closely related to its Greek etymology

– roughly 'to judge' or 'to decide'.[8] 'The crisis', according to Hippocrates, 'occurs in diseases whenever the diseases increase in intensity or go away or change into another disease or end altogether'.[9] Writing in the midst of the Antonine plague, a virulent epidemic in the second century AD, Galen restated the importance of the 'critical' phase of a disease.[10] He concluded that some crises 'are worse and more severe, and the struggle is greater', and that there might be 'warning days' preceding a crisis; in others 'it occurs suddenly without warning, not only for him who is ignorant of medicine, but also for the one skilled in it'.[11] Summaries of Galen in Hebrew and Arabic concluded that 'a crisis is unavoidably accompanied by hardness and struggle'.[12] Diseases provoked crises of differing intensity and unpredictability, but all had a tendency to produce considerable hardship before an improvement or worsening of the situation. These common themes would shape future uses of the term.

'Crisis' was common currency in Hippocratic and Galenic medical texts, but when doctors began publishing in the vernacular in the mid sixteenth century, they feared their terminology was rather obscure.[13] Writing in 1547, Christopher Langton felt 'it is necessarye to expounde this worde Crisis, which the lattyns call judicium, & in english it may be called jugement'. He noted that 'it signifieth any sudden mutation in every disease whether it be longe or short … For ether the sicke is made hole incontinent, or elles is in a greate towardnesse to health, or dieth out of hand, or finally becumeth a greate deale worse.'[14] The concept became understood by lay readers as well, such that in the 1590s, Florida, while attending to the Black Knight in his sickness, could 'ask … him whether the day of his *Crisis* had passed'.[15] By the

---

8   R. Starn, 'Historians and "Crisis"', *Past & Present*, 52 (1971), pp. 3–5; J.B. Shank, 'Crisis: A Useful Category of Post-Social Scientific Historical Analysis?', *American Historical Review*, 113 (2008), pp. 1090–1.

9   *On Affections*, quoted in Starn, 'Historians and "Crisis"', p. 4.

10   Note that the Antonine Plague had widespread political and economic consequences for the Roman Empire. See W.M. Jongman, 'Roman Economic Change and the Antonine Plague: Endogenous, Exogenous, or what?' in E. Lo Cascio (ed.), *L'Impatto Della 'Peste Antonina'* (Bari, 2012), pp. 253–63, and other papers in that volume.

11   G.M. Cooper (ed.), *Galen, De diebus decretoriis, from Greek into Arabic: A Critical Edition, with Translation and Commentary, of Hunayn ibn Ishaq, Kitab ayyam al-buhran* (Farnham, 2011), p. 102.

12   G. Bos and Y.T. Langermann (eds), *The Alexandrian Summaries of Galen's On Critical Days: Editions and Translations of the Two Versions of the JAWĀMIʿ, with an Introduction and Notes* (Leiden, 2014), p. 106.

13   The following discussion focuses on English-language works. Shank finds a similar pattern in French and Italian in 'Crisis: A Useful Category?', pp. 1091–3.

14   C. Langton, *A very brefe treatise, ordrely declaring the pri[n]cipal partes of phisick …* (1547), Book iii.

15   Italics in the original. R. Parry, *Moderatus, the most delectable & famous historie of the blacke knight: …* (1595).

turn of the seventeenth century, this had transferred into a broader political and religious analogy, reflecting contemporary perceptions of the political nation as the 'body politic' with the monarch at its head. It retained the sense that a 'crisis' was a tipping point, the result of which could be either dire or good – but maintaining the status quo was not an option. John Donne made the comparison explicitly: 'we may make a Judgment of our spiritual health; for that is the crisis of our bodily health', but elsewhere the metaphor needed no elaboration.[16]

Given the emerging religious and political connotations of the word, it is not surprising that the use of 'crisis' reached an apogee in the middle decades of the seventeenth century, used much more frequently in English books than it had been before.[17] This meaning was well understood: Francis Rous wrote specifically about the 'crisis of a soule' in *The heavenly academie* (1638); and John Sadler of the 'crisis of heaven' in *Masquarade du ciel* (1640).[18] Henry Parker bemoaned King Charles I's lack of respect for Parliament, saying 'there can be no more certaine Crisis of seducement, then of preferring private advise before publike'.[19] Effortlessly mixing his metaphors, Richard Vines saw 'the swarm is up and settles in so many places, as ... they will never be got into one hive; such symptomes doe wee put forth now that God is healing of us, and are come to such a crisis as makes our hearts to bleed'.[20] The earl of Bristol was relieved that 'the long lookt for *Crisis* of a Battail is over' in 1643, while a 1659 pamphlet expressed relief that the 'Crisis of publique affaires' was 'somewhat over'.[21] Thomas Hobbes wrote of the 'Crisis or the Catastrophe' in discourse being the 'but' in a sentence: 'he is a good natured man, *but* he hath a naughty quality'.[22] Crisis still, therefore, meant a turning

16   J. Donne, *Devotions upon emergent occasions and severall steps in my sicknes ...* (1624), p. 380.
17   Though, it has to be said, still not *very* frequently: at its peak in the 1650s, 'crisis' made up only one published word in 300,000, compared with, say, 'disease', which was one word in 15,000 at its seventeenth-century peak, or 'lord', which was one word in 800. These calculations are based on the 44,000 hand-keyed books of the EEBO Text Creation Partnership. By comparison, mid-1930s printed usage in the Google Books corpus was also about one word in 300,000, although it climbed rapidly in the later twentieth century to a 1994 peak of one word in 100,000. See http://earlyprint.wustl.edu/exploreeebotcp.html; http://www.textcreationpartnership.org; http://books.google.com/ngrams [accessed 1 March 2015].
18   F. Rous, *The heavenly academie* (1638), p. 77; John Sadler, *Masquerade du ciel presented to the great Queene of the little world* (1640).
19   H. Parker, *Observations upon some of His Majesties late answers and expresses* (1642), p. 30.
20   R. Vines, *Calebs integrity in following the Lord fully* (1642), pp. 27–8.
21   G. Newbury, *A trve and impartiall relation of the battaile betwixt His Majesties army and that of the rebells neare Newbury in Berk-shire* (1643) p. 1; Anon., *To the Right Hounourable the supreame authority of the Common-wealth of England in Parliament assembled* (1659), p. 1.
22   T. Hobbes, *The questions concerning liberty, necessity, and chance clearly stated ...* (1656), p. 29. Italics in the original.

point. The original medical definition and its related political and religious metaphors went hand in hand through into the eighteenth century.[23] Crucially the word retained its uncertainty and diversity, including questions over the severity and duration of crises. A crisis was, however, always a 'judgement' or decision point, where the situation would change for better or worse. Thomas Paine, in *The American Crisis*, thought that crises or 'panics':

> produce as much good as hurt. Their duration is always short; the mind soon grows through them, and acquires a firmer habit than before. But their peculiar advantage is, that they are touchstones of sincerity and bring things and men to light which might otherwise have lain forever undiscovered ... They sift out the hidden thoughts of men, and hold them up in public to the world.[24]

The chapters below explore how far crises reveal the underlying tensions of society, with John Singleton, for example, observing that 'only in a period of heightened danger or crisis do we discover what [people] are made of – some excel but most flounder'.

The medical roots of the term point us to more recent developments in the way that crisis has been understood and employed, with the field of medical history acknowledging the cultural significance of disease with the literary turn of the late twentieth century. As Charles Rosenberg noted in the 1980s, 'a generation of social scientists and social critics have emphasised that there is no simple and necessary relationship between disease in its biological and social dimensions ... disease is constructed not discovered'.[25] More generally, a shift towards widely cultural concerns can be seen as a discernible feature of developed economies since the 1970s. Increasing living standards have caused a shift in political culture from a 'materialist' to 'postmaterialist' focus.[26] This has in turn broadened the use of crisis because 'on any measure used, the rise of aggregate money incomes has done little or nothing to improve the sense of well-being' within the population, creating what has been termed the 'paradox of happiness'.[27] The late 1950s and early 1960s were a period of relatively high growth and improving living standards for the major industrialised economies. Yet, despite this, contemporary commentators in

---

23 Politically, crisis retained its link with the Civil Wars; it was the 'Crisis of That Great Revolution': see R. l'Estrange, *A brief history of the times, &c. ...* (1687).

24 Quoted in Starn, 'Historians and "Crisis"', p. 6.

25 C.E. Rosenberg, *Explaining Epidemics and Other Studies in the History of Medicine* (Cambridge, 1992), p. 259.

26 R. Inglehart, *Culture Shift in Advanced Industrial Society* (Princeton, 1990), pp. 3–7.

27 A. Offer, *The Challenge of Affluence: Self-Control and Well-Being in the United States and Britain since 1950* (Oxford, 2009), p. 357.

Britain believed themselves to be living through a period of national crisis, or 'decline'.[28]

Indeed, that crisis is now accepted as more metaphysical in its manifestation was shown in President Obama's 2008 inaugural address, in which the realities that 'homes have been lost, jobs shed, businesses shuttered' were identified as 'indicators of crisis, subject to data and statistics'. Obama located the real crisis in the 'less measurable ... sapping of confidence across our land; a nagging fear that America's decline is inevitable, that the next generation must lower its sights'.[29] A number of the chapters below show that the 'crisis' they examine was as much, if not more, the product of qualitative perceptions, the faltering of confidence, than determined by straightforward empirical realities. Others, however, argue for a firm, measurable basis for their definitions of crisis. Such differences demonstrate the importance of ontological considerations to any discussion on the nature and scale of crisis, both in historical studies and contemporary debate. This also opens up the potential for crisis to be seen as a constant; the normative rather than extra-ordinary state. Simon Critchley, for example, suggests that 'for a philosopher ... the real crisis would be a situation where crisis was not recognized'.[30] In Chapter 5, Paul Warde explores the pervasive nature of timber shortages in public discourses across early modern Europe, showing how crisis can become an almost ubiquitous state of mind.

The development of the conceptual range of crisis beyond its medical roots has been argued, most notably by Reinhart Koselleck, to have been a consequence of the eighteenth-century Enlightenment.[31] The disassociation between political and moral authority led to a political utopianism that in itself entailed a philosophy of history; a conceptualisation of a future that required an interpretation of the relationship between the past and the present.[32] The French Revolution, representing 'the crisis of the Enlightenment' brought with it a fundamental temporality to the concept of crisis, and this temporal dimension developed alongside the creation of history as a discipline. Such a development led to two new 'coinage uses' for crisis: 'as a permanent or conditional category pointing to a critical situation which may constantly recur or else to situations in which decisions have

28 G. Ortolano, '"Decline" as a Weapon in Cultural Politics', in W.R. Louis (ed.), *Penultimate Adventures with Britannia* (London, 2008), pp. 201–14.

29 'President Barack Obama's Inaugural Address' (20 January 2009) at http://www.whitehouse.gov/blog/inaugural-address [accessed 8 March 2015].

30 S. Critchley, 'Introduction: What is Continental Philosophy?', in S. Critchley and W.R. Schroeder (eds), *A Companion to Continental Philosophy* (Oxford, 1999), p. 12.

31 R. Koselleck, *Critique and Crisis: Enlightenment and the Pathogenesis of Modern Society* (Cambridge, MA, 1988).

32 J. Roitman, 'Crisis', *Political Concepts: A Critical Lexicon* (2011), in http://www.politicalconcepts.org/issue1/crisis/ [accessed 11 March 2015].

momentous consequences', or '... to indicate a historically imminent transitional phase. When this transition will occur and whether it leads to a worse or better condition depends on the specific diagnosis offered.'[33]

II

The frequent association between crisis, disease and death suggests at first glance that its meaning is overwhelmingly negative. Hobbes, as we have seen, used 'crisis' and 'catastrophe' in the same breath, as do many modern commentators. Some writers also recognised that crisis could bring opportunity, however; a difficult, risky period could be followed by something more positive. Indeed, Galen was positively optimistic about the nature of crisis, often referring to a 'good crisis' because 'its outcome is toward recovery in most cases'.[34] In the lull of Civil War, Nicholas Caussin pleaded 'let us make our adresses to God the founder of Safety, and the reconciler of Divisions; for when we despair he can repair, our extremity is the crisis of his opportunity'.[35] Man's lowest point, in other words, is when god displays his true colours. In a similar fashion, Marxism has seen crisis as a politically useful tool, even as it creates misery. The founding principles of Marxist communism saw periodic economic crisis as endemic to the bourgeois power structure that had overtaken Europe from the sixteenth century:

> Ever since the beginning of this [nineteenth] century, the condition of industry has constantly fluctuated between periods of prosperity and periods of crisis; nearly every five to seven years, a fresh crisis has intervened, always with the greatest hardship for workers, and always accompanied by general revolutionary stirrings and the direct peril to the whole existing order of things.[36]

In their *Manifesto*, Marx and Engels expanded on the consequences of these crises:

> And how does the bourgeoisie get over these crises? On the one hand by enforced destruction of a mass of productive forces; on the other, by the conquest of new markets, and by the more thorough exploitation of the old ones. That is to say, by paving the way for more extensive and

33 R. Koselleck and M.W. Richter, 'Crisis', *Journal of the History of Ideas*, 67, 2 (2006), p. 372.
34 Cooper (ed.), *Galen, De diebus decretoriis*, p. 102.
35 N. Caussin, *The holy court in five tomes* ... (1650), p. 6.
36 F. Engels, *The Principles of Communism*, trans. Paul Sweezy (1847), sec. 12, available at: www.marxists.org/archive/marx/works/1847/11/prin-com.htm [accessed March 2015].

more destructive crises, and by diminishing the means whereby crises are prevented.[37]

With the right inducement, workers would be expected to throw off their chains. The *Manifesto* concludes that after the abolition of private property and the system that promotes overproduction and misery, 'there will be no more crises'.[38]

Throughout much of the mid twentieth century, Marxist historians applied the term liberally to preceding stages in the progression towards abolishing property. The crisis of feudalism, for example, was seen as a prerequisite to the transition from feudalism to capitalism.[39] For Rodney Hilton the medical analogy underpinning the concept of crisis was important in its utility as an analytical concept:

> crises by definition are turning-points in the history of a social as well as of a natural organism. The organism may die; it may also survive, more or less intact; or it may survive having undergone sufficient changes to enable it to cope with changing circumstances. After the first crisis in the fourteenth and fifteenth centuries, feudalism had a long and tortured subsequent history.[40]

But which crisis was this? Was this 'first crisis' the extensive depopulation caused by the Great Famine of 1315–17, in which 10 per cent of the population of Europe died, and the Black Death of 1347–50, which killed approximately half the European population? Or was it related to the underlying political and social problems that resulted in the Peasants' Revolt of 1381 and the decline of serfdom? Or perhaps it was the longer-term consequences of these events and the mid-fifteenth-century recession? It is now more common to analyse these crises in isolation, each with its own causes and consequences rather than seeing them as symptomatic of the problems of an entire social system or agrarian regime.

If we take the first of these crises, the Great Famine, then the problems of interpretation become even more apparent. Were the effects of poor weather in the early fourteenth century enhanced by the poor productivity and declining yields of medieval agriculture and, if so, what caused this

---

37 K. Marx and F. Engels, *Manifesto of the Communist Party*, trans. S. Moore with F. Engels (1848, 1888), sec. 1, available at www.marxists.org/archive/marx/works/1848/communist-manifesto [accessed March 2015].

38 Ibid.

39 See e.g. Dobb, *Studies in the Development of Capitalism*; Hilton, *The Decline of Serfdom*; R.H. Hilton *et al.*, *The Transition from Feudalism to Capitalism* (London, 1976); S.H. Rigby, 'Historical Materialism: Social Structure and Social Change in the Middle Ages', *Journal of Medieval and Early Modern Studies*, 34 (2004), pp. 473–522.

40 R.H. Hilton, 'A Crisis of Feudalism', *Past & Present*, 80 (1978), p. 4.

decline? It has commonly been argued that there was a decrease in yields over the course of the thirteenth century because of the increasing fragmentation of peasant holdings and declining numbers of livestock owned by medieval peasants. But was this a Malthusian crisis or a crisis of feudalism? For Hilton and Robert Brenner it was the 'surplus-extraction relations of serfdom [which] tended to lead to the exhaustion of peasant production', and so it was feudalism that caused, or at least enhanced, this crisis.[41] By comparison, M.M. Postan, Jan Titow and David Farmer argued along the Malthusian and Ricardian lines of diminishing returns, and thus it was not a crisis of a social system per se but an inevitable problem facing agrarian societies in which population increase outstrips agricultural output, with 'chronic under-manuring' to blame because of poor stocking densities.[42] To confuse the issue still further, Bruce Campbell and Mark Overton have argued that medieval agriculture followed a Boserupian pattern where agricultural yields in fact did not decline during periods of population pressure in Norfolk, though this was often achieved at the expense of labour productivity.[43] Focusing upon the famine itself and inspired by Amartya Sen's work on food entitlement during the Bengal famine of 1943, Philip Slavin has more recently argued that institutional factors enhanced the crisis, with market failure during the Great Famine having 'much in common with market failure during famines in the developing world'.[44] Crisis has thus proven to be a fertile research tool in the medieval rural economy, from the 'general crisis' of the period to more specific work on individual causation and consequences.

The 'general crisis' of the seventeenth century, examined by Eric Hobsbawm in 1954 as 'the last phase of the general transition from a feudal to a capitalist economy', became another seminal Marxist episode.[45] What for Hobsbawm was only a European economic crisis, albeit with far-reaching political causes

41 R. Brenner, 'Agrarian Class Structure and Economic Development in Pre-Industrial Europe', in T.H. Aston and C.H.E. Philpin (eds), *The Brenner Debate: Agrarian Class Structure and Economic Development in Pre-Industrial Europe* (Cambridge, 1987), p. 33.

42 M.M. Postan, 'Medieval Agrarian Society in its Prime: England', in M.M. Postan (ed.), *The Cambridge Economic History of Europe*; vol. 1, *The Agrarian Life of the Middle Ages* (Cambridge, 1966), pp. 548–59; J.Z. Titow, *Winchester Yields: A Study in Medieval Agricultural Productivity* (Cambridge, 1972); D.L. Farmer, 'Grain Yields on the Winchester Manors in the Later Middle Ages', *Economic History Review*, 30 (1977), pp. 555–66.

43 B.M.S. Campbell and M. Overton, 'A New Perspective on Medieval and Early Modern Agriculture: Six Centuries of Norfolk Farming, c.1250–c.1850', *Past & Present*, 141 (1993), pp. 38–105; see also, B.M.S. Campbell, 'Arable Productivity in Medieval England: Some Evidence from Norfolk', *Journal of Economic History*, 43 (1983), pp. 379–404.

44 P. Slavin, 'Market Failure during The Great Famine in England and Wales (1315–1317)', *Past & Present*, 222 (2014), pp. 9–49; Amartya Sen, *Poverty and Famines: An Essay on Entitlement and Deprivation* (Oxford 1981).

45 E.J. Hobsbawm, 'The General Crisis of the European Economy in the 17th Century', *Past & Present*, 5 (1954), p. 33.

and consequences, took on a life of its own in the fledgling *Past & Present* journal. From a different perspective, Hugh Trevor-Roper linked economic to political tumult, arguing that the general crisis 'was a crisis not of the constitution nor the system of production, but of the state, or rather of the state to society'.[46] Thus the potency of the mid-seventeenth-century crises was because they linked economic depression and political instability. The result was an unprecedentedly acute phase of warfare and revolution, which more recent global scholarship has broadened out beyond Europe. The 1640s saw the catastrophic collapse of Ming China, resulting in a wave of hundreds of local revolts that involved more than a million people.[47]

For Hobsbawm this 'general crisis' was a necessary phase in social progression – it was the natural result of feudalism, and an inevitable transitory phase. Yet the fact that this crisis emerged across the full range of global economies and societies in the seventeenth century requires further explanation. Contemporaries, and some more recent historians, have sought its causes outside the human realm altogether. In 1649 the Welsh historian James Howell observed that 'God Almighty has a quarrel lately with all mankind ... for within these twelve years there have been the strangest revolutions and horridest things happened, not only in Europe but all the world over'.[48] Jan de Vries remarks that 'the conjuncture of seventeenth-century economic events was not easily comprehended by contemporaries; nor is it easily reconstructed by historians'.[49] But contemporaries certainly tried: the English Parliament chose to blame the Irish; the Scots Parliament blamed the witches; and a particularly bright comet that appeared in 1618 was blamed by Spanish, Russian and Indian writers. A popular Chinese encyclopedia noted that 'when comets have dominated Heaven, there have been conflicts over the succession to the throne'.[50] Geoffrey Parker lays the blame on climate change, and in particular the calamitous coincidence of 'the sunspot minimum, the volcanic maximum, and the more frequent El Niños'; 'Each of these extreme climatic events remains unparalleled; each occurred in the Little Ice Age.'[51] Why was it that in some places the general crisis of the seventeenth century brought relatively small-scale riot, but in England and China, it toppled dynasties? Hugh Trevor-Roper answers in stormy metaphor: 'In England

---

46 H. Trevor-Roper, 'The General Crisis of the 17th Century', *Past & Present*, 16 (1959), p. 61.
47 G. Parker, 'Crisis and Catastrophe: The Global Crisis of the Seventeenth Century Reconsidered', *American Historical Review*, 113 (2008), p. 1053; J.W. Tong, *Disorder under Heaven: Collective Violence in the Ming Dynasty* (Stanford, 1991), pp. 47–9.
48 J. Howell, *Epistolae Ho-Elinae*, 3 vols (London, 1650), vol. 3, pp. 1–3, quoted in Parker, 'Crisis and Catastrophe', p. 1060.
49 J. de Vries, 'The Economic Crisis of the Seventeenth Century after Fifty Years', *Journal of Interdisciplinary History*, XL (2009), p. 151.
50 Parker, 'Crisis and Catastrophe', pp. 1060–2, quoting Xie Zhaozhe's *Wu za zu*.
51 Parker, 'Crisis and Catastrophe', p. 1074.

... the storm of the mid-century, which blew throughout Europe, struck the most brittle, most overgrown, most rigid court of all and brought it violently down.'[52] Or, as Francis Bacon warned, 'So when any of the foure Pillars of Government, are mainly shaken, or weakened (which are Religion, Justice, Council and Treasure,) Men had need to pray for Fair Weather.'[53]

Crisis, then, does not necessarily produce catastrophic political or social consequences, but it sets up the necessary conditions for major change. As Nietzsche explained: 'crises clear the ground, firstly of a host of institutions from which life has long since departed and which, given their historical privilege, could not have been swept away in any other fashion'.[54] As with the diseased patient of sixteenth-century textbooks, crisis is the point at which a patient – an economy, a state – either runs inextricably towards death or makes a miraculous recovery. Both the patient and the nation, having reached this point, need to pray for the best.

The 'general crisis', apparently seeping into all areas of human life, is a recurrent theme over the *longue durée*, and the twentieth century has seen crisis conceived in the most general terms. The 1930s, in the midst of a global trade depression precipitated by the collapse of financial institutions in the USA, saw a sense of crisis seep into other areas. Edmund Husserl's *The Crisis of the European Sciences and Transcendental Phenomenology* (1936) identified a failure of the physical sciences to accord with the subjective nature of human existence. Such concern was a product of unresolved issues, 'ranging from national identity and historical purpose to the struggle over justice and the future of capitalism ... all marked by the complex interface between ideas and conflicts in a world shaped by both'.[55]

Again, the 1970s, as popularly constructed – particularly in British history – stand out as a time of almost unparalleled crisis afflicting all aspects of public life. As Norman Shrapnel remarked at the end of the decade, 'The Seventies, like the Thirties, saw crisis become a daily condition of life.'[56] In economic terms, though the 1970s did not see the levels of unemployment of the following decade, inflationary pressures affected everyone and may have served to cultivate a more general sense of alarm. Indeed, the popular perception of unfolding inflationary crisis outstripped economic realities. Tomlinson has noted that in 1974 the majority of those canvassed believed annual inflation to be running at over 50 per cent, at a time when the official

52   Trevor-Roper, 'General Crisis', p. 62.
53   Francis Bacon, *The Essayes or Counsels, Civill and Morall* ... (London, 1625, 1632), pp. 79–80.
54   Quoted in Starn, 'Historians and "Crisis"', p. 9.
55   J. Dodd, *Crisis and Reflection: An Essay on Husserl's Crisis of the European Sciences* (New York, 2004), pp. 31–2.
56   N. Shrapnel, *The Seventies: Britain's Inward March* (London, 1980).

figure was somewhere between 10 and 20 per cent.[57] Similarly, Colin Hay has posited that, contrary to the popularly constructed perception of the Winter of Discontent as a crisis demonstrating the failure of Keynesianism as an economic paradigm, 'economic performance was improving prior to the onset of crisis and it worsened significantly in the turn to monetarism in response to the crisis. The notion that this was a crisis of Keynesianism to which monetarism was a (necessary) response is difficult to reconcile with the empirical record, however central it was to the construction as it unfolded.'[58] The ambiguities, constraints and inconsistencies that have emerged from casting the 1970s in popular memory solely by 'defining characteristics' – such as 'economic disaster, terrorist threats, corruption in high places, prophecies of ecological doom and fear of the surveillance state's suffocating embrace'[59] – have led to re-evaluations of the decade that seek to recast the broad perception of crisis. One such example has argued that 'the term "social panic" might be more appropriate, given the perceived threats to the established order that characterised the decade'.[60]

III

Crisis has thus proven a useful and adaptable category for contemporary historical actors as well as for historians. But such broad conceptions of crisis, encompassing all aspects of economic and social life, risk making each instance appear unique and comparison fruitless. As de Vries puts it: 'Perhaps the concept of [the seventeenth-century] general crisis sought to achieve too much, too soon. In seeking to incorporate politics, institutions, culture, art, economy, and ecology ..., crisis enthusiasts were surely courting trouble.' He sees his role as finding a 'salvageable core, a more modest crisis on which we can build'.[61] Applying a narrower and more rigorously policed definition is one way to encourage comparison. Daniel Curtis has recently explored the concepts of 'resilience' and 'vulnerability' in a range of systematic comparisons of pre-industrial settlements, concluding that a more equitable distribution of property and power can enable a society to create more successful

57   J. Tomlinson, 'British Government and Popular Understanding of Inflation in the Mid-1970s', *Economic History Review*, 67 (2014), p. 761.
58   C. Hay, 'Chronicles of a Death Foretold: The Winter of Discontent and the Construction of the Crisis of British Keynesianism', *Parliamentary Affairs*, 63 (2010), p. 462.
59   D. Sandbrook, *State of Emergency, The Way We Were: Britain 1970–1974* (London, 2011), pp. 9–10.
60   L. Black and H. Pemberton, 'Introduction. The benighted decade? Reassessing the 1970s', in L. Black, H. Pemberton and P. Thane (eds), *Reassessing 1970s Britain* (Manchester, 2013), p. 13.
61   de Vries, 'General Crisis', p. 156.

coping strategies to protect itself from crises.[62] For Curtis, crisis can be defined in a very restricted sense, with three main markers of vulnerability: the level of population decline or stagnation after a crisis; the loss or degradation of agricultural land; and the destruction of housing and capital goods. Undoubtedly, this definition serves his quantitative comparative purpose well.

This volume takes a different approach. We do not offer a similar all-encompassing definition of crisis or a uniform approach to the subject. Instead, contributors have focused on three particular areas: the concept and nature of crisis, how societies have responded to particular crises, and the immediate and long-term consequences of decisions undertaken during a crisis. In doing so, clear themes emerge across the traditional boundaries of historical time periods and between the different 'types' of crisis around which the volume is arranged. Contrasts and similarities are evident not only in the way that the authors have used crisis as an analytical tool, in exploring different levels of society and the way different crises move at different speeds, but also in the conjunctive nature of crisis, the transformative effect it could have on economies and societies, and its tendency to provide opportunities for some sections of society while punishing others.

The contrasts between chapters in this volume begin with the concept of crisis itself – the nature and defining attributes of what constitutes a crisis and our ability to detect one. There is a strong contingent of chapters, running across the thematic structure of the volume, whose authors deploy sophisticated quantitative methodologies to detect crises. Mark Casson and Catherine Casson, for example, examine the ability to identify different types of crisis in the volatility of long-run economic data for the medieval economy – deviation of two standard deviations or more from the trend is taken to constitute a crisis. Similarly, Pamela Nightingale uses a decline of 40 per cent from the previous year in credit supply to identify credit crises in late-medieval England, while Peter Bent uses GDP data to explore the importance of the Dingley Tariff in stimulating recovery in the US economy in the 1890s. This approach represents the strong empirical focus of these chapters and the way economists have used crisis to represent a 'grave and sudden disturbance upsetting the complex equilibrium between the supply and demand of goods, services, and capital'.[63] By comparison, Alan Knight draws out the differences between objective (etic) crises and subjective (emic) crises, noting that 'a crisis which no one perceives is, arguably, no crisis at all', while Paul Warde explores the putative nature of fuel availability in the wood shortage debates of early modern Europe. In a similar fashion, John Singleton argues that a disaster is external to observation but 'for there to be a crisis, then, there must be a

62   D.R. Curtis, *Coping with Crisis: The Resilience and Vulnerability of Pre-Industrial Settlements* (Farnham, 2014), pp. 19, 270.
63   Starn, 'Historians and "Crisis"', p. 11.

recognition that something is wrong', going so far as to observe that 'crisis is a phenomenon that does not lend itself to direct measurement'. The transitional nature of the term has made 'crisis' in one sense solidly structural, in defining historical epochs, but as Janet Roitman has argued crisis can be 'an enabling blind spot for the production of knowledge. ... In that sense, crisis is not a condition to be observed ...; it is an observation that produces meaning'.[64]

Crisis as a concept can be employed to discuss anything from a purely individual issue to a transnational catastrophe, giving the term the potential for nebulousness, but also expanding its scope as a comparative tool. Crisis could hit individuals and households at any time, but the interaction between localised crises and national and international forces is clear throughout these chapters. John Martin examines the globalised market for British farmers, and the impact of an international price rise because of Russia's purchase of American grain and the decline in Peru's anchoveta harvest in 1972. Several of the chapters also explore how different levels of society interact during a crisis, not always harmoniously or successfully. Paul Warde notes how the everyday experience of poor people throughout Europe often reinforced national discourses of a timber crisis as they internalised debates surrounding wood shortages because of their own daily struggles to afford fuel. Josette Duncan explores the different layers of political governance in Malta and the often contradictory forces that were at work when responding to cholera in the nineteenth century. The British Empire had a strong vested interest in improving the sanitation of the island and so conducted a survey with this in mind. However, it was not until the local outbreak of cholera in 1865 that the survey was acted upon, and then only because the colonial government overruled local concerns surrounding costs; this makes for an interesting case study of how different levels of governance collide in responding to a crisis.

The dynamics of crises have often had a vague, unframed temporal conception. Such differences again speak to the varied way in which 'crisis' as a term is understood and employed. In Chapter 1, Alan Knight suggests that crises could move at different speeds depending upon the normal time-frame of the process in question. Political crises could last a matter of days or weeks, for example, whereas ecological crises could last for generations. John Singleton, in Chapter 2, sees crisis as an immediate phenomenon, separate from its consequence, termed a disaster, which can last much longer. For instance, Marxist historian Perry Anderson, though clear that he was analysing an immediate, contemporary 'present crisis' afflicting Britain in the 1960s, still argued this was 'not a sudden breakdown, but a slow sickening entropy'; structurally ingrained through what he perceived as an incomplete bourgeois revolution and early industrialisation in the infancy of social thought.[65]

64   Koselleck and Richter, 'Crisis' p. 374; Roitman, 'Crisis'.
65   P. Anderson, 'Origins of the Present Crisis', *New Left Review*, 23, 1 (1964), p. 50.

Though at the point of their emergence crises seem immediate, their causes are almost always claimed to have deep roots. The 2007–08 crisis has been no exception: Beenstock states that 'the seeds of this new [debt] crisis were partly planted back in 1973 when the oil price crisis broke out';[66] Castells *et al.* similarly argue that the global financial crisis was the result of 'the specific dynamics of the global informational economy' that had developed over many years.[67] The chronologies of crises are challenging in a way that demands full consideration.

Just as in the historiographical debates surrounding the general crises of the fourteenth and seventeenth centuries, the environment appears strongly as a causal agent of crises in pre-industrial societies, and yet it is often difficult to isolate individual causation in history and, as Steve Rigby has argued, often unhelpful to attempt to do so.[68] In Chapter 4, Philip Slavin discusses the role that low solar irradiance of the Wolf Minimum played in creating the cold and wet conditions that were ideal for the spread of sheep scab, a clear instance where the environment precipitated a crisis. However, even where the environment played a key factor, such as the Great European Famine of 1315–17, causes were 'interwoven with, and heavily dependent on, one another'; while the 'crisis *began* with nature [it] was *intensified* by purely endogenous factors'.[69] Thus crises are by their nature conjunctive, with a strong propensity to overlap, intersect and mutually reinforce each other. Some of these, such as famine's tendency to produce increased mortality, have often been misunderstood. For example, Morgan Kelly and Cormac O'Grada have recently highlighted the link between harvest failures and epidemic diseases, noting how 'it is only with improved public health in the twentieth century that people began literally to starve to death: before this most famine victims succumbed to epidemic disease'.[70] Others are even more complex and reveal the need for further study on crises. In Chapter 10, Pamela Nightingale details the short-term credit crises that outbreaks of pestilence often caused in late-medieval England because lenders had less confidence that they could recoup their outlay if their debtors died. Interestingly, in Chapter 3,

---

66   M. Beenstock, 'The Rise, Fall and Rise Again of OPEC', in M.J. Oliver and D.H. Aldcroft (eds), *Economic Disasters of the Twentieth Century* (Cheltenham, 2007), p. 135.
67   M. Castells, J. Caraca and G. Cardoso, 'The Cultures of the Economic Crisis: An Introduction', in M. Castells *et al.* (eds), *Aftermath: The Cultures of Economic Crisis* (Oxford, 2013), p. 5.
68   B.M.S. Campbell, 'Nature as Historical Protagonist: Environment and Society in Pre-Industrial England', *Economic History Review*, 63 (2010), pp. 281–314; S.H. Rigby, 'Historical Causation: Is One Thing More Important Than Another?', *History*, 80 (1995), pp. 227–42.
69   Slavin, 'Market Failure', p. 11.
70   M. Kelly and C. O'Grada, 'Living Standards and Mortality since the Middle Ages', *Economic History Review*, 67 (2014), p. 359.

Mark Casson and Catherine Casson show how some political crises, such as the Good Parliament of 1376 and the Peasants' Revolt of 1381, though of great importance in certain sections of society, do not appear to have spread into the wider economy to create economic crises. The conjunctive nature of crises is as much a feature of the modern economy as it was in the past, if not more so. John Martin, for example, in Chapter 6, shows the way weather can still precipitate crises in modern society because of the interconnected international food market and the ripple effect caused by an abundance or scarcity of essential consumer goods.

That historians have identified such complexity in the causes of crisis is reflected in the ways that contemporaries have apportioned blame. Although the disaster management cycle invoked in Chapter 2 is an established tool, John Singleton notes that there has not been a stage devoted to blame in previous versions of the model, even though this activity is a common component of crises and disasters. A key contributor to this blame was the fear and panic that crises induce. This was prevalent in potentially life-threatening situations, such as harvest failure and outbreaks of disease, but, as Matthew Hollow and Ranald Michie show in Chapter 12, modern financial crises are also capable of producing contagious mass panics. Similarly, cholera 'shocked nations, prompted riots and was closely connected to the political unrest of the 1830s and 1848' as Josette Duncan argues in Chapter 9, while there was also 'the fear that the poor were being infected and killed by the medical profession to steal their bodies'. In Chapter 8, Pavla Jirková identifies a series of antiplague measures that were applied in the Jewish quarter of late-seventeenth-century Prague. At one level, they reflected the overcrowdedness of this quarter, but they also had an undeniable anti-Semitic character. On the other hand, this link between epidemic disease and fear and violence is of recent origin according to Samuel Cohn (Chapter 7): only since the medical revolution of the nineteenth century have epidemics produced waves of hatred. Aside from the Black Death, during which Jewish communities were accused of poisoning food, wells and streams and rounded up and massacred in Europe, epidemics in the ancient and medieval world were not accompanied by such outbreaks of violence.[71] Even at the height of the Black Death and the Jewish pogroms, there were attempts to restrict the violence, with Pope Clement VI arguing that Jews could not be behind the disease because 'God's hidden judgement has afflicted and continues to afflict the Jews themselves'.[72]

In a sense, the apportionment of blame is a form of 'coping', but the chapters that follow trace ways that a crisis could be managed, with greater

---

71 See e.g. S.K. Cohn, 'The Black Death and the Burning of Jews', *Past & Present*, 196 (2007), pp. 3–36.
72 J. Aberth, *The Black Death: The Great Mortality of 1348–1350: A Brief History with Documents* (Bedford, 2005), p. 159.

or lesser success. Unlike in Hugh Trevor-Roper's mid-seventeenth-century metaphorical storm – when the Stuart great oak was undone by its lack of 'give' – institutions considered below often showed flexibility and creativity in responding to crisis. Pavla Jirková's chapter reveals the extensive set of documentation commissioned by the Czech authorities in response to plague in 1680. This included health passports recording where a person was travelling from, as well as deliberately limiting trade and movement, and recording those who had succumbed to the disease. Josette Duncan also shows how the Maltese colonial authorities sought to improve the sanitary conditions of the island in order to prevent further outbreaks of cholera.

Institutions could be proactive about potential crises as well as reactive. In responding to the loss of the American colonies, Anne Murphy demonstrates in Chapter 11 that the Bank of England was willing to do just enough to 'deal with the threat of reform', keeping criticism at bay and maintaining the Bank's monopoly. The Bank anticipated censure and artfully crafted a response that would satisfy its critics. Singleton highlights the difficulties facing contemporaries when formulating a response to a crisis because events are often not understood, while decision-makers 'are hampered by uncertainty, ambiguity and pressure'. Cinzia Lorandini demonstrates this adaptive decision-making in action in the nineteenth-century Tyrolean silk industry (Chapter 14): the Salvadori firm were initially innovative in their response to a disease outbreak in silkworms in the 1850s but then acted more conservatively in the face of deflation from the 1870s onward, which saw the gradual decline of the industry. 'The decline of the Tyrolean silk industry', she argues, 'can be blamed on the lack of entrepreneurial spirit among the individuals involved in the crisis.' Similarly, Hollow and Michie highlight the factors important in the ability of British banks to cope with a crisis because of changes in regulations and the lender of last resort. Mindful of the unrest that accompanied slumps in the cloth industry, John Lee shows in Chapter 13 how Thomas Wolsey and the duke of Norfolk took steps to control grain prices as well as begging clothiers not to lay off cloth-workers in the 1520s. Lee goes on to argue that the protectionist measures that some larger boroughs employed in response to the trade crisis of the 1450s/1460s only exacerbated the problem further, whereas Peter Bent (Chapter 15) contends that the implementation of the Dingley Tariff stimulated economic recovery by boosting investor confidence.

Those that could adapt, and those that were powerful or lucky, might even do well out of crisis. In his Nobel Peace Prize acceptance lecture in 2007, Al Gore offered the political cliché that 'in both Chinese and Japanese, "crisis" is written with two symbols, the first meaning "danger", the second "opportunity"'.[73] Although this anecdote appeared in American politics in

73 Available at http://www.nobelprize.org/nobel_prizes/peace/laureates/2007/gore-lecture_ en.html [accessed 20 February 2015].

the mid twentieth century, historians have long recognised that periods of crisis can give rise to opportunities for some sections of society. For example, the fourteenth and fifteenth centuries have traditionally been described as a period of crisis, recession and retrenchment in the medieval economy.[74] This is because the incomes of landlords and merchants, through whose eyes we view medieval society, generally fell as rents and prices declined and wages increased. By comparison, Thorold Rogers christened the fifteenth century as a 'golden age of the wage-labourer' in which real wages were at their highest in England before the nineteenth century because of the scarcity of labour in the period following the Black Death.[75] Revisionist assessments have emphasised the significant economic and political gains made by more skilled workers in the 1930s, and some groups of women in the 1970s, despite the severe economic conditions of those decades.[76] Though economic and social crises may be particularly damaging to some sectors or locations, they leave other areas relatively unscathed; the Latin American financial system, for example, escaped contagion in the 2007–08 North American and European crisis.[77]

Periods of crisis are thus also opportunities for economic actors who could in some way capitalise on the new economic conditions. Martin shows in Chapter 6 how some people, such as large upland sheep farmers, may have actually prospered in the warmer and drier conditions of drought and were thus able to reap the benefits of high prices.[78] This was also the case in the late-medieval cloth industry which, as Lee shows in Chapter 13, underwent structural changes that favoured the lower production costs of a few wealthy clothiers who increasingly dominated the relocated, rural industry. The mid-fifteenth-century recession, therefore, had a transformative effect on society but, just as Galen originally observed, a crisis more often than not tends towards recovery rather than death, and so there could be broader

74　M.M. Postan, 'The Fifteenth Century', *Economic History Review*, 9 (1939), pp. 160–7; J. Hatcher, *Rural Economy and Society in the Duchy of Cornwall, 1300–1500* (Cambridge, 1970), p. 148.

75　J.T. Rogers, *Six Centuries of Work and Wages: The History of English Labour* (1906), p. 326. For a reassessment of this view, see J. Hatcher, 'Unreal Wages: Long-Run Living Standards and the "Golden Age" of the Fifteenth Century', in B. Dodds and C.D. Liddy (eds), *Commercial Activity, Markets and Entrepreneurs in the Middle Ages: Essays in Honour of Richard Britnell* (Woodbridge, 2011), pp. 1–24; A.R. Bridbury, *Economic Growth: England in the Later Middle Ages* (Westport, 1983); C. Dyer, *An Age of Transition? Economy and Society in England in the Later Middle Ages* (Oxford, 2005), p. 242.

76　J. Stevenson and C. Cook, *The Slump* (London, 1979); P. Thane, 'Women and the 1970s: Towards Liberation?', in L. Black, H. Pemberton and P. Thane (eds), *Reassessing 1970s Britain* (Manchester, 2013), p. 167–86.

77　E. Ottone, 'A Non-Global Crisis? Challenging the Crisis in Latin America', in M. Castells *et al.* (eds), *Aftermath: The Cultures of the Economic Crisis* (Oxford, 2013), p. 288.

78　For an early modern comparison, see M. Overton, *Agricultural Revolution in England: The Transformation of the Agrarian Economy, 1500–1850* (Cambridge, 1996), p. 20.

positives for its survivors.[79] 'Crisis is not necessarily destructive', as Cinzia Lorandini argues with regard to the silk industry in nineteenth-century Tyrol, 'as it can offer incentives for investment and innovation. The ultimate impact of crisis is mostly determined by the manufacturers' willingness and ability to provide a firm response.'[80] Indeed, Duncan shows that the outbreak of cholera in Malta in 1865 may have brought with it initial hardship, but also prompted widespread improvements in sanitation for the whole island.

IV

The chapters in this book offer a number of new perspectives for the comparative history of crisis, and for (carefully) drawing analogies from the past that will be useful in the present and the future. Roger Middleton acknowledges that 'the current Great Recession, beginning in 2008 ... has reawakened interest in the interwar period. ... Much of this interest has inevitably taken the form of seeking to identify lessons from the Great Depression.'[81] Black and Pemberton likewise state that 'a situation of crisis akin to the 1970s, a crisis in which the state is seen at once as over-mighty and ineffectual, is apparently back, and with a vengeance'.[82] Of course, an interest in the past does not necessarily lead to a worthwhile understanding of it, and 'lessons' can rarely be straightforward. It is far easier for a politician or journalist to cherry-pick 'facts' that underpin their existing comprehension of crisis than it is to understand the past on its own terms. But, as Yueng Foon Khong's work on the escalation of US military involvement in Vietnam has shown, analogies do not simply reinforce decisions made by other means; they can be an active part of analytic processes.[83] The in-depth case studies of crises in this volume demonstrate that such events are complex and multifaceted, but similarities between the causes and responses to crises in vastly differing contexts have been striking. In emphasising these overlaps, it is not our intention to flatten the contours of history, nor do we claim that easy equivalencies can be made between the past and the present. Nonetheless, these connections deserve some attention.

It has been argued that the Black Death formed a watershed in medical

---

79   For some of the long-term effects of the fifteenth-century recession on rural society, see A.T. Brown, 'Estate Management and Institutional Constraints in Pre-Industrial England: The Ecclesiastical Estates of Durham, c.1400–1640', *Economic History Review*, 67 (2014), pp. 699–719.

80   Chapter 14, below, p. 353.

81   R. Middleton, 'Macroeconomic Policy in Britain Between the Wars', *Economic History Review* [Virtual issue], 64.VI (2011), p. 2.

82   Black and Pemberton, 'Introduction. The benighted decade? Reassessing the 1970s', pp. 1–2.

83   Y.F. Khong, *Analogies at War: Korea, Munich, Dien Bien Phu, and the Vietnam Decisions of 1965* (Princeton, 1992), pp. 252–3.

history because it 'brought about a crisis in medieval medicine which stimulated professionalism, the rise of surgery, new laws of public health and sanitation, and the development of hospitals designed not just to isolate society's sick but to try to cure them'.[84] This narrative does an injustice to medieval medical practitioners who, despite the inadequacies of medical knowledge, were far from the 'inept' and 'fatalistic' figures that an older historiography painted them as: men who 'explained it all away on purely theoretical, often fantastic, grounds'.[85] Gentile de Foligno, for instance, who died on 18 June 1348 after contracting the disease 'from too constant attendance on the sick', was known for his practical experience based upon several public dissections and autopsies, recommending that no sick person should be allowed to enter a city if he came from 'contaminated parts'.[86] Similarly, medieval landlords have been criticised for spending 'up to the hilt on personal display, on extravagant living, on the maintenance of numerous retinue, and on war', while it was only in the sixteenth and seventeenth centuries that improving farmers 'drawn to the potential of employing reason and empirical investigation in agricultural practice' set about their practice with increasing economic rationality.[87] More recently, David Stone has concluded that 'while outlook and attitudes may have changed in many ways since the Middle Ages, in economic terms medieval decision-makers were not necessarily less rational than their modern counterparts'. And Ben Dodds has shown that medieval peasants in north-east England were responsive to market fluctuations in the production and sale of their output.[88]

Many of the following chapters continue this historical reinterpretation of the medieval and early modern past, emphasising continuities in the way societies have responded to crises. Philip Slavin, for example, shows the remarkable parallels between how medieval landlords responded to outbreaks

---

84   R.S. Gottfried, *The Black Death: Natural and Human Disaster in Medieval Europe* (London, 1983), p. 110.
85   P. Ziegler, *The Black Death* (Harmondsworth, 1970), p. 71; Gottfried, *The Black Death*, p. 104; C.H. Talbot, *Medicine in Medieval England* (London, 1967), p.169.
86   J. Henderson, 'The Black Death in Florence: Medical and Communal Responses', in S. Basset (ed.), *Death in Towns: Urban Responses to the Dying and the Dead, 100–1600* (Leicester, 1992), p. 146; Aberth, *The Black Death*, pp. 47–8.
87   R.H. Hilton, 'Rent and Capital Formation in Feudal Society', in R.H. Hilton (ed.), *The English Peasantry in the Later Middle Ages: The Ford Lectures for 1973* (Oxford, 1975), p. 177; M.M. Postan, 'Investment in Medieval Agriculture', *Economic History Review*, 27 (1967), p. 578; R. Brenner, 'Agrarian Class Structure and Economic Development in Pre-Industrial Europe', in T.H. Aston and C.H.E. Philpin (eds), *The Brenner Debate: Agrarian Class Structure and Economic Development in Pre-Industrial Europe* (Cambridge, 1987), p. 31; K. Wrightson, *Earthly Necessities: Economic Lives in Early Modern Britain* (New Haven, 2000), p. 203.
88   D. Stone, *Decision-Making in Medieval Agriculture* (Oxford, 2005), p. 276; B. Dodds, *Peasants and Production in the Medieval North-East: the Evidence from Tithes, 1270–1536* (Woodbridge, 2007), pp. 132–61.

of sheep scab in 1279/80 and rinderpest in cattle in 1319/20 and reactions to the same diseases in the nineteenth and twentieth centuries. Although quarantine featured far more prominently in responses to the later outbreaks, very similar remedies of tar and sulphur were used for scab, as was a special votive prayer against rinderpest in cattle. Samuel Cohn's chapter goes even further, challenging the historiographical orthodoxy that outbreaks of diseases in past societies brought about waves of hatred towards minority groups; rather, he suggests, this was a distinctly modern phenomenon after the laboratory revolution of the late nineteenth century. He shows how 'for the US smallpox was the disease, par excellence, for hate and blame, not cholera as in Europe', despite the fact that there existed effective vaccinations for smallpox by the late nineteenth century. These two diseases, smallpox and rinderpest, are the only two infectious diseases to have been declared eradicated by the World Health Organization, the former in 1979, the latter by 2011.[89] John Martin also shows how scientific and technological improvements have created much greater consistency in agricultural output between one year and another in modern Britain because of plant breeding, the use of pesticides to control disease and the increased mechanisation of farm equipment. Although modern science has thus enabled developed countries to control certain types of medical and agricultural crises, outbreaks of disease can and do still create the same kind of fear experienced by past societies. Indeed, the foot and mouth outbreak in the United Kingdom in 2001, which resulted in the slaughter of between 6 and 10 million animals, created a level of panic and scapegoating that appears to have been largely absent from the medieval outbreaks of scab.[90] Meanwhile new strains of influenza in the twenty-first century, from H5N1 to H1N1, still have the power to induce international fear of a global pandemic.

The rhetoric of resource shortage, explored by Warde in Chapter 5 with regard to the timber crisis of early modern Europe, reappeared (as he points out) in the 1860s with logging in North America and oil crises in the late twentieth century. Moreover, there were remarkable similarities in the responses to trade slumps and financial crises from the Middle Ages through to the twenty-first century. John Lee shows in Chapter 13 how 'like the early nineteenth-century trade crises, the late medieval crises in the English cloth industry generated under-employment, unemployment, discontent and ruined many smaller manufacturers, but also enabled certain larger producers, such as the leading clothiers, to flourish'. At first glance, there

---

89   The campaign to eradicate dracunculiasis (guinea worm disease) has been ongoing since 1981 and shows the difficulty of such campaigns, although this and several other diseases are close to eradication: http://www.who.int/dracunculiasis/eradication/en/ [accessed 5 February 2015].

90   See the BBC's special reports on foot and mouth, including contemporary accusations, recriminations and mass panic: http://news.bbc.co.uk/1/hi/in_depth/uk/2001/foot_and_mouth/default.stm [accessed 1 January 2015].

would seem to be few similarities between a medieval credit crisis and the 2007–08 'credit crunch', but as Pamela Nightingale shows in Chapter 10 credit was 'extraordinarily sensitive ... to any crises which made potential creditors suspect that repayment was doubtful'. In these circumstances, such as an outbreak of pestilence, medieval merchants were reluctant to extend credit given the potential expenses and difficulties of enforcing payment from executors. Similar fears often underpinned financial crises in the nineteenth and twentieth centuries, as Hollow and Michie show in Chapter 12. Retaining investor confidence has been integral to ensuring that the collapse of one bank does not lead to bank runs; perception is as important as reality in coping with a financial crisis. Crises, at their core, are socially constructed, rather than natural phenomena: the uncertainty they engender, and the perception of insecurity, is often as important as the reality of their immediate impact. Indeed, the disaster management cycle employed by Singleton could be applied to a medieval crisis as much as a modern one. Each had similar experiences of forewarnings, sense-making, scapegoating and recovery, as many of the following chapters demonstrate.

There are few terms that can boast the semantic and analytical reach of 'crisis'. It relates to both the internal well-being of an individual and the progress of global pandemics, to the massive destruction brought on by weather or war, and to an imagined threat cooked up on a computer screen. It is precisely this wide applicability that gives us the opportunity to conduct comparisons across time, space and disciplinary boundaries. The history of crisis is still reflected in its current applicability, from its use as a turning point or judgement, to the varied pace and intensity of crises, and the link between crisis and opportunity. 'Viewed metaphorically', argues Shank, 'and treated as a rhetorical term of art rather than as a literal term of scientific and deterministic objectivity, the concept of crisis becomes a powerful tool.'[91] Crises are historical moments when profound change is possible, but they can, in Lewis Namier's words, be 'turning points when history failed to turn'.[92] Just because a crisis did not result in the transformation of society 'we need not ... pretend that the crisis did not happen'.[93] The road not taken during a crisis can, after all, be as revealing about society as the historical course of events. Crisis may be a contested concept, but it is a concept that underpins many of the key historiographical debates of the past two centuries, and remains integral to twenty-first century public discourse. How historians and historical actors have coped with crisis reveals much about both the past and the present.

---

91   J.B. Shank, 'Crisis: A Useful Category of Post–Social Scientific Historical Analysis?', *American Historical Review*, 113 (2008), p. 1098.
92   See Alan Knight, Chapter 1, below, p. 33. Namier was referring to the 1848 revolutions.
93   Hilton, 'Crisis of Feudalism', p. 4.

PART I:
CONCEPT AND METHODOLOGY

'Crisis' and the Great Depression in Latin America

ALAN KNIGHT

This is a somewhat schizoid chapter: it consists of two sections that are imperfectly linked. The first part attempts to clarify the notion of 'crisis', which is central to our discussion; it is therefore rather more conceptual in approach (though not lacking in empirical examples). The second part deals with a specific – temporally limited but geographically broad – crisis: the Great Depression of the (early) 1930s and its impact on Latin America. Apart from being a case I know something about, it has the advantage of involving a definable crisis which, being economic, can be measured, and which affected several countries, thus making possible some cross-national comparisons. Most of the second section therefore concerns, I would argue, real, objective (etic) crises; it has, unfortunately, less to say about subjective (emic) perceptions of crisis, even though – as I argue in section I – these are often independently important and worthy of study. There are two reasons for this relative omission: the data on subjective perceptions are much harder to acquire and assess (especially when they concern some twenty countries);[1] and, even if they could be acquired and assessed, their discussion would require the best part of a book rather than half a chapter. Having made that *mea culpa*, I will proceed to section I, which tackles the question of 'crisis' as an 'organising concept'.[2]

I

Some historians, even some very good ones, like to affect a bullish empiricism, claiming to avoid grand, general concepts and categories, allowing the 'facts'

---

[1] The conventional head count for the countries of Latin America, every one of which gets at least a mention in these pages.

[2] William McNeill, 'Organizing Concepts for World History', *Review*, X/2 (2002), pp. 211–29.

or the 'historical actors' to speak for themselves.[3] There are probably fewer
of them today than, say, fifty years ago. But there are also some – today much
more numerous – who use such concepts and categories without thinking
through, or clearly explaining, what they mean. In other words, they seem to
think that the concepts and categories speak for themselves, when they do not,
or when they speak in so many tongues that they are thoroughly confusing.
What are meant to be 'organising' concepts become 'disorganising' concepts.
(The worst offender in this conceptual Bedlam, in my subjective opinion, is
'modernity' – and cognate terms like 'modernism' and 'modernisation' –
which have bred like rabbits in recent years.)[4]

Of course, it would be tedious and unnecessary to preface every historical
analysis or narrative with a series of lengthy definitions, especially when
the concepts being defined are fairly clear-cut, when there is a reasonable
consensus as to their meaning, and when the analysis/narrative does not
hinge on the particular definition being used. We can usually talk about, say,
the First World War without presenting an elaborate definition of what it
precisely entails; on the other hand, a discussion of the First World War as
'total war' would require some conceptual clarification. So, too, I can usually
talk about my own focus of research – the Mexican Revolution – without
necessarily defining what a revolution is or stipulating when the Revolution
started or stopped (which in turn involves deciding what the Revolution was,
since you cannot determine the longevity of an indeterminate being).

So, at the risk of sounding a bit like Donald Rumsfeldt, I think there are:

* Concepts/categories (like 'modernity') which urgently require
  definition, but which rarely if ever receive adequate definitional clarity
  and, for that reason, obfuscate more than they clarify and should
  probably be avoided.[5] Let's call them conceptual *non-starters*. If, unlike
  me, you are a fan of 'modernity', you can substitute what I assume

3   Richard Cobb, *The Police and the People: French Popular Protest, 1789–1820* (Oxford, 1972),
pp. xvi–xvii, which is echoed, rather more prosaically, by Simon Schama, *Citizens: A Chronicle
of the French Revolution* (New York, 1989), pp. xiii–xiv.
4   This fundamental problem – which 'organising concepts' we use and how we define
and 'operationalise' them – should be distinguished from the traps of translation and 'false
friends' which, though sometimes tricky, can be negotiated. The problem is not linguistic but
methodological.
5   I should clarify that I can see the relevance and utility of 'modern(ity)' when it is used
carefully by a good historian of ideas like Jonathan Israel, who discerns a 'decisive shift' in ways
of thinking, at least among some literate elites in one part of the world (western and central
Europe and North America): *Radical Enlightenment* (Oxford, 2001), p.151. It is the mindless
proliferation of the term – now become an empty passepartout – to cover all countries and
cultures and all spheres of human life that is, to use the polite cliché, 'problematic'. For a brief
explanation, see Alan Knight, 'When Was Latin America Modern? A Historian's Response',
in Nicola Miller and Stephen Hart (eds), *When Was Latin America Modern?* (New York and
Basingstoke, 2007), pp. 91–117.

would be less contentious examples of conceptual non-starters: for example, Divine Providence or racial character.

- Concepts/categories which, for many historical purposes, are pretty self-evident and do not require definition or clarification (e.g., The First World War, the Mexican Revolution). These could be called *consensual* concepts.[6]

- Finally, there are concepts/categories which are useful, necessary and even unavoidable, but which *do* require some definition/clarification. These would include, for example, 'revolution', 'total war' and, in our case, perhaps, 'crisis'. They are, to use the cliché, *contested* concepts.

I say 'perhaps' because some people may consider 'crisis' to be either a non-starter or a consensual concept: that is, 'crisis' may be *either* a vague – even meaningless – term, best avoided; *or* it may be a simple, self-evident term which we can all happily use without need for further discussion and without fear of confusion. Personally, I do not find either of these positions convincing. I think the term has some real utility and, if we were to banish it from the historian's lexicon, the latter would be somewhat impoverished and we would probably start scurrying around looking for an approximate synonym.[7]

There is also the problem – though this is a familiar one that we can live with – that historical actors themselves may have used the term so, even if as (objective?) historians we choose to avoid it, we cannot ignore it altogether, since the (subjective) ideas and assumptions of 'our' historical actors are a matter of concern.[8] This, however, is a very different problem from that of whether we should use the term ourselves – as a considered, *ex post facto*, 'etic' category for explaining history. (The difference is very clear in the case

---

6   These, of course, are particular historical events or processes; though loose at the edges (when did the Revolution stop and start? Which socio-political processes should be included in the process and which excluded?), they are readily amenable to constructive analysis and debate, which is presumably what historiography is all about.

7   *Roget's Thesaurus* gives ten related categories under the heading 'crisis', each of which contain numerous – certainly dozens – of illustrative words/phrases (many, it is true, entirely irrelevant to our purposes). The common elements would seem to be: risk, threat, brevity and momentousness. In other words, a crisis, in common usage, denotes an event that carries threat, provokes concern and contains the potential for major change (usually for the worse).

8   So, there is a phenomenological side to the problem: as David Easton put it, 'if men define situations as real, they are real in their consequences': cited by Michel Dobry, *Sociologie des crises politiques* (Paris, 1986), p. 197. A useful survey of how the term 'crisis' and its cognates have been employed – from their Greek origins to the present – is provided by Randolph Starn, 'Historians and "Crisis"', *Past & Present*, 52 (1971), pp. 3–22. Regarding the Greek origins of the term, I would not place much faith in conclusions derived from distant etymology, since, with time and translation, the meanings of words change, sometimes profoundly (consider 'tremendous', 'sad', 'awful', and – a semantic cousin of 'crisis' – 'revolution'). It is current, or recent, usage that counts, especially careful, considered – sometimes scholarly – usage.

of Divine Providence or racial character: I assume no respectable historian would wish to invoke these as causal categories; but historical actors did so frequently, hence their – 'emic' – usage is an important matter which as historians we have to take into account and try to understand.)

So, 'crisis' is, at least potentially, a useful, even necessary term, neither irrelevant, nor straightforwardly self-evident. The wealth of examples presented would seem to confirm both points: plenty of historians feel happy using the term, but they may well be using it in different ways, which could lead to confusion, especially if we seek to establish comparisons. (Some ambitious positivists may even hope to discover the 'laws of motion' governing historical crises; to me, this would be an illusion. But denying general laws does not mean denying the utility of a concept: again, take 'revolution' or 'total war': both useful concepts, but neither, in my view, subject to general laws of process or causality.)[9] At the very least, by studying many different examples of 'crisis', we may be able to get a sense of how a cross section of historians – or social scientists more generally – use the term (use being a crucial criterion) and, even if we fail to reveal 'laws of motion', we might discern some helpful typologies (different types of crisis) and/or insightful ways of looking at crises, especially from a comparative perspective. Thus, in section II, I make a conventional distinction between *economic* crisis and *political* consequences, while also trying to assess the relative *severity* of crisis in different countries.

Finally, one reason why 'crisis' presents problems is that it is under-theorised.[10] If we were looking at, say, 'the state' we would have a wealth of sophisticated literature, including history, political theory, comparative politics, political economy and political sociology, ranging from Plato and Aristotle to, *inter alia*, Scott, Mann and Centeno.[11] 'Nation' and 'nationalism' are also pervasive concepts, which have received extensive attention from historians and social scientists, as are 'democracy' and, to a lesser extent,

9   Michael Brecher and Jonathan Wilkenfield, *A Study of Crisis* (Ann Arbor, 1997), pp. 6–11, seem confident that, on the basis of studying 412 international crises between 1918 and 1994, they can identify four phases common to crises, which form part of their 'unified model of crisis'. For a critique of stage-theories, as applied to revolutions, see Alan Knight, 'Social Revolution: A Latin American Perspective', *Bulletin of Latin American Research*, 9/2 (1990), pp. 178–80.

10   As J.A. Robinson noted in the *International Encyclopedia of the Social Sciences* some 45 years ago: 'crisis is a lay term in search of a scholarly meaning': cited in Starn, 'Historians and "Crisis"', p. 13.

11   James Scott, *Seeing Like a State* (New Haven, 1998); Michael Mann, *The Sources of Social Power* (2 vols, New York, 1986); Miguel Angel Centeno and Agustín Ferraro, *State and Nation-Making in Latin America and Spain* (New York, 2013).

'populism'.[12] So, in these cases, there is an extant literature, well-known debates, and even some possibly consensual definitions.[13]

But when it comes to 'crisis' it is a different matter. The term is common enough, in both scholarly and 'lay' usage, but a glance at the literature, including the chapters in this volume, suggest quite varied and divergent approaches.[14] For example: need a crisis be short-lived ('their duration is always brief', as Tom Paine asserted); or can crisis last, in the case of E.H. Carr's famous study, two decades, if not – in the terminology of a well-known historical debate – an entire century, if not longer?[15] Some commentators, following Paine, would wish to limit 'crisis' to short-term

12 I mention these in particular since I know something about the related debates. Plenty more could be listed: feudalism, capitalism, bureaucracy, charisma, industrialisation, liberalism, fascism, totalitarianism, authoritarianism, etc.

13 Thus, debates about democracy used to be vitiated by competing definitions, some embodying strong normative elements; my impression is that political scientists – and, to some extent, historians too – have settled on a limited, procedural definition of representative democracy, thus managing to extricate themselves from endless conceptual and normative squabbles: see, for example, Paul W. Drake, *Between Tyranny and Anarchy. A History of Democracy in Latin America, 1800–2006* (Stanford, 2009), pp. 4–5. Dr Tim Power (personal communication) confirms that this is broadly the case among political scientists (of which he is one).

14 The Bodleian Library in Oxford has 11,569 titles containing the word 'crisis'; a glance at the list reveals a huge range of meanings and contexts. The Library of Congress (online catalogue) lists 10,000 titles (but there are more). As Emmanuel Le Roy Ladurie observed, 'the word "crisis" has such a general meaning that it is becoming overworked – and, as a result, losing its usefulness': *The Mind and Method of the Historian* (Chicago, 1984), p. 270; Istvan Hont agrees that there has been a 'vast inflation in the range of instances described as "crises"', to the point where 'the notion ... is overused, generalized and trivialized': 'The Permanent Crisis of a Divided Mankind: "Contemporary Crisis of the Nation State" in Historical Perspective', in John Dunn (ed.), *Contemporary Crisis of the Nation State?* (Oxford, 1995), pp. 167–8.

15 Paine, cited in Starn, 'Historians and "Crisis"', p. 6. Compare E.H. Carr, *The Twenty Years' Crisis, 1919–29: An Introduction to the Study of International Relations* (London, 1964 [1939]); Trevor Aston (ed.), *Crisis in Europe, 1560–1660* (New York, 1967); Geoffrey Parker and Lesley M. Smith (eds), *The General Crisis of the Seventeenth Century* (London, 1978); and Thomas N. Bisson, *The Crisis of the Twelfth Century* (Princeton, 2009). Le Roy Ladurie, *The Mind and Method of the Historian*, pp. 272–3, goes further, discussing 'crises extending over several centuries', such the demographic collapse affecting Native Americans after 1492. There is, of course, a significant semantic difference between Carr's forthright 'twenty years' crisis' (which makes clear that the 'crisis' lasted two decades) and the looser formulation 'crisis of' the twelfth or seventeenth centuries (which could be taken to mean simply that the crisis was located somewhere *in* those centuries). However, both the implication – and the argument (which in Bisson's case I found quite opaque) – clearly mean that the crisis spanned *all* or *most* of those centuries and affected much of Europe (and maybe beyond); i.e. it was both temporally and geographically very extensive. E.J. Hobsbawm, who started the ball rolling, was explicit: the crisis was 'general' and lasted at least 1620–80 and, probably, 1620–1720: 'The Crisis of the Seventeenth Century', in Aston, *Crisis in Europe*, p. 14.

events or sequences of events (and I would tend to agree with them): crises have to be short, sharp and serious.[16]

But how short, how sharp, and serious in whose eyes? First, I would suggest that the timescale should be related to the process in question: politics moves fast, so political – and international – crises are likely to be more abrupt (they can blow up or blow over in a matter of days or weeks); while economic or 'eco-demographic' crises typically last longer. Thus, it usually took at least a couple of years for economies to go from boom to bust in the early 1930s. And, while the Black Death caused an unusually sudden demographic reverse in Europe, the impact of European disease on Native American populations after 1492 was protracted, consisting of a series of epidemics lasting over a century.[17]

Secondly, 'sharp' and 'serious' bring us back to the emic/etic distinction, between what the historical actors thought and what we, as historians, think. For many historical conjunctures or episodes, this distinction is key: as already mentioned, actors may believe in Divine Providence or racial character as motors of history which, I hope, we historians would not. But historians regularly and rightly advance explanations which were unknown to the actors and may even have been incomprehensible to them: first, because historians have the benefit of hindsight and know the outcome of chains of events; second, because they can unearth causal chains of which actors, close to the action and lacking information, were ill-informed or which, indeed, they could not conceivably comprehend (for example, the causes of inflationary cycles, of pandemics, demographic trends, industrial 'revolutions', and so on. Of course, the actors knew and understood a great deal that we do

16   Mattei Dogan and John Higley, 'Elites, Crises, and Regimes in Comparative Analysis', in Dogan and Higley (eds), *Elites, Crises and the Origins of Regimes* (Lanham, 1998), pp. 3–4, 6–7, see crises (chiefly political crises involving elite turnover and regime change) as 'sharp confrontations', 'abrupt and brutal challenges to the survival of a political regime', which can have 'decisive outcomes', and are therefore 'potentially major turning points in politics': pp. 3–4, 7. Consonant with this view, they question the notion that Colombia, for example, 'has been in continual crisis through the past half century', p. 6. Brecher and Wilkenfeld, *A Study of Crisis*, p. 3, identify three necessary and sufficient conditions of (international) crises: threat, 'finite time' and heightened probability of violence (though 'finite' seems an oddly lax way of flagging duration, given that all history is 'finite'); they also cite Charles F. Hermann's similar threefold definition, which includes 'surprise'. Hont, 'The Permanent Crisis of a Divided Mankind', p. 167, writes that – notwithstanding the 'permanent' in his title – 'crisis implies a moment of crucial decision in the face of acute difficulty or danger'. His stress on decision-making (which surely requires that there be alternatives on offer?) presents problems when we deal with crises – like, for example, the Black Death of the 1340s – in the face of which historical actors had few or no options: remedies were lacking and flight was futile, so 'nobody had any hope to offer': John Hatcher, *The Black Death. An Intimate History* (London, 2008), pp. 66–8.
17   Suzanne Austin Archon, *A Pest in the Land. New World Epidemics in Global Perspective* (Albuquerque, 2003).

not: they possessed 'local knowledge' and could, among other things, grasp moods and sentiments that elude historians, especially those historians – the great majority – who rely on documentary evidence).[18]

However, the emic/etic distinction is unusually slippery when it comes to crisis, or a few other comparable concepts, such as ethnicity and nationalism. The common feature of these concepts is that they all involve a heavily *subjective* element. An industrial revolution can happen irrespective of whether textile entrepreneurs and mill workers believe they are taking part in a 'revolution'. The collective outcome does not depend on a purposive commitment or belief on the part of thousands of individuals. But to experience a crisis or to build a nation requires a belief on the part of the actors. 'Crisis' depends on perception (at least in most of its usages). A crisis that no one perceives is, arguably, no crisis at all.[19] As I have suggested elsewhere, this raises some intriguing possibilities.[20]

There are crises that clearly meet both emic and etic criteria: for example, Munich or the Cuban missile crisis.[21] These tick both boxes, because the situation was at the same time objectively critical – a major war could have occurred on either occasion – and also subjectively critical (contemporaries saw the risks, feared the outcome and spoke of 'crisis').[22] True, neither crisis led to war, but either could have done.[23] Some crises, of course, have amply fulfilled their critical potential: August 1914 and September 1939, for example. These are well-known international examples, but we can also cite domestic crises. Some (for example, the Boulanger crisis of 1886–88 in France) also fizzled out;[24] they were, in Namier's famous phrase (apropos the revolutions of 1848), 'turning points when history failed to turn'.[25] But others, again,

18   A point emphasised by Hatcher, *The Black Death*, pp. x–xi.
19   Though Dobry, *Sociologie des Crises Politiques*, p. 196, citing Eberwein, refers to 'latent' crises.
20   Alan Knight, 'Historical and Theoretical Considerations', in Dogan and Higley, *Elites, Crises and the Origins of Regimes*, pp. 31–9.
21   It is not coincidental that these salient cases of both objective and subjective crises involve international conjunctures (rather than domestic political or economic upheavals): the stakes are high, the outcomes (war or peace) are often starkly binary, and the resolution, one way or the other, tends to come quickly. Domestic upheavals are likely to be more messy, protracted and even indecisive.
22   A rare instance in which I can draw upon distant personal memory.
23   Dobry, *Sociologie des Crises Politiques*, p. 14, offers, as a 'good provisional definition' of (domestic, political) crisis, 'those social processes which lead to (*aboutissant à*), or are capable of leading to (*susceptibles d'aboutir à*) ruptures in the functioning of political institutions'. So, a crisis must contain the potential for 'rupture', even if that potential is not fulfilled (e.g., Cuba) or, in the case of Munich, is postponed.
24   Robert Gildea, *Children of the Revolution: The French 1799–1914* (London, 2009), pp. 260–5.
25   Lewis Namier, '1848: Seed-plot of History', in *Vanished Supremacies: Essays on European History* (New York, 1963), pp. 21–30; though, as the title of the essay suggests, the 'seed-plot'

fulfilled their critical potential: the fall of the Bastille (1789); the overthrow and murder of President Francisco Madero in Mexico (1913); the Bolshevik seizure of power (1917); the March on Rome (1922); the Marco Polo bridge incident in northern China (1937).

There are, in contrast, fictitious crises, by which I mean widespread fears that are baseless or hugely exaggerated.[26] The Grande Peur during the French Revolution would be a classic example: the common people feared violent reprisals from an army of marauding royalists, but no such army existed.[27] Pogroms and other xenophobic massacres have often involved similar 'moral panics' – fear and outrage provoked by scare stories and stereotyping.[28] Slave societies, perhaps for obvious reasons, seem to be particularly prone to these panics (on the part of both the slaves and, a fortiori, the masters).[29] Nor should we exonerate modern liberal-democratic states: in the UK we have witnessed both minor and not-so-minor examples of crisis-driven policy premised on misconceptions, illusions and scare-mongering.[30] Indeed, it has

---

of 1848 was far from inconsequential and its consequences were not purely negative (i.e., some seeds sprouted, not all the shoots were trampled underfoot by the boots of reaction): see Roman Szporluk, 'The Making of the Modern Ukraine: The Western Dimension', Harvard Ukrainian Studies, XXV, 1/2 (2001), pp. 57–8, which dismisses the quote itself as a 'tired cliché'. Dobry, Sociologie des Crises Politiques, p. 79, offers an alternative formulation: 'moments when history hesitates', which he attributes to Le Roy Ladurie, though I could not find this phrase in the original.

26   Compare Dobry's 'crise autistique', Sociologie des Crises Politiques, p. 196.

27   Georges Lefebvre, The Great Fear of 1789 (New York, 1973).

28   For example, the violent anti-Semitism of the Crusades: Norman Cohn, The Pursuit of the Millennium (London, 1962), chap. 3. More recent British 'moral panics' may be mild in comparison; but they also involved 'exaggerating grossly the seriousness of events' in order to produce alarm and outrage (in this case, regarding youth violence and alleged 'riots'): Stanley Cohen, Folk Devils and Moral Panics (St Albans, 1973), p. 31.

29   Steve Hahn, '"Extravagant Expectations" of Freedom: Rumour, Political Struggle and the Christmas Insurrection Scare of 1865 in the American South', Past & Present, 157 (1997), pp. 122–58; Robert L. Paquette, Sugar is Made with Blood. The Conspiracy of La Escalera and the Conflict between Empires over Slavery in Cuba (Middletown, 1988). Paquette shows – contra some historians – that there was a serious challenge to the Cuban plantocracy (i.e., the rebellion was not a complete fabrication); but the authorities exaggerated the scale and severity of the threat, thus justifying draconian repression. A similar pattern – fear, hyperbole and savage repression – was evident in the 1932 massacre of Indians and leftists in El Salvador – which, though not a slave society, was similarly afflicted by severe class and ethnic tensions: Thomas P. Anderson, Matanza: El Salvador's Communist Revolt of 1932 (Lincoln, 1971).

30   A fairly minor example would be Chancellor Denis Healey abruptly going to the IMF for an unnecessary loan in 1976; a not-so-minor one would be the Weapons of Mass Destruction supposedly stashed in Iraq, which became the (official) casus belli of the Iraq invasion in 2003. The latter case is, of course, open to two interpretations: that the authorities, from Tony Blair down, genuinely believed in the threat and, 'in good faith', turned a misconceived crisis into decisive – many would say disastrous – war. Or they knew what they were doing and, in very bad faith, successfully deployed official misinformation to pursue a policy that they espoused for quite different reasons. A similar mixture of motivations – genuine overreaction as against

recently been argued that the combined influence of the security services, the state and the (allied) media can generate fears – a sense of crisis – out of proportion to any actual threat (statistical illiteracy on the part of the public plays a part, of course).[31]

We therefore need, I think, a category of fictitious or contrived or, at the very least, hyperbolic crises: those in which widespread fears are out of proportion to any objective threat. And we might wish to consider how far, in 'critical' situations of this kind, it is indeed possible to fool most of the people most of the time.[32] Does the 'wisdom of crowds' kick in, so that the fictitious/contrived/hyperbolic crisis blows over? Or can such crises lead to major changes, decisive forks in the trajectory of history? If so, fictitious crises, the product of error or deliberate obfuscation or both, can have major, even momentous, consequences. This becomes possible, of course, because 'crisis', as an emic term, denotes a public mood, a collective sentiment.

Two further questions follow. First, how prevalent must the mood be? No doubt in all societies there are minorities who, whatever the 'reality', see 'crisis' looming. We can leave aside those suffering 'personal crises' (perhaps the most common usage of the term in today's media), since these do not add up to a collective or public mood: they are individualised crises, relating to individual predicaments, and they probably do not correlate (positively) with public moods. Indeed, there are examples when the correlation, if it exists,

---

devious hype – is apparent in other cases, such as the slave and peasant rebellions mentioned above. At the time of the Munich crisis, the British authorities misconceived and greatly exaggerated the threat (to life) of aerial bombing; at the same time, it has been suggested, they deliberately stoked the fears of ordinary people: A.J.P. Taylor, *English History, 1914–45* (Harmondsworth, 1973), pp. 528, 535–6.

31 On statistical illiteracy, see Stuart Sutherland, *Irrationality* (London, 1992), chap. 5. David L. Altheide, 'Notes Towards a Politics of Fear', *Journal for Crime, Media and Conflict*, 1 (2003), pp. 37–54, argues that – in the USA, at least – 'the politics of fear is a dominant motif for news and popular culture', leading to 'the seemingly easy public acceptance of governmental proposals to expand surveillance and social control'; in this, 9/11 accelerated a trend evident at least as early as the 1980s, even though – objectively – 'we enjoy unprecedented levels of health, safety and life expectancy'.

32 Dogan and Higley, 'Conclusion', in *Elites, Crises and Regimes*, pp. 238–9, are open to the notion of subjective (emic) crises, but place great faith in the wisdom – and honesty? – of politicians who, they say, are discerning in their evaluation of crises and, whatever their casual rhetoric, know what is really going on; therefore, 'actors' perceptions (of events) ... coincide with the perception of outside observers much more than the etic/emic distinction implies'. I am not persuaded, but then I am a historian, while Dogan and Higley are political sociologists; thus, intellectual dispositions aside, they tend to deal with contemporary actors, for whom, perhaps, the etic/emic distinction is less pronounced. On the other hand, another political scientist/sociologist, Dobry, *Sociologie des Crises Politiques*, p. 23, argues that 'reality ... gives rise to misperceptions' and, especially 'in the conjunctures which interest us' (that is, political crises), '"adequate" perceptions are very rare' ('les perceptions "adequates" soient d'une fréquence très limitée').

appears to be negative.[33] But collective moods, relating to public concerns (such as revolts, revolutions, natural disasters, political upheavals, economic slumps, famines, epidemics, wars and 'rumours of wars') are another matter. Given the importance of subjective perceptions in the creation of 'crisis', it would be helpful to know what the public thinks, and what proportion of the public feels itself in the grip of crisis. After all, if it is no more than a handful of cranks on a hilltop awaiting the end of the world, it is no real crisis. The Jonestown massacre of 1978 was a crisis and a tragedy for the members of the cult, but it was hardly a collective crisis for either the USA or Guyana.

Unfortunately, when it comes to history, such questions of mood are notoriously difficult to answer, as I admit when I come to my case study. Indeed, even in this day and age, when opinion polls are both sophisticated and extensive, it is not clear that they provide unimpeachable answers to questions that are, as in this case, rather open-ended and nebulous. Polls can often tell us specifically whom voters will choose in an imminent election, but broad questions relating to 'political culture' and its components (such as 'trust' or 'legitimacy') are another matter.[34] And, in fact, 'crisis' rarely enters into the questionnaires (that I am aware of); the closest would be questions that ask about radical regime change (e.g., authoritarian versus democratic systems). Of course, people can say whether they are happy or hopeful, but that may not help much.[35] And, of course, polls are relatively recent additions to the historian's armoury; in the case I know best, Mexico, they begin to surface, very sporadically (and, I suspect, unreliably) in the 1940s; they do not become seriously useful until the 1960s; and only since the 1980s have they become common and – at least for specific electoral purposes – fairly reliable. (The chronology for other countries would, I assume, be very roughly similar, with the USA ahead of the pack by several years.)

As a result, generalisations about public mood are, for the vast sweep of human history, based on anecdotal evidence, which often means (i) generalising from particular cases and (ii) inferring mood from action. Both

33 There is a large literature on suicide in relation to social trends, such as interpersonal violence, including murder or civil war. Some negative correlations catch the eye: Finland, a relatively peaceful country, has, like the other Baltic states, very high figures of suicide, as does Denmark; while Texas, for example, ranks low in the US suicide table. See José Manoel Bertolote and Alexandra Fleischmann, 'A Global Perspective in the Epidemiology of Suicide', *Suicidologi*, 7/2 (2002), available at http://asp.info/pdf/papers/Bertolote.pdf.

34 Alan Knight, 'Polls, Political Culture and Democracy: A Heretical Historical Look', in Roderic Ai Camp (ed.), *Citizen Views of Democracy in Latin America* (Pittsburgh, 2001), pp. 230–2.

35 Polls in Mexico (the country I study most) are affected by the so-called 'Cantinflas factor' (named after the popular Chaplinesque movie star of that name): even when times are bad – and they have been very bad at several junctures in recent Mexican history – respondents tend to consider themselves happy, since they manage to insulate individual or familial feelings from collective national problems.

approaches are valid and can yield convincing results in certain circumstances. Lefebvre, I think, shows that the Grande Peur was widespread and genuine. We cannot say what percentage of the French population were fearful (and, even if there had been painstaking pollsters in 1789, would they have given us a better answer? After all, in times of crisis polling may be difficult and even dangerous).[36] Still less can we calibrate the degree of fear (are you [i] somewhat fearful [ii] very fearful or [iii] terrified out of your wits?). But we can safely conclude that there was sufficient fear across a sufficiently wide swathe of French territory to provoke widespread, consequential popular reactions; and reactions are, in a sense, better evidence than one-off replies to pollsters' questions, since they mean that the fearful put their money – or their pitchforks and cudgels – where their mouth is. The fear was real and compelling. And, as Lefebvre shows, it is possible to go further and track the progress of the fear (how it spread from place to place) and to note which regions and which groups were most susceptible.[37] So, we can say something about both the dynamics and the scope of the fear (or crisis).

Most of the history of popular collective action – a boom topic at least since the 1960s – takes this approach. It studies actions: food riots, strikes, uprisings, revolutions. These actions are, of course, accompanied by statements – some quite clear and articulate – which voice grievances and may thus communicate something of the popular mood. However, as James Scott persuasively points out, such statements cannot be taken at face value, since the 'weak' may deliberately dissimulate, not least by telling their superiors what they want to hear (especially when the weak are being hauled before a hostile court).[38] In such situations, speaking 'truth to power' is seriously risky.

That said, we can, on the basis of both actions and (sometimes) statements, draw tentative conclusions concerning perceptions of crisis. Thus, I have argued elsewhere, there is a big difference between a one-off riot in an isolated Mexican village in the (fairly tranquil) early eighteenth century – which could be called 'business-as-usual', in the form of 'negotiation-by-riot'[39] – and a concatenation of riots in several villages during the War of Independence after 1810, when the Colony was experiencing huge political, social and

36 The 1921 census in Mexico, coming after a decade of civil war, is widely reckoned to have substantially undercounted the population; a historical antipathy to officials and outsiders who came asking questions was compounded by fears of brigandage, extortion and forced military recruitment.

37 Lefebvre, *The Great Fear of 1789*, part 3.

38 James Scott, *Domination and the Arts of Resistance: Hidden Transcripts* (New Haven, 1990).

39 The notion of 'negotiation-by-riot' goes back to Hobsbawm's seminal work on popular protest: see E.J. Hobsbawm, *Primitive Rebels* (Manchester, 1974), p. 111. For a recent example: John Bohstedt, *The Politics of Provisions: Food Riots, Moral Economy and Market Transition in England, 1550–1850* (Farnham, 2010), p. 162.

ethnic upheaval.[40] What happens in a particular community may look and even sound somewhat similar (the grievances are often local, the terminology may be nostalgic and the usual suspects may be involved), but the role, of both rioters and authorities, is different, because the context is different; after 1810 it is no longer 'business-as-usual', but, rather, the 'world-turned-upside-down'. Horizons expand (for better or worse); new hopes and fears are born; and, soon, ideology and discourse catch up with action on the ground.[41] The sequence of events meets the several putative criteria of crisis: the sequence is rapid and it involves, and is seen to involve, high stakes; it is also violent and surprising.[42]

Note that this sequence is rather different from that envisaged by many analysts of popular protest, especially some political sociologists, who often posit initial *ideational* dispositions leading to action.[43] Yet, in the absence of proof of those prior dispositions (there being no polls and often little by way of reliable *vox populi* evidence) the dispositions are in fact inferred from the actions, so the argument suffers from circularity (as Dobry points out).[44] To put it crudely, we know these people were seriously disgruntled (in more refined academic discourse, they suffered 'relative deprivation' or 'status anxiety') because they proceeded to run the local landlord out of town, burn the chateau/courthouse or lynch the tax collector. That is pretty good evidence – more eloquent than a tick in a pollster's box. Of course, it tends to privilege violent, eye-catching incidents, at the expense of the more discreet 'weapons of the weak', which are harder to discern, especially for the historian. But, since we are dealing with 'crisis', this may well be appropriate. Indeed, we could suggest that one feature of crisis, especially serious, consequential, crisis (crisis *'aboutissant ... à des ruptures dans le fonctionnement des institutions politiques'*),[45] is that the 'weapons of the weak' – flight, lying, evasion, discreet footdragging – give way to boldly overt forms of protest and resistance, which subvert the status quo ante.[46]

The second and final point to raise is to ask whether there can be 'etic'

40   Alan Knight and Eric Van Young, *En torno a la otra rebelión* (Mexico, 2007).

41   Peter F. Guardino, *Peasants, Politics and the Formation of Mexico's National State: Guerrero, 1800–57* (Stanford, 1996) and the same author's *Time of Liberty: Popular Political Culture in Oaxaca, 1750–1850* (Durham, NC, 2005) convincingly describe such a transformation in late colonial and early independent Mexico.

42   Harking back to previous definitions, I take the first two criteria to be common or consensual, the second two to be optional, or contested.

43   Ted Robert Gurr, *Why Men Rebel* (Princeton, 1970); James C. Davies, *When Men Revolt and Why* (New York, 1971). Note that women did not have much to do with revolts in the 1970s.

44   Dobry, *Sociologie des Crises Politiques*, p. 54.

45   Ibid., p.14.

46   Alan Knight, 'Weapons and Arches in the Mexican Revolutionary Landscape', in Gilbert M. Joseph and Daniel Nugent (eds), *Everyday Forms of State Formation. Revolution and the Negotiation of Rule in Modern Mexico* (Durham, NC, 1994), pp. 34–6.

(objective) crises that entirely escape the ('emic') perception of historical actors – the mirror image of 'contrived' crises, in which non-events are turned into major matters of public concern.[47] Can you have a crisis which no one – or which very few people – perceive as a crisis? Again, we can discard a few cranks and heretics whom no one listens to but who, one ill-omened day, may be proven correct in their constant jeremiads.[48] In my view, for a crisis to be a crisis – to correspond to the common and reasonable meaning of the term – there must be a fairly widespread *perception* of crisis, that is, of decisive, destabilising change, usually of a negative kind. Of course, this perception may lag behind objective events. Contrary to the febrile/pathological model – which identifies mounting fever leading to complete prostration[49] – some revolutions have come as sudden surprises, while plenty of lesser revolts have also been bolts from the blue. Crisis has struck unexpectedly, piercing a veil of cosy complacency. The outbreak of the Mexican Revolution in late 1910 was such a crisis: only during the winter of 1910–11 did the sclerotic regime of Porfirio Díaz, along with its admirers and acolytes, wake up to the fact that a serious armed challenge had emerged and that the regime therefore faced a real threat, thus a real crisis, which soon proved fatal.[50] The Iranian Revolution of 1979 and the implosion of the Soviet Union and its Eastern European client-states also seem to have happened suddenly, without displaying mounting febrile symptoms or eliciting expert diagnoses of imminent demise.

I would conclude from these cases that there are crises that sneak up on unsuspecting publics and their masters; when, if you like, the objective tensions and contradictions, thus far concealed or denied, break to the surface and the public mood – suddenly but belatedly – perceives a crisis, *ex post facto*. However, if, in the face of tensions and contradictions (conditions which, after all, every country, community and organisation experiences),[51]

---

47   Dobry, *Sociologie des Crises Politiques*, p. 196, mentions 'latent crises', which seem roughly to fit the bill; but the point is not developed. Nor have I encountered any focused discussion of this point in the 'crisis' literature I have looked at.

48   We could call this the 'Private Frazer syndrome', Frazer's catchphrase – in the BBC sitcom *Dad's Army* – famously being: 'we're doomed'. I have tried, without success, to think of notable historical counterparts of Private Frazer. Cassandra, of course, does not fit, because her grim prophecies – though they went unheeded – were in fact correct.

49   Crane Brinton, *The Anatomy of Revolution* (New York, 1968).

50   Friedrich Katz, *The Secret War in Mexico* (Chicago, 1981), p. 3.

51   Dobry, *Sociologie des Crises Politiques*, p. 135, following Flanagan, offers a schematic hierarchy of social 'polarisation' involving five levels: from the bottom up, 'business as usual', 'managed tensions', 'crisis and confrontation', 'organized violence and Revolution', and 'anarchy [and the] dissolution of the polity'. Clearly, the levels merge into each other: it could be argued that 'business as usual' involves 'managing tensions', while 'Revolution' is a more extreme subset of 'crisis'; 'Revolution' also involves – to varying degrees – the 'dissolution of the polity'. Thus, we have a continuum, not a step-ladder. The greater problem is knowing how to measure these different conditions.

most people carry on regardless, blithely ignoring, discounting or 'internal-ising' those conditions, then it becomes difficult to speak meaningfully of 'crisis'. To that extent, a subjective 'emic' dimension is essential. But, as I have said, we lack survey data on which to measure this dimension, so we will often have to rest content with reasonable inference, based on scattered evidence: an objective crisis of such-and-such proportions, such as the Great Depression of the 1930s, *must* have registered as 'critical' in the eyes of many historical actors, even if their perceptions lagged behind events and the proof of those perceptions is patchy.[52]

So, to sum up these scattered thoughts: unlike many phenomena in history that we study, 'crisis' involves a subjective (emic) perception on the part of historical actors, without which we cannot speak of 'crisis', or we risk devaluing or debauching the term. In this, 'crisis' is like 'nationalism', but unlike 'industrialisation'. However, we may distinguish between 'objective' crises, in which events run ahead of the public mood and perceptions of crisis lag behind; and 'subjective' or 'fictitious' crises, in which the crisis mood is spun out of the ether, on the basis of ('in good faith') misperceptions and/or ('in bad faith') misinformation. In each case, it is desirable, if often difficult, to try to assess who perceives the crisis – a prescient (or deluded or devious) minority, or the people at large; and to trace, as Lefebvre does for the Grande Peur, the dynamics of crisis perception and transmission.

In all this, there is a presumption, I think, that the chain of events is of limited length. A lot happens in a short space of time. How short? I doubt that a fixed rule can be usefully stated, but, like Dogan and Higley, I would suggest that it is, at most, a matter of a few months or years. And I would repeat: the timescale will vary depending on whether we are dealing with fast-moving political or international crises, somewhat more sluggish economic crises or, slowest of all, socio-demographic crises. A very crude metric might be to suggest that the first could involve days or weeks (a week being 'a long time in politics'), the second could stretch to months and the third to years. One reason for insisting on the (relative) brevity of crises is that if crises are hugely protracted – recall Carr's twenty-year crisis or the 'general crisis' of the seventeenth century (perhaps also the eleventh) – they risk losing their 'critical' quality. 'Crisis' becomes a feature of 'normal', if difficult, life.[53] But then life is often difficult.

---

52   There is a degree of circularity in this argument (of the kind that underpins, for example, Davies's 'J curve' thesis, whereby subjective notions are inferred from overt actions). However, the inferences, in this case, are based on some pretty solid causal assumptions (reliable 'covering laws', we might say): that, for example, lay-offs and widespread unemployment, especially in the absence of social security, lead to hardship, discontent and – here comes the overt action – collective protest.

53   It would, of course, be possible to see the seventeenth century, for example, as a distinctive period characterised by structural problems and tensions (including politico-religious conflict,

Finally, we can also distinguish between crises that are truly consequential, which provoke major historical changes (such as France, 1789; Mexico, 1910; Europe, 1914; Russia, 1917; Europe, 1939) and those that, for all their 'critical' appearance, leave no such mark on the great scheme of things – the 'turning points when history failed to turn' (Europe 1848; perhaps also Europe 1968). Of course, 'failing to turn' is a matter of historical consequence, since it marks a major fork in the historical road, at which radical change was avoided and the status quo roughly prevailed; but it is usual to stress the significance of *positive* causality – the war or revolution that *does* happen, not the one that is averted. So, Munich is a different sort of crisis from 1914 or 1939. The Cuban missile crisis had some positive consequences, especially for Cuba, but by far the biggest was the negative one: the world was not incinerated.

II

I now make an abrupt switch to the empirical focus of this chapter: the Great Depression of the 1930s and its impact on the Americas.[54] I shall do this in a fairly schematic way, with scant narrative and a good deal of analytical summation, which may facilitate some comparisons.

First, the crisis in question was economic and exogenous. It involved a sharp decline in demand for Latin American products, as both prices and export volume contracted, on average, by over half.[55] This was coupled with a withdrawal of US capital and credit: a somewhat novel destabilising factor, since, in previous decades, 'metropolitan' recessions (which chiefly meant European and British recessions) had not resulted in capital flight, British export of capital to Latin American being counter-cyclical, whereas that of

major wars, rising state spending and ensuing fiscal confrontations); these would be manifested in sporadic moments of crisis, more severe and frequent in some countries than others: Niels Steensgaard, 'The Seventeenth-Century Crisis', in Parker and Smith, *The General Crisis of the Seventeenth Century*, pp. 26–56, offers a good resumé. Socio-demographic slumps – Europe in the fourteenth century, the Americas in the sixteenth – would also involve sudden bouts of high mortality, caused by specific epidemics, interspersed by longer periods of incremental ('non-critical') demographic change: Scott L. Waugh, *England in the Reign of Edward III* (Cambridge, 1991), pp. 85–7; Alchon, *A Pest in the Land*, pp. 69, 76, 85, 95.

54 What follows is a much abbreviated and tailored version of Alan Knight, 'The Great Depression in Latin America: An Overview', in Paulo Drinot and Alan Knight (eds), *The Great Depression in Latin America* (Durham, NC, 2014), pp. 276–339.

55 Victor Bulmer-Thomas, *The Economic History of Latin America since Independence* (Cambridge, 1994), p. 197, gives an aggregate fall in the purchasing power of Latin American exports, between 1928 and 1932, of 57%. Chile suffered the steepest fall: 83%, which contributed to a decline in GDP of 46%.

the USA tended to be pro-cyclical.[56] Unlike Britain, the USA was also fond of agricultural protection: hence the ill-advised Hawley–Smoot tariff of 1930.[57]

Latin America had been increasingly integrated into global markets during the later nineteenth century and, as the war of 1914–18 had shown, external shocks could be severe.[58] Economies that had once been struck by natural disasters, crop failures and Malthusian crises – all, in their different way, endogenous – were now vulnerable to a new type of exogenous crisis, a market and monetary crisis (such as the Wall Street crash and its consequences), which was the price to pay for global integration and the 'dependency' that this produced.[59] Large subsistence sectors still existed in several Latin American countries, as I shall note, and those sectors were, to some degree, cushioned against the worst consequences of the global economic crisis. But they were shrinking (and it would be a mistake to conflate 'rural' with 'subsistence').

The crisis was economic in that it derived from serious failings in the US economy, aggravated by US policy (we need not get involved in the thorny question of exactly which failings, what their causes were, and how policy-makers responded or should have responded).[60] And the transmission belt was economic too: the loss of demand for Latin American exports and the repatriation of US capital. There were no immediate political causes in Latin America, where a diversity of regimes and policies prevailed but, of course, there were rapid and sometimes profound political consequences (as I later suggest).

We should note, however, a systemic, global factor, which derived from the First World War: the overproduction of primary products – wheat and sugar were two key examples – which the War had stimulated and which the so-called 'return to normalcy' of the 1920s had never resolved.[61] Through the later 1920s, well before the 1929 crash, primary product prices were stagnant or falling. Thus, for several Latin American economies, export dynamism was

---

56 Though the bull market on Wall Street had also sucked capital from Latin America in 1927–29. On the fundamental significance of American versus British financial hegemony, see Charles Kindleberger, *The World in Depression: 1929–39* (London, 1973), pp. 288–305.

57 William E. Leuchtenberg, *The Perils of Prosperity, 1914–32* (Chicago, 1958), pp. 109–10.

58 Bill Albert, *South America and the First World War: The Impact of the War on Brazil, Argentina, Peru and Chile* (Cambridge, 1988), focuses on the larger economies (apart from Mexico, which was then mired in revolution anyway).

59 Elsewhere in the 'third world' this transition was less pronounced: 'the depression had much less effect [in Asia] ... than a monsoon failure would have done': A.J.H. Latham, *The Depression and the Developing World, 1914–39* (London, 1983), p. 185.

60 I have found Peter Temin, *Did Monetary Forces Cause the Great Depression?* (New York, 1976) and Michael A. Bernstein, *The Great Depression. Delayed Recovery and Economic Change in America, 1929–39* (Cambridge, 1987), particularly useful.

61 Derek H. Aldcroft, *From Versailles to Wall Street, 1919–29* (London, 1977), pp. 226–7; Bill Albert and Adrian Graves (eds), *The World Sugar Economy in War and Depression, 1914–40* (London, 1988).

lost well before 1929. For them, the Depression did not bring a sudden end to a bonanza, as it did in the USA; rather, it sent flatlining export economies into a tailspin. Compared with the USA, therefore, the shock was less severe; it was a crisis, for sure, but of less depth and, as we shall see, of shorter duration.[62]

The severity of the fall varied according to several factors, and the diversity of the Latin American economies offers good scope for comparative analysis. In terms of the external shock, a key question was a country's export basket and how it fared in the famous 'commodity lottery' of the 1930s.[63] The worst-case scenario was to be highly dependent on a single export for which demand slumped: Cuban sugar and Chilean copper were the best (that is, worst) examples. All primary product exports fared badly (and all Latin American exports were of this kind), but some did better than sugar or copper. Wheat prices had been weak for years but, compared with an industrial mineral like copper, demand was less elastic. Coffee prices slumped, but Brazil was in the unusual position of being able to curb production in order to bolster prices, to its own advantage, and also to the advantage of 'free-riders' like Colombia.[64] Silver suffered less than industrial metals, thanks to US price supports and, in the case of Mexico, to Washington's awareness that a stable and revived Mexico was in the USA's geopolitical interests.[65] Much the best ticket in the commodity lottery was oil, demand for which remained buoyant, which meant that Venezuela suffered no external shock at all. Countries highly dependent on a single export (e.g., Chile, Cuba) were particularly vulnerable; those with a more diverse basket of exports – such as Peru and Mexico – fared rather better.

An ancillary factor was what might be called 'global significant others'. Intra-Latin American trade being small, most Latin American exports went to Europe or the USA. The Depression came at a time when the USA was expanding at the expense of Europe, especially Britain (the First World

62   Thus, the Brazilian economy recovered pre-1929 levels by 1933, the Mexican by 1934 and Argentinian by 1935. In the USA, the economy had nearly (96%) recovered it pre-1929 peak by 1937, only to hit the 'double-dip' of the 'Roosevelt recession' (when GDP fell a further 4%): see Robert Higgs, *Depression, War and Cold War* (Oxford, 2006), p. 6. The US economy thus lost about a decade of growth, a (negative) record probably equalled, in Latin America, only by Chile and possibly Cuba. The Latin America data are take from several sources, principally the Oxford Latin American Economic History Database, at http://oxlad.qeh.ox.ac.uk.

63   Carlos Díaz Alejandro, 'América Latina en los años treinta', in Rosemary Thorp (ed.), *América Latina en los años treinta. El papel de la periferia en la crisis mundial* (México, 1988), p. 34.

64   Frank Safford and Marco Palacios, *Colombia. Fragmented Land, Divided Society* (New York, 2002), p. 275. Similarly, Peruvian cotton could, to some extent, free-ride on US price supports: Rosemary Thorp and Geoffrey Bertram, *Peru 1890–1977. Growth and Policy in an Open Economy* (London, 1978), pp. 175–6.

65   John Morton Blum, *From the Morgenthau Diaries. Years of Crisis, 1928–1938* (Boston, MA, 1959), pp. 494–5.

War again played a part, rapidly accelerating pre-1914 trends). As already mentioned, this had consequences for capital flows (American export of capital tending to be pro-cyclical, unlike Britain's); but it also affected exports. Mexico and Peru benefited from US price supports (for silver and cotton respectively); but Cuba suffered from US agricultural protection and the relatively harsh terms of the US–Cuban Reciprocity Treaty of 1934.[66] But Cuba had nowhere else to turn. Argentina was tied to the British market in comparable fashion but the Roca–Runciman agreement of 1933 (which made Argentina an 'honorary member of the British empire') was arguably a better deal (in part because Britain made concessions in order to protect its extensive interests in Argentine railways and public utilities).[67]

Turning to domestic economic factors, two were crucial in determining the scale and character of the Depression. First, some countries possessed large peasant/subsistence sectors, which could soak up surplus labour in times of recession and unemployment.[68] The unemployed and destitute could, in the Mexican phrase, 'return to the quelite' – literally, survive on edible wild plants.[69] There is good evidence of the subsistence cushion softening the blow in (roughly) Mesoamerica (Mexico, Guatemala, Nicaragua) and Andean America (Peru, Colombia).[70] Some governments, indeed, set out to expand the subsistence sector by means of land reform, especially in Mexico.[71] On the

66   Hugh Thomas, *Cuba or The Pursuit of Freedom* (London, 1971), pp. 693–5.

67   Peter Alhadeff, 'Dependency, Historiography and Objections to the Roca Pact', in Christopher Abel and Colin M. Lewis (eds), *Latin America, Economic Imperialism and the State* (London, 1985), pp. 368–78.

68   State social security was minimal in Latin America during the 1930s. In Argentina – among the more prosperous and 'advanced' societies – a law creating a National Board to Combat Unemployment was (belatedly) proposed in 1933, but it aroused little interest and appears to have had no impact. In part, this was because unemployment stood at less than 6% of the labour force: Peter Alhadeff, 'Public Finance and the Economy in Argentina, Australia and Canada During the Depression of the 1930s', in D.C.M. Platt and Guido di Tella (eds), *Argentina, Australia and Canada. Studies in Comparative Development, 1870–1965* (London, 1985), pp. 164–6.

69   Victor L. Urquidi, *Otro siglo perdido. Las políticas de desarrollo en América Latina (1930–2005)* (Mexico, 2005), p. 71. Quelite is a generic name for several wild spinach-like plants, which can be stewed and eaten.

70   For example, on the Atlantic coast of Colombia, banana workers who were laid off 'moved onto idle United Fruit Company properties, cleared small fields and planted foodcrops': Catherine LeGrand, *Frontier Expansion and Peasant Protest in Colombia, 1830–1936* (Albuquerque, 1986), p. 115. Peruvian peasants also retreated into subsistence, although, consonant with Chayanov's thesis, this involved systematically exploiting unpaid family labour: Vincent C. Pelosi, *Peasants on Plantations. Subaltern Strategies of Labor Resistance in the Pisco Valley, Peru* (Durham, NC, 1999), pp. 138–49.

71   After a lull in 1930–32, land reform picked up in Mexico and reached a peak under Lázaro Cárdenas (1934–40), when 18 million hectares were distributed. This extensive and precocious reform derived from the Mexican Revolution of 1910 and its powerful agrarian impulse; nevertheless, the Depression had a decisive effect by way of reviving and radicalising the programme. It is worth recalling that the FDR administration in the USA also flirted with the notion of

other hand, in societies – including rural societies – where proletarianisation had advanced more rapidly and completely, the subsistence cushion had largely lost its stuffing and the result was serious unemployment, destitution and, sometimes, militant protest: Chile would be a clear example, along with Cuba and El Salvador.[72]

The reverse side of the coin was industrialisation. The major Latin American economies already possessed significant industrial sectors, especially in textiles; in several cases, the decade of the 1890s had been – as in southern Europe – a phase of rapid growth in manufacturing. The First World War, by cutting off foreign imports, had spurred further import-substitution industrialisation (ISI), which the Depression now accelerated, especially in the larger countries where the domestic market offered greater incentives: thus, in Argentina, Brazil and Mexico.[73] By contrast, ISI made less progress in countries where the domestic market was small and shallow (e.g., Central America, Paraguay, Ecuador, Bolivia) and/or imports remained more buoyant (Venezuela and, to some extent, Peru). Latin American governments reinforced the process by raising tariffs (emulating governments in the industrialised world); but, again, this was no dramatic U-turn (as sometimes imagined); as in the USA, the Depression served to strengthen previous protectionist trends. But whereas in the USA structural conditions – allied to FDR's inconsistent policy – made industrial recovery difficult, in Latin America the rapid growth of manufacturing, via ('easy') ISI, provided the chief motor of growth, especially in Argentina, Brazil and Mexico.[74]

A final indicator of economic crisis involved labour and migration. Mexico, which had exported migrants to the USA *en masse* since 1910, now faced the repatriation of over 300,000 workers, though the Mexicans repaid the Americans in kind, forcibly expelling Chinese migrants north of the border.[75] This reversal of migration flows proved transient: with the Second

'putting a million families into subsistence farming': John A. Garraty, *The Great Depression* (New York, 1987), p. 131.

72 Simon Collier and William F. Sater, *A History of Chile, 1808–1994* (Cambridge, 1996), p. 221; Barry Carr, 'Mill Occupations and Soviets: The Mobilization of Sugar Workers in Cuba, 1917–33', *Journal of Latin American Studies*, 28/1 (1996), pp. 129–58. There are parallels here with, for example, Turkey and Egypt, where subsistence options were lacking and the state, strapped for cash, raised taxes on the rural poor: Dieter Rothermund, *The Global Impact of the Great Depression, 1929–39* (London, 1996), pp. 80–1.

73 Between 1932 and 1939 manufacturing output rose by 7.3%, 7.6% and 11.9% annually in these three countries (GDP growth, by comparison, was 4.4%, 4.8% and 6.2% respectively): Bulmer-Thomas, *The Economic History of Latin America*, pp. 219, 226.

74 'Easy' ISI was based on relatively cheap and accessible technology (e.g., textile machinery). By contrast, in the – more advanced – USA, the structural obstacles to industrial growth were more formidable: see Bernstein, *The Great Depression*.

75 Abraham Hoffman, *Unwanted Mexican Americans in Great Depression* (Tucson, 1974), chap. 8.

World War and the *bracero* programme, Mexican labour headed *al norte* in even greater numbers. But elsewhere the Depression marked a watershed: the flow of European migrants to the 'neo-Europes' of South America (Argentina, Uruguay and southern Brazil) was halted, never to be resumed. Instead, the labour demands of the factories of Buenos Aires and São Paulo were now met by mass internal migration, which would have major socio-political consequences in the decades to come. The Caribbean also witnessed major reverse migrations, as Jamaicans and Haitians were expelled from Cuba, and Haitians were expelled – and also massacred in large numbers – by the Trujillo government of the Dominican Republic.[76]

If we turn to the politics of the Depression, several points are worth stressing. First, what was, as I have said, an economic and exogenous shock soon had major political repercussions, especially since Latin American states depended heavily on foreign trade taxes and rapidly faced severe shortfalls in revenue. Governments therefore made cuts, which exacerbated the economic contraction (again, they followed global trends). Governments also found it hard to service foreign debts, so the result was a series of defaults, the main exceptions being oil-rich Venezuela (which had no foreign debt) and Argentina, which, cleaving to orthodoxy, continued to service its foreign debt, though at some cost to its domestic economy.[77]

Unable to borrow, thrown back on their domestic resources, the majority of Latin American countries were obliged to improvise. In this, the 1930s were a period of innovation and experiment, much of it successful. While pursuing a tight fiscal policy, the Argentine government – a conservative, 'oligarchic', semi-authoritarian regime – pursued a creatively expansionist monetary policy, which boosted business confidence.[78] In Mexico, too, after a brief period of orthodoxy and austerity, a new Finance Minister, Alberto J. Pani, inaugurated a policy of monetary expansion in 1932, rapidly converting the country from a metallic (silver) to paper currency, thus boosting growth (and, especially, industrialisation).[79] Mexico's early espousal of (proto-?)Keynesian

---

76 Robert Lee Turits, *Foundations of Despotism. Peasants, the Trujillo Regime and Modernity in Dominican History* (Stanford, 2003), pp. 161–80.

77 Carlos Marichal, *A Century of Debt Crises in Latin America: From Independence to the Great Depression, 1820–1930* (Princeton, 1989), p. 204. Honduras, Nicaragua and Haiti, being under US financial tutelage, also did not default.

78 Gerardo della Paolera and Alan M. Taylor, *Straining at the Anchor. The Argentine Currency Board and the Search for Macroeconomic Stability, 1880–1935* (Chicago, 2001), pp. 188–218. As the authors note, Argentina's 'precocious heterodox' approach (p. 202) bore testimony to the emergent influence of economist Raúl Prebisch – who would become a central figure in Latin American economic thinking in subsequent decades – and of the late Silvio Gesell (d.1930), a less celebrated economist, whom Keynes, no less, credited with a rare grasp of proto-Keynesian principles (my phrase, not Keynes's).

79 Enrique Cárdenas, *La industrialización de México durante la gran depresión* (Mexico, 1987).

policies was connected, in two ways, to its prior experience of social revolution: Mexico could not borrow abroad (so monetary heterodoxy carried no immediate penalties in foreign markets) and, we may hypothesise, the revolutionary regime, keen to bolster popular support, was more disposed than many in Latin America to innovate and experiment. Brazil, too, pursued an expansionist policy, not least through the mechanism of the coffee support scheme which, even if not 'Keynesian' in its original conception and rationale, had a similar reflationary effect.[80] A final case of mildly Keynesian policy was Colombia.[81] These countries had in common larger and more diverse economies (i.e., with significant industrial sectors) and governments which, whatever their political complexion, were prepared to innovate.[82] We should note that in no case was economic revival premised on arms spending; indeed, Latin America experienced only one major war in the 1930s, whose connection to the Depression remains moot.[83] The Depression did not, therefore, subvert the region's reputation for being relatively unwarlike.[84]

Proto-Keynesian policy indicated the capacity of some governments to react to the external shock, or crisis, in ways which, though 'reactive',[85] were also creative and innovative. Like FDR, they were prepared to try fresh policy initiatives. But, in contrast, many governments were buffeted by the external storms; thus, the most obvious consequence – and, I would assume, the best indicator of 'crisis', in the political realm – was the successive toppling of administrations and, sometimes, of regimes. There were thirteen coups in Latin America between 1930 and 1934, and a further seven between 1934 and 1940; Ecuador, it is said, experienced fourteen coups in the decade of the

80   Werner Baer, *The Brazilian Economy: Its Growth and Development* (Columbus, 1979), pp. 43–5 (though there is some debate about this).

81   Safford and Palacios, *Colombia*, pp. 289–90.

82   By 'political complexion' I mean the position of a given regime/administration on both a conventional left/right ideological continuum and also a democratic versus authoritarian (that is, institutional) continuum (clearly, I am assuming that these are not identical): thus, the Mexican regime was progressive but undemocratic (in the strict sense), while the Colombian was progressive and democratic; the Argentine regime was neither progressive nor democratic (also in the strict sense). In other words, economic experimentation crossed ideological and institutional boundaries.

83   The Chaco War between Bolivia and Paraguay, 1932–35: see Herbert S. Klein, *Parties and Political Change in Bolivia, 1880–1952* (Cambridge, 1969), pp. 145–98. The connection is moot in the sense that Bolivian President Salamanca may well have seen warfare as a means to distract his people from the impact of the Depression; however, there is scant evidence that, politico-psychological factors aside, war, or preparation for war, boosted the economy, whether in Bolivia, Paraguay or elsewhere in Latin America.

84   In respect of interstate warfare. The armed forces were often used for domestic purposes, of course. However, even when those purposes produced major spikes in military expenditure, that did not necessarily inject demand and dynamism into the economy, in part because military hardware was usually imported (and most soldiers were poorly paid).

85   Díaz Alejandro, 'América Latina en los años treinta', pp. 38, 40.

1930s.[86] The sequence is fairly clear, in schematic fashion: the Depression cut exports, jobs and government revenue; government cutbacks typically exacerbated the contraction; administrations were either voted out of office (thus, there were constitutional changes of administration, as in Colombia in 1930) or were turfed out by force (non-constitutionally); in some cases, the change went beyond that of personnel or party and involved a fundamental change of regime. Frequently, the shift was towards authoritarianism, involving military intervention and the ouster of either representative – even democratic – regimes, as in Argentina and Uruguay or narrow oligarchic, but civilian, regimes, as in Bolivia and much of Central America.[87] Thus historians talk of a 'dictatorial decade'; or, in Central America, of a turn towards 'authoritarian caudillismo'.[88]

However, some political change went in the other direction. In Chile an incumbent military regime was overthrown in 1932 and the crisis ushered in forty-one years of democracy. In Cuba, the Depression also led to the overthrow of an entrenched dictator (Machado) and a rapid – even revolutionary – transition to a more diverse, progressive (but also corrupt and violent) politics. A key factor was the distribution of pre-1930 regimes: the Depression tended to subvert the political status quo, so if the latter was loosely democratic (as in Argentina and Uruguay), the Depression doomed democracy; but if the status quo was civilian/oligarchic (as in Bolivia and Central America), the Depression deposed the oligarchs in favour of an authoritarian military. In Chile, the victim was authoritarianism; democracy – of an initially unstable kind – was the beneficiary.

That said, some broader conclusions can be drawn. It is impossible (for me at least) to assess, comparatively, the subjective sense of 'crisis' that affected Latin America in the early 1930s. Clearly, the external (economic) shock was severe and it had economic and – soon – social and political repercussions: protests, marches, strikes and land seizures. Countries hardest hit, such as Cuba and Chile, were in the van; political reactions, which might reasonably be assumed to stem from a subjective sense of 'crisis', reflected the severity and duration of the economic shock. Cuba narrowly avoided a major social revolution (radical mobilisation was eventually curtailed), but the old dictatorship of Machado fell and the new regime, though imperfectly democratic,

---

86   Paul W. Drake, *Between Tyranny and Anarchy: A History of Democracy in Latin America, 1800–2006* (Stanford, 2009), p. 165; Charles W. Anderson, *Politics and Economic Change in Latin America* (Princeton, 1967), pp. 219–20. It should be remembered, of course, that Latin America (conventionally defined) comprises twenty countries, so the aggregate rate of coups works out at no more than one per country per decade.

87   'Democratic' in this context means effective universal male suffrage; women did not get the vote in Argentina until 1951.

88   Drake, *Between Tyranny and Anarchy*, p. 165; Victor Bulmer-Thomas, *The Political Economy of Central America since 1920* (Cambridge, 1978), p. 67.

embodied reformist, nationalist and populist politics. Chile briefly experienced a 'Socialist Republic' in 1932 and, six years later, elected a popular front government – the only such government to achieve power outside Europe.[89]

But in most cases recovery was fairly rapid (Latin America, we could say, had a 'good' depression, certainly compared with, say, Germany or the USA); and that recovery was in part helped by innovative policies, coupled with the 'natural' recuperative powers of the economies (e.g., in respect of both subsistence agriculture and manufacturing). The prevailing sense of doom and gloom that Overy discerns – and perhaps exaggerates? – in inter-war Britain and Europe has no counterpart in Latin America that I am aware of.[90] Of course, the relative absence of interstate warfare (or the threat of such warfare) was a key factor; but, as I have argued, Latin America's economic experience was also less negative.[91]

The Depression provoked a degree of economic introversion, coupled with enhanced state intervention. The latter did not involve extensive state spending (there was growth, in some countries, but it was quite small and nothing to compare with the hypertrophied *dirigisme* of the post-war decades, especially the 1960s and 1970s). However, spending aside, governments regulated the economy to a greater degree: notably in Cuba, where sugar output was strictly controlled, or in Brazil, where the state intervened in the crucial coffee sector. Central banks augmented their power and, as import duties diminished, modest efforts were made to increase direct taxes, chiefly on income (land usually remained undertaxed). Innovative labour legislation created a new framework for the mediation (or repression) of industrial disputes (in contrast, rural class relations were less affected: only Mexico launched a radical land reform). The Depression helped stimulate more nationalist cultural policies, notably in Vargas's Brazil; and it certainly encouraged regimes to target immigrant communities (such as Mexico's Chinese or, more violently, the Haitians of the Dominican Republic). In almost all these cases, I would argue, the Depression accelerated existing trends (towards protection, direct taxation, labour arbitration, central

---

89 Collier and Sater, *A History of Chile*, pp. 221–34. On the Cuban revolution of 1933 and its aftermath, see Thomas, *Cuba*, chaps 51–8.

90 Richard Overy, *The Morbid Age. Britain and the Crisis of Civilization* (London, 2010). A good read, the book strikes me – an amateur in these Anglocentric matters – as overly dependent on literary/intellectual sources and, of course, its title involves a risky segue from Britain to 'civilization' (which, I hope, would include Latin America). I admit that my take on Latin America may be influenced by my Mexican expertise (the 1930s being, for Mexico, a decade of growth, innovation, reform and redistribution); however, I see no clouds of morbidity hanging over the region as a whole (with some grim but unusual exceptions: the torrid battlefields of the Chaco, the killing fields of El Salvador, 1932, and the bloodstained borderlands of Haiti and the Dominican Republic).

91 Of course, the same could be said of Britain, compared to Germany or the USA.

banking, nationalism or, in Mexico, land reform). It did not create something out of nothing.

This incremental expansion of the role of the state occurred under regimes and administrations of very different ideological hue: radical/populist in Mexico under Cárdenas (1934–40); liberal/progressive under López Pumarejo in Colombia (1934–38); conservative/oligarchical in Argentina during the so-called 'infamous decade' of the 1930s; authoritarian – some would say semi-fascistic – under both the Estado Novo in Brazil after 1937 and the 'military socialist' regime established in Bolivia in 1936. Thus, the Depression tended to augment the power of the state, while encouraging a measure of economic introversion (interestingly, the 1930s were a decade of politico-ideological *extroversión*, as Latin Americans eagerly followed events overseas and were influenced by them: Stalinism and fascism; the Spanish Civil War; the New Deal and Good Neighbor Policy in the USA).

None of the ensuing (economic) changes were, of themselves, revolutionary; they cannot compare to what happened in Cuba after 1959 (or Russia after 1917). Economic change, even when spurred by external shock and 'crisis', tended to be evolutionary – as, perhaps, it had to be, given the way that economies work (they can be quickly devastated, e.g., by war, hyper-inflation or doctrinaire collectivisation, but growth is necessarily incremental, even when rapid). Political change, in contrast, was more skittish and more stochastic. It could be quick and unpredictable. It depended on individual decision-making (such as Daniel Salamanca's decision to launch the Chaco War in 1932; or Enrique Olaya Herrera and Oscar Benavides' contrasting decision *not* to push the Leticia crisis towards all-out war between Colombia and Peru two years later). Political change did not follow any clear common patterns, not least because outcomes depended on the status quo ante, which varied from country to country.[92] The Depression tended to weaken incumbent governments, stimulate opposition and promote political instability; but the outcomes were, to borrow a convenient term of the economists, 'path-dependent', and they were conditioned by peculiar national circumstances – the Mexican Revolution, Brazil's federal system, Argentina's close links to Britain, or Cuba's to the USA.[93]

To put it simply, while the common causes of the crisis were economic, the

92   There is a parallel here with the debt crisis of the 1980s, which also contributed to widespread political instability and regime change in Latin America. It so happened that many of the affected regimes were military and authoritarian, so the net effect was democratising. Some observers too readily jumped to the conclusion that economic liberalisation (another consequence of the crisis) was therefore intimately and necessarily wedded to democracy. Whatever the merits of this – contentious – thesis, a good deal of the outcome was in fact random rather than deterministic.

93   Of course, 'path-dependency' – the economist's grudging tribute to history – often involves a statement of the obvious: what happened at t^1 affects what happens (later) at t^2. We

fallout, especially the political fallout, was highly varied. Economies – hence economic crises and their resolution – follow rough patterns and trends, and are subject to tight constraints. There are only so many ways to grow wheat or manufacture widgets, and then to sell the product in national or international markets. Change demands capital investment, new technology, labour inputs, effective transport and accessible markets. These may vary from case to case, country to country, but the range of variation is necessarily limited (thus, in the 1930s, the USA did not produce coffee and Latin America did not produce battleships). And change did not come overnight (a coffee bush requires four or five years to bear fruit).

Hence, the economic story is usually one of evolution, often of acceleration (or retardation); not sudden U-turns or quantums leaps. Politics, however, allows U-turns and quantum leaps; indeed, we could argue that politicians, especially in 'modern' states, with mobilised 'mass publics', feel obliged to turn and leap, that being their profession and their preference. *Quieta non movere* ('let sleeping dogs lie') may have been Robert Walpole's sage motto, but Walpole did not have mass publics to worry about. Most of his successors have opted for activism, even frenetic activism. Occasionally, as Hirschman has argued, innovation and experiment are needed, especially in 'critical' times; policymakers 'learn by doing'.[94] But such a heuristic approach – which had its successes in 1930s Latin America – needs to be intelligent, flexible and modest, not, to cite Hirschman again, the kind of manic *proyectismo* that affects many political leaders, not least in Latin America.[95]

Thus, we could say, the economic depression of the 1930s spread, like a tsunami, from its US epicentre, crashing against the shoreline of Latin America (and elsewhere). It was a common crisis, exogenous and economic, but its impact was highly variable, depending on the coastline it encountered, some places being more vulnerable, some more accustomed to oceanic buffeting. In general, the consequences were less serious than in other parts of the world. The reactions of the local people also varied: there was protest, leading to enhanced political instability, especially where economic conditions were harsh and governments stuck to counter-productive orthodoxy. Typically, the tidal wave provoked experimental responses, usually involving an acceleration of existing socio-economic trends, rather than radical or revolutionary

(historians) have been exploring 'path-dependency' for ages, just as – like Molière's M. Jourdain – we have been speaking and writing prose.

94 Albert O. Hirschman, *A Bias for Hope. Essays on Development in Latin America* (New Haven, 1971), p. 28.

95 Though usually attributed to Hirschman, who later popularised the term, 'proyectismo' – meaning an irrational attachment to grand transformative projects – seems to have been coined by the agronomist Eyler Simpson, *The Ejido. Mexico's Way Out* (Chapel Hill, 1937), p. 580, who defined it as 'the tendency to spin out of thin air tremendous programs for the accomplishment of anything and everything under the sun'.

innovations. Since these responses sometimes succeeded – in restoring growth, confidence and optimism – Latin America did not live through a 'morbid age' (or decade). Nor did it descend into systemic warfare. One general conclusion might be that Tom Paine exaggerated only somewhat when he declared that crises 'produce as much good as hurt'.[96] More specifically, we could say that most Latin American countries (or peoples, or societies), while undoubtedly confronting economic crisis in the early 1930s, contrived responses that were diverse, innovative and often successful; if they subjectively perceived 'crisis' in their lives, as many no doubt did, a combination of luck (e.g., the commodity lottery), of structural opportunities (such as ISI), and of creative endeavour produced, in most cases, recovery and reform, rather than fascism and warfare.

96   Quoted by Starn, 'Historians and "Crisis"', p. 6.

2

Using the Disaster Cycle in Economic and Social History[1]

JOHN SINGLETON

This chapter introduces the Disaster Management Cycle (DMC) and applies it to three historical cases – Hurricane Katrina, the First World War and the inter-war Depression. The objective is to demonstrate how the DMC could be used by economic and other historians. The case studies, a natural disaster, a global war and a macroeconomic collapse, are chosen to illustrate the versatility of the framework. The first section examines and differentiates between the concepts of crisis and disaster, and asks what constitutes a disaster. The second section discusses the DMC and makes some modifications to the basic framework. The remaining sections discuss the three case studies.

Crisis and disaster

The words crisis and disaster are often used interchangeably in conversation and in the media. At the same time, certain conventions have arisen around their employment to describe costly phenomena in different domains, hence 'natural disaster' but not natural crisis, and 'economic crisis' but rarely economic disaster. This state of affairs is messy and confusing, and the current chapter offers a solution by differentiating between crisis and disaster.

Crisis is defined as a period of heightened danger that poses urgent challenges to decision-makers, while disaster is defined as an event or process that generates very large costs. Disasters typically occur within periods of crisis. The crisis continues while emergency measures are taken to alleviate or respond to the disaster. Crisis is not invariably accompanied by disaster, for

1 The themes in this chapter will be developed in a monograph provisionally entitled *Crises and Disasters, 1900–2010: An Economic Perspective*, to be published by Edward Elgar.

the threat may be averted by good decision-making or luck. Most crises start before the associated disaster, although in some cases – for example, earthquakes – they may arrive simultaneously. A disaster could even begin before anyone is aware of a crisis. It was not until the 1920s that rising mortality from lung cancer became noticeable. The emergence of lung cancer – a previously rare condition – followed an increase in smoking several decades earlier. For there to be a crisis, then, there must be recognition that something is wrong.

Crisis is a phenomenon that does not lend itself to direct measurement. A crisis resolved satisfactorily may soon be forgotten. If a crisis leads to disaster, however, we might have to be content with estimating the size of the disaster. Those involved in a crisis may not know how serious it is until disaster strikes. For example, in late June 1914 it was not at all obvious that the assassination of Archduke Franz Ferdinand would produce a general European war. Measuring disasters is also problematical. Horwich regards a disaster as an event that involves 'a loss of resource value beyond some socially specified level', but does not set a particular level.[2] Barro is more precise, but perhaps too strict, defining a 'rare economic disaster' as one that reduces real GDP per capita by 15 per cent or more.[3] He lists 'economic events (the Great Depression, financial crises), wartime destruction (world wars, nuclear conflicts), natural disasters (tsunamis, hurricanes, earthquakes, asteroid collisions), and epidemics of disease (Black Death, avian flu)', as potential causes of rare economic disasters.[4] In practice, only the First World War, the Depression of the 1930s, the Spanish Civil War, the Second World War, and periods of post-war dislocation, qualify as disasters in Barro's sample of developed economies over the twentieth century.

The Centre for Research in the Epidemiology of Disasters (CRED) sets a much lower bar, defining a disaster as an event that meets one of the following criteria: '10 or more people killed; 100 or more people affected; declaration of a state of emergency; call for international assistance'.[5] By this definition there were 18,000 disasters in the world between 1900 and 2013.[6] CRED puts disasters into seven groups, spanning the natural and technological (including industrial) spheres: biological, climatological, complex, geophysical, hydrological, meteorological and technological. Macroeconomic and financial collapses are excluded, despite the vast costs and disruption they sometimes cause.

---

2   George Horwich, 'Disasters and Market Response', *Cato Journal*, 9 (1990), p. 532.
3   Robert J. Barro, 'Rare Disasters and Asset Markets in the Twentieth Century', *Quarterly Journal of Economics*, 121 (2006), p. 828.
4   Ibid., p. 828.
5   http://www.emdat.be/frequently-asked-questions [accessed 30 September 2013].
6   CRED relies on official sources and information in the public domain, and has not managed to record every disaster; consequently 18,000 is an underestimate.

Except for those working in the narrow field of the economics of natural disasters,[7] most economists struggle to distinguish between disaster and crisis. Nowhere is this more unfortunate than in discussion of 'financial crises'. After the failure of a systemically important bank or group of banks, taxpayers or depositors may endure large losses, while a credit crunch may ripple through the economy destroying jobs and businesses. How could that not be a disaster? Yet the convention is to call it a crisis. In their history of financial folly, Reinhart and Rogoff use 'crisis' rather than 'disaster' when describing episodes, some of which generated economic losses far in excess of most natural disasters.[8] The phenomena they discuss, namely internal and external debt crises, banking crises, currency crises and very high inflation, were indeed crises, for they posed serious challenges to policymakers and other economic actors. Many of these episodes also led to economic disaster. The Depression of the early 1930s, the Japanese crash of the early 1990s and the Asian financial turmoil of the late 1990s, were not just crises – they were disasters too. Another example of terminological difficulty is the chapter on 'Financial Crises' in Oliver and Aldcroft's collection, *Economic Disasters of the Twentieth Century*, which implies that a crisis is a type of disaster.[9] Conceptually, Barro's approach is preferred, for he establishes that a disaster is an event involving heavy loss, whether it originates in the macroeconomic or financial sphere, the natural world, or international conflict.

The Disaster Management Cycle

The DMC offers a framework for examining the relationship between crisis and disaster, and exploring the stages through which disasters evolve. The DMC has been 'influenced by many disciplines such as sociology, geography, psychology, civil defence, public administration and development studies'.[10] Prince's study of the explosion at Halifax, Nova Scotia in 1917, which destroyed much of the city and killed two thousand people, was a pioneering effort to describe how a community experiences and responds to disaster.[11] Three disaster phases were identified in the 1930s by Carr. During the

---

7   Eduardo Cavallo and Ilan Noy, 'The Economics of Natural Disasters: A Survey', *International Review of Environmental and Resource Economics*, 5 (2011), pp. 63–102.
8   Carmen M. Reinhart and Kenneth S. Rogoff, *This Time is Different: Eight Centuries of Financial Folly* (Princeton, 2009).
9   M.J. Oliver, 'Financial Crises', in Michael J. Oliver and Derek H. Aldcroft (eds), *Economic Disasters of the Twentieth Century* (Cheltenham, 2007), pp. 182–235.
10   Christo Coetzee and Dewald van Niekerk, 'Tracking the Evolution of the Disaster Management Cycle: A General System Theory Approach', *Jàmbá*, 4 (2012), pp. 1–9.
11   Samuel H. Prince, *Catastrophe and Social Change* (New York, 1920).

'preliminary or prodromal' period the forces leading to catastrophe build up. The disaster itself – the 'precipitating event' – ushers in the second phase of 'dislocation and disorganization'. The third phase involves 'readjustment and reorganization' on the individual, interactive and cultural levels.[12] Some disasters, for example, floods in Bangladesh, tend to recur, and in the 1970s the concept of the disaster cycle was formulated. Most disasters are preceded by warnings. An initiating or triggering event causes the disaster. Relief, rehabilitation, and reconstruction phases ensue. Finally, new precautions may be taken to prevent or mitigate future disasters. The cycle is completed by another warning.[13]

A DMC of four phases – *mitigation, preparedness, response* and *recovery* – was endorsed by the US National Governors' Association in the late 1970s. Mitigation incorporates measures to reduce the likelihood or scope of disasters, for example, by constructing flood levees. Preparedness involves accumulating emergency supplies and planning for evacuation. The response phase includes attempts to contain the disaster and relieve victims, while the recovery phase concerns the restoration of the stricken area.[14] Neal adds that the disaster phases are functional rather than temporal; activities such as relief and reconstruction overlap; and individuals or groups pass through the cycle at different speeds and experience the phases with varying intensity.[15]

Absent from previous versions of the DMC is a stage devoted to the apportionment of blame, yet this activity accompanies all disasters. A striking example is provided by the L'Aquila earthquake in Italy in 2009. Four seismologists, two engineers and a government official were convicted of manslaughter and jailed. The jury decided that they had failed in their duty to assess the risks to L'Aquila and communicate them to the public.[16] Birkland argues that official disaster reports are often designed to protect powerful actors by shifting blame elsewhere. Such 'fantasy documents' may also give the false impression that action will be taken to prevent further disasters.[17]

Behavioural aspects of the DMC are emphasised by social scientists.

12   Lowell J. Carr, 'Disaster and the Sequence-Pattern Concept of Social Change', *American Journal of Sociology*, 38 (1932), pp. 207–18.

13   A. Baird, P. O'Keefe, K.N. Westgate and B. Wisner, *Towards an Explanation and Reduction of Disaster Proneness*, University of Bradford, Disaster Research Unit, Occasional Paper 11 (1975), p. 42.

14   National Governors' Association, *Emergency Preparedness Project Final Report* (Washington, DC, 1978).

15   David M. Neal, 'Reconsidering the Phases of Disaster', *International Journal of Mass Emergencies and Disasters*, 15 (1997), pp. 239–64.

16   Times Higher Education Reporters, 'Lessons from the L'Aquila Earthquake', *Times Higher Education*, 3 October 2013. URL: http://www.timeshighereducation.co.uk/features/lessons-from-the-laquila-earthquake/2007742.fullarticle [accessed 21 October 2013].

17   Thomas A. Birkland, 'Disasters, Lessons Learned, and Fantasy Documents', *Journal of Contingencies and Crisis Management*, 17 (2009), pp. 146–56.

According to Turner, most disasters are preceded by an incubation phase marked by anomalies that jar with conventional thinking. A precipitating event initiates a crisis (a period of threat and challenge). Disaster may yet be averted if organisations respond creatively, but often they fail. A rescue and salvage stage will commence in the immediate aftermath of disaster, followed by a more reflective period including a thorough investigation of causes.[18] Stein's version has three stages: incubation, the critical period, and the aftermath. The critical period begins when a triggering event occurs that 'in the absence of remedial action, almost invariably leads to disaster'.[19] A key challenge facing actors during the critical period (which includes the impact and emergency response) is how to make sense of what is happening. If events are not understood, it will be difficult to formulate a response. Decision-makers, however, are hampered by uncertainty, ambiguity, and pressure.[20]

Several modifications discussed above are incorporated into the new version of the DMC depicted in Figure 2.1. Whereas the originators of the DMC were interested in providing a guide to disaster management policy, the current chapter is not policy-oriented; rather it focuses on observing patterns in the behaviour of policymakers and other actors. In a sense the cycle begins with reforms taken in the light of a previous disaster (the last phase of the previous cycle). Warnings or danger signals may then be issued, although they may only be recognised in retrospect. Four stages occur within the critical period, which is essentially a time of crisis when decision-makers are challenged to respond to a succession of threats. The triggering event is equivalent to lighting a fuse. It precipitates disaster unless appropriate action is taken. Decision-makers must make sense of the situation and determine how to act. If they make the right decisions then the crisis may be defused before it leads to disaster (or the disaster may at least be rendered less serious). If they make the wrong decisions then disaster unfolds. The implementation of rescue and relief measures completes the critical period. The final phases comprise the attempt to attribute blame, followed by recovery and restoration, and the enactment of measures to mitigate further disasters, including regulatory reform. That the triggering event may not be identified correctly at the time is not a drawback if the DMC is used to explain the evolution of historical processes and not as a template to guide decision-makers.

The DMC, as modified above, has some features in common with work in economics. The financial instability hypothesis of Minsky and Kindleberger is cyclical, and driven in part by misperception of risk on the part of borrowers

18   Barry A. Turner, 'The Organizational and Interorganizational Development of Disasters', *Administrative Science Quarterly*, 21 (1976), pp. 378–97.
19   Mark Stein, 'The Critical Period of Disasters: Insights from Sense-making and Psychoanalytic Theory', *Human Relations*, 57 (2004), p. 1244.
20   Ibid., p. 1251.

Figure 2.1. Revised Disaster Management Cycle

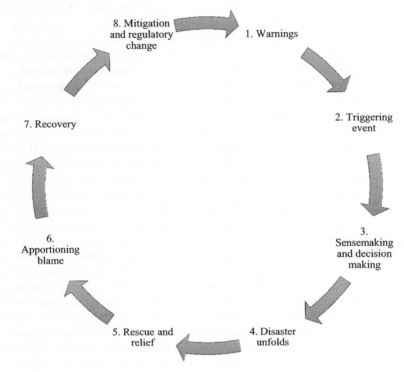

Critical phase: 2, 3, 4, 5
Source: Author's own design

and lenders.[21] The cycle is set off by an exogenous event, which induces more borrowing and lending. If borrowers and lenders become euphoric, credit growth accelerates. Loans are extended to those with no prospect of repaying unless asset prices continue to rise. After a while, borrowers and lenders may become nervous, and credit growth will slow. If an important financial institution fails, panic may ensue, sending asset prices down, and ruining borrowers and lenders. Minsky did not dwell on the reasons for the swings in sentiment that drive the cycle. Kindleberger and Aliber, however, point out that people are constrained by incomplete data, inadequate reasoning power

---

21   Hyman P. Minsky, 'The Financial-Instability Hypothesis', in Charles P. Kindleberger and Jean-Pierre Laffargue (eds), *Financial Crises: Theory, History & Policy* (Cambridge, 1982), pp. 13–39; Charles P. Kindleberger and Robert Z. Aliber, *Manias, Panics, and Crashes*, 6th edn (Basingstoke, 2011).

and changing emotions.[22] They may be carried along by mob psychology, ignoring inconvenient evidence and fearing to express dissent.

The ability of decision-makers to grasp what is happening in the critical period is crucial to disaster management. Karl Weick calls this 'sensemaking', and his approach is particularly germane to the current chapter. Weick discusses the Mann Gulch disaster in 1949. Although small, with only thirteen fatalities, Mann Gulch illustrates how a crisis (or period of heightened threat) can lead to a disaster if poorly managed. A team of smokejumpers became confused when confronted by a forest fire that did not behave as expected. In the midst of a life-threatening crisis, they rejected the advice of a more experienced but unfamiliar member of the squad and panicked. Only three survived.[23] A failure of sensemaking and human organisation turned crisis into disaster at Mann Gulch. This episode is symptomatic of what can go wrong in a threatening situation in any walk of life. In a related study, Stein compares the Apollo 13 crisis in 1970 and the Three Mile Island nuclear accident in 1979. Despite a serious malfunction during the early stages of Apollo 13's mission, Flight Control and the astronauts kept calm, worked tirelessly to make sense of their predicament, and eventually brought the spacecraft home. At Three Mile Island, however, the power station operators behaved as though they had the situation under control when in fact they did not. They ignored instrument readings that suggested the reactor was heading for meltdown, refusing to contemplate the worst. Catastrophe was avoided by sheer luck when a maintenance worker noticed a valve in the wrong position. Stein depicts Apollo 13 as an instance of creative sensemaking and Three Mile Island as the opposite. Each group reacted differently to anxiety. One was energised into searching for solutions, while the other went into denial.[24]

Tuckett and Taffler use psychoanalytic theory to explain financial bubbles and collapses, focusing on the dotcom episode of 1998–2002. In 'face of [the] uncertainty' pervading financial markets 'there is increased scope for emotional and unconscious phantasy to shape reactions to news'.[25] Internet stocks became 'phantastic objects' representing the deepest desires of investors. In their 'paranoid-schizoid' state they suppressed all doubt and made light of risk. When the markets turned against them, they resorted

22   Kindleberger and Aliber, *Manias, Panics, and Crashes*, pp. 39–45.
23   Karl E. Weick, 'The Collapse of Sensemaking in Organizations: the Mann Gulch Disaster', *Administrative Science Quarterly*, 38 (1993), pp. 628–52; Norman Maclean, *Young Men and Fire* (Chicago, 1992); Sally Maitlis and Scott Sonenschein, 'Sensemaking in Crisis and Change: Inspiration and Insights from Weick (1988)', *Journal of Management Studies*, 47 (2010), pp. 551–80.
24   Stein, 'Critical Period'.
25   David Tuckett and Richard Taffler, 'Phantastic Objects and the Financial Market's Sense of Reality: A Psychoanalytic Contribution to the Understanding of Stock Market Instability', *International Journal of Psychoanalysis*, 89 (2008), p. 392.

'to denial, to anger, and then to paranoid efforts to find scapegoats'.[26] Stein discusses the 'culture of mania' that gripped financial markets before the 2008 crash. Every setback was treated as a challenge to stake even bigger bets.[27]

The point is not that psychoanalysis beats economics, but rather that individuals and groups are only partially rational. They may engage in herd behaviour, ignore inconvenient evidence or experience wild mood swings. Only in a period of heightened danger or crisis do we discover what they are made of – some excel but most flounder. Disaster management specialists identify several types of crisis manager. Collectivists work effectively with other crisis managers, delegate tasks and adapt their plans to the changing situation. Integrators are determined to follow best practice methods; although laudable in principle this approach may lead to delays until all assets are in place. Reactives lack a consistent strategy, fail to communicate effectively and incline to autocracy. Finally, paralytics have no idea what to do and lapse into passivity.[28]

To reiterate, the terms crisis and disaster are used in precise ways in this chapter. They are not synonymous, although everyday and even some academic usage might suggest otherwise. The DMC, supplemented by work on sensemaking and behaviour during times of threat, helps us to compare different types of disaster. In the following sections, the DMC is used to shed light on Hurricane Katrina, the First World War and the inter-war Depression.

Hurricane Katrina

Since the DMC was developed with events such as hurricanes and floods in mind, it is convenient to start with Hurricane Katrina, which flooded New Orleans in 2005.

Mitigation and regulatory change
Over two centuries, levees and other defences have been built to protect New Orleans and other centres along the Mississippi from flooding caused by heavy rain and hurricanes. Hurricane Betsy was a harbinger of Katrina, overcoming New Orleans' flood defences and killing eighty-one people in 1965. The federal government reacted by introducing the National Flood Insurance Program (NFIP) to subsidise flood insurance for property

---

26   Ibid., p. 404.
27   Mark Stein, 'A Culture of Mania: A Psychoanalytic View of the Incubation of the 2008 Credit Crisis', *Organization*, 18 (2011), pp. 173–86.
28   Amanda M. Olejarski and James L. Garnett, 'Coping with Katrina: Assessing Crisis Management Behaviours in the Big One', *Journal of Contingencies and Crisis Management*, 18 (2010), pp. 26–38.

owners. Government also instituted a programme of levee strengthening and construction. Despite initial enthusiasm for this scheme – the Lake Pontchartrain and Vicinity Protection Project – work was never finished, because of the inability (or unwillingness) of some communities to provide funding. As memories of Betsy receded, so did the motivation to spend on flood defences.[29] Levee maintenance was the responsibility of local boards, resulting in haphazard standards. Take up of insurance remained low, notwithstanding NFIP subsidies.[30] Emergency response to natural disasters was overseen by the Federal Emergency Management Agency (FEMA). After the 9/11 terrorist attacks FEMA was absorbed into the Department of Homeland Security, and resources diverted to dealing with possible terrorist attacks.[31] The mechanisms in place for coping with a powerful hurricane were patchy.

Warnings

New Orleans had several near misses, including Hurricane Georges in 1998 and Hurricane Ivan in 2004. Prompted by Hurricane Georges, an exercise called Hurricane Pam was conducted. Pam demonstrated the vulnerability of New Orleans and assumed over 60,000 fatalities.[32] But the US Army Corps of Engineers persistently discounted the threat to New Orleans, maintaining that the flood defences would thwart all but a one in 200- or 300-year storm.[33] Identifying threats from hurricanes was the job of the National Hurricane Center (NHC) at Miami. Even with the technology available in 2005, forecasting was problematic because hurricanes change course and intensity unexpectedly. Whenever a tropical storm formed, the NHC issued regular forecasts of track, intensity and wind speed. It was explicit about the probabilistic nature of such forecasts, and most hurricanes that threatened New Orleans never arrived. In the case of Hurricane Katrina, however, the NHC's forecasts were accurate.[34]

29   Robert Meyer, 'Why We Still Fail To Learn From Disasters', in Erwann Michel-Kerjan and Paul Slovic (eds), *The Irrational Economist: Making Decisions in a Dangerous World* (New York, 2010), p. 126.
30   Erwann O. Michel-Kerjan, 'Catastrophe Economics: The National Flood Insurance Program', *Journal of Economic Perspectives*, 24 (2010), pp. 165–86.
31   Charles Perrow, *The Next Catastrophe* (Princeton, 2007), pp. 48–67.
32   US House of Representatives, *A Failure of Initiative: Final Report of the Select Bipartisan Committee to Investigate the Preparation for and Response to Hurricane Katrina* (Washington, DC, 2006), pp. 81–3.
33   Charles F. Parker, Eric K. Stern, Eric Paglia and Christer Brown, 'Preventable Catastrophe? The Hurricane Katrina Disaster Revisited', *Journal of Contingencies and Crisis Management*, 17 (2009), p. 209.
34   Eva Regnier, 'Public Evacuation Decisions and Hurricane Track Uncertainty', *Management Science*, 54 (2008), pp. 16–28.

Triggering event

On Tuesday 23 August 2005, at 4.00 p.m., a tropical depression formed near the Bahamas.[35] At 2.30 p.m. on Thursday 25th the storm was designated a hurricane and named Katrina. At 11.00 a.m. on Friday 26th, the NHC predicted Katrina would track in the general direction of New Orleans. At 10.00 p.m., it forecast that landfall would take place east of New Orleans on Monday. At 4.00 a.m. on Saturday 27 August the NHC projected a direct hit on New Orleans by a Category 3 hurricane.[36] News that Katrina could be on the way triggered a crisis: how would the authorities respond?

Sensemaking and decision-making

Katrina arrived with only three or so days' warning. Making sense of what was happening was conceptually straightforward in this case. Everyone knew what a hurricane could do if it went near New Orleans. The challenge was to make the right decisions with inadequate information and little time for reflection. Evacuation decisions were the responsibility of the mayor, Ray Nagin. A *voluntary* evacuation order was issued at about 1.00 p.m. on Saturday 27th. Nagin delayed the *mandatory* evacuation order until 9.30 a.m. on Sunday 28th.[37]

Why did Nagin delay? The decision to evacuate a major city is not to be taken lightly. Most hurricane threats are false alarms, evacuation is costly, and if the mayor 'cries wolf' too often he risks losing credibility.[38] When Hurricane Ivan was expected in 2004, Nagin announced a voluntary evacuation. More than half of New Orleans's residents left town, but Ivan veered east and spared the city.[39]

The embarrassment of a false alarm had to be balanced against the risk to the city. Any evacuation needed to start between 50 and 72 hours before arrival of the storm.[40] The NHC's decision-support software, Hurrevac, set precise deadlines for a decision. At 10.00 p.m. on Friday 26th, Hurrevac set a deadline of 4.00 a.m. on Saturday morning for New Orleans to decide, which

---

35   All timings converted into Central Daylight Time.
36   US Senate, Committee on Homeland Security and Governmental Affairs, *Hurricane Katrina: A Nation Still Unprepared* (Washington, DC, 2006), p. 67; Richard D. Knabb, Jamie R. Rhome and Daniel P. Brown, *Tropical Cyclone Report: Hurricane Katrina 23–30 August 2005* (Miami, 2011). http://www.nhc.noaa.gov/pdf/TCR-AL122005_Katrina.pdf [accessed 22 May 2013].
37   There are several versions of the timing of the mandatory order, but I follow US Senate, *Hurricane Katrina*, p. 68.
38   Parker *et al.*, *Preventable Catastrophe?*, p. 211.
39   US Senate, *Hurricane Katrina*, p. 24.
40   Regnier, *Public Evacuation*, p. 17.

would have given about 50 hours until landfall to implement the evacuation.[41] When faced with a tough decision and incomplete information, Nagin procrastinated.

Disaster unfolds

The eye of Katrina made landfall around 6.00 a.m. on Monday, as anticipated. New Orleans was subjected to a double attack, first from the storm surge that came up the waterways, and second from torrential rain accompanying the hurricane proper. The storm surge overtopped some levees and flood defences. Other defences, especially those that had been poorly maintained, crumbled and collapsed. The most damaging breaches occurred in canals that usually helped to drain New Orleans.[42]

Eighty per cent of New Orleans was flooded. Approximately 1,800 lives were lost, mostly in New Orleans and Louisiana. Economic activity in New Orleans ceased. Thousands of buildings were destroyed or damaged. The port closed for seven months, and the oil and gas industries were disrupted. Those lacking transport, and those unwilling to leave, were encouraged to take refuge in the Superdome and the Convention Center. About 20 per cent of the population was stranded, including the least mobile: the poor, the elderly, the disabled and the sick.

Rescue and relief

The rescue and relief effort started before Katrina arrived. The aims were to expedite the evacuation, and gather the assets and personnel needed for rescue work, patching up flood defences, restoring essential services, and feeding and caring for the displaced. Coordinating the various agencies at city, state and federal level posed a challenge. The rescue and relief operation was beset by difficulties, not least because of inadequate and damaged communication networks and bureaucratic inflexibility.[43] It took five days to evacuate the Superdome and Convention Center. Nevertheless, fatalities were far less than envisaged during the Hurricane Pam exercise.

---

41   Alex Kirlik, 'Lessons Learned from the Design of the Decision Support System Used in the Hurricane Katrina Evacuation Decision', *Proceedings of the Human Factors and Ergonomics Society 51st Annual Meeting* (Thousand Oaks, CA, 2007), pp. 253–7.
42   Peter Nicholson, 'Hurricane Katrina: Why Did the Levees Fail? Testimony of Peter Nicholson on behalf of the American Society of Civil Engineers Before the Committee on Homeland Security and Governmental Affairs, U.S. Senate, on November 2, 2006'. http://www.hsgac.senate.gov/download/2005-11-02-nicholson-testimony [accessed 19 August 2014].
43   James L. Garnett and Alexander Kouzmin, 'Communicating Throughout Katrina: Competing and Complementary Conceptual Lenses on Crisis Communication', *Public Administration Review*, 67 (2007), pp. 171–88; Perrow, *Next Catastrophe*, pp. 111–13.

Apportioning blame
CRED describes Katrina as the fourth worst natural disaster to strike the
USA between 1900 and 2014, killing over 1,800 people and causing $125
billion of damage.[44] Unlike many previous disasters, Katrina was a live media
event, and the search for culprits began immediately. President George W.
Bush was portrayed as either confused or callous. One contemporary illus-
tration showed him as Nero, fiddling while New Orleans drowned.[45] In one
public opinion survey, respondents were invited to identify the person most to
blame for the lives lost and destruction in New Orleans. For 65.5 per cent of
Democrats, the principal villain was President Bush. Republicans were more
ambivalent: 35.1 per cent identified Ray Nagin as the main culprit, and 21.6
per cent Bush.[46]

The Senate and the House of Representatives embarked on detailed
hearings. The Senate report on Katrina, subtitled *A Nation Still Unprepared*,
blamed all levels of government for underestimating the threat to New
Orleans, and a lack of leadership and poor organisation during the disaster
itself. The solutions offered were bureaucratic – to replace FEMA with a
new and stronger body, and to give greater emphasis to mitigation, disaster
preparedness, planning, and coordination.[47] *A Failure of Initiative*, the
House report, concentrated on the same themes.[48] These reports were fantasy
documents. They focused on one aspect of the disaster, namely the errors of
government, but did not address others such as why so many people lived in a
flood-prone area. The Senate report's conclusion that government needed to
do better was rather simplistic.

Recovery
Recovery was slow, but by 2012 the population of New Orleans was back
to 81 per cent of its pre-disaster level. One of the most intriguing features
of the aftermath was the debate over whether there was any point in
rebuilding New Orleans, a city in relative decline that might flood again.[49]
Conceivably, many of the former inhabitants of New Orleans would be more
productive elsewhere. Whatever the merits of rebuilding in principle, no
government could afford to abandon a major city in practice. By 2010 the
federal government had spent $45.5 billion on the recovery of New Orleans,

44   Data from http://www.emdat.be/database [accessed 1 May 2015].
45   'George W. Bush, American Nero', by Danny Hellman, September 2012. http://www.
dannyhellman.com/category_folders/politics/politics_nero.html [accessed 22 August 2014].
46   Neil Malhotra and Alexander G. Kuo, 'Attributing Blame: The Public's Response to
Hurricane Katrina', *Journal of Politics*, 70 (2008), p. 127.
47   US Senate, *Hurricane Katrina*, pp. 589, 606–15.
48   US House of Representatives, *A Failure of Initiative*, pp. xi, 359–61.
49   Jacob Vigdor, 'The Economic Aftermath of Hurricane Katrina', *Journal of Economic
Perspectives*, 22 (2008), pp. 135–54.

including improvements to flood defences, flood insurance payments, and the Road Home Program, designed to encourage families to return home and restore their properties.[50] The recovery process did not run smoothly or avoid controversy. As government funds flowed into New Orleans, the opportunities for corruption expanded. Ray Nagin was sentenced to ten years in prison in 2014 for accepting bribes while mayor, including some from firms seeking rebuilding contracts.[51] African-American groups felt that their interests were neglected and priority given to rebuilding white areas.[52]

Mitigation and regulatory change
There have been no major policy innovations since Katrina. Flood defences have been strengthened, but there remain disputes over how to pay for and manage them. The US public rewards politicians for disaster relief but soon loses interest in expensive mitigation programmes. The electorate only pays attention *after* a disaster, and even then only briefly.[53] Attempts to reform flood insurance petered out, not least because of the threat to existing interests. Further flooding has taken place along the Mississippi, and there is no reason to believe that the future will be free of disaster.

The First World War

Alan Kramer suggests that most 'Italians regarded the [First World] war as a natural catastrophe like an epidemic or an earthquake.'[54] The critical phase or crisis lasted from 1914 to 1918, and the need for sensemaking and decision-making was continuous during this period.

Mitigation and regulatory change
Attempts to make war less likely, or mitigate its impact, took various forms before 1914. Although very different at first glance, they served the same purpose as levee building along the Mississippi. Routine diplomacy, supplemented by occasional crisis conferences, aimed to defuse potential conflict.

---

50 Louise K. Comfort, Thomas A. Birkland, Beverly A. Cigler and Earthea Nance, 'Retrospectives and Prospectives on Hurricane Katrina: Five Years and Counting', *Public Administration Review*, 70 (2010), p. 672.
51 David Zucchino, 'C. Ray Nagin, Former New Orleans Mayor, Sentenced to 10 Years in Prison', *Los Angeles Times*, 9 July 2014, http://www.latimes.com/nation/nationnow/la-na-nn-ray-nagin-new-orleans-sentenced-20140709-story.html [accessed 22 August 2014].
52 Naomi Klein, *The Shock Doctrine* (London, 2007), pp. 465–6.
53 Andrew Healy and Neil Malhotra, 'Myopic Voters and Natural Disaster Policy', *American Political Science Review*, 103 (2009), pp. 387–406.
54 Alan Kramer, *Dynamic of Destruction: Culture and Mass Killing in the First World War* (Oxford, 2008), p. 240.

The rules of war and treatment of combatants and non-combatants were discussed at conferences at The Hague and Geneva, but negligible progress was made on the central issues of arms limitation and abolition of war.[55] The expansion and modernisation of armies and navies before 1914 was arguably a mixture of deterrence and provocation.[56]

Warnings

Imperial competition, nationalism and arms races on sea and land were often interpreted as portents of war. Hobson argued that competition for colonies as outlets for savings and exports would bring the great powers into conflict.[57] Novelists, particularly those based in Britain, also played on the fear of war.[58] The decade before 1914 was punctuated by diplomatic incidents and localised wars. In 1905–06 Germany encouraged Morocco to resist French influence, provoking a Franco–German stand-off. In 1908 Austria-Hungary annexed Bosnia-Herzegovina. During the second Moroccan crisis in 1911, Germany responded to French military intervention by sending a gunboat to Agadir. The First and Second Balkan Wars in 1912–13 fuelled tensions between Austria-Hungary, Serbia and Russia.[59] On several occasions before 1914 the great powers had come close to blows, but caution had ultimately prevailed. Arrangements for the mitigation of conflict, including diplomacy and deterrence, proved sufficiently effective to avert war between the major powers, but that would change in 1914.

Triggering event

The assassination of Franz Ferdinand in Sarajevo in 1914 could easily have been another near miss, just as Hurricane Katrina could have fizzled out or spared New Orleans. Sarajevo triggered a diplomatic crisis, in which Austria-Hungary demanded satisfaction from Serbia, which was blamed for the murders. Austria-Hungary was backed by Germany, while Serbia was backed by Russia and (albeit indirectly) by France and possibly Britain. A challenge had been issued to the leaders of Europe to make sense of the situation and decide on war or peace.

55   Geoffrey Best, *Humanity in Warfare* (London, 1983).
56   David Stevenson, *Armaments and the Coming of War: Europe 1904–1914* (Oxford, 1996); Jari Eloranta, 'From the Great Illusion to the Great War: Military Spending Behaviour of the Great Powers, 1870–1913', *European Review of Economic History*, 11 (2007), pp. 255–83.
57   John A. Hobson, *Imperialism: A Study* (London, 1902).
58   For example, Erskine Childers, *The Riddle of the Sands* (London, 1903).
59   Margaret MacMillan, *The War that Ended Peace* (London, 2013); Hew Strachan, *The First World War*, vol. 1, *To Arms* (Oxford, 2003), chap. 1.

Sensemaking and decision-making

Sensemaking and decision-making in 1914 were the function of 'small coteries [in each capital], most of them having fewer than ten persons', consisting of the head of state, senior ministers and the professional head of the armed forces.[60] They occupied the position of Ray Nagin and his advisers after the receipt of news that Katrina could be on the way. Each group perceived an external threat, and some discerned opportunities. All wished to enhance or preserve the power of their nation or empire. After a series of compromises and withdrawals in previous years, another compromise might have been expected, but this time decision-makers concluded that they had less to lose by fighting than by backing down. They could not have known how devastating modern warfare would be, not only in terms of casualties but also in terms of material loss and waste. There had not been a clash between first-rate European powers since the Franco–Prussian War of 1870–71. The influential Polish military theorist, Jean de Bloch, predicted stalemate and trench warfare, on the grounds that modern weapons favoured the defence,[61] but many professional soldiers anticipated lightning, although bloody, campaigns in which well-disciplined and motivated troops overcame modern technology.[62]

Political scientists model the descent into war in 1914 using game theory. In the 'asymmetric escalation game', Germany/Austria-Hungary is the challenger and Russia/France the defender. Players must decide in each round whether to compromise or escalate. In another variant, Germany is the challenger, Austria-Hungary the protégé, and Russia the defender. Germany encouraged its protégé to be intransigent by giving it a 'blank cheque'. Without German support, Austria-Hungary could have defected or collapsed. The British opted for a 'straddle' strategy, attempting unsuccessfully to restrain France while deterring Germany.[63]

We cannot know for certain why mitigation failed in 1914. Avner Offer, however, argues persuasively that there was more to 1914 than mere miscalculation, and that visceral factors played a part in the descent into war. For Europe's leaders, he suggests, the decision not to back down was infused by

---

60 Richard F. Hamilton and Holger H. Herwig (eds), *Decisions for War, 1914–1917* (Cambridge, 2004), p. xv.
61 Jean de Bloch, *The Future of War in its Technical, Economic and Political Relations* (Boston, MA, 1899).
62 Richard F. Hamilton, 'War Planning: Obvious Needs, Not so Obvious Solutions', in Richard F. Hamilton and Holger H. Herwig (eds), *War Planning 1914* (Cambridge, 2010), p. 20.
63 Frank C. Zagare and D. Marc Kilgour, 'The Deterrence-Versus-Restraint Dilemma in Extended Deterrence: Explaining British Policy in 1914', *International Studies Review*, 8 (2006), pp. 623–41; Frank C. Zagare, 'After Sarajevo: Explaining the Blank Check', *International Interactions*, 35 (2009), pp. 106–27; Frank C. Zagare, 'Explaining the 1914 War in Europe: An Analytic Narrative', *Journal of Theoretical Politics*, 21 (2009), pp. 63–95.

considerations of national and personal honour. Fighting, *whatever the cost*, seemed better than accepting another slight or abandoning an ally.[64]

Disaster unfolds

Millions of soldiers and civilians died in the fighting or from disease or starvation. Millions more were disabled and rendered incapable of returning to civilian occupations. Economic activity was disrupted, and output fell in most belligerent countries. A rising share of national output was directed to the war effort, further depressing civilian consumption.[65] Numerous civilians had to flee. The Austro-Hungarian, German and Russian emperors lost their thrones, and the Russian royal family lost their lives.

Rescue and relief

Military medicine was better than in previous conflicts, especially on the Western Front where armies were relatively well resourced and the war zone largely static. Army medical services underwent rapid expansion; their work was supplemented by voluntary agencies, including Red Cross societies. Improved methods for treating wounds, and more efficient surgical techniques, were introduced. Of equal importance was the emphasis on halting the spread of infectious disease through better hygiene.[66] The Geneva Convention established principles for treatment of wounded enemy soldiers, while the Hague Conventions set minimum standards for treatment of other prisoners. Jones notes that there was a 'mammoth charitable aid effort' to help prisoners of war.[67]

Pensions were paid to the widows and orphans of soldiers and sailors. Food availability on the home front was affected by the conscription of peasants and horses, shipping shortages, blockade, and in some cases enemy occupation. Governments struggled to ensure that food supplies were adequate, often introducing rationing systems.[68] The German occupiers could not feed

---

64   Avner Offer, 'Going to War in 1914: A Matter of Honor?', *Politics and Society*, 23 (1995), pp. 213–41.
65   Stephen Broadberry and Mark Harrison (eds), *The Economics of World War I* (Cambridge, 2005); John Singleton, 'Destruction and Misery ... The First World War', in Michael J. Oliver and Derek H. Aldcroft (eds), *Economic Disasters of the Twentieth Century* (Cheltenham, 2007), pp. 9–50.
66   Mark Harrison, *The Medical War: British Military Medicine in the First World War* (Oxford, 2010); Sophie Delaporte, 'Military Medicine', in John Horne (ed.), *A Companion to World War I* (Chichester, 2010), pp. 295–306.
67   Heather Jones, 'Prisoners of War', in Jay Winter (ed.), *The Cambridge History of the First World War*, vol. 2 (Cambridge, 2014), p. 273.
68   Thierry Bonzon and Belinda Davis, 'Feeding the Cities', in Jay Winter and Jean-Louis Robert (eds), *Capital Cities at War: Paris, London, Berlin 1914–1919* (Cambridge, 1997), pp. 305–41; Belinda Davis, *Home Fires Burning: Food, Politics, and Everyday Life in World War I Berlin* (Chapel Hill, NC, 2000).

Belgium properly, not least because of their own desperate food situation. Herbert Hoover, an American business leader, organised the Commission for Relief in Belgium, which arranged food shipments.[69] Millions of civilians were rendered homeless on the main fronts. Many refugees fled from the advancing enemy, but others, especially ethnic minorities, were removed by their own governments because of doubts over their loyalty.[70]

Apportioning blame
The quest to apportion blame began in August 1914. Whereas incompetence and neglect were at the heart of the attacks on the authorities after Katrina, the First World War was attributed by the victors to the malice of those dubbed aggressors. The German invasion of Belgium and France gave rise to accusations of atrocities against civilians.[71] In 1919, as a curtain raiser to the Paris peace conference, the Commission on the Responsibility of the Authors of the War and on Enforcement of Penalties concluded that the conflict was 'premeditated by the Central Powers', who were wholly to blame.[72] The Treaty of Versailles redrew the map of Europe, dismembering the Austro-Hungarian Empire, and taking swathes of territory from Germany. Article 231 stated that Germany and the other Central Powers were responsible for causing all of the losses suffered by the Allies after embarking upon a war of aggression. Germany signed the treaty, but objected strongly to the 'war guilt' clause. As was customary, the losing powers – primarily Germany – were presented with a large bill for damages. Germany, however, paid only a fraction of the sum demanded, and convinced many observers that it had been treated unfairly.[73] That Germany, assisted by Austria-Hungary, was *wholly* to blame for the war was a fantasy, but the notion that Germany was a victim was equally fantastic.

Recovery
Recovery involved both physical and institutional reconstruction. France and Belgium regained their 1913 levels of GDP per capita in 1922. Britain reached the same point in 1924, followed by Poland and Germany in 1926, and Austria

69 Johann den Hertog, 'The Commission for Relief in Belgium and the First World War', *Diplomacy & Statecraft*, 21 (2010), pp. 593–613.
70 Peter Gatrell, 'Refugees and Forced Migrants During the First World War', *Immigrants & Minorities*, 26 (2008), pp. 82–100.
71 Kramer, *Dynamic of Destruction*, pp. 22, 27.
72 Commission of Responsibilities, *Violation of the Laws and Customs of War: Reports of Majority and Dissenting Reports of American and Japanese Members of Commission of Responsibilities* (Oxford, 1919), p. 11.
73 Sally Marks, 'Smoke and Mirrors: In Smoke-Filled Rooms and the Galerie des Glaces', in Manfred F. Boemeke, Gerald D. Feldman and Elisabeth Glaser (eds), *The Treaty of Versailles: A Reassessment after 75 Years* (Cambridge, 1998), p. 367.

in 1927.[74] The international monetary system, based on the Gold Standard, was patched up alongside the recovery of the main European countries. But Europe had lost a decade of intensive economic growth and rising living standards.

Fighting had devastated parts of Belgium and northern France. Villages, towns, cities and industries needed to be rebuilt, coal mines repaired, farms restocked with animals and land cleared of war debris. Urban reconstruction was not completed until the 1930s.[75] Germany faced different reconstruction challenges, having been deprived of territory containing assets such as agricultural land, coal mines and steelworks. Disordered government finances led to hyperinflation, exacerbating Germany's troubles.[76] In central Europe the situation was even worse: the dismantling of empire disrupted pre-war flows of trade and finance.[77] Overall, the recovery after 1918 was brittle and incomplete, as is often the case with post-disaster recoveries: New Orleans after Hurricane Katrina being a good example. When the US economy faltered at the end of the 1920s, cracks in the European economy began to widen.

Mitigation and regulatory change
The post-war economic and political settlement aspired to the prevention of further conflict, partly by weakening the defeated powers, and partly by creating institutions that would defuse international conflict. It was anticipated that the League of Nations would be the centrepiece of the new regime. In the event, however, the League was toothless, not least because the USA declined to join.[78] The League would fail spectacularly to restrain aggression in the 1930s. In the 1920s it failed to persuade members to commit themselves to a permanent reduction in armaments, although the naval powers did agree to limit the size of their fleets.[79] In the economic sphere, the League and central banks promoted financial stability in eastern and central Europe, especially by setting up new central banks and linking national currencies to gold.[80] As a disaster, the First World War passed through essentially the

---

74   Joan R. Roses and Nikolaus Wolf, 'Aggregate Growth, 1913–1950', in Stephen Broadberry and Kevin H. O'Rourke (eds), *The Cambridge Economic History of Modern Europe*, vol. 2 (Cambridge, 2010), p. 187.

75   Hugh Clout, 'The Great Reconstruction of Towns and Cities in France, 1918–35', *Planning Perspectives*, 20 (2005), pp. 1–33.

76   Niall Ferguson, 'Constraints and Room for Manoeuvre in the German Inflation of the Early 1920s', *Economic History Review*, 46 (1996), pp. 635–66.

77   John Komlos, *The Habsburg Monarchy as a Customs Union* (Princeton, 1983).

78   Stephen Wertheim, 'The League of Nations: A Retreat from International Law?', *Journal of Global History*, 7 (2012), pp. 210–32.

79   Andrew Webster, 'Making Disarmament Work: The Implementation of the International Disarmament Provisions in the League of Nations Covenant, 1919–1925', *Diplomacy & Statecraft*, 16 (2005), pp. 551–69.

80   John Singleton, *Central Banking in the Twentieth Century* (Cambridge, 2011), pp. 57–9.

same stages as Hurricane Katrina. The DMC allows us to compare how the key actors behaved, when faced with decisions that involved high stakes and uncertainty, at parallel stages of each disaster.

The Great Depression

The Depression was a complex disaster that confounded policymakers and economists.[81] Attempts at sensemaking during the early stages of the slump were ineffective; policymakers lapsed into denial or panic because the situation was at odds with their preconceptions.

Mitigation and regulatory change

Policymakers and business leaders in the 1920s believed that good institutions would prevent or mitigate financial disaster. Their ideal consisted of the Gold Standard managed by independent central banks.[82] Membership of the Gold Standard required fiscal discipline by governments and careful attention to costs by the private sector. The US Federal Reserve was set up in 1914 to mitigate and respond to financial instability. A key central banking function was to act as lender of last resort. At the International Financial Conference in 1920, governments were urged to balance the budget, combat inflation, restore gold convertibility and confirm the independence of their central banks. New central banks were created in a number of countries, and the Gold Standard was gradually restored.[83] Disaster mitigation in the economic sphere involved a measure of international cooperation, and in that sense was equivalent to the diplomatic arrangements designed to avert global war before 1914.

Warnings

The global outlook in the late 1920s was perplexing. Euphoria gripped the USA, as consumer goods production, property prices and the stock market boomed, fuelled by credit expansion. Investors were encouraged to believe that they were better informed than ever before, and that crashes were a thing of the past.[84] Practitioners of the new art of business forecasting failed to detect signs of an impending US slump.[85] In Europe, however, there was

81 Randall E. Parker (ed.), *Reflections on the Great Depression* (Cheltenham, 2002).
82 Barry J. Eichengreen and Peter Temin, 'The Gold Standard and the Great Depression', *Contemporary European History*, 9 (2000), pp. 183–207.
83 Singleton, *Central Banking in the Twentieth Century*, pp. 50–9, 73–80.
84 Reinhart and Rogoff, *This Time is Different*, p. 16.
85 Walter A. Friedman, *Fortune Tellers: The Story of America's First Economic Forecasters* (Princeton, 2013).

unease. Unemployment was high in Britain, and the German economic recovery was fragile. The German foreign minister, Gustav Stresemann, likened the economic and financial situation in 1928 to 'dancing on a volcano'.[86] Germany's balance of payments depended on inflows of US capital. If Americans withdrew their funds (a 'sudden stop') Germany's position would be untenable. The uneven distribution of world gold reserves was another concern. Gold had drained from Europe to the USA between 1914 and 1918, leaving most European countries in a desperate plight.[87] Alarmed by perceived speculative frenzy, the Federal Reserve removed the punch bowl, and tightened monetary policy in 1928–29.[88] The situation was a new one for the fledgling central bank. US financial history, however, suggested that failure to control irrational exuberance could lead to a crash, with 1907 offering the most pertinent example.[89] It was in order to avert such wild swings that the Federal Reserve had been created. Tragically, by raising interest rates, the Federal Reserve was inadvertently setting the stage for the very disaster that it hoped to avert.

Triggering event
The Wall Street Crash, which is usually linked to monetary tightening, posed a challenge for decision-makers. The Dow Jones Industrial Average (DJIA) fell by 49 per cent between 3 September and 13 November 1929. Financial markets around the world were destabilised. US investors repatriated funds invested abroad. According to James, the crash had 'really world-historical consequences (the Great Depression, even perhaps the Second World War)'.[90] Reinhart and Rogoff concur that the 'global stock market crash [of 1929] marked the onset of the Great Depression'.[91]

Sensemaking and decision-making
Making sense of the situation was difficult. Just as there remained doubt as to whether Hurricane Katrina would strike New Orleans in 2005, or that the assassination crisis in June 1914 would result in a world war, it was far from inevitable in 1929 that a stock market crash would lead to a major slump. But the crash heightened uncertainty, prompting consumers

86   Quoted in Albrecht Ritschl, '"Dancing on a Volcano": The Economic Recovery and Collapse of Weimar Germany, 1924–33', in Theo Balderston (ed.), *The World Economy and National Economies in the Interwar Slump* (Basingstoke, 2003), p. 105.
87   Barry J. Eichengreen, *Globalizing Capital* (Princeton, 1996), p. 65.
88   James D. Hamilton, 'Monetary Factors in the Great Depression', *Journal of Monetary Economics*, 19 (1987), p. 148.
89   Reinhart and Rogoff, *This Time is Different*, p. 390.
90   Harold James, '1929: The New York Stock Market Crash', *Representations*, 110 (2010), p. 131.
91   Reinhart and Rogoff, *This Time is Different*, p. 17.

and businesses to reconsider spending plans.[92] Those that had borrowed to play the stock market were in dire straits, as were their banks. The banks responded to the threat of insolvency by cutting new lending.[93] The Federal Reserve loosened monetary policy briefly, but was largely passive in the early 1930s. Unfortunately, the central bank misread the situation, concluding that liquidity remained adequate. Although nominal interest rates fell, real interest rates rose when the price level dropped. The money supply, a much better indicator, plummeted. But the Federal Reserve stuck stubbornly to conventional ideas and methods.[94] As Meltzer puts it, 'People see most clearly what they are trained or disposed to see.' Perhaps there was an element of denial in the central bank's thinking.[95] In the same way, it could be argued that European political and military leaders in 1914 were in denial over the likelihood and consequences of war, and Ray Nagin was in denial over the need to make a speedy decision to evacuate New Orleans in 2005. Although there was more time for sensemaking after October 1929 than there was in 1914 or 2005, the results were no better.

European perceptions of the challenge varied. Britain and Germany were vulnerable to the transmission of financial turmoil from the USA, but France was insulated for several years by plentiful gold reserves and a competitive exchange rate. American funds were withdrawn and US demand for European products dropped. The situation was interpreted by Europeans as a threat to gold convertibility.[96]

We might expect professional economists to have been better placed than policymakers to make sense of the downturn. The 'business depression' was the focus of a session at the 1931 conference of the American Economic Association (AEA). Carl Snyder of the Federal Reserve blamed the Depression on the collapse of a 'speculative mania'.[97] Joseph Schumpeter, however, inclined to the view that the problem was the combination of a trough in the short-term economic cycle and downswings in the medium- and long-term cycles.[98] Compared with later generations of economists, beginning with

---

92   N.F.R. Crafts and Peter Fearon, 'Lessons from the 1930s Great Depression', *Oxford Review of Economic Policy*, 26 (2010), p. 291; Christina D. Romer, 'The Nation in Depression', *Journal of Economic Perspectives*, 7 (1993), p. 31.

93   Benjamin S. Bernanke, 'Nonmonetary Effects of the Financial Crisis in the Propagation of the Great Depression', *American Economic Review*, 73 (1983), pp. 257–76.

94   Allan H. Meltzer, *A History of the Federal Reserve*, vol. 1 (Chicago, 2003), pp. 400–13.

95   Ibid., p. 400.

96   Barry J. Eichengreen, *Golden Fetters: The Gold Standard and the Great Depression, 1919–1939* (Oxford, 1992).

97   Carl Snyder, 'The World-Wide Depression of 1930', *American Economic Review*, 21, Supplement (1931), p. 174.

98   Joseph Schumpeter, 'The Present World Depression: A Tentative Diagnosis', *American Economic Review*, 21, Supplement (1931), pp. 179–82.

Friedman and Schwartz in the 1960s,[99] most economists in 1931 overlooked or downplayed the role of monetary policy in the Depression. Reviewing contemporary economic literature on the slump by European and US authors, Watkins concluded that many interpreted the disaster as punishment for a decade of greed. Unable to grasp the economic processes behind the Depression, they resorted to a form of moralising.[100]

Disaster unfolds

Instead of bouncing back, the US economy continued to contract. Late 1930 saw the first in a series of regional banking collapses. One third of American banks failed between 1930 and 1933. The annihilation of uninsured deposits, and the public's growing preference for holding currency, slashed the money supply. Surviving banks became ultra-cautious, resulting in a credit crunch.[101] Millions lost their jobs, prices and wages fell sharply, businesses closed, and farmers and homeowners were evicted. The Gold Standard transmitted the slump to Europe and other continents.[102] US capital exports dried up, as did US demand for imported commodities and manufactures. Since nations on the Gold Standard could not use depreciation as a cushion, they faced rising unemployment. Central banks raised interest rates, creating further distress. Banks became insolvent as loans went sour. The banking failures in Austria and Germany in 1931 marked a new stage in the Depression.[103]

Rescue and relief

Policymakers' response to the Depression was inadequate. The US president in 1929 was Herbert Hoover, who had coordinated the response to the 1927 Mississippi floods. A staunch advocate of voluntary activity, Hoover's approach was to cajole business leaders and bankers to solve the Depression, but they lacked the confidence to spend and invest.[104] Federal Reserve passivity was not confined to monetary policy. Attributing banking collapses to imprudent management, the central bank declined to act as lender of last resort.[105] Such inaction by a single agency with the power to stem the tide of bank failures contrasts with the situation during Hurricane Katrina, when

---

99   Milton Friedman and Anna J. Schwartz, *A Monetary History of the United States, 1870–1960* (Princeton, 1963).

100   Myron Watkins, 'The Literature of the Crisis', *Quarterly Journal of Economics*, 47 (1933), pp. 504–32.

101   Benjamin S. Bernanke, *Essays on the Great Depression* (Princeton, 2000).

102   Eichengreen, *Golden Fetters*, pp. 222–316.

103   Richard S. Grossman, 'The Shoe that Didn't Drop: Explaining Banking Instability during the Great Depression', *Journal of Economic History*, 54 (1994), pp. 654–82.

104   William J. Barber, *From New Era to New Deal: Herbert Hoover, the Economists, and American Economic Policy, 1921–1933* (Cambridge, 1985).

105   Friedman and Schwartz, *A Monetary History of the United States*, pp. 342–59.

there was no one in overall charge of relief and rescue, and agencies struggled to coordinate their response. Both approaches were lacking in effectiveness, albeit in different ways.

Safeguarding gold reserves was the priority of economic emergency services in Europe. They assumed that the Depression would deepen in the absence of convertibility. The era of floating exchange rates in the early 1920s was still associated with hyperinflation.[106] Gold reserves could be used either to support convertibility or to bolster the banking system. Central bankers gave priority to the Gold Standard. International cooperation was intermittent. Hoover granted the Europeans a debt moratorium in 1931, but governments and central banks in Europe were reluctant to aid their neighbours.[107]

Relief work was no less important at the level of individual victims and their families. Workers in some European nations were eligible for unemployment benefits under centrally managed schemes.[108] In the USA, however, relief of the unemployed was left to local authorities and charities. Senator La Follette urged Hoover to declare the slump a 'disaster', for there was a tradition of making Federal grants to help areas affected by natural disasters, but Hoover refused to equate economic with natural disasters.[109]

Apportioning blame

After any disaster, the public, political leaders and the media search for someone to blame. In Germany, the list of scapegoats extended to the Allies, who had imposed the Treaty of Versailles and reparations (thereby reflecting back the blame put on Germany after 1918), the leaders of the Weimar Republic, Jews and bankers in general. For the British, the turmoil came to a head in August and September 1931. The Labour cabinet collapsed over new austerity proposals. A rumour was spread that Wall Street bankers had demanded welfare cuts in return for a rescue loan for sterling.[110]

Suspicion of Wall Street was also endemic in the USA. According to Carosso, the 'crash and the depression transformed the image of the investment banker from one with a halo to one with horns and spiked tail'.[111] A Detroit priest and radio broadcaster, Charles Coughlin, became a channel

106 Tobias Straumann, 'Rule Rather than Exception: Brüning's Fear of Devaluation in Comparative Perspective', *Journal of Contemporary History*, 44 (2009), pp. 603–17.
107 Eichengreen, *Golden Fetters*, pp. 277–8.
108 Barry J. Eichengreen and T.J. Hatton, 'Interwar Unemployment in International Perspective: An Overview', in Barry J. Eichengreen and T.J. Hatton (eds), *Interwar Unemployment in International Perspective* (Dordrecht, 1988), pp. 1–60.
109 Michele L. Landis, 'Fate, Responsibility, and "Natural" Disaster Relief: Narrating the American Welfare State', *Law & Society Review*, 33 (1999), pp. 257–318.
110 The rumour was inaccurate. Phillip Williamson, 'A "Bankers' Ramp"? Financiers and the British Political Crisis of August 1931', *English Historical Review*, 99 (1984), pp. 770–806.
111 Vincent P. Carosso, *Investment Banking in America* (Cambridge, MA, 1970), p. 300.

for the disaffected, calling for the 'gamblers of Wall St ... and their lieutenants
in crime' to be punished.[112] He interpreted the Depression as a conspiracy
to enrich the financial elite.[113] An investigation into Wall Street, commissioned by the Senate, found that some financial institutions had behaved
unethically, for instance by selling risky securities to naïve investors.[114] The
resulting Pecora Report was the key fantasy document to emerge from the
Depression. It was so because it dealt with surface phenomena – the ethics
of Wall Street – and not the economic processes that caused the slump. The
post-Katrina reports were equally shallow, in the sense that they focused on
details rather than the awkward question of why so many people lived in a
flood-prone city.

Recovery
Britain's departure from gold in 1931, though humiliating for policymakers, was actually a precondition for recovery. Depreciation gave a boost
to exporters and permitted the relaxation of austerity measures. Lower
interest rates prompted a housing boom. An early departure from gold was
associated with a healthier banking system because central banks could now
give priority to domestic stability.[115]

After Britain's defection, the commitment of other countries to gold could
no longer be taken for granted. London even began to attract funds from New
York. The European 'Gold Bloc', led by France, faced increasingly vigorous
competition from Britain and Japan, but pressed ahead with austerity.[116]
Global recovery would have been faster if the leading nations had agreed to
abandon gold and loosen monetary policy, but cooperation was never on the
cards. The World Economic Conference in 1933 ended in deadlock. Most
Europeans wanted to salvage the Gold Standard, but President Roosevelt,
who had succeeded Hoover, dismissed the conference as a waste of time.[117]

Roosevelt's election as president reflected dissatisfaction with Hoover's
handling of the Depression. The Roosevelt administration adopted a more
pragmatic response to the disaster. According to Eggertsson, Roosevelt's

112   Quoted in Alan Brinkley, *Voices of Protest: Huey Long, Father Coughlin and the Great
Depression* (New York, 1983), p. 117.
113   James Reveley and John Singleton, 'Re-storying Bankers: Historical Antecedents of
Banker Bashing in Britain and America', *Management and Organizational History*, 8 (2013),
pp. 329–44.
114   Michael A. Perino, *The Hellhound of Wall Street* (New York, 2010).
115   Eichengreen, *Golden Fetters*, pp. 287–316; Grossman, 'The Shoe'.
116   Nikolaus Wolf, 'Scylla and Charybdis: Explaining Europe's Exit from Gold, January
1928–December 1936', *Explorations in Economic History*, 45 (2008), pp. 383–401.
117   Patricia Clavin, '"The Fetishes of So-called International Bankers": Central Bank
Co-operation for the World Economic Conference, 1932–3', *Contemporary European History*,
1 (1992), pp. 281–311.

approach amounted to a 'regime change'.[118] The 'dogmas' of convertibility and balanced budgets were swept away. Roosevelt promised to raise the price level and restore economic activity, and people believed him. By changing expectations, he persuaded households and businesses to resume spending. He reinforced his rhetoric with action: troubled banks were supported and government spending increased. The dollar was devalued and gold flowed back into the USA, boosting the money supply.

Mitigation and regulatory change

Depression led to changes in economic policy and financial regulation. Change was dramatic in the USA (and Germany) but more subtle in Britain. Government intervention strengthened in the wake of the apparent failure of laissez-faire capitalism. The goal was to establish policies and institutions that could mitigate instability. Banking regulation and surveillance were tightened and central bank independence was superseded by a partnership with government.[119] New Deal financial reform stemmed from the desire to control perceived rogues. Banks and stockbrokers fought back, lobbying for moderate regulation. The Banking Act of 1933, commonly known as Glass–Steagall, separated commercial from investment banking, established federal deposit insurance and introduced controls over deposit rates.[120] Separating commercial from investment banking was popular with critics of Wall Street. Whether or not this measure had genuine economic merit is debatable.[121] Between 1945 and the early 1970s the developed world experienced no systemic banking collapses.[122] Eliminating risk and competition from banking came at a price, however, in the form of complacency and a reluctance to innovate.[123] The aftermath of the First World War also spawned new forms of regulation, particularly in the form of the League of Nations. The League, however, proved comparatively weak, whereas financial regulation persisted throughout the mid twentieth century, and was reinforced by the Second World War.

118 Gauti B. Eggertsson, 'Great Expectations and the End of the Depression', *American Economic Review*, 98 (2008), pp. 1476–1516.
119 Singleton, *Central Banking in the Twentieth Century*, pp. 85–90.
120 Carosso, *Investment Banking in America*, pp. 368–75.
121 Randall S. Kroszner and Raghuram G. Rajan, 'Is the Glass–Steagall Act Justified? A Study of the U.S. Experience with Universal Banking before 1933', *American Economic Review*, 84 (1994), pp. 810–32.
122 Michael Bordo, Barry Eichengreen, Daniela Klingebiel, Maria Soledad Martinez-Peria and Andrew K. Rose, 'Financial Crises: Lessons from the Last 120 years', *Economic Policy*, 16 (2001), pp. 51–82.
123 Charles Goodhart, 'The Bank of England 1970–2000', in Ranald Michie and Philip Williamson (eds), *The British Government and the City of London in the Twentieth Century* (Cambridge, 2004), p. 342.

Conclusion

The Disaster Management Cycle allows the historian to observe the behaviour of actors at comparable stages of a disaster. Those stages are common to disasters that, at first sight, might seem very different, such as Hurricane Katrina, the First World War and the Depression. In particular, the challenges of sensemaking are conceptually similar across disasters. The Mayor of New Orleans in 2005, Europe's political and military leaders in 1914 and the world's central bankers, politicians and economists in 1929–31 were all confronted by crises or threats that they struggled to comprehend, let alone respond to effectively. In each instance, they failed to avert or contain disaster. To some extent, of course, the stages of the DMC are imposed by the observer, but that must be the case with any interpretative framework that abstracts from reality.

None of the three disasters examined in this chapter was unprecedented. There had been floods along the Mississippi before, there had been wars between the great European powers before, and there had been macroeconomic contractions before, although all three were on a very large scale. Attempts had been made after previous disasters to mitigate further episodes, for example by building flood barriers, strengthening diplomacy and deterrence, and establishing central banks. Those measures proved imperfect. Warnings, in the form of near misses with hurricanes and diplomatic incidents in the early twentieth century were not fully heeded, in part because they could be ambiguous. The runes before 1929 were especially hard to read, especially in the USA. Triggering events – the formation of Hurricane Katrina, the assassination in Sarajevo and the Wall Street crash – were followed by attempts at sensemaking that fell short of grasping the magnitude and urgency of the threat. There was always an element of ambiguity as to whether these were more than routine events. The pace of events varied, being fastest in the case of Hurricane Katrina, but in all three cases there was procrastination and prevarication, and crisis was allowed to turn into disaster on an incalculable scale, certainly in the cases of the First World War and the Depression. Relief and rescue measures were often implemented tardily, if at all. In the Depression, governments chose badly, opting for austerity in the midst of deepening distress. Those involved, as well as observers, were quick to attribute blame, to incompetent officials (Katrina), German militarists (the First World War), and greedy bankers and speculators (the Depression), often glossing over the deeper causes of disasters. Recovery was rarely complete. Initial enthusiasm for rebuilding, and for setting up new arrangements and institutions to avert further disasters gradually waned, especially after 1918 and 2005. The DMC is a valuable tool for historians that aids our understanding of the behaviour of people and organisations before, during and after periods of great stress.

3

Economic Crises in England, 1270–1520:
A Statistical Approach

MARK CASSON AND CATHERINE CASSON

Introduction

This chapter examines crises in the late medieval English economy from 1263 to 1520 using a statistical approach. Historians have identified crises in different ways. Some have suggested that a crisis is best defined as an event that contemporaries themselves thought of as a crisis.[1] The subjectivity of this approach means, however, that different generations may use different criteria, so that crises at different times are not strictly comparable. An alternative is to assess crises in terms of their impacts, but the measurement of impact can also be problematic; for example, a crisis may have a substantial local impact but be insignificant nationally.[2] Furthermore, crises may impact differently on different groups of people, for example, the rich and poor, landowners and labourers.

Statistical data can generate a more comprehensive chronology of crises

---

1   See, for example, William Chester Jordan, *The Great Famine: Northern Europe in the Early Fourteenth Century* (Princeton, 1996), p. 182. For a discussion of broader attitudes towards crisis, including the significance of portents, see Chris Given-Wilson, *Chronicles: The Writing of History in Medieval England* (London, 2004).

2   For some of the difficulties in establishing the geographical impact and legacy of crises, see literature on the Black Death and the Peasants' Revolt, including R.H. Hilton, 'Introduction', in R.H. Hilton and T.H. Aston (eds), *The English Rising of 1381* (Cambridge, 1984), p. 3; R.H. Hilton, *Bond Men Made Free: Medieval Peasant Movements and the English Rising of 1381*, 2nd edn (Abingdon, 2003); P.J.P. Goldberg, *Women, Work and Life Cycle in a Medieval Economy: Women in York and Yorkshire c.1300–1520* (Oxford, 1992); J.M. Bennett, *Ale, Beer, and Brewsters in England: Women's Work in a Changing World, 1300 to 1600* (Oxford, 1996); Sandy Bardsley, 'Women's Work Reconsidered: Gender and Wage Differentiation in Late Medieval England', *Past & Present*, 165 (1999), pp. 3–29; Mark Bailey and Stephen Rigby (eds), *Town and Countryside in the Age of the Black Death: Essays in Honour of John Hatcher* (Turnhout, 2012), p. xxv.

than a collection of contemporary accounts. For England there are particularly extensive data-sets, derived from government administrative records,
which historians have examined for fluctuations in previous literature.[3]
Annual statistical data are available on a range of economic variables,
including prices, wages, output and money supply, as explained below. Time
series for some variables go back as far as 1250.

One way of identifying crises from statistical data is to search for peaks
and troughs. Identifying peaks and troughs is not so simple as it may appear,
however. Peaks and troughs in time series data are defined with reference to
the years before and the years after. A peak value over a decade is not necessarily a peak value over a century. One way of addressing this problem is to
fit an equation to the data and assess peaks and troughs with reference to
the fitted values.[4] Crises are then assessed in terms of annual deviations from
the fitted values. The 'best fit' line can be estimated by the method of least
squares. This is the essence of the approach presented in this chapter: crises
are identified by the deviations of economic variables from their fitted values.

When potential crises have been identified from statistical data, the crisis
years concerned can be compared with crisis years identified in the secondary
literature. The two lists can be matched up and discrepancies noted. The
literature on the medieval English economy has identified a good number of
crisis years, because different authors have used different criteria for identification purposes. An advantage of the statistical approach is that it provides
a consistent analysis of crises based on explicit criteria applied to publicly
available information. The judgements arrived at by statistical methods can
therefore be independently verified. Furthermore, the criteria can be adjusted
to ensure that only a limited number of crisis years are identified over any
given period, allowing the researcher to focus their attention on the most
critical situations.

Existing historiography on crises in medieval England has tended to be
fragmented, with crises often examined largely in isolation from each other
and sometimes examined using separate sources of evidence.[5] This chapter

---

3   Bruce M.S. Campbell, 'Physical Shocks, Biological Hazards, and Human Impacts: The
Crisis of the Fourteenth Century Revisited', in Simonetta Cavaciocchi (ed.), *Le Interazioni
Fra Economia e Ambiente Biologico nell'Europa Preindustriale. Secc. XIII–XVIII Istituto
Internazionale di Storia Economica 'F. Datini'* (Prato, 2010), pp. 13–22.
4   A simple example of fitting an equation to data is to draw a straight line through a scatter
diagram in such a way that the sum of the squares of the distances of the points from the line
is as low as possible. The methods described below generalise this simple principle to more
complex situations.
5   For example Ian Kershaw, 'The Great Famine and Agrarian Crisis in England 1315–1322',
Past & Present, 59 (1973), pp. 3–50; Jordan, *The Great Famine*; Michael Bennet, *Richard II and
the Revolution of 1399* (Stroud, 1999); A.J. Pollard, *The Wars of the Roses*, 2nd edn (Basingstoke,
2001).

examines the presence of crises in a set of annual observations on prices, wages, output, money supply, population and crop yields. These time series were selected because there is already an established tradition of using some of them in order to identify crises, and because they cover different aspects of economic activity. For statistical reasons all the variables except crop yields are measured in logarithms.

It would be possible to analyse these variables separately, looking first at prices, say, and then at wages, and so on. Many of these variables are closely related, however, for example, prices are correlated with wages and money supply. This chapter analyses all the variables together. It uses a simultaneous equation model of the medieval economy, which comprises three separate equations: a price equation, an output equation and a wage equation. According to this model, prices depend on wages, output and money supply, wages depend on prices, and output depends on prices and wages. There is two-way causation: for example, prices depend on wages while wages depend on prices. Where there is two-way causation, lags are used to identify the separate effects. For example, the model postulates that prices depend on the previous year's wages and wages depend on the previous year's prices. This means that the impact of wages on prices can be inferred from the correlation between current prices and past wages, while the impact of prices on wages can be inferred from the correlation between current wages and past prices.

The methods used to fit the model from the data have been published elsewhere.[6] Because of the lags, the model has a recursive structure, and this allows each of the three equations (for prices, output and wages) to be estimated independently of each other without any bias. The price equation is adapted from the price equation used by Mayhew.[7] Simultaneous equation models have been widely used for forecasting modern economies, but this model is the first of its kind to be applied to the medieval economy, so far as the authors are aware. Similarly, this is the first attempt to use the residuals from a simultaneous equation model to identify historical crises in either the medieval or modern periods.

---

6   Mark Casson and Catherine Casson, 'Modelling the Medieval Economy: Money, Prices and Income in England, 1263–1520', in Martin Allen and D'Maris Coffman (eds), *Money, Prices and Wages: Essays in Honour of Professor Nicholas Mayhew* (Basingstoke, 2014).
7   Nicholas J. Mayhew, 'The Quantity Theory of Money in Historical Perspective', in Mark Casson and Nigar Hashimzade (eds), *Large Databases in Economic History: Research Methods and Case Studies* (Abingdon, 2013), pp. 62–96.

Sources of data

Before considering the methods used to analyse the data in detail, it is useful
to consider the background to the data being used. The start date of 1263
was chosen because it is the earliest period when continuous runs of annual
data are available, while the finishing date of 1520 immediately precedes the
take-off of Tudor price inflation.[8]

Price and wage data for the study came from Allen's price and wage indices,
which are nominal sterling values expressed in logarithms.[9] The process of
auditing steward's accounts on the great ecclesiastical and monastic estates
generated a large amount of regionally representative information on prices
and crop yields. Wage information for skilled workers is recorded in the
financial accounts of cathedral building and castle building. In the case of the
wage data, missing observations were interpolated by Allen.

Price evidence suggests that a long period of stability from the time of the
Norman Conquest (and possibly earlier) was succeeded by a rise in prices
in the period 1170–1300.[10] There were several spikes in prices between 1300
and 1348, although from 1320 the underlying trend was downward. Prices
are graphed against time in Figure 3.1. The top dashed line shows the actual
level of prices, while the bottom solid line shows their deviation from a linear
trend, which was fitted by the method of least squares. The scale of prices is
shown on the right-hand axis, and the scale of the deviations on the left-hand
axis. Prices can be negative as well as positive because they are measured in
logarithms. Deviations are negative when the actual value is below trend.
Prices rose in 1348–69, and then began a further decline between 1370 and
1500, after which an upward trend resumed, which continued well into the
sixteenth century. Prices spiked in 1438 and slumped 1439–72, which is
generally regarded as a period of trade depression.[11]

The money-supply data is measured by the stock of coin, estimated from
the accounts of mints, supplemented by information from recoinages and
hoards. Mint accounts provide information on issues of new coin, while
recoinages provide direct information on stocks, and hoards provide estimates
of the physical depreciation of the stock. This chapter uses Mayhew's recent

---

8   G.R. Elton, *England under the Tudors* (Abingdon, 1991), p. 228.
9   Robert C. Allen, 'The Great Divergence in European Wages and Prices from the Middle
Ages to the First World War', *Explorations in Economic History*, 38 (2001), pp. 411–47; Robert
C. Allen, Consumer price index for London, www.nuff.ox.ac.uk/People/sites/Allen/Shared%20
Documents/Forms/AllItems.aspx [accessed 15 April 2013].
10   Nicholas J. Mayhew, 'Prices in England, 1170–1750', *Past & Present*, 219 (2013), pp. 3–39.
11   John Hatcher, 'The Great Slump of the Mid-Fifteenth Century', in Richard Britnell and
John Hatcher (eds), *Progress and Problems in Medieval England: Essays in Honour of Edward
Miller* (Cambridge, 1996), pp. 237–72.

Figure 3.1. Prices (in logarithms), 1264–1520: level and deviations from mean

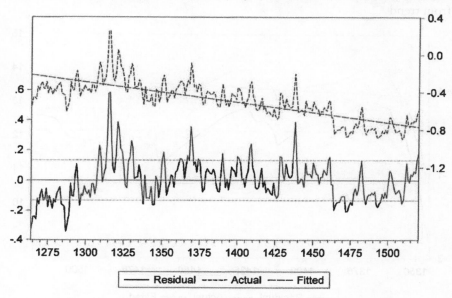

Figure 3.2. Silver coin stock (in logarithms), 1264–1520: level and deviation from trend

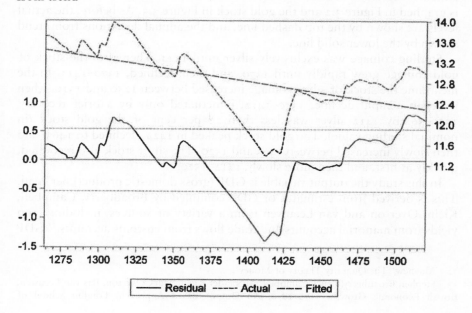

Figure 3.3. Gold coin stock (in logarithms), 1344–1520: level and deviation from trend

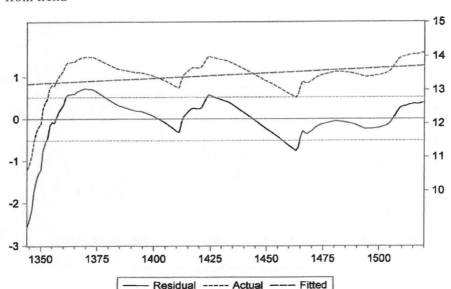

annual stock series for silver and gold coin, for 1220–1750.[12] The silver stock is graphed in Figure 3.2 and the gold stock in Figure 3.3. As before, the actual levels are shown by the top dashed line, and the annual deviations from trend shown by the lower solid line.

Sterling coinage was exclusively silver until 1344. Thereafter the stock of gold coinage grew rapidly until 1370, and then declined, 1370–1411. In the meantime the stock of silver coinage increased between 1250 and 1310, when it began a rapid decline, 1310–1412, punctuated only by a brief recovery, 1350–56. By 1412 silver was less than 20 per cent of the gold stock (in nominal sterling value). The gold stock peaked in 1424, declined to 1463, and then slowly increased between 1463 and 1520. The silver stock also recovered, quickly at first, and then more slowly, 1412–1520.

In this study the output variable is GDP (gross domestic product) per head. This is derived from estimates of GDP compiled by Broadberry, Campbell, Klein, Overton and van Leeuwen from a variety of sources, including crop yields from manorial accounts and trade flows from customs accounts.[13] GDP

12   Mayhew, 'The Quantity Theory of Money'.
13   Stephen Broadberry, Bruce Campbell, Alexander Klein, Mark Overton, Bas van Leeuwen, British Economic Growth, 1270–1870: An Output Based Approach, London School of

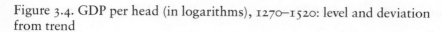

Figure 3.4. GDP per head (in logarithms), 1270–1520: level and deviation from trend

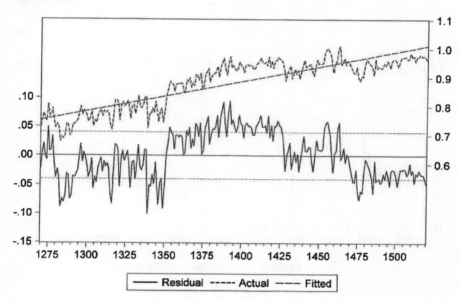

is calculated at constant prices using modern procedures for national income accounting, and this allows the series to be linked to existing post-1750 series. The output series is graphed in Figure 3.4. It shows a strongly rising trend. The most significant period of growth is after the Black Death, 1350–1420. The volatility of output tends to fall over the period, the most volatile period being before the Black Death.

Population data is a difficult data-set to establish for the medieval period, as there was no equivalent to a census, and the alternative potential sources of taxation lists and muster rolls are available only for selected years. It is also difficult to establish mortality rates from epidemics of disease from the available sources.[14] As a result, there is a wide margin between 'high' and 'low' estimates of medieval population, even though there is often broad agreement over whether population was rising or falling at any given time. The population series comes from the same source as the output series, and represents just one possible interpretation of the available evidence. Its most striking feature is the

Economics, http://www.lse.ac.uk/economicHistory/pdf/Broadberry/BritishGDPLongRun16a. pdf [accessed 15 April 2013].
14 For a fuller discussion of some of these issues, see John Hatcher, *Plague, Population and the English Economy, 1348–1530* (London, 1977).

Figure 3.5. Wage (in logarithms), 1264–1520: level and deviation from trend

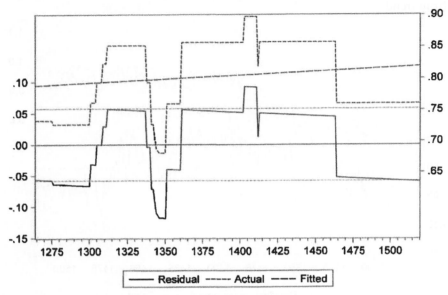

Figure 3.6. Crop yields (index for barley, wheat and oats), 1270–1470: level and deviation from deterministic trend line

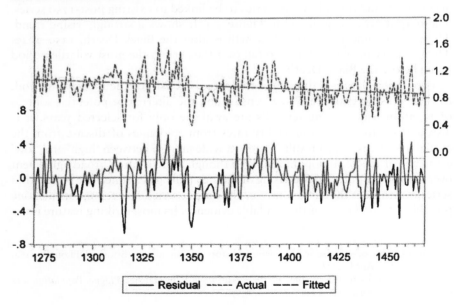

sudden fall in population at the time of the Black Death. This was followed by continued decline in the century 1350–1450, when slow growth resumed.

Wages are graphed in Figure 3.5. This gives an impression of wage rigidity which may be false. Interpolation means that if the wage level is similar at the beginning and end of a period then, in the absence of intervening observations, it is assumed to be constant throughout. Other wage series suggest greater volatility, but these rely on very small numbers of observations in intervening years, and so may reflect, not underlying variation, but random error. Periods of rigidity are interspersed with occasional periods of dramatic change. This is consistent with inertia due to custom or regulation, which occasionally breaks down under the pressure of long-run market forces. The evidence suggests that there were two main wage regimes: a low-wage regime at the beginning and end of the period, 1264–1300 and 1465–1520 respectively, and a high-wage regime, 1310–35 and 1364–1463; the main exception is a temporary but substantial drop in wages, 1336–60.

Crop yields are derived from a database compiled by Campbell, which draws upon various regional studies of manorial accounts.[15] The data comprise an index of yields for three key crops, barley, wheat and oats, 1270–1470, supplied by the author. They are graphed in Figure 3.6. Crop yields are the most volatile of the time series (high variance and low autocorrelation) and exhibit a downward trend. They are relatively high in 1264–1315, but then erratic 1315–48, with bad years in 1315–17 and 1321 and very good years in 1333 and 1338. Crop yields fall after the Black Death, but recover between 1376 and 1395, before declining, 1396–1438. There are further good years in 1458 and 1463.

Statistical methodology: identifying a crisis

In the simultaneous equation model the three variables explained by the three regressions – namely price, output and wages – are used as crisis indicators. A large deviation from the fitted value of any one of these variables is a potential indicator of crisis. Positive and negative deviations may signify different types of crisis, however. Consider inflation and deflation, for example. Inflation may signify a shortage of consumer goods, perhaps as a consequence of failed harvests. On the other hand, it could also signify a boom caused by an increase in credit and consequent shortage of building materials. Similarly, deflation could signify a depression in which labour is laid off and unemployment results. On the other hand, deflation could arise from a good harvest and an abundant supply of consumer goods.

15   Bruce M.S. Campbell, 'Three Centuries of English Crops Yields, 1211–1491', http://www.cropyields.ac.uk (2007) [accessed 11 July 2014].

When interpreting price deviations, historical context matters. In a modern industrial economy, deflation is often regarded as a symptom of depression, caused by falling demand for consumer goods, rather than as the beneficial effect of a good harvest. Similarly, inflation is associated with boom and prosperity, rather than with famine due to a bad harvest. It is essential to bear in mind that the dynamics of an agricultural economy dependent mainly on short-term credit are different from an industrial economy dependent on long-term finance. Where output is concerned there is less ambiguity, however. Crisis is likely to be associated with low output rather than high output. In an agricultural economy low output is likely to be associated with low crop yields, but in an industrial economy it is more likely to be associated with low consumer confidence. In an agricultural economy, a combination of deflation and high output may be regarded as a symptom of a good harvest, whereas a combination of deflation and low output could be a symptom of genuine economic crisis due, for example, to the export of coinage in a foreign war. On balance, in a medieval context it is appropriate to consider inflation as the more likely indicator of a crisis, but crises involving deflation certainly cannot be ruled out.

The wage data used in this study relate mainly to regulated wages set by administrators or by guilds, and therefore do not directly reflect the short-run state of the labour market. Wage changes may reflect several years

Figure 3.7. Prices (in logarithms), 1264–1520: level, fitted regression and deviation based on deterministic and stochastic trends (with one-year lag)

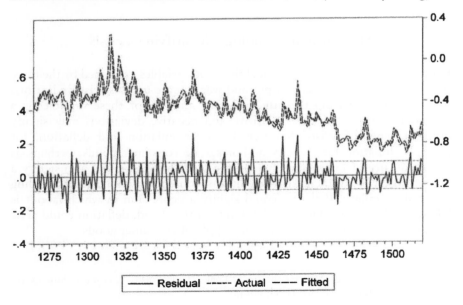

of cumulative change that have finally attracted administrative intervention. In this context the most plausible symptom of crisis is a reduction in wages, for example, to reduce unemployment and make goods cheaper, although it is possible, at least in theory, that an increase in wages might be administered in an attempt to quell social unrest.

To identify potential crises in any year it is necessary to compare the deviations of each of the three variables with some critical value. The critical value needs to be small enough that significant deviations can be found, but large enough that not every deviation suggests a crisis. An appropriate criterion is that the deviation should exceed two standard deviations, as calculated from an appropriate estimate of variance. The relevant variance can be estimated from the variance of the actual data around the fitted values. When the distribution of deviations is approximately normal, on average the deviations in about 2.5 per cent of years will appear as significantly positive, and in another 2.5 per cent of years as significantly negative. Thus potential crises will appear in either 2.5 or 5 per cent of years, depending on whether significant deviations must be either positive or negative, or can be both.

Statistical methodology: stochastic trends

There are two main kinds of trends: deterministic and stochastic. A deterministic trend is exemplified by the linear trend shown in Figure 3.1. To estimate a linear trend a variable is regressed against time and the deviations calculated from the residuals. A stochastic trend emerges when a variable depends on its own history, that is, on its own previous values. In the simplest case, the value of the variable depends just on its value in the previous year (one-year auto-regression).[16] In more complicated cases it may depend on values in much earlier years as well; in practice, however, it is not usually helpful to go back further than three years, because it becomes difficult to disentangle the effects from different years.

Where stochastic trends are present there will be autocorrelation in the residuals from a fitted linear trend. Careful examination of Figure 3.1 shows that when the deviation from trend is negative in one year it is likely to be negative in the next, and similarly for positive values. Over the period 1264–92, for example, all the residuals are negative, while over the later period 1312–25 they are all positive. Figure 3.7 introduces a stochastic trend as well. It shows the results of regressing price against time and against its own previous value. Regressing against time eliminates the deterministic trend (as in Figure 3.1), while regressing against previous price eliminates the stochastic trend.

16   Jeffrey M. Wooldridge, *Introductory Econometrics: A Modern Approach* (Andover, 2014).

Table 3.1. Estimates of the price regression, showing the effects of introducing additional explanatory variables

Explanatory variable	1. Removal of linear trend	2. Removal of stochastic trend (first-order auto-regression)	Controls applied to price variation				
			3. Removal of stochastic trend (third-order auto-regression)	4. Removal of monetary impacts	5. Removal of output and population impacts	6. Removal of wage impacts	7. Removal of crop yield impacts
Period	1264–1520	1264–1520	1264–1520	1264–1520	1264–1520	1264–1520	1264–1470
Constant	-0.225*** (0.000)	-0.050*** (0.006)	-0.049*** (0.002)	-0.404* (0.076)	0.586* (0.086)	-0.563 (0.179)	-1.486** (0.001)
Time	-0.217*** (0.000)	-0.052*** (0.000)	-0.053*** (0.000)	-0.070*** (0.000)	-0.011 (0.689)	-0.040* (0.089)	-0.150*** (0.000)
Price lagged 1 year		0.767*** (0.000)	0.933*** (0.000)	0.924*** (0.000)	0.916*** (0.000)	0.782*** (0.000)	0.601*** (0.000)
Price lagged 2 years			-0.335*** (0.000)	-0.341*** (0.000)	-0.294*** (0.001)	-0.290*** (0.000)	-0.199*** (0.008)
Price lagged 3 years			0.168*** (0.003)	0.166*** (0.004)	0.166*** (0.001)	0.065 (0.273)	0.012 (0.839)
Silver stock				0.011 (0.311)	-0.008 (0.549)	0.015* (0.0667)	0.051** (0.001)
Gold stock				0.017 (0.207)	0.026* (0.058)	0.015 (0.296)	-0.011 (0.505)
Dummy 1344				0.202 (0.268)	0.306* (0.074)	0.094 (0.616)	-0.236 (0.259)

GDP per head				−0.928*** (0.000)	−1.006*** (0.000)	−0.094 (0.719)
Population				−0.184 (0.158)	0.071 (0.634)	0.292 (0.125)
Wage lagged 1 year					0.909*** (0.000)	1.324*** (0.000)
Crop yield						−0.233*** (0.000)
R^2	0.598	0.852	0.854	0.865	0.880	0.856
Adjusted R^2	0.597	0.850	0.849	0.860	0.874	0.847
F	379.6*** (0.000)	359.3*** (0.000)	273.6*** (0.000)	168.5*** (0.000)	171.6*** (0.000)	98.5*** (0.000)
Normality	87.6*** (0.000)	68.0*** (0.000)	66.4*** (0.000)	41.1*** (0.000)	18.2*** (0.000)	19.1* (0.000)
Serial correlation	186.4*** (0.000)	4.9*** (0.008)	4.7 (0.010)	5.8*** (0.003)	2.7 (0.071)	0.8 (0.465)
Heteroscedasticity	11.5*** (0.001)	4.4*** (0.002)	3.0*** (0.005)	3.6 (0.000)	3.3*** (0.000)	1.4 (0.158)
No. observations	257	254	249	246	246	195

Note: * indicates 10 per cent significance, ** 5 per cent significance and *** 1 per cent significance. Prices, GDP, money stock, wage and population are all measured in logarithms. White robust standard errors. Normality of the residuals is tested using a Jarque–Bera test. Serial correlation is tested using a Breusch–Godfrey LM test based on an F-statistic with two lags. Heteroscedasticity is tested using a Breusch–Pagan–Godfrey test based on an F-statistic. These estimates are based on data as collected by the originators on or shortly before 1 October 2013. Some of the data series may have been revised since then. For further details, see Casson and Casson, 'Modelling the Medieval Economy'.

Comparing Figure 3.7 with Figure 3.1 shows that including a stochastic tend produces a much better fit; the variance of the residuals is much reduced, and their pattern is very different, because they change sign with greater frequency.

The relevant price regressions are shown in Table 3.1. The first column illustrates the estimation of a deterministic linear trend. The second column includes a stochastic trend based on a one-year lag. The third column includes a stochastic trend based on lags of up to three years. The inclusion of a one-year price lag raises R^2 (the proportion of the variance that is explained by the regression) from 0.598 to 0.842, but the inclusion of two additional lags increases it by only a small amount, to 0.852.

The importance of stochastic trends may be explained by the persistence of shocks. Suppose that there is a good harvest, for example. With a relatively stable population, demand remains unchanged but supply increases, and so prices will fall. Faced with lower prices, farmers may withhold some grain as seed, while speculators may buy up grain, to store for human or animal consumption in the following year. As a result, supply will be high in the following year as well, so that, other things being equal, low prices will persist. Prices may therefore exhibit inertia; according to the model, however, this inertia is due, not to institutional rigidity in the market, but rather to price adjustments that encourage speculative storage.

Statistical methodology: causation

Once the effects of persistence have been eliminated, further analysis can be carried out to ascertain the causes of shocks and so, by implication, the causes of crises. Inflation was identified above as an important symptom of crisis. According to the Quantity Theory of Money, inflation can be caused by an increase in the money supply. In this case deviations in price will be correlated with changes in money supply. If price deviations are regressed on money supply, the influence of money supply in generating crises can be determined. The residuals from this regression can then be used, in turn, to assess whether additional factors affect crises.

A simple test of the Quantity Theory is reported in column 4 of Table 3.1, where money supply is introduced into the regressions. Results for silver coinage and gold coinage are reported separately, since the two metals may have different roles. For example, when silver is the main circulating medium, and gold acts mainly as a store of value, silver will tend to have a greater impact on prices than gold. A dummy variable is also introduced to allow for unobserved foreign gold in circulation prior to the introduction of sterling gold coin in 1344. The results reported in this column suggest that neither silver nor gold has a major influence on price.

Table 3.2. Estimation of a simultaneous equation model for price, output and wages, 1264–1520

Explanatory variables	1. Price	2. Output	3. Wage	1. Price	2. Output	3. Wage
Period	1264–1520	1264–1520	1264–1520	1270–1470	1270–1470	1270–1470
Constant	-1.036** (0.017)	0.439*** (0.000)	0.129** (0.027)	-2.092*** (0.002)	0.304*** (0.000)	0.148** (0.048)
Time	-0.072*** (0.007)	0.029*** (0.000)	-0.003 (0.353)	-0.215*** (0.000)	0.020*** (0.002)	-0.008 (0.213)
Price lag 1	0.564*** (0.000)	0.068*** (0.000)	0.029** (0.034)	0.286*** (0.005)	0.034*** (0.028)	0.028 (0.104)
Price change lag 1	0.293*** (0.000)	-0.047** (0.019)	-0.002 (0.817)	0.298*** (0.004)	-0.012 (0.466)	-0.006 (0.648)
Price change lag 2	0.007 (0.929)	-0.008 (0.631)	0.002 (0.885)	0.117 (0.116)	-0.016 (0.278)	-0.000 (0.980)
Silver stock lag 1	0.037** (0.022)			0.071*** (0.000)		
Silver stock change	0.021 (0.925)			-0.025 (0.911)		
Silver stock change lag 1	-0.104 (0.734)			-0.047 (0.838)		
Silver stock change lag 2	0.014 (0.948)			0.028 (0.866)		
Gold stock lag 1	0.006 (0.715)			-0.025 (0.239)		

ctd …

Explanatory variables	1. Price	2. Output	3. Wage	1. Price	2. Output	3. Wage
Period	1264–1520	1264–1520	1264–1520	1270–1470	1270–1470	1270–1470
Gold stock change	−0.008 (0.700)			−0.033 (0.199)		
Gold stock change lag 1	−0.009 (0.278)			−0.009* (0.060)		
Gold stock change lag 2	0.004 (0.593)			0.004 (0.318)		
Dummy 1344	−0.042 (0.841)			−0.439 (0.115)		
GDP per head lag 1	−0.400 (0.170)	0.615*** (0.000)	−0.006 (0.878)	0.318 (0.445)	0.723 (0.000)	−0.026 (0.636)
GDP per head change	−1.492*** (0.000)			−0.227 (0.578)		
GDP per head change lag 1	−0.054 (0.849)	−0.107 (0.127)	−0.014 (0.768)	−0.101 (0.763)	−0.012 (0.865)	−0.002 (0.976)
GDP per head change lag 2	−0.043 (0.866)	−0.121* (0.070)	−0.003 (0.950)	−0.201 (0.535)	−0.125 (0.084)	0.043 (0.592)
Population lag 1	0.233 (0.155)	−0.150*** (0.000)	−0.052** (0.027)	0.405* (0.078)	−0.109 (0.001)	−0.074** (0.034)
Wage lag 1	0.800*** (0.000)	−0.043 (0.300)	0.896*** (0.000)	1.578*** (0.000)	−0.037 (0.365)	0.915*** (0.000)
Wage change lag 1	−0.482 (0.196)	−0.002 (0.988)	−0.076 (0.242)	−0.892*** (0.007)	−0.010 (0.908)	−0.107 (0.136)

Wage change lag 2	−0.237 (0.506)	−0.014 (0.853)	0.005 (0.910)	−0.681** (0.045)	−0.018 (0.772)	−0.021 (0.681)
Crop yield				−0.237*** (0.000)	0.074 (0.000)	−0.001 (0.788)
Crop yield lag 1				−0.018 (0.655)	−0.055 (0.000)	−0.003 (0.699)
Crop yield lag 2				−0.006 (0.868)	−0.000 (0.986)	−0.004 (0.475)
Crop yield lag 3				−0.033 (0.347)	−0.007 (0.425)	0.007 (0.362)
R^2	0.895	0.943	0.949	0.870	0.973	0.940
Adjusted R^2	0.884	0.941	0.947	0.849	0.971	0.935
F	87.0*** (0.000)	359.5*** (0.000)	402.4*** (0.000)	42.0*** (0.000)	424.6*** (0.000)	186.0*** (0.000)
Normality	28.2*** (0.000)	17.2*** (0.000)	6,063.0*** (0.000)	28.7*** (0.000)	27.7*** (0.000)	2,451.4*** (0.000)
Serial correlation	0.198 (0.821)	0.581 (0.560)	3.466** (0.033)	0.9 (0.409)	5.0*** (0.008)	5.0*** (0.008)
Heteroscedasticity	1.584 (0.055)	1.997** (0.030)	0.804 (0.636)	0.9 (0.592)	1.0 (0.428)	0.7 (0.816)
No. observations	237	249	194	183	194	194

Note: For notes on estimation methods and diagnostic tests, see Table 3.1. The correlations between the residuals 1264–1520 are as follows (probability values in brackets): price–income: 0.000 (1.000); price–wage: 0.265 (0.000); wage–income: 0.014 (0.834). For 1270–1470 the correlations are: price–income: 0.000 (1.000); price–wage: 0.329 (0.000); wage–income: 0.010 (0.891).

The Quantity Theory has other implications. With a constant velocity of circulation and a given money stock, the total value of annual transactions will be constant too, and this implies that high levels of GDP are associated with low prices, and vice versa. In the short run, high GDP could result from high output (high GDP per head) and in the long run from high population. Output and population can be included in the regression analysis; the theory predicts that high output and high population will both reduce prices. The results are shown in column 5 of Table 3.1. The negative impact of output is strongly supported, but the influence of population is weak, though of the expected sign. Note that the gold stock (but not the silver stock) now becomes significant once income is included in the regression.

One of the key assumptions of the Quantity Theory is that wages are flexible, so that the labour market can adjust to maintain full employment. But, as shown above, there is some evidence of rigidity in money wages. In this case the level of wages could influence the level of prices. Column 6 shows the effect of including wages in the regression. Wages are highly significant and have the expected effect: higher wages lead to higher prices in the following year. When wages are included, however, it appears that silver rather than gold influences prices.

Bad harvests are another explanation of inflation. Bad harvests may be the result of low crop yields. The effects of low crop yields may already be reflected in estimates of GDP; it is possible, however, that they have an independent effect as well. This is corroborated by the results in column 7, which show that low crop yields significantly increase prices. The inclusion of crop yields makes output insignificant, suggesting that agricultural output may be a more important determinant of prices than other forms of output.

Results from the simultaneous equation model

The simultaneous equation model is estimated both with and without crop yield data. Without crop yield data the period covered is 1264–1520, and with crop yield data it is 1270–1470. Both sets of results are reported in Table 3.2. The system generates three sets of residuals that are used in combination to analyse crises.

Potential crises are identified by one or more of the following symptoms occurring in any given year:
- Inflation or deflation: large positive or negative price residuals.
- Low output: large negative output residuals.
- Very high or very low wage: large wage residuals.

The results are analysed in three parts. The first part concerns just the price regressions, and is based on Table 3.3. This table is derived from Tables

3.1 and 3.2. It indicates, for each regression, the years in which inflation or deflation was more than two standard deviations from its predicted value. It shows how the years of significant deviations change as more explanatory variables are entered into the regression. Significant deviations from the mean are identified in column 1. The information in columns 2–8 is derived from Table 3.1 and the remaining information in columns 9 and 10 is derived from Table 3.2. The final column (column 10) contains all the explanatory variables used in this study.

The results may be summarised as follows:

- In 1309 unexplained inflation is identified once output and population effects are controlled for. It disappears again, however, when wages effects are introduced, and reappears after crop yields are introduced. Inflation is also identified in the final regression where crop yields are included. It was a year of good harvests but, even so, prices were well above their predicted level.

- The Great Famine is also a period of unexplained inflation. Although bad harvests lead to inflation, inflation in these years was even higher than expected. Crop failure began in 1315, became worse in 1316, but diminished somewhat in 1317. Unexplained inflation is higher in 1315 than 1316. There are signs of inflation in 1314, the year before the famine, suggesting that other forces besides famine may have been at work. Although inflation continued until 1317, this appears to have been due to persistence rather than to any new inflationary shock.

- The year 1321 also witnessed poor harvests, and once again there is unexplained inflation. The experiences of 1315–16 and 1321 suggest that prices may respond non-linearly to crop failure. This is consistent with the view that stock-piling and panic buying may have exacerbated problems. On the other hand, it could be simply that starving people became desperate for food.

- Prices fell in 1322, when harvests returned to normal, but not so quickly as might be expected. This could be because precautionary stocks of foodstuffs had been run down the previous year and needed to be replenished.

- The year 1330 shows some symptoms of high inflation, but the regression results do not suggest any obvious explanation.

- According to the full regression, prices in 1333 did not fall by as much as might be expected, given the very good harvest that year.

- In 1339, a year of bad harvests, there is some unexplained inflation, but this disappears once exceptionally low output is allowed for.

- The years 1350–51, in the aftermath of the Black Death, also witness unexplained inflation. The effect disappears in 1350 once low crop yields are controlled for, but not in 1351. In 1351 wage increases contribute to inflation.

Table 3.3. Significant residual variation in the annual money price level, analysed according to the number of explanatory variables included in the regression

	1. Deviation from mean	2. Removal of linear trend	3. Removal of stochastic trend (first-order auto-regression)	4. Removal of stochastic trend (third-order auto-regression)	5. Removal of monetary impacts	6. Removal of output and population impacts	7. Removal of wage impacts	8. Removal of crop yield impacts	9. Final result without adjustment for crop yield impacts	10. Final result with adjustment for crop yield impacts
Period	1264–1520	1264–1520	1264–1520	1264–1520	1264–1520	1264–1520	1264–1520	1270–1470	1270–1520	1270–1470
Number of observations	257	257	256	254	249	246	246	195	237	183
1264	X	−	X	X	X	X	X	X	X	X
1287		−	−	−	−	−	−	−	−	−
1288		−								
1309	+	+				+		+		+
1314	+	+		+	+	+	+	+	+	
1315	+	+	+	+	+					+
1316	+	+				+				
1317	+	+								
1321	+		+	+	+	+	+		+	
1322	+	+								
1330					+	+	+	+		

Year								
1333				+		+	−	+ + +
1338	−		−	+ +		+ +	+	+
1339				+	−	−	+ +	+ +	+ +
1340					−	+			+
1350					−		+		+ +
1351						−			+ +
1353									
1365				+	−			+	+ +	+	−
1369							+		+ + + +
1400						+		+ +	+ +
1408									−
1428							+		+ +	+
1437								+	+
1438									+
1464									−
1509	X		X		X				−

Note: A significant variation is more than double the standard deviation of the residuals from the conditional mean (predicted value) of the relevant estimated regression. X indicates that estimated residuals are not available for the year in question.

- There is a run of bad harvests in the period 1367–69, and this culminates in unexplained inflation in 1369. It is possible that destocking occurred in 1367–68, which helped to maintain price, and that there was a sharp jump in 1369 when reserves finally ran out. This is consistent with the view that each year people were expecting a better harvest, but that this did not materialise until 1370, which was too late.
- There is evidence of inflation in 1400 once wage impacts are allowed for. This may have been linked to political uncertainty surrounding the deposition of Richard II.
- The year 1408 marks the start of a run of poor harvests. Unexplained inflation appears when controlling for three-year price persistence, continues when monetary factors are introduced, but disappears when income is introduced.
- There is unexplained inflation in 1428, although it is weaker when wage impacts are allowed for.
- In 1437 there is unexplained inflation when controlling for three-year price persistence, but this disappears once monetary factors are introduced. There is much stronger evidence for inflation in the following year, however. These are two consecutive years of bad harvests.

The second part of the analysis concerns the results of the three-equation system, which are presented in Table 3.4. The focus is now on low output and on any significant change in wages. Since the aim is to identify additional years of potential crisis, years already discussed are not mentioned again. There are three years with significantly low output but no significant price effects, 1283, 1374 and 1432, and no fewer than nine years with significant changes in wages and no significant price effects: there are wage increases in 1301, 1305 and 1312, reductions in 1338 and 1341, increases in 1351, 1361 and 1403, a reduction in 1412, an increase in 1413 and a reduction in 1464.

There were poor crop yields in both 1283 and 1374, but output was still low in 1283 even when controlling for crop yields. In 1374, however, low output seems to be explained by low crop yields. In 1432 output was low even though crop yields were normal. Thus 1283 and 1432 appear to be the main years of potential crisis.

Because of the fragmentary nature of wage evidence, it may be misleading to treat each year of significant wage change as if it represented a separate crisis. There is a clear pattern of increases over the period 1301–12, decreases 1338–41, increases in 1361, and volatility 1403–13. All of the wage changes are significant before crop yields are controlled for, but when controlling for crop yields only four are significant: in 1338, 1361, 1403 and 1412. Since none of these wage changes are associated with unexpected price changes, they may be due, at least in part, to administrative action rather than to economic adjustment.

The final stage is to identify a short list of potential crisis years, and examine the events that occurred in these years. Table 3.5 lists the years selected for special study, and some of the most prominent events associated with them.

Internal disputes between the crown and the nobility provide the context to the possible crises in 1309 and 1321. The reign of Edward II is especially identified by historians of fourteenth-century England as one of crisis, and these results therefore correspond with that historiography. The key issue for Edward II's contemporaries was the favouritism that he displayed towards certain individuals, notably Piers Gaveston and the Despencers.[17] This was eventually to contribute to his deposition by Queen Isabella and Roger Mortimer.

Domestic wars have been identified as another potential source of crises by political historians. Table 3.5 shows that domestic wars have a relatively modest impact. The Welsh wars of Edward I, the Scottish wars of Edward III, and the Wars of the Roses do not seem to have precipitated any economic crises. The main exception is relatively tenuous; the defeat of Hotspur in the Welsh wars occurred in the crisis year of 1403. In addition, significant inflation occurred in 1438, the year of an Anglo–Scottish truce, but the impact is the opposite of what would be expected from cessation of war. The lack of significant impacts of the Wars of the Roses in particular supports recent historiography in the field. While earlier analysis of the Wars tended to see them as protracted and bloody, more recent assessments have emphasised the gaps in the fighting and seen the battles as interspersing peace, rather than peace being only occasional.[18]

Foreign wars appear to be more significant than domestic wars. The crises in 1338–39 follow the start of the Hundred Years' War with France in 1337 while the crisis of 1369 occurs when Edward III resumed the title of King of France.[19] A sharp reduction in wages in 1412 coincides with Henry IV abandoning Burgundy while inflation in 1428 coincides with the assault on Orleans.

Moving on to consider economic factors, the Great Famine and the Black Death both feature, but it is interesting to note the specific years that appear. For the Great Famine the major years of crop failure are included, but years when diseases of sheep and cattle were rife do not.[20] For the Black Death,

17   Michael Prestwich, *The Three Edwards: War and State in England 1272–1377* (London, 1980), p. 81 and p. 114.

18   See, for example, John Gillingham, *The Wars of the Roses: Peace and Conflict in Fifteenth-Century England* (London, 1981), pp. 1–14; Philip A. Haigh, *The Military Campaigns of the Wars of the Roses* (Stroud, 1997), pp. 1–7; A.J. Pollard, *The Wars of the Roses*, 2nd edn (Basingstoke, 2001), p. v.

19   Christopher Allmand, *The Hundred Years War: England and France at War c.1300–c.1450* (Cambridge, 1988).

20   For further discussion of this, see Philip Slavin, 'The Great Bovine Pestilence and its Economic and Environmental Consequences in England and Wales, 1318–50', *Economic History Review*, 65 (2012), pp. 1239–66.

Table 3.4. Significant residual variation in prices, output and wages in a simultaneous equation model, including a comparison between estimates for 1264–1520 that exclude crop yield variation and for 1270–1470 that include crop yield variation

Period	1. Price Fully adjusted for persistence 1264–1520	2. Output Fully adjusted for persistence 1264–1520	3. Wage Fully adjusted for persistence 1264–1520	4. Price Fully adjusted for persistence and crop yields 1270–1470	5. Output Fully adjusted for persistence and crop yields 1270–1470	6. Wage Fully adjusted for persistence and crop yields 1270–1470
Number of observations	237	249	249	183	194	194
1275		+				
1283		−			−	
1287	−			−		
1288						
1301			+			
1305			+			
1309				+		
1312			+			
1314		−				
1315	+			+		
1316		−				
1317						
1321		−				
1322						
1330				+		
1333						

Year					
1338	−	−	−	−	−
1339	−		−		−
1340					−
1341	+	+	+	−	−
1350	+	+	+	+	+
1351	+		+	+	+
1353	+				
1361	+				−
1365			+	+	+
1369		+		+	+
1374	−		−	−	
1388					+
1400	+	+	+	+	+
1403				+	
1408	−		−	−	
1412		−	−		−
1413		+	+	+	+
1428		+			+
1432		−			
1437		+	+		+
1438		+	+		+
1446					−
1454	−	+	−		−
1464	−				
1509	X	X	X		

Note: See notes to previous table. 'Income' signifies GDP per head, and 'wages' signify the money wage rate. Output deviations in 1406 and 1407 have been removed from the table because it is possible that they result from errors in the data.

Table 3.5. Possible crises in the late medieval English economy

Date	Symptoms	Context
1283	Reduction in output (not only due to poor crop yields)	Edward I calls two provincial councils, at York and Canterbury
1309	Selective evidence of inflation	Edward I dies in 1307. Piers Gaveston, favourite of Edward II, returns to England from exile
1315	Significant inflation (even allowing for variation in crop yields). Reduction in output due to low crop yields	Start of the Great Famine. Major rainfall and flooding. Ordinances make the barons the administrators of the royal revenues
1316	Inflation (before adjusting for persistence). Reduction in output due to low crop yields	Continuation of the Great Famine
1321	Selective evidence for inflation. Reduction in output due to poor crop yields	The final year of the Great Famine. Political unrest between Edward II and the nobility as the king's favourites, the Despencers, are banished, but only to be recalled in 1322
1338	Some evidence of price deflation. Reduction in wages	The Hundred Years' War with France begins in 1337
1339	Selective evidence of price inflation. Reduction in output (not due only to poor crop yields)	Edward III invades France, defeats the French at Sluys, and makes a treaty with Philip VI of France. Instability in the wool export trade
1350	Inflation (after allowing for persistence) and increase in income (after allowing for crop yield variation)	Black Death (1348–49)
1351	Inflation and wage increases	Statute of Labourers
1361	Significant wage increase	Plague reappears. Justices of the Peace Act
1369	Significant inflation	Edward III resumes the title King of France. Charles V declares war on England. Anglo–Scottish truce
1374	Low output	Dancing mania in Europe. Edward III dies in 1377

Year		
1400	Inflation after adjusting for wage impacts	Richard II is murdered, after being deposed the previous year by Henry IV. Welsh Rebellion, led by Owain Glyndwr, begins, lasting until 1415. Henry IV suppresses a rebellion of the barons. Prosperity in the cloth export trade
1403	Wage increase	King Henry IV defeats 'Harry Hotspur' (Henry Percy) at Shrewsbury
1412	Sharp reduction in wages	Henry IV abandons Burgundy and allies with Orleans in the Hundred Years' War. Arundel is appointed Chancellor and the Prince of Wales removed from the Council. Henry IV dies the following year
1428	Inflation, and reduction in output after allowing for crop yield variation	Assault on Orleans in the Hundred Years' War with France
1432	Low output	An uneventful year
1438	Significant inflation	Anglo–Scottish truce for 14 years
1446	Low output	An uneventful year

Note: The terms 'increase' and 'reduction' must be interpreted in the context of the residuals analysis. 'Increase (decrease)' signifies a positive (negative) residual exceeding two standard deviations from the predicted value.

inflation appears in the years after the Black Death, rather than the years of the plague itself.

The connection between the Black Death and inflation is not so straight-forward as may appear. Although the Black Death diminished the supply of agricultural products, it diminished the demand as well; the fall in population that reduced the labour supply also reduced the number of mouths to be fed. If the balance between demand and supply remained unchanged then there is, in principle, no reason for prices to change as well. If the money supply remained roughly constant, however, while output fell, then the Quantity Theory of Money would predict an increase in price. If monetary factors impacted with a lag, then this would explain the lag in inflation. Another reason for the lagged response could be long-term disruption to the market system, caused by the death of so many merchants and the disorganisation of civic and manorial life.

Apart from the Black Death, monetary factors seem to have had little effect. The stocks of silver and gold are of limited significance in the regression equations, and the dummy variable for the introduction of gold coinage in 1344 is mostly insignificant too. There is an unexplained increase in the wage in 1301, following the partial recoinage of 1299–1301, but this disappears once crop yields are allowed for; the direction of change is unusual too, as improvement in the quality of the currency would be expected to reduce the wage. Trade policy too appears to have little effect. There is no discernible crisis in either 1275, when Edward I introduced the 'Ancient custom' on wool (a tax on wool exports), nor in 1347 when the 'cloth custom' was introduced (although the effects of the latter may be masked by the Black Death).

Other events are also notable for their absence. The Good Parliament of 1376, which saw parliament refuse Edward III's requests for direct taxation and a lay subsidy, does not appear as a crisis. This is perhaps because its decision, while a serious attack on Edward III's authority at the time, was reversed the following year.[21] The Peasants' Revolt of 1381 does not appear to have caused a crisis. While earlier historiography on the Revolt considered it to be widespread across England and perceived it to have long-term conse-quences, there has been a move towards down-playing the scale of the Revolt and its long-term significance.[22] The results of this chapter tie in with the view that the Revolt was not a major crisis.

21   W.M. Ormrod, *The Reign of Edward III: Crown and Political Society in England 1327–1377* (Stroud, 2005), p. 37.
22   Hilton, 'Introduction', p. 3; Hilton, *Bond Men*; M. McKisack, *The Fourteenth Century* (Oxford, 1959), p. 422; M.M. Postan, *The Medieval Economy and Society* (London, 1972).

Conclusions

This chapter has shown that crises identified directly from statistical data correspond with some, but not all, of the events identified as crises in the established historiography. Both economic and political events feature in the results.

In terms of economic events, the timing of the impacts of the Great Famine and the Black Death is somewhat different from what might have been expected. Certain years of the Great Famine appear in the results, but not all. Meanwhile the immediate aftermath of the Black Death appears more prominently in the results than the high point of the disease itself. For political events, meanwhile, it can be seen that internal disputes between the crown and the nobility correspond with a number of the crises identified in the statistical analysis. In particular the results lend support to the concept of crises in the reign of Edward II. The Hundred Years' War corresponds with four of the years of crisis identified in the statistical analysis. This may be because, while the fighting took place in France, the financial element of the war had a strong impact on English citizens, as much of the literature has suggested.[23]

While the conclusions so far have discussed crises that may derive from a single dominant cause, the results also show that crises can occur from a combination of events that collectively overwhelm the capacity of institutions. This can be seen in particular with regards to the Great Famine, where the years 1315 and 1321 – identified as crisis years in the statistical analysis – both witnessed a combination of environmental and political disruption. This relationship was identified by Jordan and has been supported by recent research.[24]

From the evidence in this chapter it appears that a problem becomes a crisis when markets are not sufficiently flexible to adjust, or when political authorities are not sufficiently vigilant or decisive. It can also be noted that events whose impact is often considered by historians to have been relatively short-term, such as the Good Parliament and the Peasants' Revolt, do not appear as crises in the statistical analysis.

23   Allmand, The Hundred Years War; M.M. Postan, 'The Costs of the Hundred Years War', Past & Present, 27 (1964), pp. 34–53.

24   Jordan, The Great Famine, p. 182; Philip Slavin, 'Market Failure during the Great Famine in England and Wales (1315–1317)', Past & Present, 221 (2014), pp. 9–49. The topic is currently also being examined in a Leverhulme Major Research Fellowship (MRF-2011–2014), P.R. Schofield, The Great Famine. Dearth and Society in Medieval England c.1300, http://www. leverhulme.ac.uk/files/seealsodocs/946/MRF2011-abstracts.PDF [accessed 15 July 2014].

PART II:
AGRICULTURE AND ENVIRONMENT

4

Flogging a Dead Cow: Coping with Animal Panzootic on the Eve of the Black Death

PHILIP SLAVIN

Climatic change and animal disease

In the space of seventy years, England and other parts of the British Isles were devastated by no less than three major biological catastrophes of panzootic/ pandemic proportions. First, there was an outbreak of scab, a highly acute and transmissive form of dermatitis, caused by faeces and bites of sheep mites (*Psoroptes ovis*), which ravaged English flocks between 1279 and 1281.[1] Although the major wave of scab was over by 1281, there were minor recurrent outbreaks of scab well into the 1320s (in particular, in 1282–87, 1297–1305, and 1314–17). In 1319–20, England was hit by a major cattle pestilence, most likely rinderpest (a highly viral disease, caused by the RPV virus), which killed about 62 per cent of bovine stocks within less than a year.[2] The rinderpest crisis was followed by two minor and local outbreaks of bovine disease, whose nature is unclear, in 1324–27 and 1333–34. Finally, between late 1348 and early 1350, England was devastated by human pestilence, the Black Death, which is now established to have been a bubonic plague caused by a biovar of *Yersinia Pestis*.[3] In order to understand this sudden rise of pathogens and

---

1 That it was scab is apparent from various references in manorial documents. See, for instance, the National Archives (henceforth, TNA), SC 6/929/19, SC 6/938/2, SC 6/761/11 and SC 6/1007/10.

2 T. Newfield, 'A Cattle Panzootic in Early Fourteenth-Century Europe', *Agricultural History Review*, 57 (2009), pp. 155–90; P. Slavin, 'The Great Bovine Pestilence and its Economic and Environmental Consequences in England and Wales, 1318–50', *Economic History Review*, 65 (2012), pp. 1239–66.

3 K. Bos, V.J. Schuenemann, G.B. Golding, H.A. Burbano, N. Waglechner, B.K. Coombes, J.B. McPhee, S.N. DeWitte, M. Meyer, S. Schmedes, J. Wood, D.J.D. Earn, D.A. Herring, P. Bauer, H.N. Poinar and J. Krause, 'A Draft Genome of Yersinia Pestis from Victims of the Black Death', *Nature*, 478 (27 October 2011), pp. 506–10.

the decline in health of both animals and humans, it is vital to appreciate the wider environmental context of the period. As recent studies have shown, shifts and fluctuations in ecological regimes tend to have a profound impact on the biological attributes of living organisms.[4]

It is generally accepted that, around 1270, some major climatic changes were under way. After some 200 years of mild and warm climate (aka, 'Medieval Climate Anomaly', MCA), when average annual temperatures were similar to those of c.2000, the climate of the North Atlantic region entered a new transitional phase, lasting for approximately 150 years and leading to the commencement of a new climatic *longue durée*, commonly known as the Little Ice Age (LIA) (c.1420–1850; naturally, there is much debate about its chronology). This transitional phase from the MCA to LIA, itself a part of a much broader global climatic shift, is a highly complex and still under-appreciated phenomenon. The MCA was marked by a positively strong North Atlantic Oscillation (NAO),[5] provoking strong winter Westerlies and causing mildly wet and relatively warm weather in north-western Europe and arid conditions in the Mediterranean and North Africa. Around 1270, however, there was a shift to a new and highly unstable regime, characterised by high amplitude of annual sea and air temperature and a great degree of variance in year-to-year precipitation index. In other words, each year temperature and precipitation varied a great deal. There was a gradual weakening of the NAO, to the point that by the 1430s the NAO became negative, causing stormy and cold weather, which were dominant for the duration of the LIA.[6] In addition, the solar irradiance levels declined, reaching the abysmally low *minimum* between c.1280 and 1340 (the 'Wolf Minimum').[7] During this period, the levels of solar irradiance were approximately 36 per cent below average for the period of 1000–1500. Piecemeal weakening of the NAO on the one hand and the depressed solar irradiance meant gradual cooling.[8] It was in this climatic context that the scab outbreak originated. The wet and increasingly cold

4   For instance, T. Ben Ari, S. Neerincx, K.L. Gage, K. Kreppel, A. Laudisoit, H. Leirs and N.C. Stenseth, 'Plague and Climate: Scales Matter,' *PLoS Pathog* 7:9 (2011), e1002160. doi:10.1371/journal.ppat.1002160.g002.

5   Roughly speaking, the North Atlantic Oscillation (NRO) is the difference in atmospheric pressure of sea levels between the 'Icelandic Low' and the 'Azores High' cyclones.

6   A.G. Dawson, K. Hickey, P.A. Mayewski and A. Nesje, 'Greenland (GISP2) Ice Core and Historical Indicators of Complex North Atlantic Climate Changes during the Fourteenth Century', *Holocene*, 17 (2007), pp. 427–34; A.G. Cage and W.E.N. Austin, 'Marine Climate Variability during the Last Millennium: The Loch Sunart Record, Scotland, UK', *Quaternary Science Review*, 29 (2010), pp. 1633–47.

7   G. Delaygue and Edouard Bard, 'An Antarctic View of Beryllium-10 and Solar Activity for the Past Millennium', *Climate Dynamics*, 36 (2011), pp. 2201–18.

8   B.M.S. Campbell, 'Panzootics, Pandemics and Climatic Anomalies in the Fourteenth Century', in B. Herrmann (ed.), *Beiträge zum Göttinger Umwelthistorischen Kolloquium 2010–2011* (Göttingen, 2011), p. 186.

winters presented the ideal conditions for the spread of scab: scab mites like damp and cold weather, and it is in those conditions that they act and mate aggressively.[9] It is hardly surprising that the recurrent outbreaks followed the main wave in the subsequent decades: the period between the 1280s and 1320s was marked by excessively low radiance levels and cold weather.

Outside of north-western Europe, the climatic shift was equally pronounced. Around the Pacific Rim, the MCA was characterised by the dominance of La Niña, resulting in low precipitation levels along the west coast of the Americas and south Asian monsoons. During the 1280s, the monsoon levels declined considerably and the last two decades of the thirteenth century saw unprecedentedly dry and cold years in the Pacific and Central Asia.[10] It was precisely around the same time that the first signs of mass cattle mortality were reported in various parts of Eurasia, and it seems that the cattle pestilence was a disaster on a global scale. According to the fourteenth-century Chinese chronicle *Yuan Shi*, there were recurrent outbreaks of cattle plague among the cattle of Mongol nomads between 1288 and 1331. There were also similar outbreaks of panzootics in northern China in 1288, 1301, 1306 and 1335. The mortality was accompanied by exceptionally cold winters with heavy snowstorms.[11] Similarly, the cattle plague prevailed in other parts of the Mongolian Empire. In the Ilkhanate, the cattle mortality emptied the royal treasury of Gaykhatu Khan (1291–95).[12] Two Persian chroniclers, Al-Makrizi and Badr ad-Din al-'Aini, relate that all cattle died in the days of Tohtu Khan, the Khan of the Golden Horde (1291–1312).[13] Such weather anomaly presented the ideal condition for the appearance and spread of the virus responsible for the cattle pestilence. It is most likely that from the Mongols, the cattle disease came to Europe through the Russian steppes. The Russian chronicles speak of great cattle mortality in 1298 and 1309.[14] Various Russian chronicles report exceptionally dry years of 1298–1300 and 1309.

9 P. Bates, 'Sheep Scab (*Psoroptes ovis*)', in I.D. Aitken (ed.), *Diseases of Sheep*, 4th edn (Oxford, 2007), p. 323.

10 Campbell, 'Panzootics, Pandemics', pp. 186–9, 192, 196, 199; R. D'Arrigo *et al.*, '1738 years of Mongolian Temperature Variability Inferred from a Tree-Ring Width Chronology of Siberian Pine', *Geophysical Research Letters*, 28 (2001), pp. 543–6.

11 *Yuan Shi* (Beijing, 1995), vol. 2, pp. 310, 436, 468 and vol. 3, p. 826. I am grateful to Ilia Mozias for his reading and translation of the Chinese sources; Elizabeth Endicott, 'The Mongols and China. Cultural Contacts and the Changing Nature of Pastoral Nomadism (Twelfth to Early Thirteenth Centuries)', in Reuven Amitai and Michal Biran (eds), *Mongols, Turks and Others. Eurasian Nomads and the Sedentary World* (Leiden, 2005), pp. 461–81.

12 David Morgan, *The Mongols* (Cambridge, MA, 1987), p. 165.

13 The account is given, for instance, by Badr ad-Din al-'Aini (1361–1451): *Istoriya Kazakhstana v Arabskikh Istochnikakh*, ed. and trans. V.G. Tizengauzen (Almaty, 2005), p. 359.

14 *Patriarshaia ili Nikonovskaia Letopis'*, in Polnoe Sobranie Russkikh Letopisej 10 (Saint Petersburg, 1885), p. 171; *Moskovskij Letopisnyj Svod Kontsa XV Veka*, in Polnoe Sobranie Russkikh Letopisej 25 (Moscow, 1949), p. 159.

By c.1316, the cattle pestilence reached Central Europe, where its presence is attested in Bohemia and eastern German lands. By 1318, the pestilence ravaged northern France, the Low Countries and parts of northern Italy. In the same year, cattle mortality is reported in Denmark.[15] Finally, by Easter 1319 the disease had reached England.

Scab of 1279–80 and rinderpest of 1319–20

Unlike the bovine pestilence, however, the scab outbreak seems to have been on a local scale, confined to the British Isles. The available sources, both statistical and textual, provide contradictory information about the origins, seasonality and geography of the dissemination of scab disease in England. For instance, William Rishanger, a contemporary chronicler, stated that scab had been brought by a diseased Spanish ewe, imported into Northumberland by a certain wealthy Frenchman in 1274/5.[16] Some historians went as far as interpreting it as the first reference to *merino* sheep in England.[17] This story, as well as its interpretation, can be both dismissed as a *curiosum* outright, for three reasons: (1) there is no evidence of the import of Spanish sheep (let alone the North African *merino* ones, unknown in Europe until 1339) into England in the late thirteenth century; (2) no manorial account provides any evidence of large-scale sheep mortality in 1274/5; (3) there are no references, to my best knowledge, to scab outbreak in either Spanish kingdoms, or in France. Some other chronicles report sheep mortality under 1276 and 1277.[18] Finally, according to *Louth Park Chronicle*, the disease broke out in 1279 in Lindsey (Lincolnshire).[19] It seems that this contradiction of chronology would have left us in the shadows if we did not have the manorial accounts with their remarkably accurate and detailed information.

In addition to indicating the mortality rates, calculated by deflating the

---

15   The geographic spread of the pestilence in northern Eurasia has been surveyed in Newfield, 'Cattle Panzootic', pp. 159–63. In northern Italy, the pestilence is mentioned in the *Chronicon Parmense*. See Bonazzi, Giuliano (ed.): Chronicon Parmense. Ab Anno MXXXVIII usque ad Annum MCCCXXXVIII, *Rerum Italicarum Scriptores* 9/9 (Città di Castello 1902–04), p. 157. I am thankful for Martin Bauch of the German Historical Institute in Rome for this reference.
16   H.T. Riley (ed.), *Willelmi Rishanger Chronica et Annales*, Rolls Series (London, 1865), p. 84.
17   G. Fleming, *Animal Plagues: Their History, Nature and Prevention* (London, 1871), p. 79.
18   Thus, Barlings Chronicle *sub* 1276 (W. Stubbs (ed.), *Chronicles of the Reigns of Edward I and Edward II*, vol. 2, Rolls Series (London, 1883), p. cxvii); Annals of Waverley *sub* 1277 (Annales monasterii de Waverleia, in H.R. Luard (ed.), *Annales Monastici*, vol. 2 (London, 1864), p. 388.
19   A.R. Maddison (ed.), *Chronicon Abbatie de Parco Ludae. Chronicle of Louth Park Abbey with appendix of documents*, Lincolnshire Record Society, I (Lincoln, 1891), p. 18.

number of deceased animals by the total number of animals stocked in a given year, the accounts specify whether the animals died 'before lambing' (in case of ewes), 'between lambing and sheering', or 'after sheering', thus implying the seasonality of mortality. In the vast majority of cases, sheep panzootic is mentioned in the 1279–80 accounts, running between the two Michaelmases. This, however, does not mean that the disease arrived in England sometime after Michaelmas 1279. In fact, the first reference to scab is found in the East Meon (Hampshire) portion of the 1231–32 Winchester Bishopric pipe roll, noting 32 'scabious' ewes (out of the total 1,075), for whose medication was spent 2.5d.[20] Similarly, a minor and local incidence of scab is reported in the East Knoyle (Wiltshire) portion of the 1272–73 Winchester Bishopric pipe roll. In that year, 208 out of 1,691 ewes and 463 out of 962 lambs died and 3.5d was spent on sulphur 'to heal ewes with scab'.[21] It should be noted, however, that these were isolated and minor episodes, affecting neither the size, nor health of the Winchester sheep flocks. In fact, the sheer size of the Winchester Bishopric flock rose from 27,561 to 29,618 animals during the 1272–73 accounting year, reaching its pre-Black Death maximum.[22] It is possible that the 'scab' of 1232 and 1272 was, in fact, a different disease, but it is equally possible that if it was indeed 'scab' as we understand, then it may imply that the disease had existed in England in an enzootic form for at least several decades. It was not until 1279 that we hear again about scab, this time of disastrous proportions. According to several 1278–79 accounts from Norfolk and Essex demesnes, the disease hit some East Anglian manors in early 1279, before lambing, commencing in late February or early March.[23] The vast majority of fatalities, however, occurred during the 1279–80 accounting year. A systematic consultation of all the available surviving accounts from that year (60 in number, recording almost 34,000 animals) reveals that about 52 per cent of all deaths occurred during the period between October 1279 and February 1280 (judging by the number of ewes that died before lambing). Those high figures are hardly surprising: the cold and damp months of autumn and winter provided the most ideal conditions for mite mating and aggressive behaviour. Moreover,

---

20 Hampshire Record Office (henceforth, HantsRO) 11 M59/M1/14, membr. 9v; noted in M. Stephenson, 'The Productivity of Medieval Sheep on the Great Estates 1100–1500' (Unpublished University of Cambridge PhD Thesis, 1987), p. 81 (who mistook the 32 ewes for 32 wethers).
21 HantsRO, 11 M59/M1/37, membr. 5v; noted in R. Trow-Smith, A History of British Livestock Husbandry to 1700 (London, 1957), p. 156.
22 HantsRO, 11 M59/M1/37. Between 1274 and the outbreak of scab in 1279, there were, on average, 24,581 sheep on the Winchester Bishopric estates. In 1282, there were only 11,062 sheep. The 1273 figures were not attained again until 1376 (HantsRO, 11 M59/M1/37–42 and 11 M59/M1/128).
23 Norfolk Record Office (henceforth, NRO), DCN 60/33/6; TNA, SC 6/837/13, and Canterbury Cathedral Archives (henceforth, CCA), DCc/BR/Bocking/2.

during those months, sheep tended to be densely concentrated in sheepcotes, and the close contact between animals would encourage the transmission of the disease. About 80 per cent of all fatalities occurred by June 1280, by the time of shearing. In other words, there was hardly any wool left to be shorn. By Michaelmas 1280, the first wave of the panzootic in England was, more or less, over, even though scab was still ravaging some manors during the 1280–81 accounting year.[24]

At the same time, the panzootics wreaked havoc in eastern Ireland and south-eastern Wales during that year, as both manorial accounts and narrative evidence suggests.[25] There is no textual evidence for the outbreak of scab in either Gaelic Ireland, or anywhere in Scotland. It is possible that the relative isolation of the Gaelic Highlands, where sheep farming has always played an enormously important role, accounted for this silence. Until proven otherwise, however, such assumption shall remain a mere hypothesis. It is clear, however, that the disease seems to have spread westward from the east coast, judging from the fact that the earliest references are found in Norfolk and Essex accounts. If this was indeed the case, then there seems to be a striking similarity in geographic dissemination of scab and rinderpest forty years later. While there is no doubt that in the case of the bovine pestilence, the westward movement was caused by the spread of the disease from either Holland or France, it is unclear what accounted for the similar geographic dissemination in the case of scab. One possible factor could be that the eastern counties were both more commercialised and far more densely populated than the western ones. This fact may imply frequent movement of flocks from place to place on the one hand and close physical contacts between animals on the other. As we have seen, unlike the cattle pestilence, the continental origins of the 1279 outbreak are unclear, given the total lack of references in continental sources.

In reference to mortality rates, the accounts are careful in distinguishing between those sheep that died and infected animals that were either butchered or sold, 'because of the disease'.[26] The significance of this distinction will be discussed later in the chapter. It appears that out of 33,559 sampled sheep, 14,616 animals (44 per cent) were reported as dead and a further 1,559 animals were sold or butchered. This inflates the mortality rate figure to 48 per cent. Naturally, these are average figures and the mortality rates varied

---

24 Thus, Westminster Abbey Muniments (henceforth, WAM) 25,579; CCA, DCc/BR/Lalling/2; CCA, DCc/BR/Elverton/4; TNA, SC 6/1007/10; Longleat House Muniments 10,599.

25 As indicated in the manorial accounts from Ballysax (county Kildare) (TNA, SC 6/1237/1) and hinted in the Annals of Inisfallen *sub* 1281 (S. Mac Airt, *The Annals of Inisfallen MS. Rawlinson B. 503* (Dublin, 1951), p. 375. For the Welsh evidence of scab, see P.M. Remfy (ed.), *Annales Cambriae* (Castle Studies Research and Publishing, 2007), p. 258.

26 TNA, SC 6/761/11; SC 6/929/19.

from manor to manor. Thus, Whitchurch (Hampshire), lost 89 per cent of its animals (1,100 out of 1,240 sheep), while Halvergate (Norfolk) lost only 15 per cent of its sheep (38 out of 253 animals).[27] Some flocks seem to have hardly been affected by the panzootic at all.[28] There were several possible factors standing behind those variances in mortality rates. First, as we shall see, wethers were more prone to the disease and therefore, grazing manors (namely, those consisting solely of wethers), were more likely to end up with higher mortality rates. Second, as David Stone has shown, managerial decisions played an enormous role in the success or failure of sheep farming and it is, therefore, possible that high mortality rates reflect careless and inefficient management of flocks.[29] In any event, a much more thorough investigation is required, in order to establish a clear correlation between the variances in mortality rates and other variables. Unfortunately, the scope of the present chapter does not allow this kind of exercise.

Just as in the case of the rinderpest of 1319–20, the scab of 1279–80 tended to discriminate across genders and age groups (Table 4.1 and Table 4.2). Thus, it killed more male than female animals: about 54 per cent of all succumbed sheep were male, while the proportion of female sheep that died in the panzootic was about 41 per cent. This calculation does not account for lambs, because in most cases the accounts did not specify their gender. Also, as the tables indicate, young animals, especially yearlings, but also lambs, were at a higher risk than mature animals. While it is hardly surprising that younger animals tend to be more prone to various pathogens and diseases, it is somewhat puzzling that male animals, chiefly wethers, were more exposed to scab than ewes. This is in sharp contrast with the outbreak of rinderpest in 1319–20, when cows fell in much greater numbers than oxen.[30] After all, both cows and ewes spend considerable amount of time pregnant and lactating (nine and five months, respectively), which tends to compromise their immune system and make them more susceptible to various pathogens. There are two possible explanations to that conundrum. First, one has to account for the physiological differences between wethers and oxen. Unlike oxen, which perform various physical tasks as draught animals, wethers are non-working animals, doing little except grazing and folding. This may imply a weaker immune system and resistance to diseases. Second, wethers grow longer and heavier fleeces than sexually active sheep. This encourages

27   HantsRO, DC/J1/3; TNA, SC 6/936/7.
28   At Wheathampstead (Hertfordshire), only 13 out of 175 ovids seem to have died in the course of the 1279–80 year, and it is unclear if those animals died of scab at all (Hertfordshire Record Office, M94).
29   D. Stone, 'The Productivity and Management of Sheep in Late-medieval England', *Agricultural History Review*, 51 (2003), pp. 18–20.
30   Slavin, 'Bovine Pestilence', p. 1247.

Table 4.1. Ovine mortality rates during the 1279–80 scab outbreak in England

	Total sheep	Deaths through murrain		Total losses (through scab + butchery + 'panic sales')	
	(Heads)	(Heads)	(As %)	(Heads)	(As %)
All animals	33,559	14,616	43.6%	16,175	48.2%
Female animals (excluding lambs)	11,800	4,332	36.7%	4,811	40.8%
Male animals (excluding lambs)	12,709	5,845	46.0%	6,824	53.7%
Mature, sexually active animals (ewes and rams)	11,107	4,106	37.0%	4,590	41.43%
Immature animals (hoggets and gimmers)	5,930	3,025	51.0%	3,189	53.8%
Lambs	7,742	3,955	51.1%	3,999	51.7%
Neutered animals (wethers)	8,780	3,578	40.8%	4,445	50.6%

Source: Manorial accounts database. As of March 2015, the manorial accounts database consists of over 30,000 demesne accounts running between 1208 and 1530, covering nearly 3,000 demesnes around England, as well as parts of eastern Western and eastern Ireland.

Table 4.2. Bovine mortality rates during the 1319–20 rinderpest outbreak in England

	Total cattle sampled	Deaths through murrain		Total losses (through murrain + butchery + 'panic sales')	
	(Heads)	(Heads)	As %	(Heads)	(As %)
All animals	7,605	4,277	56.2%	4,734	62.3%
Female animals (excluding calves and yearlings)	2,107	1,343	63.8%	1,574	74.7%
Male animals (excluding calves and yearlings)	4,057	2,137	52.7%	2,316	57.1%
Mature, sexually active animals (cows and bulls)	2,067	1,410	68.2%	1,639	79.3%
Immature animals (bullocks and heifers)	1,001	548	54.7%	597	59.7%
Calves and yearlings	1,442	839	58.2%	883	61.2%
Neutered animals (oxen)	3,095	1,537	49.7%	1,674	54.1%

Source: Manorial accounts database.

the spread of scab, either through direct contact with live mites, or through shearing combs and cutters. Intriguingly, wethers, sexually neutered animals, died in much larger proportions than sexually active ewes and rams. After all, it would be expected that physical contacts between the animals during the breeding season (October) would increase mortality rates. One possible explanation to this paradox is that in most cases, the panzootic struck after the mating season.

The toll of rinderpest was higher: as Table 4.2 indicates, about 56 per cent of cattle and oxen died through murrain, but the mortality rate figure is inflated to 62 per cent, when we account for the panic sales and butcheries of infected animals. Just as in the case of scab, fatality rates varied from place to place. For instance, at Culham (Berkshire) and Sutton-under-Brailes (Warwickshire) entire bovine stocks perished.[31] On the other hand, at Pittington (Durham) and Sedgeford (Norfolk), local animals were spared altogether.[32] As I have shown elsewhere, there seems to have been a strong negative correlation between crop yields during the famine years (1315–17) and mortality rates of oxen and cattle on the same demesnes in 1319–20. Here, crop yields serve as a proxy for fodder resources, whose shortage had undoubtedly weakened the bovine population and made it prone to various pathogens.[33] As noted above, rinderpest attacked female animals more aggressively than the male ones: as many as about 75 per cent of cows and heifers (with the mortality rates of cows alone, not accounting for heifers, standing at the overwhelming 80 per cent) succumbed, in comparison with male animals, whose average mortality rates stood at 57 per cent. As we have seen, cows spent much of their time in pregnancy and lactation, and this fact undoubtedly weakened their immune system. Unlike wethers, which were at a higher risk than sheep, oxen seem to have been the least prone to the pathogen, certainly much less than cows. Apart from being stronger than both cows and bulls, oxen are generally better fed than non-draught cattle, in terms of crop allowance and fodder intake. This might have strengthened their immune system and made them more resistant to pathogens than other cattle.

Responses to animal diseases: religious

The murrains of 1279–80 and 1319–20 were catastrophes of unprecedented proportions. Apart from creating biological and economic vacuums, they undoubtedly had a psychological impact on local communities. How did local

31   HantsRO, 11 M59/M1/74, membr. 16r and 11 M59/M1/75, membr. 15r; and Gloucestershire Record Office, 1099/M31/36.
32   Durham Cathedral Archives, Enrolled Accounts, 1319–20; NRO, DCN 60/33/6.
33   Slavin, 'Bovine Pestilence', pp. 1244–7.

lords and tenants respond to the crisis? Roughly speaking, we may distinguish between two kinds of human responses to the outbreaks of animal panzootics and the crisis they created: 'religious' and 'managerial'. Let us start with religious responses. In late-medieval England, rural life was closely interwoven into the cultural and religious norms, values and beliefs of tenants, parish priests and lords. Because of this fact, some earthly topics found their way into the very heart of peasant religiosity: liturgy. The fear of crop failures and outbreaks of local animal diseases, omnipresent reality in the countryside, is reflected in votive masses, said on special occasions to ward off various disasters. Although various forms of prayers and charms against animal mortality existed since late Antiquity, there was no special mass against scab. The outbreak of 1279–80 led to a creation of a new liturgical practice around 1280, included in the Cartulary of Eynsham Abbey (Oxfordshire).[34] The new practice included several liturgical segments. First, a mass in honour of the Holy Spirit was sung. Afterwards, sheep were to be gathered together in a sheepcote and the priest was to read several Gospel passages, sprinkling holy water at the end of his reading. Finally, the priest said a charm in the mixture of medieval French and Latin. The charm depicts a young maid sitting on a sea isle, protecting her sheep from pox and scab. The shepherdess is visited by God, who assures her that her sheep will never be attacked by those diseases. The ceremony ends with the traditional votive mass against animal mortality (*Missa contra mortalitatem/pestem animalium*).[35] The fact that an altogether new liturgical practice had been created undoubtedly implies the tremendous emotional impact the scab outbreak had upon local communities. Generally speaking, the vast majority of liturgical practices, known and used in medieval Catholic rite, had been devised by the end of the first millennium and comparatively few innovations had been introduced after the year 1000. Indeed, new liturgical practices were created as a response to a new threat or condition that was largely unknown beforehand and that no existing prayers or ceremonies were deemed effective against. Such examples of later liturgical additions included the introduction of new votive masses 'against the Heathen', following the loss of the Holy Land to Saladin in 1187, the subsequent Crusading failures and the Turkish threats in the later Middle Ages.[36] The scab outbreak was yet another example of a new liturgical practice, to aid the faithful in warding off an imminent and unknown threat: as we have seen, it appears that scab had been largely unknown in England

34   H.E. Slater (ed.), *Eynsham Cartulary*, vol. 1 (Oxford, 1907), p. 18. Slater dates the charm to c.1270, but it is most likely that it was composed shortly after the outbreak of 1279–80.
35   W.C. Jordan, 'Charms to Ward Off Sheep and Pig Murrain', in M. Rubin (ed.), *Medieval Christianity in Practice* (Princeton, 2009), pp. 67–75.
36   The topic has been extensively studied in Amnon Linder, *Raising Arms: Liturgy in the Struggle to Liberate Jerusalem in the Late Middle Ages* (Turnhout, 2003).

before the 1270s.[37] It is true that there were several episodes of sheep pox in the early thirteenth century, but these all seem to have been local outbreaks, of minor proportions and consequences.[38] Although the new charm intended to cure the disease, its suggestion to concentrate all the diseased sheep in a single edifice would have resulted in a faster spread of the disease.

Conversely, no new liturgical practices were created in the case of the 1319 rinderpest outbreak, despite its disastrous proportions. This, however, is hardly surprising: unlike scab, cattle mortality had been reported on numerous occasions long before 1319, and this fact is reflected in the existence of a traditional votive mass against animal mortality (*Missa contra mortalitatem/pestem animalium*), which had originated in late Antiquity and has been found in numerous medieval liturgical books since the eighth century.[39] In England, this mass is found in various missals since at least the eleventh century.[40] The mass indicates what the manorial documents do not: the contemporary perception of the causes of the cattle pestilence. Draught animals were installed by God to assist humans in their labours as necessary means to be fed and sustained. The murrain was brought about by God as a punishment for numerous human sins; its destruction would also mean the destruction of humans. The curse could be removed by God's power only, through 'sacrifice', namely through mass. Through the penance and prayer of the repentant, God would stop the destructive disease among the animals.[41] There can be little doubt that during the disastrous years of 1319–20, the votive mass against animal mortality has been recited extensively in both aristocratic households and parish churches. After all, cattle pestilence was a menace to both the seigniorial and peasant economies.

37   Stephenson, *Productivity*, pp. 80–4; M. Stephenson, 'Wool Yields in the Medieval Economy', *Economic History Review*, 41 (1988), p. 381.

38   M. Page, 'The Technology of Medieval Sheep Farming: Some Evidence from Crawley, Hampshire, 1208–1349', *Agricultural History Review*, 51 (2003), p. 149.

39   Thus, in the Gelasian Sacramentary: L. Mohlberg (ed.), *Liber Sacramentorum Romanae Aeclesiae Ordinis Anni Circuli (Cod. Vat. Reg. Lat. 316/Paris Bibl. Nat. 7193, 41/56 (Sacramentarium Gelasianum)* (Rome, 1981), p. 202.

40   For instance, Nicholas Orchard (ed.), *The Leofric Missal*, Henry Bradshaw Society, 114 (London, 2002), p. 344; J. Legg (ed.), *The Sarum Missal edited from Three Early Manuscripts* (Oxford, 1916), p. 411.

41   The *oratio* (supplication prayer) goes as follows (all translations from Latin are mine): 'Oh God, Thou hast granted compassion for the toils of men and even of the brute animals, we humble petitioners implore you, through our Lord Jesus Christ, that you not permit us to lose those things that we need without which the human condition is not sustained.' The *oratio* was followed then by the *secreta* part, whose most common form was: 'Oh Lord, pleased with the sacrifice offered, apply Thy power mildly in our time.' The *post-communio* (post-communion) part contained the following formula: 'We beseech, oh Lord, through these holy rituals that we undertake, to avert all errors from Thy faithful and drive away the destruction of furious diseases that attack animals, so that Thou shalt favour with Thy kindness those corrected one, that you deservedly scourge as erroneous ones.'

Responses to animal diseases: managerial

Although to most late-medieval people, votive litanies and charms were considered a valid and reasonable response, there is no doubt that the same people realised that additional means of purely anthropogenic nature had to be used, to cope with the situation. To begin with, there were attempts to cure animals with medicaments. In the early fourteenth century (and indeed until the development of the anti-rinderpest vaccine in the 1950s), cattle pestilence was an incurable disease, and this must have been a known fact to contemporaries, given the fact that not a single infected animal recovered. Scab, on the other hand, could still be treated, albeit with limited success. It should be borne in mind that scab was a new disease, and Walter of Henley, an author of an influential late-thirteenth-century agricultural treatise (composed around 1286) omitted scab, despite mentioning pox and liver fluke and suggested cures for those diseases.[42] Consequently, local tenants, manorial officials and lords had little or no idea how to combat scab. The manorial accounts provide a unique glimpse into various experimentations undertaken by manorial officials in the late thirteenth and the early fourteenth centuries. As early as 1273, during the local outbreak at East Knoyle (Wiltshire), local shepherds applied sulphur and locally produced butter.[43] The 1279–80 and early 1280s accounts from the estates of Winchester Bishopric and Winchester Cathedral Priory report purchases of various biological and chemical medicaments, including pig lard, ox fat, grease, horse salve, butter, oil, verdigris, quicksilver and copperas. It appears that biological and chemical components were usually mixed.[44] As some accounts indicate, applying medicaments incurred additional expenses (Table 4.3). At Whitchurch (Hampshire), a person was hired for 2s to spread fat on sick sheep.[45] There were 1,240 sheep, out of which 1,100 died of scab. Such a remarkable waste of fat, in face of the high mortality rates, may appear as a sign of ineffective management at Whitchurch. On the other hand, several demesnes did not report to have spent any money on medicaments at all. This, however, does not mean that those demesnes did not apply any medicaments: one should bear in mind that in many instances, manorial officials applied locally produced substances, such as lard and fat, which were not accounted for in the account rolls. Because of this underrecording, it is difficult to establish a correlation between the mortality rates and the expenditure on medicaments. Thus, no treatment was used on the Michelmersh flocks (Hampshire), while at Easton (in the same county), local manorial officials spent rather generously

---

42   D. Oschinsky (ed.), *Walter of Henley and other Treaties on Estate Management and Accounting* (Oxford, 1971), pp. 185–7, 338 and 380–3.
43   HantsRO, 11 M59/M1/37, membr. 5v; noted in Trow-Smith, *British Livestock*, p. 156.
44   HantsRO, DC/J1/3, *passim*; Trow-Smith, *British Livestock*, p. 156.
45   HantsRO, DC/J1/3.

Table 4.3. Types and costs of medicaments used against scab on sheep farming demesnes of Winchester Cathedral Priory, 1279–80

	Medicament	Sheep, total	Mortality rates	Expenditure on 10 sheep (in d)	Spread weight per 10 sheep (in lbs)
Barton Priors	locally produced butter	2,030	73.5%	0.00	0.00
Chilbolton	nothing reported	538	38.5%	0.00	0.00
Crondall	nothing reported	649	36.8%	0.00	0.00
Easton	unspecified medicament	925	49.3%	1.21	
Houghton	fat (*unctum*)	262	42.0%	2.11	0.84
Hurstbourne Priors	quicksilver, horse salve, etc.	1,656	73.7%	1.07	0.43
Littleton	nothing reported	547	44.6%	0.00	0.00
Long Sutton	fat (*unctum*)	342	86.8%	0.96	0.38
Michelmersh	nothing reported	740	49.9%	0.00	0.00
Silkstead	locally produced butter	489	80.4%	0.00	0.36
Whitchurch	fat (*unctum*)	1,240	88.7%	2.85	1.14
Wonston	fat (*unctum*)	1,748	54.9%	1.88	0.75
Alton Priors	fat (*unctum*)	558	28.7%	0.84	0.34
Enford	hard fat (*cepum*)	1,233	39.5%	0.24	0.10
Stockton	locally produced pig lard	432	55.8%	0.00	0.58
Average				0.74	0.38

Source: HantsRO, DC/J1/3.
Note: All the manors, except Alton Priors, Enford and Stockton (all in Wiltshire) are in Hampshire.

on the sick sheep. In both instances, nearly half of sheep had perished in the panzootic and the lion's share of fatalities occurred before June 1280. This might imply that the Michelmersh officials stood totally confused in the face of the outbreak and, having had no prior experience in dealing with scab, could not think of any solution.

The main innovation to scab treatment came in the first decade of the fourteenth century, possibly in conjunction with the minor outbreak of 1304–05 and the ascension of Henry Woodlock as the new bishop of Winchester (1305–16). In addition to the traditional medicaments, increasingly large amounts of tar were being purchased, gradually ousting the former, to the extent that by the 1320s a mixture of tar and grease became the primary treatment against scab.[46] It should be noted that tar is still widely used as an anti-scab medicament by present-day British farmers.

It is unfortunate that the accounts do not specify if the application of the medicaments had any effect on the ovine health and if any animals managed to recover. The continuous purchases of various substances, during minor and local outbreaks in the subsequent decades, may suggest that they might have worked in some cases. In some instances, however, local farmers and manorial officers seemed to have been sceptical of their ability to cure the infected animals. Instead, they chose to get rid of the diseased animals through either 'panic sales' or 'panic slaughter'. This was a widespread strategy during both the scab and rinderpest outbreaks. The manorial accounts were careful in specifying that animals were sold because of the 'fear of disease', or because 'they were likely to die', thus distinguishing between panic sales and butcheries of morbid and contagious animals and ordinary sales of healthy beasts and routine butcheries of older livestock.[47] For instance, 18 wethers out of 52 and 44 ewes out of 87 were sold 'because of scab' at Langley Marish (Bucks).[48] Similarly, 34 out of 36 oxen were sick and sold en masse for £10 4s 6d at Wisbech Barton (Cambs).[49] As we shall see below, the sale prices of diseased animals were considerably lower than those of the healthy ones. Unfortunately, the accounts do not specify who bought the diseased animals, but judging by their abysmally low prices on the one hand, and the fact that

46   Page, 'Medieval Sheep Farming', p. 149.
47   WAM 22,109, 25,636, 26,416, 27,854 and 32,533; CCA, DCc/BR/Barksore/25, Mersham/9, Ruckinge/8, Great Chart/32, Lydden 41–42 and Ebony/32; Merton College Archives, MCR 5549; Lambeth Palace Library (henceforth, LPL), ED/379.
48   TNA, SC 6/761/11.
49   Cambridge University Library, Ely Diocesan Records (henceforth, CUL, EDR), D8/1/4. Similarly, 52 out of 62 animals were sold at Llantrissent (Monmouthshire) in the summer of 1320 (TNA, SC 6/923/28). The panic sales were especially numerous on Kentish demesnes of Canterbury Cathedral, as well as some manors of Westminster Abbey (for instance, LPL, ED/379–384, CCA, DCc/BR/Eastry/48 and Hollingbourne/29–31; WAM 8,429–8,433, 22,110–22,117).

no diseased animals are reported to have been purchased by manorial authorities, it is likely that the purchasers were manorial tenants. In some instances,
manorial officers decided to slaughter morbid animals, to avoid further
causalities. For instance, at Lower Halstow (Kent), 32 ovids were butchered,
because of their disease.[50] Similarly, at Westerham, in the same county, 27
bovine animals were slaughtered, 'because they were likely to die'.[51] Similar
butcheries were undertaken at Eltham (Kent) and Hendon (Middlesex),
during the 1319–20 panzootic.[52] Overall, 'panic sales' and 'panic butcheries'
accounted for no more than 5–6 per cent of all animal losses during both the
scab outbreak and the cattle panzootic.[53]

Was that strategy profitable? In order to answer this question, it is essential
to analyse the price movement of sheep and cattle, during the respective
panzootics. In both instances, high morbidity levels of livestock drove down
the prices. During the accounting year 1279–80, an average price of one
diseased ewe and wether stood at 1s (falling from 1s 6d for a healthy animal
in the previous year), while in 1319–20 the value of a sick ox and cow was
4s (compared with 15s and 12s, which were the respective prices of healthy
animals in 1318–19).[54] There is no doubt that the fall in cattle prices was
steeper compared with the sheep ones because of both the debilitated and
potentially contagious state of the animals, and the fear and risk aversion
of their potential buyers. Sheep, on the other hand, were dying in smaller
proportions, and it is possible that scab might have been considered a curable
disease, unlike cattle pestilence. This fact explains a relatively non-aggressive
fall in sheep prices. Naturally, prices varied from case to case. For instance,
at Walton (Suffolk), 44 wethers and 27 ewes were sold for 28s 9d (at 5d per
animal), while at Ospringe (Kent), two wethers were marketed for 1s 6d each.
In both cases, the animals were designated as sick.[55] It should be noted that
in many cases, the accounts did not specify if the sold sheep were morbid or
healthy animals, but it is apparent that panic sales of sick animals dragged
down the average, while healthy animals were selling for higher prices,
because of their rarity.[56] Likewise, the manorial reeves did their best to sell the

50   CCA, DCc/BR/Barksore/2.
51   WAM 26,416.
52   WAM 27,854 and 32,533.
53   Slavin, 'Bovine Pestilence', p. 1247.
54   The calculations for healthy animals derive from D. Farmer, 'Prices and Wages', in H.E.
Hallam (ed.), *The Agrarian History of England and Wales*, II: *1042–1350* (Cambridge, 1988),
pp. 803–5, while the prices of diseased animals derive from all the available manorial accounts
for the crisis years.
55   TNA, SC 6/893/32 and 1007/10.
56   Farmer, who did not distinguish between healthy and sick animals, reported 14s and 9s, as
average respective prices of oxen and cows in 1320. The calculations for healthy animals derive
from Farmer, 'Prices and Wages', p. 805.

meagre amounts of wool produced by both healthy and sick animals. Clearly, scab damaged the quality of wool, and it is hardly surprising that the wool of infected animals was selling for abnormally low prices, compared with fine quality produce. Thus, at Quickbury (Essex), 74 fleece weighing 86 lbs was sold for only 14s 8d (at 2s 4½ d per stone), while an average price of wool made of seemingly healthy animals stood at 4s 8d per stone in that year.[57] Obviously, the manorial officials could not pursue a similar strategy during the cattle panzootic and vend bovine by-products (first and foremost, milk and meat): unlike scab, when, despite physical debilitation and skin irritation, some poor-quality wool can still grow on diseased animals, rinderpest renders milk, meat and hides useless.[58] Therefore, there is no doubt that during the scab outbreak of 1279–80, the manorial reeves managed, in many instances, to convert both morbid sheep and their damaged wool into cash, to be invested in healthy animals once the initial wave of the panzootic was, at least temporarily, over. During the rinderpest of 1319–20, on the other hand, the profit seems to have been much less pronounced: not only bovine by-products could not be marketed, but also the selling prices of diseased cattle were abysmally low.

The massive losses of sheep in 1279–80 and oxen and cattle in 1319–20 created a biological and energy vacuum, which had to be temporarily filled by introducing alternative sources of power and production. In the case of the sheep panzootic, local lords and their tenants lost an important source of manure (even though there is no evidence that the harvests of 1280 and 1281 failed),[59] as well as producers of meat, milk, wool and parchment, while the cattle pestilence meant massive losses of draught power (both as 'tractors' and haulers), as well as the supply of milk, meat, manure and hides. With the exception of goats, no animal could substitute sheep as a wool producer. Replacing sheep with goats, however, was not an option, given the low levels of goat population (and popularity) in late-thirteenth-century England, and the fact that goats produce a much coarser type of wool.[60] On the other hand, draught energy, meat, milk and manure could easily be derived from other animals. Indeed, quite a few demesnes opted to augment the proportion of

57   TNA, SC 6/839/26; Farmer, 'Prices and Wages', pp. 808–9.
58   T. Newfield, 'A Great Destruction of Cattle: The Impact and Extent of Epizootic Disease in Early Fourteenth-Century Northwestern Europe' (unpublished MA thesis, University of Toronto, 2005), p. 57.
59   The composite yields for 1280 and 1281 stood at 2 and 11 per cent above average. The calculations derive from Bruce Campbell's database of late-medieval crop yields, 1211–1492: Bruce M.S. Campbell (2007), Three Centuries of English Crop Yields, 1211–1491, http://www.cropyields.ac.uk [accessed April 2015].
60   C. Dyer, 'Alternative Agriculture: Goats in Medieval England', in R.W. Hoyle (ed.), People, Landscape and Alternative Agriculture: Essays for Joan Thirsk, Agricultural History Review Supplement Series, 3 (Exeter, 2004), p. 35.

both carthorses and stots (ploughing horses), to take up the slack for the shortage of oxen as draught animals. On the estates of Winchester Bishopric, the sheer number of horses rose from some 280 during the 1310s to almost 500 in 1320–21. Accordingly, the plough-horse prices went up from about 12s 9d in 1319 to 16s in 1320, reflecting the increased demand for that animal.[61] In terms of livestock density, it implied an impressive rise from about 3 to 5.5 horses per 100 acres. Similar augmentation of horse power during the early 1320s has been reported on the estates of Canterbury Cathedral Priory, Norwich Cathedral Priory, Westminster Abbey, Ely Bishopric and other estates.[62] It should be noted, however, that the expansion of the horse into traction was a temporary phenomenon and, by the late 1320s, when ox population levels returned, more or less, to their pre-pestilence levels, horse numbers returned to their pre-1319 levels.[63]

The loss of meat could be compensated by the augmentation of either beef cattle stocks or pig herds in the case of 1279–80 and by the expansion of either sheep or pig stocks during the crisis of 1319–20. A close analysis of the manorial accounts reveals that the lords and their officials focused more on the expansion of cattle, rather than swine. Thus, between 1280 and 1286, the bovine stocks of Canterbury Cathedral estates were augmented by approximately 40 per cent, while their swine herds grew by about 20 per cent.[64] Similar expansion of cattle and swine was seen on several demesnes of Westminster Abbey.[65] There are several factors accounting for the preference of cattle over swine. First, cattle are more versatile, rendering both beef and milk. Second, there is the ratio between relative price and produce yields. In the 1280s, one cow was selling for around 7s 6d (namely, five times more expensive than one ewe), yet it was capable of rendering about 10 times as much milk and about 12 times as many meat calories as an average ewe. On the other hand, one pig, selling for 2s 8d per head (1.75 times the price of a ewe), was rendering about 3 times as many meat calories and no consumable milk.[66] Finally, one has to account for the availability of necessary resources for the augmentation of swine herds, namely sufficient woodland pasture or legume acreage, in case of stall feeding. Indeed, in some cases swine could graze in open fields, but the expansion of such space, especially in the context of human population growth, could have been a costly and at times impossible option. One apparent advantage of swine over cattle was their fast

61   Farmer, 'Prices and Wages', pp. 803–5.
62   The calculations derive from the manorial accounts database.
63   Slavin, 'Bovine Pestilence', pp. 1253–4.
64   The calculations derive from the manorial accounts database. See also B.M.S. Campbell, 'Agriculture in Kent in the High Middle Ages', in S. Sweetinburgh (ed.), *Later Medieval Kent 1220–1540* (Woodbridge, 2010), pp. 51–3.
65   The calculations derive from the manorial accounts database.
66   The prices derive from Farmer, 'Prices and Wages', pp. 803–5.

reproductive cycle: usually, one sow produced ten piglets in two litters each year.[67] This fact prompted some demesne managers to augment their swine herds as a short-term strategy, prevailing in the early 1280s. Once enough heifers reached their maturity and turned into cows, the numbers of pigs shrank once again. For instance, such strategy was undertaken by the reeves of Kinsbourne (Herts) and Knightsbridge (Middlesex), both belonging to Westminster Abbey.[68]

Much grimmer was the situation in 1319–20. To reach the pre-pestilence levels of meat and milk production, it would be necessary to substitute each dead cow with ten ewes. This was an impossible task for most lords: assuming that there were some one million cows in England on the eve of the pestilence, and some 750,000 were lost to the murrain, then it would require some 7.5 million ewes to take over. Given that there were approximately 5 million ewes (out of the total 15 or so million sheep), to increase their flocks by more than half within a short period of time was not an option. In fact, very few demesnes managed to take up the slack by expanding their sheep flocks sufficiently. Even the demesnes of such wealthy lords as Canterbury Cathedral Priory and Westminster Abbey could not maintain pre-1319 levels of dairy output.[69] Therefore, the ratio between the available bovine and ovine dairy force did not change as drastically as that within the draught sector, in the aftermath of rinderpest.

Certainly, the shift to an alternative mode of livestock husbandry was only a temporary option. To ensure the recovery of the wool industry after the scab outbreak and dairy production after the cattle pestilence, manorial officials had to do their best to replenish the ovine flocks and bovine stocks after each respective catastrophe. In both cases, the restocking of animals was a slow and costly process. As Figure 4.1 indicates, it took about twenty years to replenish the bovine stocks and as many as thirty years to restock the ovine flocks. In both cases, the process was hindered by several minor (and in some instances, local) episodes of disease: sheep flocks were attacked by the recurrent outbreaks of scab in 1283–85, 1289, 1296, 1301–02, 1306, 1308–09 and 1313–17, even though the latter might have been a combination of scab and liver fluke, while oxen and cattle were hit by minor outbreaks in 1324–27 and 1333–34.

Roughly speaking, there were three main channels of replenishment: inter-manorial transfer, trade and biological reproduction.[70] Inter-manorial transfers of healthy animals were related in most cases to the demesnes that

---

67   B.M.S. Campbell, *English Seigniorial Agriculture, 1250–1450* (Cambridge, 2000), p. 165.
68   WAM, WAM 8,764–8,771 (Kinsbourne) and WAM 16,372–16,376 (Knightsbridge).
69   Slavin, 'Bovine Pestilence', pp. 1253–4.
70   One should also add, primarily in the case of the 1319–20 outbreak, tenancy dues, which contributed only marginally to the replenishment process. See, Slavin, 'Bovine Pestilence', p. 1254.

Figure 4.1. Replenishment rates of sheep (1279–1311) and oxen and cattle
(1318–50) on English demesnes

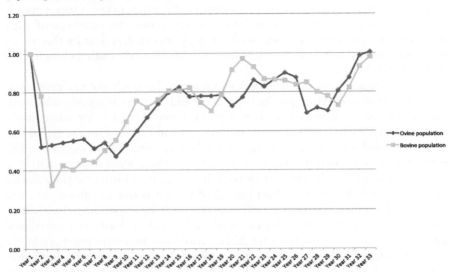

Source: Manorial accounts database.

either incurred light losses or no losses at all. Thus, in 1280 the officials of
Agney (Kent), where only 10 per cent of sheep had died, sent 105 healthy
lambs to Lydden, in the same county.[71] Likewise, in 1320, the reeve of
Sedgeford (Norfolk), a demesne entirely spared by the cattle pestilence,
dispatched eight cows and six calves to the nearby demesnes of Gnatingdon
and Thornham, in addition to giving one cow 'to the poor'.[72] It is likely that
this clause reflects the impact of the rinderpest crisis on the tenant economy,
but unfortunately there are no comparative data to quantify the losses within
the tenant livestock sector.[73] Securing new animals from local markets was
more challenging because of the shortage of healthy animals. Still, some
manorial accounts indicate that such transactions took place. For instance,
at Quickbury (Essex), local officers purchased one wether, nine ewes, three
hoggets and two gimmers, at some point in late 1280 or early 1281.[74] Generally

71   CCA, DCc/BR/Agney/4.
72   NRO, DCN 60/13/21.
73   Some possible implications of the rinderpest crisis on the tenant economy have been laid
out in Slavin, 'Bovine Pestilence', pp. 1260–3.
74   TNA, SC 6/839/27. The account indicates that those animals were purchased before
lambing.

speaking, sheep purchases were rare and few in the immediate aftermath of the scab panzootic. The volume of sheep sales increased slightly after c.1284, but they never grew into large-scale transactions. Even such wealthy lords as the Bishop of Winchester and Winchester Cathedral Priory opted to regain their flocks through biological reproduction. On the other hand, the 'panic sales' of diseased cattle during the 1319–20 panzootics were followed, almost immediately, by 'panic purchases' of healthy animals, chiefly oxen. Thus, the Kentish demesnes of Canterbury Cathedral Priory managed to replenish their ox stocks by 1328, through extensive purchases. A similar strategy was undertaken by the reeve of Wisbech Barton (Cambridgeshire), achieving the pre-1319 levels within ox stocks by 1331.[75] The large-scale and extensive transactions related to oxen are hardly surprising, for two reasons. First, a comparatively long reproduction cycle in cows implied longer restocking, prompting manorial reeves to seek an additional channel of replenishment. Second, restocking oxen as fast as possible was most crucial for human well-being: with no sufficient draught power, the threat of low yields, malnutrition (or possibly famine) was quite real. This was especially true in 1321–22, when the composite net crop yields of the 1321 harvest were 34 per cent below average.[76] A slower restocking of sheep, on the other hand, only meant less cash deriving from wool sales.

It should be said, however, that livestock trade was undertaken on a strictly local or regional level, and long-distance trade in animals was extremely rare in pre-Black Death England.[77] In most cases, the oxen and cattle were purchased at nearby markets and fairs. Unless aided by purchases and inter-manorial transfers, the particularly high mortality rates of the two panzootics imply that it would have taken at least 11 and 17 years, respectively, to achieve the pre-1279 levels of sheep population and the pre-1319 levels of bovine population, through biological reproduction only. This is, of course, if no intermittent diseases broke out and if manorial business went as usual. Naturally, this implied that in the first few years after the scab outbreak, younger sheep occupied a disproportionally large share within local flocks. In the 1280s, the share of immature sheep (hoggets, gimmers and lambs) rose from about 24 to 40 per cent. Also, to keep the pace of reproduction, the manorial officers had to restock ewes faster than wethers. By 1292, ewes had reached about 82 per cent of their pre-1279 level, while wethers attained only 72 per cent. One clear implication of the predominance of immature sheep and ewes was that the levels of wool and mutton production, in both relative

---

75   CUL, EDR, D8/1/4.
76   The calculation derives from Bruce Campbell's database of late-medieval crop yields, 1211–1492: Bruce M.S. Campbell (2007), Three Centuries of English Crops Yields, 1211–1491, http://www.cropyields.ac.uk [accessed April 2015].
77   Slavin, 'Bovine Pestilence', p. 1254.

and sheer levels, were low. This was, nevertheless, the most efficient strategy the demesne managers could think of.

Conversely, in the case of the 1319–20 crisis, biological reproduction had several drawbacks. First, with some rare exceptions, cows and heifers bear only one calf. Second, cow pregnancy lasts around nine months. Third, cows and heifers usually have only three opportunities each year to get pregnant. Fourth, only some 75 per cent of all cows were fertile each year in the early fourteenth century. All those factors made the restocking process through biological reproduction challenging. Finally, most demesnes suffered from a dearth of bulls capable of inseminating cows for five years after the panzootic. All these facts made the restocking process especially challenging.[78] Because of the imminent threat of being left with no draught animals, the manorial officials had to ensure that they replenished the ox stocks first. Within the ovine sector, on the other hand, there were no working animals, whose shortage could deeply impact the availability of food resources for humans. This fact freed the manorial reeves of their concern to secure mature animals through purchases. It should be noted, that despite the animal shortage, reeves were still able to 'control' younger bovine populations by selling, transferring, and butchering immature animals. On the other hand, very few lamb sales have been reported during the 1280s and in most cases young ovids were either retained on the demesnes, or transferred to other manors.[79] One factor accounting for that was the fact that ovine flocks were periodically attacked by minor outbreaks of scab during the following decades and eliminating young animals would imply that the restocking process would have been even longer.

Conclusions

There is no question that animal panzootics were a serious blow to the pre-Black Death English economy, whose fortunes, meanwhile, were turning for the worse, because of both environmental and institutional factors. Although local incidences of both ovine and bovine diseases were common before both the scab and rinderpest outbreaks, the events of 1279–80 and 1319–20 were on an altogether different scale. With animals succumbing and dying in unprecedentedly high proportions, local producers had to act as quickly and efficiently as possible to cope with the crisis and to prevent a potential famine and economic slump. Devoid of either theoretical knowledge or practical experience in struggling with such a challenge, they had to put

78   Ibid.
79   This is not to say that no sales of lambs ever occurred. For instance, in 1284, 4 out of 189 lambs were sold at High Clere (Hampshire), before shearing: HantsRO, 11 M59/B1/43, membr. 9v.

their faith in various methods. Some of those methods were clear trial-and-error experiments, while other methods were used during previous smaller outbreaks. As we have seen, in 1273, six years before the scab outbreak, the shepherds of East Knoyle (Wiltshire) applied sulphur and locally produced butter, to cure diseased sheep.

A close analysis of the available evidence reflects the highly eclectic mentality of late-medieval agricultural producers. On the one hand, the victims of the crisis turned to various liturgical practices, both old and new. In particular, the creation of a new 'macaronic' charm against sheep scab around 1280, shortly after the national outbreak of the panzootic, indicates the impact of the disaster on liturgical practices. Despite the very impractical advice of the charm to gather all the diseased sheep in a single sheepcote, there is no doubt that this religious practice was deemed an efficient response to the scab outbreak. On the other hand, the same producers were determined to cope with the crises in more practical ways.

Although the two disasters were similarly devastating in their magnitude, it appears that it did not take long for the lords and peasants to realise that while the cattle pestilence was an incurable disease, there was still a chance of recovery in the case of scab. It is hardly surprising, then, that demesne managers invested sums of money on various medicaments to cure scabious sheep, or possibly to prevent the expansion of scab within flocks. Conversely, there is not a single piece of evidence that manorial officials attempted to apply medicaments on diseased cattle and oxen.

If medicaments had limited or no effect on the health of the animals, the demesne managers attempted to get rid of the potentially sick animals to avoid further casualties, either through slaughter or sales. Judging by the comparatively low occurrence of 'panic butcheries', selling diseased animals was always the preferred strategy of the two, given that there were always buyers, most likely manorial tenants. This was particularly true in the case of the scab outbreak, when manorial officials still managed to sell infected sheep for reasonably good prices. Clearly, this indicates that scab was not considered a terminal disease and there has always been some hope in recovery. In the case of rinderpest, however, there was little hope of selling diseased cattle and the profits were, therefore, minimal. Nevertheless, the fact that the manorial officials managed to sell diseased and potentially contagious animals reveals their commercial mentality.

Intriguingly, modern farmers reacted to later outbreaks of panzootic very similarly to their medieval forefathers. Recurrent scab outbreaks between 1865 and 1895 led to the enactment of a series of scab orders in 1898, 1905, 1907, 1914, 1920, 1928 and 1948. Some measures suggested in those orders had striking similarity to those employed by late-medieval shepherds. Thus, the 1928 order prescribed, among other things, tar acid and tar oil dip, as well as arsenic and lime sulphur. The orders also required compulsory destruction of infested animals, where treatment failed. In addition, the orders suggested isolation of healthy animals: a measure seemingly not taken by late-medieval manorial officials. Eventually, all of those measures contributed to the temporary eradication of scab in 1952 (it returned to England in 1973).[80] Equally striking is the similarity between measures attempted by early-fourteenth-century lords and tenants and those undertaken by cattle farmers during the 1865–67 outbreak of rinderpest in Britain, which claimed 6 per cent of the national bovine stock. In accordance with the Cattle Diseases Prevention Bill, enacted in February 1866, farmers were required to slaughter diseased animals and were encouraged to do the same with those animals that were in contact with the disease. Truly striking, however, is the fact that during this outbreak, a special votive prayer against cattle mortality, whose contents were closely based on the same Latin mass uttered by fourteenth-century lords and tenants, was said in parish churches and cathedrals across the country. Unlike the 1319–20 outbreak, the 1866 bill placed severe restrictions on cattle movement and importation.[81] Perhaps the single biggest difference between the late-medieval and modern outbreaks is the fact that while in the case of the former, the burden of coping with the disaster befell on the shoulders of producers, while in the case of the latter, farmers and government joined forces to solve the crisis.

Despite the relatively commercialised nature of the English economy in c.1300, and particularly of its arable sector, livestock markets were comparatively underdeveloped. As we have seen, sheep and cattle trade was confined primarily to a local or regional level, while long-distance trade in livestock was extremely rare. Despite the virtual lack of long-distance livestock trade, the diseases were still able to spread fast and easily across vast geographic regions. This fact meant that securing large numbers of healthy animals from potentially panzootic-free regions was a challenging, if not impossible task. Because of this fact, the most obvious strategy to replenish the decimated animal cohorts was to rely on the biological cycle of reproduction. As we have seen, this was a long and painful process in both instances. To avoid grain scarcity, the demesne managers began the replenishment process of bovine stocks with oxen, at the expense of cattle. This meant that beef and, most importantly, dairy industries were depressed for at least fifteen years.[82] This fact had some harsh consequences for human diet and health.[83] Within the

80   The history of anti-scab legislation is surveyed in K.W. Page, *Control of the Sheep Scab Mite. Veterinary Pesticides Symposium. Society of Chemical Industry. 31st March–2nd April 1969*. University of London Scientific Monograph, 33 (London, 1969).

81   S.A. Hall, 'The Cattle Plague of 1865', *Medical History*, 6 (1962), pp. 45–58.

82   Slavin, 'Bovine Pestilence', pp. 1258–60.

83   S. DeWitte and P. Slavin, 'Between Famine and Death. Physiological Stress and Dairy Deficiency in England on the Eve of the Black Death (1315–50): New Evidence from Paleoepidemiology and Manorial Accounts', *Journal of Interdisciplinary History*, 44 (2013), pp. 37–60.

ovine sector, on the other hand, the preference was given to ewes, to ensure fast biological reproduction. Although this had an impact on wool and mutton productivity, it also supplied local sheep farmers with fresh milk and healthy young animals. This was especially crucial given the recurrent nature of scab between c.1280 and 1320.

With dramatic changes in wider climatic and bio-ecological regimes towards the end of the thirteenth century, English lords and peasants became increasingly vulnerable to new economic challenges, totally unfamiliar to them or their predecessors. A piecemeal decline in land productivity, as reflected in crop yield statistics,[84] and mass livestock mortality were undoubtedly great blows to the socio-economic and biological well-being, whose population continued rising into the early fourteenth century, reaching perhaps about 5.25 million around 1300.[85] In those circumstances of widespread poverty and socio-economic restrictions, the massive losses of oxen (providing traction energy, beef and hides), cattle (providing meat, milk and hides) and sheep (supplying meat, milk, wool and hides) could have most tragic consequences, if not acted upon quickly. As the manorial accounts indicate, demesne managers reacted fast and employed several strategies, to save the situation. Nevertheless, despite the immediate reaction, the replenishment process, in both instances, was slow, because of the reliance on biological reproduction and lack of the commercial alternative. This fact added an additional burden to the impoverished pre-Black Death society, whose economic performance and living standards showed omnipresent signs of constraints and crisis.

84   The calculations derive from Bruce Campbell's database of late-medieval crop yields, 1211–1492.
85   Estimates on pre-Black Death population of England vary a great deal. The debate is summarised in S. Broadberry, B. Campbell, A. Klein, M. Overton and B. Van Leeuwen, *British Economic Growth, 1270–1700* (Cambridge, 2015), pp. 3–22.

5

Early Modern 'Resource Crisis': The Wood Shortage Debates in Europe

PAUL WARDE

Permanent crisis?

Fear of wood shortage was ubiquitous in early modern Europe.[1] It was expressed in the fifteenth century and the nineteenth century; it could be found from the Kingdom of Naples and the states of the Iberian peninsula to the Swedish north, from the British Isles in the west to the Kingdom of Poland in the east. It appears to have been no respecter of clime nor of the extent of wood cover. While it varied in intensity and form from place to place, the scarcity of timber and fuel was claimed everywhere. How can one evaluate this relentless sense of crisis? Indeed, can we take such permanent claims to crisis seriously at all?

There are, of course, many ways to frame a crisis. In this regard, the early modern period was no different from debates around 'energy crisis' or 'peak oil' in the twentieth century and today.[2] One can argue that the perception of crisis is sufficient to validate it, but where perceptions are contested, the argument falters. One can make arguments about the levels of privation experienced amounting to a 'crisis', yet such experiences are rarely absolute, and always relate to expectations. Does one have to heat one's home (the peoples of the far north do not)? Do you have to cook or consume hot drinks? Certain foodstuffs require it, but over time diet can adapt. This seems to have been the case in England, where bread was more common in fuel-poor regions of the south, but oat pottage was more widespread nearer coalfields;

1   Paul Warde, 'Fear of Wood Shortage and the Reality of the Woodlands in Europe, c.1450–1850', *History Workshop Journal*, 62 (2006), pp. 28–57.
2   See, for example, Peter Z. Grossman, *U.S. Energy Policy and the Pursuit of Failure* (Cambridge, 2013); E. Streissler, 'Die Knappheitsthese – Begründete Vermutungen oder vermutete Fakten?', in H. Siebert, *Erschöpfbare Ressourcen* (Berlin, 1980), pp. 9–36.

and where Frederic Eden suggested in the 1790s that what we now call 'fuel
poverty' explained a southern preference for cheese while northerners could
consume more beef.[3] Similarly, a crisis in one firm or industry from high costs
of fuel could be viewed as part of a desirable and efficient reallocation of
resources to another firm or industry. The perception of crisis was relative
to one's prior life and observations of the condition of one's peers and
neighbours; even physical experience is felt in accordance with habituated
norms and the immediate possibilities for change.

The fact remains that whatever the 'reality' of crisis, which must be investigated on a case-by-case basis sensitive to needs and expectations, the rhetoric
of crisis was pervasive and found across the social scale. This in itself suggests
deep structural reasons for the 'wood crisis' that made such claims plausible.
Early modern Europe was an 'organic economy', that is, its energy supplies
were overwhelmingly derived from plant matter to which there were fairly
narrow limits of productivity set by climate and soil.[4] Only a few regions of
coal production in Britain, and the peat lands of the North Sea littoral and
British Isles escaped this brute fact. Energy, both thermal and muscular (i.e.
channelled through human limbs and animal traction), required land, and the
productivity and area of that land set a basic constraint to supply. Equally,
technological limitations meant that fuel could not be affordably transported any great distance, especially in the absence of water, as this in turn
put heavy demands on fodder for pack or draught animals, and human time.
Indeed, a long-distance trade in firewood or charcoal (a less bulky processed
form that could also generate higher temperatures) was extremely rare and
was conducted to only a few urban centres such as Madrid, generally under
the auspices of governments that did not pay a market rate.[5] Consequently,
agricultural production and fuel supplies both competed for space and were
generally subject to a pervasive but inadequate localism, as many settlements
were dependent on the immediate vicinity for their basic needs. In a world
highly subject to the vagaries of weather and climate change, where road
transport and navigation could easily be impeded, markets functioned very

3   Craig Muldrew, *Food, Energy and the Creation of Industriousness: Work and Material
Culture in Agrarian England, 1550–1750* (Cambridge, 2011), pp. 100–1; David Zylberberg,
'Plants and Fossils: Household Fuel Consumption in Hampshire and the West Riding of
Yorkshire, 1750–1830', York University (Toronto) PhD (2014), pp. 194–220.
4   E.A. Wrigley, *Continuity, Chance and Change: The Character of the Industrial Revolution
in England* (Cambridge, 1988); E.A. Wrigley, *Energy and the Industrial Revolution in England*
(Cambridge, 2010); Astrid Kander, Paolo Malanima and Paul Warde, *Power to the People:
Energy in Europe over the Last Five Centuries* (Princeton, 2013); Rolf-Peter Sieferle, *The
Subterranean Forest: Energy Systems and the Industrial Revolution*, trans. M.P. Osman
(Knapwell, [1982] 2001).
5   Jesús Bravo Lozano, *Montes para Madrid. El abastecimiento de carbón vegetal a la villa y
corte entre los siglos XVII y XVIII* (Madrid, 1993).

imperfectly and political uncertainty was frequent, the possibility of interruptions to supply was never far away. Equally, as populations grew it was
difficult for land productivity to keep pace, pushing local societies closer to
the limits of sustainable supply for their habitual needs.

The limits and fears attendant on the 'organic economy' were one
reason for a sense of 'permanent crisis'. Another was the diversity of
demands placed upon wood itself, and the ensuing competition for space
and resources. Wood is a product with many qualities, and was used for a
very wide range of purposes. Fuel was the largest one by far, but in many
regions timber also provided the primary means of construction, and was
the sole basis of shipbuilding until the second half of the nineteenth century.
Land transport was formed of wood too, as were ploughs and the body of
agricultural equipment. As well as tools, tableware, cutlery and furnishings,
the essential means of packaging and storage, barrels, casks and numerous
forms of bucket, were also made from wood.[6] The largest inputs of wood
products into international trade were in the highly processed form of tar
and pitch (for caulking vessels of all sizes) and potash (an alkali input into
industrial processes). These multifarious uses required different qualities
of wood, whether in the species of tree itself or the manner in which it was
grown and harvested. The choice to manage a forest in a particular way (for
fuel, for example) might be exclusive of other potential uses of the wood (for
timber), while more specialised demands could not easily be met in one place,
stimulating a restless search for secure supplies, as was found with mast
timbers. There was thus potential for any one of these particular uses, which
might also compete with alternative employments of the land and trees, to
experience a scarcity of supply that might easily become ramified into claims
of a general shortage.

A crisis in the supply of wood was hence eminently plausible to many.
There were structural features of the economy, and the ecology of the trees,
that perennially made such crises a distinct possibility. Yet the *proximate*
causes of a perceived crisis could be highly variable, although often acting in
combination. To help disentangle the reasons why we find the persistent, even
hackneyed mantra of 'wood shortage', this chapter will proceed by identifying a series of 'ideal types' of crisis in which the supply of wood played
a central role. As we will see, many of them were not necessarily directly
connected to any change in the availability of wood itself, but must be set
against the inherent plausibility of a general crisis of supply, alongside what
were, sometimes, real shifts in demand or output. No 'ideal type' of crisis

---

6 Harvey Green, *Wood. Craft, Culture, History* (London, 2006); Fernand Braudel, *The
Structures of Everyday Life: The Limits of the Possible* (London, 1981); Joachim Radkau,
Wood: A History (Cambridge, 2012).

thus operated in isolation, and particular sequences of events tended to build up from the ramifying forces generated by a range of fears and tensions.

'Wood shortage' has been debated extensively among historians in various guises. John Nef argued that 'timber famine' was a stimulus to the expansion of coal use and industrialisation in sixteenth-century England, although subsequent historians have tended to dismiss this idea.[7] The rise of modern forestry was long lauded by foresters as saving society from travails brought on by earlier wasteful habits. In the words of renowned forest historian Kurt Mantel, 'Forestry was born of the wood crisis.'[8] This view was developed further by germanophone historians from the 1970s, who saw wood scarcity as a structural crisis in the traditional economy that, as in Nef's view, led to innovation, fossil fuel use, and industrialisation.[9] Objectors, inspired to a large degree by Joachim Radkau and drawn primarily from social history, argued that the heightened rhetoric of wood shortage, especially in the eighteenth century, represented sectional interests and reflected struggles for control of resources rather than broader questions of their availability. Rocketing wood prices, it was pointed out, might come from market failures and privileged allocation of resources rather than genuine bottlenecks in supply.[10] That voices from the past often represent their own narrow interests

7   J.U. Nef, *The Rise of the British Coal Industry* (London, 1932); George Hammersley, 'The Charcoal Iron Industry and its Fuel, 1540–1740', *Economic History Review*, 26 (1973), pp. 593–613; Michael W. Flinn, 'Timber and the Advance of Technology: A Reconsideration', *Annals of Science*, 15 (1959), pp. 109–20; John Hatcher, *The History of the British Coal Industry*, vol. 1, *Before 1700: Towards the Age of Coal* (Oxford, 1993); R.C. Allen, 'Was There a Timber Crisis in Early Modern Europe?', in Simonetta Cavaciocchi (ed.), *Economia e energia* (Florence, 2003), pp. 469–82; Paul Warde and Tom Williamson, 'Fuel Supply and Agriculture in Post-medieval England', *Agricultural History Review*, 62 (2014), pp. 61–82; J.-C. Debeir, J.-P. Deléage and D. Hémery, *Energy and Civilization Through the Ages* (London: Zed Books, [1986] 1991), pp. 94–6.
8   G. Schröder-Lembke, 'Waldzerstörung und Walderneuerung in Deutschland in der vorindus-triellen Zeit', *Zeitschrift für Agrargeschichte under Agrarsoziologie*, 35/2 (1987), p. 21.
9   Sieferle, *The Subterranean Forest*; Rolf-Jürgen Gleitsmann, 'Rohstoffmangel und Lösungssttategien: das Problem vorindustrieller Holzknappheit', *Technologie und Politik*, 16 (1980), pp. 104–54; Rolf-Jürgen Gleitsmann, 'Aspekte der Ressourcenpolitik im historischer Sicht', *Scripta Mercaturae*, 15 (1981), pp. 33–89; H. Etzold, 'Probleme bei der Wärmeenergiegewinnung am Vorabend der industriellen Revolution in Preußen', *Jarbuch. für Wirtschaftsgeschichte* (1989/4), pp. 77–8.
10   Joachim Radkau, 'Holzverknappung und Krisenbewußtein im 18. Jahrhundert', *Geschichte und Gesellschaft*, 4 (1983), pp. 513–43; Joachim Radkau, 'Zur angeblichen Energiekrise des 18. Jahrhunderts: revisionistische Betrachtungen über die "Holznot"', *Vierteljahrschrift für Sozials- und Wirtschaftsgeschichte*, 73 (1986), pp. 1–37; Joachim Radkau, 'Warum wurde die Gefährdung der Natur durch den Menschen nicht rechtzeitig erkannt? Naturkult und Angst vor Holznot um 1800', in Hermann Lübbe and Elisabeth Ströker (eds), *Ökologische Probleme im kulturellen Wandel* (Paderborn, 1986), pp. 47–78; Joachim Radkau, 'Das Rätsel der städtischen Brennholzversorgung im "Hölzernen Zeitalter"', in Dieter Schott (ed.), *Energie und Stadt in Europa: von der vorindustriellen 'Holznot' bis zur Ölkrise der 1970er Jahre*. Beihefte der Vierteljahrschrift für Sozials- und Wirtschaftsgeschichte, 155 (Stuttgart, 2007), pp. 43–75;

is hardly to be disputed; and as already noted, there is no clear relationship between the local general availability of wood and the rhetoric of crisis. Indeed, some fierce conflicts erupted in areas obviously well catered for.[11] This does not mean, however, that arguments about crisis and shortage were necessarily ill-founded (if we want to make such a judgement in hindsight), purely instrumental, cynical, deluded, or that they could not have had the effects on innovation attributed to them. The fact that some consumers were privileged does not, by itself, undermine the claim that all consumers were justified in fearing belt-tightening. The question remains to understand the prevalence of such arguments and assess their effects.

A wood shortage crisis 'occurs' in the historical record because a number of voices claim the existence or imminence of such a thing, whether in court cases, printed literature, petitioning, or actions such as wood theft. In that sense, of course, all crises relate to perceived penury regarding wood, and in most cases fuel. In this chapter, however, I will examine three *proximate* causes by which such perceptions become articulated. All three cases *may* involve instances where people suffered from cold, dietary limitation, or incapacities to build or work. But this was not *necessarily* so. Equally, in the way that one cannot harness energy without matter, the manner in which the physical experience or possibility of wood shortage emerged in the historical record was always mediated through the social milieu in which it was articulated. The three types of crisis addressed here are of *allocation*, *entitlement* and *the state*. In the first instance, of *allocation*, a crisis emerges because of disputes over political rights to a fuel supply and the way resources are *distributed* through processes of political decision-making. This was particularly frequent in disputes over common rights, but also the privileging of some industrial consumers. Fundamentally, fairness and political process was at stake in such disputes. In the second instance, of *entitlement*, a crisis emerged because of a lack of spending power that prevented people from obtaining the supplies they needed. This could result from either a fall in supply (and higher prices) or a reduction in income. While the response might be to demand institutional reform, such crises did not necessarily call

Bernd-Stefan Grewe, *Der versperrte Wald. Ressourcenmangel in der bayerischen Pfalz (1814–1870)* (Köln, 2004); Bernd-Stefan Grewe, '"Man sollte sehen und weinen!" Holznotalarm und Waldzerstörung vor der Industrialisierung', in Frank Uekötter und Jens Hohensee (eds), *Wird Kassandra heiser? Die Geschichte falscher Ökoalarme* (Stuttgart, 2004), pp. 24–41; Christoph Ernst, *Den Wald entwickeln. Ein Politik- und Konfliktfled in Hunsrück und Eifel im 18. Jahrhundert* (München, 2000); M. Grabas, 'Krisenbewältigung oder Modernisierungsblockade? Die Rolle des Staates bei der Überwindung des "Holzenergiemangels" zu Beginn der Industriellen Revolution in Deutschland', *Jahrbuch für europäische Verwaltungsgeschichte*, 7 (1995), pp. 43–75.
11 Richard Hölzl, *Umkämpfte Wälder. Die Geschichte einer ökologischen Reform in Deutschland 1760–1860* (Frankfurt, 2010).

into question the political order and practices of distribution as the *cause* of the crisis. Thus while allocation and entitlement crises might be intimately interconnected in many cases, we may distinguish them as ideal types. Finally, there were crises of the *state*, where wood shortage was perceived to put the government under existential threat, whether through commercial and social disruption from lack of fuel, or lack of timber for naval construction. How responses to such perceptions played out might again be related to crises of allocation or entitlement, or indeed might actually cause them, as we shall see.

Before moving on to a more detailed analysis, however, we must consider the issue of *scale* – how a sense of crisis that rested in the end on the essentially local experience and economic horizons of the majority of Europeans was so easily translated into national debates that bore a remarkably similar stamp across all of the continent's political borders.

Crisis and scale

The issue of scale can be considered in relation to both space and time. Crisis could be local but projected onto much broader scales; or be articulated as a problem for the polity as a whole, even if not experienced locally. Equally, a crisis could be current and immediate; perceived as the vanguard of worse to come; or predicted by Cassandras when others thought that plenty would reign.

At the most basic level of organisation we find households. Individual households were always subject to flux, according to the life cycle, the frequent occurrence of sudden mortality, and disruptions to commerce or from the weather. Especially in regions of impartible inheritance, settlements tended to develop a relatively stable core of prosperous farmers with enduring lineages, surrounded by a more ephemeral population of smallholders and labourers with a high turnover who in addition to a lesser degree of economic security often did not possess full, or any rights to the resources of the commons.[12] The potential for familial crisis was thus ever-present for large sections of the population, arguably to a degree sufficient to represent the norm. Such micro-crises, viewed on the larger scale, might be interpreted morally, providentially, or ascribed to fate. Yet from the point of view of the poor, the constant fragility of their circumstances could be interpreted through wider discourses, expressing grievances and contesting the distribution of resources in terms of

---

12   Martina de Moor, Leigh Shaw-Taylor and Paul Warde (eds), *The Management of Common Land in North-west Europe, c.1500–1850* (Turnhout, 2002); for Swedish examples, see also Jonas Lindström, *Distribution and Differences. Stratification and the System of Reproduction in a Swedish Peasant Community 1620–1820* (Uppsala, 2008).

national debates. In turn, they could testify to the truth of putative threats to wider society through their own experience.

Something similar could be argued about larger settlements. Moments of crisis in villages where open conflict emerged over access to resources were generally episodic. Indeed, they related not only to resource availability itself but wider changes in governance, either within the community or in their relations with lords.[13] As wood was by and large obtained locally or not transported more than a few miles, any 'crisis' was, for the most part, necessarily local. However, these discrete events could easily be seen as emblematic of more general trends, every local conflict read as a sign of a gathering storm. Cities faced particular vulnerabilities, given that the scale of population demanded imports of wood from further afield. Equally, many cities, especially in central Europe, were essentially independent polities that were confronted with the need to negotiate with neighbours to facilitate commerce. Some, like Freiburg im Breisgau or Nuremberg, managed to maintain their own large woodlands close to the city.[14] This was not the case for the wood-poor, such as Amsterdam (said to be 'standing on Norway') or even more so Venice, both requiring large amounts of wood for construction, to maintain the piles on which the very city stood, and shipbuilding.[15] Potential supply bottlenecks required the maintenance of either secure avenues of trade, over sea or via river-rafting, or obtaining guaranteed reserves distant from the city, which in turn antagonised peasants who had traditionally exploited the land. This could generate similar kinds of confrontations between the needs of city and country that are familiar in modern times (especially in the provision of water supplies), but also on a global scale between a majority urban population and raw materials supplied from elsewhere.[16]

As nation-states became consolidated over this period, and sought supplies of timber to underpin their military power, especially naval, alliances and

13   Paul Warde, 'Imposition, Emulation and Adaptation: Regulatory Regimes in the Commons of Early Modern Germany', *Environment and History*, 19 (2013), pp. 313–37.

14   Heinz Brandl, *Der Stadtwald im Freiburg* (Freiburg, 1970); E. Schubert, 'Der Wald: wirtschaftliche Grundlage der spätmittelalterlichen Stadt', in Bernd Herrmann (ed.), *Mensch und Umwelt im Mittelalter* (Stuttgart, 1987); Rolf Kiess, 'Bemerkungen zur Holzversorgung von Städten', in J. Sydow (ed.), *Städtsche Versorgung und Entsorgung im Wandel der Geschichte* (Sigmaringen, 1981), pp. 76–98.

15   Jaap R. Bruin, 'The Timber Trade. The Case of Dutch–Norwegian Relations in the 17th Century', in A. Bang-Andersen, B. Greenhill and E.H. Grude (eds), *The North Sea. A Highway of Economic and Cultural Exchange. Character-History* (Stavanger, 1985), pp. 123–35; Jason W. Moore, '"Amsterdam is Standing on Norway", Part I: The Alchemy of Capital, Empire and Nature in the Diaspora of Silver, 1545–1648', *Journal of Agrarian Change*, 10 (2010), pp. 33–68; Karl Appuhn, *A Forest on the Sea: Environmental Expertise in Renaissance Venice* (Baltimore, 2009).

16   For example, Harriet Ritvo, *The Dawn of Green: Manchester, Thirlmere and Modern Environmentalism* (Chicago, 2009).

coercion came into play. States sought to both secure adequate supplies domestically, to reduce risk, and projected their influence overseas: most notably in the case of the penetration of the Baltic by Dutch and English fleets.[17] As well as seeking to keep the flow of Baltic timber open, access to timber became part of Britain's imperial web, building many vessels on the east coast of America before independence, and at the beginning of the nineteenth century reserving teak woodlands for use at the new naval base of Bombay.[18] Venice began to regulate the wood market on its *Terrafirma* to secure supplies for the city at the beginning of the fifteenth century. Between the 1460s and 1550s it acquired over forty woodlands reserved for its own use, especially for the Arsenal.[19]

Different *timescales* also came into play in the definition of crisis. They had greatest power when arguments placing events into longer-term trends made the effects of narratives mutually reinforcing. From the point of view of consumers, most crises in fuel supply were immediate, such as a long spell of freezing weather that increased demand and could both push up prices and trigger waves of crime. As ever, these were experienced differentially within society, compounding inequalities. Yet such events, triggered by variable weather and possibly more frequent in certain decades due to climate change, could again be interpreted as a sign of a gathering long-term crisis of supply, in much the same way that spikes in the oil price are viewed (and debated) today. Actuality generated anticipation of worse to come, while anticipation of crisis made it more likely to interpret events as a prophecy made actual.

Different qualities of wood operated according to different timescales themselves. Timber required a long time to grow, possibly up to a century. If a shortage was perceived, the provision of a local remedy could take generations. Restrictions on the use of larger timbers, and the reservation of promising trees for landlords or naval authorities, tended to emerge early.[20] Deliberate plantations for fuel or other small-diameter wood were rarer; and as this was mostly obtained in western and central Europe through the coppicing or pollarding of deciduous trees, a new crop would take the best

17   Robert Greenhalgh Albion, *Forests and Sea Power: The Timber Problem of the Royal Navy 1652–1852* (Cambridge, MA, 1926).
18   Richard Grove, *Green Imperialism: Colonial Expansion, Tropical Island Edens, and the Origins of Environmentalism, 1600–1860* (Cambridge, 1995).
19   Appuhn, *A Forest on the Sea*, pp. 81, 83, 100, 110–11, 114.
20   Warde, 'Fear of Wood Shortage'; Richard Hoyle, 'Redefining Copyhold in Sixteenth-century England: The Case of Timber Rights', in Peter Hoppenbrouwers and Bas van Bavel (eds), *Landholding, Land Tenure and Land Markets in North-west Europe, c.1200–1850* (Brepols, 2004), pp. 250–64; Per Eliasson and Sven G. Nilsson, 'Rättat efter skogarnes aftagende – en miljöhistorisk undersökning av den svenska eken under 1700- och 1800-talen', *Bebyggelsehistorisk Tidskrift*, 37 (1999), pp. 33–64.

part of a decade to produce. Unsurprisingly, while some remedies for shortage involved restrictions on consumers to limit the rate of exploitation, those that sought to enhance future supplies had be couched in terms of posterity and benefits that accrued to future generations. As the German jurist and forestry official Noé Meurer put it in 1576, measures were required so that, 'not they alone, but also their descendants, heirs and children, will always have from their woods what they need (*die Notdurft*) for building and burning'.[21] An English pamphleteer of the 1610s raged against those who felled woods, 'desiring to become heyres of their owne time, without respect had to such heyres as shall succeed them'.[22] Wood became a matter of intergenerational justice.

On longer horizons, the decline of wood supply was also understood to be an ancient and troubling aspect of the advance of civilisation. The primeval landscape was reckoned to have been a great forest (stereotypically allowing squirrels to traverse the country without leaving the boughs), and hence deforestation was a trajectory that seemed bound up with the existence of society itself. Hans Carl von Carlowitz published what is considered to be the first true text of 'forest science' in 1713, citing Tacitus and Caesar to show how Germany had once been swathed in deep forest. He saw the great woodlands of Germany as residuals of the ancient Hercynian forest, undone by the advance of agriculture.[23] Most countries had their equivalent tales. In poet Michael Drayton's extraordinary *Poly-Olbion* of 1613, the woods and rivers of England are given a reproachful voice, making deforestation a commentary on the state of the nation and excessive desire:[24]

> But mans devouring hand, with all the earth not fed,
> Hath hew'd her timber downe. Which wounded, when it fell,
> By the great noise it made, the workmen seem'd to tell
> The losse that to the Land would shortlie come thereby,
> Where no man ever plants to our posteritie.[25]

---

21 Noé Meurer, *Jag und Forstrecht* (Frankfurt.a.M, 1576), p. 5; Paul Warde, *Ecology, Economy and State Formation in Early Modern Germany* (Cambridge, 2006), p. 325; see also Joachim Allmann, *Der Wald in der frühen Neuzeit* (Berlin, 1989), pp. 103–4.

22 Arthur Standish, *New directions of experience authorized by the Kings most excellent Majesty, as may appeare, for the planting of Timber and Fire-wood* (London, 1614), p. 2.

23 Hans Carl von Carlowitz, *Sylvicultura oeconomica oder haußwirtschaftliche Nachricht und naturmäßige Anweisung zue Wilden Baum-Zucht nebst gründlicher Darstellung wie zu förderst durch göttliches Benedeyen dem attenthalben und insgemein einreissenden grossen Holz-Mangel* ... (Leipzig, 1713), pp. 3–5.

24 Andrew McCrae, 'Tree-Felling in Early Modern England: Michael Drayton's Environmentalism', *The Review of English Studies*, 260 (2012), pp. 410–30.

25 Cited in McCrae, 'Tree-felling'.

Allocation crisis

We can now turn to the 'types' of crisis that were more proximate causes of anxiety and conflict. The first of these were allocation crises; this was driven not by a scarcity of wood per se, although this was usually evoked, but a question about how those with authority over wood reserves should distribute it among the population. These disputes were particularly prominent, as might be expected, where a large proportion of woodland was the property of the state, municipal or communal government, or subject to common rights. Questions of access then immediately translated into the obligations and functioning of political institutions.

In the drawing up of village by-laws regarding wood, the problem of overcutting and disorder were often cited as spurs to action. Sometimes this was because old rules had been forgotten or fallen into abeyance, a relatively frequent occurrence in Germany during and after the Thirty Years' War. While framed in terms of the diminution of wood supply, however, many disputes that ended up in higher courts related to how wood was allocated between households, and referred to changes in village life that put pressure on previous arrangements. Firewood might be granted from the village common according to rights held by every resident male inhabitant; to families; or to particular homesteads. In-migration or the subdivision of homesteads and houses between families led to a desire from some for more restrictive arrangements, removing equal rights held by all resident families, and denying newcomers rights altogether. Multiple families living in a single house, for example, would still receive only one lot of wood instead of each household hearth being given one lot. Disputes of this nature seem particularly common in the late sixteenth and early seventeenth century, and doubtless reflected population growth, but also the specific living arrangements that accommodated that growth.[26] They turned, in the end, on how membership of village societies was conceived, as a mutual alliance of equals, or a functioning hierarchy in which unequal allocations reflected differentiated roles.

Central to these disputes in Germany were arguments about what constituted 'necessity' or *Notdurft*, a basic legal right to have access to the resources to function as a household. Did this entail equality, or did it require differentiation, and if so, by what criteria? A typical means of giving wealthier households larger shares was to allocate them according to the category of service they provided lords, whether with a plough-team of horses and oxen,

---

26 Warde, 'Imposition'; Paul Warde, 'Law, the "Commune" and the Distribution of Resources in Early Modern German State Formation', *Continuity and Change*, 17 (2002), pp. 183–211.

or labouring only with their hands.[27] As late as the 1750s the German economic writer Johann Gottlieb von Justi noted that private property, which he saw as deriving from labour invested in the property, was only justified if no one was excluded from being able to supply their needs.[28] That such a claim was legally admissible meant that it enjoyed wide application, as it was one of the means by which peasants could legitimately contest exclusion from wood resources before higher courts and in petitions. The process of restricting wood rights and increased commercialisation of the whole economy tended, consequently, to increase the use of claims to rights to *Notdurft* or necessity, even though we were rarely, in fact, dealing with autarkic subsistence economies. Indeed, in the village of Ebersberg in 1606 peasants claimed the right for wood to sell, because they needed the income to purchase grain.[29] As Andy Wood has pointed out, common rights could provide the raw material to engage in market relations, as much as screen people from them.[30] Often, as with other claims to customary rights, such claims on lords were associated with holding a tenancy in a manor.[31]

Allocation was not only an issue between households; on the grander scale, domestic fuel consumption was set against the needs of industry. Indeed, it was the realisation that allegations of wasteful use of wood and shortage cast against industrial concerns, and by industrialists against peasants, that have led some historians to argue that the whole 'problem' of shortage was merely a chimera used by different interest groups to secure cheaper supplies for themselves. When Simon VI of Lippe in northern Germany, for example, told his subjects to use beech for building rather than scarce oak, this was almost certainly because he could reap the rewards of selling oak to the valued Dutch markets. It might well be rises in *demand*, or the need to remain competitive, that prompted a desire to reserve cheap wood reserves for industry and lower general consumption, as in the case of Lippe's salt-processing and distilling industries; more usually, iron-smelting stood at the centre of contestation.[32] In Nuremberg by contrast, protection for consumers

27 Paul Warde, 'Common Rights and Common Lands in South-west Germany, 1500–1800', in Martina de Moor, Paul Warde and Leigh Shaw-Taylor (eds), *The Management of Common Land in North West Europe ca.1500–1850* (Turnhout, 2002), pp. 195–224.
28 Hölzl, *Umkämpfte Wälder*, p. 65.
29 Stefan von Below and Stefan Breit, *Wald – von der Gottesgabe zum Privateigentum. Gerichtliche Konflikte zwischen Landesherren und Untertanen um den Wald in der frühen Neuzeit* (Stuttgart, 1998), pp. 65, 128.
30 Andy Wood, *The Memory of the People: Custom and Popular Senses of the Past in Early Modern England* (Cambridge, 2013), p. 157.
31 For a series of examples from England and Wales see Nicola Whyte, 'An Archaeology of Natural Places: Trees in the Early Modern Landscape', *Huntington Library Quarterly*, 76/4 (2013), pp. 506–8.
32 Ingrid Schäfer, '*Ein Gespenst geht um.*' *Politik mit der Holznot in Lippe 1750–1850. Eine Regionalstudie zur Wald- und Technikgeschichte* (Detmold, 1992), pp. 53, 140–77; Denis

emerged as early as 1340 as industrial uses were barred from its Reichswald by the Emperor.[33] This was the case with Tudor woodland legislation, which was partly an effort to triangulate a trio of demands from domestic hearths, iron-making and shipbuilding. Timber for construction was of quite a different form from firewood, although supply of timber trees could be achieved by leaving isolated 'standards' uncut to grow to maturity among coppices. In maritime states, however, governments fretted as to whether they could easily source timbers of sufficient dimensions in reasonable proximity to shipyards. Numerous states enacted rules reserving regions of wood for the navy, or commanding the preservation of trees above a certain girth for purveyors. In Sweden, officials stamped trees in woodland and meadow. The reaction of Swedish peasants, who now enjoyed nothing of the tree but its shadow that diminished the sward on their pastures, was to whittle the stamp deeper, causing rot to set in, killing the tree.[34] As we have seen, one of the policies widely enacted to reduce wood consumption and preserve woodlands was to 'reserve' woods, whether for particular uses, or excluding competing ones (like grazing, the collection of litter for stalls, or indeed wood-cutting during seasons of the year to encourage game).[35] The policy of 'reserves' would later be extended to colonial India and beyond.[36]

Entitlement crisis

The second ideal type identified is that of *entitlement*. This is used in the sense developed by Amartya Sen in his study of famine, that the cause of starvation may not be a collapse in the supply of a good, but in the entitle-ments of certain consumers to obtain it.[37] Entitlement failure could come from institutional changes, and be related to disputes over allocation, but equally through the operation of the market, where a decline in income and/or increase in the price of wood might render it unaffordable. At its simplest, it meant that wood cost more than the consumer could easily afford (or so they perceived it), which might be a result of supply relative to demand, but also

Woronoff (ed.), *Forges at Forêt. Recherches sur la consummation proto-industrielle de bois* (Paris, 1990); Etzold, 'Probleme'.

33   Joachim Radkau, *Holz – wie ein Nahrstoff Geschichte schreibt* (München, 2007), p. 104.

34   Eliasson and Nilsson, 'Rättat efter skogarnes auftagende', pp. 46–51.

35   An explicit formulation of the challenges of the multi-use forest can be found in Ernst, *Den Wald entwickeln*.

36   Gregory A. Barton, *Empire, Forestry and the Origins of Environmentalism* (Cambridge, 2002); S. Ravi Rajan, *Modernising Nature. Forestry and Imperial Eco-development 1800–1950* (Oxford, 2006).

37   Amartya Sen, *Poverty and Famines: An Essay on Entitlement and Deprivation* (Oxford, 1983).

factors such as the transport infrastructure. Rising wood prices, particularly in the latter part of the eighteenth century, could be interpreted as indicating the imminence of a wood shortage without anybody actually lacking wood, although people must have reduced their demand for wood, or other goods, in response. This issue of *entitlement* is to be distinguished from *allocation* in that the crisis did not necessarily relate to decisions by political bodies to which the sufferers had a claim to participation or petition, but a change in circumstances of particular groups. While allocation crises could call the legitimacy of political arrangements directly into question, entitlement crises, while certainly being equally political, did not necessarily question more generally the legitimacy of distribution. Certainly institutional decisions could alter 'entitlements', such as the more vigorous and legalistic policing of common rights, excluding those who had previously been allowed to gather wood on sufferance, or introducing payment for the use of a resource that had previously been given gratis. Both of these became more frequent as wood itself rose in price over time. But those who had no direct claim to wood through common rights or ownership of woodland were vulnerable to shifts in their real income, especially as prices rose.

Waves of wood theft were a clear indicator of such crises, often associated with cold years (the rise in demand itself an indicator that people did not usually heat their homes for much of the year) when any traditional allowances proved insufficient. Desperation and even threats could elicit some sympathy from foresters who knew the privation peasants were enduring.[38] Although theft was sometimes for resale, it was widely considered a legitimate satis-faction of needs, seeing 'the so-called forest crimes as trivial and insignificant injuries to property'.[39] Indeed, such action might also be based on a sense of entitlement derived from popular memories of greater access to the woods in previous generations.[40]

It was sometimes recognised, as in consultation for a new Danish forest law in 1733, that setting tight-fisted fuel allowances for the wider populace would simply induce crime. Where access to wood via property or common rights was limited to tenant farmers or minimal allowances in Crown woodlands, the result was a large section of the populace, rural and urban, left without easy access to fuel and hence vulnerable to crises of *entitlement*, even if they were not disputing the basic order of property rights. The consequence was noted by the Governor of Nykøburg on the Danish Island of Falster in 1686; in the town, firewood could only be obtained from thieves.[41] Such pressures

38 Warde, *Ecology*, pp. 329–32.
39 Forester Neebauer in 1803, cited in Hölzl, *Umkämpfte Wälder*, p. 105.
40 See the discussion in Wood, *Memory of the People*, pp. 166–87.
41 Bo Fritzbøger, *A Windfall for the Magnates. The Development of Woodland Ownership in Denmark, c.1150–1850* (Odense, 2004), pp. 118–19, 228.

were compounded by the great waves of enclosure and sales of Crown land that lapped over Europe after 1770.[42] The apogee of these crises came with the 'forest wars' of Germany, peaking in the 1830s and 1840s. While these were a period of hunger with rapid population growth, the previous decades had also seen widespread curtailment of common rights, and the gradual transformation of the woodlands under the authority of state forestry administrations. Between 1835 and 1861, on average the number of forest offences per year equated to a fifth of the entire population in the Bavarian Palatinate, peaking at a third in 1842–43. It was in this last year that Marx wrote on these events in the *Rheinische Zeitung*, arguing that the law was simply enforcing the interests of the propertied over those of the excluded.[43] Ironically, what for some was the solution to the wood crisis threw others into immediate penury, and challenged the bounds of property and authority. However, underpinning the anxieties of the time was the fact that wood prices were clearly advancing more rapidly than the general price level, itself driven by demographic growth causing downward pressure on real wages.

Crise d'état

At the beginning of the early modern period, the primary concern of central government was maintaining orderliness, as well as building the wherewithal to defend or project the interests of the ruler. Hence legislation regarding resources tended to stress the social dislocation that would come with wood shortages, and aimed to maintain systems of arbitration and regulation among the different users of the woodland. Measures tended to be 'negative', prohibiting overuse and monitoring areas to prevent crime and malfeasance. As time went on, government ambitions became more transformatory: to stimulate development and plan ahead for the needs of future generations. Because of the difficulties of easily purveying large amounts of timber to naval dockyards (which does not necessarily mean there was a more widespread shortage of timber), shipbuilding, largely for military purposes, was an area where maritime states felt the need to intervene in their woodlands and wood-pastures.

Hence John Evelyn, who was invited by the Royal Society to produce a document on the state of the nation's woodlands after the Commissioners of the Navy submitted concerns in 1662, and who published the famous *Sylva* in 1664, could proclaim, 'our *Forests* are undoubtedly the greatest *Magazines*

---

42   Marie-Danielle Demelas and Nadine Vivier (eds), *La propriété collective 1750–1914* (Rennes, 2003).

43   Grewe, *Der versperrte Wald*, p. 74; Warde, 'Fear of Wood Shortage', pp. 28–57.

of the *wealth*, and glory of this *Nation*; and our *Oaks* the truest *Oracles* of the *perpetuity* of our *happineß*, as being the only support of that *Navigation* which makes us fear'd *abroad*, and flourish at *Home*'.[44] Of course Evelyn was following the brief, but he almost certainly meant it. A century later, when the Liverpool shipwright Roger Fisher published *Heart of Oak: the British bulwark* after the Seven Years' War in 1763, he was mining a rich seam of cliché already found in Evelyn.[45] Similarly, concerns over the limited stores of timber available to the navy in the late 1780s and early 1790s prompted hand-wringing over the state of the woodlands, and led to a major survey of Crown forests, and the attempt to compile a wider imperial inventory of timber resources.[46] The linking of naval prowess, national fortune and timber supplies was not simply a British concern, however, but could be found all along the Atlantic and North Sea littoral.[47]

Such sentiments provided background and plausibility to moments when 'wood crises' erupted closer to the heart of government, as shortages were seen to threaten the state itself. In fact, viewed in terms of the wood supply, such 'crises' could only ever be ephemeral, as perceived wood famine was not amenable to short-term solutions. There was usually some other proximate cause that had drawn public debate towards the issue, and in time attention would move on. Early Jacobean England, for example, experienced a 'paper crisis' in that a series of shrill warnings about wood shortage do not appear to have any great effects on the ground, but were the consequence of surveying work done on the Crown estates as part of a revenue drive by the new government. When, in the words, of one surveyor, 'I found lamentable scarcitie, and exceeding abuses', their condition was slotted into a general discourse of deforestation and neglect.[48] The projects of the gentleman Arthur Standish published between 1611 and 1616 to foster a systematic national scheme to avert the 'generall destruction and waste of woods in this kingdom' won the imprimatur of James I but had no practical impact.[49]

---

44 John Evelyn, *Sylva, or, A discourse of forest-trees, and the propagation of timber in His Majesties dominions* (London, 1664), p. 111; Beryl Hartley, 'Exploring and Communicating Knowledge of Trees in the Early Royal Society', *Notes and Records of the Royal Society of London*, 64 (2010), pp. 229–50.
45 Cited in Simon Schama, *Landscape and Memory* (London, 1995), p. 167.
46 Fredrik Albritton Jonsson, *Enlightenment's Frontier: The Scottish Highlands and the Origins of Environmentalism* (New Haven, 2013), pp. 157–8; *House of Commons Journal*, 43 (1788), pp. 559–97; *House of Commons Journal*, 44 (1789), pp. 551–619.
47 For example, see John T. Wing, 'Keeping Spain Afloat: State Forestry and Imperial Defense in the Sixteenth Century', *Environmental History*, 17 (January 2012), pp. 116–45.
48 Rooke Church, *An olde thrift newly reuiued Wherein is declared the manner of planting, preserving, and husbanding yong trees of diuers kindes for timber and fuell* (London, 1612), fol. 1.
49 Arthur Standish, *The commons complaint* (London, 1611), p. 1; Arthur Standish, *New directions of experience*; Arthur Standish, *Directions of experience authorized by the Kings*

In the 1650s and 1660s, attention returned to the woods, with particular attention to the Royal Forests, traditional stores for the navy. This reflected political events in the new Commonwealth. First, the selling off of the forests was entertained for several years as an expedient to pay arrears to the army; indeed, timber-felling was frequently used in strife-torn regions to pay off debts or tax arrears.[50] Secondly, the series of naval wars with the Dutch saw national marines fluctuate wildly in size due to seizures of vessels by privateers, and the English found themselves barred from the Baltic. Hence Silvanus Taylor, who published another plea for setting up national timber reserves (and enclosure) to ensure future supplies, noted that some could object to his project by arguing, *'if our Plantations fail, yet our trade will fetch both Timber and Ships at all times, as the* Hollanders *now do that have no Timber growing, for it's usually said, that though trade be sick, it will never die'.* But Taylor asserted that if one was at war with the Dutch, who controlled access to the timbers reserves of northern Europe, this was no answer.[51] On the other hand, the royalist Evelyn could utilise the Commonwealth regime's attempts at a sell-off, and the deleterious results of pursuing royalist opponents for indemnities leading to timber sales from their estates, to blame the Protectorate for the state of the nation's timber stock bequeathed to the Restoration, as 'late prodigious *Spoilers*, whose furious devastation of so many goodly *Woods* and *Forests* have left an Infamy on their *Names* and *Memories*'.[52] These paper crises left no mark on policy but gave apparent long-term trends an urgency or a scapegoat via contemporary politics.

In France, the influence of contemporary politics was similar, but the effects more lasting. Efforts to reform the royal and communal forests under the *surintendent des forêts* Fleury in the 1600s, and more famously by Colbert in the 1660s, were largely driven by the need to improve royal finances, driving a narrative of *crise forestière*.[53] Indeed, we might see these events as a manifestation of a more 'general crisis' of the seventeenth century as states sought

---

most excellent Majesty, as may appeare, for the planting of Timber and Fire-wood, with the least waste and losse of ground (London, 1616).

50 Winfried Schenk, 'Forest Development Types in Central Germany in Pre-Industrial Times. A Contribution by Historical Geography to the Solution of a Forest History Research Argument about the "Wood Scarcity" in the 18th Century', in Simonetta Cavaciocchi (ed.), *L'uomo e la foresta* (Florence, 1996), pp. 201–23; Winfried Schenk, *Waldnutzung, Waldzustand und regionale Entwicklung in vorindustrieller Zeit im mittleren Deutschland* (Stuttgart, 1996).

51 Silvanus Taylor, *Common-good: or, the improvement of commons, forests and chases, by inclosure, wherein the advantage of the poor, the common plenty of all, and the increase and preservation of timber, with other things of common concernment* (London, 1652); see, for an account of the period, Sara Morrison, 'The Stuart Forests: From Venison Pie to Wooden Walls', University of Western Ontario PhD (2004).

52 Evelyn, *Sylva*, p. iii.

53 Andrée Corvol, 'La belles futaies d'antan', in Andrée Corvol (ed.), *La Forêt malade. Débats anciens et phénomènes nouveaux XVIIe–XXe siècles* (Paris, 1994), pp. 21–3.

to keep revenue in step with rapidly increasing expenditure. Standardising cutting cycles and management regimes across woodlands made it easier for Crown officials to arrange sales and leases, while the rhetoric of a devastated forest suited many parties: the legislators, property-holders who wanted charges and services on their property to be reduced, and potential buyers who expected it to depress prices. In practice, the reforms were far from fully realised and only became widely implemented after a century, but the impact was not negligible.[54]

Forestry as 'crisis discipline'

The cumulative effect of these 'crises', from a household and community to national level, was to develop and refine a discourse of scarcity, and a disaster to be expected with varying degrees of imminence, familiar right across the social scale and ever-ready to be pressed into service. As we have seen, this reflected structural aspects of resource provision in the early modern world, but also created a common discourse around wood resources that were in fact quite diverse. In truth, the ease of procuring massive timbers for the mast or keel of a ship, or bent to the particular shape desired by a shipwright, did not have anything much to do with the availability of coppice-wood for domestic hearths. But the knowledge that this language had political effect, and wide legitimacy, provided an incentive to use it – and indeed may have undermined the arguments of those who did not.

Wood was not, of course, the only source of fuel. Turf and peat were widely used alternatives in northern Europe, the former consisting of clods of earth cut from the surface that were thick with the roots of plants such as gorse that could be burned; the latter was the dried-out cuttings of peat bogs, both lowland and upland, in which plant matter had been crushed and preserved in anaerobic conditions over thousands of years.[55] Both were significant fuels in the British Isles, while peat dominated in the Dutch Republic, with extraction and distribution managed commercially on a large scale.[56] Yet exploitation ate into finite reserves and tended to push the cutting frontier away from settlements; despite some encouragement of substitution, it had limited scope

54 Andrée Corvol, 'La decadence des forêts. Leitmotiv', in Corvol (ed.), *La Forêt malade*, pp. 8–13; Andrée Corvol, *L'homme er l'arbre sous l'Ancien Regime* (Paris, 1984).
55 Warde and Williamson, 'Fuel Supply'.
56 On the Dutch use of peat, see C. Cornelisse, *Energiemarkten en energiehandel in Holland in de late middeleeuwen* (Hilversum, 2008); M.A.W. Gerding, *Vier eeuwen turfwinning. De verveningen in Groningen, Friesland, Drenthe en Overijseel tussen 1550 en 1950* (Wageningen, 1995); J.W. de Zeeuw, 'Peat and the Dutch Golden Age. The Historical Meaning of Energy Attainability', in *Afdeling agrarische Geschiedenis Bijdragen* 21 (1978), pp. 3–31.

beyond those areas where it was, in any case, the prevalent fuel.[57] Coal was widely recognised as a potential alternative in Britain, Germany and France, and imported into the Netherlands. Efforts at technological adaptation were widespread, especially in heavy consumers of fuel such as the salt industry. However, while most intensive users of fuel in Britain had already adopted coal as the primary fuel in the seventeenth century (iron-smelting being the notable exception), such efforts had limited success where coal reserves were distant and transport costs remained high.[58] Of course, a final recourse was economising on fuel and the introduction of more efficient wood-fired technology. The Prussian state made significant efforts to stimulate such behaviour, and led by example in its own military and systems of purveyance, including the setting up of departments to control timber and firewood provision in 1764 and 1785 respectively. These laboured, however, under the contradictory goals of seeking to raise revenue from sales and keep industrial costs down while supposedly reducing consumption, and seem to have had little effect regarding the 'crisis', which did, however, provide a justification for their existence.[59]

This has led some historians, most notably Joachim Radkau, to argue that in many cases the 'wood shortage' debates were largely a scare story with little basis in reality. The rhetoric acted to disguise the real interests of those who wanted power over wood resources, whether the state, or industry (and we might add at a village level the more prosperous magistrates and holders of common rights), and if supply crises existed they were really 'institutional crises' generated by failures to effectively distribute the resource. The escape from the crisis was simply to stop talking about it. Even the move to coal-based industrialisation in Germany has been attributed to powerful forces dominated by the state steering development to their benefit, rather than a necessity for modern economic growth, although most economic historians view such efforts as having rather limited affect before the mid nineteenth century.[60] Certainly, the claim of a wood crisis (*Holznot*) was

57   On Germany, see Grabas, 'Krisenbewältigung', pp. 54–5, 67; Etzold, 'Probleme', p. 86.

58   Hatcher, *British Coal Industry*; M. Fessner, 'Salz und Kohle: die Salinenbetriebe bei Unna in Westfalen als Förderer des märkischen Steinkohlenbergbaus im 17. Und 18. Jahrhundert', in Westermann, *Vom Bergbau*, pp. 51–75.

59   Grabas, 'Krisenbewältigung', pp. 60–3; see also C.S. Bartel, 'Umschwünge in der Entwicklung des Oberharzer Bergbaureviers um 1630, 1760 und 1820 im Vergleich', in E. Westermann (ed.), *Vom Bergbau – zum Industrie revier* (Stuttgart, 1993), p. 163.

60   Radkau, *Holz*, pp. 150–2; see also Schäfer, '*Ein Gespenst geht um*'; however, a critique was developed by Grabas, who noted that import barriers actually kept coal more expensive in northern Germany than would otherwise have been the case: Grabas, 'Krisenbewältigung', pp. 48, 68–9; on the more orthodox view in economic history, see Toni Pierenkemper, 'Die schwerindustriellen Regionen Deutschlands in der Expansion: Oberschlesien, die Saar und das Ruhrgebiet im 19. Jahrhundert', *Jahrbuch für Wirtschaftsgeschichte*, 33 (1992), pp. 37–56.

'An argument used almost as variously as was wood itself'.[61] Nevertheless the trope was employed by those who had no obvious interest in doing so, including governments who won no significant incomes from the woodlands. As early as 1504 arguments were made for a parliamentary act in Scotland as being needed, 'considering that the wood of Scotland is utterly destroyed',[62] while that passed under Henry VIII in 1543 evoked 'the great decaye of Tymber and Woodes', meaning, 'a great and manifest likelihood of scarcity'.[63] In 1495 a state ordinance of the Duchy of Württemberg bewailed 'the great shortage of wood for fuel and building', and almost innumerable examples could be piled up from across the continent.[64]

The sixteenth and early seventeenth centuries established it as one of the fundamental duties of a ruler – and responsibility to be imposed on their subjects – to guard against 'the occurrence of wood shortage or clearances of the woodlands', a line usually accompanied by a list of suggested measures, 'else the wood shortage will be found in almost every place'.[65] Under Peter the Great widespread, draconian and doubtless unenforceable restrictions on wood use, especially regarding large timbers, were found in Russia too.[66] By the mid eighteenth century, this prognosis of crisis had moved into the present tense as German authors could claim that they wrote to aid the 'bringing to an end of the frequent complaints because of the wood shortage to be found in nearly every place.'[67] Indeed, 'In our times ... if good counsel does not prevail in time, it may be that in many regions of our fatherland the wood shortage will press even more than the shortage of bread, and finally draw after it the end and downfall of entire places.'[68] By the end of the century a Prussian forester could declare, 'It appears utterly redundant to repeat proof that the consumption of wood is greater than the increase and increment with us.'[69]

But why did it appear so? The instinct of the modern historian is to blame Malthusian pressures on the land, or, in a less dramatic version of the story, a structural crisis of institutions unable to cope with demographic pressure

61   Radkau, 'Das Rätsel', p. 70.
62   T.C. Smout, Alan R. Macdonald and Fiona Watson, *A History of the Native Woodlands of Scotland* (Edinburgh, 2005), p. 38. Although, on p. 45, the authors express the suspicion that this was the view of a monarch eager to supply his needs more cheaply.
63   35. Hen VIII c. 17.
64   Warde, *Ecology*, p. 175.
65   Veit Ludwig von Seckendorff, *Teutscher Fürsten-Staat* (Jena, [1655] 1737 edn), pp. 471, 474.
66   V.V. Alexejev, Y.V. Alexejeva and V.A. Shkerin, 'Russian Forest: Its Dimensions and Use', in Cavaciocchi (ed.), *L'uomo*, pp. 1088–9.
67   Johann Gottlieb Beckmann, *Gegründete Versuche und Erfahrungen der zu unsern Zeiten höchst nöthigen Holzsaat, zum allgemeinen Besten* (4th edn, Chemnitz, [1755] 1777), p. 8.
68   Wilhelm Gottfrid Moser, *Grundsätze der Forst=Oeconomie* (Frankfurt and Leipzig, 1757), p. 5.
69   Friedrich August Ludwig von Burgsdorf, cited in Sieferle, *Subterranean Forest*, p. 141.

on the old systems of distribution.[70] But the discourse of the age itself was different. It was people who were to blame – not their numbers, but their habits: '... everywhere bare mountains and clear-cut forests reveal to everyone their poverty of wood and accuse their inhabitants of bad housekeeping before the Creator'.[71] The crisis was, in this view, not the result of demand outstripping the intrinsic resources of the land, but the failure of people to harness those resources to their full potential. True, there were also many efforts to encourage conservation and efficiency, reducing demand through switching to coal, use of better stoves, or simply stimulating what we have called above an 'entitlement crisis': 'better set the price somewhat higher ... Nothing serves better to spur people to think of all sorts of means to do with less than necessity.'[72] A liberal and influential minority of foresters around the turn of the nineteenth century, notably von Hazzi in Bavaria and Pfeil in Prussia, argued that high prices would stimulate a supply response and greater wood production.[73] But by and large it was foresters and central government officials who presented themselves as saviours, a pattern found in France, the German states, Denmark and Sweden, and Russia. The rhetoric was also present but became less strident and frequent in England and the Netherlands, which had access to major imports of timber and whose fuel supplies came to be dominated by peat and coal. Forestry became a 'crisis discipline', no longer simply managing reserves for the needs of rulers and arbitrating disputes among the users of the woods, but a repository of expertise that could haul society away from collapse; in the rhetoric of its practitioners that multiplied rapidly after 1750, it was on a mission.

Wood shortage in Enlightenment discourse was often not so much a problem of environmental *degradation*, although this certainly features as an argument, but a brake on development. This was articulated by von Carlowitz in his famous work of 1713, written specifically out of a concern that wood supply could not keep up with the demands from the mining and metallurgical industries of Saxony. The production of the mines was 'through God's blessing inexhaustible', but 'wise men' had long been led to 'prophesying' that wood supplies could not keep up with the supply of metal, so that 'a future wood-shortage' would bring the mines into decline, and 'the flourishing commerce might be inhibited'.[74] Indeed various authors articulated the notion that industry did not lead to inevitable resource exhaustion,

---

70 Grabas, 'Krisenbewältigung', pp. 45, 47.
71 Zedler, cited in Sieferle, *Subterranean Forest*, p. 141.
72 Möller, cited in Sieferle, *Subterranean Forest*, p. 150.
73 Heinrich Rubner, *Forstgeschichte im Zeitalter der industriellen Revolution* (Berlin, 1967), pp. 112–13.
74 He added the shortage, although Europe-wide, was particularly marked in the vicinity of mines; and also that the English had to import ship-timber from America at high prices. Von Carlowitz, *Sylvicultura*, pp. 7, 44, 52–3.

but could provide the prompt for higher standards of management. 'The good condition of the woodlands depends on the economic and sustainable use of the same,' argued von Justi in 1758, but this in turn required demand for the wood.[75] As we have seen, a few liberal foresters anticipated the market mechanism providing the answers, but it was more commonly thought that foresters would work under state direction as part of a general programme of development. In fact, another contrast between the north-west of the continent and the regions of most energetic forestry regulation in central and northern Europe was the large areas of woodland under state control, often supplying industries considered strategic.[76]

The main problem, then, was argued to be the ignorance of the masses, and indeed the form of ownership most associated with them: commons. 'Common rights are the first and most important cause of neglect of everything that might serve to conserve and foster the forests and leads to negligence and damage in every action in the common woods,' proclaimed Danish clergyman Hvass in 1761, joining a cacophony of similar excoriating judgements across Europe.[77] Or as von Carlowitz put it, 'It is mostly people who are themselves guilty, when infertility is found in the earth ...',[78] and the poorly yielding commons gave people the limited but too-easy means to stay in ignorance and penury. The answer was enclosure and subjection to the professional forester. The legal possibility of such a move was, as we have seen, established in the sixteenth and seventeenth centuries, but the Enlightenment would bring both the means, in a much larger printed literature and the emergence of educational institutions, and the idea of the forester and professional transformer of the land for the 'public good'. As Büchting wrote in his 1756 *Entwurf der Jägerei* (Treatise on Hunting), 'If every district had the fortune to be managed by people well-versed in forestry, it is sure no wood shortage would arise, as experience shows.'[79] By the 1750s this was not in dispute among foresters, although authors in the field produced large and sometimes catty works as to why their own methods were better than their rivals'. It was a debate increasingly played out in print and employing

75 'Kommt der gute Zustand der Wälder auf den wirtschaftlichen und nachhaltigen Gebrauch derselben an.' Johann Heinrich Gottlob von Justi, *Staatswirtschaft oder systematische Abhandlung aller Oekonomischen und Cameralwissenschaften, die zur Regierung eines Landes efodert [sic] werden* (Leipzig, 1758), p. 227; see Hölzl, *Umkämpfte Wälder*, on view of decay in remote areas of Bavaria.

76 Rubner, *Forstgeschichte*, pp. 66, 121–4.

77 Fritzbøger, *Windfall for the Magnates*, p. 31.

78 Von Carlowitz, *Sylvicultura*, p. 106.

79 'Wenn alle Reviere das Glück hätten, von forstverständigen Leuten verwaltet zu werden, so rise gewiß kein Holzmangel ein; doch stehet auf die Erfahrung'. Cited in Beckmann (1777), preface, p. 13.

an ever-more technical language, instilling expectations of the broad skill set the modern forester should have. 'In these times whoever as a student wants to come to be called a cameralist or an economist (*Oekonomen*), should be ashamed if they are afraid of algebra.'[80]

This move towards mathematical abstraction on the one hand did not mean a withdrawal from the particularities of local condition on the other. On the contrary, it went hand in hand with ever higher expectations of local knowledge and engagement, as it was recognised that detailed environmental knowledge was required for any transformation to be effected. This was especially the case with the followers of Wilhelm Pfeil, who headed the leading forestry school at Eberswalde in Prussia from the 1820s to 1840s: 'We lay great value on the observation of Nature, on the study of trees and their natural behaviour, of the careful consideration of all circumstances under which one works (*wirtschaftet*).' Foresters partook of the increasing stress on fieldwork in the botanical sciences. 'Ask the tree', proclaimed Pfeil, 'how it wants to be raised; it will teach you better than the books can.'[81] Yet this still represented a clear break with the forester and indeed peasant of the past, because experience had to be combined with 'learning and instruction'.[82] The new *Forstwissenschaft* followed von Carlowitz by putting at its heart the 'artificial' regeneration of the forest by systematic planting, getting the sustainable maximum out of the ground. Such deliberate re-afforestation had been practised since the fourteenth century but now became a generalised ambition.[83] 'Because this sowing is precisely the single and indispensible means, by which the great retreat of wood can be repaired.' After all, continued J.G. Beckmann in 1756, if natural rejuvenation was sufficient, how come that loss of wood was 'so large and notable'?[84]

Conclusion

Belief in wood crisis was a structural element of the early modern world, and could be evoked as a possibility as soon as the costs of obtaining any *particular kind* of wood supply appeared to be rising. This could come about for all sorts of reasons, to do with the opportunity cost of labour, transport infrastructure, political struggles, information costs (such as finding the

---

80   He was citing Kästner. G.U. Däzel, *Ueber Forsttaxierung und Ausmittelung des jährlichen nachhaltigen Ertrages* (München, 1793), p. ii.
81   Karl Hasel and Ekkehard Schwartz, *Forstgeschichte. Ein Grundriss für Studium und Praxis* (3rd edn, Kassel, 2006), pp. 343–4; Rubner, *Forstgeschichte*, p. 126.
82   Moser, *Grundsätze*, p. 11.
83   Schröder-Lembke, 'Waldzerstörung'.
84   Beckmann, *Gegründete Versuche*, p. 13.

right-shaped piece of timber), or indeed rising demand and dwindling supply. Hence each community, or on a grander scale, state, experienced an episodic articulation of the 'crisis' without it ever really going away, depending on local circumstances both institutional and economic. In literature, legis-lation and historiography the theme of wood shortage and crisis is certainly more prevalent in the German states, a fact probably due to the extent of political fragmentation and the sheer number of states and jurisdictions. This context also provided, however, multiple poles of development for forestry in a land with a tradition of proactive territorial and municipal government. Consequently Germany emerged as a driving, though not the only, force in the emergence of modern forestry.

The forester could thus be presented as saviour, and professional forestry became the gatekeeper of environmental management by which a wide variety of skills were inculcated, from formal mathematical training to intimate knowledge of the soil and ground. Other individuals might possess some of these skills, but without the full set they were found wanting by the new professionalism. The evidence that foresters provided for their necessary remedy to the wood crisis was ... the indisputable and widely articulated wood crisis, which itself was evidence that traditional methods had not worked. It should be noted that the emergence of 'scientific forestry' was not simply a 'paper crisis', which was able to assert its own criteria for expertise and authority in the face of local knowledge. Many contributors to the emerging *Forstwissenschaft* had already worked long years in the woods and were themselves practising foresters; they often described what they did as much as proclaimed the new, but in doing so they also prescribed the path for those that came after them. The wood crisis, whether 'real' or not, was the necessary condition for the emergence of forestry in its modern form, because that crisis was what provided the new discipline with its justification and impetus.

In a few regions of Europe, substitute fuels were found that had long been employed. In fact, in most cases the dissolution of the old, largely locally orientated wood economy, a phenomenon of the nineteenth century, was not a failure of supply, but the opening up to competition from the products of coal-fired regions, and the railways that emerged from them in the 1830s. These rapidly made old wood-fired industries uncompetitive and gave popula-tions access to fossil fuels. The expanding output of the new, often monocul-tural woods of scientific forestry was now used for pit-props, railways sleepers and the building trade. And almost overnight, the rhetoric of wood shortage was cast aside, only to reappear across the Atlantic by the 1860s with the rapid logging out of North America, and late transposed on to global fears of resource shortages in the twentieth century.[85]

85   Michael Williams, *Deforesting the Earth. From Prehistory to Global Crisis* (Chicago, 2003), pp. 386–95.

6

The International Crisis of 1972–77: The Neglected Agrarian Dimension

JOHN MARTIN

Introduction

The international crisis of the mid-1970s ushered in an economic collapse the magnitude of which, in terms of its effects on the downturn in economic activity and increase in unemployment, was the worst crisis since that of the Great Depression (1929–32). Unlike previous recessions, where the downturn in economic activity had been accompanied by precipitous price falls, particularly for agricultural commodities, the mid-1970s constituted a period of 'stagflation'.[1] Not only was the British economy enduring its longest and most pronounced decline in manufacturing production since the 1930s, but this was accompanied by unprecedented peacetime levels of retail price inflation (RPI), which peaked at in excess of 27 per cent in 1975.[2] Price increases were even more pronounced in the case of the staple components of the British diet – bread and potatoes – the cost of which more than trebled in the space of five years. Not surprisingly, these strongly inflationary pressures, coupled with the decline in industrial production, led to a significant increase in unemployment and either stagnating or falling living standards even for those fortunate to still be in work. Under these circumstances the Labour government toiled to deal with the crisis, and in 1976 the Chancellor of the Exchequer Denis Healey was forced to go 'cap in hand' to the International Monetary Fund (IMF) to secure a $3.9 billion loan, the largest to that date ever granted by the institution.[3]

---

1   For a detailed analysis of the magnitude in the fall of individual agricultural commodities during the Great Depression, see J.H. Kirk, *Agriculture and the Trade Cycle* (London, 1933), p. 79; C.P. Kindleberger, *The World in Depression, 1929–1939* (London, 1973), p. 86.
2   A.K. Cairncross, 'The Heath Government and the British Economy', in S. Ball and A. Seldon (eds), *The Heath Government, 1970–74: A Reappraisal* (London, 1996), p. 107.
3   The widespread view that the Labour government had to be 'bailed out' by the IMF loan is challenged by a number of writers who argue that the 1976 crisis in the financial exchange

The dominant narratives about the causes of the crisis stress the role of three interrelated external seismic shocks: the currency instability that followed the collapse of the Bretton Woods agreement, the unprecedented increase in the price of oil as a result of the OPEC (Oil Producing and Exporting Countries) crisis, and the inflationary pressures precipitated by the commodity price explosion.[4] In contrast, scant attention has been paid to the importance of the agrarian dimension to the crisis, namely the contribution of weather-induced changes in agricultural production and the food price inflation that characterised the 1970s. This study challenges the conventional wisdom, that the crisis was primarily precipitated by the collapse of the Bretton Woods agreement and the OPEC oil crisis. It argues that there was another vitally important, but neglected causal factor contributing to the international crisis, in particular weather-induced disruptions to food supply, which were responsible for the unprecedented levels of food price inflation. In addition to exploring the conventional explanations for the international crisis this chapter also considers the impact of the Russian 'great grain robbery' of 1972 and the collapse of the anchoveta harvest, as well as the effects of the West European drought of 1975–76.

Taking into account the multitude of different factors contributing to the crisis, it is not surprising that the role of the weather in dislocating agricultural production has merited scant attention. However, this neglect reflects in part a fundamental and long-term issue, that western European historians have in general given very limited credence to the impact of the weather in determining the fortunes of the agricultural sector.[5] This is not necessarily surprising given that, on a comparative basis, the weather in Europe has historically had considerably less impact on agricultural productivity than in other areas of the world. Moreover, since the medieval period there has been a long-term decline in fluctuations in annual production. Even in the late eighteenth century yearly fluctuations in the order of 15 per cent or more in Britain were considered the norm, whereas by the post-Second World War period a 10 per cent change from one year to the next was deemed exceptional. By comparison, weather patterns have a considerably more profound impact on yearly agricultural production in countries such as the USA and

---

markets was really a speculative spasm unrelated to market fundamentals. See M. Artis and D. Cobham, 'Summary and appraisal', in M. Artis and D. Cobham (eds), *Labour's Economic Policies, 1974–79* (Manchester, 1991), p. 276.

4   Ibid., p. 4.

5   Geoffrey Parker makes a similar point and links it to American climate-change denial. Geoffrey Parker, 'Crisis and Catastrophe: The Global Crisis of the Seventeenth Century Reconsidered', *American Historical Review*, 113 (2008), pp. 1053–79. On the role of the environment, see also, for example, B.M.S. Campbell, 'Nature as Historical Protagonist: Environment and Society in Pre-Industrial England', *Economic History Review*, 63 (2010), pp. 281–314.

Russia.[6] Indeed, in sub-Saharan Africa, a drought can not only lead to a harvest failure for just one year but a famine lasting several years as the malnourished, and less productive, population resort to killing their draught animals and consuming the seed corn reserved for the following crop.[7]

Even in Britain the weather has historically played a key role influencing agricultural productivity and in turn the level of economic activity and prosperity.[8] This was particularly evident in medieval England when, as Hoskins' analysis has shown, a wet spring and summer would significantly delay the planting of crops, reducing crop yields while also encouraging the spread of a variety of illnesses in livestock. Conversely, prolonged droughts or even simply dry weather would also affect crop and livestock production.[9] By the onset of the agricultural depression of the 1870s, the ready availability of low-priced cereals and refrigerated meat ensured that the country continued to be well supplied with food irrespective of weather-induced fluctuations in domestic agricultural production. Despite the threat to food security posed by the country's abnormal dependence on imported food in the First and Second World Wars, the importance of the weather as a causal factor in determining the level of food supply continued to attract less attention from both policy-makers and the academic community.

This neglect of weather-induced fluctuations in domestic food supply in Britain became even more apparent during the post-Second World War period when, as a result of the scientific and technological revolution, there was much greater consistency in agricultural output between one year and the next. Nearly half of the increase in crop yields and grassland productivity that has taken place since the Second World War is the result of genetic improvements developed by plant breeders.[10] The decline in the variability of yields between one year and another also reflected improvements in disease control following the development of herbicides to control weed infestation and fungicides to combat diseases such as mildew, a fungus disease that spreads rapidly during periods of hot humid weather. This also reflected increased mechanisation where fields could be ploughed and the soil worked down to a suitable tilth even during prolonged dry periods. In order to insulate the country from the

---

6   M. Atkin, *Agricultural Commodity Markets: A Guide to Futures Trading* (London, 1989), p. 127.
7   M.H. Glantz (ed.), *Drought and Hunger in Africa: Denying Famine a Future* (Cambridge, 1987), pp. 37–58.
8   For the historic variations in crop yields in England, see, for example: W.G. Hoskins, 'Harvest Fluctuations and English Economic History, 1480–1619', *Agricultural History Review*, 12 (1964), pp. 28–46; and C.J. Harrison, 'Grain Price Analysis and Harvest Qualities, 1465–1634', *Agricultural History Review*, 19 (1971), pp. 135–55.
9   Hoskins, 'Harvest Fluctuations', pp. 28–46.
10 P. Palladino, 'Science, Technology and the Economy: Plant Breeding in Great Britain, 1920–70', *Economic History Review*, 69 (1996), p. 116.

volatility in agricultural production and prices that characterised international markets and to promote long-term peacetime security for British farmers, the post-war Labour government had passed the 1947 Agriculture Act.[11] This landmark legislation committed the state to providing 'stability and efficiency' in the form of guaranteed prices for the main agricultural commodities.[12] This was accompanied with the introduction of a five-year plan, which set ambitious targets for the main review commodities in an effort to increase agricultural output by 20 per cent.[13] Agriculture was therefore largely insulated from the volatile international prices that had characterised the pre-Second World War period. Having guaranteed prices and assured markets for their products, ensured that British farmers had a vested interest in maximising their output and productivity. As an incentive to become more efficient, increases in guaranteed prices undertaken in the Annual Price Review did not cover all of the increased costs of production that had been incurred.[14]

As a result, by the early 1970s, successive governments and Ministry officials in Britain tended to pay scant attention to the possibility that prolonged periods of dry weather, or abnormally bad weather, would seriously disrupt domestic food production. Little attention, for example, was devoted to ways of alleviating droughts by the use of irrigation.[15] Such systems were used by only a small number of farmers and were confined almost exclusively to high-value intensively farmed horticultural crops. It was commonly regarded that summer droughts were so infrequent that having irrigation equipment was not cost effective for most agricultural crops in Britain, with the exception of potatoes and sugar beet, and even then such expenditure had only been undertaken by a small number of farmers.[16]

The agricultural dimension to the international crisis of the mid-1970s has been overlooked by British policymakers as well as the academic community. Instead they have tended to focus on the manifestations of the economic crisis and the way it was further exacerbating Britain's underperformance as a manufacturing nation in relation to that of its industrial competitors.[17] Given

11   J.K. Bowers, 'British Agricultural Policy since the Second World War', *Agricultural History Review*, 33 (1985), p. 66.

12   J. Martin, *The Development of Modern Agriculture: British Farming since 1931* (Basingstoke, 2000), pp. 69–76.

13   E.H. Whetham, 'The Agricultural Expansion Programme 1947–51', *Journal of Agricultural Economics*, 11 (1955), p. 313.

14   Martin, *The Development of Modern Agriculture*, pp. 69–76.

15   In 1973 less than 3 per cent of the potato crop was irrigated, see: *Farmer and Stockbreeder*, 8 May 1976, p. 8.

16   Irrigation was only really deemed cost effective in respect of potatoes, sugar beet and horticultural production, B. Wilson, 'Freak Drought that may Change British Farming', *Farmer and Stockbreeder*, 31 July 1976, p. 8.

17   J.F. Wright, *Britain in the Age of Economic Management* (Oxford, 1979), pp. 174–83.

the magnitude of the crisis contemporary studies tended to portray an apocalyptic vision of Britain's prospects. Internal strife was widespread while with the spread of nationalism in Northern Ireland, Scotland and Wales the very future of the UK appeared to be in jeopardy. Historical accounts of the 1970s can be broadly divided into two main schools of thought. Those on the right tended to focus on the shift from Keynesian demand management in Britain to more of a free market approach to managing the economy – what was to become the precursor of Mrs Thatcher's free market reforms.[18] Conversely, those historians of a more left-wing disposition tended to focus their interest on the effects of the industrial unrest and strife, which was centred on the old staple industries, which was to culminate in the year-long miners' strike of 1985.[19] This polarised approach invariably led to a neglect of interest in what was perceived as the more mundane issue of the reasons for the unprecedented increase in food prices in the 1970s. For example, academics such as Brian Burkett and Mark Bainbridge have stressed the effects of Britain's entry into the EEC in accentuating the food price inflation of this period.[20]

The aim of this chapter is to address this omission by investigating the reasons for the agrarian crisis of the early 1970s, in particular the extent to which weather-induced changes to food production contributed to the economic problems that Britain experienced during the period 1972–77. In particular it will explore the effects of weather on agricultural production, and prices. Finally, it will consider the impact of the Western European drought of 1975–76 which constituted the longest driest and hottest period in Britain in the twentieth century.

The international crisis of 1973–74

The international crisis of 1973–74, which significantly affected the industrialised nations, is primarily attributed to a series of external seismic shocks, the effects of which were felt almost simultaneously in the early 1970s and brought the world trade boom and economic prosperity of the previous decades to an abrupt end. The most obvious long-term cause of the international crisis was the currency instability that followed the collapse of

---

18   D. Marquand, 'The Paradoxes of Thatcherism', in Robert Skidelsky (ed.), *Thatcherism* (London, 1988), p. 165; A. Gamble, *The Free Economy and the Strong State: The Politics of Thatcherism* (Basingstoke, 1988), p. 81; A. Gamble, S. Walkland and J. Hayward, *The British Party System and Economic Policy: Studies in Adversary Politics* (Oxford,1984), p. 73.

19   L. Loach, 'We'll be right here to the end ... and after: Women in the Miners' Strike', in H. Benyon (ed.), *Digging Deeper: Issues in the Miners' Strike* (London, 1985), pp. 169–79.

20   B. Burkett and M. Bainbridge, 'The Performance of British Agriculture and the Impact of the Common Agricultural Policy', *Rural History*, 1 (1990), p. 265.

the Bretton Woods agreement.[21] This had been established by the USA in 1944 in order to ensure currency stability by maintaining exchange rates by linking currencies to the convertibility of the US dollar to gold. The aim was to restore the multilateral basis of world trade and cooperation between countries and to prevent the competitive currency devaluations and trade protectionism caused by the Great Depression (1929–32). The breakdown of the Bretton Woods system in 1972 was ultimately precipitated by the decision of the USA to finance its rising spending by expansionary monetary policies rather than by increasing tax levels. The outcome was a continuing rise in the US balance of payments and an acceleration in world inflation, which led to the rest of world, specifically Europe, being unwilling to acquire dollar balances.[22] Currency stability was brought to an abrupt end on 15 August 1971, when the USA unilaterally terminated the convertibility of the dollar to gold.[23] As currency exchange rates were no longer fixed, there was a decline in the value of the pound sterling in relation to the dollar, which in turn further increased the price that Britain had to pay for imported agricultural commodities, which were priced in dollars on the international markets. The collapse of equity markets that accompanied the international recession prompted institutional and even some private investors to acquire speculative long positions in the futures markets in order to take advantage of the rising prices for agricultural commodities.[24]

The second seismic shock was the end of the world trade boom in the early 1970s. The expansion of world trade during the post-war period was also facilitated by the favourable terms of trade (the value of manufactured goods in relation to raw materials including agricultural commodities), which shifted in favour of the manufacturing nations of the world. Along with the continued increase in world demand for manufactured goods, Britain derived immense benefits from the increasing supply of relatively low-priced food, which was readily available in the 1950s and 1960s. Imports of food such as grain continued to flood into Britain not only from the USA but also from agriculturally dominated Commonwealth countries such as Australia and New Zealand.[25] However, the food surpluses and low prices were replaced by

21   G. Zis, 'The International Status of Sterling', in M. Artis and D. Cobham (eds), *Labour's Economic Policies, 1974–79* (Manchester, 1991), p. 105.

22   Ibid., p. 105.

23   A. Seldon, 'The Heath Government in History', in S. Ball and A. Seldon (eds), *The Heath Government, 1970–74* (London, 1996), p. 12.

24   D.J.S. Rutledge, 'Trading Volume and Price Variability; New Evidence on the Price Effect of Speculation', *International Futures Trading Seminar Proceedings*, vol. 5 (Chicago, 1978), pp. 160–74, reprinted in B.A. Goss (ed.), *Future Markets: Their Establishment and Performance* (London, 1986).

25   M. Butterwick and E. Neville Rolfe, *Food, Farming and the Common Market* (Oxford, 1968), pp. 33–9.

food shortages and unprecedented price rises on an international scale in the early 1970s. The main cause of the rise in worldwide agricultural commodity prices was weather-induced reductions in agricultural production. This was accompanied by a commodity price explosion in precious metals, principally gold, precipitated in part by currency instability and the collapse of equity markets.[26]

Another seismic shock and key contributory cause of the international crisis of 1973–74 was the Arab–Israeli or Yom Kippur war of 1973. Following the US decision to rearm Israel in the conflict, OPEC imposed a trade embargo on the shipment of oil to many Western countries, including Britain, the USA and Canada. This led to oil prices increasing by 420 per cent between 1972 and 1974. This in turn had an impact on agricultural production as a result of the increase in the price of petrochemicals, which were used extensively in artificial fertilisers and herbicides. The OPEC crisis affected food supplies indirectly in Brazil, the world's leading exporter of cane sugar. Higher oil prices encouraged a shift to utilise corn and sugar in the fermentation of ethanol for use in motor vehicles as well as for human consumption. The USA had come to see cheap sugar products as a birthright. Even those consumers who might have turned to the newest artificial sugar substitute, cyclamate, quickly returned to the real thing when the US Food and Drug Administration pulled cyclamate off the market in 1969 after reports that it might cause cancer.[27] Between 1966 and November 1974, raw sugar made the astonishing climb from 1.4 cents to 66.5 cents per pound. By the end of 1972, there had been four straight sugar seasons with record crops. Yet consumption actually outpaced supplies in 1972, literally eating into sugar inventories over the next year. The 1973–74 sugar season began with extremely tight supply conditions worldwide; demand continued to rise. As a result, between January 1972 and September 1974, there was a fourfold increase in the price of raw sugar.[28]

However, even before the White House published the 'Presidential Proclamation' of 1975 limiting sugar imports into the USA to seven million tonnes, the speculative bubble in the futures markets, which peaked at over 66 cents per pound, was over. Investors, including Arab oil money, had switched their interest to other agricultural commodities. Rutledge's analysis rejects the view that 'speculative activity destabilises price' and 'that movements in trading volume, represent a response to rather than a cause of, movements in price variability'.[29]

26 Atkin, *Agricultural Commodity Markets*, p. 127.
27 S.L. Inhorn and L.F. Meisner, 'Irresponsibility of Cyclamate Ban', *Science*, 167 (1970), p. 1436.
28 Food and Agriculture Council, *The State of Food and Agriculture* (hereafter FAO), 1974, p. 9.
29 Rutledge, 'Trading Volume and Price Variability'.

In order to explain the price rises in agricultural commodities that occurred in the early 1970s, it is important to take into consideration that the late 1960s and early 1970s witnessed a gradual but nevertheless discernible shift among many of the leading food-exporting countries to their food stocks. The run-down in inventories or grain stockpiles was particularly evident in North America, which for 20 years or more had acted as final reserve against food shortages elsewhere. By the late 1960s a number of initiatives, such as federal acreage restriction programmes, were implemented to rationalise the carryover of grain stocks from one year to the next in an effort to reduce the burgeoning cost of agricultural support, and as part of a general need for budgetary cuts.[30] A similar but slightly less pronounced reduction in the level of grain stocks was also evident in other food-exporting countries such as Canada, Australia and New Zealand.

At the time the prevailing consensus was that international food surpluses were likely to prevail for the foreseeable future and that there was little need to maintain expensive stockpiles of food in the event that another world war might break out. This was also underpinned by the fact that by the 1960s there had been a marked decline in the variability of agricultural output between one year and the next. This improved consistency of yearly production was attributable to a combination of factors, including improved levels of crop husbandry, better technical understanding of plant requirements and enhanced mechanisation. Harvest failures of the type and magnitude that had characterised earlier decades were deemed to be increasingly isolated and disparate events, which would only affect underdeveloped countries.

The most important reason for the increase in food prices in the early 1970s was the weather-induced decline in agricultural production. Fluctuations in yearly world agricultural production were a common feature of the world food situation. Often regional deficits were, at least in part, offset by more abundant harvests in other areas of the world. What differentiated 1972 from previous periods was the simultaneous decline in agricultural production in most of the major food-exporting and food-importing countries.[31] This rise in agricultural commodity prices was in stark contrast to the precipitous fall in food prices that had taken place during the Great Depression.[32] The emergence of food surpluses coupled with a shift to tariff protection meant that by 1931 Britain had literally become the world's largest free trade area for agricultural produce, and as a result a dumping ground for the food surpluses

30   Zis, 'International Status of Sterling', p. 105.
31   While not all countries experienced an actual physical decline in production, the rise fell short of the underlying trend rate even in those countries that did experience an increase, FAO, 1974, p. 11.
32   Kindleberger, *The World in Depression*, p. 86.

in the international economy. In contrast, it was food shortages, rather than food surpluses, that marked the international crisis of the 1970s.

The origins of this crisis first became apparent in 1971 when droughts in Australia and New Zealand affected agricultural production and exports. This culminated in 1972, which is described by a number of meteorologists as 'the year of climate anomalies'.[33] In 1972, there were droughts in Russia, Central America, the Sahelian zone of West Africa, India, the People's Republic of China and Kenya as well as parts of the grain-growing belt of Australia.[34] Collectively this weather-induced agricultural disruption meant that, for the first time in more than twenty years, global food production and reserves declined. Grain production in the USA, which was the world leading grain exporter, also declined in the dry summer of 1972, although grain exports increased as a result of rising world demand coupled with the trade liberalisation policies pursued by the Nixon administration to bolster farmers' incomes in the run-up to the 1972 election.[35] The high volume of exports meant that wheat stocks in both the USA and Canada were at their lowest level since 1952, when the Korean War had precipitated a commodity price explosion.[36] Cereal production in the grain-exporting countries of the southern hemisphere, notably Australia and Argentina, experienced a 20 per cent decline in 1972.[37]

In terms of affecting the international grain trade the most significant shortfall in grain production in 1972 was evident in Russia as a result of a major drought. Historically the country had experienced considerable fluctuations from year to year in the amount of grain harvested. Most Russian cereal production is undertaken in drought-prone dry-land or semi-arid regions where crop yields are susceptible to even minor reductions in rainfall levels.[38] This resulted in considerably greater volatility in yields than in Europe, where the rainfall is not only substantially greater but also more predictable, and crop production more consistent. In most years cereal production in Russia would be sufficient to supply the country's own needs, and during exceptionally favourable growing seasons even produce an export surplus. Higher than normal summer temperatures during 1971 and 1972, coupled with

---

33   M. Glantz, *Currents of Change: El Nino's Impact on Climate and Society* (Cambridge, 1996), p. 32.
34   G. McKay and T. Appsopp, 'Global Interdependence of the Climate of 1972', *Proceedings of the Mexican Geophysical Union Symposium on Living with Climate Change*, Mexico City, May 1976, pp. 79–86; Glantz, *Currents of Change*, p. 32.
35   K.A. Ingersent and A.J. Rayner, *Agricultural Policy in Western Europe and the United States* (Cheltenham, 1999), pp. 10–20.
36   FAO, 1974, p. 73.
37   Ibid., p. 21.
38   For a detailed analysis of this, see C. Henry Smith, *Smith's Story of the Mennonites* (Newton Abbot, 1981), pp. 263–5.

lower than average levels of precipitation, led to a 14 per cent reduction in Russian grain production in 1972. Previous shortfalls in production in the 1950s had resulted in the enforced reduction in domestic consumption, and by the slaughtering of livestock, in order to reduce demand for cereals. But in 1972 with détente, the thawing of the Cold War, there was an opportunity for Russia to increase its purchases of grain from the USA from 300,000 metric tonnes in 1971 to in excess of 15 million in 1973. The trade negotiations with the USA in the autumn of 1971 illustrated that it was now the intention of Russia not only to import grain, in the event of harvest shortfall, but also in order to facilitate their ambitious long-term plan to expand livestock production.[39] With a food production shortfall of this magnitude the Russian efforts to alleviate their shortfall by purchasing wheat and corn from the USA in turn exacerbated the scarcity and price of these commodities on the international markets, an activity that was called the 'great grain robbery 1972'.[40] This was accompanied by China also purchasing large quantities of grain at the same time, which amounted to a further 15 per cent of US grain exports. Unlike previous purchases by Russia and China, which had been secured mainly by making formal agreements with the US administration, in 1972, much greater use was made of the futures markets to purchase grain. Speculative open interest in the number of grain contracts on the futures markets increased rapidly during 1972–73, with the Russian purchasers taking physical delivery of the grain, rather than simply closing out their positions.

The volume of exports surprised the US farmers, resulting in an unprecedented upsurge in international wheat prices, which virtually trebled in the space of 18 months, while maize and soybean prices had considerably more than doubled in the same period.[41] These price rises were further exacerbated by the decline in yields of corn and other cereals in the USA as a result of early frosts. In spite of a relatively good cereal harvest in Britain both in 1972 and 1973, as the country was a net importer of grain, the price rises in the international markets invariably impacted on British domestic prices.

As Table 6.1 shows, cereal prices increased rapidly in the early 1970s: wheat prices rose from an average of £24.10 per tonne for the 1971 harvest to £59.32 per tonne for the 1973 harvest; barley prices rose from £24.60 to £55.05 in the same period. As a result, British grain prices rose considerably above the prices for cereals, which were provided by the guaranteed price system that

---

39   FAO, 1974, p. 69.
40   The term refers to the way Russian grain purchasing companies were summoned to Moscow and instructed to embark upon a buying campaign of US grain. Not wishing to share their good fortunes with their competitors, they purchased large quantities of grain using the futures markets at what the Americans thought with the benefit of hindsight were knock-down prices. US grain exports to Russia grew from 0.3 million tons in 1970/1 to 3.4 million tons in 1971/2 and to 15 million tons in 1972/3.
41   FAO, 1974, p. 13.

Table 6.1. Annual average market price for wheat, barley and oats, 1970/1 to 1976/7 (£ per tonne)

	Wheat	Barley	Oats
1970/1	27.5	28.9	24.9
1971/2	24.1	24.6	20.5
1972/3	35.2	30.7	26.7
1973/4	59.3	53.1	48
1974/5	58.6	59.1	56.6
1975/6	66.6	66.2	61.4
1976/7	85	83.2	76

Source: Ministry for Agriculture, Fisheries and Food (MAFF), *Agricultural Statistics* (HMSO, 1978), p. 183.

had been an integral part of the agricultural support system since the 1947 Agriculture Act. Hence, for virtually the first time since 1947, it was no longer necessary for the Ministry of Agriculture to provide deficiency payments to compensate domestic cereal producers for the difference between the market prices they received and the guaranteed price.

Livestock production, not only in Britain but in the rest of the world, was also affected by the increased prices for cereals. This was further compounded by a shortage of fishmeal, which was, in Britain, one of the most important sources of protein used in animal feed, particularly for intensive pork and poultry production, a rapidly expanding sector. Prices for fishmeal increased from $150 per tonne in 1969 to $305 per tonne in 1972, peaking in the following year at $520 per tonne.[42]

The higher prices caused by the shortage of fishmeal was primarily the result of El Niño-induced climate anomalies of 1972, which led to a worldwide decline in fish catches, the effects of which were particularly pronounced in Peru's anchoveta harvest, the species that was used to produce most of the fishmeal. By the late 1960s the country had become the world's leading fishing nation, harvesting in excess of 20 million tonnes a year of anchoveta, which was dried and processed into fishmeal. By 1970-71 fishmeal production was in the region of 11 million tonnes per year, whereas by 1972-73, output had collapsed to little more than 4 million tonnes.[43] Peru's exports of fishmeal were initially maintained by drawing on its stocks. By 1973, these had largely

42 'The Effects of El Nino still Damaging Feed', *Farmers Weekly*, 1 February 1974.
43 Glantz, *Currents of Change*, p. 32.

been exhausted and a major shortage of fishmeal emerged, as other fishmeal-producing countries became increasingly unable to meet the deficit.

The failure of the anchoveta harvest reflected not only the effects of El Niño but also the overfishing that had been taking place in Peru since the early 1960s. Since its initial inception in the 1950s, the production of fishmeal had expanded rapidly, and by its heyday, in 1969, was accounting for almost one third of the country's foreign exchange earnings. Given its importance in generating income from overseas, which was essential in order to improve the country's infrastructure, successive governments in Peru had paid scant regard to managing the country's vitally important resource, allowing it to expand largely unfettered and oblivious to the warnings about the extent to which fish stocks were being exhausted.[44] The overexploitation of this finite resource had profound implications for intensive livestock across the world.

The reduction in the supply of fishmeal led to a worldwide shortage of protein-rich animal feed, which encouraged a switch to soybeans as an alternative, the price of which increased from £58 per tonne in 1972 to more than £192 per tonne in 1973.[45] As a result farmers in the USA were switching from growing wheat to soybeans in spite of the rapid increase in cereal prices. In an effort to encourage farmers in the USA to increase cereal production and to conserve soybeans for their own use, in 1973 the US government halted certain shipments of grain to Russia and Iran as well as imposed restrictions on export sales, in an effort to ensure 'an adequate but not excessive' flow of grain to 'traditional customers'.[46] The net result was that British livestock farmers, who mainly depended on imported fishmeal or soybeans as a source of protein to feed their animals and chickens, were forced to endure a dramatic increase in their costs of production. Ironically, the ready availability of cheap imported fishmeal and soybeans in the 1950s and 1960s had discouraged British farmers from growing field beans as a source of protein, the acreage of which reached an all-time low of little more than 100,000 acres in the late 1960s. This lack of interest in growing beans led to it being regarded as a 'Cinderella crop' by plant breeding institutes in Britain who had made little attempt to develop more productive strains that could compete with higher-yielding and more profitable cereal crops.[47]

This dramatic worldwide rise in the price of agricultural commodities coincided with Britain joining the European Economic Community and becoming part of the Common Agricultural Policy (CAP). Under this regime the guaranteed prices system based on deficiency payments would now be

44   Ibid., p. 32.
45   Peter Hardy, 'Soya Meal', *Hansard* 3/7, vol. 859 (1973), cols 84–5.
46   FAO, 1974, p. 10.
47   Palladino, 'Science, Technology and the Economy', p. 116; D.A. Bond, 'Recent History and Varieties of Field Beans in the UK', *JRASE*, 146 (1985), pp. 144–59.

replaced by a system of intervention prices whereby farmers could sell their surplus produce to intervention boards during periods of low prices for specific commodities. As agricultural prices were considerably higher in the rest of the EEC than Britain, it is not surprising that contemporary accounts tended to regard this as one of the main causal factors for the British food price inflation of this period. For example, academics such as Brian Burkett and Mark Bainbridge have pointed out the effects of Britain's entry into the EEC in accentuating the food price inflation of this period.[48] While food prices were in fact considerably higher than in Britain, the plan was a five-year period of transition before parity was achieved, and the continuation of the 'green pound exchange' ensured that agricultural prices continued to remain considerably lower in Britain.[49]

The rationale for focusing on regarding Britain's entry into the EEC as the main reason for higher food prices appeared to many to be self-evident given the overwhelming cost of the European agricultural support system. In 1972 two thirds of the of EEC's budget was spent on agricultural support, only half of which was derived from import levies, the rest being funded by national budgets according to a scale of contributions laid down in Article 200 of the Treaty of the Communities Budget.[50] The cost of maintaining the CAP was less onerous on countries with large agricultural populations such as Germany, Italy and France, which had a much higher proportion of their labour force employed in agriculture, and thus financial support for agriculture was regarded as a form of social welfare for those engaged in farming activities.[51] While it is tempting to attribute the high food prices in Britain to the adoption of the CAP, it is important to take into account that, by this time, world grain prices were unusually above the intervention prices provided by the CAP. The world shortage of temperate foodstuffs caused prices for cereals and sugar to rise above EC target prices, which would have encouraged countries to source their food supplies from the EC, but this did not materialise because of policy changes.

Import levies, which the EC had historically used to limit the imports of these commodities into Europe, were rapidly replaced by export taxes in an effort to prevent food being sold to the rest of the world. The outcome was that inflation particularly for basic commodities, such as bread and sugar in Britain as well as the rest of the EC, was at record levels. The prices for these basic staple foods would have been even higher if it had not been for the introduction of food subsidies. The CAP's historical adherence to import

48　Burkett and Bainbridge, 'The Performance of British Agriculture', p. 265.
49　C. Ritson and S. Tangermann, 'The Economics and Politics of Monetary Compensatory Amounts', *European Review of Agricultural Economics*, 6 (1979), pp. 119–64.
50　D. Swann, *The Economics of the Common Market* (London, 1995), pp. 246–56.
51　R. Danziger, *Political Powerlessness: Agricultural Workers in Post-War England* (Manchester, 1988), p. 55.

restrictions and export subsidies in an effort to prevent the influx of cheap food from the rest of the world undermined Britain's relationship with its Commonwealth suppliers. If Britain had not joined the EEC in 1973, then it would still have been possible for it to import food from Commonwealth suppliers, including Australia, which supplied cereals, meat and sugar, and New Zealand, which provided lamb, butter and other dairy products.[52]

This decline in the level of food imports from Commonwealth suppliers in the 1970s was not simply the result of Britain's entry into the EEC. By the early 1970s, even if there had been no restrictions on Britain importing food from the Commonwealth, there was no longer a large surplus of low-priced food that could easily be imported into the country. This was partly a result of the weather-induced reduction in agricultural output, which had already affected Australia and New Zealand, and the rising world demand for agricultural produce. As EC Commissioner George Thomson explained:

> It is a modern myth to imagine that there are great reservoirs of cheap New Zealand dairy produce, of cheap Canadian wheat and Australian produce ready to flood our supermarkets but blocked by the dam of Community Food Taxes.[53]

The higher world prices coupled with the reduced level of food production in New Zealand, for example, had ensured that by 1973 the country underfulfilled its quota for butter imports to Britain by 21 per cent and cheese by nearly 33 per cent.[54]

Although there was a limited revival in world food production in 1973, this did little to alleviate the gravity of the food crisis. The US government embarked upon an ambitious plan to lift the restrictions on its compulsory set-aside programme, which had determined how many acres of each crop individual farmers could grow. However, the area planted for wheat for harvest in 1973 was only slightly higher because of unfavourable weather in the previous autumn.[55] Given the higher fertiliser and herbicide prices that prevailed as a result of the oil crisis farmers were preferring to grow soybeans, which being legumes did not require nitrogen fertiliser or such expensive herbicide treatment. By the start of the 1974–75 season, wheat stocks in the main exporting countries – Argentina, Australia, Canada and the USA – were reported to be 'abnormally small', amounting to a mere 25 million tonnes, the lowest recorded since 1951–52.[56] Taking into account the increase in

---

52   Martin, *The Development of Modern Agriculture*, p. 139.
53   A. Sampson, *Anatomy of Britain* (London, 1962), p. 341.
54   Ibid.
55   FAO, 1974, p. 75.
56   Ibid., p. 21.

the world's population, world wheat supplies were now considerably worse than those that had prevailed at the height of the Korean War, representing little more than one month's world consumption.[57] As the FAO lamented in its 1974 report, '1975 will be the successive third year in which food supplies depend perilously on current harvests'.[58]

The West European 1975–76 drought

Consumer food prices in Britain and the rest of Europe were also profoundly affected by the West European drought of 1975–76.[59] On a world scale of extreme climatic events, the West European drought was a rather mundane affair, barely meriting a footnote in the annals of meteorological history. While the European drought did not directly lead to widespread crop failure, loss of livestock or widespread starvation or even malnutrition of the population its effects were still very significant.[60] In the twentieth century the longest period of dry weather on record was from May 1975 to August 1976. As research by John Rodda and Terry Marsh has shown, there had been no corresponding comparable period of dry weather of this magnitude by a considerable margin since the 1850s.[61] Indeed a prolonged period of dry weather of this magnitude was deemed to be so unusual that one contemporary account predicted that it would not be repeated for another thousand years.[62] Precipitation in most areas was little more than 50 per cent below normal while June, July and August 1976 were the hottest summer ever recorded and crop yields were significantly reduced.[63] In most regions the amount of rain falling in the spring of 1976 was insufficient to remedy the moisture deficit in the soil, and during the warm, dry

---

57   Ibid.

58   Ibid., p. 8.

59   In an effort to limit the impact of the rise in agricultural prices on food prices the Labour government had introduced subsidies on bread, butter, cheese, flour, milk and tea. In 1974–75 the cost to the exchequer was over £900 million. See M. Artis and D. Cobham, 'The Background', in Michael Artis and David Cobham (eds), *Labour's Economic Policies, 1974–79* (Manchester, 1991), p. 4.

60   S. Carter, 'The Effects of the Drought on British Agriculture', in *Scientific Aspects of the 1975–6 Drought in England and Wales* (London, 1978), p. 45.

61   Terry Marsh, 'The 1975–76 Drought – A Retrospective Appraisal', in John Rodda and Terry Marsh (eds), *The 1975–76 Drought: A Contemporary and Retrospective Review* (Wallingford, 2011), p. 41.

62   S. Condon, 'Drought Minister who Brought a Downpour', *The Telegraph*, 16 May 2006; C.E. Wright, 'Once in 1,000 years', *Water*, November 1976, pp. 2–6.

63   A hotter summer in terms of the average temperature for the period covering May to September inclusive was recorded in 2006. It was a five-month period that eclipsed every comparable period since the seventeenth century. J. Prior and M. Beswick, 'The Record Breaking Heat and Sunshine of July 2006', *Weather*, 62 (London, 2007), pp. 174–82.

Figure 6.1. Rainfall in the UK between May 1975 and August 1976

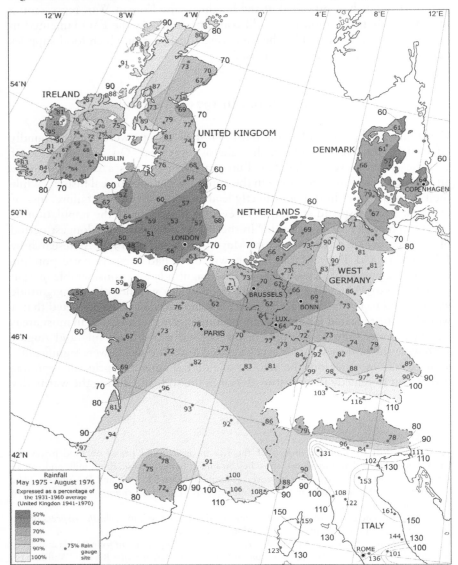

Source: H.C. Pereira, Scientific Aspects of the 1975–76 Drought in England and Wales (London, 1978).

Table 6.2. Agricultural yields, 1970–76 (tonnes per hectare)

	1970–74	1975	1976
Wheat	4.5	4.3	3.8
Barley	3.8	3.4	3.4
Oats	3.9	3.4	3.2
Sugar beet	36.1	24.8	30.8
Potatoes	31.5	22.1	20.8

Source: MAFF, *Agricultural Statistics* (HMSO, 1978).

weather of May and June spring-sown cereals, potatoes and sugar were being worst affected; winter-sown cereals, which were dominated by wheat, were less affected. The continuing drought led to early ripening of the cereal crop, with widespread reports of the earliest start to the grain harvest in living memory.

Spring-sown barley, which dominated the barley acreage in the 1970s, bore the brunt of the drought, with national yields being 30 per cent below normal. Spring germination of the crop was uneven, particularly on the heavier soils where the crop had been sown in cloddy, very dry seedbeds, which resulted in many of the grains being slow to germinate because of the lack of moisture. The drought ensured there was little crop growth during the crucial May growing period. The decline in output obscured the fact that the quality of the grain was reduced. There were widespread reports of samples of barley consisting primarily of pinched or small, shrivelled grains. The amount of straw produced per acre was also well below normal. In traditional livestock areas of western England and Wales, where straw was used for livestock bedding, the reduced amount of locally grown straw caused shortages and high prices for many livestock farmers.

The effects of the dry weather in the summer of 1975 on British agricultural output were mixed. As Table 6.2 shows, the dry summer of 1975 had reduced cereal yields by about 10 per cent, while sugar and potato yields had declined by in excess of 30 per cent. The continuation of dry weather in the autumn and winter made the harvesting of these crops easy, although in 1975 there were reports of the taproots of sugar beet snapping in the ground because of the dry conditions. This in turn led to a reduction in the harvestable yield. There was also bruising of potatoes in the dry soil conditions.

Conversely, the dry weather provided ideal conditions for harvesting both cereal and grass in the form of hay and silage. Hay crops were good, although in some regions were slightly lighter than usual. The dry weather did adversely affect potato yields and other root crops such as sugar beet, mangels, swedes and turnips. The dry autumn of 1975 enabled a record acreage of winter wheat to be sown in good conditions at the optimum time of the year, with land that might normally have been planted with spring barley now being sown with winter wheat. The problem of autumn planting in 1975 was the prevalence of cloddy seedbeds, an issue that was partly addressed by the increasingly common practice of the sown fields being rolled after planting in order to break down the clods.

The most dramatic effect was on the potato crop. Although crops were planted early in the spring of 1975 the onset of dry weather in June hit a critical period in the growing season. In 1975 less than 3 per cent of the potato crop was irrigated.[64] As a result there were high prices for seed potatoes in the following year, which led to farmers slightly reducing the amount of seed potatoes they planted per acre. They were planted early in good condition in the expectation of high yields but even early in the season growth was adversely affected by the lack of moisture, while the hot, dry weather, which continued virtually unabated through May, June and July, further reduced yields. Conversely, wet weather in October meant that harvesting was severely delayed, with 55 per cent of the main crop still unharvested at the end of October compared with 25 per cent in the previous year.[65] Storage problems occurred with those potatoes that had been harvested, with growers trying to sell crops as soon as possible rather than put them into store. This led to a short-term overloading of the market in the late autumn and early winter, which exacerbated the shortfall in supplies in the spring, leading to unprecedentedly high potato prices, higher than at any previous period.

By the end of January 1976 potato ware prices averaged in the region of £160 per tonne.[66] By April, however, spot prices for Pentland Crown were averaging in excess of £220 per tonne, with the £300 per tonne mark being topped for some loadings.[67] These benefits were not, however, immediately evident to those growers selling on forward contracts to processing outlets, where the price of the potatoes had been agreed prior to the onset of the drought. This was at least part alleviated by making extra payments to growers to compensate for low yields.[68] The potato received most attention from domestic policymakers: the Potato Marketing Board (PMB) regulated production by determining the acreage that growers could plant each year and by regulating the riddle size to ensure that in years of abundance a smaller proportion of potatoes could be sold as ware.[69] Conversely, in poor growing

64   *Farmer and Stockbreeder*, 8 May 1976, p. 8.
65   *Farmers Weekly*, 13 November 1976, p. 49.
66   *Farmer and Stockbreeder*, 7 February 1976, p. 11.
67   *Farmer and Stockbreeder*, 8 May 1976, p. 18.
68   *Farmer and Stockbreeder*, 3 January 1976, p. 7.
69   EEC controls over potatoes consisting of artificially removing surpluses in years of overproduction in order to provide a safety net for growers were not that dissimilar from the controls

years, the PMB directed farmers to extend the permitted riddle size, which allowed more potatoes to be sold as ware, thus helping to reduce any price spikes that would be caused by shortages.[70] The problem in 1975 and 1976 was that yields were considerably lower than those that would have been achieved in a more typical growing season. But following the abnormally low yields for potatoes, which were considerably below the 10-year average, the PMB's institutionalised mechanism for regulating supply in line with demand was ineffective, resulting in widespread potato shortages and the most dramatic rise in potato prices since the reintroduction of the PMB in 1954.[71] These potato shortages not only caused considerable hardship to consumers, but also forced them to economise in consumption as well as to switch to alternative foods such as rice. Even as early as February 1976 the PMB's figures indicated that potato consumption was 15 per cent lower than a year earlier, while the National Federation of Fruit and Potato trades suggested that the figure was nearer 25 per cent.[72]

In the harvest year of 1976, wheat and barley prices were nearly three times the levels that had prevailed in 1971, while oat prices had risen by in excess of 250 per cent. The substantially higher grain prices, particularly those that prevailed in 1976, reflected the shortfall in Western European production and stocks, and especially the poor grain harvest in France.[73] This was further compounded by the impact of the drought in the winter wheat-growing states of America, in particular parts of west Kansas, Oklahoma, Colorado, Nebraska and southern Texas.[74] While the USA only grew 16 per cent of total world wheat production in 1975 it accounted for 53 per cent of total wheat exports.

Sugar beet yields were also adversely affected by the dry weather, particularly in 1975 when the lack of precipitation reduced yields to a mere 24.8 tonnes per hectare as compared with an average yield of 36.1 tonnes per hectare for 1970–74. Sugar beet yields were higher in 1976 than 1975 as result

---

implemented by the PMB. The main difference was that quotas on production were deemed contrary to the EEC.

70   In order to maintain prices the PMB would also in years of good harvests purchase ware potatoes from farmers and these would be diverted for animal feed. The Board had experienced difficulties in regulating production by enforcing quotas and preventing price spikes, particularly at the end of the season. For a detailed analysis of its early history, see G.C. Allen, *Agricultural Marketing Policies* (Oxford, 1959), p. 293.

71   Given the history of the Irish potato famine of the mid-1840s it would be inappropriate to claim that the potato shortages of 1975–76 were unprecedented. Indeed the potato shortages caused by the abnormally cold weather in early 1947 forced the government to introduce a quasi-rationing system for potatoes.

72   *Farmer and Stockbreeder*, 7 February 1976, p. 6.

73   In 1975, Russia produced only 132 million tonnes of grain compared with the official target of 215 million tonnes. See *Farmer and Stockbreeder*, 24 January 1976, p. 18.

74   'Why Grain Prices are Rising as Crop Prospects Improve', *Farmer and Stockbreeder*, 6 March 1976, p. 13.

of the wet weather in the autumn, which enabled the crop, which had been short of water during the summer, to grow rapidly, with yields averaging 30.8 tonnes per hectare, although sugar content was considerably lower than normal. The wet weather also made harvesting more difficult than usual, with dirt tares in the harvested beet being considerably higher than usual. Yield fluctuations of this magnitude, although exceptional, were not however unique. In 1974 the crop had only produced 23.6 tonnes per hectare as a result of a wet spring, which had led to late planting, and the wet autumn and winter had led to fields not being harvested. Sugar beet producers derived fewer benefits as the guaranteed prices paid by the British Sugar Corporation did not rise to the same extent as those for cereals and potatoes. In 1975 sugar beet growers received on average about 28 per cent more per tonne than in the previous year. The increase reflected both the increase in EEC prices and the reductions in the Green Pound Exchange rate.[75] Although similar increases in sugar beet prices were achieved in the following year, these were not of the magnitude of the increased returns obtained by potato growers.[76] By 1977, the world's sugar shortage was well and truly over. Three straight bumper crops of sugar cane assured plenty of sugar in the world, and had resulted in a precipitous collapse in prices on international markets, ensuring that the EEC was once again imposing import restrictions on raw sugar.

High prices for arable crops, in particular potatoes and cereals, also impacted on the livestock sector, particularly prices for store cattle and store lambs. Historically, many arable farmers had purchased cattle not only to provide manure but also as a means of utilising arable by-products such as straw and chat potatoes, and providing a means of selling some of their cereals on the hoof.[77] In 1975, the weather was ideal for hay and silage making, with high-quality fodder going into store. Although there were widespread reports in the farming press of low yields of fodder, nationally yields were only slightly below those achieved in previous years.[78] The fodder situation was, however, worse in the following year when it became necessary to feed livestock fodder that had been conserved for the winter in order to compensate for the lack of grass on pastures, which had been affected by the hot, dry weather. Even relatively drought-resistant lucerne was affected, with yields on the light sandy soils of the Brecklands at Elveden, Suffolk being reduced by some 30 per cent.[79]

As Table 6.3 shows, turnips and swedes were less affected by the dry weather

75   Cmnd 6392, *Annual Review of Agriculture* (HMSO, 1976), p. 3.
76   Cmnd 6703, *Annual Review of Agriculture* (HMSO, 1977), p. 3.
77   *Farmers Weekly*, 22 October 1976, p. 59.
78   Ministry for Agriculture, Fisheries and Food (MAFF), *Agricultural Statistics* (HMSO, 1978), p. 52.
79   'Every Year's a Dry Year for Elveden', *Farmers Weekly*, 19 November 1976, p. 70.

Table 6.3. Crop yields, 1970–76 (tonnes per hectare)

	1970–74	1975	1976
Hay	4.3	3.7	4.3
Turnips and swedes	47.7	46.7	33.2
Mangels and fodder beet	67.8	59.6	56.6

Source: MAFF, Agricultural Statistics (HMSO, 1978), p. 51.

in 1975. Indeed average yields of 46.7 tonnes per hectare compared very favourably with the five-year average, which had benefited from the very good growing seasons for these crops in 1973 and 1974. In contrast, yields plummeted in 1976 as a result of flea beetle damage exacerbated by the prolonged dry spell in the summer. In contrast to sugar beet, which had benefited considerably from the late autumn rains, swedes and turnips were too far advanced to benefit.

Livestock production was also affected. This was particularly evident in the case of milk production, where yields fell as a result of the shortage of fodder caused by the dry weather, and the fact that the cows tended to rest during the heat of day, further reducing the amount of grass they consumed. Milk production in August 1976 was the lowest level for eight years for that month.[80] A similar pattern was also evident in the case of beef and sheep production, with livestock in the lowlands, particularly in the south-eastern part of England, being worst affected. The contrast between the drought-parched south of England and the rest of Britain was denoted as 'spectacular'.[81] Indeed Harry Thompson, a dairy farmer in Penrith, Cumbria had managed to produce 30 per cent more silage than his existing clamp could cope with, requiring him to stack the surplus in a temporary clamp.[82]

In the traditionally wetter and cooler western parts of England and Wales, where grass growth was less affected, including many upland areas, the livestock benefited from the warmer and drier conditions, which had a smaller effect on grass growth than in the lowlands while reducing the incidence of diseases such as liver fluke and foot rot in sheep. Hill sheep were in good condition and the higher prices yielded many benefits for livestock farmers in these marginal areas whose main source of income was the sale of cattle and sheep for fattening on lowland farms. The main beneficiaries were those producing the larger store cattle and lambs. The smaller stores originating from the upper hills were in less demand.[83]

80 Sampson, Anatomy of Britain, pp. 30–2.
81 Farmer and Stockbreeder, 21 August 1976, p. 6.
82 Ibid.
83 Farmer and Stockbreeder, 27 September 1975, p. 13.

On 5 August 1976 a Drought Bill was rushed through Parliament granting the water authorities the power to limit or even cut off water supplies. This was followed on 24 August by the appointment of Denis Howell as the 'drought Supremo' or Minister of Drought. Ironically, on the August Bank holiday heavy and prolonged rainfall fell on the parched ground, which had become iron hard in places. This led to widespread flooding, and Howell was now hailed as the Minister of Flooding. The rain brought the drought but not the water-saving measures to an abrupt end.

It was not until the September rains that there was a revival in grass growth. The abnormally wet spell that followed led to the subsequent persistence of near-saturated soil moisture conditions, which restricted harvesting opportunities for potatoes and sugar beet and resulted in extensive poaching of grass fields, particularly those on the heavier soils. Such conditions adversely affected dairy production as well as cattle and sheep production. The rains did, however, assist the recovery of the sugar beet crop, which was able to achieve compensatory growth in the autumn. The rain came too late for the potato crop, however. The excessive summer heat coupled with moisture shortages produced potatoes unsuitable for eating. Even potato crops that had been irrigated were still affected by the high temperatures.[84] More importantly, the wet autumn led to difficulties in harvesting the crop, with some areas reporting that only half of the crop had been harvested by early November, in comparison with a more normal autumn when virtually all of the crop would have been harvested. This led to difficulties in storing the crop for the winter. As a result by the spring of 1977 potato prices were between six and seven times higher than usual, which played a major part in the food price inflation.[85]

The rise in prices for agricultural commodities, an integral part of the international crisis of 1973–74, was exacerbated by the European drought, and this in turn contributed to Britain's financial woes. In spite of the reduction in crop yields that occurred as a result of the drought of 1975–76 for arable farmers in particular, this decline was considerably more than offset by the higher prices they received for their produce. According to Bowers and Cheshire, between 1972 and 1977 the net income of farmers increased by in excess of 60 per cent, and in a similar way higher farming incomes that resulted from the food shortages of the Second World War were responsible for transforming farmers from their virtual peasant status of the eighteenth century to an exalted and romanticised position.[86] Such figures relate to the total income of the 'national farm' and make no attempt to differentiate

84   Carter, 'The Effects of the Drought', p. 45.
85   *Farmer and Stockbreeder*, 7 February 1976, p. 11.
86   J.K. Bowers and P. Cheshire, *An Economic Critique: Agriculture, The Countryside and Land Use* (London, 1983), pp. 52–60.

between the ways it affected different groups of farmers. There were, of course, some marked variations between one group of farmers and another in the extent to which their income increased.[87] The main beneficiaries were the large arable farmers, particularly owner-occupiers who derived unprecedented benefits from the rapid increase in commodity prices and were able to generate windfall profits. In order to reduce tax, this prompted investments in new machinery and other forms of infrastructure, including a number of farmers who, in order to take advantage of the enhanced level of grant aid, constructed reservoirs to store water to be used to irrigate root crops in the event of another dry summer.[88] Companies supplying irrigation equipment were by July 1976 reporting record orders.[89]

Smaller farmers, notably livestock farmers whose main source of income was derived from milk production or intensive pig and poultry production, were particularly affected by the higher prices for animal feeding stuffs.[90] Livestock farmers in upland areas, whose main source of income was the rearing of store cattle and lambs for sale to be fattened on lowland arable farms, benefited from the dry summers in two main ways. First, the dry weather was good for their animals, enabling them to grow quicker. Secondly, the higher incomes received by arable farmers in the lowlands encouraged them to pay more for the store cattle they purchased, which were to be fattened on arable by-products.

One of the unforeseen and indirect consequences of the international crisis of the 1970s was its impact on land prices, which, in nominal terms, virtually doubled in the 1970s. The magnitude of the increases was unprecedented, dwarfing the increases in prices that had taken place during previous periods of high food prices such as during the French and Napoleonic wars (1793–1815) or the First or Second World Wars. Richard Body has attributed the capitalisation of land values to the implementation of the EEC agricultural support system coupled with its favourable capital grant policies.[91]

The land price rises were generated primarily by the economic and financial crisis of the 1970s, which had led to collapse of equity markets

87   Cmnd 6703, *Annual Review of Agriculture* (HMSO, 1977), p. 1.
88   Ibid.
89   B. Wilson, 'Freak Drought that May Change British Farming', *Farmer and Stockbreeder*, 31 July 1976, p. 8.
90   Bowers and Cheshire, *Agriculture*, p. 61.
91   R. Body, *Agriculture: The Triumph and the Shame* (London, 1982), pp. 124–5. See also W.B. Traill, *Land Values and Rent; The Gains and Losses from Farm Support Programmes*, Department of Agricultural Economics Bulletin, 175 (Manchester, 1980); W.B. Traill, 'The Effect of Price Support Policies on Agricultural Investment, Employment, Farm Incomes and Land Values in the UK', *Journal of Agricultural Economics*, 33 (1982), p. 381; D.R. Harvey and J.K. Thomson, 'Cost Benefits and the Future of the Common Agricultural Policy', *Journal of Common Market Studies*, 24 (1985), p. 4.

and the desire, by city institutions in particular, to purchase land and other fixed assets that were appreciating rapidly in value.[92] During periods of high inflation, such as those that prevailed in the mid-1970s, the real rate of interest on mortgages was negative, underpinning the desire to invest in fixed assets that were appreciating in value. Moreover, unlike investments in assets such as precious metals and antiques, land was able to generate rental income. Even Harvey, who was one of the leading exponents of the land capitalisation thesis, openly acknowledged that during the international crisis of the 1970s, land was regarded as the 'ultimate inflation hedge', while government support policies reinforced this.[93]

Competition among large institutions and companies for high-grade land in the favoured arable regions of south-east Britain was very acute, particularly during periods such as 1973–74 when share prices appeared to be in free fall.[94] This was also fuelled by the building boom of the early 1970s, which had produced massive capital gains accruing to those farmers who had sold land for commercial development. Given the need to reinvest in land in order to take advantage of roll-over benefits, the demand for land was very buoyant at a time when few farms were coming on to the market. The speculative boom was largely confined to 1972–73. By the following year not only were prices lower but only 100,000 hectares of land was sold in England and Wales, the lowest amount since 1945 and less than 1 per cent of the total.[95] Institutions had become much more selective, seeking to secure only fairly large, easily managed estates of 1,000 acres and preferably in the south or east of England, and which were capable of growing a variety of arable crops.[96] This speculative boom in land fuelled mainly by institutional demand caused by the collapse of equities made it difficult for farmers to acquire land to expand their own farming activities. As a result, even those arable farmers who had benefited from the higher grain and potato prices had difficulty in expanding their holdings. The higher prices meant it was even more difficult than in the past for outsiders to enter the industry.[97] The classic idea postulated by Joseph Schumpeter that economic recession initiates a phase of 'creative destruction', which in turn brings about restructuring and recovery, did not apply to British agriculture during the 1970s crisis.[98]

92   *Farmer and Stockbreeder*, 10 July 1976, p. 10.
93   Harvey and Thomson, 'Cost Benefits and the Future', p. 6.
94   Cmnd 6392, *Annual Review of Agriculture* (HMSO, 1976), p. 9.
95   Martin, *The Development of Modern Agriculture*, p. 153.
96   *Farmer and Stockbreeder*, 10 July 1976, p. 10.
97   Ibid., p. 10.
98   Joseph Schumpeter, *The Theory of Economic Development*, 16th edn (New Brunswick, NJ, 2012).

Conclusion

The economic crisis of the 1970s, which marked the end of the post-war world trade boom and heralded a watershed for not only post-war Britain but also the other industrialised nations of the world, has traditionally been attributed to a series of external economic shocks. However, it is evident that this international crisis was also underpinned by the effects of weather-induced changes in agricultural production that took place across most of the world in 1972. In particular, the 1972 decline in world grain production, which coincided with the collapse of the anchoveta harvest, precipitated an unprecedented rise in the price of agricultural commodities and in turn domestic food prices.

Not surprisingly, these strongly inflationary pressures, particularly clear in the price of food, coupled with the most pronounced downturn in economic activity since the Great Depression, led to a significant increase in unemployment in Britain and either stagnating or falling living standards, even for those fortunate to still retain their jobs. In stark contrast to the Great Depression, when agricultural commodity prices and food prices collapsed, the 1970s crisis was accompanied by rapidly rising agricultural prices.[99] These inflationary pressures were further exacerbated by the effects of the 1975–76 drought, which impacted particularly on the southern part of England, the main cereal and potato area of the country. This case study of the crisis of the 1970s reveals the extent to which industrially advanced countries, including Britain, still depended on a benign climate to sustain agricultural production and in turn their economic prosperity. As this study shows, food prices in Britain were not simply dependent on the state of the domestic harvest, but were also significantly influenced, even determined by, weather-induced changes in agricultural production that were taking place in the rest of the world. Food price inflation was a major factor exacerbating the difficulties Britain experienced in the mid-1970s.

In an era of potential climate change, coupled with growing world population and increasing dietary standards in many parts of the world, achieving food security will invariably be even more problematic in the future than in the past. Weather-induced challenges to food security are even more likely to reoccur in the future. The 2011 *Climate: Observations, Projections and Impacts* report predicts that within the next few decades Britain will experience a significant increase in the incidence and intensity of droughts, floods and storm damage.[100] By 2040, it is anticipated that

99   For a detailed analysis of the magnitude in the fall of individual agricultural commodities during the Great Depression, see J.H. Kirk, *Agriculture and the Trade Cycle* (London, 1933), p. 79.
100   Met Office, *Climate: Observations, Projections and Impacts* (London, 2011), p. 1.

summers in southern England could experience temperatures of up to 3 degrees Centigrade hotter than at present, accompanied by a 20 per cent drop in summer rainfall. A similar scenario is also envisaged by the *Review on the Economics of Climate Change*, which predicts that average global temperatures could increase by 2–3 degrees with fifty years.[101] Indeed the report even postulates that a temperature increase of 5–6 degrees is a real possibility. Such forecasts are also supported by the fact that, since 2002, Britain has experienced three significant droughts (2003, 2004–06, 2010–12) interspersed with damaging flood episodes.[102] A number of global studies have postulated a rather optimistic outlook for the impact of climate change in Britain, primarily due to its historic capacity to import food to compensate for any weather-induced deficit in domestic production.[103] However, this investigation of the 1972–77 crisis suggests that if a weather scenario of this magnitude was to reoccur it would have profound British and global implications. Given these predictions, it is evident that the agrarian dimension to the economic, political and social crises that have occurred in the past and are likely to reoccur in the future clearly merits more detailed attention than it receives at present.

101   N. Stern, *Review on the Economics of Climate Change* (London, 2006), p. 3.

102   T. Marsh, S. Parry, M. Kendon and J. Hannaford, *The 2012 Drought and Subsequent Extensive Flooding* (Oxford, 2012), p. 44.

103   M. Falenmark, J. Rockstrom and L. Karlberg, 'Present and Future Water Requirements for Feeding Humanity', *Food Security*, 1 (2009), pp. 59–69; Wu Wenbin *et al.*, 'Scenario-Based Assessment of Future Food Security', *Journal of Geographical Sciences*, 21 (2011), pp. 3–17.

PART III:
DEATH AND DISEASE

7

Coping with Epidemic Crises, from Antiquity to the Present

SAMUEL K. COHN, JR

I

Over the past sixty years or more, historians have seen epidemics as crises that invariably give rise to hate, violence, and the stigmatisation of the 'Other'. As René Baehrel held in his classic article in *Les Annales*, 1952, big epidemics have always sparked hate and class enmity, and such reactions are part of our 'structures mentales ... constantes psychologiques'.[1] With the eruption of HIV/AIDS in the 1980s, these conclusions gained force from a wide variety of well-known scholars across disciplines. According to Carlo Ginzburg, 'the prodigious trauma of great pestilences intensified the search for a scapegoat on which fears, hatreds and tension of all kind could be discharged'.[2] By the reckoning of Dorothy Nelkin and Sander Gilman, 'blaming has always been a means to make mysterious and devastating diseases comprehensible and therefore possibly controllable'.[3] Roy Porter concurred with Susan Sontag: when 'there is no cure to hand and the 'aetiology ... is obscure ... deadly diseases spawn sinister connotations'.[4] More recently, from earthquake-wrecked, cholera-hit Haiti, Paul Farmer has proclaimed: 'Blame was, after all, a calling card of all transnational epidemics.'[5]

As these examples suggest, the AIDS experience of the 1980s and 1990s

1 René Baehrel, 'La haine de classe en temps d'épidémie', *Annales: E.S.C.*, VII (1952), pp. 351–60.
2 Carlo Ginzburg, 'Deciphering the Sabbath', in B. Ankarloo and G. Henningsen (eds), *Early Modern European Witchcraft: Centres and Peripheries* (Oxford, 1990), p. 124.
3 Dorothy Nelkin and Sander L. Gilman, 'Placing Blame for Devastating Disease', *Social Research*, LV (1988), pp. 362–78.
4 Roy Porter, 'The Case of Consumption', in J. Bourriau (ed.), *Understanding Catastrophe* (Cambridge, 1992), p. 179.
5 Paul Farmer with J.S. Mukherjee, *Haiti After the Earthquake* (New York, 2011), p. 191.

swayed historians and social scientists to stress the possibilities and power of epidemics to provoke hatred and blame. In addition, scholars have introduced at least implicitly a historical dynamic to this supposed universal 'fact' of collective psychology: when the causes and cures of epidemic disease are unknown, hatred of the other becomes more likely and more pronounced.[6] By this logic, the 'decline of magic' in the sixteenth, the scientific revolution in the seventeenth, the Enlightenment of the eighteenth and ultimately the laboratory revolution of the late nineteenth century made diseases progressively more comprehensible. Consequently, epidemics' need for scapegoats ought to have waned from early modernity on,[7] and before breakthroughs in modern Western medicine the disease–hate nexus should have been more potent and especially in Antiquity and the Middle Ages. This chapter challenges this current scholarly consensus.

For Antiquity, the chronological patterns of the disease–hate nexus appear to have been the opposite of what historians presently presume.[8] Historians have interpreted the most famous of ancient pandemics, the fifth-century BC Plague of Athens, as illustrative of the supposed premodern proclivity for blame. From origins in Ethiopia, this plague spread rapidly to Greece, entering the port of Piraeus. According to Thucydides, inhabitants here claimed that Peloponnesian soldiers at war with Athens spread the disease by poisoning cisterns.[9] However, no more is heard of these accusations once the disease

---

6   From the general literature, similar remarks can easily be found; for instance, Julia Irwin, 'Scapegoats and Epidemic Disease', in J.P. Byrne (ed.), *Encyclopedia of Pestilence, Pandemics, and Plagues* (Westport, 2008), pp. 618–20: 'Throughout history, societies have created scapegoats … innocent … to rationalize and explain the origins and course of disease outbreaks' (vol. 2, p. 618). For further examples, see my 'Pandemics: Waves of Disease, Waves of Hate from the Plague of Athens to A.I.D.S.', *Historical Research*, 85 (2012), pp. 535–6.

7   For instance, Niall Johnson, *Britain and the 1918–19 Influenza Pandemic: A Dark Epilogue* (London, 2006), pp. 152–3, cites approvingly Susan Sontag and others on the supposed universal, timeless tendency to name diseases after other peoples and nations and that such naming meant blaming. Yet when he turns to the influenza pandemic of 1918–19, often called, 'the Spanish Flu', he must admit that no evidence appears of blaming or abusing Spaniards for the disease. He then concludes that such blaming becomes 'especially true with sexually transmitted diseases' (p. 153). On the supposed tendency of sexually transmitted diseases to stir hate, see William Eamon, 'Cannibalism and Contagion: Framing Syphilis in Counter-Reformation Italy', *Early Science and Medicine*, 3 (1998), pp. 1–31; and the interesting parallels between syphilis and AIDS in Laura J. McGough, *Gender, Sexuality, and Syphilis in Early Modern Venice: The Disease that Came to Stay* (Basingstoke, 2010), pp. 150–1.

8   For instance, Frank M. Snowden, *Naples in the Time of Cholera, 1884–1911* (Cambridge, 1995), p. 151, relying on K. Thomas, *Religion and the Decline of Magic: Studies in Popular Belief in Sixteenth and Seventeenth Century England* (London, 1971).

9   Thucydides, *History of the Peloponnesian War*, Books I and II, ed. and trans. Charles Forster Smith, Loeb Classical Library (London, 1928), 2.48, p. 343; and see James L. Longrigg, 'Epidemic, Ideas and Classical Athenian Society', in Terence Ranger and Paul Slack (eds),

reached Athens, levelling a third of the population,[10] and where Thucydides begins his detailed account of the disease's social and psychological consequences.[11] As mortalities mounted in Athens, the failure to find any reports of inhabitants blaming any foreigner or belligerent 'Other' for the spread of the disease is all the more surprising given that the epidemic devastated Athenians but, according to Thucydides, failed to afflict their enemies, the Peloponnesians, 'to any extent'.[12]

Despite the fragmented survival of early registers and written sources, epidemics fill the annals of Antiquity and the Middle Ages. Livy alone recorded at least fifty-seven of them, mostly from 490 to 165 BC.[13] The modern historian to pay the greatest attention to the representation of diseases in Antiquity, R.P. Duncan-Jones, leaves the impression that blaming was the usual outcome of ancient plagues, because, as he argues, 'societies' had 'no effective medical explanation' for them.[14] Yet he mentions only a handful of cases, and when we examine the texts, they all prove problematic as evidence of scapegoating the other. His first example is the best – the Peloponnesians' poisonings at Piraeus – but, as we have seen, it did not result in blaming Peloponnesians or any other 'Others' once plague gained momentum in upper Athens.[15] A second case comes from Livy: deaths among the Roman ruling class in 329 BC were pinned on wealthy Roman matrons convicted of poisoning. But Livy was sceptical, calling it 'a false story'.[16] Moreover, if in fact it were an epidemic disease (and there is no claim that it was), its spread was limited to a small number among Rome's ruling class, and the alleged poisonings were not sparked by ethnic or class hatred.[17] As Livy comments, even those who found the matrons guilty believed their acts to have been ones 'of madness rather

Epidemics and Ideas: Essays on the Historical Perception of Pestilence (Cambridge, 1992), pp. 21–2.

10   Thucydides, *History of the Peloponnesian War*, p. 343.

11   Ibid., 2.53, p. 353.

12   Ibid., 2.53, p. 355; instead, with mortality rates rising and the defeat of the Athenian navy at hand the Athenians turned inward and placed the blame on their esteemed leader, Pericles, for his decision to continue the devastating war with Peloponnesia and his failure to sanction his countrymen's desires to negotiate with the enemy; ibid., 2.57–9, pp. 359–61.

13   Thus this would amount to thirty-eight epidemics mentioned by Livy within these years. According to R.P. Duncan-Jones, 'The Impact of the Antonine Plague', *Journal of Roman Archaeology*, 9 (1996): 'Major epidemics are so frequent in Roman annalists that contemporaries must have found them relatively commonplace' (p. 109). Actually, overwhelmingly, they come from one author alone, Titus Livy (59 BC–AD 17) and his massive *Ab Urbe Condita*, even though only 35 of his original 142 books survive.

14   Duncan-Jones, 'The Impact of the Antonine Plague', p. 115.

15   Ibid., p. 115.

16   Titus Livy, *Ab Urbe Condita*, Loeb Classical Library, various editors, 14 vols (London and Cambridge, MA, 1919–), 8, 18.

17   Duncan-Jones, 'The Impact of the Antonine Plague', p. 115.

than deliberate wickedness'. In a third case, one of 184 BC,[18] Roman rulers attempted to justify their crushing of a shepherds' rebellion around Rome by accusing them of mass poisoning. The sources, however, do not record any epidemic that then accompanied these alleged acts. The same goes for two further incidents in Rome during the reigns of Domitian (AD 81–96) and Commodus (AD 180–92) of criminals, who randomly poisoned others with needles, but again, these acts were not connected to any supposed epidemic disease that may have been spreading contemporaneously.[19]

To evaluate the socio-psychological reactions to pestilential crises in past time,[20] I have thus far found over two thousand descriptions of epidemics before the sixteenth century.[21] While ancient authors seldom described the symptoms or epidemiological traits of diseases, they regularly pointed to the palliative nonmedical measures populations took to confront these crises. Yet, despite this attention, hardly any ancient author hints that a population or government blamed an outsider, the poor or the rich, of wilfully spreading disease. Instead, when a plague was particularly severe or mysterious, populations turned to their oracles and sacred texts. The answers received show that they saw the causes lodged in the heavens or brought on by themselves and not by any 'Other'. To placate the gods they called for united communal action with vows to stage games,[22] build chapels,[23] declare work-free holidays,[24] or mass prayers at shrines with wealthy matrons sweeping temple floors with their hair.[25] In several incidences, the Romans offered sacrifices to the gods, and on occasion these sacrifices specified the inclusion of humans as well

---

18   Ibid., p. 115.
19   Ibid., p. 115. The criminal poisoning during Commodus's reign paralleled a severe epidemic in Rome, but the source of these incidents, Dio Cassius's *Roman History*, book 73, does not suggest that the two were related.
20   Perseus 4.0, last updated in 2007, accessed 30 July–3 August 2011. The Perseus collection, however, is weak in the number of Greek and Roman texts it has thus far downloaded for late antiquity. For instance, it does not include the histories of Cassius Dio (c.155–c.229) or Paolo Orosius (c.383–c.420), which recorded several epidemics in the first centuries after Christ. I used keyword searches (epidemic, pandemic, plague, pestilence, pestilential, disease, poison and variants of these words). Individual deaths, metaphorical usage, and legendary plagues that are difficult to pin down chronologically, such as ones in the Bible, were discarded from my tallies. I have supplemented the Perseus searches with ones for Livy in the Brepols Library of Latin Texts (A), finding six further epidemics, and have added two from Paulus Orosius, *Seven Books of History against the Pagans*, trans. A.T. Fear (Liverpool, 2010). The online Loeb Classical Library was not yet available when conducting this research.
21   For Antiquity I have at present the following chronological distribution: seventh century BC (2); sixth (0); fifth (19); fourth (14); third (14); second (16); first (2); first AD (5); and five in which the date cannot be determined.
22   Livy, 4.25; 27.23, and 27.4.
23   Livy, 4.30.
24   Livy, 1,31; 40.19; 41.21; 41, pos. 256.
25   See Livy, 3.7, vol. 2, pp. 24–8, in 462 BC.

as animals. But in no case did our authors, ancient governments, or their populations attribute blame to these victims or to the social or ethnic groups they may have represented.[26]

Instead of igniting class violence, plague often came to the rescue, as in 433 BC when an epidemic 'afforded a respite' from strife between plebs and patricians in Rome. The Romans offered vows to Apollo to build a temple for the people's health and strove to import corn from Sicily to avert famine. By these communal offerings, unity was temporarily achieved.[27] In 403 BC a plague dumbfounded Romans; their doctors could point to no causes and knew no cures. The mystery did not, however, induce blame or persecution (as the historiography would now predict). Instead, Rome's coping with the crisis took the opposite turn; for eight days, lavish festivities were celebrated to propitiate the gods:

> throughout the City the front gates of the houses were thrown open and all sorts of things placed for general use in the open courts, all comers, whether acquaintances or strangers, being brought in to share the hospitality. Men who had been enemies held friendly and sociable conversations with each other and abstained from all litigation, the manacles even were removed from prisoners during this period, and afterwards it seemed an act of impiety that men to whom the gods had brought such relief should be put in chains again.[28]

For late antiquity, historians have asserted that the Pestilence of Cyprian, AD 252–266, incited Romans to persecute Christians.[29] Yet the sources show little evidence of it. For a variety of reasons, Romans threatened to throw Cyprian to the lions, but his abundant surviving letters do not suggest that the persecution of Christians stemmed from the plague named after him. His tract on the plague describes the signs and symptoms of the disease and claims that 'many of us died from it', but fails to mention any persecution

---

26 Diogenes Laertius, *Lives of Eminent Philosophers*, ed. Tiziano Dorandi (Cambridge, 2013), 1.10 (c.600 BC); and Livy, 40.19 (181 BC).

27 Livy, 4.25.

28 Livy, 5.3: as with Antiquity, so with the Middle Ages, new and mysterious epidemics failed to spark blame and hatred. Instead, they led to charity and created temporary unity rather than division, as with the early Middle Ages' first pandemic, that of plague, in 541. The eye-witness historian of the Byzantine court, Procopius describes the traditional adversaries of Constantinople unifying in their effort to bury the plague dead, turning to charity or staying at home to tend the sick and the dead, Procopius of Caesarea, *History of the Wars: Book I: The Persian War*, ed. H.B. Dewing, Loeb Classical Library (London, 1914–35), pp. 451–65.

29 Dionysius Stathakoupolos, 'Plagues of the Roman Empire', in *Encyclopedia of Pestilence*, II, p. 536.

that supposedly ensued from it.[30] Instead, this plague ended the persecutions of Emperor Valerius and inaugurated one of the longest periods of Roman tolerance of Christianity. It lasted to Diocletian's edict of 303, when a decade-long persecution – Christendom's bloodiest, the so-called 'Great Persecution' – ensued. Yet no plague then was lurking behind the scenes to trigger it.[31]

The rise of Christianity, nonetheless, brought a new ingredient to the disease–hate relationship. Relying on Old Testament precedent, Christian writers could view plagues positively as God's vengeance to punish their persecutors. By Paulus Orosius's account, the Romans understood the plague of 253 as God's fury against their Roman rulers, and it prompted an about-face in their policies, ending their half-century of persecution.[32] Similarly, the early-fifth-century church historian Sozomen interpreted the pestilence of 363 as the 'manifest token of God's displeasure brought down against Julian the Apostate's persecution of the church', and in 409 a plague following Alaric's siege of Rome was 'Divine wrath sent to chastise [the Romans] for their luxury, debauchery, and manifold acts of injustice'.[33] Yet before the Black Death of 1348, I have found few instances when an epidemic spurred a community to persecute the outsider or for that matter any social group from within.

Agobard, bishop of Lyon, reported a story that circulated around 810. Grimoald IV, duke of the Beneventans, had allegedly sent some of his people to spread a special dust on fields, mountains, meadows, and springs of northern Europe to kill the cattle of his enemy, Charlemagne. Many were apprehended and confessed to have scattered the poisonous dust.[34] But this was an epidemic of cattle, not men, and was a matter of warfare, not of

---

30   *De mortalitate*, pp. 297–314, in *Corpus Scriptorum ecclesiasticorum Latinorum*, III, pt 1: *S. Thasci Caecili Cypriani opera omnia* (Vienna, 1868). Graeme Clarke, 'Christianity in the First Three Centuries', in A. Bowman, P. Garnsey, and A. Cameron (eds), *Cambridge Ancient History*, vol. 12, 2nd edn (Cambridge, 2005), pp. 589–671, conjectures that 'one can imagine' that Cyprianus would have been 'popularly blamed' for the plague (p. 647). He supplies no evidence, however, for it.

31   Clarke, 'Christianity in the First Three Centuries', pp. 649–52. The later Christian chronicle of the ten persecutions from Nero to Constantine's Edict in 313 does not allude to any persecution stemming from the eruption or spread of plague. Instead, the relationship was the other way around: the Romans paid for their persecutions by God's vengeance, served on them in the form of plagues; see Orosius, *Seven Books of History Against the Pagans*, trans. Roy J. Deferrati (Washington, DC, 1964), 7.26, pp. 364–6.

32   Orosius, *The Seven Books of History Against the Pagans*, pp. 316–17.

33   *The Ecclesiastical History of Sozomen, Comprising a History of the Church, from A.D. 324 to A.D. 440*, trans. E. Walford (London, 1855), book VI, ch. 2 and IX, ch. 6, pp. 247 and 412–13.

34   Paul Dutton, *Charlemagne's Mustache and Other Cultural Clusters of a Dark Age* (Basingstoke, 2004), pp. 170–1, 185. I wish to thank Jennifer Davis for this reference.

internal anxieties leading to the persecution of outsiders or insiders living within the affected society. In 1172 the Venetian doge claimed that those on their occupied island of Chios (Scio) in the Aegean Sea revolted against tax rises by poisoning wells to kill off Venetian soldiers, but there were no claims of them spreading any epidemic other than the poisoning itself.[35] More significant was the 1321 slaughter of lepers in southern France, partly instigated by the king himself on grounds that they were poisoning wells. But, even though this may have been the blueprint for the mass murder of Jews in 1348–51, no new epidemic, a sudden increase in leprosy, or of any other disease sparked these atrocities. Moreover, despite presumptions that lepers were universally feared, despised, and persecuted through the Middle Ages, we hear of no other mass riots or even of smaller acts of collective violence against lepers during the Middle Ages or during the early modern period. Instead, as Zachary Gussow was first to stress and which more recently has been underscored by the detailed research of François-Olivier Touati, Carole Rawcliffe, and Luke Demaitre, medieval persecution of lepers was a myth created by nineteenth-century politicians and governments to justify their own brutal segregation and treatment of lepers.[36]

Certainly, Europe's most deadly and devastating disease, the Black Death of 1347–51, unleashed horrific mass violence against 'Others' – the murder of Catalans in Sicily, clerics and beggars at Narbonne, and especially pogroms against Jews with over a thousand communities annihilated down the Rhineland, into Austria, Spain, and France – even if these massacres did not occur everywhere the plague struck.[37] Prominent historians have claimed that these Black Death slaughters established patterns of violence and blame that continued to reignite through the late Middle Ages and early modern period.[38] Yet subsequent strikes of plague in late medieval and Renaissance Europe

35   Marino Sanuto, *Vitæ Ducum Venetorum italice scriptæ ab origine urbis, sive ab Anno CCCXXI usque ad Annum MCCCCXCIII*, cols 599–1252 in Ludovico Muratori (ed.), *Rerum Italicarum Scriptores*, 28 vols (Milan, 1723–51), XXII, p. 501.

36   Zachary Gussow, *Leprosy, Racism, and Public Health: Social Policy in Chronic Disease Control* (Boulder, 1989); François-Olivier Touati, *Maladie et société au Moyen Age: La lèpre, les lépreux et les léproseries dans la province ecclésiastique de Sens jusqu'au milieu du XIVe siècle*, Bibliothèque du Moyen Age, 11 (Paris, 1998); Carole Rawcliffe, *Leprosy in Medieval England* (Woodbridge, 2006); and Luke Demaitre, *Leprosy in Premodern Medicine: A Malady of the Whole Body* (Baltimore, 2007). Also, see the numerous reflections on the charitable treatment and integration of lepers into communities across the British Isles during the Middle Ages to the sixteenth century in Rawcliffe's *Urban Bodies: Communal Health in Late Medieval English Towns and Cities* (Woodbridge, 2013).

37   See my 'The Black Death and the Burning of Jews', *Past & Present*, 196 (2007), pp. 3–36.

38   See, for instance, Joshua Trachtenberg, *The Devil and the Jews: The Medieval Conception of the Jew and its Relationship to Modern Anti-Semitism* (New Haven, 1943), pp. 106–7; and Yosef Hayim Yerushalmi, *The Lisbon Massacre of 1506 and the Royal Image in the Shebet Yehudah* (Cincinnati, 1976), p. 7.

failed to spark such waves of hatred against Jews or any other minorities – (a
trend historians have yet to reflect upon).[39] Virulent and widespread pestilence
such as the pan-European one of 1399–1400 (for central and northern Italy
one of the most devastating plagues of the Middle Ages), instead, harkened
back to earlier patterns of coping with epidemic crises as seen in Antiquity,
provoking not hatred but peace movements across much of central and
northern Italy and into Provence aimed at ending regional and city-state strife
and at bringing different classes and factions together in peace. Unlike the
flagellant processions of 1349, these ones were backed by orthodox leaders of
the church and heads of state such as Giangaleazzo Visconti, Grand Duke of
Milan, and were filled with 'hope and joy'.[40]

II

By contrast with the previous centuries of Antiquity and the Middle Ages,
early modernity with its scientific breakthroughs and rise of naturalistic
explanations was a fillip for increased blaming and scapegoating as witnessed
with the trials of supposed plague spreaders from the early sixteenth century
to those of 1656–67. Such accusations, torture, and execution were not
limited to cities beneath the slopes of the Alps – Milan, Geneva, and Lyon
– as Yves-Marie Bercé has argued, and these urban incidents were not the
consequence of supposed primitive 'ideas and fantasies' of ancient magic
suddenly pried loose from their isolated mountain hollows.[41] Accusations
of plague-spreading erupted also in places much further removed from
the Alps, such as in Toulouse, Rouen, Palermo, Messina, Madrid, Rome,
and other places presently awaiting studies. More importantly, the ideas,
sentiments, and impulses behind them had nothing to do with imported
magic or folkloric backwardness. The instigators and theorists, instead, were
university-educated judges and physicians and included intellectuals at the
cutting edge of medical science and culture (Fortunato Fedeli, Jean Bodin,

---

39   An exception occurred for parts of Poland around Kraków and Miechów in 1360–61 during
the second wave of plague. However, these were areas that had escaped plague in 1348–51. In
effect, 1360 was these regions' 1348; see my *The Black Death Transformed: Disease and Culture
in Early Renaissance Europe* (Oxford, 2002), p. 232.
40   On the contagion of this peace movement through the towns and regions of northern and
central Italy, see, for instance, *Chronicon Fratris Hieronymi de Forlivio ab anno MCCCXCVII
usque ad annum MCCCCXXXIII*, ed. Adam Pasini, *Rerum Italicarum Scriptores*, XIX/5
(Bologna, 1931), pp. 4–5; and Daniel E. Bornstein, *The Bianchi of 1399: Popular Devotion in
Late Medieval Italy* (Ithaca, 1993), esp. pp. 70–83.
41   Y.-M. Bercé, *Les semeurs de peste*, in *La vie, la mort, la foi, le temps: Mélanges offerts à
Pierre Chaunu*, ed. J.-P. Bardet and M. Foisil (Paris, 1993), pp. 85–94.

Paracelsus, Athannasius Kircher, and, in Milan, members of one of Europe's most advanced health boards).[42]

Yet even with this new plague-propelled collective violence, neither Jews nor any other minority were the targets.[43] Given the means of transmitting plague through items of clothing (as understood by contemporaries), Jews who specialised in second-hand clothing could have easily been the accused and persecuted. But rarely were they even said to have spread the disease.[44] Instead, the trials singled out a wide variety of individuals, who seldom were the poor or plague cleaners and gravediggers or geographical outsiders as with Spanish soldiers in Milan, as historians have claimed.[45] In the most studied case – that of Milan during its last plague of 1630–31, later dramatised by Alessandro Manzoni's *I Promessi sposi* – the targets of the city's tribunals began with native and skilled artisans and professionals – Milanese barber-surgeons, scissor-makers, tailors, and dyers – and ended with indigenous and

---

42   Ibid., pp. 21, 25, 37–8, 45, 64, 79. Also, see Paolo Preto, *Epidemia, paura e politica nell'Italia moderna* (Bari, 1987), pp. 11–17, 43, for other physicians and intellectuals. Even the great enemy of folk and religious superstition of the eighteenth century, Ludovico Muratori (*Del governo della peste, e delle maniere di guardarsene … divio in Politico, Medico, ed Ecclesiastico …* [Rome: per Girolamo Mainardi, 1743]), accepted Milan's official story and condemned 'enorme delitto', 'funesta memoria', 'inumani carnefici' of the plague spreaders.

43   After 1349, the only incidents of anti-Semitic riots sparked by plague in Italy that Paolo Preto (*Peste e società a Venezia nel 1576* [Vicenza, 1978], pp. 52–3) has uncovered from archives and published sources were in Udine in 1511, when Jews were chased from town after the cessation of plague, and in 1556 when Jews were accused of bringing the plague to Padua. In addition to these, a local Mantuan chronicle asserts that the plague of 1463 was carried there by Jews from Ferrara. But as with Padua no action appears to have been taken against them by state officials or the populace, Andrea Schivenoglia, *Cronaca di Mantova dal 1445 al 1484*, ed. Carlo d'Arco (Mantua, 1857), p. 32.

44   For this recrudescence of persecution associated with plague, see William Naphy, *Plagues, Poisons and Potions: Plague-spreading conspiracies in the Western Alps c.1530–1640* (Manchester, 2002). Naphy finds that the first signs of scapegoating during plague at Geneva were sparked only in 1545 (p. 57). For Italy, see Preto, *Le grandi pesti dell'età moderna 1575–77 e 1630–31*, in *Venezia e la peste 1348/1797* (Venice, 1979), pp. 125–6; Preto, *Peste e società a Venezia*, chap. 2; Preto, *Epidemia, paura e politica*; A. Pastore, *Crimine e giustizia in tempo di Peste nell'Europa moderna* (Bari, 1991); and *Processo agli untori*, eds G. Farinelli and E. Paccagnini (Milan, 1988). According to Preto, *Epidemia, paura e politica*, accusations of intentional plague-spreading were 'wholly absent from the fifteenth and most of the sixteenth century, not only in Italy but across Europe' (p. 10). Also, see Paul Slack, *The Impact of Plague in Tutor and Stuart England*, 2nd edn (Oxford, 1990), pp. 293–4; and Paul Slack, 'Responses to Plague in Early Modern Europe: The Implications of Public Health', pp. 111–31, in Arien Mack (ed.), *Time of Plague: The History and Social Consequences of Lethal Epidemic Disease* (New York, 1991) esp. p. 117, who finds such scapegoating rare in England. For Italy, moreover, the plagues of late Cinquecento amounted to only anticipations of what would become much more widespread during Italy's last early modern plagues of the 1630s and 1656–57. On these late-sixteenth-century anticipations, see Samuel Cohn, *Cultures of Plague: Medical Thinking at the End of the Renaissance* (Oxford, 2010), pp. 3, 101, 119, 271–2, and 277.

45   See, for instance, Naphy, *Plagues, Poisons and Potions*.

wealthy bankers, members of the clergy,[46] and included the aristocrat Don Giovanni de Padilla, son of one of Milan's highest-ranking officials.[47] At Milan, not a single Jew was accused; nor do I know of any Jews tried or executed for plague-spreading in other Italian towns or in France during the plagues of the sixteenth or seventeenth century. Nor were there any repeats of the 1348–49 plague-inspired massacres of Jews or of any other innocents.[48] The one exception present in the historiography – the massacre of the 'New Christians' at Lisbon in April 1506 – is mistaken. None of the surviving chronicles or administrative records point to the plague (which had struck Lisbon over six months earlier) as the trigger of this anti-Semitic slaughter or specifically led to the accusation of *conversos* as plague spreaders. Instead, a New Christian's scepticism over a Dominican-orchestrated miracle sparked the riots that massacred two thousand or more in three days.[49]

III

With the nineteenth century and the spread of cholera into Europe, things would change: modernity, instead of decoupling the disease–hate nexus, increased its toxicity. Under strikingly different political regimes and social contexts, cholera set off waves of social violence against the rich, doctors, hospital workers, and government officials in its first major tour of Europe and America, 1830–37.[50] Its provocation of hate covered a more extensive

46   See the example of the Servite friar Giacinto condemned to death, perhaps by an ecclesiastic tribunal; Fausto Nicolini, *Parte III: La Peste 1629–1632*, in *Storia di Milano*, diretta di G. Treccani degli Alfieri, X (Milan, 1957), pp. 497–557, at p. 527.

47   *Processo agli untori*, pp. 76, 150, 480.

48   See note 42.

49   For those who suppose that sudden outbreaks of plague sparked this anti-Semitic massacre and normally led to the slaughter of Jews, see Bercé, *Revolt and Revolution in Early Modern Europe*, p. 19; Yerushalmi, *The Lisbon Massacre of 1506*, pp. 7–8, 18, and Ami Isseroff, 'Lisbon Massacre', in *Zionism and Israel – Encyclopedic Dictionary: Zionism and Israel on the Web Project*, 31 March 2009. In fact, none of the contemporary sources describing the Lisbon massacre hints that plague was its trigger; the humanist Damião de Gois, writing a half-century after the massacre, perhaps goes further, claiming that 'the most honourable' citizens of Lisbon, because of the plague, had left the city and therefore were not around to protect the 'New Christians': 'Nestes dia perecerão mais de mil almas sem aver na cidadequem ousasse de resistir, pola pouca gente de sorte que nella avia por estarem os mais dos honrados fora, por caso da peste' (*Chronica do feliccissimo rey dom Emanuel da gloriosa memoria* ... (Lisbon, 1619), p. 142). On several of these sources, see François Soyer, 'The Massacre of the New Christians of Lisbon in 1506: A New Eyewitness Account', *Cadernos de Estudos Sefarditas*, 7 (2007), pp. 221–43.

50   In Sicily, major insurrections of peasants, miners, unemployed workers, and vagabonds swept through the cities of Messina, Siracusa, Catania and the countryside, threatening the stability of the Neapolitan regime. See F. Maggiore-Perni, *Palermo e le sue grandi epidemie*

terrain than that even of the Black Death in Europe alone. Whereas Black Death pogroms of 1347–51 centred on German-speaking lands, spilling into parts of France, Spain, and the Low Countries, the myths, accusations, and popular violence sparked by the cholera epidemic of 1830–37 spared few, if any, countries of Europe, east or west, from autocratic Russia to sophisticated Paris and democratic Manchester and Edinburgh. Moreover, the patterns of hate were broadly similar across these diverse regions. The same myths, conspiracies, and class prejudices emerged. Physicians and journalists may have laid their prejudices bare, blaming the spread of the disease on the ignorance of the poor and on their uncivilised and uncouth habits. But the poor and marginal outsiders, as with the Irish in London, Liverpool, Glasgow, and New York City or the tribal Asiatic Sarts in Ashkend, were the ones to riot, accusing the rich of orchestrating a vast Malthusian plan to kill them off and others living in poverty, and thereby ending population pressure.[51]

Moreover, unlike the Black Death, cholera's dance with social loathing did not suddenly cease with its first performance; instead, subsequent waves in the 1850s to its sixth in 1910–11 continued to provoke hate and collective violence, that is, after John Snow had mapped its mode of transmission in 1854 and Koch had cultured the bacillus in 1884.[52] To date, no one has compared these waves of cholera to measure or evaluate changes in their

---

dal XVI al XIX secolo (Palermo, 1894), p. 226; Alfonso Sansone, Gli avvenimenti del 1837 in Sicilia (Palermo, 1890); and Preto, Epidemia, paura e politica, pp. 121–64; Franco Della Peruta, Mazzini e i rivoluzionari italiani: Il 'partito d'azione' 1830–1845 (Milan, 1974), pp. 220–77.

51   These generalisations are based on online newspaper searches in the Library of Congress's 'Chronicling America', Readex's 'America's Historical Newspapers', the 'British Newspaper Archive', the National Libraries of Australia's 'Trove' Collection, Gallica's collection of French newspapers, and the ProQuest Collections of The Times, The Scotsman, The Guardian, and The Observer. For problems in keyword searches with online newspaper archives, especially with varying degrees of character recognition (OCR), see Ian Mulligan, 'Illusionary Order: Online Databases, Optical Character Recognition, and Canadian History, 1997–2010', The Canadian Historical Review, 94 (2013), pp. 540–69. The literature on cholera disturbances is large; see especially R.J. Morris, Cholera 1832: The Social Response to An Epidemic (London, 1976); Michael Durey, The Return of the Plague: British Society and the Cholera 1831–2 (Dublin, 1979); and Michael Holland, Geoffrey Gill, and Sean Burrell (eds), Cholera & Conflict: 19th Century Cholera in Britain and its Social Consequences (London, 2009); R.E. McGrew, Russia and the Cholera 1823–32 (Madison, 1965); Peter Baldwin, Contagion and the State in Europe, 1830–1930 (Cambridge, 1999), chap. 2; Alfonso Sansone, Gliavvenimenti del 1837 in Sicilia; and Charles E. Rosenberg, The Cholera Years: The United States in 1832, 1849, and 1866 (Chicago, 1962).

52   Riots against doctors and surgeons accused of spreading cholera erupted in Le Var, the region of Toulon, Arles, and Auriol in southern France in 1884 (Baehrel, 'Epidémie et terreur: histoire et sociologie', Annales historiques de la Révolution française, XXIII (1951), pp. 114–15, 128); riots at Puerta del Sol in Madrid continued to June 1885, when angry crowds captured the queen (Bernard Vincent, Le cholera en Espagne au XIXe siècle, in J.P. Bardot, P. Bourdelais, P. Guillaume, F. Lebrun, and C. Quétel (eds), Peurs et terreurs face à la contagion (Paris, 1988), pp. 54–5); and major revolts erupted in Italy during its last significant wave of cholera in 1910–11.

social repercussions, the character of the conspiracies, protests, or levels of social violence. The assumptions have been that they declined dramatically after the first wave and lingered on only in backward corners of Europe and Asia.

Although the first wave of cholera may have sparked the most violent rioting in the USA, France, and Britain, this was not the case in Russia or even Italy, and in Spain, Portugal, Germany, Hungary, and elsewhere cholera still ignited serious rioting and destruction until the end of the nineteenth century. At Santa Cruz de Santiago, the capital of the Canary Islands, for instance, disregard of quarantine regulations by the Captain-General and Civil Governor coming from Spain on 21 August 1885 mobilised the local population into street fighting: bombs exploded, all the local authorities resigned *en masse* and hundreds fled into the interiors of the islands.[53]

More dramatic, violent, and numerous were the cholera riots down the Volga and into Asiatic Russia that continued until its last cholera wave in the 1910s. At Astrakhan, Saratof, Ashkend, Nizhny-Novorgrod, Hughesovka (present-day Donetsk), and other towns, armed crowds estimated as great as ten thousand attacked counts, governors, doctors, and health workers; burnt police stations and hospitals; stoned judges to death, and dragged patients from their beds, under the illusion that they were saving them from being poisoned or buried alive by physicians, pharmacists, or state officials. For short periods, rioters took over municipalities. Cossacks and local troops had to be called in; deaths mounted on both sides. During the pandemic of 1892, cholera riots spread even more widely than in 1830–37, from China, through Afghanistan, into Syria, Asia Minor, Persia, Poland, Hungary, Bavaria, and into Italy (and not just in the Mezzogiorno). One of the largest of the Italian cholera riots occurred in 1893 among organised workers in industrial Livorno.

The next and last significant cholera wave in Italy, that of 1910–11, provoked more collective violence still, despite the fact that by then the disease posed few mysteries. To be sure, these riots concentrated in the south, principally in Puglia and Calabria. Here, even in small towns, as with Mola di Bari and Massafra, crowds of two to three thousand besieged hospitals and town halls, destroyed archives and hacked mayors and judges to death. For the most part, the old myths of elites purposefully spreading the disease with poisons to cull the poor persisted, and aroused labourers and particularly women to acts of collective violence. These riots, however, were not restricted to the south; they flared in towns outside Rome, such as Segni, at Pontedra in Tuscany, and, according to a *Lancet* correspondent, at Venice in 1910.[54]

---

53   *Sacramento Daily Record-Union*, 22 August 1885, front page.
54   For Segni, see *La Stampa*, 17 October 1911, 4 'Una ripetizione dei fatti di Verbicaro: Il Municipio di Segni incendiato dalla popolazione'. In addition, it was widely reported principally from Milanese correspondents in the foreign press: see, *The Scotsman*, 17 October 1911,

Even the seventh cholera wave of the El Tor isolate that remains alive today[55] continues to provoke prejudice, blame, and riots, despite case fatalities falling below 1 per cent.[56] As with classic cholera, blame and its conspiracies continue to cut along class lines. When cholera reached Peru in 1991, government officials accused the poor of spreading the disease by their 'pig-like' habits, and the poor retaliated with mass demonstrations against state officials.[57] A year later the Venezuelan government blamed cholera's spread on the poor's uncouth habits, especially their diet of crabs; the poor accused the government and multinationals of poisoning their food (especially their crabs) to kill them off;[58] and most recently, in Haiti, those homeless from the earthquake rioted against UN troops, who unintentionally carried cholera to the island from Nepal.[59]

IV

Cholera was not the only disease to spark social violence and hatred in the nineteenth and twentieth century. Despite the vast literature on smallpox through the ages, scholars have yet to study the social protest, violence, and inhumanity that this disease unleashed. Attention on this score has been largely limited to the politics of anti-vaccination campaigns[60] and to a few incidents of biological warfare, most infamously Jeffrey Amherst's

p. 8: 'Cholera Riots at Segni; Anger of ignorant Populace'; *The Times* (London), 17 October 1911, p. 5, 'Cholera Riots in Italy: A Town Hall Sacked', and in the Australian press, for instance, *The Maitland Daily Mercury* (New South Wales), 17 October 1911, p. 5. For Pontedra, see Frank M. Snowden, *Naples in the time of Cholera 1884–1911* (Cambridge, 1995), p. 239; and for Venice, *Lancet*, 22 July 1911, p. 274.

55   A. Mutreja, et al., 'Evidence for Several Waves of Global Transmission in the Seventh Cholera Pandemic', *Nature*, 477 (7365) (24 August 2011), pp. 462–5; and 'Global Epidemics and the Impact of Cholera', *WHO Website*: Health Topics: Cholera (2013).

56   Marcos Cueto, 'Stigma and Blame during an Epidemic: Cholera in Peru, 1991', in Diego Armus (ed.), *Disease in the History of Modern Latin America: From Malaria to AIDS* (Durham, NC, 2003), p. 269.

57   Ibid., pp. 281–3.

58   Charles Briggs, 'Theorizing Modernity Conspiratorially: Science, Scale, and the Political Economy of Public Discourse in Explanations of a Cholera Epidemic', *American Ethnologist*, 31 (2004), pp. 164–87, esp. pp. 164–72. On crabs as an alternative host of *Vibrio cholera*, see Christopher Hamlin, *Cholera: The Biography* (Oxford, 2009), p. 275.

59   Farmer, *Haiti after the Earthquake*.

60   See, for instance, the excellent article by David Arnold, 'Smallpox and Colonial Medicine in Nineteenth-century India', in David Arnold (ed.), *Imperial Medicine and Indigenous Societies* (Manchester, 1988), pp. 45–66. For opposition to earlier inoculation as in the 1721 epidemic against the Boston physician, Bolyston, see Ola Elizabeth Winslow, *A Destroying Angel: The Conquest of Smallpox in Colonial Boston* (Boston, MA, 1974), p. vi.

distribution of smallpox-infested blankets to Amerindians in 1763,[61] but scholars have yet to analyse this disease's social violence – how populations coped with it – especially in comparison with other diseases.[62]

Even more than with cholera, smallpox riots and violence against its victims cut against the grain of the expected progression of the dampening of hate with scientific advances in understanding and preventing disease. Before inoculations and vaccines had been discovered, and when the disease was probably the principal cause of the New World's drastic depopulation and when it returned to haunt the Old World in a more deadly strain in the sixteenth and seventeenth century,[63] no examples come to light of smallpox spreading blame or sparking deadly social violence against foreigners, religious minorities, or other 'Others'. Moreover, I know of no examples from Antiquity (as with the Antonine plague, AD 166–72, assuming that it was smallpox) or during the Middle Ages when the disease provoked social loathing.[64]

Instead, smallpox's power to inflict blame and persecution increased and became prominent only during the last two decades of the nineteenth and the opening ones of the twentieth century, that is, contemporaneously with the laboratory revolution.[65] For the two places I have studied with online newspapers, the USA and Britain, the watershed was the mid nineteenth century and especially the smallpox epidemic of 1881–82, after effective

61   Among other places, see Victoria Harden, 'Smallpox', in *Encyclopedia of Pestilence*, II, pp. 647–50; Michael B.A. Oldstone, *Viruses, Plagues & History*, 2nd edn (Oxford, 2010), p. 72; John Duffy, 'Smallpox and the Indians in the American Colonies', *Bulletin of the History of Medicine*, 25 (1951), pp. 324–41, at p. 324; and John Duffy, *Epidemics in Colonial America* (Port Washington, NY, 1953), pp. 244–5.

62   Traders and governments repeated such savage acts on Indian reservations of the Southwest into the twentieth century. And in the 1890s, second-hand clothiers sent the cheap wares of smallpox victims to be sold to blacks in the USA; *Daily Dispatch* (Richmond, VA), 8 February 1892.

63   Ann Carmichael and A.M. Silverstein, 'Smallpox in Europe before the Seventeenth Century: Virulent Killer or Benign Disease?', *Journal of the History of Medical and Allied Sciences*, 42 (1987), pp. 147–68.

64   See Walter Scheidel, 'Germs for Rome', in Catharine Edwards and Greg Woolf (eds), *Rome the Cosmopolis* (Cambridge, 2003), pp. 158–76; Duncan-Jones, 'The Impact of the Antonine Plague'; Vivian Nutton, *Ancient Medicine* (London, 2004), chap 2.

65   I have thus far found only four incidents of collective violence sparked by smallpox in Colonial America. These were anti-inoculation riots – the firebombing of Cotton Mather's house in Boston on 13 November 1721, because of his support of Dr Zabdiel Boylston's inoculation campaign, two riots at Norfolk, Virginia, 1768 and 1769, and one on Cat Island, near Marblehead, Massachusetts, in 1773. For the Marblehead incident, see *The Massachusetts Spy*, 26 November 1800, and for the others, a retrospective essay in *The Boston Journal*, 24 November 1901, p. 4; Pauline Maier, *From Resistance to Revolution: Colonial Radicals and the Development of American Opposition to Britain, 1765–1776* (London, 1972), pp. 4–5; Frank L. Dewey, 'Thomas Jefferson's Law Practice: The Norfolk Anti-Inoculation Riots', *The Virginia Magazine of History and Biography*, 91 (1983), pp. 39–53, esp. pp. 40–1 and 43–4; and Patrick Henderson, 'Smallpox and Patriotism', in ibid., 73 (1965), pp. 413–24.

preventative measures with state-run vaccination programmes had become well established, smallpox being the first epidemic killer that could be controlled through medical intervention before the laboratory revolution. In the USA, smallpox spawned social violence and splintered the social fabric of communities more than cholera or any other disease. Like cholera, smallpox hatred cut along class lines, but here the instigators of violence and their targets changed sides. With smallpox violence, the good and well-heeled citizens comprised the mobs, some of whom came from the highest echelons of society, as with those responsible for the Staten Island torching of its smallpox hospital and thirty-one other buildings for their care in the fall of 1858. The mob's ringleaders were the brother of Commodore Vanderbilt and Ray Tompkins, chief of the fire department but, more alarmingly, also son of a vice president of the USA. On the other side of smallpox stigmatisation and social violence were usually the poor, blacks, immigrant Chinese, Jews, Mormons, and tramps, who became double victims, of the disease and of persecution for its spread. Unlike cholera riots, smallpox violence tended to be on a smaller scale and turned on the victims themselves (as opposed to the declared intentions of the cholera mobs who claimed to be rescuing the afflicted from the demonic hands of doctors and the state). For the USA smallpox was the disease, par excellence, for hate and blame, not cholera as in Europe, and historians have yet to recognise this fact. Space allows only a few descriptions of these individualistic or small group acts of inhumanity that begin to flood US newspapers only by the epidemic of 1881–82:

January, 1882: 'A colored man in Louisa Co. [Virginia] infected with smallpox was repulsed from the hospital at the muzzle of a shot-gun.' He returned to his home, seven miles distant, on foot, 'and was considerate enough to carry in his hand an improvised smallpox flag as a warning to people not to approach him'.[66]

January, 1882: Headline: 'A Hard story to believe comes from the Christian town of Jersey City.' 'A man seized with a malignant type of smallpox was refused admission to the police station, and died on the sidewalk.'[67]

January, 1882: At Minnesota a Norwegian who lives a mile and a half from that place, and in whose family are two cases of small-pox, made his appearance on the streets, causing a stampede. A physician drove him out of town by threatening to shoot him.[68]

66   National Republican (Washington, DC), 2 January 1882, p. 2.
67   The Columbus Journal (Columbus, NB), 4 January 1882, p. 2.
68   The New Ulm Weekly Review (New Ulm, MN), 4 January 1882, p. 2.

January, 1882: Pittsburgh: 'A smallpox hospital is on a boat kept anchored on the river. People living on the bank opposite object to its proximity and a conspiracy to cut it lose and sink it has been unearthed. The newspapers are now moralizing as to whether or not such measures would be justifiable.'[69]

January, 1882: 'The body of a five-year old child was found on Saturday in the South Fordham Woods, near Jerome Ave ... New York [City]. It was covered with sores and is supposed to be that of a smallpox victim, thrown out to avoid the quarantine that would follow.'[70]

June, 1882: 'Several Nevada towns have banished the redskins from their midst and ordered them to return no more ... Fear of smallpox epidemic was the alleged cause for the ukase.'[71]

December, 1882: 'They have enlightened quarantine ideas at Austin [Texas]. Two children were attacked with smallpox and the city authorities resolved to isolate them. So they pitched a tent on the bank of the Colorado ... hoisted a yellow flag over it, and that tent is Austin's smallpox hospital. For there the children were carried and there they now are. A wet norther, which is liable to ensue any day, would test the humanity of such hospital arrangements.'[72]

Perhaps these headlines might well suggest small-town yellow journalism, groveling in horrific tales to boost newspaper sales, an Oprah Winfrey show of the 1880s. Yet, such stories are almost entirely unique to smallpox. They rarely, if ever, appear with reports of epidemic cholera, yellow fever, influenza, typhus, polio, or any other disease I have thus far researched. During numerous yellow fever epidemics from Philadelphia in 1793 to Pensacola in 1905 and flu pandemics, such as the Russian one in 1889–90 or the Great One of 1918–19, the emotional appeals from often the very same newspapers were different. Headlines, editorials, and interviews on these epidemics featured physicians, nurses, and others, acting with extraordinary compassion, courage, and self-sacrifice in their care of the afflicted. Many of these, as with the fifty-four nurses 'worn by long hours of brave fighting against the influenza' at the Philadelphia General Hospital on 12 October 1918 had refused to quit work even after being stricken with the disease, and the headlines celebrated their bravery: 'Five Nurses Die: Martyrs to Duty: 54 Ill of Influenza: Refuse to quit work.' Or take stories during yellow fever epidemics as with one in 1878 from

69   *The Waco Daily Examiner* (Waco, TX), 24 January 1882, p. 2.
70   *The Cambria Freeman* (Ebenburg, PA), 27 January 1882, p. 2.
71   *Nebraska Advertiser* (Brownville, NB), 23 June 1882, p. 7.
72   *The Waco Daily Examiner* (Waco, TX), 24 December 1882, p. 2.

The Memphis Appeal, a newspaper whose racist inclinations in other places are easy to detect:

> the man in charge of a Memphis cemetery came to the spot where the grave was to be dug and informed the negroes that they would not receive any extra pay for the extra work they were doing after six. ... The negroes, more humane than he, and indignant at such an exhibition of brutality before the husband and children [of the deceased] replied that sometimes they worked for friendship. They dug the grave, lowered the casket ...[73]

The near absence of such praise of altruism and courage was not peculiar to the press's presentation of the smallpox epidemic of 1881–82. A search for those proclaimed as 'martyrs' to save the afflicted in numerous smallpox epidemics across the millions of newspaper pages contained in the *Chronicling America* online archive of the Library of Congress from its earliest entries in 1836 to its present end point of 1922, produces not a single hit.

The newspapers, moreover, reveal much further the prejudices aroused by smallpox, both in their reporting and even more so in their own endorsement of such attitudes. Their stories turned on the supposed ignorance of German immigrants, 'the anti-vaccination Bohemian', 'the superstitious Italian', 'the black tramp', 'the Russian Jew', 'the Chinese coolie', 'the uncivilized redskin', and ubiquitously 'the unclean foreigner' as the cause of smallpox's origins and spread. Again, a few examples:

> 'The Chinese bring with them customs and systems which displace our civilization ... and in addition bring contagious disease. There have been already outbreaks of the smallpox on Chinese account in several parts of the country. ... We hear of the small-pox first in those places where Chinese are congregated. ... The mechanism for its dissemination throughout the country is now furnished by the Mongrol nucleus in every state ...'[74]

> 'There is, however, a considerable class of our population who have an unreasonable, a superstitious hostility to vaccination. It comprises the Bohemians, the most ignorant of the Germans, and some of the lowest of the Italians. Of these there are enough to start a smallpox epidemic. ... To the prejudices of such people the prevalence of the disease at Chicago and St Louis, and now in California, is undoubtedly due.'[75]

> 'Smallpox has assumed an epidemic form in Chicago ... raging furiously in the uncleanly haunts of the foreign population. ... No doubt filth and

73   *The Memphis Appeal*, p. 194.
74   *The Daily Astorian* (Astoria, OR), 8 January 1882.
75   *The Sun* (New York City), 12 December 1882, p. 2.

frowsy ways of living have much to do with it. ... If the tenement houses could be "flushed" as the sewers are, such a process would also tend greatly to the diminution of danger.'[76]

'The prevalence of smallpox does not appear to intimidate in the least the adventurous spirit of tramps that infest this country. Fearless of danger they move from one place to the other, little caring whether they spread disease or fall victims themselves. ... the prevalence of disease in its different forms can be traced to this method of transmission.'[77]

Against this blanketing of propaganda across America, statistics compiled at the time tell another story about the Chinese and the immigrant. In Hawaii, the Chinese had the lowest fatality rate of any group, accounting for less than 10 per cent of smallpox cases and less than 5 per cent of the deaths. At the New York harbour of Castle Garden over 100,000 immigrants arrived from 1 January to 1 April 1882: of these, 20 cases of smallpox were discovered.[78]

In addition to these prejudices and acts of individual cruelty, smallpox in America provoked a greater number of collective acts of violence than any other disease. Again, such incidents of large-scale collective violence begin to mount only with the breakthroughs of the laboratory revolution and the epidemic of 1881, and they reached a crescendo between 1896 and 1904. Moreover, their social composition and the targets of attack and blame were strikingly different from cholera riots. Again, some stories:

January 1882: 'A case of smallpox recently discovered in Topeka hotel caused no little excitement. The Board of Health at once hired a building on the outskirts of [town] for a pest-house, but before the city authorities could get possession, the business men of the First Ward hired the building over again. ... They then notified the authorities that they could not have the place for a smallpox hospital, and that any attempt to bring a patient over the river would be resisted by force, armed men being stationed on the bridge. Fearing bloodshed, the mayor revoked the authorization of a pest-house.'[79]

May 1882: 'The Piutes Indians now acknowledge that there is smallpox among them. ... The people have burned all the Indian camps and relics.'[80]

---

76   *The Sacramento Daily Record-Union*, 18 October 1882, p. 2.
77   *The Columbian* (Bloomsburg, PA), 3 February 1882.
78   *The Saturday Press* (Honolulu, HI), 22 October 1882, p. 2; *The Sun*, 30 April 1882, front page.
79   *The Iola Register* (Iola, KN), 27 January 1882, p. 6.
80   *Sacramento Daily Record-Union*, 5 May 1882, front page. It is not clear here who 'the people' were, and I have yet to find another description of this incident. I am presuming that

On June 6 [1893] a mob of twenty-five masked men gathered at midnight about the west end pest-house, where three new smallpox patients were taken yesterday. The leader warned Health Officer Boyd not to keep the patients in the building. They came armed with Winchesters and threw rails at the Chief of Police.[81]

On 4 May [1894] at Miles Switch, near Eldorado, Arkansas, a mob burnt the hut, where a doctor had isolated 'a negro' ill with smallpox 'and cremated the colored man. By some reports the mob shot him first.'[82]

'April 3 [1896]. William Haley, colored, is in the Memphis hospital, badly beaten and wounded with bullets in three places. He had been mobbed by whitecaps because of smallpox in his family several months ago.'[83]

But even with smallpox epidemics in America, the victims of prejudice and collective violence were not always the 'Other'; instead, the disease could violently wedge communities apart.

'In Mississippi a negro woman supposed to have smallpox goes to church; she is run off and the next day her dead body is found. Ann Hughes, suspected of having smallpox, was brained with a bed slat by panic stricken negroes at Columbus, Mississippi.'[84]

Nor were the perpetrators always the well-heeled. Other smallpox riots turned citizens and even the underclass against municipal and state authorities much the same as with the vast majority of cholera riots. From 19 March 1899 to the end of the month, papers across America reported the Mexican riots on the Texas border at Laredo against smallpox quarantine that amounted to three separate battles over several days against municipal and health authorities that required the intervention of federal marshals and ultimately the military.

it was not the Indians themselves; otherwise, the article would have said that they burned their own camps and not 'all the Indian camps'.
81   *The Evening World* (Brooklyn, NY), 6 June 1893.
82   *Alexandria Gazette* (Alexandria, VA), 5 May 1894, p. 2; *The Omaha Daily Bee* (Omaha, NB), 5 May 1894, front page; *The Times* (Richmond, VA), 6 May 1894, p. 4; *The Sun* (New York), 6 May 1894, front page; *The New York Tribune*, 6 May 1894, front page; *The Salt Lake Herald*, 6 May 1894, p.3; *The Warren Sheaf* (Warren, MN), 10 May 1894; *The Richmond Planet* (Richmond, VA), 12 May 1894, p. 3; *The Perrysburg Journal* (Perrysburg, OH), 12 June 1894, p. 2; and *The Daily Herald* (Brownsville, TX), 16 May 1894, p. 2. The last of these denied the veracity of the report, charged that it was Northern propaganda, since no Southern paper had reported it. As the list above indicates, this was not the case.
83   *The Star* (Reynoldsville, PA), 8 April 1896.
84   *Gazette* (Raleigh, NC), 18 September 1897, p. 4; 'Southern Pick Ups'.

When US marshals went to arrest the ringleaders, the 'mob' stoned them and fired on them. The health officers resumed their work, but were soon met 'by another mob of 500 or 600 Mexicans, many of them armed'. The Governor of Texas was called on to intervene and he called on the War Department to send in troops. Two days later a third battle ensued. Five hundred Mexicans assembled against the quarantine. At least two were killed and a captain of the State Rangers seriously wounded. Further US troops had to be dispatched.[85]

In May 1900 a mob of men and boys, about two thousand, refused six smallpox patients being brought and treated at a smallpox hospital at Turtle Creek, eight miles east of Pittsburgh. The mob took possession of the town. When the police and firemen were called in, the crowd cut the fire hoses, pelted the firemen with stones, and beat them with clubs.[86]

In March 1901, 'a mob' of Italians, estimated at 300 by several papers, 400 by others, destroyed a building erected by the health authorities to accommodate smallpox patients, at Orange, New Jersey. The police guard around the building was overpowered. Many of the rioters were 'armed with axes', and after the police had been driven off, 'the structure was quickly hewn down'.[87]

Despite widespread press coverage of these and other smallpox riots at the end of the nineteenth and opening years of the twentieth century in North America, the scholarly literature has analysed only two of them. One, at Montreal, stretched over three months from 28 September to 31 December 1885, and comprised various protests against compulsory vaccination, forcible removal of victims to smallpox hospitals, and quarantine boundaries. These divided sharply the more elite English-speaking citizens from the working-class French Canadians, and resulted in the latter attacking and destroying buildings in the city centre and staging a siege of city hall. The military ultimately had to be summoned to restore order.[88] The other was a series of smallpox riots that continued from 6 to 29 August 1894, when 'mobs' of Pomeranian and Polish women at Milwaukee, Wisconsin, armed with

85 *The Seattle Star*, 25 March 1899; also many other papers in the America's Historical Newspapers collection, reported these incidents, from Idaho to Washington, DC.

86 Many papers reported the riot; for the detailed descriptions, see *The Scranton Tribune* (Scranton, PA), 14 May 1900, and *The Times* (Washington, DC), 15 May 1900, front page.

87 *The Daily Journal* (Salem, OR), 11 March 1901; *Albuquerque Daily Citizen* (Albuquerque, NM), 11 March 1901; *The Salt Lake Herald*, 12 March 1901; *The Times* (Richmond, VA), 12 March 1901; *Adams County News Ritzville* (Washington territory), 13 March 1901; *Warren Sheaf* (Warren, MN), 13 March 1901; *The New York Times*, 10 March 1901.

88 Michael Bliss, *Plague: A Story of Smallpox in Montreal* (Toronto, 1991). In addition, these incidents were covered by newspapers in Canada, across the USA, in Britain, and Australia.

baseball bats, potato mashers, clubs, bed slats, and butcher knives, patrolled streets against health inspectors who attempted to remove smallpox patients to hospitals.[89] The class confrontations of these two well-studied smallpox revolts resemble those provoked by cholera. However, the two were uncharacteristic of smallpox riots, which reversed the class lines of struggle, with the disease's underclass of victims having become double victims – of disease and of violent social prejudice.

V

As the contrast in the social violence between cholera and smallpox indicates, the crises posed by different epidemic diseases could provoke radically different responses from communities within the same place and period. However, greater differences are found between these two diseases on the one hand and equally big or bigger killers such as yellow fever and influenza, and especially, the Great Pandemic of 1918–19 on the other. Space does not allow an adequate investigation of these latter two diseases and their modes of coping. But, as suggested above, these big killers rarely provoked any social violence, scapegoating or inhumanity towards health carers or state officials as seen with cholera or the disease's victims as seen with smallpox. Certainly, the difference did not rest on yellow fever or influenza posing fewer mysteries than cholera or smallpox during the late nineteenth or early twentieth century. Yellow fever's mechanisms of transmission were not discovered until the twentieth century, and its causal agent not until 1927. Discovery of influenza's virus came later (1933), and an effective vaccine was not developed until the 1950s. Even with racial and sectional tensions stretched to their limits on the eve of the Civil War as at New Orleans in 1853 during one of the worst epidemics in US history, yellow fever brought communities together. It encouraged charity from the north and prompted tolerance across class and race. The absence of social loathing and violence is all the more surprising given yellow fever's patterns of immunity. Overwhelmingly, its victims were recent immigrants and the poor, more so than with cholera or any other disease of nineteenth-century America or Europe.[90] Moreover, because of

---

89   Judith Walzer Leavitt, 'Politics and Public Health: Smallpox in Milwaukee, 1894–1895', in Leavitt and Ronald L. Numbers (eds), *Sickness and Health in America: Readings in the History of Medicine and Public Health* (Madison, 1978), pp. 403–13; first published in *Bulletin of the History of Medicine*, 50 (1976), pp. 553–68; and Judith Walzer Leavitt, *The Healthiest City: Milwaukee and the Politics of Health Reform* (Princeton, 1982). Also, see Susan Craddock, *City of Plagues: Disease, Poverty, and Deviance in San Francisco* (Minneapolis, 2000), pp. 87, 108.
90   On its patterns of immunity and effects on immigrant populations, see John R. Pierce and Jim Writer, *Yellow Jack: How Yellow Fever Ravaged America and Walter Reed Discovered Its*

resistance gained from millennia of exposure in West Africa, many Southern blacks possessed greater immunity to it than whites – a fact that could have stirred suspicion and fuelled mounting racism as had happened in 1348–51, when Jews were alleged to have escaped the Black Death and therefore killed for it.[91] Instead, whites solicited blacks to provide basic services for the mostly white yellow fever-afflicted. Blacks volunteered and were praised for their efforts and sacrifices: racial tensions eased.[92]

Another case in point is the Great Influenza of 1918–19, which in absolute numbers felled more than any single pandemic in world history.[93] That it provoked no major riots or religious and sectarian hatred is more remarkable still. In 1918 its symptoms, seasonality, and the age structure of victims differed radically from any flu epidemic past or future, marking it as a new and mysterious disease.[94] In addition, this pandemic exploded in the midst of war frenzy and nationalistic hatred. In the USA, the great influx of immigrant workers fleeing Europe and the upsurge of racial and class tensions added fuel to the socio-economic toxins soon to spark the longest and bloodiest race riots in US history, and a hysterical red scare across America.[95] Yet this general milieu of hate failed to influence influenza. Instead, the pandemic eased social tensions. With public services near collapse and unburied bodies left in heaps, elites, and especially women, in cities such as New York, Washington, Philadelphia, Boston, and El Paso entered ghettos, opened soup kitchens, and fed the poor, Mexicans, and other minorities. They joined motorcades, donated their automobiles as ambulances, scrubbed the floors of the poor,

Deadly Secrets (Hoboken, NJ, 2005), pp. 15, 38, 47. In 1853, 7,000 of the 8,000 to 11,000 victims at New Orleans were recent immigrants, in the main, the poor Irish; John Duffy, *Sword of Pestilence: The New Orleans Yellow Fever Epidemic of 1853* (Baton Rouge, 1966), p. 95.

91   See Preto, *Epidemia, paura e politica*, p. 9; and Brian Pullan, 'Plague and Perceptions of the Poor in Early Modern Italy', pp. 101–23, in *Epidemics and Ideas*, p. 117.

92   For New Orleans, 1853, Pierce and Writer, *Yellow Jack*, p. 38; for Memphis in the epidemic of 1878, Margaret Humphreys, *Yellow Fever and the South* (New Brunswick, NJ, 1992), p. 7. Mary Crosby, *The American Plague: The Untold Story of Yellow Fever. The Epidemic that Shaped Our History* (New York, 2006), p. 79, alleges that blacks' immunity 'had been fuel for racism for decades' but supplies no evidence for it.

93   Carol Reeves, 'Influenza', in *Encyclopedia of Pestilence*, I, pp. 304–13; and Tom Quinn, *Flu: A Social History of Influenza* (London, 2008).

94   Johnson, *Britain and the 1918–19 Influenza Pandemic*, p. 122. It decimated those in good health and in early adulthood, failing to conform to flu's usual 'U' curve of death that killed predominantly infants and the elderly. Instead, in 1918–19 it triggered pneumonia much more often than with any pandemic of flu before or since, and inflicted much higher fatality and mortality rates, attaining mortalities as high as 40 per cent in places such as the Western Samoa, other Polynesian islands, and several settlements in northern parts of Canada. Among other places, see Alfred Crosby, *America's Forgotten Pandemic: The Influenza of 1918*, 2nd edn (Cambridge, 2003; first published 1976). In the USA it was called that 'strange prostrating malady'; see *The New York Tribune*, 12 September 1918.

95   Crosby, *America's Forgotten Pandemic*, p. 65.

served as orderlies, cooks, and cleaners, cared for orphans and afflicted infants, thereby putting their lives at stake against this disease that they knew was highly contagious, in fact more so than cholera or smallpox.[96] And unlike smallpox, no proven vaccine was then known and previous hereditary exposure guaranteed no immunity. With the flu pandemic, charitable organisations cut across accustomed denominational lines; people of all kinds 'thrust themselves into the presence of lethal disease'.[97] Despite the bombardment by the medical profession, notices across newspapers blaming 'sneezers, coughers, and spitters' for spreading the disease and with special local ordinances passed against them, the Great Influenza failed to fuel any stories of personal or collective prejudice, callous selfishness, and inhumanity towards victims, as seen with smallpox. Instead, articles in many of the very same newspapers portrayed and celebrated men and especially young women as the heroines and martyrs of the Great Influenza, who had risked and in many cases sacrificed their lives caring for afflicted strangers.

VI

In conclusion, crises created by epidemic diseases across history did not invariably spur hatred, a search for scapegoats, or acts of violence against 'the Other'. Some diseases, such as smallpox in America and cholera in Europe, have been much more likely to provoke blame and violence than other epidemic diseases. Yet historians have rarely analysed the socio-psychological consequences of diseases comparatively, or shown that communities have coped with crises of yellow fever and influenza, differently. Instead of diseases of hate, these were epidemics of compassion and heroic self-sacrifice that inspired acts of martyrdom, despite the mysteries of their transmission or the character of their agents. Even those diseases to provoke blame and social violence against others have shown a wide variety of instigators and victims. The dominant members of society did not inevitably persecute 'the Other'; in fact, more usually, it was the other way around. In conspiracies and trials against supposed plague spreaders in early modern Europe as at Milan in 1630, the accusations came predominantly from impoverished women, while the victimised stretched from solid male artisans to bankers and governors. With cholera this class alignment of hatred sharpened: marginal communities of immigrants, as with the Irish in England, the Asiatic Sarts in European Russia, the proletariat in Munich and Livorno, impoverished fig growers in

---

96 These conclusions are based on evidence from hundreds of newspapers included in the online newspaper archive of The Library of Congress, *Chronicling America*, from September to November 1917 (3,440 pages investigated).
97 Crosby, *America's Forgotten Pandemic*, p. 82.

Puglia, and striking fishermen in Naples and Taranto manned the barricades, burnt hospitals and City Halls, attacked physicians, nurses, pharmacists, policemen, mayors, and judges. Smallpox's class conflict, on the other hand, usually cut in the opposite direction: the 'better' citizens, who could include physicians, merchant princes, and heads of fire departments, formed the mobs, burnt smallpox hospitals and viciously maimed or killed smallpox victims. Finally, recent assumptions about when diseases in history have been most likely to spur hate and blame, need rethinking: the key variable does not seem to have been the newness or mysteriousness of the disease or the medical establishment's inability to prevent or cure it. Otherwise, epidemics in Antiquity and the Middle Ages would have been the ones most prone to blame, hate, and social violence, and they were not. Instead, with few exceptions such scapegoating developed later with early modernity and became most intense just before or shortly after the late-nineteenth-century laboratory revolution. The one epidemic disease to pose the fewest mysteries by the nineteenth century as far as effective preventive measures go was smallpox, and it – not cholera – became America's disease par excellence for violence and the vicious blaming of the 'Other' – 'the black', 'the tramp', 'the Bohemian', 'the Coolie', 'the redskin'. Coping with epidemic crises displays a wide array of emotional and social reactions over time and across diseases: their enigmas are still to be unravelled.

8

Plague Year 1680 in Central Europe:
Using Czech Plague Registers to
Monitor Epidemic Progression[1]

PAVLA JIRKOVÁ

This chapter focuses on a number of aspects of the epidemiological crisis that affected the countries of Central Europe at the turn of the 1670s and 1680s. The plague epidemic, which older writings state resulted in the death of almost 20,000 people in Vienna in 1679, spread to the countries north of Austria, and other countries within the Habsburg composite state.[2] Its main wave swept through Moravia in 1679, with the population of Bohemia and Silesia struck by the epidemic a year later. The fact that unique sources have survived in the National Archive in Prague, however, narrowed our research to looking at the method by which the Kingdom of Bohemia faced up to the epidemiological crisis in 1680.[3] This chapter will give a more detailed summary of the course and nature of the plague epidemic in Bohemia, with particular attention paid both to the actual working of the information system based on the sending of lists of the dead, and to the extent of infection

1   This study has been written with financial support given by the Czech Science Foundation's 'Restrictive Plague Policies and the Prevention of Demographic and Economic Crisis in the Early Modern Czech Lands' project (registration number GAČR 13–35304S), undertaken by the Economics Institute of the Czech Academy of Sciences (the joint workplace CERGE-EI). I thank Prof. Richard M. Smith, Prof. Sheilagh Ogilvie and Dr Janine Maegraith, all from the University of Cambridge, and Dr Alexander Klein from the University of Kent, as well as Prof. John Henderson from the University of London, for their encouragement, assistance in obtaining an access to the library resources, and their interest in Central European history research.
2   F. Mareš, 'Veliký mor v letech 1679–1680', *Sborník historický*, 1 (1883), pp. 397–419 (especially p. 407).
3   National Archive, Prague (hereafter referred to as NAP), archival holding Archiv pražského arcibiskupství I. (hereafter referred to as APA I.), inventory No. 3753–4, signature C 142/6a–b, boxes 2229–30, unfoliated. Ibid., archival holding Stará manipulace (hereafter referred to as SM), inventory No. 842, signature E 2/4–8, boxes 659–60.

in the country, together with a microanalysis of demographic information on the structure of the population who died. A third set of problems, looking at the existence of the early modern monitoring system from the perspective of political arithmetic and in economic terms will only be touched upon in this chapter, although it will be explored further in later stages of this research.

An interdisciplinary debate continues to re-evaluate and revise the present positions in the field. As the social historian of medicine Mary Lindemann stated:

> We are now ... much less sure about the economic consequences of plague than we once were. Did real wages climb in response to a shortage of workers? Did fertility bounce back? Did areas recover quickly or only slowly from the plague? Did it contribute to the rise or decline of serfdom? None of these questions has received a fully satisfactory answer.[4]

In 2010, Samuel K. Cohn revised our ideas of the epidemiological contexts of plagues at the end of Renaissance with his research on cultures of plague.[5] In 2011, Keith Wrightson published a book describing the impact of the plague epidemic on the city of Newcastle-upon-Tyne in 1636, from the perspective of a young scrivener living at the time, Ralph Tailor.[6] In 2012, Paul Slack published an introduction to the history of plague in England and other European countries.[7] Slack sums up his results covering nearly thirty years of research on the demographic, social and economic impacts of epidemics, and updates the latest developments in the field. The listed works are accompanied by many others, which study the character and course of plague epidemics in the early modern age in various parts of Europe, from the British Isles to the Mediterranean and to the Baltic Sea.[8]

4   M. Lindemann, *Medicine and Society in Early Modern Europe* (Cambridge, 2010), p. 58.
5   S.K. Cohn, *Cultures of Plague: Medical Thinking at the End of the Renaissance* (Oxford, 2010).
6   K. Wrightson, *Ralph Tailor's Summer: A Scrivener, His City, and the Plague* (New Haven, 2011).
7   P. Slack, *Plague: A Very Short Introduction* (Oxford, 2012).
8   L. Clark and C. Rawcliffe (eds), *The Fifteenth Century XII: Society in an Age of Plague* (Cambridge, 2013); K.W. Bowers, *Plague and Public Health in Early Modern Seville* (New York, 2013); K.-E. Frandsen, *The Last Plague in the Baltic Region, 1709–1713* (Copenhagen, 2010); A.P. Cook and N.D. Cook, *The Plague Files: Crisis Management in Sixteenth-Century Seville* (Baton Rouge, 2009); A.L. Moote and D.C. Moote, *The Great Plague: The Story of London's Most Deadly Year* (Baltimore, 2004); R.M. Smith, 'Plagues and Peoples: The Long Demographic Cycle 1250–1670', in P. Slack and R. Ward (eds), *The Peopling of Britain: The Shaping of a Human Landscape* (Oxford, 2002), pp. 177–209; S. Scott and C.J. Duncan, *Biology of Plagues. Evidence from Historical Populations* (Cambridge, 2001).

I

At the end of summer 1679, the population of Bohemia were confronted with the increasing likelihood of an outbreak of plague in the country and the inherent implications of travelling from the afflicted region south of Bohemia. During the autumn, controls on Bohemia's borders, especially with Austria and Moravia, were tightened. The city of Prague's first specific order was given in August 1679 which, for example, limited entry to persons from an afflicted territory to the city's gates. Particular attention was paid to the many people arriving from Austria and Moravia. If they were unable to show a valid health passport, they were to be taken to designated sites in front of Prague's gates to undertake a 40-day quarantine. Streets were ordered to be cleaned both for the Christian population and in the Jewish ghetto.[9]

As part of 'Praecauirung' ('precaution'), a 'Conferenz' took place in Prague, which was a meeting between Prague's governors and provincial doctors and surgeons to give expert opinions in discussions on quarantine measures. In the end, the provincial doctors and surgeons of the kingdom of Bohemia prepared an (undated) recommendation for the Czech proconsulate and the highest national authorities containing 34 points for preventing the introduction of the disease to Prague, or to mitigate its course.[10] It mentions, for instance, setting up a lazaretto outside the city's walls, isolating the sick from the healthy, banning the operation of spas and inns and special measures for the Jewish population. In terms of the focus of this chapter, however, the very first point is of particular interest. The Bohemian doctors and surgeons spoke of the duty to send notes with a list of the dead from every Prague parish, to be delivered to the Bohemian Chamber. At the same time, the persons who were to prepare these reports and be responsible for the whole matter were to be determined.

Already by August 1679, the governors of the regions lying in South and East Bohemia were informed of the intention of Leopold I, Emperor and King, to flee from the plague to Prague.[11] They were encouraged to allow the monarch smooth passage through their land. Leopold I was welcomed to Prague in September 1679, but the threat of the disease spreading forced him to move to East Bohemia. Once the plague epidemic was in full flow in Bohemia in 1680, the Emperor returned to Austria via Linz. A Czech equivalent of the infection rules issued in Vienna (1679) and Silesia (1680) was preserved as a draft document consisting of almost 100 pages.[12]

One of the defensive precautions against the spread of infections was the

---

9   NAP, SM, inventory No. 842, signature E 2/5, box 659.
10   Ibid.
11   Ibid.
12   Ibid., signature E 2/4, box 659.

issuance of so-called health passports ('*foedus sanitatis*').[13] The city councils issued passports to those citizens setting out to travel beyond the borders of the country, with these serving as proof that the traveller came from a region unaffected by plague. These documents were inspected at state borders and at city gates by appointed guard patrols. According to the proposal of the plague rules, the identity of travellers for whom the passports had been issued was also to be verifiable with additional data relating to age, physique, hair, nose, eyes, clothing and characteristic features on their face or hands. In practice, the passports mostly contained the name of the traveller, their destination and dates, plus the nature of any goods and brief information on the traveller's appearance.[14]

The first steps were taken in August 1679 that were to lead to the removal of the part of the Jewish population living in the ghetto in Prague's Old Town to the village of Libeň lying outside the city walls.[15] A reduction commission was founded whose job it was to make a list of Jews in cooperation with Jewish elders, and according to the level of taxes actually paid in order to determine people who were to be expelled to Libeň. The reason for this measure was the marked overpopulation of Prague's Jewish ghetto, and with news of the plague in nearby Austria, this caused fear that the Jewish town might become a potential focus of the plague as a result of the unsuitable hygiene conditions inherent in the overpopulated ghetto (according to the reduction commission's report, there were roughly 22 people per building) and also in the nature of many Jews' livelihood. Trading activities required a higher mobility of the Jewish population within and outside the state, where furthermore the epidemiological situation could not be checked by Bohemian authorities.

Overpopulation in those city neighbourhoods in which the Jewish population lived was an issue that also affected other European cities. Cohn refers to this problem, for example, in Padua, Italy, in relation to the plague year of 1576 in documents of Canobbio, a notary.[16] Canobbio relates the higher mortality of the Jewish population to the poor social conditions in which the Jews were living (overcrowding, insufficient fresh air and dirty water). Canobbio, however, avoids coming to a conclusion that would sound

13   V. Schulz, *Příspěvky k dějinám moru v zemích českých z let 1531–1746. Z archivu Muzea království českého* (Praha, 1901), pp. 104–5, 114, 116.
14   Around ten health passports were preserved in the archives researched, either originals or copies, and these had been issued for persons from the upper classes of early modern urban society (councillors and traders). NAP, SM, inventory No. 842, signature E 2/5 and E 2/9, boxes 659–60.
15   Ibid., signature E 2/5, box 659. Ibid., archival holding Česká dvorská kancelář (hereafter referred to as ČDK), inventory No. 1024, signature IV T 1, boxes 793–4. J. Prokeš, 'Úřední antisemitismus a pražské ghetto v době pobělohorské: redukční a extirpační pokusy z let 1679 až 1729', *Ročenka Společnosti pro dějiny Židů v Československé republice*, 1 (1929), pp. 41–224.
16   Cohn, *Cultures of Plague*, p. 119.

anti-Semitic. In contrast, the method for dealing with the problem in Prague around 1680 (appointing a reduction commission and a plan to evict the Jews) was closer to an anti-Semitic approach, at least in regards to the approach of the authorities documented in the sources studied.

Under the influence of various circumstances, the registration of the dead continued until March 1680, when the reduction commission published an alarming fact about the level of overpopulation in the Jewish town. It found that 7,113 people older than ten years of age were squeezed into 318 buildings.[17] The reduction commission decided to move more than a third of the Jews to Libeň. In April, however, the plague epidemic broke out in full in Prague and the long-planned removal did not take place in the end. The number of plague victims markedly increased from spring 1680. In April, 347 Jews died, in May 494, June 545, July 857 and in August 373.[18]

Extra surveillance, or at least special attention, was also meant to be paid to the Jewish population according to the concept of the plague rules issued in Bohemia in 1680.[19] Rules determined for the Jewish population in the Prague ghetto were stated in 12 points at the very end of the regulations. The number of Jews of both gender were to be added together, and those exceeding the given number to be 'expelled from Prague'. Other regulations applied to banning the arrival of Jews in the ghetto and the admittance of Jews from the nearby village of Libeň into the city gates, which was above all meant to prevent the arrival of Jews escaping from countries infected by the plague. There were a number of points restricting Jewish trade. Jews were banned from offering goods and making sales in buildings and churches in the Christian parts of Prague, the import of goods from suspicious (infected) places was forbidden, and if the plague turned up in the ghetto, then its market fair was to be closed. Moreover, measures described in more detail in the section for the Christian population were to be followed.[20] If, despite all these measures, the plague was to break out in the ghetto, the Jewish town was to be closed with nobody else allowed to enter under threat of beheading.

On the basis of his years of research into the plague, Cohn points out that there was a reduction in labelling the Jewish population and other social minorities as 'scapegoats of plague' after the end of the Black Death and their punishment for allegedly spreading disease.[21] This perspective is also seen in Cohn's finding that medical documents discussing the plague written in Italy during the sixteenth century only rarely related the spread of disease

---

17   NAP, ČDK, inventory No. 1024, signature IV T 1, boxes 793–4.
18   Ibid., SM, inventory No. 842, signature E 2/7, box 659.
19   Ibid., signature E 2/4, box 659.
20   Ibid.
21   Cohn, *Cultures of Plague*, p. 3. S.K. Cohn, 'The Black Death and the Burning of Jews', *Past & Present*, 196 (2007), pp. 3–36.

to the religion or traits of the Jewish section of the population.[22] In the case of Prague, many of the preventive measures applied not only to the Jews but also to the Christian part of Prague's population, whether in regard to quarantine and medical measures, the ordered clean-up, burial taking place generally outside the city walls, restriction of mobility and trade and other regulations. Nevertheless, it is clear that the authorities dedicated to the Jews paid particular attention to antiplague measures. As Cohn demonstrated through these medical documents, in comparison to Italy in the sixteenth century, attempts at avoiding an epidemiological crisis in Bohemia – at least in terms of official procedures – were much more anti-Jewish in focus. The sources studied demonstrate that the measures planned were not implemented primarily in order to improve the living and other social conditions of the Jewish population themselves, but rather with the objective of eliminating the potential danger the situation could constitute for Prague's Christian majority.

The first plague deaths were reported in Bohemia in autumn 1679 in regions in South Bohemia. These were still, however, isolated individuals and small groups of the population. We have clear proof of the numbers of deaths in Prague for the period from April 1680, however the assumption for deaths through plague for the months prior also appears to be valid. During the next two months, the infection had spread to eight regions. The maximum mortality rate was measured in the summer months of 1680. During autumn, there was a gradual drop in individual plague deaths. During the winter months of 1680–81, the plague disappeared completely.[23]

The situation which Prague's Old Town found itself in during the plague in 1680 was described by town council members themselves as dismal. Many of the houses in the city were emptied of inhabitants twice or even three times over.[24] There was a particular reason for the town council's interest in specifying plague victims in terms of rough location and date of death and other specific criteria. This information was required not just by the Emperor and King, Leopold I, and senior government institutions, but also by the Archbishopric of Prague, to which the Catholic parishes in Prague belonged.

The Old Town Council used the information on Prague's abandoned houses in its statement to the Prague Archbishopric on 11 April 1681. In total, the plague resulted in the loss of 3,794 lives there in 1680. According to a

---

22   Cohn, *Cultures of Plague*, pp. 3, 251, 233. According to Cohn, Andreas Gabrielli, a doctor practising in Genoa, and Silvano Razzi, a Florentine theologian, are among the few Italian authors whose works are anti-Semitic in nature.

23   E. Čáňová, 'Mor v Čechách v roce 1680', *Sborník archivních prací*, 31 (1981), pp. 265–339 (especially p. 275). NAP, APA I., inventory No. 3753–4, signature C 142/6a–b, boxes 2229–30, unfoliated.

24   Ibid., inventory No. 3753, signature C 142/6a, box 2229, unfoliated.

postscript, the Old Town councillors sent the same information to Emperor Leopold I. Town councils operating in the two remaining parts of Prague, Prague New Town and the Lesser Quarter, also responded to the orders of the Prague Archbishopric dated 3 February 1681.[25] A total of 6,577 deceased can be counted, separated by place of funeral (a parish or around the lazaretto). Lesser Quarter councillors (also representing Hradčany) stated that a total of 1,681 people had succumbed to the plague in that part of the city. The number of plague victims given by the councillors of all the separate Prague towns reached a final total of 12,052 people, as is also confirmed by the preserved overall summary for Prague as a whole.[26] Prague, as the capital of the Kingdom of Bohemia, thus itself became the focus of the epidemic and lost almost a third of its population according to available estimates.[27]

II

The Archbishopric of Prague initiated a registration project to record the number and character of plague victims in an effort to document how many people entrusted to the care of the Catholic faith died, and to list their place of residence and personal characteristics. I believe that the inception and scope of this project may also be linked to the process of recatholicisation, which increased in intensity after the battle of Bílá Hora in 1618 and whose main objectives were achieved during the second half of the seventeenth century. The existence of a mortal disease in the country was unquestionable and the strengthening Catholic Church, whose power in the state was far from negligible at the time, wanted to understand the situation caused by the epidemiological crisis in the country. The appeal to conduct registration, addressed to the vicarages and parishes belonging to the administration of the Archbishopric of Prague, was made after incidence of the plague in the country had ended, specifically on 3 February 1681.

The councillors of Prague's towns were also required to send overviews of plague victim numbers to acting government authorities of Emperor Leopold I. There were two likely motivations for the monitoring system initiated by the state, which may be inferred from the changing character of state needs and interests in the course of the crisis. Decrees issued before the arrival of the main wave of the epidemic, and during its course and culmination, were to serve above all as a source of information about the character of the disease's spread, while also identifying its current scope. Particularly at the beginning

25   Ibid.
26   Ibid.
27   See section III.

Figure 8.1. Schematic map of Bohemia in 1680: regions according to approximate plague mortality (%)

Regions	Plague mortality (%)
Praha	30.1
Vltavský	16.1
Podbrdský	14.4
Kouřim	13.0
Slaný	6.8
Rakovník	6.5
Čáslav	3.1
Boleslav	1.5
Chrudim	1.3
Bechyně	1.2
Prácheň	1.2
Plzeň	0.1

of 1680, the decrees leading to the compilation of lists of the deceased can be considered a preventive measure of sorts, which would ideally have contained the epidemic in its early stages. As the intensity of the epidemic grew in 1680, the lists would have provided a current overview of the situation in the country and distinguished infected and uninfected locations. The second reason for which the ruling authorities introduced the monitoring system was the need to analyse the size and character of the deceased population in terms of their obligations within the state tax system. This phase of the monitoring system was approached only after the plague ended in 1681.

In the second half of February and during March 1681, reports from individual dioceses and parishes in Bohemia were received by the Prague Archbishopric.[28] They provide a detailed summary of the portions of the population that died of the plague during the summer and autumn of 1680 (and also partially autumn 1679 and winter 1680/81), divided by region, diocese and parish, town or village. In accordance with instructions, church administrators of separate parishes recorded not just the total number of plague

---

28   Ibid., inventory No. 3753–4, signature C 142/6a–b, boxes 2229–30, unfoliated.

deaths, but also partially the structure of the deceased population. Plague registers frequently mentioned the names of the deceased people as well as their demographic profile, for instance: gender, approximate age, symptoms and length of illness, marital and family status, and social rank. The reports on numbers of dead were prepared as tables or structured lists.[29] The plague registers from the year 1681 produced at the Prague Archbishopric's bidding contain data about the capital city of Prague and eleven regions. This means that approximately two thirds of the territory of Bohemia is covered by this source.[30] The information acquired relates to around three quarters of the vicarages that existed within the territory of the regions from which lists were sent. These lists of the dead cover on average almost 70 per cent of parishes in each vicarage from which the reports were sent. This value should be considered the absolute minimum.[31]

III

We can achieve a picture of the plague dynamics by considering estimates of the population living in different regions. Data in confessional lists of 1678 were used as a basis for determining the size of the population living in individual regions, to which the estimated number of children not of the age of confession was added (approximately 30 per cent of the population).[32]

29   The source materials mentioned are known in Czech historiography as a result of the study of Eliška Čáňová from 1981: Čáňová, 'Mor v Čechách v roce 1680', pp. 265–339. The author added the abbreviated edition of the examined documents to the paper, which gives a brief overview of the course of the plague in 1680, and this became an alternative source of information that supplemented my research. However, Čáňová created a simplified version of the demographic information provided by the plague registers. For these reasons, a study of archived materials is essential.

30   Due to the amount of extant material, the analysis presented in this chapter is based solely on plague registers from the data collected by the church authorities. The next phase of the grant project will take into account the systematic analysis of the list of deceased persons, initiated by state institutions. The grant project as a whole will use the parish death records, but these will be presented as another partial output.

31   The identity of the parishes recorded in the plague lists was checked according to the parish organisation that operated in 1678.

32   J.V. Šimák, Zpovědní seznamy arcidiecése pražské z let 1671–1725. Boleslavsko, Kouřimsko, Chrudimsko, Čáslavsko (Praha, 1909), pp. 157, 383, 475, 491, 657, 673, 681, 707; J.V. Šimák, Zpovědní seznamy arcidiecése pražské z let 1671–1725. Bechyňsko, Vltavsko, Podbrdsko, Prácheňsko (Praha, 1928–29 and 1931), pp. 175, 303, 381, 475, 487, 493; J.V. Šimák, Zpovědní seznamy arcidiecése pražské z let 1671–1725. Plzeňsko a Loketsko, Žatecko, Slánsko, Rakovnicko. Praha s okolím. Kladsko (Praha, 1935 and 1937–38), pp. 161, 173, 185, 197, 493, 537; O. Placht, Lidnatost a společenská skladba českého státu v 16.–18. století (Praha, 1957), pp. 290–1. For Prague, records of confession lists have been preserved so sporadically that other sources were used to estimate the population (see below). Šimák provides the data on confession

Table 8.1. Estimates of plague mortality within the regions of Bohemia in 1679–80

Regions	Plague mortality (%)	Population estimates (1678)	No. of deaths
Praha	30.1	40,000	12,052
Vltavský	16.1	24,813	4,005
Podbrdský	14.4	21,600	3,120
Kouřim	13.0	74,676	9,715
Slaný	6.8	34,307	2,332
Rakovník	6.5	16,340	1,066
Čáslav	3.1	63,377	1,950
Boleslav	1.5	110,254	1,633
Chrudim	1.3	99,956	1,306
Bechyně	1.2	176,680	2,068
Prácheň	1.2	92,621	1,086
Plzeň	0.1	132,141	129

Subsequently, the percentage of deaths compared to the population size in individual regions was determined (see Table 8.1). We can see how in Bohemia, the Central Bohemia region headed up by Prague is profiled as the region that was overwhelmingly the worst affected by the plague epidemic. An estimate of the size of the population living in Prague in the mid seventeenth century is based on studying the *Berní rula* (Taxation Rule, 1654), which is the first complete inventory of tax liabilities of the Bohemian population, and comes to a total of 33,800 people (of whom 7,800 were members of the Jewish community).[33] Higher values for the estimated population size were determined when data on numbers of births registered by Prague's registries were used.[34] In order to determine an estimated size of the population living in Prague in 1679–80, we use the rough data of 40,000 people at the end of the 1670s. The death of 12,052 Prague citizens, then, represented a loss to the

lists in Plzeň and Loket regions together. As he also gives detailed information on vicarages in Plzeň region, we take into account only the records from confession lists coming from vicarages in this region.

33 L. Fialová, 'Vývoj obyvatelstva Prahy v letech 1650–1800 na základě matrik', *Historická demografie*, 30 (2006), pp. 219–76 (especially p. 234).

34 Ibid., p. 235. The sum of 39,520 people as an approximate size of the population of Prague in the decade 1671–80 corresponds to a crude birth rate expressed as 45 per thousand.

political, economic and administrative centre of the Kingdom of Bohemia of up to 30.1 per cent of the population.

The loss of almost a third of Prague's population is not out of step with the course and nature of plague epidemics in other European cities in the early modern period. Sutherland provides an overview of plague mortality in London during the largest epidemics in the course of the sixteenth and seventeenth centuries. On the basis of the bills of mortality he argues that the Great Plague in London in 1665 killed 17.6 per cent of the population, whereas some of the previous epidemiological crises even took 20 or more per cent of the total population of London (24.0 per cent in 1563, 22.6 per cent in 1603 and 20.1 in 1625). According to Sutherland's results, the London plagues in 1593 (14.3 per cent), 1578 (7.8 per cent) and 1636 (7.5 per cent) showed a lower mortality rate.[35] According to Wrightson, the 'catastrophic mortality' that accompanied the 1636 plague epidemic in Newcastle was responsible for a roughly 47 per cent fall in the city's population.[36] Wrightson speaks of this mortality crisis as 'the most devastating cull experienced by any English city in this period', which confirms the conviction of Shrewsbury made in 1970 that it was one of the severest plague epidemics ever to have afflicted an English city.[37] Scott and Duncan state in *Biology of Plagues* that the largest plague epidemics of the sixteenth and seventeenth centuries were linked to an urban environment and their occurrence was affected by the population density. Plague mortality often reached values ranging from 30 to 50 per cent. Their own research confirmed that between the years 1596–98, about half of the population of the market town of Penrith situated in north-west England was wiped out.[38] Scott and Duncan also determined that somewhere between 33 and 38 per cent of the population died in the Derbyshire village and parish of Eyam during the plague in 1665/6.[39] Cohn examines the plague crisis in 1575–78 in Italy on the basis of the plague tracts from Milan, Padua, Venice and Verona, which show that one third of the population succumbed to the disease in Milan. In Venice, plague victims made up one quarter to one third of the population.[40] Alexander estimated the population losses

---

35 I. Sutherland, 'When Was the Great Plague? Mortality in London, 1563–1665', in D.V. Glass and R. Revelle (eds), *Population and Social Change* (London, 1972), pp. 287–320; P. Slack, *The Impact of Plague in Tudor and Stuart England* (London, 1985), pp. 150–1.
36 K. Wrightson, *Ralph Tailor's Summer*, p. 38.
37 Ibid. See also J.F.D. Shrewsbury, *A History of Bubonic Plague in the British Isles* (Cambridge, 1970), p. 384.
38 Scott and Duncan, *Biology of Plagues*, pp. 146, 389–90. The high mortality at Penrith in 1596 was also caused by famine, but there were substantial population losses even in the two years following (1597–98) caused by the plague epidemic.
39 Ibid., pp. 279–80.
40 Cohn, *Cultures of Plague*, pp. 21, 116, 125, 167.

in Moscow during the year of the plague in 1771. The sources he used to stipulate plague mortality mention 20 per cent losses in the population. Using an alternative source type, this share exceeds even 30 per cent.[41]

The proximity of the capital city of Prague, which over the course of the epidemic lost almost a third of its population, had an impact on the epidemiology of surrounding regions in Central Bohemia, which suffered a loss of life of up to one sixth. Most affected were the areas lying south and south-east of Prague, that is, in the direction from which the plague had arrived from Austria and Moravia. If we consider the number of deaths recorded compared to an estimated figure for the population living in these regions, we discover that immediately after Prague, the largest death rate was seen in the region of Vltavský (16.1 per cent), Podbrdský (14.4 per cent) and Kouřim (13.0 per cent). Regions lying close to Prague in the west (the regions of Slaný and Rakovník) were less affected by the plague, although even here the death rate came to almost 7 per cent.

From a geographical point of view, the northern part of Central Bohemia can be characterised in summary as lowland country on the junction of the two longest Bohemian rivers: the Vltava and the Elbe. The landscape of the southern part of Central Bohemia, from where the Vltava River flows from the south towards Prague, can be considered a basin region with the appearance of gentle upland areas. The geographic profile of Central Bohemia (especially the lack of high mountains), and also the presence of the capital city and copious trade routes was an important factor that led to the marked spread of the plague infection within this territory.

Those regions that neighboured the Central Bohemia regions, and stretched out further towards the borders with surrounding countries, were much more distant from Prague and its surroundings. This geographic distance from the epidemic's centre reduced the possibility that the plague affected such regions to its full extent. The population living in eastern, northern, southern and western Bohemia were spared the worst impact of plague, where it killed up to 3 per cent of the population. This maximum was achieved in East Bohemia in the Čáslav region (3.1 per cent). Together with the neighbouring region of Chrudim (1.3 per cent), this was the main communication route from the infected Moravia, and consequently from Vienna. In the parts of North Bohemia for which we have records (the region of Boleslav), an average of just 1.5 per cent of the population succumbed to the plague. In South Bohemia, the likelihood of dying from the plague was also very low, as seen in the 1.2 per cent loss of the total population. It is, furthermore, interesting to note that this same value was determined for both regions lying in South Bohemia, for the regions of Bechyně and Prácheň. The

41   J.T. Alexander, *Bubonic Plague in Early Modern Russia: Public Health and Urban Disaster* (Baltimore and London, 1980), pp. 257–8, 260, 302.

region of Plzeň in western Bohemia was almost spared the harmful consequences of the epidemic (at just 0.1 per cent population loss), which is why
government offices were moved from Prague to this area. In comparison with
the low-lying territory of Central Bohemia, the surrounding regions are at
higher elevations without the presence of lowland areas. In these regions,
there are some basins, but also extensive belts of highland and mountains.
These mountains are mainly located in close proximity to the borders with
other states, or Moravia as another state within the Bohemian Crown. In
addition to the distance from the capital city, the geographical nature of
these regions also resulted in a sparser network of roads and trade routes and
particular isolation of some localities. It can be assumed, then, that there is a
relationship between the low proportion of plague victims in regions outside
Central Bohemia and the geographical profile of these areas described and
the difficult-to-traverse terrain. Only further research will bring clear conclusions here, however.

These summaries of the number of deaths through plague in all vicarages
and regions in Bohemia that are recorded in the reports prepared for the
Archbishopric of Prague correspond to a total of 40,462 dead. Can we
determine the approximate proportion of the recorded numbers of deaths
and the size of the population living in the second half of the seventeenth
century? The *Berní rula* gives an estimate of around one million people
living in Bohemia, and according to confessional lists made every year before
Easter, we can estimate the size of the population (after inflating by 30 per
cent to account for children below the age of confession) in Bohemia in 1672
at 1,267,241 people, and in 1682 at 1,408,531 people.[42] If we take Placht's
research into account based on confessional lists, we can give a rough value
of 1,400,000 as the size of the population in Bohemia around the year 1680.
The proportion of documented numbers of deaths as a result of the plague
compared to the approximate size of the population then comes out at 2.9
per cent, but we can assume that the proportion of the population to die as a
result of the plague must have been higher. A third of Bohemia's territory did
not fall under the Archbishopric of Prague.[43] Moreover, there are no lists of
the dead preserved for the region of Žatec, and within the other regions, data
is missing for individual parishes. In reconstructing death registers, Maur and
Fialová came to the conclusion that the natural population growth in Bohemia

---

42   Placht, *Lidnatost*, p. 316; L. Dokoupil, L. Fialová, E. Maur and L. Nesládková, *Přirozená
měna obyvatelstva českých zemí v 17. a 18. století* (Praha, 1999), p. 87; L. Fialová et al., *Dějiny
obyvatelstva českých zemí* (Praha, 1996), p. 117.
43   Two bishoprics lying in the north (Bishopric of Litoměřice, 1655) and east (Bishopric of
Hradec Králové, 1664) of Bohemia did not come under the Archbishopric of Prague. Also not
subject to the Archbishopric of Prague was the area lying around the town of Cheb in the very
west of the country and the territory of Kłodzko lying near Bohemia's northern borders.

in 1680 was positive, but nevertheless very low – just 450 people. The evidence that there was a mortality and epidemiological crisis is also illustrated by the fact that over the whole period of 1651–1700 with the exception of 1680, the natural annual population growth did not fall below 16,924 people, and on average reached a level of 25,738 people (including the plague year of 1680, the annual natural population growth comes to 25,232 people).[44]

IV

The extensive evidence contained within the sources allows us to document the plague's impact on the demographic structure of Bohemia in great detail. This is best illustrated in a case study on the progress of the plague in the vicarage of Poděbrady situated in Central Bohemia. As far as ecclesiastical division is concerned, the vicarage of Poděbrady was part of the Kouřim region.[45] The centre of the vicarage, the town of Poděbrady on the river Elbe, was located around 50 kilometres east of Prague. It was a flat, lowland region with a large area of cultivated agricultural land, but was also close to the main trade routes in the country. The Poděbrady vicarage included a total of 15 parishes and represented a total of 133 locations altogether (towns and villages).[46] Data on numbers of deaths are described according to these individual locations, which are the smallest land units in the lists. In keeping with general findings on the hard-hit areas of Central Bohemia, we can see high plague mortality in Poděbrady in 1680.[47] Altogether, there are records of a total of 3,902 deceased.[48] Table 8.2 gives exact figures.

The value of the sources, which include the church lists of plague victims, lies in allowing us to differentiate the deceased population in terms of gender and age (see Table 8.3). The age criteria for the deceased are specified in the studied sources as following: adults, children (up to the age 14 according to the

---

44   Dokoupil et al., Přirozená měna, pp. 123–4.

45   According to the administrative disposal of Bohemia (as the map shows), the town of Poděbrady belonged to the Hradec region.

46   NAP, APA I., inventory No. 3753–4, signature C 142/6a–b, boxes 2229–30, unfoliated. J.V. Šimák, Zpovědní seznamy arcidiecése pražské z let 1671–1725. Boleslavsko, Kouřimsko, Chrudimsko, Čáslavsko (Praha, 1909), pp. 358ff.

47   Note that the Kouřim region, which included the Poděbrady vicarage according to the ecclesiastical division, was one of the worst-affected areas following the capital Prague. Church lists estimate the number of plague victims in the Kouřim region at 9,715.

48   The original church lists for the Kolín parish (town, village and imperial palace) include records of deaths from the plague in 1679. Numerical figures relating to this period were not taken into account in this microanalysis. This case study also did not include the Jews who died of the plague in the Kolín parish in 1680.

Table 8.2. Number of plague victims within the parishes of the vicarage of Poděbrady in 1680

Parish names	Type of parish seat	Plague mortality (%)	Population estimates (1678)	Deaths
Kolín	town	33.6	3,543	1,191
Sluštice	village	31.1	2,079	646
Solopisky	village	21.9	1,366	299
Kouřim	town	15.1	2,431	366
Dobřichov	village	12.6	1,121	141
Sadská	small town	12.1	1,770	215
Skramník	village	10.5	1,781	187
Poděbrady	town	7.7	3,886	298
Nymburk	town	7.3	2,659	193
Plaňany	small town	6.3	1,389	88
Český Brod	town	4.6	1,350	62
Zásmuky	small town	2.1	1,289	27
Kolín (domain)	village	–	–	51
Nová Lhota	village	–	–	15
Břístaví	village	–	–	123

prevailing customs of early modern Czech society) and unspecified persons.[49] For the total number of deaths for which the gender can be specified (3,788 people, 97 per cent), just under half of the dead were male and 51.1 per cent were female. How does this finding relate to the normal gender balance within the population of Bohemia in the seventeenth century? According to research on the demographic structure of the population of Bohemia in the mid seventeenth century, it was found that the proportion of females was greater than that of males, particularly in the 15 to 29 years age group with a ratio of 3:2. Moreover, a higher proportion of women were recorded in towns and cities in comparison with rural areas. For the population in the 30 or above age category, the predominance of females was no longer so clear, and

49 Two additional age groups are detailed in regard to the predictive value of the sources, which in a small number of cases defines the group of children between 8 and 14 years, and a group of unmarried youth.

Table 8.3. Plague victims within the vicarage of Poděbrady in 1680, according to gender and age ratio

Groups	No. of deaths	All groups (%)	Gender specified (%)	Male (%)	Female (%)	Age specified (%)	Adults (%)	Children (%)
Adult male	773	19.8	20.4	41.7	–	19.9	48.4	–
Adult female	788	20.2	20.8	–	40.7	20.3	49.3	–
Boys up to age 14	1,073	27.5	28.3	57.9	–	27.6	–	46.9
Girls up to age 14	1,143	29.3	30.2	–	59.1	29.4	–	49.9
Children	11	0.3	–	–	–	0.3	–	0.5
Children up to age 8	62	1.6	–	–	–	1.6	–	2.7
Unmarried youth	37	0.9	–	–	–	0.9	2.3	–
Male	8	0.2	0.2	0.4	–	–	–	–
Female	3	0.1	0.1	–	0.2	–	–	–
Persons	4	0.1	–	–	–	–	–	–
Total (No.)	3,902	3,902	3,788	1,854	1,934	3,887	1,598	2,289
Gender specified vs. total (%)	–	–	97.1	–	–	–	–	–
Male vs. female (%)	–	–	–	48.9	51.1	–	–	–
Age specified vs. total (%)	–	–	–	–	–	99.6	–	–
Adults vs. children (%)	–	–	–	–	–	–	41.1	58.9

from 40 years of age the proportion of men in the population was higher than women. Yet boys also made up the majority of births.[50]

Research into the gender-specific mortality within the plague epidemics in the early modern period in some other countries have various findings. Scott and Duncan submitted a brief but illustrative overview of the results of early modern epidemics in England: 'Women were said to be more susceptible to plague than men in parts of Europe, although apparently the reverse was seen in England.'[51] Nevertheless, Slack refers to a higher number of female deaths compared with male deaths in the epidemics in Barnstaple and Chelmsford, and Stratford-upon-Avon. A predominance of female victims is also demonstrated by Scott and Duncan for the plague at Penrith in 1597–98 (roughly 58 per cent women compared with 42 per cent men). Research on plague epidemics in England undertaken by M.F. Hollingsworth, T.H. Hollingsworth and Hirst in contrast documents a higher proportion of males among plague victims. Schofield and Bradley acquired data on the basis of their research of the famines in Colyton and Eyam, showing an equal proportion of male and female plague victims.[52] Höhl found an almost equal gender ratio of adult deaths through plague in Hildesheim, Germany, in 1609–10 (roughly 49 per cent men and 51 per cent women).[53] According to Zapnik, significantly greater numbers of adult women died compared with adult men during the plague of 1710 in another former Hanseatic city in north Germany, Stralsund (the data give a proportion of roughly 61 per cent women compared with 39 per cent men).[54] The predominance of women over men in the part of the population that succumbed to the plague was demonstrated also by Frandsen in the case of the Copenhagen parishes in 1711. As he says, in the Vor Frue parish the predominance of the female element is apparent among both adults and children (55 per cent of women compared with a 45 per cent representation of men).[55] The gender ratio for adult deaths in Holmen's parish (Skibskirkegården cemetery) was similar. For children, the predominance of females was even more marked (65 per cent of girls compared to 35 per cent of boys).[56] According to vital statistics for Moscow Guberniia, facilitated

---

50   E. Maur, 'Problémy demografické struktury Čech v polovině 17. století', *Československý časopis historický*, 19 (1971), pp. 839–70 (especially pp. 847–50); Fialová et al., *Dějiny obyvatelstva*, p. 106.

51   Scott and Duncan, *Biology of Plagues*, p. 139.

52   Ibid.

53   M. Höhl, *Die Pest in Hildesheim. Krankheit als Krisenfaktor im städtischen Leben des Mittelalters und der Frühen Neuzeit (1350–1750)* (Hildesheim, 2002), p. 302.

54   J. Zapnik, *Pest und Krieg im Ostseeraum, Der 'Schwarze Tod' in Stralsund während des Großen Nordischen Krieges (1700–1721)* (Hamburg, 2007), p. 241.

55   Frandsen, *The Last Plague*, p. 358.

56   Ibid., p. 370.

by Alexander, the gender ratio for the dead in the plague year of 1771 was mostly balanced, with a slight predominance of male victims (52 per cent).[57]

As can be seen, a balanced gender ratio can be found in many places in Europe for victims of early modern plague epidemics, but a predominance of one or the other gender is sometimes observed. The examples detailed suggest that where the ratio was not balanced, a predominance of female plague victims was more marked (values of around 55 per cent to 60 per cent female victims). As stated above, the gender profile of plague victims in the region studied in Bohemia is one of the European regions with an almost balanced representation of male and female dead. The slight predominance of female victims is somewhat more marked for the group of children (48.4 per cent of boys compared with 51.6 per cent of girls) than for the group of adults (49.5 per cent of men compared with 50.5 per cent of women). Although women made up the majority of the living population for the 15 to 29 years age group, in contrast for those who died from plague there was a slight majority of women outside this age group too (in the group of children up to 14 years, and also among adults among whom those older than 30 years were also naturally counted).

The basic division of plague victims by their age group is available in 99.6 per cent of cases. Almost 60 per cent of the population who succumbed to the epidemic within the vicarage of Poděbrady were children. Research into the demographic structure of the Bohemian population in the mid seventeenth century all comes to the conclusion that roughly 30 per cent of the living population were children.[58] We can see that the proportion of child deaths in the vicarage of Poděbrady is almost double the proportion of children in the population. In Scott and Duncan's book, the age structure of plague victims is also noted in the context of research conducted by mainly English researchers: 'It is generally agreed that those aged in their mid-40s and above were less likely to die during a plague outbreak, which might suggest a previous exposure and immunity to the disease.'[59] Their own research of plague victims at Penrith in 1597–98 does not document a marked predominance of any age groups, although the authors concede to a lower mortality for those aged over 45 years. M.F. Hollingsworth and T.H. Hollingsworth demonstrate a higher mortality for those aged 4–44 in the parish of St Botolph's without Bishopsgate in London. Scott and Duncan also note the results of Hirst's research, which deem those aged 10–35 to be the group most affected, while children aged 5–10 were least susceptible to plague deaths. Pollitzer deems adolescents and adults no older than 45 years to be the group

---

57   Alexander, *Bubonic Plague*, pp. 258–9.
58   Maur, 'Problémy demografické struktury Čech v polovině 17. století', pp. 844–6.
59   Scott and Duncan, *Biology of Plagues*, pp. 138–9.

most susceptible to the plague.[60] In contrast, Zapnik demonstrates a high proportion of children (49 per cent of children compared with 51 per cent of adult men and women) in the plague deaths in Stralsund, Germany, in 1710.[61] According to Höhl's data, the structure of plague victims in Hildesheim in 1609–10 also demonstrates a higher number of victims of a young age: 28.3 per cent of adults, 27.3 per cent of children, 34.1 per cent of sons and daughters, 8.7 per cent servants and 4 per cent of unspecified persons.[62] Absolute numbers of plague deaths in Holmen's parish in Copenhagen in 1711, published by Frandsen, again testify to a high proportion of children among the dead. In percentage terms, the proportion of children here was 51 per cent, with the remaining 49 per cent being adult victims. In another of the Copenhagen parishes (Vor Frue parish), in contrast, adults were predominant (71 per cent) over children (29 per cent).[63] Alexander describes the age structure of males who died from the plague in Moscow Guberniia in 1771 as follows: roughly half of the plague victims (48.7 per cent) were adolescents and adult men aged 11–50. From figures for the absolute number of deaths in various age categories, we can determine that the proportion of children aged 1–10 of the total number of dead here in 1771 came to 20 per cent.[64]

When we summarise the results of the research mentioned, the proportion of children among those who died of the plague varies depending on location. A proportion of roughly 20 to 60 per cent of child victims appears to be marked, even if we consider the possible distortion of results through any regional differences in determining the age range for children. In relation to research of age-specific mortality in the vicarage of Poděbrady in Bohemia, we can state that the almost 60 per cent proportion of children among the dead is so far one of the highest to have been determined in European regions.

V

The sources used in this research offer valuable evidence of historic demographic processes in early modern Central Europe, comparable in some ways to the well-known 'bills of mortality' created in London and its immediate surroundings from the mid fifteenth century. These lists were to inform state authorities and the population of the numbers of deceased (especially plague victims) up to a certain date and place. In international discussions, historians usually term this sort of data collection so-called

60   Ibid.
61   Zapnik, *Pest und Krieg*, p. 241.
62   Höhl, *Die Pest in Hildesheim*, p. 299.
63   Frandsen, *The Last Plague*, pp. 358, 370.
64   Alexander, *Bubonic Plague*, pp. 258–9.

'early warning systems' monitoring the progress of an epidemic in a country. These 'bills of mortality' were created in printed form and on a weekly basis. A summarised annual list was published at the end of each year and included causes of death.[65]

Traditionally, the Western European historical community has paid a lot of attention to London's 'bills of mortality'. In particular, there should be mentioned Slack's contribution to the topic of state government and information usage in seventeenth-century England.[66] As well as the most well-known English bills of mortality, similar sources from other places in Europe have also been studied. These include work by Carlo M. Cipolla, who studied the bills of mortality from Florence.[67] The impact of these bills of mortality on the history of population, statistics and epidemiology in west Europe has been extensive. John Graunt (1620–74) used a series of London's bills of mortality for his famous book, *Natural and Political Observations Made upon the Bills of Mortality*, in 1662.[68] English historiography's interest in Graunt's work illustrates his importance as the founder of demographics and one of the pioneers in the field of epidemiology, as well as statistics and probability. Graunt's friend, William Petty, one of the founders of political economy, followed on from his work in developing political arithmetic in a number of papers.[69] Graunt's research also contributed to the work of the Huygens brothers, Lodewijk and Christiaan, from Holland, who used it in their study of probability theory.[70] Study of the archive material to date does not suggest that the Czech 'bills of mortality' were subjected to systematic statistical analysis when they were created by Czech church or state institutions. Nevertheless, more detailed results are expected from the planned study of sources preserved in the centre of the Habsburg monarchy, in Vienna, where data on the extent of the plague may have been sent.

Prevention of the spread of plague in the early modern period generally involved interventions in the economic sphere such as banning markets from

65   A. Rusnock, *Vital Accounts: Quantifying Health and Population in Eighteenth-Century England and France* (Cambridge, 2008), pp. 18ff; S. Usherwood, 'The Plague of London, 1665', *History Today*, 21:5 (1971), pp. 316–21.
66   P. Slack, 'Government and Information in Seventeenth Century England', *Past & Present*, 184 (2004), pp. 33–40. See also P. Slack, 'Measuring the National Wealth in Seventeenth-Century England', *Economic History Review*, 57 (2004), pp. 607–35.
67   C.M. Cipolla, 'The Bills of Mortality of Florence', *Population Studies*, 32 (1978), pp. 543–8.
68   W.F. Willcox (ed.), *John Graunt, Natural and Political Observations Made Upon the Bills of Mortality* (Baltimore, 1939); Rusnock, *Vital Accounts*, pp. 15–39; I. Hacking, *The Emergence of Probability: A Philosophical Study of Early Ideas about Probability, Induction and Statistical Inference* (Cambridge, 2006), pp. 102–10; A. Hald, *A History of Probability and Statistics and Their Applications before 1750* (New York, 1990), pp. 81–105.
69   Rusnock, *Vital Accounts*, pp. 15–39; Hacking, *The Emergence of Probability*, pp. 102–10; Hald, *A History of Probability*, pp. 104–5.
70   Hald, *A History of Probability*, pp. 106–15.

being held in towns and villages, which blocked trading from occurring in the country. In order to reduce the spread of infection, outsiders were restricted from entering the gates of cities, or from travelling into the country. The restrictions in movement affected not just goods, but also traders and other people travelling beyond their country's borders.[71]

Another issue is the level of mortality crisis and its consequences for the economic vitality of the state. The acquisition of numerous details about the deceased is particularly relevant here, based on specific regions or locations and a specific date. A no less important finding is the structure of the deceased population in terms of different demographic criteria (gender, age, family and social status). From a purely economic perspective, all these findings give us a picture of the specifications of the process that occurred during the epidemic, that is, to the fall in the number of productive contributors in the country. For this reason, the data provided by the Czech plague registers is most valuable, data that was initiated by state authorities (and church institutions to a lesser extent). This is because the system for collecting data about the deceased was not just carried out to monitor the progress of the epidemic in space and time, but also (and perhaps above all) to document the situation in the country in terms of the numbers of deceased and living contributors. On this basis, the governing institutions could, for example decide on levels of taxation for the population.

It is extremely important that this point is not merely considered at a theoretical level. It is noteworthy that only a very small proportion of the Czech plague registers contain some details regarding the property situation of the deceased, or even the quantitative data related to the tax collected from specific persons (differentiated by name).[72] These records mention among others the amount of tax to be collected, which, de facto, represents the tax arrears for the specific person. As well as the number of taxpayers, the population able to work was also important information for the state. At least on the basis of the case study carried out on the Czech plague registers, the greatest level of mortality can be attributed to the youngest age group including not just children but also servants.[73] This aspect should also be considered in terms of the work and economic potential of the new generation of the Czech population at the end of the seventeenth century.

On the basis of the actual level of knowledge of the Czech plague registers, I expect that, at least on the theoretical level, the methods used for monitoring the epidemiological crisis in Bohemia in 1680 matched the procedures known in Western Europe in the early modern period. The disease information

71 See Section II.
72 For instance, NAP, SM, inventory No. 842, signature E 2/6, box 659, fols 43–50, 157–65.
73 Compare ibid., signature E 2/8, box 660, fols 57–60.

system and plague registers suggest some sort of 'modern' rationality existing in the country in which, at the same time, the 'second serfdom' represented the dominant economic system.[74] Moreover, there seems to be one specific aspect of the Czech plague registers that overreaches the scope of London's 'bills of mortality' and the method of data collection used in England in the early modern period. This is the extensive geographic scope of Czech plague registers in comparison with the 'bills of mortality' covering only the City of London and its surroundings. From a geographical perspective, the Czech plague registers extend not only over the capital city, but also nearer (the regions of Slaný, Boleslav or Kouřim) and farther (the region of Plzeň) regions located at distances of hundreds of kilometres from Prague.

To conclude, I would like to emphasise the importance of the Czech plague lists in broadening our knowledge of the crisis management conducted by the church and state institutions using data on individual identities of the thousands of plague victims. Moreover, on this basis we can obtain detailed information on contagion dynamics and specific patterns of plague mortality in early modern Bohemia. These results may contribute to European historical discussion about the plague issues that suffers from a lack of systematic research on plague epidemics in Central Europe. The mentioned documents should not be perceived as a sort of church register of deaths, as this was usually put together with birth and marriage registers every year. The plague registers are authentic documents created in connection with clerical or government attempts to limit upcoming crises or monitor the actual situation. In short, the early modern Czech plague registers are unique sources whose worth is reflected in their technical precision as well as in the huge geographic field of interest they supply.

---

74 A. Klein and S. Ogilvie, 'Occupational Structure in the Czech Lands Under the Second Serfdom', *Economic History Review*, early view online (2015); A. Klein, 'The Institutions of the "Second Serfdom" and Economic Efficiency: Review of the Existing Evidence for Bohemia', in S. Cavaciocchi (ed.), *Schiavitù e servaggio nell'economia europea. Secc. XI–XVIII [Serfdom and Slavery in the European Economy. 11th–18th Centuries]* (Firenze, 2014), pp. 59–81; S. Ogilvie and J. Edwards, 'Women and the "Second Serfdom": Evidence from Early Modern Bohemia', *Journal of Economic History*, 60 (2000), pp. 961–4; S. Ogilvie, 'The Economic World of the Bohemian Serf: Economic Concepts, Preferences, and Constraints on the Estate of Friedland, 1583–1692', *Economic History Review*, 54 (2001), pp. 430–53.

9

'Two Words … Good Sanitation': Colonial Medical Responses to the Cholera Epidemics of 1865 and 1888 in Malta[1]

JOSETTE DUNCAN

On 28 June 1865 the vessel *Wyvern* landed in Malta from Alexandria, carrying 302 passengers. All passengers disembarked in one lazaretto building, among them a man on the verge of collapse. He died instantly on the landing jetty. Another eleven passengers were treated for Asiatic cholera, eight of whom succumbed to it in the subsequent days. These were the first few deaths of Asiatic cholera reported to have been imported to Malta in the 1865 epidemic.[2] It was a common story, certainly among countries with thriving sea ports. Since 1813, the Maltese islands had been under British dominion, and for several decades during the nineteenth century they served as an entrepôt depot for trading vessels in the British Empire. Malta's harbours were crucial to trading vessels from the Mediterranean, Europe and British Asia, as well as to the British military and navy, with thousands of soldiers based in the Maltese garrisons. Under British dominion, Malta was transformed into a 'fortress colony'. It became an indispensable British possession for safeguarding the British Navy in the Grand Harbour; for enforcing maritime quarantine on vessels, troops, passengers and goods; and as a coaling station for vessels travelling further east.[3]

---

1 Salvatore Pisani's last recommendation in his 1887 report was: 'prophylactic measures for the future – I may sum them up in two words – GOOD SANITATION.' Salvatore L. Pisani, *Report on the Cholera Epidemic in the Year 1887* (Malta, 1888), p. 21 [his emphasis].

2 John Sutherland, *Report on the Sanitary Condition of Malta and Gozo with Reference to the Epidemic Cholera in the Year 1865* (London, 1865), pp. 18–19.

3 Henry Frendo, *Party Politics in an Island Fortress: The Maltese Experiment* (Malta, 1979); Henry Frendo, *Europe and Empire: Culture, Politics and Identity in Malta and the Mediterranean (1912–1946)* (Malta, 2012); Robert Holland, *Blue-Water Empire: The British in the Mediterranean since 1800* (London, 2012); Desmond Gregory, *Malta, Britain, and the*

Its geographical position and trading importance made the Maltese islands vulnerable to bouts of contagious diseases like cholera, which visited Europe from time to time. Ever since Asa Briggs's appeal to historians to investigate cholera in 1961, the historiography of cholera in England, Europe, India and around the world has grown.[4] Yet these historical works went further than simply investigating cholera as an epidemic. Historians began to explore not only cholera but also the impact that pandemics and infectious diseases had on the historical transformation of societies. Historians such as Charles Rosenberg, Anthony S. Wohl, Dorothy Porter, Richard Evans and Margaret Pelling have investigated the social, economic and political responses to contagious diseases like cholera in order to explore how changes and reforms were both caused and determined by epidemics.[5] Others such as R.J. Morris and Michael Durey studied cholera's impact on 'social cohesion'. Morris claimed that studying cholera was to 'watch the trust and cooperation between different parts of the society strained to the utmost'.[6] Yet this view was contested by historians like Margaret Pelling who suggested that the impact of cholera was far less momentous than tuberculosis or fevers. She concluded that cholera had almost no lasting impact on the political history of the countries.[7]

These works were the catalysts for the expansion of the historiography of public health where historians explored the different aspects of epidemics: social classes, the medical profession, religious organisations and politics. Furthermore, the historiography of cholera in the nineteenth century widened its scope beyond Europe and England. The study of cholera expanded in the 1980s to include works on how epidemics could influence the developments of imperialism and colonialism. In particular, India (where cholera was

European Powers, 1793–1815 (London, 1996); Dennis Angelo Castillo, The Maltese Cross: A Strategic History of Malta (Westport, 2006); Stefan Goodwin, Malta, Mediterranean Bridge (Westport, 2002).

4 Asa Briggs, 'Cholera and Society in the Nineteenth Century', Past & Present, 19 (1961), pp. 76–96.

5 Charles Rosenberg, 'Cholera in Nineteenth-Century Europe: A Tool for Social and Economic Analysis', Comparative Studies in Society and History, 8 (1966), pp. 452–63; Richard J. Evans, 'Epidemics and Revolutions: Cholera in Nineteenth-Century Europe', Past & Present, 120 (1988), pp. 123–46; Anne Hardy, 'Cholera, Quarantine and the English Preventive System, 1850–1895', Medical History Journal, 37 (1993), pp. 250–69; Dorothy Porter, Health, Civilization and the State: A History of Public Health from Ancient to Modern Times (London, 1999), pp. 1–9; Margaret Pelling, Cholera, Fever and English Medicine 1825–1865 (Oxford, 1978); Anthony S. Wohl, Endangered Lives: Public Health in Victorian Britain (Cambridge, 1983); Warwick Anderson, Colonial Pathologies: American Tropical Medicine, Race and Hygiene in the Philippines (Durham, NC, 2006); Charles L. Briggs and Clara Mantini-Briggs, Stories in the Time of Cholera: Racial Profiling during a Medical Nightmare (Berkeley, 2003).

6 As quoted in Evans, 'Epidemics and Revolutions', p. 126.

7 Ibid., pp. 126–7.

endemic) received increasing attention from historians.[8] More recently, Pamela Gilbert's work on Britain showed how cultural histories of cholera could illustrate the different meanings acquired by cholera in particular national contexts.[9] Peter Baldwin's classic work on the role of contagion explains how cholera influenced modern political institutions.[10] Recently *Cholera: The Biography* by Christopher Hamlin seems to have aimed at a new agenda, demanding that historians 'trace continuities and discontinuities in archaeologies of cholera knowledge' in a bid to refocus historians' attention towards general global shifts of cholera, instead of emphasising various local, regional or international epidemics.[11]

The 1830–32 cholera outbreaks were the most devastating for England during the nineteenth century, and they became the centre of historians' attention.[12] In England, the last cholera epidemic took place in 1866, after which further epidemics were prevented. As Anne Hardy claims, a combination of good quarantine systems and national preventive sanitary measures must have been pivotal in the stemming of cholera cases in England after 1866.[13] The debate on how cholera was transmitted was still raging during the mid nineteenth century, and it was still not clear whether quarantine or sanitary measures (or a combination of both) were effective against the incursion of cholera. So, while England got away unscathed, the rest of the world (Asia, Africa, the Americas and Continental Europe) was not as fortunate.

This disease shocked nations, prompted riots and was closely connected to the political unrest of the 1830s and 1848. Revolts were experienced all over Europe, from Russia to England. In England riots took place in big cities such as Exeter, Glasgow, London, Manchester and Liverpool. There was also a fear that the poor were being infected and killed by the medical profession to steal their bodies for medical research. In Liverpool, the rioters feared

8 Notably: David Arnold, 'Cholera and Colonialism in British India', *Past & Present*, 113 (1986), pp. 118–51; Mark Harrison, 'Quarantine, Pilgrimage, and Colonial Trade: India 1866–1900', *Indian Economic & Social History Review*, 29 (1992), pp. 117–44; Mark Harrison, 'A Question of Locality: The Identity of Cholera in British India 1860–1890', in David Arnold (ed.), *Warm Climates and Western Medicine: The Emergence of Tropical Medicine, 1500–1900* (Amsterdam, 1996), pp. 133–59.
9   Pamela K. Gilbert, *Cholera and Nation: Doctoring the Social Body in Victorian England* (Albany, 2008).
10 Peter Baldwin, *Contagion and the State in Europe, 1830–1930* (Cambridge, 2005).
11   Christopher Hamlin, *Cholera: The Biography* (Oxford, 2009); Bill Luckin, 'Book Reviews, *Cholera: The Biography*', review of Christopher Hamlin, *Cholera: The Biography*, Biographies of Disease Series (Oxford, 2009), *Medical History Journal*, 54 (2010), pp. 544–6.
12 Michael Durey, *The Return of the Plague: British Society and the Cholera, 1831–32* (Dublin, 1979); R.J. Morris, *Cholera 1832: The Social Response to an Epidemic* (London, 1976); Pelling, *Cholera, Fever*.
13 Hardy, 'Cholera, Quarantine', pp. 250–69.

'Burking' and tried to prevent medical officials from entering houses or from removing bodies from houses.[14]

The British were deeply concerned about the spread of cholera throughout the British Empire. British authorities in England and India were constantly under pressure from European powers to contain cholera within India where it was endemic. Despite their efforts, the 1865 epidemic was brought into Europe from India. European powers blamed Indian pilgrims for the spread of cholera in Europe, on their way to Mecca. Muslim pilgrims travelled to Mecca from all over Asia and Africa. Cholera spread to Aden Port and also to Jidda (modern Jeddah) by Indian pilgrims, and Mecca itself suffered a big cholera pandemic in 1865. Surviving pilgrims returned to their countries, travelling along the Nile into Egypt, Ethiopia and Sudan, and further afield to Syria and Palestine, spreading the disease. Thus, Muslim pilgrimages became the targets for regulation and control, and British authorities in India were frequently blamed for refusing to enforce stricter control over the pilgrims.

The 1865 epidemic reinforced the belief that cholera was circulated by human contact. The competing theory, which postulated that unsanitary conditions and water pollution were the causative agents for the spread of cholera, was also very popular with the medical profession and government policymakers.[15] This medical dilemma was central to the understanding of cholera by administrators and politicians, and was the cause of many disagreements between British authorities and Continental powers. John Snow's 1857 theory (that cholera could be transmitted to the human body by ingesting polluted water) had by then gathered supporters including Munich sanitation expert Max von Pettenkoffer. However, countries like Italy remained contagionists in their approach, giving increasing attention to quarantine and sanitary cordons.

Contagion theory was prevalent in the beginning of the nineteenth century. On the one hand contagionists believed that direct person contact spread invisible 'poisons' and the only way of safeguarding populations was to enforce military cordons. On the other extreme were the anti-contagionists who believed in the miasmatic theory that noxious airs arising from decayed matter made the air insalubrious. These noxious airs, in the right atmospheric conditions, generated epidemic diseases. To the anti-contagionists

14 Evans, 'Epidemics and Revolutions', explains how the movement of people and armies across Europe due to civil and political unrest could have caused cholera to spread easily. He does not believe that cholera was a causative agent for people to revolt but it was rather the result of mass population movement to avoid the repercussions of the revolutions. Coupled with this was the population's distrust towards the medical profession and the state. For more on the Liverpool case, see Geoffrey Gill, Sean Burrell and Jody Brown, 'Fear and Frustration – the Liverpool Cholera Riots of 1832', *The Lancet*, 358 (2001), pp. 233–7.

15 Jo Hays, *Epidemics and Pandemics: Their Impacts on Human History* (Santa Barbara, 2005), pp. 267–71.

the solution was clear: to clean the filth.[16] The different approaches towards preventive measures against Asiatic cholera, coupled with increasing emphasis on better sanitary conditions for Muslim and Hindu pilgrims, dominated most of the discussions during the International Sanitary Conferences in the nineteenth century.[17] These conferences were convened by European powers between 1851 and 1894 to discuss the dangers of cholera for Europe, and were tasked with the responsibility of finding solutions as to how borders could be secured against cholera without the need to resort to traditional methods of quarantine. Thus, understanding the way cholera was propagated was essential for the success of the Sanitary Conferences. These discussions were not only essential for the contagionism/anti-contagionism debate, but also for political and economic manoeuvrings, which were in reality the true motivation behind these conferences. Often, during the discussions in the conferences, political rivalry prevented the members from reaching a consensus on the best prophylaxis against cholera. Such disagreements in the medical and political camps made an international medical standardised action difficult to implement.[18]

The question of quarantine was always behind these political rivalries. Quarantine in the Mediterranean had existed for centuries before the establishment of British colonies in the nineteenth century. Britain found Mediterranean quarantine difficult to manage. Italy and France claimed to manage quarantine better than other countries, and they were prepared to inflict punitive quarantine on British ships if London was seen as neglectful of its Mediterranean quarantine stations. Quarantine in the Mediterranean could have easily offset the power that the British fleet and the imperial authorities enjoyed. The issue of quarantine, therefore, became a major political conflict during the International Sanitary Conferences.

Cholera became the scourge of the nineteenth century. With multiple

16   In-between these two extremes were the 'contingent contagionists'. Influenced by both arguments, they claimed that an individual's contagiousness depended on factors ranging from climate to personal cleanliness. Nancy Krieger, *Epidemiology and the People's Health: Theory and Context* (Oxford, 2011), pp. 68–9; also see works such as: Peter Baldwin, *Contagion and the State in Europe 1830–1930* (Cambridge, 2004); Erwin Ackerknecht, 'Anti-Contagionism between 1821 and 1867', *Bulletin of the History of Medicine*, 22 (1948), pp. 562–93; Elsbeth Heaman, 'The Rise and Fall of Anticontagionism in France', *Canadian Bulletin of Medical History*, 12 (1995), pp. 3–25; Christopher Hamlin, 'Predisposing Causes and Public Health in Early Nineteenth-Century Medical Thought', *Social History of Medicine*, 5 (1992), pp. 43–70.
17   Works such as: Valeska Huber, 'The Unification of the Globe by Disease? The International Sanitary Conferences on Cholera, 1851–1894', *The Historical Journal*, 49 (2006), pp. 453–76; M. Liverani and R. Coker, 'Protecting Europe from Diseases: From the International Sanitary Conferences to the ECDC', *Journal of Health Politics, Policy and Law*, 37 (2012), pp. 916–34; Norman Howard-Jones, *The Scientific Background of the International Sanitary Conferences, 1851–1938* (Geneva, 1975).
18   Huber, 'The Unification of the Globe', pp. 453–6.

epidemic bouts from the 1830s until the 1920s, it was universally dreaded. Every epidemic needed immediate action to counteract it and long term plans to prevent future outbreaks. The latter was the most important for many European powers, which needed better coping mechanisms to deal with cholera. This chapter will explore whether sanitary reforms in Malta were used as coping mechanisms against cholera. Was cholera the catalyst for sanitary reform and cleaner water supply? Or were sanitary reforms hastened by the belief that it was the best prophylaxis against cholera? Standing in the middle of the Mediterranean and ruled by the British, Maltese politicians during the 1870s were unsure whether sanitary reforms were as effective against a cholera epidemic as quarantine was against other epidemics like the plague.

From 1863 onward the Maltese government became more engaged with reforming the drainage and water supply systems while maintaining strict quarantine on people and goods segregated in the lazaretto. This was at a time when European countries in the International Sanitary Conferences agreed that land-based quarantine and sanitary cordons were futile against the cholera pandemic. They deemed that a country that based its defences only on land-based quarantine and policed cordons was condemning its people and increasing the likelihood of fear and panic among the population.[19] This chapter will focus on the 1865 and 1887 cholera bouts and the role these played in the implementation of the sanitary reforms in the towns and villages of Malta. While discussing these reforms, this chapter will also focus on the internal political situation in Malta, and will explore how sanitation reform became embroiled in the local fight for better political representation. It will show how crisis prompted important changes that had wider ramifications and consequences.

The history of the sanitary reform in Malta is mainly covered by two Maltese historians. Paul Cassar in his *The Medical History of Malta* gives a brief account of the major issues discussed in the Council of Government and how drainage works and water supply were ultimately completed.[20] Henry Frendo briefly mentions the sanitary reform to illustrate the political clashes between the government and opposition in the Council of Government in 1879. Frendo explains how this political turbulence, together with the 'language question' in Malta, contributed to better political representation for the Maltese.[21] This chapter will explore the reasons behind the need for such

---

19 Frank M. Snowden, *Naples in the Time of Cholera 1884–1911* (Cambridge, 1995), pp. 81–4.

20 Paul Cassar, *The Medical History of Malta* (London, 1964).

21 The 'language question' in Malta started in the 1870s when the imperial government proposed that English should be taught in primary schools and Italian studied as an optional subject. The Italian language was the language of the administration, the law courts and the

a reform, the relevance that such reforms had in a British Mediterranean, and the role that the 1865 and 1887 cholera epidemics played in pushing forwards these reforms.

Malta under British dominion

An outline of the island's colonial history and its politics is necessary in order to understand the context for the drainage and water reforms. The British connection with Malta started in 1800 when the French were driven out by Nelson's fleet. Technically, Malta was not conquered, but ceded to the British by the Maltese in 1800. The British subsequently withheld ruling rights over the Maltese and denied them any administrative or legislative power.[22] Instead, all legislative power was placed in the hands of the Governor. In lieu of being given a representative system where a Governor ruled with a local assembly (as was customary in the West Indies and later adopted in Canada, Australia and New Zealand), Malta was given the status of a Crown Colony, meaning that the Maltese could not take legislative or financial decisions, and the colony was ruled by the Governor on behalf of the British Government.[23]

In 1849 a new constitution was granted to Malta by which the number of the official members was greater than the elected ones. This meant that the new elected members were perpetually outvoted. In the 1860s the elected members asked for more control in domestic matters, particularly control of the treasury. In 1864, as a gesture of goodwill from a Liberal government in England, it was decreed that in domestic matters, the opinion of the elected members of the Council of Government should be given special consideration. This was called the 'Cardwell Principle' and its aim was to stop Governors from running roughshod over the wishes of the elected members in the Council of Government.[24]

university. The pushing forward of the English language over the Italian created a storm among those in favour of *italianita* (the learning of Italian culture, language and arts). The majority of the elected members in the Council of Government opposed the government's suggestions, and politicians in Malta were divided between the Reformers and the anti-Reformers. These opposing camps were instrumental in the creation of the first two political parties in Malta. For more on this subject, read Frendo, *Party Politics*.

22 Frendo, *Party Politics*, p. 3.

23 Peter J. Marshall, *The Cambridge Illustrated History of the British Empire* (Cambridge, 1996), pp. 152–4.

24 The 'Cardwell Principle' was named after Lord Cardwell (Secretary of State for War). Although most of the Cardwell Principles were in general reforms for the British army, the one bestowed on Malta was aimed at respecting the spirit of the Letters Patent of 1848 and at giving more weight to the arguments presented in Council by elected members. John J. Cremona, *The Maltese Constitution and Constitutional History since 1813* (Malta, 1994), pp. 7–14.

Cholera: social transformation

Similar to those in other countries, the cholera epidemics in Malta could not be described as having caused demographic crises. Compared with other diseases such as tuberculosis, typhus, smallpox, influenza and diphtheria, cholera had a far lower mortality rate. Humans ingested the cholera bacillus through water or food infected with faecal matter.[25] Cholera could kill after a few hours or up to three days from the onset of the first symptoms. This is why cholera was a 'shock disease': the symptoms came on suddenly, killed people within a few hours, and moved rapidly from one area to another while sometimes missing entire towns and villages.[26]

The importation of the 1865 cholera epidemic in Malta was attributed to the vessel *Wyvern* coming from Alexandria. However, in his report, John Sutherland (physician and promoter of sanitary science) claimed that a previous, less virulent cholera epidemic had already passed the island with no fatal cases reported. A second wave of cholera hit Malta later in 1865, this time with fatal consequences. This epidemic lasted 155 days until 11 November 1865. In a population of 118,596 inhabitants, there were 2,362 cases (19.9 per thousand) with 1,479 deaths (12.5 per thousand) among the civil population. Out of 7,469 troops, there were 203 cases (27.2 per thousand) of cholera with 145 deaths (19.4 per thousand).[27] John Sutherland, in the 1867 report claimed that 'in so far as it relates to its proportionate mortality, [the 1865 cholera] must be classed among the most mortal on record'.[28]

The next major cholera bout in Malta took place in July 1887. The first few cases appeared in the villages of Żabbar and St Julian's and in the towns of Cospicua and Valletta. Each day, as the cholera epidemic progressed, new cases were reported in each village and town. The disease spread through Malta, with the highest number of deaths (twelve people) being reported on 10 August. The Chief Government Medical Officer, Salvatore L. Pisani, claimed that many deaths occurred unnecessarily owing to the reluctance of people to receive medical attention as soon as the symptoms of diarrhoea set in.[29]

The 1865 cholera bout was deemed by Sutherland as the 'most mortal on

25 Pisani, *Report on the Cholera Epidemic*, p. 4.
26 Wohl, *Endangered Lives*, p. 119.
27 Morbidity rate refers to the number of individuals in poor health during a given time period while mortality rate (or death rate) is a measure of the number of deaths in a population, scaled to the size of that population.
28 Sutherland, *Report on the Sanitary Condition … Cholera Malta*, p. 8.
29 Pisani, *Report on the Cholera Epidemic*, pp. 4–16; National Archives Malta (hereafter NAM), General Miscellaneous Report, *Final Report made to the Central Committee Appointed by His Excellency the Governor to check the Spread of Cholera by order of the Central Sub-Committee, on 30th December 1887* (Malta, 1887), GMR 316.

Table 9.1. Morbidity and mortality figures for both 1865 and 1887 cholera epidemics in the towns and villages of Malta

Towns	Population (1861)	Population (1887)	Cases (1865)	Cases (1887)	Deaths (1865)	Deaths (1887)	Deaths per 1,000 (1865)	Deaths per 1,000 (1887)
Valletta	23,993	26,124	454	43	282	40	11	1.5
Floriana	5,791	6,858	76	15	48	10	8	1.5
Senglea	6,887	8,283	99	15	64	10	9	1.2
Cospicua	10,933	12,479	175	67	122	43	11	3.4
Vittoriosa	5,712	6,885	175	14	107	6	18	0.9
Total	53,316	60,629	979	154	623	109	11.7	1.8
Villages	58,939	76,161	1,203	470	724	352	12.3	4.6
Overall total	112,255	136,790	2,182	624	1,347	461	24	6.4

Source: Sutherland, *Report on the Sanitary Condition ... Cholera Malta*, p. 8; Pisani, *Report on the Cholera Epidemic*, p. 13.
Note: The table also shows the death rate per thousand of the population for both epidemics.

record', and it had a higher death rate than the 1887 cholera epidemic. For 1887, Pisani reported 461 deaths out of 624 cases of cholera, giving a death rate of 74% for the civilian population. In particular, Table 9.1 shows that the death rate (per thousand) in the urban areas during the 1887 cholera was much lower than that of the 1865 epidemic. However, it is clear that the death rate in the villages was significantly higher than the death rate in the urban areas during the 1887 epidemic. This difference between the death rates in the urban and rural areas did not exist during the 1865 cholera bout.

The sanitary reforms in the towns resulted in a lower death rate during the 1887 cholera epidemic compared with the 1865 one, providing a coping mechanism against the cholera crisis. By 1887, the belief in sanitary reform as a prophylaxis was widely accepted in Europe. The British methods of sanitation and the sanitary surveillance of international shipping earned them the respect of other European nations.[30]

In 1887, Maltese medical opinion was in favour of these reforms. Indeed, Pisani's last recommendation in his 1887 report was: 'prophylactic measures for the future – I may sum them up in two words – GOOD SANITATION'.[31] At the behest of the government, physicians such as John Sutherland, Captain Galton, Salvatore Pisani, Antonio Ghio and Gavino Gulia wrote reports suggesting approaches to reduce incidence of infection and improve general sanitary conditions on the island. These reports were frequently consulted by members of the Council of Government during their sessions. This shows that although the medical profession was not involved directly into the policy-making of the island, the local medical opinion influenced and shaped health policies in Malta.

British Army sanitary reforms and the Maltese sanitary reform

In Britain, the concept of public health arose as a response to growing urban populations, increasing poverty and high levels of infectious diseases. The health of the people had become a matter of increasing state concern. From the 1840s onward, the state provided public health measures even when there were no major outbreaks of diseases. Edwin Chadwick's famous report of 1842 was motivated by the state of poverty and disease experienced by many families after the cholera bouts of the 1830s. Chadwick's reforms took a different approach from previous models of reform;[32] he insisted that better sanitation and water supply would reduce disease and poverty, thus reducing

30   Hardy, 'Cholera, Quarantine', p. 268.
31   Pisani, *Report on the Cholera Epidemic*, p. 21 [Pisani's emphasis].
32   Anne Hardy, 'The Public in Public Health', in Christian Emden and David Midgley (eds), *Beyond Habermas: Democracy, Knowledge and the Public Sphere* (New York, 2013), pp. 87–9.

government expenses for poor relief.[33] In 1843, a Royal Commission was asked to look into the details of the sanitary situation of fifty of the largest towns in England. It reported back that more could be done to improve the sanitary conditions of some of the towns. Their report gave broad suggestions towards the improvement of public health. After further work and yet more delays, the Public Health Act was passed in 1848.[34] The Act argued that since sanitary problems such as lack of water and defective sewerage affected the general population, local and national governments should work together to solve these issues as a nation.

Edwin Chadwick's sanitary reform was largely devoid of medical analysis or intervention from the medical profession. The shift from public health as a sanitary project to the idea of medical management occurred in the second half of the nineteenth century when John Simon (pathologist and surgeon at St Thomas' Hospital) was appointed chief health administrator and later medical officer to the General Board of Health in 1855.[35] Simon believed that the health of the people or the community was part of the social, economic and political developments in the country. The work of the Medical Officers of Health has been characterised as 'an era of preventive measures'. Away from the central power of Whitehall, the MOHs were responsible for the sanitation of their communities.[36]

Parallel to this work, yet intrinsically part of it, were the reforms of the Army that took place in the aftermath of the Crimean War (1854–56). Two of the most celebrated reformists were Florence Nightingale and Sidney Herbert who worked tirelessly to improve the sanitary condition of the army, both at home and in the colonies.[37] The first Baron Sidney Herbert of Lea was a Tory politician who became the Secretary to the Admiralty in 1841. When the Crimean War started, Herbert was spokesman for the army in the House of Commons. In October 1854, Herbert wrote to Nightingale asking her to visit Scutari with a small group of female nurses; thus began the legendary expedition of Florence Nightingale.[38]

In 1857, a Royal Commission on the Sanitary State of the Army was set up. Herbert presided over the commission. The report found that the 'total

33   Christopher Hamlin and Sally Sheard, 'Revolutions in Public Health: 1848 and 1998?', *British Medical Journal*, 317 (1998), p. 558.
34   Ibid., pp. 558–89.
35   Porter, *Health, Civilisation*, pp. 119–20.
36   Sally Sheard and Liam J. Donaldson, *The Nation's Doctor: The Role of the Chief Medical Officer 1855–1998* (Oxford, 2006), pp. 4–5.
37   Jharna Gourlay, *Florence Nightingale and the Health of the Raj* (Aldershot, 2003), p. 24.
38   H.C.G. Matthew, 'Herbert, Sidney, first Baron Herbert of Lea (1810–1861)', *Oxford Dictionary of National Biography* (Oxford, 2004); online edn, May 2009 [last accessed July 2014].

mortality in the army was nearly double ... that of the civil population'.[39]
This report prompted the establishment of four other subcommissions. The
first commission found that both barracks and hospitals were overcrowded,
lacking ventilation, good drainage or adequate water supply. The same
commission extended its work to the sanitary condition of the Mediterranean
stations.[40] The second subcommission was tasked with the reorganisation of
the army medical department and with framing a new code of regulations for
both hospitals and sanitary services of the army. The third subcommission
was charged with the organisation of a school at Chatham for the instruction
of military hygiene and army medical services. Lastly, the fourth subcommission was asked to reorganise the army medical statistics, which until then
were incomplete and sparse.[41]

One royal commissioner, who worked both as an Inspector to the General
Board of Health (set up following Chadwick's campaign), and as part of
the Royal Commission investigating the Sanitary State of the Army, was
John Sutherland.[42] In 1861 he accepted the invitation to analyse the health
and sanitary conditions of the Mediterranean barracks. As a result, in 1863
he published a detailed report on Malta, Gibraltar and the Ionian Islands.[43]
This report analysed the sanitary condition of the military hospitals and
barracks, including the health of the civilian areas surrounding the barracks
or hospitals. Sutherland observed that it was not possible to separate the
sanitary conditions of the troops from that of the civil population owing to
the proximity of the barracks to the civilian dwellings. He claimed that all
military hospitals in Malta were in a bad condition, the sanitary state of the
hospitals was dire, the drainage system was almost universally defective and
the water supply not nearly enough for the demands of the civil population

39   Florence Nightingale, *Army Sanitary Administration and its Reform under the Late Lord Herbert* (London, 1862), p. 3.
40   Nightingale worked tirelessly for the reforms in the Army, including the armed forces in India. In 1859 a royal commission was set up as a sanitary commission for the Indian Army. The report was published in 1863. For more about the Indian sanitary reform, see Gourlay, *Florence Nightingale*.
41   Nightingale, *Army Sanitary Administration*, pp. 3–6. William Farr, 'The Health of the British Army and the Effects of Recent Sanitary Measures on its Mortality and Sickness', *Journal of the Statistical Society of London*, 24 (1861), pp. 472–84; Hew Strachan, 'The Early Victorian Army and the Nineteenth-Century Revolution in Government', *English Historical Review*, 4 (1980), pp. 784–5.
42   Stephen Halliday, 'Commentary: Dr John Sutherland, Vibrio Cholerae and "Predisposing Causes"', *International Journal of Epidemiology*, 31 (2002), pp. 912–13. Sutherland, born in Edinburgh in 1808, qualified as a physician from the University of Edinburgh in 1831. He was initially involved in preparing the first Royal Commission report about the health of the army in English barracks and hospitals.
43   John Sutherland, *Report of the Barrack and Hospital Improvement Commission on the Sanitary Condition and Improvement of the Mediterranean Stations* (London, 1863).

and the garrisons. Among many changes, Sutherland proposed that new military hospitals be built in Malta, that drainage was to be connected and water supply provided for the garrisons. He recommended numerous other changes in the latrines of the barracks and the married soldiers' quarters, and advised that more recreational facilities be installed in the barracks.[44]

In 1865, the cholera hit Malta and, soon after, John Sutherland was again sent to the island to report on the sanitary conditions of the island following the epidemic.[45] In 1867 he presented another report focusing on the civilian sanitation and how the civil population had fared throughout the cholera epidemic. In this report Sutherland attempted to underpin the importance of sanitary reforms and the increasing irrelevance of land-based quarantines:

> my sole object is to place on record corrected statements of these events ... so that a decision may be arrived at as to whether the public health of Malta is to be protected in future by sanitary improvements or by restrictions on commerce.[46]

Sutherland's 1867 report was preoccupied with the correct methods of house ventilation, house construction, the analyses of water samples and defective drainage. By 'plac[ing] on record corrected statements' of cholera stories, Sutherland aimed at some clarification on the propagation of cholera in Malta.[47]

In the space of a decade, the army sanitary reform, as initiated in England following the Crimean War, placed Maltese sanitary conditions in the limelight. It was to be the first step towards achieving healthier garrisons, towns and villages in Malta. This reform took decades to complete, well into the twentieth century. The seed for reform was sown in Malta by the need to provide better sanitary conditions for the troops. As historian David Arnold has stressed, military needs remained an important motivation behind widespread civilian sanitary reform. Whereas the needs of the civilian population were a concern for the colonial governments, the local endemic illnesses that endangered naval or army lives were of paramount importance to the British authorities.[48] It was clear that the reforms in Malta were not initiated in the first place to safeguard the Maltese population from endemic fevers and pandemics like cholera. However, given the restricted geographical location of the military barracks, any drainage and water reforms had to

---

44   Ibid., pp. 1–22.
45   Sutherland was also tasked with doing the same in Gibraltar. For more information, see John Sutherland, *Report of the Sanitary Condition of Gibraltar with Reference to the Epidemic Cholera in the year 1865* (London, 1867).
46   Sutherland, *Report on the Sanitary Condition ... Cholera Malta*, p. 59.
47   Ibid.
48   David Arnold, *Imperial Medicine and Indigenous Societies* (Manchester, 1988), p. 19.

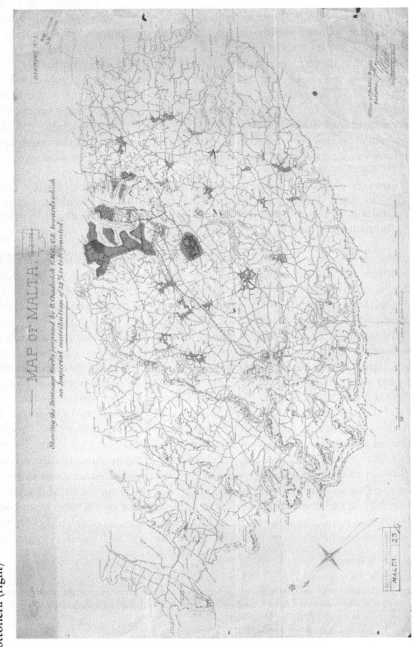

Figure 9.1. Map of Malta showing an arrowed line depicting the 1870s drainage reform in Valletta (centre) and Cottonera (right)

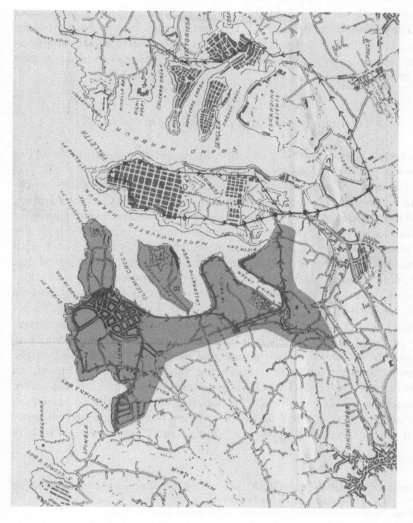

Source: TNA CO 1047/547, Map of Malta showing the Drainage Works as proposed by Osbert Chadwick, C.M.G., C.E.
Note: The lightly shaded parts and the arrowed line around Sliema, Manoel Island and Ta' Xbiex Creek (left) indicate the areas to be reformed as proposed in Chadwick's report.

encompass the civilian housing surrounding the barracks. Barracks were typically situated in the most densely populated part of Malta: the Grand Harbour and Marsamuscetto Harbour, encompassing the Three Cities, namely Cospicua, Senglea and Vittoriosa (see Figure 9.1). Reforming the drainage and bringing a better water supply to this area meant better social conditions for thousands of Maltese citizens, albeit only as a by-product of the army sanitary reforms. Further cholera crises had to be averted by providing better health and social conditions. Thus better social conditions were not the goal, but merely a means to an end: a means to avoid further cholera crises.

Drainage works and political manoeuvres

For the better part of two decades the discussion on sanitation in Malta concentrated on 'provisions to reform drainage'. This constituted the first part of the sanitary reform. Constructing a timeline for the drainage works of Malta is thus crucial to understand why the local elected Council members opposed these reforms. Up to the beginning of the 1860s there were numerous discussions about the health of the Mediterranean stations, specifically the harbours, ports and garrisons but never about drainage.[49] The British government did not offer significant subsidy for the drainage works in Malta, and the financial burden inflicted on the Maltese government was greater than its revenues, hence the reforms took much longer to complete and became embroiled in local politics, causing rancour among local politicians.

Some small sanitary improvements had started in 1865: twenty sewer ventilators were to be built at the height of eight or ten feet above the roofs of the houses.[50] This seems to be the first real initiative towards the drainage and sewage reforms in Malta. Following Sutherland's 1865 report, in December 1867, Governor Patrick Grant confirmed to the Colonial Office that the renowned civil engineer John Lawson was in Malta to report on the best and most economical means of carrying out the proposed improvements of the existing drainage system.[51] Sutherland's report appears to have

---

49   National Archives UK (hereafter TNA), CO 158/178, Inspector General for the Hospitals to Lieutenant Col. Pocklington, 29 November 1855.

50   *Maltese Council of Government Debates*, 1879, sitting no. 87, col. 21.

51   TNA CO 158/212, correspondence between the Governor and the Secretary for the Colonies, 6 December 1867. John Lawson was a civil engineer (1824–73) primarily interested in sanitary engineering. In 1867 Lawson was employed by the Colonial Office to report on Malta's sanitary reform, but this seems to have been an isolated case. His work was mainly focused on reforms for major cities in England. John Lawson; 'Obituary John Lawson 1824–1873', *Minutes of the Proceedings of the Institution of Civil Engineers*, 38 (1874), pp. 315–17.

instigated correspondence between colonial authorities in England and Malta, discussing the merits of a reform in the drainage scheme of Valletta, Floriana and the Three Cities. It is clear, therefore, that the move towards a sanitary reform had commenced as early as 1867, at least a decade before the discussion started in the Council of Government in Malta. This was one of the sticking points between the elected members in the Council and the government. The Maltese government was later accused by the elected members of planning sanitary and drainage reform without consulting the Council: indeed British authorities in Malta only disclosed their plans about a major sanitary reform when the first financial vote was required to commence the works.

Various drainage schemes were proposed to the colonial office. However, little else was done by the local authorities until 1869. In March 1869, the Governor sent a long dispatch to Earl Granville (Secretary for the Colonies) explaining that Lawson's scheme had stopped, owing to the local coffers being short of money.[52] In his correspondence to Granville, Grant explained that in order for the public to benefit from these works, the project had to be finished in three years. Lawson's estimates were that, for the first year, the Maltese government would vote the sum of £25,000 and a further £30,000 per annum in the following two years.[53] John Lawson's estimate amounted to £85,000 exclusive of the works for water supply and for internal house fittings such as water closets. The sum needed for a good supply of water was estimated at £37,300 and the house fittings were to amount to around £200,000, to be shouldered by house owners, private households, taverns and other commercial buildings.[54] Therefore, this scheme was to cost the islanders (directly or through taxes) the staggering sum of £322,300. In comparison, the island's total revenue for the year 1869 was £154,488 9s 11d. The sum to be paid by the islanders for the sanitary reform was almost double the revenue of the entire island for one year.[55]

The discussions between Grant and Granville indicate that money matters were also of concern to the local Governor. Granville felt that the War Department and the garrisons in Malta were the primary beneficiaries of this drainage scheme.[56] In September 1872, the new Governor, Charles van Straubenzee, reported back to the Earl of Kimberley (the Secretary for the Colonies) that owing to a lack of communication (and assurance of payment)

---

52   TNA CO 158/218, correspondence between the Governor and Earl Granville, 29 March 1869.
53   Ibid.
54   TNA CO 158/239, correspondence between John Fowler and Sir Victor Houlton, 3 February 1874.
55   Blue Books Malta, 1869.
56   TNA CO 158/218.

from the Admiralty and the War Office on the subject of financial aid, he was loath to approach the Council with this project.[57] Long years had passed since 1869, and the War Department and the Admiralty would still not commit to pay part of the expense. The lack of funds continued to be the major hurdle keeping the government from approaching the Council with this project, fearing that the elected members would dismiss it immediately on grounds of insufficient funds. Van Straubenzee needed urgent confirmation of imperial financial aid.[58]

Finally, after confirming the commitment of the War Department and the Admiralty, in June 1875 the Maltese government presented the estimate for this project to the Council. As feared by the Governor, the elected members reportedly postponed voting for the funds for several sittings, claiming that the government had yet to solve the question of the formation of a Sanitary Office first.[59] Since 1873, the elected members had been proposing a resolution 'for the creation of a 'Sanitary and Statistical Office' before launching into any heavy expense for Sanitary objects'.[60] The government opposed this resolution over three sittings. The Crown Advocate, Adrian Dingli, claimed that there was no need for a new Sanitary Office as the Police Physicians were more than adequately qualified to perform their sanitary duties. Despite the protests of the elected members, the motion on the Sanitary Office was passed by the official majority of the Council, creating a Sanitary Office under the direct rule of the Crown Advocate, rather than under the control of a British professional health officer as suggested by the elected members.[61]

The fight over the Sanitary Office was another setback for the elected members. Their opinions were disregarded and the vote was rushed through by the official members. The fight over the Sanitary Office was viewed by the official members as a tactic by the elected members to delay the discussion on the sanitation reform. When finally presented in the Council, after the delays caused by the setting up of the Sanitary Office, the drainage question was opposed by the elected members on financial grounds. After numerous debates, the official majority forced the drainage scheme through the Council and the money was voted towards its commencement. This showed that the local Governors and the government cared little about the 'Cardwell Principle' of 1864: public money was voted against the express wishes of the elected members.

Politically, the drainage question was the catalyst that brought to a head

---

57   TNA CO 158/232, correspondence between Governor Charles van Straubenzee and Earl of Kimberley, 17 September 1872.
58   TNA CO 158/234, correspondence between Governor Charles van Straubenzee and Earl of Kimberley, 30 January 1873.
59   TNA CO 158/242, Improvement of Drains in Government Houses, 24 June 1875.
60   Cassar, *Medical History*, pp. 280–2.
61   Ibid., p. 278.

the crisis between elected and official members. The first vote for £3,000 to continue the drainage works in the Three Cities was pushed through on 21 December 1877 with a majority of one from the government's side. This was done with the sanction of the Colonial Secretary Lord Carnarvon on 27 November 1877, when he approved 'of the official majority being used (if unavoidable) for the purpose of carrying ... [the drainage reform] out'.[62] Another £7,000 and £22,000 were then passed by the votes of the official members on 10 March 1879 against the unanimous opposition of the elected members.[63] The drainage works could now start, and by the 1880s they were almost completed.[64]

The elected members' reasons for not supporting the sanitary works in 1879 were threefold. They first objected to the highhanded way that the imperial and local governments organised the drainage reform without involving the representatives of the electorate. Secondly, they resented the financial burden on the local revenues and the accruing debts that the local government had to shoulder for this project. Thirdly, there was the problem of the water supply that was to flush the drainage system of the Three Cities, Valletta and Floriana. They argued that without the water supply scheme the drainage system could not operate efficiently. The water supply scheme had yet to be drawn up and extra money voted for it, adding to the financial burden imposed on the population.

The political crisis in the Council of Government did not improve during the following two decades.[65] In 1887, the British government decided to issue a new constitution, designed to create a new representative system in Malta. The elected members were granted limited autonomy to decide on the question of finance and other local matters but the colonial authorities reserved the power to intervene. This was not enough for the elected members: they wanted absolute authority to decide on all local issues, but this was not the colonial government's intention.[66] From the start this constitution did not work. By the 1890s the elected members fell into a cycle of resigning whenever

---

62   TNA CO 158/247, correspondence between Governor van Straubenzee and Earl Carnarvon, 27 November 1877.

63   Sigismondo Savona, The Petition of the Maltese to the House of Commons – A letter Addressed to H.M. Principal Secretary of State for the Colonies (Malta, 1880), pp. 18–19; TNA CO 158/252, The Drainage Reform Scheme, 13 March 1879.

64   See Figure 9.1, line with arrows around Valletta and Cottonera.

65   Here the 'political crisis' refers to the complete confusion reigning in the Council of Government. The elected members frequently resigned, the Council was dismissed and elections were re-held. For some years the Council was the battleground between the elected members and the official Government members, and when the Council was not sitting, the Governor took over the temporary rule of the islands. During this period, relations between Malta and the Secretary of State were soured, to say the least.

66   Cremona, The Maltese Constitution, p. 15.

they felt they were being held in contempt by official members of the Council. The Council would then declare new elections and after a considerable delay new elected members would sit in the Council. This meant that for long periods Malta was governed by the prerogative of the Governor himself.[67] This period also saw a shift in imperial policies from a liberal one to a more direct approach: the British in Malta insisted on enforcing the use of the English language, particularly in the educational system and public sector. This created tensions between official and elected members. The debate on sanitary reform slipped into the background as the 'language question' became the main bone of contention between elected members, imperial and local governments.

Cholera crisis of 1887

In order to complete the sanitary reforms in Malta, a good water supply scheme was necessary, complementing the drainage reforms already carried out. The water supply project for Valletta and Floriana had also become embroiled in politics from the beginning of the 1880s. By this time two rival political parties had emerged. The first, the *Partito Nazionale*, was led by Fortunato Mizzi, and the other, the *Partito Riformista*, was headed by Sigismondo Savona. In less than four years Malta had gone through three contested elections, during which the popularity of the *Partito Nazionale* continued to rise and the British in Malta found themselves opposing a major political party with widespread support.

Nonetheless, the government plans for the water supply scheme were carried out. On December 1887, a new memorandum was sent to the Earl of Kimberley detailing a scheme proposed by Lt Tressider of the Royal Engineers in Malta to use fresh water to flush the drainage. Meanwhile, a letter sent by Governor Borton to Kimberley in 1882 revealed the shift (albeit temporary) in the elected members' disposition towards these works. The debate over the language question was less heated than a decade before, and the animosity between the official and elected members had lessened.

Furthermore, much of Europe understood by this time the importance of sanitation and sanitary works in relation to cholera epidemics. The debate as to whether the drainage reforms were necessary or beneficial for Malta was no longer relevant. It was clear that the drainage reforms would be useless without an adequate water supply. Governor Borton explained that 'all the members of the elected bench received the proposition with ... good-will, and ... unanimous ... desire that an application should be made to the

---

67 Holland, *Blue-Water Empire*, p. 122.

imperial government ... to contribute towards their share of the proposed expenditure'.[68] Yet, in December 1883, Borton reported that it was necessary to use the official majority to pass the vote for the remaining working expenses of the drainage, as the elected members expressed their wish to oppose both votes, though no reasons were given.[69] The political scene had started to change in 1886, both in Malta and in the Colonial Office. In the span of two years, the colonial secretary had changed four times: historian Henry Frendo suggests that there was a different and more sympathetic response to the elected members in Malta on the part of the colonial government after 1886.[70]

While in Malta the political scene was changing rapidly, in the Maghreb, fresh concerns about a new cholera epidemic arose. By 1883, Egypt was in the grip of another cholera epidemic. The French and the Germans accused the British of allowing cholera to slip into Egypt from India and lax quarantine measures on their vessels. British, French and German medical commissioners descended on Egypt, each trying to determine how cholera had been introduced into the country. The German expedition was led by Robert Koch, who later embarked for India to study the cholera there in more detail. While in India, Koch felt confident that he had identified the comma bacillus (Koch's bacillus) as the cholera germ and successfully made the connection between water infected with the bacillus and the outbreak of cholera among villagers. He also made the link between the cholera found in India, in Egypt and eventually in France, confirming that cholera was indeed imported from India into Europe.[71] Despite this finger-pointing among European powers, the 1885 International Sanitary Conference reiterated the importance of sanitary reform in all countries, and warned that reliance on cordons and land-based quarantines was only practised by countries guilty of neglecting the sanitary conditions.[72]

In Malta, sanitary reform was in full swing, with both sides of the Council (elected and official members) supporting the reforms. The elected members showed signs of cooperation with the Maltese government, and by 1888 Governor Simmons was anxious to implement the reforms as soon as possible because 'the majority of the elected members are in favour of carrying out the proposed schemes with as little delay as possible'.[73] This change of heart and policy also explains the limited resistance or any controversy over Osbert

68   TNA CO 158/263, Flushing Drains of Valletta and Floriana with Fresh Water, 27 December 1882.
69   TNA CO 158/266, Divisions on Votes on Drawback and Drainage Reports Use of Official Majority, 20 December 1883.
70   Frendo, *Party Politics*, pp. 48–9.
71   Mariko Ogawa, 'Uneasy Bedfellows: Science and Politics in the Refutation of Koch's Bacterial Theory of Cholera', *Bulletin of the History of Medicine*, 74 (2000), pp. 671–95.
72   Snowden, *Naples*, p. 85.
73   TNA CO 158/287, Water Supply to Villages, 9 May 1888.

Chadwick's reports to improve the water system of Malta after 1885.[74] Up to this point rural areas were largely forgotten, and their only source of potable water was the rainwater gathered in cisterns for domestic use. When the water supply ordinance was presented to the Council in May 1886, the ordinance was carried forward and Chadwick's suggestions adopted.[75] Following the cholera epidemic of 1887, it was clear from the subsequent report of the Chief Government Medical Officer Pisani and the Cholera Committee Reports, that the villages and rural areas would not have suffered such a high mortality rate had there been a better water supply.[76] Chadwick suggested that new infiltration galleries and pumping stations be constructed. Public cisterns thought to be polluting the water were emptied and decommissioned while others were cleaned and protected. Water was brought to the public taps in the main squares of the villages and towns from where the public could access water. In 1897 Chadwick made further suggestions and the system of infiltration galleries and shafts was extended further (as shown by the shaded area, extenuated by the arrowed line, in Figure 9.1).

As in the 1865 outbreak, the 1887 epidemic helped the Maltese Government and imperial authorities in Malta stay the course for sanitary reform. The reforms were already under way and the urban areas (including the garrisons) were already benefiting from a clean water supply together with adequate flushing of the drainage system. Pisani's report of 1888 indicated that the high mortality rate among the villages could have been avoided had similar sanitary precautions been taken in the rural areas. Thus, as in the 1865 epidemic, the 1887 cholera bout pushed the Maltese government to continue with their efforts towards completing the sanitary reform and to bring better sanitation conditions to all the villages in Malta.

Conclusion

The need for a sanitary reform for the naval and military services in Malta began as part of an imperial agenda. Triggered by the larger army sanitary

---

74   Osbert Chadwick became a civil engineer and consequently a Consulting Engineer for the Colonial Office. He worked on the sewage and water systems of Grenada, Malta, Hong Kong, Mauritius, Trinidad, Kingston, Jamaica and many other places. Anonymous, 'Obituary; Osbert Chadwick CMG', *Minutes of the Proceedings Institution of Civil Engineers*, 196 (1914), p. 357.
75   Frendo, *Party Politics*, p. 46.
76   Pisani, *Report on the Cholera Epidemic*, NAM GMR 316, General Miscellaneous Reports, *Final Report made to the Central Committee appointed by His Excellency the Governor to check the spread of Cholera by order of the Central Sub-Committee, on 30 December 1887*; NAM GMR 270 General Miscellaneous Reports, *Cholera Committee Reports Submitted to His Excellency the Governor* (Malta, 1888). The Cholera Committee was presided over by the Chief Government Medical Officer, Pisani, and one of the members was Osbert Chadwick.

reorganisations within the British Empire, the reform in Malta was initially to safeguard the barracks, the soldiers and their families. This was not unique to Malta: safeguarding the health of the military was always of paramount importance for British authorities. Sutherland's 1863 report highlighted the urgency of this change. The 1867 report illustrates the importance of a widespread sanitary reorganisation, one that encompassed the whole region around the Grand Harbour and Marsamuscetto Harbour. Civilian dwellings would benefit from the same drainage works and water supply installed for the barracks. Yet, despite the support of the official members in the Council of Government and the support from some of the physicians in government employ, the elected members of the Council opposed these schemes for more than a decade.

It is not clear whether the British imperial authorities would have acted on the 1863 Sutherland report alone. The 1863 report highlighted many problems within the garrisons but the first sanitary improvements started in Malta in February 1865.[77] This may be seen as the first real initiative towards the drainage and sewage reforms on the island. Although the first sanitary improvement were not linked to the 1863 Sutherland report, it shows that local authorities were aware of, and indeed acted upon some minor sanitary issues. Thus it can be argued that, despite the 1863 report, it was the cholera outbreak of June 1865 that prompted British authorities to finally act against the appalling conditions found in the barracks. Both cholera epidemics, and their subsequent reports, reinforced the authorities' belief in the proposed plans for reforms.

When the plans for the sanitary reform were finally in place, the elected members refused to vote the initial funds needed to commence this project. By pushing the financial vote through the Council without the consent of the Maltese elected members, the government (at the bidding of the imperial authorities) broke the tenuous agreement (i.e. the Cardwell Principle) that had given elected members more control in the Council. While many would have agreed that a sanitary reform of the urban areas in Malta was beneficial and necessary, the elected members felt that this project, and the way it was pushed forward by the government, undermined their already limited political representation. The local politicians used sanitary reform as political leverage, and took the opportunity to own the 'drainage question' in the absence of medical consensus on the provenance of contagious diseases like cholera.

The 1887 cholera epidemic provided the impetus to extend the reforms towards the rural areas of Malta. The beneficial aspects of the sanitary reform were, by this time, clear to the medical profession in Malta as well as the politicians. This was also in tandem with the prevailing medical understanding

77 *Maltese Council of Government Debates*, 1879, sitting no. 87, col. 21.

of all European countries. Better sanitation was also encouraged by the International Sanitary Conferences. Thus, after 1887 medical indecision could no longer be used as leverage against national sanitary reform in Malta, nor was there any political motive to do so.

The multiple factions within Malta over the implementation of the sanitary reform plans show the complex nature of local politics within a British colony. The cholera epidemics were the crises that impelled action from the imperial rulers and helped authorities stay their course with national sanitary reforms throughout the nineteenth century. Furthermore, good sanitation practices in Malta proved to be the best coping mechanisms against the cholera crisis during the nineteenth century.

Together with the 'language question', sanitary reform was instrumental in the creation of political parties, which grew large enough to bargain for better political representation as a British colony. It was difficult to separate the sanitary question from contemporary politics and the struggle of Maltese politicians for better political representation. Once the imperial government strengthened its imperial policy and supervision, Maltese politicians became more agitated. This action triggered multiple political reactions among Maltese politicians, yet most importantly, sanitary reform was itself the catalyst for political change. When in 1886 the colonial government became more sympathetic towards Maltese demands, the elected members in the Council released their grip on the sanitary question and stopped using it for political leverage. Sanitary reform in Malta was essentially part of a bigger power struggle between colonised and coloniser, and both sanitary reform and the 'language question' need to be understood and studied as part of a bigger struggle for political representation.

While this is the story of a medical crisis that brought with it a social crisis, it is also a story of political discontent in a British colony. Binding both together are the sanitary reforms that stemmed from the 1863 Sutherland report and the 1865 cholera epidemic report and resulted in the withholding of the constitutional rights of the elected members in the Council. While the cholera epidemics were not as catastrophic as tuberculosis and other fevers, the cholera crises act as a prism through which Maltese society, its political and colonial milieux can be understood. In an age when the aetiology of cholera was unclear and the correlation between sanitation and cholera was tenuous at best, local and British authorities in Malta insisted on drainage reform and a better water supply for the urban regions of Malta, triggering local political discontent and shaping the constitutional development of a Mediterranean British colony.

PART IV:
FINANCE AND BANKING

10

The Impact of Crises on Credit in the Late Medieval English Economy[1]

PAMELA NIGHTINGALE

Introduction

The complex financial instruments that contributed to the banking crisis and 'credit crunch', which plunged the economy of the Western world into recession in 2008–09, would seem to have little in common with the use of credit in late medieval England. Yet when medieval merchants asserted that 'the best ware is ever-ready money', it was not because they deplored credit, despite its possible taint of usury, but because they had to rely on it too much, and experience taught them that in crises it was unlikely to meet their needs.[2] Even at its highest, the volume of the medieval English coinage is thought to have been worth no more than £2.3 million.[3] Since this could only be increased by an improved balance of trade bringing more gold and silver to the mint, and it had to finance an economy with a GDP that has been estimated at £4 to £5 million, this meant that even in normal circumstances there was a shortage of coin, and various forms of credit, as well as barter, had to fill the gap.[4] The numerous actions for petty debts recorded on manorial and borough court rolls, the loans and credit of much higher amounts recorded on those of the royal government, and the debt cases heard in the central courts, show how at every level of society credit was used to meet personal needs, and to provide

1   I am grateful to the Leverhulme Trustees, and to the Economic and Social Research Council (award no. 000271010) for financing my calendaring of the Statute Merchant and Staple certificates and the Extents on Debt in the National Archives.
2   J. Scattergood, *Politics and Poetry in the Fifteenth Century* (London, 1971), p. 336.
3   M. Allen, *Mints and Money in Medieval England* (Cambridge, 2012).
4   N. Mayhew, 'Modelling Medieval Monetisation', in R.H. Britnell and B.M.S. Campbell (eds), *A Commercialising Economy: England, 1086 to 1300* (Manchester, 1995), p. 58, Table 4.1; B.M.S. Campbell, 'The Agrarian Problem in the Early Fourteenth Century', *Past & Present*, 188 (2005), pp. 15–16.

the investment and liquidity necessary for agriculture, trade and industry to flourish, for governments to function, and for armies to fight wars.

Historians have identified volatility in prices, wages and incomes as characteristic of economic crises.[5] Since credit was so crucial to the economy, it seems likely that it would also reflect crises by volatile changes, which included sudden, severe, falls in the number and value of transactions. How common were such occasions in the medieval English economy, and what effect did they have on long-term trends in credit? Since the only banks in medieval England were concerned chiefly with financing overseas trade, and were run by alien merchants in London, the provision of domestic credit depended mainly on the financial resources of local people, or of trading partners in nearby towns or in London. As the number and wealth of English merchants grew in the fourteenth century, so they accounted for more of the creditor class, and fewer were clerics, officials and landowners. However, since all creditors, whatever their status, were risking their own money, their first concern was to assess the likelihood of repayment. This was particularly true of merchants because cash flow was vital to their businesses, and they were likely to be enmeshed in multiple debts to others that could bankrupt them if their own debtors defaulted. Caution therefore normally characterised their decisions. Consequently there was little chance that credit would create financial bubbles, and far more likelihood that its volatility would reflect decisions to withhold it in any crises that made repayment doubtful.

Such crises might occur for various reasons, and could affect demand for credit, as well as the willingness of creditors to supply it. However, the general shortage of coin meant that creditors always held the upper hand, and it was their decisions that mainly determined whether credit expanded or contracted. They were particularly influenced by any threats to the circulation of coin since this affected the likelihood of repayment. As merchants supported the English government's opposition to expanding the currency by debasement, any serious fall in the output of the mints, or drain of coin to pay for campaigns in Europe, was likely to make creditors more wary of financial commitments.[6] When the supply of bullion from the continent diminished, either because rival mints were prepared to pay merchants a higher price for it, or, more intractably, because the existing mines had become exhausted, the output of the English mints might fall to a trickle, as they did in the early fourteenth century. Similarly, any events that reduced the wool exports that earned the bullion, such as disease in sheep flocks, or interruptions of

---

5 M. and C. Casson, 'Economic Crises in England, 1270–1520: A Statistical Approach', Chapter 3 above.
6 N.J. Mayhew, 'From Regional to Central Minting', in C. Challis (ed.), *A New History of the Royal Mint* (Cambridge, 1992), pp. 135, 145–6, 148.

trade through war, and disputes with Flanders, were likely to reduce both the demand for credit and the willingness of creditors to advance it.

Other factors could also undermine creditors' confidence in repayment. Bad harvests would cause food prices to rise, and create the possibility of famine, which would reduce the demand for other goods. Attacks by the Scots on the border counties occurred nearly every year between 1296 and 1346, and were a continuing threat to the northern economy.[7] Political instability caused by factions among the nobility, or by weak kings, could lead to civil war and undermine confidence in the rule of law, in the safety of trade and in the enforcement of debts. No threat, though, could match the fear caused by the unpredictable, repeated onslaughts of plague, which made the period after 1348 quite different from that which went before. Although there had been years of high mortality earlier, especially during the famine of 1315–18, the scale of that inflicted by the Black Death in 1348–49 was unprecedented in English experience. The frequent return of plague in subsequent years contributed to the failure of the population to recover, and also created a psychological climate that undermined confidence in investment.[8] Clearly it exacerbated the volatility of credit, but did it also determine its main trends?

Interpreting the evidence

The extent to which crises affected credit in the late medieval English economy can only be analysed by taking a sample of debts that covers the entire kingdom. The 36,595 statute merchant and staple certificates of unpaid debt in the National Archives provide such a sample between the years 1284 and 1530.[9] Although they mainly record mercantile activity, they do not exclude private loans. Also they reflect the rural, as well as the urban economy, since landowners and peasants in every village were involved in the cash economy and in trade, and they too depended for their livelihood, and often for their survival, on the availability of money and credit.[10] Unfortunately, historians' assessments of the certificates have long suffered from the views that M.M.

7 P. Nightingale, 'Finance on the Frontier: Money and Credit in Northumberland, Westmorland and Cumberland in the Later Middle Ages', in Martin Allen and D'Maris Coffman (eds), *Money, Prices and Wages: Essays in Honour of Professor Nicholas Mayhew* (London, 2014).
8 On the general background and interpretive problems of the medieval English economy, see R.H. Britnell, *Britain and Ireland, 1050–1530: Economy and Society* (Oxford, 2004); J. Hatcher and M. Bailey, *Modelling the Middle Ages: The History and Theory of England's Economic Development* (Oxford, 2001).
9 The National Archives, Classes C.241 and C.131.
10 C. Briggs, *Credit and Village Society in Fourteenth-Century England* (Oxford, 2009), *passim*.

Postan published in an article on credit in 1930.[11] From a very limited investigation of some early London statute merchant rolls, and ignoring the related statute merchant and staple certificates, Postan concluded that by the later fourteenth century the system was recording mainly penal bonds that were used to enforce contracts, rather than ordinary credit. He thereby missed the fact that because the Statute Staple of 1353 provided a cheaper and more efficient system for registering and enforcing debts in those towns where staple courts were established, they were able to attract almost all mercantile business in their localities. In London the city's statute merchant registry lost most of its mercantile business to the Westminster staple court, even though both registries sent their certificates of default to Chancery for enforcement. This means that the certificates issued by both systems have to be analysed together.

Their huge bulk has deterred other historians from investigating the evidence independently, and they have been content for the most part to repeat Postan's views, and to dismiss the statistical value of the certificates.[12] However, a full analysis of them shows that penal bonds account for no more than 3.2 per cent, and were more commonly under 2 per cent, of the total, and are easily recognised and discounted. It is also clear that all classes of people, both clerical and lay, from nobles to husbandmen, recorded debts in the registries, even though their common use by merchants for debts of high value raised their average considerably above those recorded on borough, or manorial court rolls. Although the certificates show only the debts that were unpaid, it appears from comparing them with surviving original rolls of different dates, from the London and Coventry registries, that they represent fairly consistently about one fifth of those that were originally registered.[13] The consistency of this figure is explained by the speed with which creditors reacted to any threats to repayment by withdrawing credit. This is confirmed

11   M.M. Postan, 'Private Financial Instruments in Medieval England', *Vierteljahrschrift für Sozials- und Wirtschaftsgeschichte*, XXIII (1930), reprinted in *Medieval Trade and Finance* (Cambridge, 1973), pp. 28–64.

12   The most recent, albeit inaccurate, exponent of Postan's views on this subject is J.L. Bolton, in *Money in the Medieval English Economy, 973–1489* (Manchester, 2012), pp. 275–80, and in 'Was There a "Crisis of Credit" in Fifteenth-Century England?', *British Numismatic Journal*, 81 (2011), pp. 144–64. For my refutation of his claims, see P. Nightingale, 'A Crisis of Credit in the Fifteenth Century, or of Historical Interpretation?', *British Numismatic Journal*, 83 (2013), pp. 144–64.

13   For a detailed discussion of the Statute Merchant certificates and the evidence that they represent c.20 per cent of the debts originally registered, and possibly 7 per cent of the total credit used in late medieval England, see P. Nightingale, 'Money and Credit in the Economy of Late Medieval England', in D. Wood (ed.), *Medieval Money Matters* (Oxford, 2004), pp. 51–71, reprinted in P. Nightingale, *Trade, Money and Power in Medieval England* (Aldershot, 2007), XV, and id.,'Gold, Credit, and Mortality: Distinguishing Deflationary Pressures on the Late Medieval English Economy', *Economic History Review*, 63 (2010) p. 2, notes 10–11.

by significant falls in the number of transactions on those surviving London rolls that coincide with economic recessions.

Furthermore, the value of the certificates as evidence of crises and trends in credit nationally, and not just in registered credit, is confirmed by similar trends visible in other sources. These include the outlawries for debt recorded on the Patent Rolls, the gifts of goods and chattels given as security for debt, which are recorded on the Close Rolls and on the London Plea and Memoranda Rolls, and the records of debt cases that came before the central law courts of King's Bench, and Common Pleas, and the London Mayor's Court, as well as from those recorded in towns like Colchester, Exeter and Coventry, and from some rural manorial courts.[14]

If one identifies crises of credit by the most serious falls of 40 per cent or more in the value of the certificates in any one year, then the contrast is clear between the few in the fourteenth century, and the far more numerous ones in the fifteenth (Figure 10.1). In the 115 years between 1285 and 1399 only four years are marked by falls of 40 per cent or more. These were 1295, 1318, 1349 and 1365.[15] There were also two years, 1362 and 1375, that saw falls of 30–40 per cent. By comparison, the 130 years after 1400 include fourteen when there were falls of 40 per cent or more, and another six when the falls were between 30 and 40 per cent. These indicate that the Black Death ushered in a period of much greater volatility of credit. There are also considerable differences in its main trends in these two periods. In the years 1285 to 1294, it was stable, or increasing. The war against France then initiated a marked decline in 1295–99 before there was a return to high growth between 1300 and 1311. Legislation under the Ordainers, which was influenced by their desire to win mercantile allies in their political struggles with Edward II, then decreed that from 1311 to c.1322 only creditors and debtors who were merchants could use the registries, and in most cases that restriction seems to have lasted up to 1327 or 1330. This meant that the number of certificates fell significantly in that period, with falls in value most notable in the years of agrarian crisis between 1314 and 1322.

After the restriction to merchants ceased, the number of certificates grew markedly in the next two decades, but they plunged both in number and value by approximately one third in 1349–51 with the arrival of the Black Death. Despite this initially severe fall, the certificates subsequently maintained fairly stable figures in the following decades until a drop of 27 per cent in value in 1398 proved to be the prelude to a fall of 32 per cent in their total for the first

---

14   P. Nightingale, 'England and the European Depression of the Mid-Fifteenth Century', *Journal of European Economic History*, 26 (1997), pp. 639–40, 644–8.

15   The dates cited from 1285 to 1311 refer to the date of repayment since the date of registration is not recorded on many of the certificates in this period. It usually occurred within the previous six months. After 1311 they are the dates of registration.

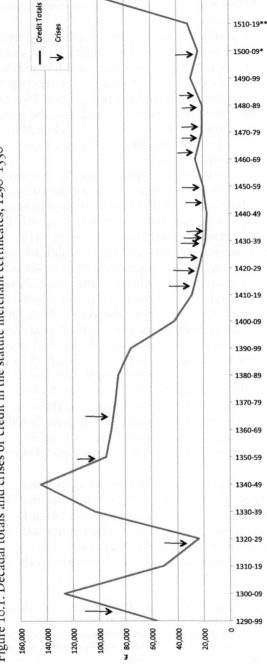

Figure 10.1. Decadal totals and crises of credit in the statute merchant certificates, 1290–1530

Sources: National Archives, Classes C.241 and C.131 certificates.

Note: The totals exclude sums of 1,000 marks or more, and include sums for missing certificates identified from Class C.131. The years 1311–30 record only mercantile credit. *Five years only. **Four years only.

decade of the fifteenth century. Thereafter the decadal totals dropped steadily to their lowest point in the 1440s. Some recovery began in the late 1450s and continued in the 1460s, but fell back in the next two decades.[16] Only in the 1490s did credit begin to increase consistently, although growth is then partly obscured until the 1520s by some years of missing certificates. In view of the overwhelming impact of the Black Death on these trends in 1348–49, one must ask how much other individual years of crisis contributed to them.

Crises before the Black Death

Crises are not noticeable in the first ten years of the certificates between 1284 and 1294. Even though the amount of bullion brought to the mints was declining from 1289, and there is evidence that general prosperity was waning, previous high mintages had increased the currency sufficiently to maintain a reasonable circulation at least until 1294.[17] In the ten years 1285–94 the certificates record average annual credit of £6,287, which did not vary much from year to year until it fell abruptly by 49.5 per cent in 1295. This was a year when a bad harvest, following a previous poor one, sent food prices to a height not previously recorded since 1272.[18] There is evidence to show that bad harvests made peasants more reluctant to lend money, but they probably mattered less to those creditors who registered larger sums in the statute merchant registries, since many of them were landowners who must have profited from the higher prices their grain fetched.[19]

Far more significant for them was what happened to the wool they produced and sold, and to prices and taxation, after Edward I declared war on France in June 1294. Edward promptly seized all the wool in the realm as a royal prise, and in November 1294 raised the export duties on it by three marks (£2), or 47 per cent of the average value of a sack. Merchants responded by attempting to force the growers to accept lower prices. They met resistance, wool remained unsold, and exports fell to little more than half their level in 1290.[20] These events reduced both the demand for credit, as

16 Nightingale, 'England and the European Depression', pp. 644–8.
17 E.M. Carus-Wilson and O. Coleman, *England's Export Trade, 1275–1547* (Oxford, 1963), p. 37. Wool exports are largely unrecorded between 1290 and 1294. M. Allen, 'The Volume of the English Currency, 1158–1470', *Economic History Review*, 54 (2001), p. 607, Table 2; Campbell, 'Agrarian Problem', p. 16.
18 E.H. Phelps Brown and S.V. Hopkins, 'Seven Centuries of the Prices of Consumables, Compared with Builders' Wage Rates', *Economica*, 23 (1956), reprinted in E.M. Carus-Wilson (ed.), *Essays in Economic History*, II (1966), Appendix B, p. 93.
19 P. Schofield, 'The Social Economy of the Medieval Village in the Early Fourteenth Century', *Economic History Review*, 61 (2008), pp. 53–61.
20 Carus-Wilson and Coleman, *England's Exports*, pp. 389.

well as the willingness to grant it, and caused the slump in the number and value of the certificates. A contributing factor was the fall in alien investment, which had been declining since the 1280s as the Italian firms found it harder to obtain the silver they needed for purchases of wool. The outbreak of war with France exacerbated their difficulties as it severed their links with the Champagne fairs where they were accustomed to borrow money. As a consequence, the Riccardi, who had financed the king, were bankrupted in 1294, while the certificates indicate that alien credit as a whole fell that year to less than 5 per cent of the whole.[21]

Falling exports earned less bullion, and caused the output of the London mint to fall by a third in 1295–96.[22] The Canterbury mint closed for lack of bullion in 1296, while the amount brought to the London mint plunged between September 1297 and October 1298 to the lowest value since records began in 1220. Credit fell again in 1297 after Edward I seized wool worth £14,000, and private treasure worth another £10,000, in the attempt to pay his troops and allies on the continent. These measures, and repeated heavy taxation of the laity and clergy, drained £350,000 in coin from the country to finance the French war.[23]

To maintain the circulation of coin necessary for trade, merchants imported quantities of foreign imitation sterlings from 1298.[24] The reputation of sterling coins for their high silver content had encouraged foreign mints for some years to produce imitations. These had been of reasonable quality, but the new wave of imitations, known as pollards and crockards, contained up to one third less silver than the sterling standard, and their wide distribution reduced confidence in the coinage and increased the general reluctance to give credit.[25] As a consequence, the total recorded in the certificates in 1298 fell in value by 25 per cent, despite the truce with France in October 1297. As sound money became scarcer, and the economy contracted, creditors were obliged to extend the average time they took to foreclose after default from one year, eight months in 1295, to three years, eight months in 1299. Only when the king demonetised the pollards and crockards and ordered a recoinage in 1300 did confidence recover, and credit in the certificates rose in value by 47 per cent that year.

It was not, though, until 1304, when silver from the newly discovered mines of Kutna Hora in Bohemia began to flood into England, that the certificates

---

21 P. Nightingale, 'Alien Finance and the Development of the English Economy, 1285–1311', *Economic History Review*, 65 (2012), pp. 7, 9, 11, 13–14.

22 C. Challis (ed.), *A New History of the Royal Mint* (Cambridge, 1992), Appendix I, p. 676.

23 W.M. Ormrod, 'The Crown and the English Economy, 1290–1348', in B.M.S. Campbell (ed.), *Before the Black Death* (Manchester, 1991) p. 183.

24 Nightingale, 'Alien Finance', p. 14.

25 N.J. Mayhew, *Sterling Imitations of Edwardian Type* (Royal Numismatic Society Special Publication, 14, 1983), p. 24.

show that credit grew consistently until the Ordainers in 1311 restricted the system to merchants only. Previously it was likely that only one party would be a merchant, while many certificates did not record merchants at all.[26] By 1310 the currency had reached a size of c. £1.5 to £1.9 million, and it was probably even larger at £1.8 to £2.3 million by 1319.[27] Since Edward II did not export coin to finance wars in Europe, its size was probably sufficient to maintain credit at a reasonable level for some years despite the reduced supply of new silver to the mints in the second and third decades. Additionally, much wool was now purchased with imported foreign gold coins, which English wool merchants also used in their own dealings with each other. These enabled them to release silver coin from savings.[28]

The restriction of the registries to mercantile creditors and debtors between 1311 and c.1330 inevitably reduced the number of certificates, but they also declined because of several adverse events that reduced the demand for mercantile credit. Wool exports fell in 1315–16 when the renewal of war between France and Flanders affected the Flemish cloth industry, and at the same time excessive rainfall between 1315 and 1318 created a Europe-wide famine, with high mortality. Furthermore, hostilities in 1317 between Flemish sailors and men of the Cinque ports hindered the full establishment of peaceful relations in 1318, with consequent effects on exports and credit.[29] Although there was an improvement in 1319, bad harvests in 1321–22, and high mortality among creditors, prevented any speedy recovery.[30] However, 1318 was the only year that stood out in this period for its sharp fall of 43 per cent in mercantile credit, almost certainly because of a decline of 21 per cent in wool exports following disease among the flocks.

Crises after the Black Death

None of these crises, though, had an impact comparable with the arrival of plague in 1348, which cut the population by up to one half, sparing neither rich nor poor, and thus reducing the numbers of likely debtors and creditors. It also made people temporarily fearful of travelling to towns to negotiate, as

---

26 Challis (ed.), *New History of the Royal Mint*, Appendix I, p. 677; P. Nightingale, *A Medieval Mercantile Community: The Grocers' Company and the Politics and Trade of London, 1000–1485* (London, 1995), pp. 123–33.

27 Allen, *Mints and Money*, p. 344, Table 10.12.

28 P. Nightingale, 'Gold, Credit, and Mortality', pp. 5–6.

29 T.H. Lloyd, *The English Wool Trade in the Middle Ages* (Cambridge, 1977), pp. 108–9.

30 Carus-Wilson and Coleman, *England's Exports*, p. 42; Challis (ed.), *New History of Royal Mint*, Appendix I, p. 678; P. Nightingale, 'Some New Evidence of Crises and Trends of Mortality in Late Medieval England', *Past & Present*, 187 (2005), p. 53.

well as register credit, and also made them less confident that their debtors would live to repay them. The combined effect of mortality and fear reduced the number of transactions in the certificates by 46 per cent in 1349, and then in 1350 by another 30 per cent. The demographic impact of the Black Death on the economy has naturally suggested to historians that repeated high mortality from plague must also have been the main cause of the recurring crises, and exceptional volatility of credit, which becomes evident in the certificates in subsequent years. Was it, though, the prime reason for the long-drawn-out trend of falling credit that the certificates reveal in the fifteenth century, and for the fact that by the end of the series it was not until the 1520s that they recovered the number and value they had in 1310?

Despite the initial huge fall of the population in 1348–49 it seems doubtful whether subsequent mortality crises were chiefly responsible for this pattern, because the certificates show that if there were no other adverse circumstances, the effect of plague on credit was usually short-lived. Moreover, they confirm that the decade after 1348–49 was one of returning growth and increased prosperity per head. Besides inheriting the land, businesses, and money of those who died, survivors of the plague gained from an export boom in wool, and from increasing exports of cloth, which brought more silver flooding into the country, and an abundant supply of coin. Combined with the shortage of labour, this created a rapid inflation of wages and prices. Wages of agricultural workers increased in purchasing power by 24 per cent in the 1350s.[31] Credit followed suit. Although the loss of population reduced the number of transactions and the total value of the certificates in that decade by 35 per cent below that of the 1340s, the average value of each rose from £38 in the 1330s, to £44.50 in the 1340s, and then to £57 in the 1350s.[32]

Moreover, there were years when the certificates indicate that there were serious falls in credit for reasons other than high mortality. In 1356 the total fell by 32 per cent, and did not recover for another two years. At the same time London's share of credit surged to 45 per cent of the whole. It appears that the reason for both movements was the government's decision in 1353 to respond to difficulties experienced by English merchants in Flanders by temporarily banning denizen export of wool, and by obliging aliens to buy their exports in eight English towns, which were designated as staples.[33] Since London was the only staple that was a port it gained more trade than the

---

31   Output increased from £62,909 in gold and £6,143 in silver coins in 1359–60, to £207,869 in gold and £6,020 in silver in 1360–61: Challis (ed.), *New History of Royal Mint*, Appendix I, pp. 680–1; Nightingale, 'New Evidence of Crises and Trends of Mortality', p. 47; G. Clark, 'The Long March of History: Farm Wages, Population, and Economic Growth, England 1209–1869', *Economic History Review*, 60 (2007), p. 116 and Figure 5.

32   Nightingale, 'Gold, Mortality and Credit', p. 7, Fig. 4.

33   Lloyd, *Wool Trade*, pp. 206–8.

others, while the ban on denizen exports reduced both the demand for credit and the ability of provincial English merchants to provide it.

Furthermore, the impact on credit of plague's second visitation, which is normally dated to 1361–62, is not clear-cut, even though deaths recorded for creditors rose to 14 per cent in 1362, and remained high at 10.4 per cent in 1363, compared with their normal average of 3.3 per cent.[34] Although the certificates dropped in value in 1361 by 12 per cent, they rose again in 1362, probably because of an abnormally high output of gold coin in the previous two years, and equally high wool exports in 1361–62, especially from London.[35] Demand for credit in the certificates actually fell more, by 35 per cent, in 1363–64, when merchants reduced their exports in protest against higher duties imposed by the Calais staple.[36]

The total plunged even further in 1365, by 45 per cent, even though the death rate among the creditors was less than half that of 1362–63, and no national plague was recorded. Again the most significant feature was the sharp fall in the share of Londoners, and this, too, was most likely the result of another temporary ban on denizens exporting wool for three and a half months between 31 January and 17 May 1365.[37] Although 1368 was reportedly the year of the third plague, it was in 1370 that the creditors' mortality rose to 7 per cent, and the value of their certificates fell by 17 per cent. The renewal of the war with France in 1369 most likely contributed more than mortality to this fall by causing a ban on denizen wool exports until August 1370.[38]

A fourth national outbreak of plague, traditionally ascribed to 1375, almost certainly began in London earlier, since the mortality rate of the creditors rose in 1374 to nearly 6 per cent. This time the total value of the certificates fell by 30 per cent, but recovered the following year. There was then another drop of 35 per cent in 1376, which reflects a fall in wool and cloth exports, particularly from London. This most likely happened because of London's conflicts with the Crown, and the political uncertainties and factional divisions in the city's own politics, which were connected with the summoning of the Good Parliament that year.[39] London was also the setting for an even greater political crisis in June 1381 when the Peasants' Revolt brought three days of fire, destruction and death to its streets, and set citizen against citizen, in a crisis that almost overthrew the royal government. However, the rebels' occupation was brief, and although several counties were

34 Nightingale, 'Some New Evidence of Crises and Trends of Mortality', pp. 40–1, 47.
35 Challis (ed.), *New History of Royal Mint*, Appendix I, p. 680.
36 Lloyd, *Wool Trade*, pp. 210–12.
37 Ibid., p. 213.
38 Carus-Wilson and Coleman, *England's Exports*, p. 50; Lloyd, *Wool Trade*, pp. 216–17.
39 Carus-Wilson and Coleman, *England's Exports*, p. 51; Nightingale, *Medieval Mercantile Community*, pp. 243–7.

involved in the rebellion it did not extend much beyond the month of June. Nonetheless, the shock to financial confidence is clear from the fall in the number of the Westminster staple certificates from the ten relating to debts registered in May, to none for any registered in the month between 27 May and 28 June. The London registry similarly issued none for that period. The revolt, though, made little change in the pattern of certificates throughout the rest of the country, and, overall, they indicate that credit fell in 1381 by only 26 per cent below the total for 1380.

The limited impact of these lesser crises helps to explain why the average annual value of the certificates in 1390–94 was, at £8,437, little short of the average of £8,974 for 1350–54, despite considerable volatility and mortality in the interval. It seems that after the first great onslaught of plague had reduced the size both of the population and of the economy, interruptions of the wool trade, and political crises, explain as much as epidemics, the occasionally severe, but nonetheless, temporary, falls of credit visible in the certificates. These did little to alter trends in which the total values fell modestly each decade by about 4.4 per cent in the 1360s and 1370s, and then by a mere 2.6 per cent in the 1380s.

The introduction of a gold coinage in 1344 had helped to sustain credit by increasing the amount of coin per head from a level of 4–7 shillings in 1300, to about 5–9 shillings in 1351.[40] Ransoms and booty from successful campaigns in France additionally made the 1350s and early 1360s years when there were high mintages of both gold and silver coins, while the new outbreaks of plague continued to raise wages. Thus, although the recurrence of plague prevented the population from recovering its former size, its effect on the distribution of wealth, combined with the expansion of the currency, and the growth of cloth exports, enabled peasants and townsmen to increase both their own purchasing power and their scope for individual enterprise. This kept domestic trade and manufactures buoyant in these decades, and so created a fairly constant demand for credit. Those crises that did occur were clearly not sufficiently deep or protracted to offset these favourable developments.

One countervailing trend, though, which became more obvious from the 1350s, was the increased concentration of credit in London. The flow of bullion and trade from the continent had always made the city the dominant financial centre, and even before the Black Death it accounted for 20 to 30 per cent of the credit recorded in the certificates. By the 1340s they record debtors of Londoners in every county except Cumberland, Westmorland, and Rutland. However, in the 1350s Londoners' share of the credit in the certificates grew to 40 per cent, and from the 1390s to 50 per cent. Several factors

40   Allen, 'Volume of the English Currency', pp. 606–7.

contributed to it. Principal among these was the city's geographical position, which gave it access through the Thames Valley to an extensive hinterland, as well as the shortest sea-route to the continent. This mattered particularly after 1362 when Calais became the principal home of the overseas wool staple. Its choice strengthened London's advantages in the export and distributive trades, and increased its merchants' ability to accumulate greater amounts of capital, and to give more credit over a wider area than could provincial towns and ports. London's greater financial resources, and far-reaching trading links, also made it a magnet for the enterprising, who could now exploit the new demand for labour created by plague, to escape from their villages to seek greater freedom and a higher standard of living in the city's crafts and trade. These factors determined that when the economy plunged into recession in the fifteenth century, London was able to increase its share of credit in the certificates to 60 per cent by the 1450s, and to 85 per cent by the 1480s.

Falling trends of credit

A deteriorating trend in credit is first marked in the certificates of the 1390s when the total fell 11.5 per cent below that of the previous decade, and did not again reach the level of 1390 until 1518. There was no significant mortality among the creditors in the 1390s, and no reports of serious outbreaks of plague. The fall in credit, though, did coincide with a significant decline in the output of silver coin from the London mint. This in turn was influenced by diminishing supplies of bullion from Europe. Despite the introduction of gold coins, silver mattered most in the everyday transactions in the economy, since gold nobles were of too high a value to be used much in the retail trade. As the kingdom's stock of money was increasingly dominated by gold, a spreading trade depression becomes visible in falling totals of credit in the certificates.

In the first decade of the fifteenth century the certificates plunged in value by 44 per cent, and the general fall in transactions was evident even in the Cambridgeshire villages of Oakington and Willingham.[41] Although plague was recorded in 1400, 1406 and 1408, and mortality among the creditors was high, no one year reveals a fall of 40 per cent or more in credit. It is likely, therefore, that its contraction reflected mostly the shortage of silver coin caused by the plunging output of the London mint. Whereas in the 1380s the mint's output of silver coin had averaged £2,500 a year, it dropped sharply in

41 C. Briggs, 'The Availability of Credit in the English Countryside, 1400–1480', *Agricultural History Review*, 56 (2008), p. 9, Table 2.

the 1390s and in 1405–06 fell to only £101, then to £80 in 1406–07, while in the following year it struck a mere £8-worth of silver coin.[42]

In the second decade there were two years, 1412 and 1419, that were marked by severe falls of credit in the certificates. Their value plunged by 51 per cent in 1412, and did not recover until 1429.[43] Plague was reported, but since there was only 2 per cent of mortality among the creditors, and wool and cloth exports were not affected, it is likely that the severity of the fall is explicable more by anxieties caused by the recoinage of 1412, which reduced the weight of the gold noble and the penny respectively by 16.7 and 10 per cent. This was the only way Henry IV had of responding to the desperate shortage of silver, but it meant that debtors could repay in coin of lower intrinsic value than that of their original debt, and imports became more expensive.[44] In 1419 credit fell by 45 per cent, with the fall most conspicuous in London's share, from 47 to 27 per cent of the total. It was probably due to plague, as soldiers returning after Agincourt brought back new infections with their booty, and the creditors' mortality rate rose to 12 per cent in 1417, and reached 13.3 per cent in 1418. Recovery came, though, by 1422.

Similar outbreaks of plague recurred repeatedly in London, and also nationally, in the next three decades. They created the same volatile pattern of sudden, severe falls of credit in the certificates, followed by fairly speedy recoveries. In the thirty years from 1420 there were six occasions when the national total in the certificates plunged by 40 per cent or more. The first, in 1423 occurred when the creditors' mortality had risen to 6.45 per cent, but it was also likely to have been influenced by the reopening of the Calais mint from July 1422, which diverted bullion from London.[45] Recovery came in 1425. The second occasion coincided with another outbreak of plague in 1427, and 5 per cent mortality among the creditors. Recovery followed the next year.

The third, in 1430 differed from the others because although the total value of credit in the certificates fell by 53.7 per cent, and mortality among the creditors reached 7.7 per cent, there was no corresponding fall in London's share, which in fact grew to nearly 62 per cent. Furthermore, unlike the relatively brief effects of mortality crises, the certificates did not recover their value of 1429 until 1460. There can be little doubt that the main cause of the crisis was not mortality but the enactment in September 1429 of the parliamentary legislation known as the bullion and partition ordinances, which was designed to bring more bullion to the English mint. They ended the

42   Challis (ed.), *New History of Royal Mint*, p. 682.
43   There are certificates for another £2,215, but these clearly relate to penalties for the performance of another obligation.
44   Challis (ed.), *New History of Royal Mint*, pp. 172–3.
45   M. Allen, *Mints and Money*, pp. 272–3.

normal arrangement by which wool was sold in Calais on credit, and obliged customers to pay the entire price in gold or silver coin when the bargain was struck. Also, the rules about partition meant that individual wool merchants were only paid when all the wool taken to Calais was sold.[46] This arrangement favoured the Londoners, with their greater financial resources, at the expense of provincial merchants. However, the consequence of all these changes was a significant drop in wool exports nationally, and of credit, in 1428–30.[47]

By contrast, the three other critical years in this period conformed with the pattern of sudden falls in credit and swift recoveries previously associated with high mortality. In 1433 the total in the certificates fell 70 per cent below that of the previous year. At the same time, the mortality of the creditors rose to 6.89 per cent, and London's share of recorded credit fell to 28 per cent of the whole as plague struck the city.[48] Little wool was also exported that year, and cloth exports from London also fell. However, as with previous mortality crises, the level of credit substantially recovered the following year.[49] Plague and famine in 1438 caused credit to fall again by 30 per cent. The creditors were too rich to be affected by famine but their mortality was high at between 6.25 and 9 per cent in 1439–41. It was also high in 1445, 1447 and 1449. However, 1444 was the only year in that decade when the total in the certificates fell by more than 40 per cent. The cause appears to have been falling wool and cloth exports from London, which significantly reduced the mint's output of both gold and silver coin.[50] Recovery followed the next year. The third major crisis of this period occurred in 1450. It was probably the result of a serious outbreak of plague that began in London the previous year, when there was a death rate among the creditors of 11.1 per cent.[51] Credit in the certificates fell by 48 per cent, and there was also another sharp fall in London's cloth exports. However, both recovered the following year, and by 1452 were expanding vigorously.[52]

Despite the severity of these mortality crises, in four of them, those of 1427, 1433, 1444 and 1450, credit recovered within one year, and from that of 1419 within three years. It also began to rise generally in the certificates of the 1450s, and reached heights in 1457–58 that had not been seen since 1429, despite the political crises and conflicts caused by the Wars of the Roses. This decade also saw evidence of agricultural recovery, including

46 Lloyd, *Wool Trade*, pp. 260–2.
47 Carus-Wilson and Coleman, *England's Exports*, pp. 58–9.
48 R.S. Gottfried, *Epidemic Disease in Fifteenth-Century England: The Medical Response and the Demographic Consequences* (Leicester, 1978), p. 47, Table 2.2.
49 Lloyd, *Wool Trade*, p. 261.
50 Challis (ed.), *New History of Royal Mint*, Appendix I, p. 683.
51 Gottfried, *Epidemic Disease*, p. 48.
52 Carus-Wilson and Coleman, *England's Exports*, pp. 97–8.

renewed expansion of sheep flocks.[53] It was aided by the absence of national epidemics, but it also coincided with a greater output of silver coin by the London mint.[54] This, though, proved to be temporary, and a renewed shortage of coin led Edward IV to carry out another devaluation in 1464 by a further weight reduction of 20 per cent. Plague also returned that decade in major epidemics, as well as in several lesser ones. National outbreaks were recorded in 1463–64 and in 1467, and mortality among the creditors was high at 7.4 and 6.45 per cent in 1465–66.[55] The pestilence of 1467 probably began the previous year in London because the capital's share of credit in the certificates fell then from 70 to under 40 per cent, and failed to recover in 1468. Instead the outbreak developed into a nationwide epidemic, which caused the total credit in the certificates to fall in 1468 by 50.5 per cent. This time it did not recover to its previous height for another six years. Nonetheless, the total for the decade still showed a rise of 23.5 per cent above that of the 1450s.

The number of epidemics increased in the 1470s, and they help to explain why credit in the certificates fell overall in that decade by 20 per cent. There was a single annual fall of 40 per cent in 1474, probably because of the flux, or dysentery, of the winter of 1473–74.[56] In 1479–80 occurred what has been called 'the fifteenth century's most severe outbreak of epidemic disease', a description that finds support in the fall of credit in the certificates of that year by 60.6 per cent.[57] There followed a brief recovery until another fall of 55 per cent occurred in 1488. Since there was no reported plague that year it is likely that this fall, coming after another in the previous year, was caused by the anxieties of the Merchant Adventurers about whether Henry VII would renew the commercial treaty made in 1478 with the ruler of the Low Countries, which affected their exports of cloth. Henry delayed until February 1489, and the Adventurers' fears no doubt explain why denizen cloth exports from London plunged in 1486–88, and credit with them.[58] That, though, proved to be the last crisis indicated by the certificates before they end in 1530, apart from a lesser fall of 36 per cent in 1523, which coincided with Henry VIII's extravagant spending on his French campaign, and a forced loan.

---

53   Nightingale, 'England and the European Depression', pp. 644–8; John Oldland, 'Wool and Cloth Production in Late Medieval and Early Tudor England', *Economic History Review*, 67 (2014), p. 28.
54   Challis (ed.), *New History of Royal Mint*, Appendix.
55   Gottfried, *Epidemic Disease*, p. 42.
56   Ibid., pp. 45, 148–9.
57   Ibid., p. 45.
58   A.F. Sutton, *The Mercery of London* (Aldershot, 2005), pp. 319–20; Carus-Wilson and Coleman, *England's Exports*, p. 109.

Short and long-term changes in credit

This brief survey shows that nine of the major crises in credit after 1350 – those in 1419, 1423, 1427, 1433, 1444, 1450, 1468, 1474 and 1480 – were linked with epidemics that had the most severe effects on London. These outbreaks reduced both the demand for, and supply of, credit because merchants would retire to the countryside to escape the pestilence, and creditors were also deterred by the possibility their debtors would die before they had repaid their loans, forcing them to wait for executors to settle estates, and to satisfy competing claims. The more that credit was concentrated in London, and the more plague became endemic there, the more volatile mercantile finance was likely to be.

Nonetheless, even though plague undoubtedly contributed in these years to a falling or stagnant population, it cannot be said that it was responsible for the most serious and long-lasting crises that shaped the trends of finance and credit. The certificates indicate that apart from the epidemics of 1467–68, 1474 and 1479–80, the recurrence of plague normally affected credit for usually no more than a year, unless there were other, economic, or political reasons, for it to fall. This was because whenever plague returned for a few months, commercial activity was delayed, rather than lost. By contrast, those crises that caused credit to fall for economic, or political reasons, were likely to last much longer. This explains the outcome of the five crises in the same period that were not linked with plague, and from which credit did not speedily recover. After its fall in 1398 by 27 per cent, the devaluation of the coinage in 1412 influenced its severe fall by 51 per cent, from which it did not recover until 1429, only to fall again in 1430 by 54 per cent, with no full recovery before 1460. Again, this was a brief respite, before the total plunged again in 1461 by 59 per cent, and did not recover until after 1500. Within that extended period there occurred a further fall in 1479 by 60.6 per cent, from which there was no recovery until 1486. Taken together, these falls amounted to a persistent serious decline of credit from 1398 that was not specifically related to high mortality, but nonetheless indicated major depressions of economic activity.

Many of these extended periods were related to falls in wool exports. Cloth exports began to influence demand for credit more in the fifteenth century, but were not predominant until cloth overtook wool as the more valuable export in the 1460s.[59] Even then, most of the proceeds of cloth sales were not remitted as bullion and taken to the mint, because the mercers invested them in the Low Countries in ever-growing imports of linen, to earn the profits of a double trade.[60] Exports of wool, therefore, continued to be crucial

---

59   M. Bonney, 'The English Medieval Wool and Cloth Trade: New Approaches for the Local Historian', *The Local Historian*, 22 (1992), p. 26.
60   Sutton, *Mercery of London*, pp. 155–8, 295–302; Oldland, 'Wool and Cloth Production', p. 41.

earners of bullion. The sensitivity of credit to them arose not because most of the certificates directly reflect wool purchases, although some obviously did. Rather, it reflects how merchants' perceptions of the link between wool exports and the output of the mint affected general sentiment in the London money market about the availability of coin. It therefore influenced general views on how likely it was that credit would be repaid, and so affected the willingness to grant it.

Political crises also contributed to the pattern. The conflicts and upheavals that brought Edward IV to the throne explain the plunge of 59 per cent in credit in 1461 as rival Yorkist and Lancastrian supporters awaited the outcome of the three crucial battles that determined the deposition of Henry VI before they would commit themselves financially.[61] Similarly, the prospect of further political upheavals after Edward's defeat by Warwick in 1469, the restoration of Henry VI the following year, and then Edward's return and victory in 1471 sent it falling again. Such crises were not long-lasting, but they contributed to delayed recoveries.

A fuller explanation of the pattern must also take into account the underlying monetary trends that exacerbated these crises. It was Europe's depleted silver stocks, and the export of English coin to finance the French war, followed by the threat to the currency of the debased pollards and crockards, which had extended the credit crisis of 1295 up to 1300. Similarly, the sharp, and prolonged fall in bullion imports from 1315 contributed to that of 1318 by reducing the output of coin from the mints, which shook mercantile confidence. Whereas after the catastrophe of the Black Death, the decadal totals of credit had been buoyed up by high mintages of gold and silver coin until the 1390s, subsequently their decline became much more precipitate and prolonged, and crises became more frequent, and recoveries usually slower.

The change can be linked with falling supplies of bullion from that decade. By 1422 the amount of silver coin per head had fallen to only about one fifth of what it had been in 1351, and as late as 1470 it had still not recovered that earlier level. Furthermore, the number of gold coins in the currency totalled less than half their value in 1422.[62] The provinces were the chief sufferers as London's share of credit in the certificates grew from 43 per cent in the 1380s to 50 per cent in the 1390s, and reached almost 80 per cent in the 1470s. Consequently, even when new supplies of silver began to reach the mints Londoners were in the strongest position to employ them to expand their own trade and credit, at the expense of provincial competitors.

---

61 Nightingale, *Medieval Mercantile Community*, pp. 516–17.
62 Allen, *Mints and Money*, p. 344, Table 10.12.

Coping with falling coin and credit

How did people cope with declining supplies of coin and credit over such long periods? Parliamentary petitions made the royal government well aware of the effect that shortages of silver coin had on the economy and on popular discontents, but it had little means of alleviating them. It could not print money, and in the long-term interest of preserving the high reputation of sterling abroad, which mattered also to English merchants, it was determined to avoid the continental choice of expanding coinages by debasing them. It had, therefore, to strike more coins of lower weight from the same amount of metal. Even these changes increasingly required parliamentary approval.[63]

Laws had been passed since the thirteenth century to protect England's supply of bullion by regulating foreign exchange, by restricting payments by letters of exchange, and by prohibiting the export of precious metals and coin without a royal licence. These were supplemented from 1340 by requirements that wool exporters should deliver specified amounts of bullion to the mint. From 1429 these rules were stiffened by various measures first to prohibit, and then to regulate sales of wool on credit at the staple.[64] Although some of these measures did help to increase supplies of bullion, their success was limited, while those that forbade wool sales on credit proved counter-productive by reducing trade. A less controversial way of increasing the supply of bullion was by raising the price that the mint offered for it so as to attract merchants away from rival European mints, and to persuade holders of old, heavier coin in England to exchange theirs. Edward IV did this in 1464–66, and, as a result, credit increased substantially in 1465–67. The improvement, though, was brief as mercantile confidence was undermined by a new outbreak of plague, and by the political intrigues and disaffection that led to Warwick's rebellion and the defeat of Edward IV in 1469.

Even without such crises, any remedial measures to improve the flow of bullion to the mints could only be short-term while Europe as a whole suffered from widespread bullion famines, particularly of silver. Henry VII tried to attract more to his mints in 1489 by reducing the king's seigniorage and moneyers' charges.[65] This measure succeeded in doubling credit in the certificates the following year. More significantly, this time growth was maintained, with only a few breaks in the next decades, primarily because

---

63 Challis (ed.), *New History of Royal Mint*, pp. 144–5.

64 J.H. Munro lists all the relevant legislation in 'Bullionism and the Bill of Exchange in England, 1272–1663: A Study in Monetary Management and Popular Prejudice', in F. Chiapelli (ed.), *The Dawn of Modern Banking* (London, 1979), reprinted in J.H. Munro, *Bullion Flows and Monetary Policies in England and the Low Countries, 1350–1500* (Variorum, 1992), IV; Appendices B, C, E.

65 Challis (ed.), *New History of Royal Mint*, pp. 195–7.

the supply of bullion, especially of silver, was increasing in Europe. Until this was sufficient to ease credit generally, membership of a trade fraternity that could pledge financial support, might help an aspiring borrower, but because merchants were usually indebted to each other in complex, multiple trans-actions, illiquidity could cause bankruptcies to occur in quick succession, with a consequent disruption of markets and widespread loss of commercial confidence.[66]

Even in recessions, money could still be borrowed at high interest rates by those willing to pay them, who could also offer security in lands and valuables. Such opportunities for profit attracted London merchants like Gilbert Maghfeld, who, because his own debtors could not repay him, found it easier to give up trade and to lend his capital instead to the nobility, who could offer jewels or lands as security, and pay a handsome return by way of interest.[67] Other creditors recorded from the 1430s in the Close Rolls and in London's Plea and Memoranda rolls, gifts of goods and chattels, some as modest as a hood, or tools, which they accepted as security for loans. Despite such attempts to maintain credit, many sources make it clear that the falling number of prosecutions for defaults reflect its continued reduction. Although merchants continued to trade by juggling payments in kind with those for which they could obtain coin, and by negotiating to offset one debt against another, wool producers still demanded advance payments of up to 40 per cent of the total price in coin, and were likely to refuse to deal with small wool-broggers like John Heritage, who could not provide them.[68] The conse-quence was that a shortage of coin meant that at best transactions slowed, financial crises became more common, and they expanded more frequently into recessions.

Only when the output of the mints increased persistently, as it did at the beginning of the sixteenth century, do the certificates record a permanent rise in the trend of credit. Confidence grew with the volume of the coinage to the extent that in 1520 John Heritage concluded that he could risk exploiting the new liquidity by venturing into money-lending.[69] There is, though, no evidence to support J.L. Bolton's claim that a form of paper money had developed in late medieval England, which 'more than made up for a shortage of coin', through the circulation of negotiable bonds.[70] Although such bonds could be legally assigned, they were not automatically negotiable because they were no more than personal I.O.U.s unsupported by any issuing authority, and so were not comparable with royal gold and silver coins of intrinsic fixed value.

66 Nightingale, 'A Crisis of Credit in the Fifteenth Century?', p. 153.
67 Nightingale, 'Money and Credit in the Economy of Late Medieval England', pp. 56–9.
68 C. Dyer, A Country Merchant, 1495–1520 (Oxford, 2012), pp. 97–8, 101–2.
69 Ibid., p. 96.
70 Bolton, 'Was there a "Crisis of Credit" in Fifteenth-Century England?', pp. 157, 162.

Moreover these bonds only had a limited circulation in London, and were unknown in the provinces. They were therefore simply another form of credit, geographically circumscribed, and subject to exactly the same limitations as other credit, in their dependence on confidence that individual borrowers had the means to repay.[71]

Conclusions

This chapter has shown that credit, like modern stock markets, was extraordinarily sensitive in the Middle Ages to any crises that made potential creditors suspect that repayment was doubtful. This sensitivity brought volatility to the financing of the medieval economy and thereby exacerbated crises that occurred for a variety of reasons. So crucial was credit to a system of payment that had to rely on an inadequate supply of coin that its prolonged contraction could be as damaging as the warfare, political turmoil, bad harvests, heavy taxation and interruption of wool exports that threatened prosperity more directly. One must, though, distinguish between crises that had short-term effects on credit, and those that caused major changes in long-term trends. Once plague became a common occurrence the former were much more numerous. But although plague inspired most fear, the certificates show that after the shock of its first devastating effects on the population, even the most serious of its recurrences rarely affected levels of credit for more than two years. There were always people to take over the businesses of those who died, even if it meant that capital and enterprise became concentrated in fewer hands, and increasingly in London.

Far more influential on the overall pattern of credit, and on the contribution it made to the economy, were creditors' perceptions of the amount of silver coin in circulation. Without some certainty that the mints were replenishing the silver needed to maintain liquidity, London merchants like Gilbert Maghfeld lost the confidence to commit their resources to trade, and would lend only to the rich who could give security in land or jewels.[72] Young people also had little hope of marrying and increasing the population without loans to set up separate households and to acquire and stock farms. It is therefore significant that new supplies of silver coin coincide with the expansion not just of credit, but also of the population in the early sixteenth century.[73] Once

---

71 Nightingale, 'A Crisis of Credit?', pp. 150–3.
72 P. Nightingale, 'Money and Credit in the Economy of Late Medieval England', in D. Wood (ed.), *Medieval Money Matters* (Oxford, 2004), pp. 58–9.
73 Nightingale, 'England and the European Depression', pp. 648–50; J. Langdon and J. Masschaele, 'Commercial Activity and Population Growth in Medieval England', *Past & Present*, 190 (2006), pp. 39–42, 73–81.

monetary and demographic growth resumed, the impact of individual crises on credit diminished, because the more powerful financial currents were able to lift the economy over the obstacles that had previously delayed its recovery. Confidence replaced uncertainty, stimulating investment and enterprise, and thereby prevented any crises that occurred from deepening and coalescing into further decade-long recessions. Finally, this analysis has shown how credit, as revealed by the statute merchant and staple certificates, reflected the crises and trends in the real economy, a reflection which, by its very closeness, helps to validate the evidence that the certificates provide.

11

Dealing with the Threat of Reform: The Bank of England in the 1780s

ANNE L. MURPHY

The 2008 financial crisis and its fallout has prompted an extended examination of what John Turner has called the 'cadavers' of past banking crises.[1] The common denominators in this work are the search for commonalities of cause, the identification of 'preventative measures' and the consideration of why reforms enacted in the aftermath of crisis fail to prevent their periodic recurrence.[2] With regard to the latter, Youssef Cassis has explored the question of how crises have impacted on financial architecture, how they have shaped banking firms and their governance, increased or decreased levels of state intervention and provoked shifts in financial and political power relationships. He concludes, perhaps unsurprisingly, that the record of taking advantage of the opportunities for positive reform presented by financial crises has been mixed. Greater levels of state interference and forced changes in governance and regulation have often missed important targets; the use of non-standard financial instruments, those notorious derivatives that did so much damage in 2008, are a particular candidate, of course.[3] The complexity of such instruments makes them difficult to regulate and, when regulation is introduced, the markets develop new instruments and strategies in part to circumvent controls. Even when the targets for regulation are clear, outcomes are compromised by horse-trading and collusion and conflict among key players. The window for real change can be surprisingly short-lived. Demand

---

1 John D. Turner, *Banking in Crisis: The Rise and Fall of British Banking Stability, 1800 to the Present* (Cambridge, 2014), p. 4.
2 Ibid., p. 3; see also Charles W. Calomiris and Stephen H. Haber, *Fragile by Design: The Political Origins of Banking Crises and Scarce Credit* (Princeton, 2014); Youssef Cassis, *Crises and Opportunities: The Shaping of Modern Finance* (Oxford, 2011); Piet Clement, Harold James and Herman Van der Wee (eds), *Financial Innovation, Regulation and Crises in History* (London, 2014).
3 Cassis, *Crises and Opportunities*, p. 157.

for regulation, for example, is usually highest in the immediate aftermath of a crisis. Thereafter, motivation can dissipate quite quickly. As is becoming ever more clear the further we move away from 2008, understanding and acting upon opportunity for reform leading from crisis is not straightforward.

The history of British public and private finance during the long eighteenth century would certainly seem to bear out this pessimistic view. Although economic and financial crises were regular, in a period of almost continuous and very costly war, the state was too dependent on the financial markets, and indeed financiers, for reform to be considered seriously. Moreover, even from the early eighteenth century, the monied men asserted their power in this respect, warning the state that they and the financial markets they supported were necessary for the maintenance of public credit. It was an argument that was convincing since no regulation was enacted against the financial markets during the long eighteenth century.[4] Yet, discussion of regulation and reform of Britain's financial architecture was considerable and always increased in response to crisis.

This chapter will consider perhaps the most prominent and wide-ranging of those crisis points: not the commonly cited South Sea Bubble of 1720 but rather the loss of the American colonies during the early 1780s. As Hoppit notes, the financial crises of the early eighteenth century tended to be limited in geographical scope and economic impact.[5] Those of the later eighteenth century were more far-reaching, and the crisis that accompanied the final years and ending of the War of American Independence encompassed not just public and private finance but seemingly the political system and the nascent empire. Responses to this crisis were limited by a lack of will to facilitate political change, but the system of public finance did become a target for reform. Indeed, the 1780s can offer us an example of successful change prompted by economic and political crisis, notably in reform of the public finances and that troublesome monied company, the East India Company. Yet, in spite of the precedent set by these reforms and its central place in Britain's financial and economic architecture, the opportunity for serious reform of the Bank of England was missed. It is the aim of this chapter to explore the reasons why this was so and how eighteenth-century bankers reacted under threat. Section I will discuss the contexts in which discussions about reform emerged. Section II will explore the construction and agenda of an internally appointed Committee of Inspection at the Bank. Section III will consider the findings and outcomes of the Committee's work.

---

4   A.L. Murphy, 'Financial Markets: The Limits of Economic Regulation in Early Modern England', in P.J. Stern and C. Wennerlind (eds), *Mercantilism Reimagined: Political Economy in Early Modern Britain and its Empire* (Oxford, 2014), pp. 263–81.

5   J. Hoppit, 'Financial Crises in Eighteenth-Century England', *Economic History Review*, 39 (1986), p. 56.

I

The development of a system of managing public debt through the issuance of long-term instruments, such as annuities, began in England during the 1690s and was motivated by William III's wars against Louis XIV's France.[6] From the first, the schemes adopted were devised, managed and promoted by private projectors. Their long-term success is evident with hindsight but, even in the 1690s with debt at relatively low levels, many contemporaries regarded the indebtedness of the state and the supposed profiteering from the nation's exigencies as highly problematic. Concern, especially that of the landed elites, tended to increase as successive conflicts with continental rivals placed more strains on the public purse. Early criticism of the handling of the public finances naturally alighted on the supposed advantages gained by financiers from wartime constraints and the troublesome political connections between the monied men and the state. But more broadly, the imagined diversion of political power away from the landed interest and into the hands of the monied men was resented. Likewise many feared that the secondary market that had grown up to support the exchange of government debt would encourage speculation, disrupt markets, and divert men away from honest trade.[7]

By the mid eighteenth century, as a result of the War of the Spanish Succession (1702–13) and the War of the Austrian Succession (1740–48), debt levels had risen significantly. One of the most outspoken critics of the government's handling of public finances, David Hume, argued at that time that either the nation must destroy the public debt or public debt would destroy the nation. Debt would limit the amount of specie in circulation, increase taxes, raise prices, oppress the poor and transfer wealth to either the idle and unproductive rich or to foreigners. Indeed, any increases in public debt merely served to put wealth into the hands of those:

> Who have no connexions with the state, who can enjoy their revenue in any part of the globe in which they chuse to reside, who will naturally bury themselves in the capital or in great cities, and who will sink into

---

6 P.G.M. Dickson, *The Financial Revolution in England: A Study in the Development of Public Credit, 1688–1756* (London, 1967); A.L. Murphy, *The Origins of English Financial Markets: Investment and Speculation before the South Sea Bubble* (Cambridge, 2009).

7 For a more complete discussion of these arguments, see Dickson, *Financial Revolution*, pp. 15–35. For alternative analyses of the contemporary debate regarding England's early modern financial system, see P. Brantlinger, *Fictions of State: Culture and Credit in Britain, 1694–1994* (London, 1996); A. Finkelstein, *Harmony and the Balance: An Intellectual History of Seventeenth-Century English Economic Thought* (Michigan, 2000); J.G.A. Pocock, *Virtue, Commerce and History: Essays on Political Thought and History Chiefly in the Eighteenth Century* (Cambridge, 1985).

the lethargy of a stupid and pampered luxury, without spirit, ambition or enjoyment.[8]

The ultimate consequences, according to Hume, of the accumulation of the public debt was that the nation would eventually tire of indebtedness, resulting either in default or repudiation or in schemes based on the reduction of interest or deliberate inflation, which would ultimately destroy public credit. Directly influenced by Hume, Adam Smith was equally pessimistic:

> ... an apology is made for the public debt. Say they, tho' we [owe] at present 100 millions, we owe it to ourselves, or at least very little of it to foreigners. It is just the right hand owing the left, and on the whole can be little or no disadvantage. But [it] is to be considered that the interest of this 100 millions is paid by industrious people, and given to support idle people who are employed in gathering it. Thus industry is taxed to support idleness. If the debt had not been contracted, by prudence and oeconomy the nation would have been much richer than at present.[9]

Indeed, commentators were never reluctant to criticise the management of the nation's finances. Their criticisms were many and various but, as the previously noted comments from Hume and Smith suggest, they chiefly amounted to a more sophisticated version of those earlier arguments and, in particular, to the ideas that the taxes required to service the debt were injurious to the underlying economy of Britain, and that the nature of the debt encouraged the idle at the expense of the industrious. Underpinning all of these criticisms was the warning that uncontrolled debt would lead to economic, and undoubtedly political, crisis. Only a very few suggested, like James Steuart, that:

> Public debts do not so much affect the prosperity of the State as private debts do that of the debtor. The interest of a private debtor is simple and uncompounded; that of a state is so complex, that the debts they owe, when due to citizens, are on the whole rather advantageous than burdensome: they produce a new branch of circulation among individuals, but take nothing away from the general patrimony.[10]

None of these arguments were beneath the notice of Parliament. Indeed it was regularly confronted directly with comment and criticism in the forms of

---

8   David Hume, *Of Public Credit* (London, 1752), pp. 357–8, cited in Takuo Dome, *The Political Economy of Public Finance in Britain, 1767–1873* (London, 2004), p. 1.
9   Adam Smith, *Lectures on Jurisprudence* (1762–63 and 1766), cited in Dome, *Political Economy of Public Finance*, p. 41.
10 James Steuart, *An Inquiry into the Principles of Political Oeconomy* (London, 1767), p. 625, cited in E.L. Hargreaves, *The National Debt* (London, 1930), p. 81.

petitions or other submissions to the Exchequer. Moreover, as Hoppit shows, the level of legislation considered in relation to public finance, especially after the Seven Years' War, indicates that the public purse was an 'ever-present concern'.[11] A 'spirit of checking upon the executive' had also become ingrained since 1688, when the Glorious Revolution placed greater financial power in Parliament's hands.[12] Such scrutiny was obviously encouraged partly by necessary interest in expenditure via the civil list, the grant given to the sovereign to cover his household expenses, and by the increasing disquiet over the feared imminence of state bankruptcy. In the former case, investigations were prompted by rising costs, which could only be explained, given the known parsimony of George III's household, by inefficiency and waste in government departments and only controlled by demanding a greater degree of scrutiny of the business of government. In the latter, one of the main consequences was the compilation of a number of reports detailing the development and state of the public finances. The first, written by James Postlethwayt in 1759, entitled *The history of the public revenue from the revolution in 1688 to Christmas 1753*, covered a variety of topics including the progress of the national debt, the terms on which it had been raised, a comparison of the expenses of the great wars to date, an examination of the efficiency of the sinking fund and the histories of the Bank of England, East India and South Sea companies. Postlethwayt concluded his account with a practical plan for reducing all the public funds into one.[13]

Such reports, however, gained little real currency until a crisis point was reached. That crisis began with the unprecedented expense of the American War of Independence. The subsequent failure of the conflict and the loss of the colonies galvanised public and political opinion. Economic and political strain is, of course, a characteristic of most conflicts but whereas heavy cost might be bearable in victory, it was regarded as catastrophic in defeat. Furthermore, by the late 1770s the country was facing not just a financial crisis, with the symptoms of economic and political decline seeming to be everywhere. As Gilmour notes, the late 1770s and early 1780s saw 'invasion scares, ... industrial riots, religious disturbances, near revolt in Ireland, denunciation of the Crown in Parliament, a reform movement in the country, a government so feeble that it seemed bound to collapse, fluctuating ministries and almost every symptom of discontent and decay'.[14] The potential losses

---

11   J. Hoppit, 'Checking the Leviathan, 1688–1832', in D. Winch and P.K. O'Brien (eds), *The Political Economy of British Historical Experience, 1688–1914* (Oxford, 2002), p. 269.
12   Ibid.
13   J. Postlethwayt, *The history of the public revenue from the revolution in 1688 to Christmas 1753 ...* (London, 1759).
14   I. Gilmour, *Riot, Risings and Revolution: Governance and Violence in Eighteenth-century England* (London, 1995), pp. 342–3.

from the defeat did not seem to be limited to the American colonies. Ireland and India also baulked against British misrule.[15] Military defeat, financial failure and political discord put Britain's nascent empire at risk. There was no question in contemporary minds that a crisis point had been reached and, as is often the case in the midst of crisis, this put the question of reform high on the agenda.

The moment of reformist zeal that occurred during the 1780s has been well-documented but is usually described as little more than an aspiration. The argument is made that the French Revolution thereafter brought the concept of reform, especially institutional reform, into disrepute. During the Wars with Revolutionary and Napoleonic France the reform agenda changed and diversified becoming, under Evangelical influence, somewhat more practical. This was met with some success in the abolition of the slave trade in 1807. But, even if abolition showed that change was possible even under an unreformed parliamentary system, the imperative for political change did not entirely disappear.[16] Action, however, had to wait until the 1830s.

Nonetheless, looking beyond the question of parliamentary reform shows that there were indeed elements of real reform taking place in the 1780s and these were targeted on the financial system. Finance and the monied men were, at this time, obvious targets for the country's ire. They were assumed to have profited while the country struggled, and to have profited not just from honest business in the country's service but from exploitation of the country's need. Thus, one pamphlet elucidated:

> Reports are gone about of the immense profusion of the public Treasury; of the enormous emoluments of some places; of large sums not accounted for; of a vast expense in favouring contractors, ... and providing for a useless set of men in order to keep up an extravagant parliamentary influence under the direction of the Crown.[17]

At the beginning of 1780 a motion brought by the Opposition was debated in the House of Commons that called for a committee of disinterested members of the House to examine the public expenditure. It called specifically for the abolition of sinecures, positions offering pay and position but requiring little work, as a matter of economy and the reduction of excessive emoluments for the work that was being done.[18]

---

15   A. Burns and J. Innes (eds), *Rethinking the Age of Reform: Britain 1780–1850* (Cambridge, 2003), p. 7.
16   Ibid., pp. 1–2.
17   British Library Add. MSS, 38213, fol. 137: Extract from a letter from a Gentleman in Norfolk to his friend in London, quoted in J.E.D. Binney, *British Public Finance and Administration, 1774–1792* (Oxford, 1958), p. 8.
18   Binney, *Public Finance*, pp. 8–9.

The motion was lost but the argument (that reform of the administration of public expenditure was necessary) was won. Under pressure Lord North, the prime minister at the time, appointed a statutory commission to examine the public accounts. The commission had two advantages over the committee previously proposed. First, it was the child of the sitting administration rather than the opposition and, secondly, a commission could be invested with the power to call documents and examine witnesses.[19] As Binney argues, these reforms might also be seen as a proxy for the more sweeping political reforms that would not be a viable proposition until well into the nineteenth century. Arguably, administrative reform, being less contentious, did not evoke the same kind of passions and was thus easier to implement.[20]

The Commission for Examining the Public Accounts sat between 1780 and 1787, and the six commissioners produced a total of fifteen reports that resulted in reform of all aspects of Britain's public finances. The principles followed by the Commission were those of removing opportunities for the misuse or misappropriation of positions or funds; eliminating corruption; and improving the effectiveness and efficiency of the various branches of revenue and expenditure. All principally addressed the public concerns that had emerged during the crisis of the 1780s, and demonstrate that crisis was viewed not just as the consequence of a failed conflict but rather the way that conflict had been managed at an administrative level. The exploitation of the system was one of the greatest concerns along with the notion that some had profited from the conflict and had perhaps had an interest in prolonging a lost cause. Although the work of reforming the public finances was arguably to extend over the following century, if not longer, as Binney argues, the Commission represented the 'dividing line between the ancient and the modern'.[21] It also arguably represents a clear example of successful reform prompted by financial and political crisis. Yet, one highly significant element of Britain's financial architecture remained untouched by the Commission. Although it had the power to examine all branches of the public revenue and expenditure, the Bank of England did not come under its jurisdiction.

On some levels this is not surprising since the Bank was a privately owned company answerable to its shareholders and subject to periodic renewals of its charter that would have allowed the government to terminate dealings with the Bank had it become dissatisfied with its performance. However, the Bank was at the same time effectively an integral part of the system of state finance, and untangling it from its public role would have been highly complex and unlikely. Moreover, the East India Company, also a private company was, at this time, under Parliamentary scrutiny. This would result in the imposition

19   Ibid., p. 9.
20   Ibid., p. 5.
21   Ibid., p. 282.

of the Board of Control in 1784: a government committee appointed to supervise the East India Company's affairs and prevent shareholders from interfering in the governance of India. The Board was the culmination of long years of concern about the Company's activities in India but did impose control over the Company's domestic affairs and sought to bring to an end the political manipulation of the Company's shares.[22] That certainly set a precedent for interference in the Bank's business, and the Bank's intimate connections to the financial stability of the state would undoubtedly have provided a valid excuse for the interference had the Bank's performance been less than satisfactory.

Moreover, while the Bank might have escaped the attention of the Commission, it had not escaped very severe criticism from some commentators.[23] Lord North, in 1781, certainly argued that the Bank 'from long habit and the usage of many years, was a part of the constitution' of England or 'if not part of the constitution, at least it was to all important purposes the public exchequer'. He went on to assert that 'by prudent management, by judicious conduct, wise plans, and exact punctuality in establishing its own credit, [it] had contributed very essentially to establish the national credit, a matter equally advantageous to this country both at home and abroad'.[24] But in this speech North was seeking to defend the Bank and argue for the renewal of its charter. Other commentators took a rather more dim view of the Bank's purpose, the management of its business and its value to the state. Notably, the Bank's close relationship to the state was deemed to be less than healthy, and the fact that monied men seemed to prosper, especially during wartime as the nation's hardship was played to the financiers' advantage, was resented. As Bowen notes, in this respect the critics of the 1780s were drawing on and reiterating concerns that had been common since the 1690s but had, prior to this point, not been pressing enough to prompt action.[25]

Criticisms manifested themselves in the calls for the establishment of a rival bank or, at the very least, the removal of the Bank of England's monopoly. There was a particular objection that the renewal of the Bank's charter in 1781 had been rushed through Parliament. One critic, the Whig MP David Hartley, pointed out that the scheme to renew the charter had been brought to the Commons with no prior notice. He wanted to know why the scheme was rushed through with such urgency when the Bank's charter still had more

---

22   H.V. Bowen, *The Business of Empire: The East India Company and Imperial Britain, 1756–1833* (Cambridge, 2008), p. 73.
23   H.V. Bowen, 'The Bank of England during the Long Eighteenth Century, 1694–1820', in R. Roberts and D. Kynaston (eds), *The Bank of England: Money, Power and Influence 1694–1994* (Oxford, 1995), p. 9.
24   Lord North, Speech of 13 June 1781 in the Committee of Ways and Means, quoted in Bowen, 'Bank of England'.
25   Bowen, 'The Bank of England', p. 9.

than five years to run. Hartley asked why there was a need for such secrecy and how it was that Parliament was not given the chance to consider such things properly. He went on to assert that the charter had been given to the Bank too cheaply. The charter, he argued, had a value and should, therefore, be offered to the highest bidder. In a pamphlet addressed to the Lord Mayor of London he reckoned that the renewed Bank charter should be valued as a 'beneficial lease of £240,000 a year for twenty-five years' and thus be costed at £1.5 million.[26] Others joined the chorus of disapproval. Sir George Savile argued that the 'public had an estate to sell' and was selling it too damned cheap.[27]

Ultimately none of these arguments affected the progress of the Bank's charter but with direct political reform not on the agenda, where critics were making the best inroads in their attacks were on the issues of administration and organisation, and with the idea that corruption could be cleared out from the bottom up. This period of crisis and the links between a corrupt and failing financial system and military defeat arguably placed the Bank of England directly in the firing line. It was part of a system of public finance that had failed the country during the War of American Independence. It prospered while the state suffered. Its monopoly protected it against rivals and the competition that might have lowered its revenues and thus the state's costs.

II

It was in the context of increasing criticism of, and investigation into, the state of the public finances that the Bank of England appointed its own Committee of Inspection. In March 1783 the Court of Directors appointed three of its own number, Mr Bosanquet, Mr Dea and Mr Winthrop, 'to inspect & enquire into the mode & execution of the Business as now carried on in the different departments of the Bank'. The Inspectors were to be permitted to 'meet at such times as may be most convenient to themselves and they are hereby impowered to inspect the management of every Office together with all such Books & Papers as they may think necessary'.[28]

There is unfortunately no 'smoking gun' that will allow us directly to connect the appointment of the Committee with the Commission for Examining the Public Accounts or anxiety about the crisis in public finances.

26   David Hartley, *Considerations on the proposed renewal of the Bank Charter* (London, 1781), p. 19.
27   J.H. Clapham, *The Bank of England: A History* (2 vols, London, 1945), I, p. 181.
28   Bank of England Archives [hereafter BEA], Minutes of the Committee of Inspection, M5/212, fol. 1.

As is usual in such documents, the Minutes of the Bank's Court of Directors and those of its Court of Proprietors were less than forthcoming about the reasoning behind decisions. With regard to the Committee of Inspection, the Minutes record only its appointment along with a brief account of its remit.[29] There was clearly no ambiguity in its establishment or discussion in the Court since the draft of Committee's remit, which is preserved in the Bank's archive, is a fair representation of what was eventually recorded in the Court's minutes. The very few alterations made on the document represent changes in wording rather than alterations in purpose or scope.[30] Moreover, the Committee's various reports tended to pass without specific notice being taken in the Minutes of the Court of Directors, although the members of the Committee were, as their task drew to a close, thanked for their 'indefatigable labour, attention and assiduity ... and very judicious observations and recommendations'.[31]

Nevertheless several factors do point to the direct connection between the Bank's appointment of its own Committee and the Commission for the Examination of the Public Accounts and, through that connection, allow us to regard the appointment of the Committee as a response to the crisis of the 1780s. Perhaps most importantly, two members of the Court of Directors at the Bank of England (Richard Neave and Samuel Beachcroft) served as Commissioners for examining the Public Accounts.[32] Richard Neave was a director between 1763 and 1811, a long-serving member of the all-important Committee of the Treasury and Governor of the Bank between 1783 and 1785, hence at the time when the Committee of Inspection was appointed. Samuel Beachcroft was a director of the Bank between 1760 and 1796, and Governor from 1775 to 1777, and he too sat on the Committee of the Treasury. Both men were, therefore, in positions of considerable influence at the Bank, and it is likely that they influenced the appointment of the Committee and had a hand in the design of its brief.[33]

The details of that brief seem to have been consistent with that pursued by the Commissioners for Examining the Public Accounts in every respect. Just as the Commissioners were given authority to call for departmental papers and take evidence from public officials, the Bank's Committee was given the

---

29 BEA, G4/23, Minutes of the Court of Directors, 14 April 1779 to 2 October 1783, fols 352–3.

30 BEA, G6/115, Court of Directors' Papers, fol. 15.

31 See, for example, BEA, G4/24, fol. 26; G4/24, fol. 43.

32 Both Neave and Beachcroft were appointed to the Committee to Examine Public Accounts by virtue of their mercantile background, viewed by Lord North as an essential ingredient in the Committee and one that, as Binney argues, might make them good judges of the reasonableness of contract prices. Binney, *Public Finance*, p. 13.

33 John Torrance, 'Social Class and Bureaucratic Innovation: The Commissioners for Examining the Public Accounts, 1780–1787', *Past & Present*, 78 (1978), p. 60.

freedom and power to 'inspect the management of every Office together with all such Books & Papers as they may think necessary ... [and] to call before them all or any of the Servants of the Bank for such information as they shall require'.[34] Equally, both Committees were empowered not just to inspect but also to make recommendations of changes that would improve the efficiency and economy of the respective businesses. The working practices of the two Committees were also similar. Both followed a practice of inspecting one department after another and publishing their findings and recommendations as they went along.[35]

With respect to the practical agenda of the Committee of Inspection, similarities can be seen with that of the Commission for Examining the Public Accounts. Of course, the Commissioners were dealing with a system mired in tradition and held back by amateurism and sinecurism. The Bank on the other hand, although affected by systems that had grown lax, was on the whole fit for purpose and staffed by men who had been promoted on the basis of time served and merit.[36] The Bank's Committee, therefore, was not quite so concerned with ensuring that all posts were associated with a useful duty and that each officer was personally executing the duties of his place, factors that were of primary interest to the Commissioners for Public Accounts. Yet, as will be demonstrated below, the Bank's Committee did examine closely the duties and workload associated with each post, and they took care to ensure that all staff were attending at the proper times. The Bank, therefore, followed the same agendas as the state-appointed Commission. It was responding to crisis in the financial system but also clearly seeking to circumvent any state interference that might have been the consequence of that crisis.

III

The Inspectors pursued their task over the course of an entire year. From March 1783 to March 1784 they visited offices, interviewed a great number of the Bank's servants from relatively lowly clerks and porters to the chief cashier and chief accountant, and explored options for adjustments and reforms in working practices. Their reports demonstrate that they had three chief concerns, all of which seem to be consistent with the reforming agenda of the Commissioners for Public Accounts: ensuring that each clerk had a well-defined role and was fulfilling that role; ensuring efficiency and

---

34 Ibid., p. 56; BEA, M5/212, fol. 1.
35 Torrance, 'Social Class and Bureaucratic Innovation', p. 66; BEA, M5/212; M5/213, *passim*.
36 Certainly initial employment in the Bank was likely to have been influenced by personal connections with the directors or prominent customers, but all staff were tested prior to employment and incompetent men were unlikely to have risen far.

effectiveness in the Bank's business; and rooting out corruption. In this way the chief criticisms of those who had identified crisis with financial and administrative incompetence would be addressed. The Bank of England would be able to prove that it had dealt with any elements that might lead to poor performance, poor value for taxpayers' money or exploitation of the country's need either for the gain of the directors of the Bank or the benefit of individual employees.

The concern with ensuring each clerk had a well-defined role was made manifest in every aspect of the Inspectors' work, from their observation of specific working practices *in situ* to their interrogation of specific clerks. In each office their investigation began with drawing up a list of those who occupied the office and the establishment of the contours of the working day. Thus Abraham Newland presented evidence about the work of the tellers in the banking hall in which he noted that they were ten in number and gave a detailed list of their duties.[37] Later, Mr Campe, the senior in-teller, was summoned before the Committee to give further specifics of the work undertaken by him and his colleagues. He testified that the hours of work were from 9 a.m. to 5 p.m. with each man being allowed an hour and a half for lunch. Lunch was strictly timed to ensure cover at all times.[38] In common with the vast majority of his colleagues, Campe informed the Inspectors that he had 'no reason to complain of the attendance of the Clerks in his department, or of their exceeding the time for which he occasionally gives them leave to be absent'.[39] The aim here was obviously to demonstrate that jobs at the Bank were not sinecures.

With regard to attendance and performance of allocated tasks, the Inspectors found little to complain of with regard to the junior men. Nonetheless, they were disappointed to find:

> a practice that strikes us a very extraordinary one, which is, that the Chiefs of the two great departments, & the Heads of most of the Offices throughout the Bank, are the first to quit the House, some at a certain hour; & others as soon as their particular part of the business is over; leaving the charge of every thing to the vigilance & honesty of the junior Clerks (frequently such as are very young in Office).[40]

Naturally, the Committee were quick to recommend that such practices be curtailed, noting that in 'any situation of Trust a compleat superintendence is desireable, it must be more immediately necessary where the Trust is of

37   BEA, M5/212, fol. 3.
38   Ibid., fols 30–5.
39   Ibid., fol. 36.
40   BEA, M5/213, fol. 173.

such infinite importance'.[41] Their willingness to censure the senior men in a document that, although not public, was presented for the scrutiny of the Court of Directors is testament to the seriousness with which the Inspectors undertook their tasks. They did not just pay lip service to the notion of reform, they were willing to demand change.

In the same spirit, although it is not officially recorded in the Inspectors' reports, they also looked beyond the reports offered by the heads of departments and offices. Notably, Samuel Bosanquet, one of the members of the Committee of Inspection, recorded his views of the Bank's servants in a private notebook as the Committee made their rounds. He seems to have sometimes found them wanting. Of Mr Gardner he wrote, 'a poor hand, obstinate and prejudiced to the old mode ...', as well Mr Gardner may have been after serving 39 years in the Bank![42] Another cashier, Mr Boult, was noted to be 'an old gentleman, allmost worn out, [and] not very sharp'.[43] Others, however, were clearly more able and open to the idea of reform. Mr Walsh of the 3 per Cent Consols Office was noted to be 'very intelligent, very able, and the only one fit for a head yet seen'.[44] Mr Walton of the 3 per Cent Reduced Consols Office was pronounced to be a 'very clever hand, very sensible and capable'.[45]

Following their inspections, the Committee also made recommendations for the future that reflected their close consideration of the abilities of the Bank's staff. They made it clear that they expected the Bank's directorate to take more notice of the capabilities of the permanent staff suggesting that they 'pay great attention to the abilities & characters of those they nominate, & at the time of election, to their performances'. Moreover, the directors were asked to reconsider the practice of promotion on seniority, 'which, though a fair and equitable rule to govern promotion, generally, will not apply in all cases, nor ought it to be resorted to where particular talents are required'.[46] As with the Commission for Examining Public Accounts, therefore, the response to crisis did drive some administrative change and improvements to efficiency.

With regard to the Inspectors' second motivation, that of ensuring efficiency, there were much more clear links with the agenda of the Commissioners for the Examination of the Public Accounts. Torrance argued that one of the Commissioners' goals was to implement a bureaucratic system of organisation in which 'speed, precision, impartiality, uniformity

41 Ibid., fol. 174.
42 BEA, M5/471, Memorandum book of Samuel Bosanquet, 1783–91, unpaginated.
43 Ibid.
44 Ibid.
45 Ibid.
46 BEA, M5/213, fols 174–5.

and accountability' were paramount.[47] The Bank's Inspectors evinced similar concerns. Specific observation was made of working practices and procedures in an attempt to eliminate waste and inefficiency and reduce the opportunity for errors. For example, early in the Committee's enquiries they discovered inefficiencies in the Bill Office. The system at that time saw clerks recording bills of exchange under their due date in a ledger, filing them under the name of the customer and then retrieving due bills from the files when needed, a system that was clearly unnecessarily complex. Hence, a recommendation was made that bills of exchange should henceforth be filed according to the day on which they fell due rather than by the name of customer, and a new filing cabinet was ordered to be built for the purpose.[48] Many such examples of alterations in procedures in order to effect efficiencies can be found in the Committee's Reports. At one point they even went so far as to recommend that the Bank's internal layout be changed so that related offices could be moved closer together.

The Inspectors' third motivation, that of rooting out corruption, was by no means the least of their concerns and created the greatest problems. The main problems identified point to perennial complaints against financiers that they exploit their positions for personal financial gain. In the eighteenth-century Bank's case this manifested in two examples of malpractice: clerks in offices dealing with securities acting in the market for themselves or as jobbers and brokers, and the giving and taking of gifts between clerks and customers and junior and senior men within the Bank.

Clerks in the transfer offices dealing in Bank stock and securities for themselves or acting as brokers and jobbers was certainly not a new problem. Rules preventing clerks from acting in the markets were well established long before the Inspectors began their investigations. Paid involvement in the financial market was banned by the Bank for a number of reasons. It distracted the clerks, led to problems with the jobbers and brokers, and was incompatible with the Bank's attempts to assert its distance from the market and its probity and integrity. As the Committee of Inspection asserted, clerks who did indulge were in danger of having their minds seduced 'from regular employment in an easy service, & attaching them to objects inviting though dangerous ...'.[49] They also placed the Bank at risk of accusations of allowing, or even encouraging, profiteering from the nation's emergencies. But it seems that the rules were commonly flouted. Hence, when the Committee took testimony from the clerks themselves, Mr Aldridge confessed that he had now and again acted as a broker but had never jobbed. Mr Windsor said he had acted as a broker and although he had not jobbed recently, 'he has now

47   Torrance, 'Social Class and Bureaucratic Innovation', p. 58.
48   BEA, M5/212, fols 19–20.
49   Ibid., fols 173, 154.

& then sold & bought a little stock which he has held for his friends'. Mr Crockford allowed that 'he had made Bargains in Stock for time, both on his own account & on that of his Principals'.[50] Mr Brown also admitted to acting as a broker occasionally 'but in a very trifling way'. In fact, nearly all the clerks interviewed admitted some involvement in the market.

They all also, like so many officials who are caught out, attempted to claim that they did not know of any orders that proscribed such behaviour.[51] In the case of the Bank's clerks, this seems disingenuous at best. Samuel Beachcroft's governor's diary, which covered the period from 1775 to 1777, contained a number of references to anonymous informers against clerks acting as jobbers and brokers, suggesting that this kind of activity was brought to the Bank's attention on a regular basis. Moreover, Beachcroft's disapproval was passed on to the clerks. He recorded in his diary:

> Upon an anonymous letter from the stock brokers & jobbers, Mr Pearce & Mr Pemberton were call'd in & reprimanded for dealing in Stocks by the Brokers transferring stock into their names & retransferring said stock by way of cloak to the brokers name, upon their promising never to act again in the same manner they were forgiven ... Mr Stonehouse & Mr Jewson were call'd in & order'd to acquaint every clerk in each of their departments that if they were found acting as brokers in future they would certainly be discharged.[52]

Mr Beachcroft's admonishments seem to have made little impact. Both Pearce and Pemberton were still employed by the Bank in 1783 when the Committee of Inspection convened, and both confessed to still being involved in the financial markets.[53]

Transfer office clerks, therefore, did have opportunities for taking advantage of their positions to generate additional earnings. Indeed, from the evidence of the Committee of Inspection it appears that stock-jobbing and broking were practised with worrying regularity by clerks who were, of course, in the right place at the right time. It is impossible to know how much these activities yielded. Some men undoubtedly dabbled occasionally in the markets, making a few pounds here and there. Others, especially those operating in partnerships with brokers, might have made significant profits. All such activity, though, pointed to precisely what the Commission for Examining Public Accounts had tried to root out of the Treasury and Exchequer: men who were failing to perform the roles for which they were being paid and instead were using privileged positions to make money from the public finances.

50 Ibid., fols 67, 84, 85.
51 Ibid., fol. 96.
52 Ibid., fol. 76.
53 Ibid., fols 111, 109.

Equally problematic were both the level of gratuities available to clerks and the opportunities to improve their positions or working lives through the making of presents to senior staff. Again this indicated that the public finances depended on a system of corruption that undermined not just the working environment but also the entire edifice of public finance. The Inspectors were evidently conscious of such concerns. They questioned each clerk about the level of gratuities received, and their answers made it clear that there was an understanding that this was a much more contentious issue than trading in securities. Hence Mr Laverick of the Accountants Office, interviewed on 19 November 1783, stated that although he had been 21 years in the Bank, he had seen 'no Gratuities whatever received from the Publick in this Office, nor did he ever hear of a Clerk making any present to the Heads of the Office for leave of absence or other indulgence'.[54] Mr Payne, the Chief Accountant at the time, was even more adamant, stating:

> That there were not any whatsoever received by him from the Publick; that some trifling ones have now & then been offered, but he has allways refused them, conceiving it totally inconsistent with his Station, to accept of any, as it is undoubtedly his duty to do the business of the Publick with the Bank, without receiving any emolument from them for so doing.[55]

Other men spoke of trifling presents. Mr Collins of the G cash book stated that Mr Steers, the Chancery broker, gave a guinea to each of the three clerks who worked the book at Christmas.[56] But these men had relatively little direct contact with customers, and interviews with men working in offices providing front-line services told quite a different story.

Mr Rogers, head of the Discount Office, told the Committee that although nothing was ever asked for, customers made gifts at Christmas to the amount of '3 or £400 in one year, in other years it has not exceeded £200'. Mr Rogers received all gifts and distributed them at his discretion according to the clerks' seniority.[57] Mr Clifford of the Drawing Office told a similar story of presents being made and the senior clerks overseeing division of the funds, as did Mr Etheridge of the Bullion Office.[58] Corporate customers also made presents to the Bank's clerks. Thus, the Bank of Scotland sent £60 per year which, after the Chief Cashier took 20 guineas, was distributed to the clerks in the Drawing offices, the Bill Office and the Chief Cashier's office.[59]

It also eventually emerged that there was some resentment of the way

---

54 Ibid., fol. 5.
55 Ibid., fol. 21.
56 BEA, M5/212, fol. 108.
57 Ibid., fols 59–60.
58 Ibid., fols 85, 132.
59 Ibid., fol. 147.

gratuities were distributed. In Samuel Bosanquet's notebook there is reference to a letter to the Committee detailing complaints about the manner of distributing the gratuities in the Drawing Office and alleging that the Committee had been given false information about the amount of gratuities received.[60] There were also clearly some concerns of preferential treatment being given to some customers at the Bank, and the Committee of Inspection were clearly concerned with ensuring that customers were not purchasing good service with presents of cash. The Committee's report notes one particular example of a bank draft for £5,500 that had been refused because the account was short by just £38. This was regarded as an error by the Bank's directors who would have clearly preferred to see the customer accommodated. It was clear that previously when such circumstances had occurred the draft had been provided and, at the very least, it was expected that the customer be informed personally before a refusal issued. The issue for the inspectors was never quite made clear but seemed to hinge on the fact that the customer in question did not generally offer Christmas boxes to the clerks, and it seemed likely that this was the reason his situation had been handled poorly.[61]

The clerks were much clearer about the problems of gratuities than they were about dealing in securities. Yet, here the Bank was on much more problematic ground when responding. It is clear that it understood quite well the value of gifts and gratuities in oiling the wheels of business. The Bank, for example, always paid New Years' gifts to officials at the Exchequer and the Treasury. At the end of December 1782 this amounted to 340 guineas.[62] Equally the Committee of Inspection's response to the question of gratuities was very pragmatic. There was a clear acknowledgement from the Inspectors of the difficulty of regulating the practice of receiving gratuities and fees. In their final report they noted:

> we must leave to the consideration of the Court, how far the practice of receiving money from the Publick under the name of Gratuities ... is an evil that can be prevented altogether: for at the same time, that we express our particular disapprobation, of the introduction & continuance of a custom, not only disgraceful in itself; but liable to occasion dissatisfaction & heart-burnings amongst the Clerks themselves, from the unequal distributions in some of the Offices; & what is a matter of much more serious consequence, to give rise to partialities & unjust preferences, towards the Publick ... yet we have found it so firmly established, so operating as part of the legal emoluments of Office, handed down to the Clerks from their predecessors, that we think it requires, not only solemn deliberation but an accurate & nice Judgement, to determine whether it were wiser to endeavour at abolishing

60 BEA, M5/471, unpaginated.
61 BEA, M5/212, fols 216–17.
62 BEA, G4/23, fol. 332.

the practice altogether; or to regulate it, by excluding the Chiefs from any participation, & ordering equal distributions amongst the inferior Clerks.[63]

With hindsight, it is clear that, although the Inspectors were very keen to make changes that improved efficiency, they merely tinkered around the edges of some things, like gratuities and fees, which might have been viewed as part of the system of corruption. At the end of their report, while they did make some criticisms, essentially they claimed to be very happy with what they had found. And in the end the conclusion they offered was:

> When we contemplate the immense importance of the Bank of England not only to the City of London, in points highly essential to the promotion and extension of its Commerce, but to the nation at large, as the grand Palladium of Public Credit, we cannot but be thoroughly persuaded that an object so great in itself and so interesting to all ranks of the community must necessarily excite care and solicitude in every breast, for the wise administration of its affairs.[64]

The Inspectors evidently believed that the changes they promoted demonstrated 'wise administration' and justified the 'care and solicitude' of the nation. But, if we return to the criticisms made of the Bank during the 1780s, it becomes clear that the agenda for reform pursued by the Inspectors, while addressing the supposed problems of inefficiency and corruption in the management of the public finances, did not in any way address the concerns of the Bank's more ardent critics. There was no consideration of the nature of its monopoly and no overt justification of the nature or cost-effectiveness of its service to the state. The Bank essentially adopted a borrowed agenda for change, one that fit a general pattern of concern with the administration of public finance but did not address the role of the Bank within Britain's financial architecture. Indeed, the reform agenda of the 1780s was purely inward-looking. Real reform of the Bank of England would require an outward-looking approach and a proper response to the needs of the broader financial system, and that would not come until the nineteenth century with the financial crises of 1825 and subsequently.

IV

The kinds of questions that were being asked of the financial system and the monied companies in the wake of the crises of the 1780s were not very

---

63 BEA, M5/213, fols 158–9.
64 Ibid., fol. 178.

different from those that are being asked today or in the aftermath of most financial crises. Was the system fit for purpose? Were those who ran the system exploiting the country's need to line their own pockets? Were levels of remuneration appropriate, and did the ability to create earnings over and above one's salary impact on behaviour?

These questions produced a solid agenda for reform in respect of the EIC and the public finances. Moreover, no one could have predicted during the appointment of the Commissioners for Public Accounts quite how necessary their reforms would be. The wars against Revolutionary and Napoleonic France placed a tremendous strain on the public purse, and levels of long-term debt rose from c. £250 million at the end of the War of American Independence to £844 million by 1819. That Britain was able to withstand such significant levels of indebtedness was testament not only to the willingness of the public to invest in the state but to the army of administrators who developed, during the later part of the eighteenth century, from John Brewer's 'gifted amateurs' to a professional class of bureaucrats.[65] As Binney argues, it was the Commissioners for Public Accounts who effected this change, dragging the system of administering the public finances into the modern era.[66] And there can be little doubt that the Bank of England's own agenda for putting its house in order during the 1780s should be thought of as part of this process.

But the Bank also had its eye on the bigger picture. The debate about corruption in the system of public finance had, if nothing else, increased the willingness of the state to scrutinise and reform its administration. The Bank was undoubtedly considered part of that administration. Arguably, therefore, the Bank in putting its own house in order was pre-empting a likely state-ordered examination of the nature and methods of its business. In doing so, the Bank demonstrated, as it did so often, its ability to play the political game, and showed how it was able to survive throughout the eighteenth century in spite of potential rivals and social and political hostility. But it did not reform, not at this time. Arguably, it did not have to because it could answer all the questions that were raised by the crisis of the 1780s: it was generally efficient and fit for purpose, its positions were not sinecures and the corruption of its clerks was on a small scale. It also did not reform because it was coping with the crisis at hand, it needed only to answer the questions that were asked in the wake of the loss of the American colonies. At that time was not required to look to wider issues nor to anticipate the crises that were to come. Perhaps that is the problem with all agendas for reform born in the wake of crisis: they are about coping, not innovating or anticipating.

---

65   J. Brewer, *The Sinews of Power: War, Money and the English State 1688–1783* (London, 1994), p. 250.
66   Binney, *Public Finance*, p. 282.

12

Bursting the Bubble: The 2007 Northern Rock Crisis in Historical Perspective

MATTHEW HOLLOW AND RANALD MICHIE

Introduction

On the morning of Friday 14 September 2007, the British public awoke to the news that Northern Rock (at that time, the UK's fifth largest mortgage lender) was in severe financial difficulties and had formally asked for financial support from the Bank of England.[1] Spooked by these reports, and anxious about the safety of their deposits, many of those with savings in Northern Rock hurriedly took the decision to withdraw their money from the bank.[2] Long queues quickly began to form outside many Northern Rock branches as beleaguered cashiers struggled to cope with the large numbers of anxious depositors desperately trying to withdraw their savings (a situation not helped by the fact that Northern Rock's website also collapsed due to the volume of traffic it received).[3] Meanwhile, in the City, shares in Northern Rock plunged by almost 40 per cent in less than a day.[4] In the end, the panic was only brought to a halt when the Chancellor of the Exchequer, Alistair Darling, gave a taxpayer-backed guarantee the following Monday that all existing deposits at Northern Rock would be protected.

Unsurprisingly, this dramatic (if brief) run on Northern Rock generated a huge amount of interest both in the UK and throughout the financial world.

---

1   The story itself had actually been broken the night before on television by Robert Peston on the BBC's *Ten O'Clock News*.
2   Subsequent estimates indicated that over £1 billion (over 5 per cent of all of Northern Rock's retail deposits) was withdrawn on 14 September 2007.
3   House of Commons Treasury Committee, 'The Run on the Rock: Fifth Report of the Session 2007–08', vol. 1 (London, 2008), p. 55.
4   BBC News, 'Timeline: Northern Rock bank crisis' (5 August 2008). Available online at: http://news.bbc.co.uk/1/hi/business/7007076.stm [accessed: 9 July 2014].

Without question, a great deal of this interest was down to the fact that – on a superficial level at least – the short-lived panic, with its accompanying images of anxious-looking depositors waiting in long queues to withdraw their money, seemed to hark back to an era of banking and financial instability far removed from our own.[5] This was an impression that was also actively reinforced by the national and international press who, in subsequent reports, quickly fell into the habit of describing the Northern Rock crisis in almost routine terms as 'the UK's first bank run in 150 years'.[6]

Given this widespread awareness of the uniqueness of the Northern Rock crisis in recent British history, it is perhaps surprising that more has not been written on the long-term historical roots of the crisis.[7] Instead, much of the writing on the events of September 2007 has been produced (seemingly) with the sole intention of pinpointing the chief 'culprits' in the build-up to the crisis.[8] More often than not, these sorts of knee-jerk pieces tend to overlook the unique record of British banks in delivering a trusted banking system for almost 100 years, along with the lessons that can be gained from this long historical experience.[9] Moreover, they have also tended to write about the events of September 2007 more in global terms, rather than looking at the crisis within a specifically British framework.[10]

The aim of this chapter is to start redressing these gaps in the literature by providing a longer-term perspective that seeks to identify those features that contributed most to the absence of mass panics and withdrawals in the British financial sector prior to 2007. Among the key issues it will explore are: the extent to which British banks became more resilient during the twentieth century; the degree to which cooperation between different

5 H.S. Shin, 'Reflections on Northern Rock: The Bank Run that Heralded the Global Financial Crisis', *Journal of Economic Perspectives*, 23 (2009), pp. 101–2.

6 It is not entirely clear which analyst or commentator first coined this catchy phrase, but it certainly seems to have stuck, developing into something of an unquestioned truism and routinely cropping up not only in newspapers, but also in academic journals and government reports. See, for example, *The Economist*, 20 September 2007; *The Observer*, 30 December, 2007; *The New York Times*, 19 October, 2007; *The Metro*, 16 November, 2007; *The Daily Mail*, 14 June 2008; A. Milne and G. Wood, 'Shattered on the Rock? British Financial Stability from 1866 to 2007', Paper presented at the conference in honour of Ted Balbach, Federal Reserve Bank of St Louis (3 March 2008); Treasury Committee, 'The Run on the Rock'.

7 See Christopher Kobrak and Mire Wilkins, *History and Financial Crisis: Lessons from the 20th Century* (London, 2014) for a recent attempt to redress this imbalance.

8 Howard Davies, *The Financial Crisis: Who is to Blame?* (London, 2010).

9 Conversely, those studies of British banking undertaken prior to the events of 2007 largely ignore the possibility of bank runs in Britain, and treat failure as the product of exceptional circumstances operating at the level of the individual bank.

10 This lack of interest in the uniquely British historical background to this most recent crisis is something that has also recently been picked up on by John D. Turner in his latest book, *Banking in Crisis: The Rise and Fall of British Banking Stability, 1800 to the Present* (Cambridge, 2014).

organisations helped ward off panics; and the changes that have taken place in the regulatory frameworks within which British banks operate. In addition, it will also consider what regulatory and crisis management lessons we can take from this remarkably long, crisis-free era in British banking. In this way, it is hoped that this chapter will be of relevance both to historians and to policy-makers as they seek to move forward from this most recent crisis in the British banking sector.

Historical perspectives on the crisis

Before moving on to look at why the British banking sector was able to remain so stable for so long, it is worth first pointing out that, despite the claims of the British press, the Northern Rock crisis of 2007 was in fact not the first bank run to take place in Britain for over 150 years. In 1878, for example, a large number of small commercial banks (notably, the Caledonian Bank in Scotland) as well as the much larger London and County Bank were affected by runs on their deposit accounts during the general panic that engulfed the financial sector following the failure of the City of Glasgow Bank.[11] Similarly, a number of chaotic bank runs also took place in London in 1892 following the collapse of the Liberator Building Society and the subsequent revela-tions about its fraudulent mismanagement, with the Birkbeck Bank suffering particularly heavy losses during the panic.[12]

Looked at from a wider perspective, factual inaccuracies of this sort can be seen to be indicative of a kind of general languor regarding the historical roots of the most recent global financial crisis (of which the Northern Rock crisis was but one element). This lack of awareness of the uniqueness or otherwise of the crisis of 2007–08 has been particularly apparent not only in the mainstream press, but also in the field of modern economics which, as Martin Daunton has suggested, has tended to 'exclude historical insight from its purview'.[13] This, in turn, has led to a somewhat paradoxical situation in which both too many and too few parallels have been drawn with previous

---

11   A.A. Mahate, 'Contagion Effects of Three Late Nineteenth Century British Bank Failures', *Business and Economic History*, 23 (1994), pp. 102–15.
12   David McKie, *Jabez: The Rise and Fall of a Victorian Rogue* (London, 2005), pp. 99–121; E.J. Cleary, *The Building Society Movement* (Woking, 1965), pp. 140–4; Matthew Hollow, 'Strategic Inertia, Financial Fragility and Organisational Failure: The Case of the Birkbeck Bank, 1870–1911', *Business History*, 56 (2014), pp. 751–8; Herbert Ashworth, *The Building Society Story* (London, 1980), pp. 44–5.
13   Martin Daunton, 'History and the Financial Crisis', *History and Policy*, 1 July 2011. Available online at: http://www.historyandpolicy.org/policy-papers/papers/history-and-the-financial-crisis [accessed: 7 October 2014].

crises, with the result being that the reader is left no clearer as to the historical significance of the events of 2007–08.

Of course, this is not meant to be a criticism of those policymakers and economists charged with the task of trying to make sense of this latest crisis. As Kobrak and Wilkins note, 'those living through events rarely have sufficient perspective to judge the historical import and duration of what they are experiencing'.[14] Instead, it is meant more as a critique of the academic community as a whole for not doing more to provide these practitioners with the sort of rigorous and in-depth scholarly analyses of previous banking and financial crises that they require to make informed and reasoned conclusions.

Thankfully, however, it does appear as if the academic community is beginning to wake up to the need for more historically informed discussion of the events of 2007–08. Notable contributions in this respect have come from Reinhart and Rogoff,[15] Ahamed,[16] and Cassis,[17] who have all in their own way helped broaden and deepen our understanding of the historical roots of the 2007–08 crisis.[18] Nevertheless, even with the publication of these new studies, there still remain a great many under-explored areas in the history of financial and banking crises. Moreover, while studies of the sort mentioned above have certainly contributed greatly to our understanding of the historical precedents for the 2007–08 crisis, they have tended to adopt global, rather than nationally specific, frameworks.

This chapter will go some way to filling this gap in the literature by focusing specifically on the British experience of the 2007–08 crisis (manifest most clearly in the 2007 Northern Rock crisis). Unlike previous works, its main focus will not be on the immediate causes of the crisis itself, but rather on the longer-term factors that helped prevent such crises from happening in the years prior to 2007. In this respect our thinking is very much in line with that of Daunton, who suggests that: 'we need to understand the circumstances in which institutions were created, so that we are aware of their problems adapting to new circumstances'.[19] Such an approach, we suggest, will not only help provide a fuller picture of the causes of the 2007 Northern Rock crisis, but will also be of more value to current debates that are ongoing regarding the redesign and reshaping of the British financial sector in the future.

---

14   Christopher Kobrak and Mira Wilkins, 'The "2008 Crisis" in an Economic History Perspective: Looking at the Twentieth Century', *Business History*, 53 (2011), p. 176.

15   Carmen M. Reinhart and Kenneth S. Rogoff, *This Time is Different: Eight Centuries of Financial Folly* (Princeton, 2009).

16   Liaquat Ahamed, *Lords of Finance: The Bankers who Broke the World* (London, 2009).

17   Youssef Cassis, *Crises and Opportunities: The Shaping of Modern Finance* (Oxford, 2011).

18   Of course, it would be neglectful at this point to ignore the huge contribution made by Charles Kindleberger's *Manias, Panics and Crashes* (first published in 1978) to the historical literature on financial crises.

19   Daunton, 'History and the Financial Crisis'.

Banking crises and financial crises

One final thing that needs to be done before moving on to consider some of the longer-term factors responsible for the 2007 Northern Rock crisis is to first outline what exactly is meant when the terms 'financial crisis' and 'banking crisis' are used in this chapter. The chief reason for this is that the two terms can be – and often are – used quite interchangeably in both popular and academic discourse. Part of the reason for this, of course, is that the two do frequently go hand in hand – as evidenced recently by the extensive liquidity support that both the UK and US governments had to provide to their respective banking systems in the wake of the 2007–08 global financial crisis.[20] Nevertheless, despite these close links, there are some notable differences between the two terms that need to be dealt with before we can start investigating the long-term historical roots of the 2007 Northern Rock crisis.

First, it is necessary to appreciate that, though the two terms can sometimes be used to describe the same event, the concept of 'a financial crisis' is generally taken to be the far more expansive of the two terms. For instance, according to Raymond Goldsmith, a financial crisis can be considered to be 'a sharp, brief, ultracyclical deterioration of all or most of a group of financial indicators – short-term interest rates, asset (stock, real estate, land) prices, commercial insolvencies and failures of financial institutions'.[21] Similarly, in Martin Wolfson's 1993 text *Financial Crises*, a financial crisis is defined as any situation in which there is a sudden, intense and unmet demand for money.[22]

The upshot of having such expansive definitions is that the label of a 'financial crisis' is invariably applied to a quite varied assortment of different economic and financial phenomena (not all of which necessarily involve bank failures or bank runs). Notable examples in this respect include: the bursting of so-called 'asset bubbles'; sudden changes in credit volume; severe disruptions in financial intermediation; breakdowns in the supply of external financing to various actors in the economy; and large-scale balance sheet problems (of firms, households, financial intermediaries and sovereigns, etc.).[23]

By contrast, the term 'banking crisis' generally tends to get applied to a far

---

20   Luc Laeven and Fabian Valencia, *Resolution of Banking Crises: The Good, the Bad, and the Ugly*, IMF Working Paper 10/146 (2010), p. 9. Available online at: https://www.imf.org/external/pubs/cat/longres.cfm?sk=23971.0 [accessed: 7 October 2014].

21   Raymond W. Goldsmith, 'Comment on Hyman Minsky's *The Financial Instability Hypothesis: Capital Processes and the Behaviour of the Economy*', in Charles P. Kindleberger and J.P. Laffargue (eds), *Financial Crises: Theory, History and Policy* (Cambridge, 1982), p. 42.

22   Martin H. Wolfson, *Financial Crises: Understanding the Postwar US Experience* (London, 1993), p. 148.

23   Stifin Claessens and M. Ayhan Kose, *Financial Crises: Explanations, Types and Implications*, IMF Working Paper 13/28 (2013), p. 5. Available online at: http://www.imf.org/external/pubs/ft/wp/2013/wp1328.pdf [accessed: 7 October 2014].

fewer range of economic phenomena. Indeed, more often than not, when the phrase a 'banking crisis' is used, it is usually intended to refer to one specific type of market event: a mass-withdrawal bank run. Various theories have been put forward to explain these mass panic withdrawals; however, perhaps the most famous is that provided by Diamond and Dybvig, who argued that a bank run can best be understood as a kind of self-fulfilling prophecy brought about by the fact that deposit-taking banks act as intermediaries between borrowers who want long-maturity loans (such as businesses or homeowners) and depositors who want to be able to withdraw their savings at short notice.[24] Under ordinary circumstances, they suggest, this combination of highly liquid liabilities (deposits) and highly illiquid assets (loans) does not present a problem since it is rare that all of a bank's depositors will want to withdraw their money at the same time. However, if, for whatever reason, large numbers of depositors decide to withdraw their money at the same time, then the bank may run short of liquidity and be forced to start liquidating some of its long-maturity loans (usually at heavily discounted prices). Naturally, if a bank is forced to engage in this sort of fire-selling of assets, its business will suffer and – if the withdrawals persist – it might ultimately be forced to close for good (resulting in significant losses for those with money still left in the bank). Given the threat of such a potentially negative outcome, they argue, it is highly probable that if an individual depositor sees enough other depositors rushing to withdraw their money, they will also rush to withdraw their money for fear of being the last one in the queue.[25]

While in theory such mass panic withdrawals can happen independently of economic fundamentals (i.e. because of a false rumour), it is generally the case that bank runs happen alongside or in conjunction with wider downturns in market conditions (particularly if people believe they may affect the value of the assets on their bank's books).[26] On the other hand, because of their importance to the working of the economy, it is also the case that a run on one bank may affect the confidence of depositors at other banks and lead to a general loss of confidence in the financial sector as a whole – thereby leading to a full-blown financial crisis.[27] For these reasons, therefore, it can actually often be very hard to distinguish between a banking crisis and a financial crisis (or, indeed, to work out which one caused which).[28] Moreover, because

24   D.W. Diamond and P.H. Dybvig, 'Bank Runs, Deposit Insurance, and Liquidity', *Journal of Political Economy*, 91 (1983), pp. 401–19.
25   Ibid., pp. 411–13.
26   Gary Gorton, 'Banking Panics and Business Cycles', *Oxford Economic Papers*, 40 (1988), pp. 751–81.
27   A. Mahate, 'Contagion Effects of Three Late Nineteenth Century British Bank Failures', *Business and Economic History*, 23 (1994), pp. 102–15.
28   Charles P. Kindleberger, *Manias, Panics and Crashes: A History of Financial Crises*, 4th edn (London, 2000), pp. 3–4.

the two are often so intrinsically linked, it often makes little sense to try to analyse one independently of the other.[29]

Bearing all this in mind, therefore, we have decided to adopt a fairly flexible approach to terminology in this chapter. While our primary area of interest is in the history of banking crises – understood by us to mean those situations where 'a country's corporate and financial sectors experience a large number of defaults and financial institutions and corporations experience a large number of defaults and financial institutions and corporations face great difficulties repaying contracts on time'[30] – we have not neglected to take into consideration the impact that financial crises of differing forms have had on the evolution and development of the British banking sector over the last three centuries. It is our belief that this more expansive approach will help provide a fuller and more complete understanding of why the British banking sector was able to remain so stable for so long.

A 'once in a lifetime' event?

One explanation that has frequently been put forward to explain the severity of the 2007–08 banking crisis, both in Britain and elsewhere, is that the crisis itself was a one-off, 'once-in-a-lifetime event'.[31] According to this line of thought, the reason why institutions such as Northern Rock failed so spectacularly during the crisis was because the financial pressures they were placed under during this period were greater than in any previous era. However, a more detailed reading of the recent history of the British (and global) financial system would seem to undermine such explanations. For one thing, major financial crises did in fact occur regularly throughout the late nineteenth and twentieth centuries. Prior to the crisis caused by the outbreak of the First World War in 1914, for instance, there were major crises of global significance in 1873, 1890 and 1907, which, in terms of severity, easily ranked alongside that of 1866.[32] Yet, unlike in 1866 (or 2007), these major financial downturns did not result in any significant loss of confidence on behalf of the British public in the national banking system.

Similarly, one could also turn to the financial crisis that began with the Wall Street Crash of 1929 and lasted until, at least, 1932. In most historical

---

29   Kobrak and Wilkins, 'The "2008 Crisis" in an Economic History Perspective', pp. 176–8.
30   Luc Laeven and Fabian Valencia, *Systemic Banking Crises: A New Database*, IMF Working Paper 08/224 (2008), p. 5. Available online at: https://www.imf.org/external/pubs/ft/wp/2008/wp08224.pdf [accessed: 7 October 2014].
31   Layna Mosely and David A. Singer, 'The Global Financial Crisis: Lessons and Opportunities for International Political Economy', *International Interactions*, 35 (2009), p. 420.
32   Kindleberger, *Manias, Panics and Crashes*, pp. 131–4.

accounts, it is still considered to be the most severe financial crisis the world has ever seen.[33] Between 1929 and 1932 numerous bank runs took place around the world, forcing governments to intervene to prevent systemic collapse. Indeed, it was in response to these thousands of bank failures that the US government decided to introduce deposit insurance through the Glass–Steagall Act of 1933, separating deposit taking and investment banking in the process.[34] By contrast, British banks managed to largely escape the fallout from the financial crisis of 1929–32, even though the British economy did experience a severe downturn during this period.[35] The result was a high degree of self-congratulation among British bankers at the time:

> The strength of the British banks has been amply demonstrated during the last few years of crisis and depression. During that period there has not at any time been any hint of failure or even of real anxiety for their safety.[36]

Of course, flagging up the damage done by past financial crisis is in no way meant to detract from the severity of the global financial crisis of 2007–08. Clearly, this most recent financial crisis has been a particularly bad one, both for Britain and the world economy as a whole. For instance, in one report it has been estimated that, in Britain, the output loss between 2008 and 2010 that can be attributed to the crisis stood at approximately 24 per cent.[37] Nevertheless, this output loss was still significantly lower than in a number of other countries – like Portugal (37 per cent) and Iceland (42 per cent) – and was also in line with that suffered by a number of other major Western economies – such as France (21 per cent) – which did not suffer any major panic withdrawals during this period.[38] These different experiences not only undermine the suggestion that it was the severity of the financial downturn of 2007–08 that explains the Northern Rock crisis, they also suggest that specific national factors related to the unique way that each respective banking system is regulated and structured also need to be taken into consideration when assessing why and when financial crises take place.

33   J.K. Galbraith, *The Great Crash, 1929* (Harcourt, 1997).
34   Reinhart and Rogoff, *This Time is Different*, pp. 233–8.
35   Ranald C. Michie, 'A Financial Phoenix: The City of London in the Twentieth Century', in Y. Cassis and E. Bussierre (eds), *London and Paris as International Financial Centres* (Oxford, 2000), pp. 15–41. It should not be forgotten that the crisis was of sufficient magnitude to force Britain to abandon the Gold Standard in 1931.
36   C.W. Taylor, 'The Case against the Nationalisation of the Banks', *Journal of the Institute of Bankers (JIB)*, 56 (1935), p. 374.
37   Laeven and Valencia, *Resolution of Banking Crisis*. Output losses are computed as the cumulative difference between actual and trend real GDP, expressed as a percentage of trend real GDP for the period 2008–10.
38   Ibid.

Structural factors

Unlike on much of the continent, banking in Britain was never dominated by state owned monopolies. Instead, banking facilities were largely provided through partnerships and companies that were privately owned. The one major exception was the Bank of England which, though it was also privately owned until 1946, was at least as responsive to the wishes of government from its formation in 1694.[39] During the early years of the eighteenth century, the British banking sector was mostly comprised of small-scale enterprises run either as sole proprietorships or partnerships by wealthy local businessmen. However, by the end of the century, the industry had become much more consolidated (see Figure 12.1). This decline was largely due not to failure, but to takeovers and mergers, particularly from the late nineteenth century onward. The eventual upshot was a far more concentrated banking sector, dominated by a handful of large banks.[40]

To get some sense of this transformation, in 1870, the five largest banks controlled 25 per cent of deposits in England and Wales; by 1910, they controlled 43 per cent; and by 1920, they controlled 80 per cent.[41] Indeed, by 1922, retail banking in England and Wales was effectively under the control of only five banks – Barclays, Lloyds, Midland, National and Provincial and Westminster.[42]

From a structural perspective, these population changes certainly had a significant effect upon the resilience of the banking sector as a whole. Most obviously, it meant that the market came to be dominated by a handful of large banks, which were not only able to spread their risks more widely,[43] but were also better able to project a public image of stability and security:

> ... a large bank, conducted on the principle of limited liability, with vast resources, issuing audited balance sheets and subjected to a rigorous system of inspection, inspires confidence and support.[44]

In addition, these large banks also enjoyed an advantage over their competitors in the sense that they could also employ, train and supervise their staff

---

39 David Kynaston, *The City of London*, vol. 3, *Illusions of Gold* (London, 2000), pp. 33–6.
40 M. Davies, *The Origins and Development of Cartelisation in British Banking*, Institute of European Finance, Bangor (1993), pp. 26–31.
41 F. Capie and G. Rodrik-Bali, 'Concentration in British Banking, 1870–1920', *Business History*, 24 (1982), pp. 286–7.
42 Scotland and Ireland had their own banks but, again, a small number dominated.
43 M. Billings and F. Capie, 'Financial Crisis, Contagion and the British Banking System between the World Wars', *Business History*, 53 (2011), p. 211.
44 J.F. Dunn, 'Banking in 1837 and in 1897 in the United Kingdom, India and the Colonies: A Comparison and a Contrast', *JIB*, 19 (1898), p. 380.

Figure 12.1. UK bank population, 1694–2008

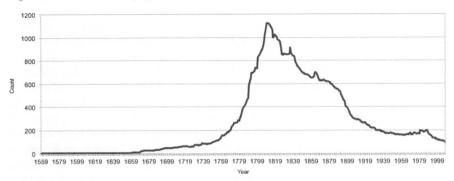

in such a way that their behaviour could be monitored and controlled, so avoiding both excessive caution and excessive risk-taking.[45]

Nevertheless, it should not be assumed that large banks were immune from those risks that could lead to failure. The City of Glasgow Bank, which failed in 1878, had been a large joint-stock bank with numerous branches. Similarly, the existence of large joint-stock banks did not prevent a number of them failing in Australia in 1892 during a financial crisis. In addition, it is also worth remembering that, unlike smaller organisations, large banks suffered from extended lines of communication and problems of authority within both hierarchal and devolved structures. In addition, the range and complexity of financial activity undertaken in the large head offices of these banks also exposed them to new and dangerous risks. As one commentator put it in 1892: '... like a chain, a bank is only as strong as its weakest link'.[46] Significantly, it was risks of this sort that were identified by Haldane and May as being the key factors in explaining the recent 2007–08 banking crisis. In their view, banks had become so large and complicated that it was impossible for management to properly oversee what was taking place within the organisation:

> There has been a spectacular rise in the size and concentration of the financial system over the last two decades, with the rapid emergence of 'super-spreader institutions' too big, connected or important to fail.[47]

45   J.B. Attfield, 'The Advantages, or Otherwise, of the Establishment of Branches by Bankers, From the Point of View (a) of the Bankers; and (b) of the General Interests of the Community', *JIB*, 13 (1892), pp. 450–67.
46   Ibid., p. 469.
47   A.G. Haldane and R.M. May, 'Systemic Risk in Banking Ecosystems', *Nature*, 20 (2011), pp. 353–4.

Empirically, this conclusion was based on research conducted by the Bank of England that suggested that the dominance of a small number of banks had grown considerably since 1960.[48] However, this research could only reach this conclusion by including Scottish banks in the data-set used, which is a misreading of the historical situation. Until the takeover of NatWest by the Royal Bank of Scotland and the merger between the Bank of Scotland and the Halifax Bank, the banking operations of these two countries remained separate. Among the large English banks only the Midland and Barclays had Scottish operations, and they disposed of them both; while among the Scottish banks only the Royal Bank of Scotland had an English branch network, and it was relatively small. Moreover, as outlined above, English banking in 1960 was already dominated by eight banks, among which five constituted the top group by a considerable margin. Indeed, the only significant merger that took place after 1960 was that between National Provincial and Westminster in 1968, and what that achieved was to bring the combined activities of these two banks up to a scale that allowed them to compete effectively with the other three large banks.[49]

Moreover, it would be wrong to assume that British banks did not face any form of competition over this period. Building societies increasingly attracted savers with attractive rates on deposit accounts, using the money to help fund the purchase of houses on mortgage.[50] New financial institutions – later known as 'secondary banks' – also catered for those borrowers unable to obtain loans from their banks, especially by providing instalment credit for the purchase of cars and consumer durables or finance required by commercial property companies responding to demands for offices.[51] The eventual upshot from this unregulated lending was a credit bubble ending with a financial crisis in 1973–74, in which the 'secondary banks' were either closed or absorbed by the existing banks.[52]

Competition of this sort only increased further with the ending of exchange controls in 1979 and the deregulation of the London Stock Exchange in 1986 (an event often referred to as the 'Big Bang').[53] The consequence of this was

48 R. Davies, P. Richardson, V. Katinaite and M. Manning, 'Evolution of the UK Banking System', *Bank of England Quarterly Bulletin (BEQB)*, Q4 (2010), pp. 322–5.
49 Forrest Capie, *The Bank of England: 1950s to 1979* (Cambridge, 2010), p. 328.
50 Cleary, *The Building Society Movement*, pp. 244–71; Ashworth, *The Building Society Story*, pp. 194–201.
51 C.J. Montgomery, 'The Clearing Banks, 1952–77: An Age of Progress', *JIB*, 98 (1977), pp. 89–91.
52 'The Secondary Banking Crisis and the Bank of England's Support Operations', *BEQB*, 18 (1978), pp. 232–3; D. Vander Weyer, 'The Threats and Opportunities Facing British Banks: A 10 Year View', *JIB*, 101 (1980), p. 72.
53 P. Augur, *The Death of Gentlemanly Capitalism: The Rise and Fall of London's Investment Banks* (London, 2000), pp. 329–30.

that the distinction that had previously existed in Britain between retail and investment banking increasingly began to erode. Instead, British banks faced renewed competition from aggressive investment banks and foreign banks located in London, which were now able to lend to UK residents without restrictions.[54] The ending of exchange controls also meant that it was no longer possible for the UK government to use British banks as a tool of monetary policy, and so it gradually removed the controls that it had previously imposed on them. The large UK banks subsequently used this opportunity to compete more aggressively for both deposits and loans – something that created much concern at the Bank of England.[55] These concerns were also echoed by Grady and Weale who, in a careful study of British banking between 1960 and 1985, warned that the environment within which banks were operating was becoming more volatile, in terms of interest and exchange rate fluctuations.[56] Matters were further complicated during this period by the fact that British building societies were also granted greater freedom to compete with banks. These freedoms included the right to convert themselves into banks – something that a number took the opportunity to do from the late 1980s onward.[57] The result was to blur the distinction between the long-established large retail banks and the newly converted building societies in the eyes of the public.[58]

Regulatory changes

Another important question to consider when looking at the long-term causes of the 2007 Northern Rock crisis is whether or not the gradual weakening of regulatory controls helped to create the possibility for such a crisis to unfold. Perhaps the most obvious place to start in this respect is with the Bank of England. Founded in the late seventeenth century in order to provide funds to support the government, the Bank of England certainly did not begin its life as a regulatory organ. Indeed, for the first hundred-or-so years of its existence, its duties were largely confined to managing the national debt and overseeing the government's gold reserves.[59] However, as the financial sector

---

54   R. Pringle, 'The Foreign Banks in London', *JIB*, 99 (1978), p. 48; 'Foreign Banks in London', *BEQB*, 26 (1986), pp. 368–9.

55   C.W. McMahon, 'The Current Financial Scene', *JIB*, 102 (1982), p. 7.

56   J. Grady and M. Weale, *British Banking, 1960–85* (London, 1986), pp. 22, 25, 28, 35, 198, 201–2.

57   Mark Boleat, *The Building Society Industry*, 2nd edn (London, 1986), pp. 209–11.

58   L. Williams, 'The Banks and their Competitors', *JIB*, 101 (1980), p. 143; 'The Development of the Building Societies Sector in the 1980s', *BEQB*, 30 (1990), pp. 502–10.

59   R.C. Michie, 'The City of London and the British Government: The Changing Relationship', in R.C. Michie and P.A. Williamson (eds), *The British Government and the City of London in the Twentieth Century* (Cambridge, 2004), pp. 31–55.

grew during the nineteenth century, and as people began to better understand the workings of the monetary system, so the pressure on the Bank of England to assume greater responsibility for the stability of the system increased. In 1802, the English economist Henry Thornton exhorted the Bank to play a more active role in ensuring that the money supply was allowed to 'vibrate only within certain limits'.[60] He also pushed the Bank to provide more support to struggling financial institutions during periods of financial distress.[61]

These calls appear to have the desired effect and, by the middle of the nineteenth century, the Bank of England was slowly coming to assume a far more active role in the regulation of the British banking sector.[62] In investigating the role of the Bank of England, however, it is important to distinguish between intervention in the face of insolvency and that driven by problems of liquidity. In the nineteenth century, the Bank of England was involved in the rescue of a small number of banks that had got into financial difficulty. In the financial crisis of 1836–37, for example, it provided a loan to Esdaile and Co., a London private bank, so that it could wind up its affairs, and the same condition was imposed on the Northern and Central Bank, based in Manchester with 40 branches, which was lent a total of £1.4 million. In 1890, the Bank of England coordinated the rescue of the private merchant bank, Baring's, and provided assistance to the Birkbeck Bank, allowing both to continue in operation.[63] It again came to the fore with the intervention to save Williams and Deacons Bank – which played a pivotal role in providing financial services to the cotton textile industry in north-west England – in the early 1930s and then again in the Secondary Bank Crisis in 1973–74.[64] Throughout all of this, the government was kept at arm's length, even after the Bank of England was taken into state ownership in 1946.[65]

From 1979 onward, however, the internationalisation and diversification of the British banking community posed increasing problems for the Bank

60   Henry Thornton, *An Enquiry into the Nature and Effects of the Paper Credit of Great Britain* (London, 1802), p. 259.

61   Similar arguments were also made by Walter Bagehot. See: W. Bagehot, 'The Currency Problem', *Prospective Review* (1848), reprinted in N. Stevas (ed.), *Collected Works of Walter Bagehot*, vol. 9 (London, 1986), p. 267.

62   Forrest Capie, '200 Years of Financial Crises: Lessons Learned and Forgotten', Paper prepared for meeting of the Economic History Research Group in Madrid (February 2012).

63   Hollow, 'Strategic Inertia', p. 755.

64   By contrast, the Bank of England took no responsibility for building societies and these were left to fail as circumstances dictated.

65   R.W. Barnett, 'The History of the Progress and Development of Banking in the United Kingdom from the Year 1800 to the Present Time', *JIB*, 1 (1880), pp. 611, 620, 624, 631; Barry Ritchie, *We're With The Woolwich, 1847–1997* (London, 1997), pp. 20–1, 41, 57, 112; Billings and Capie, 'Financial Crisis', pp. 196–7; 'The Secondary Banking Crisis and the Bank of England's Support Operations', *BEQB*, 18 (1978), pp. 230–6; L.S. Dyer, 'The Secondary Banking Crisis', *JIB*, 104 (1983), pp. 46–8.

of England in assessing the financial health of each bank and whether intervention to prevent a failure was required.[66] In response, Tony Blair's newly elected Labour government decided to reshuffle the regulatory system by creating the Financial Services Authority (FSA) in 1998. The result of this was that the Bank of England had to share regulatory responsibilities with the FSA and the UK Treasury when deciding what to do if a bank or other financial services provider got into difficulties.[67]

Right from the start, this was a move that was opposed by many inside (and outside) the Bank of England, who argued that banking was unlike other forms of business and so required the attention of a single organisation that understood its unique characteristics.[68] Whether or not this is case, it is clear that this division of regulatory responsibilities proved far from effective during the 2007 Northern Rock crisis. Indeed, one of the main problems during the whole Northern Rock debacle was the fact that it took so long for any sort of decisive action to be taken.[69] This delay not only created uncertainty, it also allowed doubt to creep into investors' minds about whether or not their savings would be protected.[70]

Another important element to take into account when trying to understand the long-term causes of the 2007 Northern Rock crisis are the changes that took place in British securities markets over the course of the twentieth century. During the nineteenth century, British banks had responded to the ever-present threat of a liquidity crisis (i.e. when an otherwise solvent bank does not have the liquid assets necessary to meet its short-term obligations) by establishing an active interbank money market through which cash could be redistributed between banks at short call, as and when they might need it.[71] Because of the many benefits that it afforded to British banks, this interbank money market rapidly grew in size and sophistication, attracting specialist intermediaries in the form of bill brokers or discount houses. These maintained daily contact with particular banks, either to borrow money

66 Grady and Weale, *British Banking*, pp. 36–9, 51–7.

67 R.C. Michie, '"Too Big To Fail": UK Financial Services Reform in History and Policy', *Economic Affairs*, 32 (2012), pp. 11–16.

68 'Are Banks Still Special? Speech by Eddie George, Governor of the Bank of England', *BEQB*, 37 (1997), p. 114; 'Financial Regulation: Why, How and By Whom. Speech by the Deputy Governor of the Bank of England', *BEQB*, 37 (1997), pp. 107–10.

69 L. Scialom and S.O. Ndong, 'Northern Rock: The Anatomy of a Crisis, the Prudential Lessons', in R. Bliss and G. Kaufman (eds), *2007–08: The Year of Crisis*, vol. 2 (Palgrave, forthcoming).

70 Treasury Committee, 'The Run on the Rock', p. 303.

71 As the name suggests, the basic principle of an interbank money market was that banks facing a shortage of cash (because of large withdrawals) could borrow from those banks with surplus funds due to an increase of deposits – hence, maintaining the stability of the system as a whole.

at interest (promising to repay the following day) or to buy and sell bills of exchange at a discount to their face value. As Bagehot observed, by 1873:

> All country bankers keep their reserve in London. They only retain in each county town the minimum of cash necessary in the transaction of the current business in that country town. Long experience has told them to a nicety how much this is, and they do not waste capital and lose profit by keeping more idle.[72]

Thanks to this vibrant money market, Britain's banks were able to retain only the minimum amount of cash that was required to meet normal requirements, safe in the knowledge that in the event of a sudden liquidity crisis they would be able to balance their overall position through the use of funds from the London money market.[73] The benefits of this system were vividly highlighted during the Australian banking crisis of the 1890s, when the large British joint-stock banks (with access to the interbank market) were able to weather the downturn much better than their equivalents in Australia (who did not have access to such a market).[74] Though the London money market was damaged by both world wars and the difficult international conditions in-between – which destroyed the use of the bill of exchange for commercial and financial transactions – a replacement was found in the shape of UK Treasury Bills. These were issued in large quantities by the British government to finance its short-term borrowing and were used by the discount houses as collateral in interbank borrowing and lending.[75]

With the removal of liquidity as a threat to their survival (as long as they maintained the confidence of the financial community and the Bank of England), British banks were able to focus much more on questions of solvency when making loans. At the start of the War in 1914, British banks, on average, kept 15.3 per cent as cash with another 12.6 per cent as money at call, making a total of 27.9 per cent that was immediately accessible. This total did then fall slightly during the War to 21 per cent, at which level it remained for the rest of the inter-war period, standing at 22.2 per cent in

---

72   W. Bagehot, *Lombard Street: A Description of the Money Market* (London, 1873), pp. 11, 13.
73   Overall, the ratio of cash/near cash to total assets for London-based banks grew from 23 per cent of all assets in the mid-1860s to 40 per cent in the early 1890s – the level at which it remained until the First World War. See M. Collins and M. Baker, *Commercial Banks and Industrial Finance in England and Wales, 1860–1913* (Oxford, 2003), pp. 74–5, 125 [Collins includes all such assets including loans to stockbrokers using securities as collateral].
74   N. Cork, 'The Late Australian Banking Crisis', *JIB*, 15 (1894), p. 200.
75   F. Whitmore, *The Money Machine* (London, 1930), p. 35; N.F. Hall, 'The Control of Credit in the London Money Market', *JIB*, 59 (1938), pp. 64–70; N. Crump, 'The Evolution of the Money Market', *JIB*, 59 (1938), pp. 291–301; 'Commercial Bills', *BEQB*, 1 (1960–61), p. 27; R.J. Clark, 'British Banking: Changes and Challenges', *JIB*, 89 (1968), pp. 468–78.

Table 12.1. Joint-stock banks: assets and liabilities, 1911–38

	1911/14	1921/24	1938
Deposits	£483 m.	£1,601 m.	£2,348 m.
Cash	£74 m.	£233 m.	£362 m.
Money at call	£61 m.	£102 m.	£160 m.
Investments	£70 m.	£342 m.	£664 m.
Bills and advances	£320 m.	£1,015 m.	£1,263 m.
Cash as % of deposits	15.3%	14.6%	15.4%
Money at call as % of deposits	12.6%	6.4%	6.8%
Investments as % of deposits	14.5%	21.4%	28.3%
Bills and advances as % of deposits	66.3%	63.4%	53.8%
Cash and money at call and investments as % of deposits	42.4%	42.3%	50.5%

Note: The data for 1911/14 and 1921/24 are taken from the tables in Sir D. Drummond Fraser, 'British Home Banking since 1911', *JIB*, 46 (1925). Those for 1938 are from the tables in N. Crump, 'The Evolution of the Money Market', *JIB*, 59 (1938).

1938. On the surface, this would suggest that British banks had become more vulnerable to a liquidity crisis, but it must be remembered that this drop was almost entirely in the proportion of money that was lent out at call. In its place had grown the share taken by investments which, as a result of the First World War, were mostly in holdings of UK government debt. These securities were highly liquid as they were easily bought and sold and readily acceptable as collateral for a loan. Taken collectively therefore the total kept by banks as cash, money at call and investments remained very high between 1911 and 1938 (see Table 12.1). This, in turn, made British banks highly resistant to the various economic, financial and monetary challenges that rocked the system during this era, including: the outbreak of the First World War in 1914; the Wall Street Crash in 1929; the departure from the Gold Standard in 1931; the depression of the 1930s; and the approach to war evident by 1938.

There was, however, a weakness in the interbank market, which was the possibility that the discount houses themselves might fail to meet their commitments, either to pay for the bills they had agreed to buy or repay their loans on demand. Such a situation was a distinct possibility if they were unable to match their lending and borrowing commitments during the course of the day. In order to protect against this threat, the Bank of England increasingly assumed the role of lender of last resort to the discount houses. Yet, the Bank of England was not the only financial institution that was in a position to do this. Prior to its collapse in 1866, Overend and Gurney was also attempting to compete with the Bank of England as lender of last resort, having noted the profits that could be made from being in that position. Its failure removed a potential competitor and left the Bank of England free to develop its role as lender of last resort.[76] What emerged after was a situation in which the major British banks kept accounts at the Bank of England through which they could make payments to and receive payments from each other. These accounts were available to the Bank of England to lend out as and when required (as, for instance, when providing the discount houses with the money they needed to meet any shortfall). Rather than the Bank of England treating the emerging joint-stock banks as potential rivals, therefore, what evolved between 1866 and 1914 was a situation in which it assumed a role as their lender of last resort. In turn, the discount houses kept the Bank of England fully informed of the financial position of every bank and client, allowing it to remain fully informed of all significant developments in the City.[77]

The role played by the Bank of England as lender of last resort remained unaltered despite its nationalisation at the end of the Second World War. Moreover, because of its role as lender of last resort to the discount market, the Bank of England was also increasingly able to expand or contract the credit that British banks could provide and so aid the operation of monetary policy. Over time, however, these actions undermined the attraction of the discount market for Britain's banks. Instead, they began to switch to alternative money markets in London that operated without Bank of England restrictions. Increasingly, these markets operated not on the basis of the UK pound, but on the US dollar (partly because of the decline of the former and the rise of the latter as an international currency).[78] Indeed, as early as 1962, it was reported that 'there is available in London an exceptionally broad range of opportunities for the employment of funds overnight'.[79]

76 For a recent book that explores the relationship between the Bank of England and other participants in the London money market, see David Sunderland, *Financing the Raj: The City of London and Colonial India, 1858–1940* (Woodbridge, 2013).

77 W.J. Aitchison, 'On the Ratio a Banker's Cash Reserve Should Bear to his Liability on Current and Deposit Accounts, as Exemplified by the London Clearing Joint Stock Banks; and on the Relation of the Clearing Banks to the Bank of England,' *JIB*, 6 (1885), pp. 300–8; W. Fowler, 'Banking Reserves', *JIB*, 21 (1900), p. 246.

78 Catherine R. Schenk, *The Decline of Sterling: Managing the Retreat of an International Currency, 1945–1992* (Cambridge, 2010); W.T.C. King, 'War and the Money Market', *JIB*, 58 (1947), pp. 47–61; 'Commercial Bills', *BEQB*, 1 (1960–61), p. 27; R.J. Clark, 'British Banking: Changes and Challenges', *JIB*, 89 (1968), pp. 468–78; R.S. O'Brien, 'The Euro-Currency Market', *JIB*, 92 (1971), pp. 245–9; C.J. Montgomery, 'The Clearing Banks, 1952–77: An Age of Progress', *JIB*, 98 (1977), pp. 89–91.

79 'Inflows and Outflows of Foreign Funds', *BEQB*, 2 (1962), pp. 93–9; 'Bank Liquidity in the United Kingdom', *BEQB*, 2 (1962), p. 248.

The emergence and growth of these alternative (and unsupervised) money markets was something that caused much concern within the Bank of England:

> For the Bank to have a reasonable chance of balancing the market, it is important that the system's overall daily surplus of cash should be channelled through to the discount houses before the Bank's final operating decisions are taken.[80]

As it was, the discount market itself disappeared in 1986, leaving the Bank of England to provide lender of last resort facilities directly to British banks in the case of a liquidity crisis.[81] What emerged in its place was an international interbank market which, though located in London, operated on the basis of the US dollar and had no single lender of last resort. By 2007, the size of this interbank market had reached $3.7 trillion, with British banks heavily engaged.[82] This not only left British banks far more vulnerable to the threat of a liquidity crisis, it also created a power vacuum in terms of who was responsible for propping up and supporting the system in the event of such a crisis.

Conclusion

In this chapter we have adopted a longer-term historical perspective to help explain why the British banking sector was able to remain almost completely free from mass panic withdrawals for such a long period prior to the events of September 2007. As we have shown, one reason behind this lack of contagious mass panics was the inbuilt resilience of British banks as they became larger and more diversified from the late nineteenth century onward. With scale came the ability to diversify assets and liabilities, move money internally, and recruit, train, supervise and pay high-quality staff. Scale also encouraged a collective mentality that led banks to balance competition and cooperation, especially when faced with adversity. By contrast, after 1979, the growth of a more competitive environment destroyed this willingness to cooperate, while the growing complexity of each bank made its rescue by another increasingly difficult.[83]

---

80   'The Role of the Bank of England in the Money Market', *BEQB*, 22 (1982), pp. 89–90.
81   'Banking Statistics Review', *BEQB*, 32 (1992), pp. 318–20.
82   John Singleton, *Central Banking in the Twentieth Century* (Cambridge, 2011), pp. 236–7; Richard S. Grossman, *Unsettled Account: The Evolution of Banking in the Industrialized World since 1800* (Princeton, 2010), pp. 96, 168, 285, 286–9.
83   The takeover of HBOS by Lloyds Bank, for instance, proved a disaster for the latter as it exposed the former to huge losses.

Another difference apparent in 2007 was that the public could no longer distinguish between a failing bank and the rest of the sector, so making a liquidity crisis into a solvency one. Even though the Northern Rock was one of the smallest banks in the UK – being geographically focused in the north-east of England and undertaking a highly specialist mortgage lending business – it was classified by the media and the public as being the same as the major retail banks that were at the centre of the payments system.[84] That was true of the Royal Bank of Scotland (which owned NatWest), but was not true of the Northern Rock.[85] Banks similar to the Northern Rock had failed in the past without causing contagion (primarily because they were seen as different). This change in attitude can be largely attributed to developments in the 1980s – notably Big Bang – which allowed banks to cover the whole range of financial activity, leading to mergers between retail and investment banks. Another factor was the freedom given to building societies to convert into banks and adopt highly aggressive (and volatile) funding models.

Finally, it is also worth remembering that the Northern Rock crisis began as an issue over liquidity, not solvency. During the nineteenth century and early years of the twentieth century, British banks had been able to respond to these sorts of crisis by turning to the Bank of England-supported London discount market, which provided them with the facilities to cover temporary imbalances. By contrast, in 2007, the main source of temporary funds for organisations such as the Northern Rock was the London interbank market. Though located in Britain, this market operated on the basis of the US dollar and had no lender of last resort. Compounding this situation were the regulatory changes that had been introduced by Labour in 1997–98, which divided responsibility for banks and their stability between the Bank of England, the new FSA and the UK Treasury. This meant that in the face of a liquidity crisis (such as the one that gripped the Northern Rock in 2007), responsibility was divided both domestically (between these three regulatory bodies) and internationally (between all the different central banks with a stake in the London interbank market). The ensuing delays that were caused by this division of responsibilities were costly as this created the opportunity for the media to spread the story that the Northern Rock Bank was in difficulty. The result was a liquidity crisis, so bursting the bubble of confidence that had long surrounded British banks.

84   S. Shimizu, 'Discourse Analysis of the Media Evaluation of the Northern Rock Crisis Management', Paper presented at the Sheffield Political Economy Research Institute 2012: The British Growth Crisis: The Search for a New Model (2012).
85   Treasury Committee, 'The Run on the Rock', p. 53.

PART V:
TRADE AND INDUSTRY

13

Crises in the Late Medieval English Cloth Trade

JOHN S. LEE

Introduction

During the course of the later Middle Ages, cloth became England's key export commodity. These exports stimulated economic growth in particular localities, and some individuals amassed huge fortunes as a result of this trade. Yet this reliance on the sale of a single commodity in overseas markets placed the same localities in a particularly vulnerable position when their trade was disrupted. Like modern industrial communities, at such times of market disruption, they faced the prospects of underemployment and unemployment. Two major periods of dislocation in England's trade occurred during the 1450s/1460s and 1520s, when cloth exports fell dramatically, and the cloth industry contracted. Failed diplomacy and warfare at the end of the 1440s, combined with a severe contraction across the agricultural and industrial sectors and monetary shortages, led to a major slump in cloth exports. In the 1520s, political embargoes disrupted exports while repeated taxation hit investment. This chapter will consider these two episodes as crises, as they had serious economic, political and social consequences, both short and longer term. In the short term, the falls in cloth exports led to unemployment and unrest. The trade crisis of the mid fifteenth century helped spark Cade's revolt, which centred on Kent, but drew textile workers from Essex, Suffolk and Wiltshire. The trade crises of the 1520s, while not as severe as the mid-fifteenth-century slump, generated protests from cloth-making communities in Suffolk, and passive resistance elsewhere. In the longer term, the two crises hastened significant structural changes in the spatial distribution of cloth-making, mercantile capital and marketing.

England's overseas trade principally consisted of exports of wool, cloth, lead, tin and pewter, in return for imports of raw materials, foodstuffs and manufactured goods. The most important markets were in the Low Countries, but there were other major trading links with the Baltic, France, Spain,

Figure 13.1. English cloth exports, 1350–1544

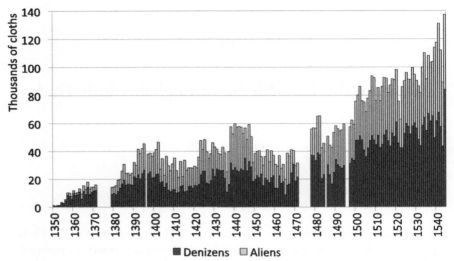

Source: A.R. Bridbury, *Medieval English Clothmaking: An Economic Survey* (London, 1982), pp. 118–22.

Portugal and the Mediterranean.[1] English merchants traded in a Europe-wide market influenced by general economic trends, many of which remain difficult to discern despite recent research. The English population, which probably halved as a result of the Black Death and subsequent epidemics, finally began to recover at some point in the later fifteenth or early sixteenth century, but the timing and extent of this growth is uncertain.[2] While there appears to have been a general rise in standards of living in the later medieval period, with a shortage of labour pushing up wage rates, the extent of these gains has been debated.[3] There is also no consensus on the degree to which monetary factors, including Europe-wide shortages of bullion, affected the medieval

1   J.L. Bolton, *The Medieval English Economy* (London, 1980), pp. 287–95; R.H. Britnell, *Britain and Ireland 1050–1530: Economy and Society* (Oxford, 2004), pp. 326–33.
2   J. Hatcher, *Plague, Population and the English Economy, 1348–1500* (London, 1977).
3   Recent debates are summarised in J. Hatcher, 'Unreal Wages: Long-Run Living Standards and the "Golden Age" of the Fifteenth Century', in B. Dodds and C.D. Liddy (eds), *Commercial Activity, Markets and Entrepreneurs in the Middle Ages: Essays in Honour of Richard Britnell* (Woodbridge, 2011), pp. 1–24, and Christopher Dyer, 'A Golden Age Rediscovered: Labourers' Wages in the Fifteenth Century', in M. Allen and D. Coffman (eds), *Prices, Money and Wages* (London, 2014), pp. 180–95.

economy, and contributed to a widespread downturn across virtually all economic sectors during the mid fifteenth century.[4]

These general economic trends impacted on the English cloth trade. Domestic demand is difficult to quantify, but the evidence generally points to a growing and widening market in cloth, particularly in the later fourteenth century. After 1350 peasant clothing was transformed by changes in fashion, including the introduction of closer-fitting clothing, loose outer garments, and more vivid colours. Complaints that lower classes were wearing 'outrageous and excessive apparel' were first raised formally in sumptuary legislation in 1363, which attempted to regulate clothing according to social status.[5] The home market has been estimated as requiring at least 160,000 cloths, bringing overall production to nearly a quarter of a million cloths by the beginning of the sixteenth century.[6] Foreign demand for English cloth is better documented through customs accounts. By the mid fourteenth century the English textile industry had virtually captured the home market, and aided by customs duties on wool exports, it gradually penetrated the overseas markets of Gascony, the Mediterranean, Baltic and Low Countries. Customs payable on wool exports were initially introduced in 1275, but raised significantly in the 1330s to finance the war with France, and by the later fourteenth century they markedly discouraged the export of English wool and enabled English cloth-makers to source wool more cheaply than their foreign competitors.[7] Exports grew dramatically from less than 2,000 cloths in 1350 to over 50,000 by 1440, to 75,000 by 1500, and nearly 140,000 by 1544 (see Figure 13.1). This growth was, however, subject to several setbacks, including the two trade crises examined in this chapter, namely the great depression of the mid fifteenth century, and the impact of political embargoes and taxation in the 1520s.

---

4 J.L. Bolton, *Money in the Medieval English Economy 973–1489* (Manchester, 2012); J. Hatcher, 'The Great Slump of the Mid-Fifteenth Century', in R.H. Britnell and J. Hatcher (eds), *Progress and Problems in Medieval England: Essays in Honour of Edward Miller* (Cambridge, 1996), pp. 237–72.

5 R. Horrox (ed.), *The Black Death* (Manchester, 1994), pp. 340–2.

6 C. Dyer, *Standards of Living in the Later Middle Ages: Social Change in England, c.1200–1520* (Cambridge, 1989), pp. 176–7; C. Dyer, *A Country Merchant, 1495–1520: Trading and Farming at the End of the Middle Ages* (Oxford, 2012), p. 17. See also John Oldland, 'Wool and Cloth Production in Late Medieval and Early Tudor England', *Economic History Review*, 67 (2014), pp. 39, 41. A standard English broadcloth was about 24 yards long by 1½ or 2 yards wide.

7 These fiscal policies gave the English cloth industry a cost advantage of 25–30 per cent: J.H. Munro, 'The Symbiosis of Towns and Textiles', *Journal of Early Modern History*, 3 (1999), pp. 37–40; Britnell, *Britain and Ireland*, pp. 327–9.

The mid-fifteenth-century crisis

During the middle of the fifteenth century the English cloth trade experienced a sharp and prolonged downturn. English cloth exports fell from an annual average of 56,000 cloths in the period 1441–45 to 29,000 in 1461–65, and fewer than 20,000 cloths were exported in 1465, lower than any other year of the fifteenth century (see Figure 13.1).[8] This decline in the quantities of commodities traded was accompanied by falls in prices. Customs valuations on unfinished broadcloth were on average 20 per cent lower in the 1450s and 1460s than in the preceding two decades, so in value terms exports may have declined by two thirds.[9]

The mid-fifteenth-century crisis in the cloth trade was so severe and prolonged because it formed part of a widespread European depression that lasted from about 1445 to 1465 and affected most sectors of the economy. The causes of this general economic depression are complex, but appear to have included a reduction of domestic expenditure, resulting from political uncertainty, together with declining overseas trade and contracting demand in foreign markets. Monetary factors also appear to have contributed, with the total stock of coin in circulation shrinking. The worst year of the European bullion famine was probably 1464–65, when a series of Florentine banks collapsed, and English cloth exports reached their nadir.[10] This falling demand across Europe was compounded by trade embargoes and warfare. The cloth trade suffered from a ban on imports of English cloth imposed by the Burgundians in 1447–52 and 1464–67; the renewal of England's war with France, resulting in the loss of Normandy and then Bordeaux; and a revival of conflict with the Hanseatic League, leading to the expulsion of Hansard merchants from England in 1468–74, damaging English trading links in the Baltic, Scandinavia and Iceland. Cloth exports recovered slowly, aided by the restoration of commercial relations with Burgundy and peace with the Hanse in 1474 and France in 1475. By 1476–80, average cloth exports had finally returned to the levels of 1441–45, but they had become increasingly focused on the London–Antwerp trading axis.[11]

Parliament was informed in 1449 that the Burgundian cloth ban was causing extensive unemployment and unrest in the cloth trade:

---

8   A.R. Bridbury, *Medieval English Clothmaking: An Economic Survey* (London, 1982), pp. 119–21.

9   Hatcher, 'The Great Slump', p. 243.

10   R.H. Britnell, 'The Economic Context', in A.J. Pollard (ed.), *The Wars of the Roses* (Basingstoke, 1995), pp. 41–6; P. Spufford, *Money and its Use in Medieval Europe* (Cambridge, 1988), p. 360.

11   Bolton, *Medieval English Economy*, p. 293; J.H. Munro, *Wool, Cloth and Gold: The Struggle for Bullion in Anglo-Burgundian Trade 1340–1478* (Toronto, 1972), pp. 138–47.

many Clothmakers, men Wevers, Fullers, Diers, and women Kembers, Carders, and Spynners, and other Biers and Sellers therof ... such of theym as can not do noon other occupations, become as ydell pepull, whiche provoketh them to synne and myschevous lyvyng.[12]

Simmering unrest erupted the following year with Cade's rebellion, which began as a petition against Henry VI's insolvent and corrupt administration, but was fuelled by the slump in the cloth trade. Cloth-workers were prominent among the rebels, although despite Shakespeare's assertion that 'Jack Cade the clothier means to dress the commonwealth, and turn it, and set a new nap upon it',[13] there are no reliable details about the origins or livelihood of their leader, John or Jack Cade. The rebels occupied London and secured commissions from the king to sit in judgement on some of the hated ministers and royal servants. The uprising, however, descended into disorder with robberies, murders and burnings; the Londoners took up arms in response, and a settlement was reached. After Cade's death, his corpse was beheaded and quarters were sent to be displayed at Norwich, Salisbury and Gloucester – three prominent cloth-making towns that were centres of the disturbances.[14] There was a general correlation between areas of disorder during Cade's revolt and areas of cloth production, which included Wiltshire and neighbouring parts of Dorset and Hampshire, Kent, Essex including Colchester, Hadleigh in Suffolk, Norwich, Newbury and Hungerford in the Thames valley, the area around Gloucester, and probably Winchester and Coventry.[15]

A series of uprisings took place in the textile-producing areas of the Cotswolds. In the leading cloth-making centre of Salisbury, Robert Hungerford, Lord Moleyns, a prominent member of the duke of Suffolk's clique, was attacked at the George Inn on 3 June 1449. At the end of November, 300 men were said to have converged on Salisbury, and the city chamberlains paid 2s 6d to repair the mace at the time of the insurrection.[16] William Aiscough, bishop of Salisbury, was murdered at Edington in June 1450, and most of those subsequently indicted came from within six miles of this village in the west Wiltshire textile area. Disorder also broke

---

12 *Rotuli Parliamentorum*, 6 vols (London, 1777–1832), V, p. 150, no. 20, quoted in Munro, *Wool*, p. 141, n. 40.

13 2 Henry VI, Act IV, Scene 2, lines 4–6.

14 I.M.W. Harvey, 'Cade, John (d.1450)', *Oxford Dictionary of National Biography* online edition (hereafter *ODNB*).

15 J.N. Hare, 'The Wiltshire Risings of 1450: Political and Economic Discontent in Mid-Fifteenth Century England', *Southern History*, 4 (1982), pp. 25–7.

16 A.D. Brown, *Popular Piety in Late Medieval England: The Diocese of Salisbury, 1250–1550* (Oxford, 1995), p. 15; M. Hicks, 'Hungerford, Robert, third Baron Hungerford and Baron Moleyns (c.1423–1464)', *ODNB*.

out in the Wiltshire textile centres of Devizes, Wilton, and Malmesbury, as
well as at Sherborne (Dorset), Crawley (Hampshire), and at Wells where
Bishop Beckington hired Welshmen for the cathedral's defence. Nearly
a quarter of those indicted in Wiltshire worked in the cloth trade.[17] This
reflected the general downturn in the cloth industry. Falling rents and court
profits were evident in Wiltshire cloth-making communities such as Castle
Combe, Trowbridge and Hindon.[18] The rebels merged political and religious
grievances with their economic concerns about the dislocation in the cloth
trade. The bishop of Salisbury was one of the most hated men in Suffolk's
circle, and there had been long-running struggles between the citizens of
Salisbury and their lord, the bishop, and between the residents of Sherborne
and their lord, the abbot.[19]

The mid-fifteenth-century slump hit the textile industries of Suffolk and
Essex, and textile workers from both counties were evident in Cade's revolt.
Cade may have been in Bury St Edmunds in May 1450, shortly before moving
to London. The 15 townsmen from Hadleigh indicted for their part in Cade's
revolt included four fullers, three weavers and a mercer. The vicar of Melton
complained of being attacked 'in the grete trobull tyme' by a gang of parish-
ioners whom he described as 'desciples and of the affynyte of the grete traytor
John Cade'.[20] The 'men of Essex' delivered Thomas Mayn of Colchester,
identified as the keeper of Colchester castle, to Cade while he was in London
in July 1450, and Mayn was beheaded. A spate of disturbances persisted for
two months or more across Essex. Among the key figures were weavers from
Great Tey and Bocking, lying west of Colchester.[21] As in Wiltshire, the crisis
in the textile trade may have been the flashpoint for the disturbances, but the
rebels nursed a complex mixture of political, social and religious grievances.

Industrial unrest could also generate xenophobia. In July 1450, textile
workers in Romsey (Hampshire) rose against their Genoese masters, who had
established a cloth-finishing industry in the locality. The Genoese imported
unfinished cloth, from England and the Netherlands, through Southampton
and dispatched it to Hampshire villages to be fulled and dyed, before
exporting the finished cloth to the Mediterranean. Over a thousand broad-
cloths had been carried to Romsey and then back to Southampton in 1441. In
the atmosphere of general lawlessness in 1450, the textile workers marched on
Southampton but the mayor and citizens protected the Italian colony. There

---

17   I.M.W. Harvey, *Jack Cade's Rebellion of 1450* (Oxford, 1991), p. 128; J.N. Hare, *A
Prospering Society: Wiltshire in the Later Middle Ages* (Hatfield, 2011), pp. 203–5.
18   J.N. Hare, 'Growth and Recession in the Fifteenth-Century Economy: The Wiltshire Textile
Industry and the Countryside', *Economic History Review*, 52 (1999), p. 20.
19   Harvey, *Cade*, pp. 121–4.
20   Ibid., pp. 118–19.
21   L.R. Poos, *A Rural Society after the Black Death: Essex, 1350–1525* (Cambridge, 1991),
pp. 255–9.

were also riots against the Italians in London in 1456–57, which led the Italian community to contemplate migrating to Southampton and Winchester.[22] These riots may have been sparked by the jealousies of urban artisans during periods of economic difficulty.

Unrest continued to linger during the 1450s and beyond. Thomas Bright, a fuller from Canterbury, was accused of raising a rebellion in Kent in 1452. John Percy, a tailor from Erith in north-west Kent, led a revolt in 1456, and nearly a third of those indicted were from the cloth trades, comprising tailors, weavers, fullers and clothiers.[23] In 1453 the Percy family's cause in Yorkshire was supported by the citizens of York and rural textile workers, including tailors, fullers and dyers, whose interests had been damaged by the commercial recession.[24] Unrest against the newly established government of Edward IV in 1463–64 stretched across the west Cotswolds and Vale of Gloucester, including cloth-making centres such as Stroud and Tetbury, and one of the instigators was a fuller, Robert White.[25] White was accused of being a Lollard, a movement that emphasised vernacular scripture and denied the efficacy of many late medieval Catholic teachings. Prosecuting authorities often chose to conflate Lollard beliefs with more general anticlericalism, so it is difficult to ascertain the precise impact of these beliefs, but Lollard teachings seem to have been particularly prevalent in textile-producing centres with their literate craftsmen who had established links with towns and ports. In 1431, there were gatherings in Salisbury and Abingdon where subversive religious literature was distributed, and weavers and a dyer were among those implicated.[26] But while heresy and dissent were more intense in cloth towns, so too, paradoxically, was the practice of orthodox piety, as the wealth generated by the cloth trade provided funds to invest in church-building, chantries and guilds.[27]

As a consequence of the mid-fifteenth-century crisis, several trends in the cloth trade became more pronounced: locational changes, marked by a general shift from larger towns to smaller urban centres and rural areas; organisational changes, with the control of production in fewer hands and the division of labour within manufacturing; and changes in mercantile credit and

22 Harvey, *Cade*, pp. 127–8; A.A. Ruddock, *Italian Merchants and Shipping in Southampton 1270–1600* (Southampton, 1951), pp. 162–86.

23 Britnell, 'Economic Context', p. 57; Harvey, *Cade*, pp. 170–3.

24 R.A. Griffiths, 'Local Rivalries and National Politics: The Percies, the Nevilles, and the Duke of Exeter, 1452–55', *Speculum*, 43 (1968), p. 617.

25 R.H. Hilton, *The English Peasantry in the Later Middle Ages: The Ford Lectures for 1973 and Related Studies* (Oxford, 1975), pp. 71–2.

26 Harvey, *Cade*, pp. 23–7. J.F. Davis, 'Lollard Survival and the Textile Industry in the South-east of England', *Studies in Church History*, 3 (1966), pp. 191–201; Hilton, *English Peasantry*, p. 72; S. McSheffrey and N. Tanner (eds), *Lollards of Coventry, 1486–1522*, Camden Fifth Series, 23 (2003), p. 25.

27 Brown, *Popular Piety*, pp. 222, 259.

marketing. The timings of these trends are difficult to identify precisely, but it appears that it was during the most difficult trading years of the mid-fifteenth-century crisis that the higher relative costs of manufacturing cloth in larger towns, compared with production in smaller urban centres, became more apparent, hastening these changes. It was also during the crisis years that the lower production costs of the larger cloth-makers, who tended to be located in the smaller urban centres, gave them the greatest competitive advantages over smaller producers, and these lesser producers declined as profits became more difficult to achieve. The trade crisis of the mid fifteenth century provided the economic environment in which entrepreneurs could thrive.

The years after the mid-fifteenth-century slump saw important locational changes in the textile industry. In the later fourteenth century, cloth production had centred on a few major towns including York, Norwich, Coventry, Salisbury and Colchester. Each town produced its own speciality and used a readily accessible port for its cloth exports. York produced broad-cloths exported through Hull; Norwich manufactured worsted shipped via Yarmouth; Coventry specialised in blue woollen cloths exported through the ports of the Wash; Salisbury made rays (striped cloths) shipped through Southampton; and Colchester specialised in middle-grade russet cloth shipped from its own port and Ipswich.[28] During the second half of the fifteenth century, cloth production increasingly moved out of the larger towns and became concentrated in more rural localities, most notably in the Stour valley of Suffolk, the Stroud valley of Gloucestershire, western Wiltshire, east Devon, and parts of Kent, Hampshire and Berkshire. There was also growth in certain small towns in the West Riding of Yorkshire, as well as around Kendal, and the Welsh border. Many of these localities also developed their own specialities. Western Wiltshire became noted for white woollen broad-cloths, the Stroud region was known for Bristol red, and Newbury developed as a centre for making narrow cloths known as kerseys.[29]

The new cloth-making centres increasingly sold and exported their cloth through London, as merchants in the capital came to dominate marketing and credit networks. Following disruption to other overseas markets, cloth exports became increasingly directed to the London–Antwerp market, and gradually focused on higher-priced, heavier cloths.[30] There were also several key developments within internal distribution networks, including the expansion of regional fairs, the development of a permanent London cloth market, and the rise of provincial chapmen, which were related to the trade crisis of the mid fifteenth century. These reflected attempts to reduce transaction costs in the wake of the crisis and the growth of London mercantile influences.

28   Britnell, *Britain and Ireland*, p. 352.
29   R.H. Britnell, *The Closing of the Middle Ages? England, 1471–1529* (Oxford, 1997), p. 213.
30   Oldland, 'Wool and Cloth Production', pp. 35–6.

During the later fourteenth and early fifteenth centuries, fairs of the leading provincial towns such as Colchester and Salisbury had provided outlets for locally produced cloth. Following the restructuring of textile manufacturing after the mid-fifteenth-century crisis, with production increasingly dominated by smaller towns and rural areas, regional fairs such as those in Somerset and Yorkshire attracted cloth producers. Several London companies prohibited their members from attending provincial fairs, in theory forcing provincial merchants to travel to London, but the impact of these measures seems to have been limited, and by the late fifteenth century the Haberdashers' Company had become successful through trading at fairs. By the beginning of the sixteenth century, two fairs had developed into major cloth markets: St Bartholomew's Fair, London, and Stourbridge Fair, Cambridge. John Stow, writing in the later sixteenth century, described St Bartholomew's Fair as one to which 'the Clothiers of all England, and Drapers of London repayred'. Yorkshire traders from Heptonstall, Halifax and Huddersfield bequeathed booths at St Bartholomew's Fair in the sixteenth century. By the 1520s a regular contingent of cloth-makers from south Suffolk attended Stourbridge Fair, known as the 'Hadleigh men'. Drapers and mercers of Coventry and London also held booths at the fair. These were supplemented by cloth merchants from other regions, including two 'kendalmen' in 1523–24 and traders from Ipswich and Bristol in the 1550s.[31] Another element of this increasing market integration was the development of a permanent London cloth market at Blackwell Hall, which had been acquired by the city in 1395–96. By the early sixteenth century, this market appears to have developed specialised salesrooms for particular commodities, including 'a hall called Colchester Hall within Blackwell Hall', where John Boswell, cloth-maker of Colchester, took cloths to sell in 1528.[32]

The contraction of trade in the mid fifteenth century increasingly led small provincial traders known as chapmen to deal directly with London whole-salers either in the city or at the fairs, with whom they could barter cloth produced in the countryside for raw materials and luxury goods imported through the capital. Debt cases show that London grocers, mercers and haber-dashers increasingly used chapmen to distribute their wares.[33] Chapmen from

---

31   J.S. Lee, 'The Role of Fairs in Late Medieval England', in M. Bailey and S. Rigby (eds), *Town and Countryside in the Age of the Black Death: Essays in Honour of John Hatcher* (Turnhout, 2012), pp. 411–14; J.S. Lee, *Cambridge and its Economic Region, 1450–1560* (Hatfield, 2005), pp. 124–8.

32   R.H. Britnell, 'The Woollen Textile Industry of Suffolk in the Later Middle Ages', *The Ricardian*, 23 (2003), p. 88; R.H. Britnell, *Growth and Decline in Colchester, 1300–1525* (Cambridge, 1986), p. 177.

33   P. Nightingale, *A Medieval Mercantile Community: The Grocers' Company and the Politics and Trade of London 1000–1485* (New Haven and London, 1995), pp. 365–8, 439–40; D. Keene, 'Changes in London's Economic Hinterland as indicated by Debt Cases in the Court

Wells supplied London merchants with West Country cloth and purchased dyes, mordants, spices and fine imported fabrics. On his death in 1446, the York chapman Thomas Gryssop owed debts to a capmaker, spicer and two mercers, all from London, and had probably purchased his 'London coffyrs', 'London pursez', 'London glassez' and London belt from them.[34]

After the trade crisis of the 1450s/1460s, it was increasingly London merchants who provided credit to finance industrial and commercial expansion in the textile industry. Greater access to capital gave London merchants a key competitive advantage over their provincial rivals. Monetary factors appear to have contributed to the mid-fifteenth-century slump, although their precise role remains open to debate. Mints across Europe reduced their output of coin and the total stock of coinage in circulation fell significantly leading to a 'bullion famine'. Contemporaries described problems with money supply during the 1460s. The anonymous writer of 'A Trade Policy', who may have worked in the cloth industry, writing shortly before 1464, complained that silver was in such short supply that manufacturers paid their workers half in money and half in goods at inflated prices, which the workers were then supposed to sell to make up their earnings. A statute of 1465 described how labourers in cloth-making were driven to take a great part of their wages in 'pins, girdles, and other unprofitable wares' and ordered cloth-makers to pay all labourers in lawful wages and payment.[35]

Monetarist historians have argued that the availability of credit was directly linked to fluctuations in the supply of bullion brought to the mint by overseas trade. When this supply was reduced, as in the mid fifteenth century, credit was dependent on merchants' cash reserves, the extent to which merchants were willing to invest in trade, and the degree to which they could substitute the exchange of goods for cash settlements. Trade recessions encouraged hoarding, the contraction of credit and higher interest rates.[36] Although it has been suggested that in theory credit should have dried up everywhere in line with the decline in money supply, and perhaps even more so in London because the money economy was more developed there, the evidence suggests that the money shortages gave Londoners, with their access to the capital's

of Common Pleas', in J.A. Galloway (ed.), *Trade, Urban Hinterlands and Market Integration c.1300–1600* (London, 2000), p. 74; J. Davis, '"Men as March with Fote Packes": Pedlars and Freedom of Movement in Late Medieval England', in P. Holden (ed.), *Freedom of Movement in the Middle Ages: People, Ideas, Goods* (Donington, 2007), pp. 137–56.

34   D.G. Shaw, *The Creation of a Community: The City of Wells in the Middle Ages* (Oxford, 1993), p. 93; J. Raine (ed.), *Testamenta Eboracensia*, iii, Surtees Society, 45 (Durham, 1864), p. 105.

35   4 Edw. IV, c. 1: *Statutes of the Realm*, II, p. 406; Bolton, *Money*, p. 270.

36   Spufford, *Money*, p. 347; P. Nightingale, 'England and the European Depression of the Mid-Fifteenth Century', *Journal of European Economic History*, 26 (1997), pp. 634–43.

superior credit facilities and greater supplies of capital, a major advantage over merchants in provincial towns.[37]

From the mid fifteenth century onward, London merchants increasingly financed provincial cloth production. Between 1449 and 1451, Henry Archer of London gave over £156 in credit to a dyer to establish a dye house in St Neots, and supplied materials from London as well as vessels and implements for the craft.[38] In the 1470s John Kendall, cloth merchant of Bridgwater, with a business associate from Dorset, borrowed £60 from William Collet, London mercer, and subsequently extended smaller sums of credit to traders including a Welsh tailor and merchant from Melcombe Regis.[39] These credit links were not created by the great slump of the mid fifteenth century, but seem to have been intensified by it. Rural and small-town clothiers were establishing direct marketing and credit links with London merchants, bypassing provincial towns.

The relocation of cloth production following the mid-fifteenth-century crisis also appears to have been a response to restrictive legislation promulgated by craft guilds and civic governments in larger towns in the interests of urban self-protection. This encouraged capital and enterprise to move to smaller towns where these structures of governance were absent. In many larger urban centres, craft guilds restricted working hours, fixed wage rates, controlled quality, and required contributions for membership, feasts and entertainments. Urban guilds imposed harsh penalties for poor workmanship: dyers at York producing faulty work were to be fined 40d for their first offence, 6s 8d for their second, and were to be expelled from the city on their third offence. This insistence on high standards by the guilds made urban products expensive in competition with cloths produced in the countryside. Craft guilds and town governments also tended to reinforce small units of production, restricting attempts to agglomerate manufacturing. Ordinances made at Colchester in 1418 specified that apprenticeships in weaving and fulling should be at least five years long, and no burgess should practise the craft of weaving and fulling together. The weavers of Bury St Edmunds were prohibited from possessing more than four looms each in 1477. The cappers of Coventry restricted each master in the city to two apprentices at a time in 1496. Smaller towns lacked these structures – guilds and guildhalls in places such as Lavenham were social and religious organisations with no authority over craft production.[40] Residents in the larger established towns

---

37 Bolton, *Money*, pp. 307–8; P. Nightingale, 'Monetary Contraction and Mercantile Credit in Later Medieval England', *Economic History Review*, 43 (1990), pp. 560–75.
38 Nightingale, *Grocers' Company*, p. 486.
39 R. Goddard, 'Surviving Recession: English Borough Courts and Commercial Contraction: 1350–1500', in R. Goddard, J. Langdon and M. Muller (eds), *Survival and Discord in Medieval Society: Essays in Honour of Christopher Dyer* (Turnhout, 2010), p. 76.
40 Bolton, *Medieval English Economy*, pp. 265–7; Britnell, *Closing*, p. 224; Britnell, *Growth and Decline*, pp. 185–6, 238–40.

also faced heavier costs of self-government to maintain the urban fabric and the administrative apparatus of the borough. These costs could be more easily avoided in villages and smaller towns.[41] Nightingale has also suggested that coins were needed less for wages in the countryside than in towns, as workers could be paid more readily in kind, and this may have been particularly advantageous during monetary shortages in the 1460s.[42]

Some larger boroughs responded to the trade crisis of the 1450s/1460s and the subsequent restructuring of cloth production by introducing their own protectionist measures, which exacerbated the problem further. In mid-fifteenth-century Ipswich, the town government compelled merchants to weigh their merchandise at the common crane and pay tolls. Fullers and clothiers were required to sell their cloth only on market day at the Moothall. Canterbury's council attempted to stimulate cloth-making in 1506 by forbidding the sale of wool out of the city and by agreeing that the mayor and each of his brethren should have two whole cloths woven during the next year, and members of the council one cloth each. With the benefit of hindsight, such measures were adopted 'at precisely the wrong time'.[43] They formed significant disincentives to non-residents contemplating producing cloth in the town, as they could operate elsewhere with few if any of these restrictions.

The accounts of a tax called ulnage, levied by the Crown on sales of cloth, help to quantify the extent of the shifts in the production and marketing of cloth following the mid-fifteenth-century crisis. The returns need to be used cautiously, as some later accounts included names that bore no relation to those paying the fees.[44] In the 1390s, Somerset and Wiltshire, recording annually over 12,000 and 7,000 cloths respectively, were the two leading counties in cloth production. The industry within these counties and neighbouring parts of Hampshire and Dorset at this time was predominantly urban. Salisbury accounted for 89 per cent of production in Wiltshire, Sherborne 87 per cent of that in Dorset, and Winchester 77 per cent of that in Hampshire. By 1467, however, there had been a major shift from Salisbury to rural parts of west Wiltshire, which now accounted for 77 per cent of the cloth production in the county. Similarly in Suffolk, where cloth-making had

---

41   R. Britnell, 'The Economy of British Towns 1300–1540', in D.M. Palliser (ed.), *The Cambridge Urban History of Britain*, i: 600–1540 (Cambridge, 2000), pp. 332–3.

42   P. Nightingale, 'Gold, Credit, and Mortality: Distinguishing Deflationary Pressures on the Late Medieval English Economy', *Economic History Review*, 63 (2010), p. 1092.

43   L.F. Salzman, *English Industries of the Middle Ages* (Oxford, 1923), p. 232; N.R. Amor, *Late Medieval Ipswich: Trade and Industry* (Woodbridge, 2011), pp. 149–50, 170–1.

44   E.M. Carus-Wilson, 'The Aulnage Accounts: A Criticism', *Economic History Review*, 2 (1929), reprinted in E.M. Carus-Wilson, *Medieval Merchant Venturers* (London, 1967), pp. 279–91; A.R. Bridbury, *Economic Growth: England in the Later Middle Ages* (London, 1962), pp. 33–5; P. Merrick, 'Taxing Medieval Cloth', *The Local Historian*, 32 (2002), pp. 218–33.

grown faster than anywhere else in England between the 1390s and 1460s, the location of production had shifted from Bury St Edmunds to Lavenham, Hadleigh, Bildeston and Long Melford. Ipswich's share of cloth production in Suffolk fell from between 7 and 10 per cent to less than 2 per cent.[45]

While the ulnage accounts do not enable the chronology of this spatial change in cloth production to be pin-pointed more precisely, other evidence reveals that the trend had started before the mid-fifteenth-century slump. Cloth-making was already developing in some small towns in the later fourteenth century, such as the Suffolk centres of Hadleigh, where about a fifth of the male inhabitants were working in textiles in 1381, and Kersey, which had given its name to a type of narrow fabric by 1376, and accommodated a cloth market and cloth hall in 1398–99. The village of Castle Combe in west Wiltshire had become a major cloth-making centre by the early fifteenth century.[46] Nonetheless, the mid-fifteenth-century trade crisis appears to have intensified this shift significantly, as the general trend was for production to peak in the larger towns during the early fifteenth century, and to decline thereafter, and for production in smaller centres to grow during the second half of the fifteenth century. In Colchester the industry peaked around 1410–15 with another cycle of growth around 1443–44, but fell away thereafter. The cloth-making towns of York and Coventry seem to have declined in prosperity after the 1440s. During the trough of the mid-fifteenth-century recession there were few opportunities for expansion, but some small centres of production were still able to prosper, such as Bisley near Stroud in Gloucestershire where the textile industry generated growth between 1447 and 1459. In the new cycle of expansion in cloth-making that began during the 1470s, growth centred on certain small towns and rural communities.[47]

Closely aligned to the movement of cloth production from large towns into smaller towns and villages, and also stimulated by the mid-fifteenth-century crisis, was the concentration of production into fewer hands. Again in a more difficult economic environment, those with the lowest production costs were better able to withstand the crisis. The concentration of production was a particular feature in Suffolk where there was a move away from cheaper and lighter cloths, which could be woven by a single weaver, to heavier and slightly higher-quality broadcloths, which needed larger looms operated by two people, and required more wool. More capital-intensive production

45 Hare, 'Growth and Recession', pp. 3–13; Amor, *Ipswich*, p. 168.
46 Britnell, 'Woollen Textile Industry', p. 86; E.M. Carus-Wilson, 'Evidences of Industrial Growth on some Fifteenth-Century Manors', *Economic History Review*, 12 (1959), pp. 190–205, reprinted in Carus-Wilson, *Medieval Merchant Venturers*, pp. 151–67.
47 Not all the smaller textile centres benefited, though: there is evidence for contraction in the small Stour Valley towns of Sudbury, Clare, Dedham and Stoke by Nayland: Britnell, *Britain and Ireland*, pp. 352–3; Britnell, *Growth and Decline*, pp. 190, 251–2, 257, 262.

encouraged larger-scale rather than smaller-scale producers, who could minimise their overheads and deal in bulk. The division of labour within the manufacturing processes also became more pronounced. Between 1463 and 1478, the share of cloth sales in Lavenham made by the leading five cloth-sellers rose from 35 to 83 per cent, while the total number of cloth-sellers halved. This industrial concentration was more evident in small towns like Lavenham than in the older cloth-making boroughs, which generally comprised smaller individual producers, and where craft guilds and urban governments often restricted the concentration of production. In 1478 the three leading merchants in Lavenham sold more than twice as many cloths as Colchester's leading seller.[48]

Admittedly, there had been earlier examples of concentrated production, including individuals working in the major cloth-making towns. In Colchester, some men with access to raw materials and fulling mills had employed other men in the 1390s. A few York merchants also directly employed outworkers from an early date. Robert Holme's will of 1396 included bequests to five dyers, including one from Pontefract, while Thomas Clynt left money in 1439 to fullers and dyers in Tadcaster who had worked for him, and to others in the city and suburbs of York.[49]

Nonetheless, by the early sixteenth century, a handful of wealthy clothiers, mostly based in smaller towns, were dominating production in several cloth-making districts, and organising production through an emerging system of outworking. These textile workers included artisans working in their own homes, live-in domestic servants and part-time labourers who maintained small holdings.[50] Thomas [ii] Spring (d.1486) of Lavenham left 100 marks (£66 13s 4d) to be distributed among 'my spinners, weavers and fullers'.[51] Thomas Paycocke (d.1518) of Coggeshall left bequests to weavers, fullers, shearmen, combers, carders and spinners, though precisely how many of these workers he employed is uncertain.[52] At Wells, John Tyler made bequests to 'his weavers and tuckers' in 1512, and John Mawdleyn, assessed on £200 worth of goods in 1524, was described a generation later by John Leland as 'late a

48   M. Bailey, *Medieval Suffolk: An Economic and Social History* (Woodbridge, 2007), pp. 274–6; Britnell, 'Woollen Textile Industry', p. 99; Britnell, *Growth and Decline*, p. 184; N.R. Amor, 'Merchant Adventurer or Jack of all Trades? The Suffolk Clothier in the 1460s', *Proceedings of Suffolk Institute of Archaeology and History*, 40 (2004), pp. 414–36.

49   Britnell, *Growth and Decline*, pp. 77, 186; J. Kermode, *Medieval Merchants: York, Beverley and Hull in the Later Middle Ages* (Cambridge, 1998), p. 205.

50   Bailey, *Suffolk*, pp. 293–4.

51   P.R. Schofield, 'Spring Family (per. c.1400–c.1550)', *ODNB*.

52   E. Power, 'Thomas Paycocke of Coggeshall: An Essex Clothier in the Days of Henry VII', in E. Power, *Medieval People* (London, 1924), pp. 152–73; R.H. Britnell, 'Paycocke, Thomas (d.1518)', *ODNB*.

great clothiar yn Wellys'.[53] This concentration of industrial entrepreneurship was a marked feature of the later fifteenth and early sixteenth centuries.

The mid-fifteenth-century crisis therefore greatly intensified a number of trends that were already apparent – the movement of cloth production from large towns to smaller centres, the concentration of cloth production in fewer hands, and an increase in market integration and credit networks focused on London. In each case these appear to have been attempts to reduce the costs of production and marketing in a period of severe commercial downturn and monetary shortage. The crisis also prompted the adoption of protectionist measures by some larger towns, which only served to further increase the tendency to locate cloth-making outside their boundaries.

The crisis of the 1520s

The English cloth trade recovered in the late fifteenth century and by 1500 exports had reached new heights. The transitions that had been accelerated by the crisis of the 1450s/1460s were not reversed: the industry continued to be based predominantly in smaller towns with larger producers taking a key role. During the 1520s, however, the cloth trade experienced another series of disruptions. The industry was hit by falling demand following poor harvests across Europe in 1520 and by the impact of repeated taxation in England in 1522–25 coupled with a trade embargo with the Low Countries. More difficulties followed in 1527, caused by grain shortages, and in 1528, with the expectation of a trade war with the Low Countries. The impact of this period of disruption, while less severe than that of the mid fifteenth century, was still significant. Total cloth exports fell by 23 per cent between 1520 and 1521, by 17 per cent between 1521 and 1522, and by 5 per cent between 1525 and 1526, and these shocks led to unemployment and unrest in cloth-making districts.

In 1520 harvests were poor, and demand across Europe contracted, with high grain prices in Flanders, famine in Castile and Portugal, and the diversion of huge sums of money from trade to warfare by the French king Francis I and Holy Roman Emperor Charles V. Following the wet summer of 1520, a bad harvest and rising grain prices, Mayor John Bond of Coventry conducted a survey of the number of people and the quantities of grain available within his city, as well as bringing nearly 100 quarters of wheat to augment supplies. Coventry's cloth industry was experiencing a downturn, and it was reported that underemployed craftsmen were playing bowls or quoits and 'levyng ther besynes at home that they shuld lyve by'. Several English towns reviewed or

---

53 L. Toulmin Smith (ed.), *The Itinerary of John Leland*, 5 vols (London, 2nd edn, 1964), I, p. 145; Shaw, *Creation of a Community*, pp. 72–3.

reissued regulations relating to baking and brewing and introduced legislation to control begging and vagrancy around this time.[54]

The Amicable Grant of 1525 was more severe than any other tax proposed
in the sixteenth century. Following loans in 1522, retrospectively converted
into grants, and two subsidies assessed in 1524 and 1525, the Amicable Grant
was to be levied on valuations of personal wealth compiled back in 1522
rather than on valuations made in 1525. The total raised in taxation between
1522 and 1527 has been estimated as accounting for one third of the coinage
in circulation.[55] Taxation reduced demand within the economy, and cloth
producers were not immune from the effects. The impact of repeated taxation
leading to falling investment, unemployment and insolvent townspeople was
expressed by the poet John Skelton, who described the impact of the forced
loans of 1522 on the huge personal wealth of Thomas [iii] Spring (c.1456–
1523), clothier of Lavenham:

> Now nothynge but 'pay, pay!'
> With, 'laughe and lay downe,
> Borowgh, cyte, and town!'
> Good Sprynge of Lanam
> Must counte what became
> Of his clothe makynge.
> He is at suche takynge,
> Though his purs wax dull,
> He must tax for his wull
> By nature of a new writ.
> My lordys grace nameth it
> A 'quia non satisfacit!'[56]
> In the spyght of his tethe
> He must pay agayn
> A thousande or twayne
> Of his golde in store.
> And yet he payde before
> An hundred pounde and more,
> Whiche pyncheth him sore![57]

54   J.S. Lee, 'Grain Shortages in Late Medieval Towns', in Dodds and Liddy (eds), *Commercial
Activity*, pp. 63–80; C. Phythian-Adams, *Desolation of a City: Coventry and the Urban Crisis
of the Late Middle Ages* (Cambridge, 1979), pp. 54–5.
55   R.W. Hoyle, 'Taxation and the Mid Tudor Crisis', *Economic History Review*, 51 (1998),
pp. 649–75.
56   'because it is not enough'.
57   John Skelton, 'Why Come Ye Nat to Courte?', in J. Scattergood (ed.), *John Skelton, The
Complete English Poems* (Harmondsworth, 1983), pp. 302–3; Greg Walker, *John Skelton and
the Politics of the 1520s* (Cambridge, 1988), pp. 112–14.

Taxing the capital of clothiers and merchants forced them to reduce the scale of their trading activities and created unemployment. The greatest opposition arose in Suffolk, around the cloth-making centres of Lavenham and Sudbury, where clothiers had laid off their workers, but there was also passive resistance in Warwickshire, Berkshire, Wiltshire and Kent.[58]

The chronicler Edward Hall relates how after being assessed for the tax in 1525, the clothiers 'called to them their spinners, carders, fullers, wevers & other artificers ... and saied, sirs we be not able to set you a woorke, our goodes be taken from us'.[59] In Norwich it was feared that the tax would draw all the money out of the city, preventing clothiers from paying their workers.[60] Hall thought that the rebels numbered 4,000, but another chronicler, Ellis Griffith, reports that 10,000 gathered at Lavenham (Figure 13.2).[61] Meeting with a group of the protesters from Lavenham and Brent Eleigh, the dukes of Norfolk and Suffolk were told that their protests were 'only for lack of worke soo that they knewe not howe to gett theire lyvinge'. They advised Cardinal Wolsey that 'a great parte of this shire and of Essex ... Cambridgeshire the Towne of Cambridge and the scolers there' were ready to assemble on the ringing of bells and were thought to have gathered 20,000 men. Griffith thought that the rebels in Lavenham had links with men in the towns of Kent.[62] Henry VIII abandoned the grant, realising that his monarchy needed the support of the tax-paying classes, and perhaps also aware of contemporary events elsewhere in Europe, as following his account of the Amicable Grant, the chronicler Hall remarked that 'in this trobelous season the uplandishe men of Germany ... rose in a great number ... and rebelled against the princes of Germany'.[63] Over one third of the rebels indicted for participating in the Suffolk uprising against the Amicable Grant in 1525 were textile workers. The largest number came from the cloth-making centres of Lavenham, Waldingfield and Long

58   A. Fletcher and D. MacCulloch, *Tudor Rebellions*, rev. 5th edn (London, 2008), p. 25; G.W. Bernard, *War, Taxation, and Rebellion in Early Tudor England: Henry VIII, Wolsey, and the Amicable Grant of 1525* (Brighton, 1986), pp. 136–48; D. MacCulloch, *Suffolk and the Tudors. Politics and Religion in an English County 1500–1600* (Oxford, 1986), pp. 291–7.

59   E. Hall, *The Union of the Two Noble and Illustre Famelies of Lancastre and Yorke* (London, 1809), p. 699.

60   British Library (BL) Cotton MS Cleopatra F.VI, fol. 268.

61   Historical Manuscripts Commission, *Report on Manuscripts in the Welsh Language* (London, 1898), I, p. ii.

62   BL Cotton MS Cleopatra F.VI, fol. 260, partly printed in J.S. Brewer, J. Gardiner and R.H. Brodie (eds), *Letters and Papers, Foreign and Domestic, of the Reign of Henry VIII* (21 vols and Addenda, London, 1862–1932), IV, pt 1, no. 1323, p. 583; *Manuscripts in the Welsh Language*, I, p. ii.

63   Hall, *Union*, p. 702, quoted in Fletcher and MacCulloch, *Tudor Rebellions*, p. 26.

Figure 13.2. Church of St Peter and St Paul, Lavenham

Rowland Suddaby, 1941. © Victoria and Albert Museum, London

Between 1485 and 1540, fifty donors bequeathed nearly £3,000 for the fabric of Lavenham church, the majority of whom worked in the cloth trade. They included legacies for the tower from clothiers Thomas [ii] and Thomas [iii] Spring, and the Spring chapel, built by Alice, widow of Thomas [iii].

The chronicler Griffith noted that during the trade crisis of 1525, the bells in the newly completed church tower were to be rung to summon support for the rebel cause, but a rich townsman removed the clappers, preventing greater numbers from assembling and enabling negotiations to proceed.

This watercolour is from the 'Recording Britain' collection. The artists were commissioned to illustrate buildings, scenes and places that captured a sense of national identity at a time of threatened crisis, from bomb damage and invasion, in the early 1940s.

Melford.[64] They included Thomas Sprunte, dyer of Lavenham, who had been assessed on goods of £30 and lands worth 10s in 1522, but whose wealth had fallen to just £5 by 1524. The crisis in the cloth trade, combined with repeated taxation, had increased levels of poverty. In Lavenham, the proportion of the poor may have increased threefold in 1525. Wage earners numbered over half the taxable population there but owned less than 3 per cent of property, and many were probably out of work in 1525.[65]

With tax collections abandoned, the immediate crisis was averted but tensions increased again after another disastrous harvest in 1527. After disturbances in Stowmarket, the duke of Norfolk sought reassurance from the wealthier inhabitants of Lavenham that there was no similar unrest there.[66] The Crown ordered a national survey of grain stocks. The commissioners who carried out this survey also investigated cases of persons who refused to sell their corn in the open market and enforced statutes concerning beggars, alehouses and unlawful games. The few surviving returns show that shortages were particularly acute in Ballingdon (Essex), a poor suburb of the cloth-manufacturing town of Sudbury. Cloth-making centres that had moved away from arable cultivation and were more dependent on the grain market were particularly vulnerable at times of grain shortage, as demand for cloth fell when food prices rose. Such problems were to become especially acute during the severe harvest failures of the late 1590s in cloth-making areas of Essex, Devon and Westmorland.[67]

Another scare arose in 1528 when the London cloth market collapsed in the expectation of a trade war with the Netherlands. Merchants withdrew from the market, and clothiers were again forced to lay off their employees. Hall describes how merchants had been unable to venture to Spain since the previous April, and consequently:

> the Clothiers of Essex, Kent, Wiltshire, Suffolk & other shires which use clothmakyng, brought clothes into Blackwell Hall of London, to be sold as thie wer wont to do: fewe merchantes or none bought any cloth at all. When the clothiers lacked sale, then thei put fro theim their spinners,

---

64   Two notable exceptions were Sir John Spring and Thomas Jermyn, the son and son-in-law of the clothier Thomas [iii] Spring, who acted to restrain the population in 1525: Schofield, 'Spring Family'.

65   J.F. Pound, 'Rebellion and Poverty in 16th Century Suffolk: The 1525 Uprising against the Amicable Grant', *Proceedings of the Suffolk Institute of Archaeology*, 39 (1999), pp. 317–30.

66   *Letters and Papers*, IV, pt 2, no. 3703, p. 1659.

67   Lee, 'Grain Shortages'; David Dymond, 'The Famine of 1527 in Essex', *Local Population Studies*, 26 (1981), p. 37; P. Slack, 'Mortality Crises and Epidemic Disease in England, 1485–1610', in C. Webster (ed.), *Health, Medicine and Mortality in the Late Sixteenth Century* (Cambridge, 1979), pp. 53–4.

carders, tuckers & such other that live by clothworkyng, which caused the
people greatly to murmor, and specially in Suffolke.[68]

Humfrey Monmouth, a London draper and cloth exporter, explained in a
letter of May 1528 how the interruption of trade with Burgundy had hit his
own sales. He traded with 'divers clothe-men in Suffolk, and in other places',
who if they did not receive their payments, 'cannot set the poore folks aworke'.
He was accustomed to sell 400–500 cloths to strangers every year, 'yet since
Chrystmas, I have sold but xxii clothes, nor I send over none, nor no man
axeth for none'.[69] Monmouth's letter illustrates the trading links between
London merchants, Suffolk clothiers and their wage-dependent employees.

Cardinal Wolsey's strategy in 1528 was to apply pressure on the London
merchants. The French ambassador reported in February that merchants
had 'conspired' not to buy from the peasants, but after being threatened
by Wolsey, had promised that at the next Wednesday market 'there shall
not remain a crown's worth of merchandise'.[70] Perhaps noting the duke of
Norfolk's suggestion to Wolsey that he 'might cause the London merchants
not to sufer so many clothes to remain at Blackwell Hall unbought',[71] the
cardinal ordered the London merchants to buy from the clothiers, and when
they refused, he threatened that the king would buy their cloths and they
would lose their liberty.[72]

Mindful of the unrest only three years before, the duke of Norfolk worked
hard to avoid similar disturbances erupting in East Anglia during 1528. In
March he reported that offenders had been imprisoned at Norwich, Bury and
Ipswich. Later that month he met with forty of the most substantial local
clothiers, and persuaded them to resume work and take back servants they
had laid off.[73] In April, he controlled grain prices and enforced the sale of
grain stored at Colchester, as well as begging clothiers not to lay off cloth-
workers.[74] But in May, the duke wrote to Wolsey again, reporting that local
clothiers were complaining that unless they could sell their cloths in London,
they would be unable to keep their workers for more than a fortnight or
three weeks – 'The scarcity of oil alone, they say, will compel them to give up

68   Hall, *Union*, p. 745.
69   J. Strype, *Ecclesiastical Memorials relating chiefly to Religion*, 3 vols in 6 parts (Oxford,
1822), I, pt 2, no. 89, p. 367, quoted in Britnell, 'Woollen Textile Industry', p. 94.
70   *Letters and Papers*, IV, pt 2, no. 3930, p. 1749.
71   Ibid., no. 4044, p. 1769.
72   Hall, *Union*, pp. 745–6; S.J. Gunn, 'Wolsey's Foreign Policy and the Domestic Crisis
of 1527–8', in S.J. Gunn and P.G. Lindley (eds), *Cardinal Wolsey: Church, State and Art*
(Cambridge, 1991), pp. 149–77.
73   *Letters and Papers*, IV, pt 2, no. 4044, p. 1769.
74   MacCulloch, *Suffolk*, p. 298.

making cloth, unless some come from Spain.'[75] This suggests that the trade dispute had also hit imports of raw materials essential to the cloth-making process.

The collapse of the cloth market in 1528 led to simmering unrest in other textile regions. William Lord Sandys reported in March that no cloth-workers would be permitted to discharge workers in Hampshire, and he hoped that Berkshire and Wiltshire would be equally well managed. Unlawful assemblies were reported at Westbury and Devizes.[76] A Colchester clothier wrote that he could not sell a cloth even at half the cost price and that the merchants said they would not buy until the commons rose and complained to the king.[77] In April 1528, Archbishop Wareham of Canterbury received a petition from the inhabitants of Kent who were 'impoverished by the great dearth of corn'. By May there were reports of seditious behaviour by textile workers in Goudhurst and Cranbrook, two prominent centres of cloth-making in the Weald of Kent, and John Andrew of Cranbrook, clothier, was sent to Wolsey to tell 'the whole truth'.[78] Sir Henry Guildford warned Wolsey that the clothiers of Kent were about to lay off workers due to the depressed state of the market: 'The clothiers complain that they have so little sale that they will not be able to keep as many men as formerly, and if they are compelled to abandon their trade great numbers will be left idle.'[79] Nationally, exports fell from 99,500 cloths in 1528 to under 82,000 by 1532, before recovering again. Yet despite these pockets of unrest, there were no major disturbances. The monarchy was in a far stronger position than in the 1450s, and was able to use the aristocracy in the provinces to prevent unrest spreading.

The locational shifts in cloth production that had begun during the early fifteenth century, grew markedly following the crisis of the 1450s/1460s, and remained evident during the later fifteenth century, also intensified after the crises of the 1520s. While the ulnage accounts no longer provide figures to quantify the distribution of cloth-making, the observations made by the antiquarian John Leland as he travelled across England between 1539 and 1545 show the changing distribution of the cloth industry. Leland remarked on the prominence of cloth-making in a number of small centres in Gloucestershire, Somerset and Wiltshire, but found declining production in the larger towns of Bath and Coventry, and at Bridgnorth (Shropshire), Berkeley and Thornbury (Glos.), where 'now idelnes muche reynithe'. In

---

75 *Letters and Papers*, IV, pt 2, no. 4239, p. 1868.
76 Ibid., no. 4043, p. 1796; no. 4058, p. 1799; no. 4085, p. 1807.
77 Ibid., no. 4129, p. 1826.
78 Ibid., no. 4173, pp. 1843–4; no. 4287, p. 1886; no. 4301, p. 1891; no. 4310, pp. 1893–4; M. Zell, *Industry in the Countryside: Wealden Society in the Sixteenth Century* (Cambridge, 1994), pp. 153–7.
79 *Letters and Papers*, IV, pt 2, no. 4276, p. 1881.

Yorkshire, he observed that Wakefield, Bradford and Leeds 'stondith most by clothing', but found the industry in decay at the older manufacturing centres of Beverley and Ripon.[80] A statute of 1534 sought to prevent cloth-making in rural Worcestershire because of the decline of neighbouring towns.[81]

Similarly the trend towards the concentration of production in the hands of entrepreneurs intensified, and as in the mid fifteenth century, the difficult trading conditions of the 1520s hastened this trend. Complaints from weavers in Kent and Suffolk in the 1530s reveal complex and differentiated industries. Around 1536, the Kentish weavers asked that no clothier use more than one loom, that clothiers pay for work by spinners and weavers in ready money and not in goods, and requested a procedure for arbitrating disputes between clothiers and weavers. The weavers of Suffolk and Essex, including those of Ipswich, Hadleigh, Lavenham, Bergholt, Colchester and Dedham, complained in 1539 that master weavers were unemployed because clothiers now had looms, weavers and fullers working in their own houses. Employers could also reduce their labour costs in small towns and rural areas, beyond the oversight of craft guilds and civic authorities. The city of York attributed the competition from clothiers in the West Riding to the fact that they were able to offer lower wages to their workers.[82]

Clothiers whose enterprise absorbed a significant proportion of trade could be found in most cloth-making regions in the second quarter of the sixteenth century. Several left lasting monuments to their wealth, adorned in some cases with merchant marks or scenes from their trade. In Devon, John Greenway (d.1529) added an ornate chantry chapel decorated with a frieze of merchant ships to Tiverton parish church, while on the aisle built as a chantry chapel for John Lane (d.1529) at Cullompton church, angels clutch teasel-frames and cloth shears.[83] In Wiltshire, William Stumpe of Malmesbury, Thomas Horton of Bradford, Trowbridge and Westwood, James Terumber, Alexander Langford and Thomas Bailey of Trowbridge, and Robert Long and Walter Lucas of Steeple Ashton were specifically mentioned by John Leland for the fortunes that they had made in the cloth industry and their investment in local churches and houses.[84] Many of these clothiers had London trading links. In the 1530s, Thomas Kytson, mercer and Merchant Adventurer of

---

80   J.S. Lee, 'The Functions and Fortunes of English Small Towns at the Close of the Middle Ages: Evidence from John Leland's *Itinerary*', *Urban History*, 37 (2010), pp. 3–25.

81   R.H. Tawney and E. Power (eds), *Tudor Economic Documents* (3 vols, London, 1924), i, pp. 173–5.

82   *Letters and Papers*, XI, no. 520, p. 210; XIV, pt. 1, no. 874, pp. 408–9. Zell, *Industry*, p. 154; B. McClenaghan, *The Springs of Lavenham and the Suffolk Cloth Trade in the XV and XVI Centuries* (Ipswich, 1924), pp. 15, 54–7; Britnell, *Closing*, p. 224.

83   E. Carus-Wilson, 'The Significance of the Secular Sculptures in the Lane Chapel, Cullompton', *Medieval Archaeology*, 1 (1957), pp. 104–17.

84   Lee, 'Functions and Fortunes', p. 15.

London, bought most of his broadcloth from Wiltshire and Somerset clothiers for cash, ensuring regular supplies and competitive prices.[85]

Some clothiers were even starting to concentrate production on a single site. In Berkshire, John Winchcombe (c.1489–1557), a prominent Newbury clothier, who supplied Thomas Cromwell with 1,000 pieces of cloth in 1539, was long remembered as an innovator who put his workers together in a single workshop.[86] The dissolution of the monasteries offered potential factory sites. Clothier William Stumpe (c.1497–1552) installed broad looms in several of the former buildings of Malmesbury Abbey. When John Leland visited in the early 1540s, he reported that 3,000 cloths were being made there every year. The city of Oxford negotiated with Stumpe in 1546 to establish a similar project at Osney Abbey, which they hoped would provide work for 2,000 people, but nothing came of this.[87] At Gloucester, Alderman Thomas Bell converted the house of the Blackfriars into a weaving-house, and reportedly provided employment to over 300 people in 1538. A cloth-maker of Burford offered to spend 100 marks a week in wages to cloth-makers in Abingdon in return for securing two fulling mills and other property of the former abbey. The former friaries at Northampton and Canterbury were also proposed as places where cloth-making could be set up.[88] These industrial capitalists, investing in plant and buildings for manufacture and managing one or more production processes in centralised workshops, were building upon the structural changes accelerated by the crises of the 1520s.

Conclusion

The trade crises of the mid fifteenth century and the 1520s were of different magnitudes but both had similar effects on the English cloth trade. The two crises sparked unemployment and protests, and hastened structural changes in the spatial distribution of cloth production, in the organisation of the industry, and in marketing networks. The lower costs of production enabled

85 Cambridge University Library, Hengrave Hall MS 78(2): The Boke of Remembraunce, 1529. C.J. Brett, 'Thomas Kytson and Somerset Clothmen 1529–1539', *Proceedings of Somerset Archaeology and Natural History Society*, 143 (2001), pp. 29–50; C.J. Brett, 'Thomas Kytson and Wiltshire Clothmen, 1529–1539', *Wiltshire Archaeology and Natural History Magazine*, 97 (2004), pp. 35–62.
86 A.F. Pollard, 'Winchcombe, John (d.1520), clothier, and Winchcombe, John (c.1489–1557), clothier', rev. E. Kerridge, *ODNB*; C. Jackson, 'Boom-Time Freaks or Heroic Industrial Pioneers? Clothing Entrepreneurs in Sixteenth- and Early Seventeenth-Century Berkshire', *Textile History*, 39 (2008), pp. 145–71.
87 H. Miller, 'Stumpe, William (c.1497–1552)', *ODNB*.
88 *Letters and Papers*, XIII(1), no 332, pp. 113–14; no. 415, p. 154; XIV, no. 42, p. 21; no. 423, p. 170; J. Youings, *The Dissolution of the Monasteries* (London, 1971), pp. 178–9.

larger cloth-makers to survive the crises better than smaller producers, prompting the concentration of production in the hands of clothiers. These entrepreneurs increasingly based their production in certain small towns and villages, leading to a locational shift, generally away from larger towns, which tended to accommodate smaller producers and were restricted by the regulations of guilds and civic governments. Marketing and credit networks became increasingly aligned with London, which may have been better able to withstand the widespread economic slump of the mid fifteenth century. The central importance of London mercantile links within the cloth trade by the 1520s was recognised by the king's chief minister, who tried to manipulate them in an attempt to resolve the crisis.

The crises of the 1450s/1460s and 1520s played important roles in the economic development of the cloth industry. Both events helped create a more volatile industrial sector than in previous centuries, because of the increased dependence on overseas markets, and the reliance on mercantile investment decisions based on where labour and other factors of production were cheapest.[89] The trends which the crisis of the mid fifteenth century stimulated made the industry more vulnerable to the crises of the 1520s. Governments had to face the consequences of communities dependent on the fortunes of distant markets for their livelihoods. Such communities could also be associated with religious and political dissent, and contemporaries tried to use these crises to secure political concessions. The attempt to force political change through Cade's revolt was unsuccessful, but the rebels secured the cancellation of the Amicable Grant in 1525. While other sectors and regions within the late medieval economy were susceptible to instabilities in overseas markets, like the coal, lead and iron industries of County Durham, which were all exported through Newcastle-upon-Tyne, these did not result in any notable discontent and disturbances.[90] Nationally, these mineral- and metal-based industries generated much less employment and their exports were far less valuable than those of the cloth industry.[91]

Interesting parallels can be drawn, though, between the two trade crises in the woollen cloth industry in the later Middle Ages and two crises in the same industry in the early nineteenth century. In the early 1810s, when diplomatic manoeuvres hit European and North Atlantic markets, 'cloth

89   R.H. Britnell, 'Urban Demand in the English Economy, 1300–1600', in Galloway (ed.), *Trade*, p. 21.

90   I.S.W. Blanchard, 'Commercial Crises and Change: Trade and the Industrial Economy of the North-East, 1509–1532', *Northern History*, 8 (1973), pp. 64–85; R.H. Britnell, 'The English Economy and the Government, 1450–1550', in J.L. Watts (ed.), *The End of the Middle Ages? England in the Fifteenth and Sixteenth Centuries* (Stroud, 1998), pp. 90–4.

91   The Bishop of Durham's most successful coal mine in the fifteenth century employed only 10 people: A.T. Brown, *Rural Society and Economic Change in County Durham: Recession and Recovery, c.1400–1640* (forthcoming, Woodbridge, 2015), chap. 1.

halls and warehouses were piled high with unsold goods, short-time working gave way to enforced unemployment, and dislocation and distress were widespread throughout the manufacturing counties'. Protests included the Luddite machine-breaking disturbances.[92] Another collapse of overseas markets in 1837 generated unemployment and protest in the form of the Anti-Poor Law movement. As a contemporary newspaper, the *Leeds Mercury*, observed in 1840, in a depression, prices 'are only remunerating to a few, that is, the largest capitalists, whose resources enable them, in a season of general embarrassment, to absorb an unusual and extraordinary share of the current business'.[93] Like the early-nineteenth-century trade crises, the late medieval crises in the English cloth industry generated underemployment, unemployment and discontent, and ruined many smaller manufacturers, but also enabled certain larger producers, such as the leading clothiers, to flourish.

92 D. Gregory, *Regional Transformation and Industrial Revolution: A Geography of the Yorkshire Woollen Industry* (London, 1982), pp. 37–8, 244.
93 Quoted in Gregory, *Regional Transformation*, p. 218.

14

The Roots of Decline: The Tyrolean Silk Industry and the Crises of the Second Half of the Nineteenth Century

CINZIA LORANDINI

Introduction

Economies are recurrently faced with crises that differ in their origins and nature, size and duration. In economic historiography a wide range of manifestations are labelled 'crises', among them financial collapses and downturns in the real economy, related to supply or demand, covering a short period or extending into the long run. At times crises are responsible for the decline of regional economies or specific industries, whereas in other circumstances they promote a restructuring process able to turn stagnation into renewed growth. The outcome depends to a large extent on whether or not the main actors are willing and able to react: that is, on a mix of incentives and capabilities that influences investment and innovation.

Drawing on evidence concerning the Tyrolean silk industry in the second half of the nineteenth century, this study explores the impact of crises of different types on the industry's structure and dynamics, and the reaction of the local producers. In this context, the term 'crisis' broadly denotes an abrupt and profound change in the economic and institutional framework that requires an adequate response from businesses if they are to survive. From the mid nineteenth century onward, the Tyrolean silk industry underwent two major periods of crisis: the first one was caused by pebrine, a highly contagious epidemic that erupted in the 1850s and raised the mortality rate among silkworms to unprecedented levels for almost two decades; the second one was related to the deflation of the 1870s, whose direct and indirect consequences were felt until the early 1890s. Although the first phase was predominantly marked by the silkworm disease and the ensuing shortage in the industry's primary inputs, other critical junctures emerged throughout the period, namely the commercial crisis of 1857/8, the wars of 1859 and 1866 – the latter combined with a financial crisis – and the Franco–Prussian war of 1870. The second period of crisis was mostly characterised by a sharp and enduring fall in the price of silk amid the deflationary pressure that started with the stock market collapse of 1873. The subsequent change in the trade policy of the European countries, along with the social provisions introduced in Austria in the 1880s, contributed to worsening prospects for the Tyrolean silk industry, which faced growing competition from foreign producers both on the home market and abroad. The local silk industry ultimately fell into decline, and, by the turn of the century, it had been largely dismantled.

This study is based on the premise that the decline of the Tyrolean silk industry can only be understood by taking into account the consequences of the many crises that punctuated the second half of the nineteenth century. To this end, the chapter draws on several sources: historiography on the silk industry at both local and international levels;[1] contemporary statistical reports, especially those compiled by the local chamber of commerce and industry, which was established in 1850 in Rovereto – the most important centre for silk manufacture in the region – with competence over Trentino as a whole;[2] and first-hand evidence from a leading family business, the Valentino e Isidoro Salvadori firm of Trento.

The Salvadori firm, whose origins can be traced back to the late seventeenth century, was one of the oldest merchant houses in Tyrol, and it had specialised since the 1780s in the manufacturing and trading of silk, activities that were carried on until the demise of the business towards the end of the nineteenth century.[3] In the 1850s, the ownership and direction of the business were in the hands of the last representative of the fifth generation, Valentino Salvadori

1   I would like to thank the editors and Andrea Leonardi for their comments on an earlier draft of this chapter. The research reported here is part of a project financed by the Fondazione Cassa di Risparmio di Trento e Rovereto. Two major references are Giovanni Federico, *An Economic History of the Silk Industry, 1830–1930* (Cambridge, 1997), and Andrea Leonardi, 'Il setificio austriaco tra crisi ed intervento pubblico (1870–1914)', *Studi Trentini di Scienze Storiche*, I: 63 (1984), pp. 361–400; II: 64 (1985), pp. 67–126.
2   Most data are drawn from the following reports: *Rapporto statistico della Camera di commercio e d'industria in Rovereto per l'anno 1870* (Rovereto, 1871); *Relazione statistica della Camera di commercio e d'industria in Rovereto per l'anno 1875* (Rovereto, 1876); *La trattura della seta nel Trentino: cenni storici e statistici* (Rovereto, 1878); *Relazione statistica della Camera di commercio e d'industria in Rovereto per l'anno 1880* (Rovereto, 1881); *Camera di commercio e di industria in Rovereto: mezzo secolo* (Rovereto, 1902). To be noted is that although these statistical data are useful for drawing an overall picture of the silk industry throughout the period, they must be taken with some degree of caution, as proven by inconsistencies between some of the figures reported.
3   For a brief overview of the Salvadori firm's operation across two centuries, see Cinzia Lorandini, 'Looking beyond the Buddenbrooks Syndrome: The Salvadori Firm of Trento, 1660s–1880s', *Business History* (forthcoming, 2015).

(1799–1885),[4] who was assisted by a trusted agent, Giacomo Tolt, whose family had been employed by the Salvadori for over a century. The firm's correspondence and accounting books, including balance sheets and shipment ledgers, enable detailed analysis of the firm's performance throughout the period, and provide useful insights into its business strategies. The Salvadori Archives thus offer a rare opportunity to combine information from institutional sources with micro evidence from a single case study, namely the case of a long-established firm, which initially proved to be one of the most innovative, but then behaved conservatively, and finally ceased to operate.[5]

As emerges from the account of the Tyrolean silk industry provided in the next section, against the backdrop of a rather traditional manufacturing process with scant technological improvements until the mid nineteenth century, the Salvadori firm stands out as a prominent actor. Furthermore, this merchant house played by no means a minor role in the collective endeavour of the Tyrolean producers to handle the pebrine crisis – as revealed in the third section, which deals with the challenges raised by the silkworm epidemic and provides insights into the many critical junctures that arose on the demand side during the same period. As for the consequences of the pebrine epidemic, what emerges is that, besides curtailing the basic input factors necessary for the manufacture of silk, the epidemic fostered a selection process among the producers and accelerated modernisation of the reeling mills. By contrast, the thrust to innovate did not seem to involve the throwing process until much later and to a lesser extent. Once the pebrine issue had been resolved, as discussed in the fourth section, the Panic of 1873 and the ensuing 'great deflation' raised further challenges; and combined with Austrian policy, they were responsible for a deterioration in the profitability of the silk business. This time the local producers proved unable to react adequately, and the silk industry fell into decline. As summed up in the conclusion, this study shows that a crisis is not necessarily destructive, as it can offer incentives for investment and innovation. The ultimate impact of crisis is mostly determined by the manufacturers' willingness and ability to provide a firm response.

The silk industry in Tyrol in the mid nineteenth century

In the mid nineteenth century, Tyrol was one of the main silk-producing areas in the Habsburg Empire. The output of cocoons was the highest after that of the adjoining regions of Lombardy and Veneto, whose territories were

4 Valentino's elder brother and partner in the business, Isidoro (1783–1848), died a few years earlier.
5 Since the Salvadori Archives are currently under rearrangement, the references reported here are the old ones.

destined to be detached from the Habsburg dominion by the 1860s. The Tyrolean silk industry was mostly located in the southern, Italian-speaking part of the region, namely the area corresponding to Trentino, and it was of utmost importance for both the number of workers involved and the value of the silk exported. The production process, which started with the cultivation of mulberry trees and the breeding of silkworms, involved two 'industrial' phases: reeling, whereby the raw silk was unwound from the cocoons immersed in basins full of hot water; and throwing, i.e. the process of twisting the raw silk into threads suitable for weaving. By contrast, the manufacture of silk fabrics was uncommon in Tyrol.

The reeling of silk took place after the cocoons had been harvested, in plants endowed, in some cases, with up to dozens of basins, though most of them had only a few basins. The wide dispersion of the manufacturing units across the countryside makes it difficult to determine the size of the reeling industry. According to data from the Rovereto Chamber of Commerce, in 1850 there were 245 silk-reeling mills in Trentino – considering only the plants with at least six basins – and 5,304 basins.[6] This last estimate is not far from the 5,479 basins mentioned in a statistical report published in 1852, which stated that 9,892 workers were engaged in the reeling of silk, producing about 2,800 quintals of raw silk.[7] Evidently these data did not include the many peasants engaged in the raising of silkworms who directly processed the cocoons in their own basins, resulting in the manufacture of small quantities of poor-quality silk. The overall number of these single basins is difficult to determine even approximately, but it probably amounted to some thousands.[8]

This situation was the result of the significant development of silk-reeling in the previous decades, which had been accompanied to only a limited extent by modernisation of production techniques. Even most of the larger factories still employed traditional technologies, namely fire-heated basins, which required two women per basin: a master reeler, called the *maestra*, who unwound the thread from the cocoons, and a younger assistant, called the *menaressa*, who turned the reel on which the silk was rolled up. The spread of steam-reeling – the new system patented in 1805 by the Frenchman Gensoul, whereby the basins were centrally heated by a steam boiler – was still limited. Compared with fire-reeling, steam-reeling was more efficient because it made it possible to save up to two thirds of the fuel. Moreover, since the temperature

---

6   *La trattura*, p. 34.

7   See Agostino Perini, *Statistica del Trentino*, I (Trento, 1852), p. 716. The author himself argues that the data must be treated with caution. It is worth noting that, in about the same period, the number of reeling mills in Lombardy exceeded 3,000. See Giovanni Frattini, *Storia e statistica della industria manifatturiera in Lombardia* (Milano, 1856), pp. 55–7.

8   [Antonio Tambosi], 'Brevi considerazioni sul passato, il presente e l'avvenire della sericoltura nel nostro paese', *L'agricoltore*, 12 (1883), no. 12, p. 2.

in the basin was kept steady and the yarn was not dirtied by the soot from the fire, the silk produced was of better quality.[9]

In about 1850, there were fewer than forty steam-reeling mills in Trentino – although they accounted for 40 per cent of all basins[10] – and the majority of them still relied on manual movement of the reels. This latter system, in fact, was largely predominant until the late 1840s also in the factories of other Italian regions.[11] Only a few manufacturers in Tyrol went so far as to use steam for the mechanical movement of the reels, and Valentino Salvadori was one of the pioneers.[12] In fact, the Salvadori firm had already been engaged in the reeling of silk, but this activity had been abandoned in the late eighteenth century. It was not until the end of the 1840s that the decision was taken to reintroduce this operation into the business. To this end, a modern steam-reeling mill was built, with all necessary equipment provided by the Philip Taylor et fils company of Marseilles and assembled by a French technician.[13] The new plant, which came into operation in 1850 in Calliano – a village near Rovereto – was endowed with 120 basins, which made it one of the largest in the region. Indeed, in that period only a handful of silk-reeling firms, all of them equipped with steam heating, had brought one hundred or more basins under one roof.[14] Apart from the Salvadori firm's plant, only two other reeling mills used steam for movement of the reels. This had two major advantages: it saved labour, and the more constant motion of the reels improved the evenness of the silk.[15] The quality of the silk was further improved, in the Salvadori reeling mill, by the system of covering the reels, which the Salvadori firm was the first to introduce in Tyrol, doing so in the early 1850s. Besides ensuring better silk due to rapid drying before the material was rolled up on the reels,

9   To be noted, however, is that this innovation became entirely viable only after the boilers were improved in the 1830s. Federico, *An Economic History*, p. 104.

10   *La trattura*, p. 34.

11   Federico, *An Economic History*, p. 107.

12   The Bettini firm of Lizzana, near Rovereto, was the first to introduce steam-reeling in 1818. It also played a pioneering role in the use of steam for the mechanisation of reeling, which was adopted in 1845, followed by Trentini in 1847 and Salvadori in 1850. See Johann Jakob Staffler, *Tirol und Vorarlberg, statistisch, mit geschichtlichen Bemerkungen* (Innsbruck, 1839), p. 365, and *La trattura*, p. 22.

13   Archivio di Stato di Trento, Archivio Salvadori (hereafter ASTn, AS), sc. 18, b. 55, letters from Philip Taylor and fils, 1848–50. Philip Taylor 'the elder' (1786–1870) was a British machine designer who emigrated to Paris and then moved to Marseille, where he started an engineering workshop for the manufacture of steam engines and boats. In 1847 the establishments in Provence were grouped under the firm name of Philip Taylor & fils. See Olivier Raveux, 'Un technicien britannique en Europe méridionale: Philip Taylor (1786–1870)', *Histoire, Économie et Sociétés*, 19 (2000), p. 263.

14   These firms were the following: Bettini in Lizzana (240 basins), Tacchi in Rovereto (188), Ciani in Trento (154), Trentini in Vigolo Vattaro near Trento (130), Chimelli in Pergine (100), and Tambosi in Trento (100). Data from *La trattura*, pp. 48–87.

15   Federico, *An Economic History*, p. 107.

this technology enabled silk to be reeled also on wet and rainy days.[16] Hence, at that time the Salvadori house stood out as one of the most technologically advanced and innovative merchant-manufacturers in the Tyrolean silk industry, so that it was able to face the upcoming crisis more effectively.

The silk that was not exported in the raw state was processed into silk yarns in water-powered throwing mills. There were two main types of yarn: tram (*trama*), which was made of two threads twisted together; and organzine (*organzino*), which had a higher value and consisted of two or three threads twisted separately and then twisted again jointly. Most of the Tyrolean throwing mills were located in the Rovereto area, whose manufacturers had earned a good reputation on the European markets for the thinness and evenness of their silk,[17] even though it hardly reached the quality of the Milanese silks, let alone those of Piedmont which were regarded as the best and profited from a close relationship with the Fabrique Lyonnaise. The Tyrolean mills, still endowed with the old 'circular' machines made of wood,[18] were not suitable for the processing of silk yarns with a high degree of twist like those demanded on the French market. Indeed, the Salvadori firm, which had throwing mills in Trento and Calliano,[19] produced organzine of the so-called *andante* quality, with a lower degree of twist compared with the *strafilati*, the manufacture of which required a modern throwing machine built of iron.[20] This was the so-called 'squared' throwing machine, which had been developed in eighteenth-century France and was more expensive than the old 'circular' machine, but had the advantage of increasing the speed of the spindles, and therefore boosted productivity. The 'cylindrical' machine, invented in the 1820s in the UK, further improved throwing technology, although the increase in speed to some extent reduced the silk's quality.[21]

By the early 1850s, the 'squared' machine had been widely adopted by the Lombard silk manufacturers, who were renowned for their *strafilati* and exported over half of their silk to Switzerland and Germany, and almost one fifth to Lyon.[22] By contrast, the Tyrolean thrown silk was marketed almost exclusively in Vienna, Switzerland and the Rhineland, whereas Milan and

---

16   *La trattura*, pp. 24–5.

17   Staffler, *Tirol und Vorarlberg*, pp. 366–7.

18   Robertino Ghiringhelli, 'La lavorazione della seta nel Roveretano nell'età della Restaurazione. Vicende ed aspetti', Atti della Accademia Roveretana degli Agiati 234 (1984), fol. A, pp. 189–239, here: p. 233.

19   The Salvadori's throwing mill in Calliano was one of the two largest in Tyrol in the late 1830s. Staffler, *Tirol und Vorarlberg*, p. 366.

20   ASTn, AS, vol. 1174, p. 383, Letter to Edoardo Martorelli of Milan, 29 Nov. 1858; p. 415, Letter to Henry Palluat et Cie of Lyon, 29 Dec. 1858.

21   For more details, see Federico, *An Economic History*, pp. 140–1.

22   Frattini, *Storia e statistica*, pp. 58, 67.

Lyon mostly imported raw silk from Tyrol.[23] This is supported by evidence from the Salvadori firm, whose shipments to Milan and Lyon consisted of raw silk, while the firm's organzines were particularly appreciated by the German manufacturers. More precisely, over the entire period, the bulk of the silk was shipped to the Gebrüder Frickenhaus firm of Elberfeld, which sold it to the Rhenish manufacturers on behalf of the Salvadori firm. The close connection with the German firm secured an important market outlet for the Salvadoris' silk, and it did not represent a significant constraint at least until the early 1870s. Thereafter, however, the other destinations further lost weight, and the development of an almost symbiotic relationship with the Frickenhaus was to the detriment of the search for market alternatives, which probably reduced the Salvadori firm's ability to cope with the crisis.

Overcoming the pebrine crisis (1854–72)

The quantity of silk exported and its price were subject to fluctuations from one year to another, depending on market dynamics and the outcome of the cocoon harvest. In particular, the supply of cocoons was deeply affected by climatic conditions, which influenced the time of ripening of the mulberry leaves, and the growth and development of silkworms. Irrational breeding practices were partially responsible for frequent diseases among silkworms, exacerbated by their propensity to contagion, thus adding further uncertainty to the harvest outcome. Among the various diseases that infected the silkworms, pebrine was by far the most durable and severe. Indeed, with harvest losses that reached 60–80 per cent in some years, mortality rates among silkworms were such to threaten the survival of Mediterranean sericulture.[24] The epidemic first appeared in France in the 1840s and reached northern Italy in the early 1850s. It then spread progressively eastward, inflicting a severe shock on the silk industry, whose primary inputs were severely curtailed.[25] In 1855 the first Tyrolean farms were infected, and by 1858 the contagion had spread throughout the region.[26]

The pebrine was so called from the Provencal word *pebre*, i.e. pepper, due to the black spots that resembled grains of pepper and covered the skin of the

23   Staffler, *Tirol und Vorarlberg*, p. 368; Ruggero Cobelli, 'L'industria serica nel Trentino', *Giornale di agricoltura, industria e commercio del regno d'Italia* (1877), no. 3, p. 8.
24   Roberto Tolaini, 'Una discontinuità nella storia del setificio italiano: la pebrina e il rinnovamento dell'industria serica', *Proposte e ricerche*, 53 (2004), p. 27.
25   On the pebrine epidemic and its consequences for the silk industry, see Federico, *An Economic History*, pp. 36–41.
26   On the pebrine crisis in Tyrol, see Alessandra Pisoni, *Il filo perduto: la bachicoltura trentina dell'Ottocento tra ripresa e declino* (Trento, 1997), pp. 77–145.

infected silkworms. There was much discussion among contemporaries, both silkworm breeders and academics, about the nature and vehicles of the disease, whose origins were traced to several factors. The main explanations included the nourishing of the silkworms with spoiled mulberry leaves, seasonal vagaries, and the unhealthy air of the closed rooms in which the silkworms were raised. Further theories pointed to the presence of cryptogams or microscopic insects, with the latter hypothesis more closely approaching the actual cause.[27] Indeed, a micro-organism, called *Nosema bombicys*, was discovered in the bodies of infected silkworms, and it was responsible for the disease. When contracted during the silkworms' lives, the pebrine did not prevent them from weaving the cocoons; it only reduced the number of eggs produced by the moths used for reproduction. But the parasite was inevitably transmitted to the eggs, whose silkworms were consequently infected from birth, and most probably bound to die. The problem was aggravated by the contagiousness of the pebrine, which was so severe that almost all the female moths exposed to the disease bore the parasite, since the corpuscle was easily transferred by dust, insects, the breeders' hands, and the tools employed to handle the silkworms.[28] Even though the disease remained incurable, following scientific research, and especially Louis Pasteur's discoveries, a preventive method was devised, which made it possible to separate the disease-free eggs from the infected ones by means of a microscopic selection. The so-called 'cellular system' was introduced in Italy in the late 1860s; however, several years passed before Pasteur's system became widely adopted.[29]

Initially, because the breeders could not ascertain whether or not the eggs were healthy, the only means to counter the dramatic consequences of the epidemic was to obtain silkworm eggs from non-infected areas, although this did not necessarily ensure a successful harvest, due to problems of acclimatisation, unfavourable weather, or the poor quality of imported eggs. This search was conducted by specialised traders called *semai*, who travelled first through the Mediterranean basin, then through the Balkans, and finally to Asia, to purchase eggs on behalf of landowners and silkworm raisers.[30] Sometimes these latter organised themselves into associations, as in the case of the Comitato seme-bachi, which was established in Trento in 1858 in order to import healthy eggs into Trentino by organising expeditions to non-infected areas.[31] To this end, besides benefiting from a loan granted by

27 Ibid., pp. 96–102.
28 Ibid., pp. 80–1.
29 For his contribution to developing an effective method to counter the disease, Pasteur received a prize of 5,000 gulden from the Austrian government in 1872. Ibid., p. 141.
30 See Claudio Zanier, *Semai: setaioli italiani in Giappone (1861–1880)* (Padova, 2006), pp. 20–3.
31 On the operation of the Comitato seme-bachi, see Luigi Canella, 'Contributo per la storia dell'industria serica austriaca', in *Programma della i.r. Scuola media di commercio in Trento alla fine dell'anno scolastico 1900–1901* (Trento, 1901); and Pisoni, *Il filo perduto*, pp. 114–37.

the Tyrolean government, the special committee collected the necessary funds among the silkworm raisers and landowners who joined the initiative. In 1859 and 1860, silkworm eggs were purchased in Bucharest, but unfortunately the cocoon harvest proved disastrous. The committee was reorganised, and the Salvadori firm's agent, Giacomo Tolt, became one of its members.[32] At that time, the committee had already established close cooperation with a local priest, Giuseppe Grazioli, who was responsible for the search for healthy eggs. In fact, Grazioli's first expeditions to the Balkans, Asia Minor and the Caucasus region were far from successful. Finding eggs of good quality and immune from pebrine proved to be a demanding task. Furthermore, attempts to reproduce healthy eggs from the imported ones failed, so that the breeders were forced to resort to further imports. Nevertheless, Grazioli's endeavours enabled local sericulture to survive.

In the end, the salvation of Mediterranean sericulture took the form of Japanese eggs, which proved to be more resistant to pebrine, and whose imports into Europe boomed from the mid-1860s onward.[33] Similarly, the turning point for Tyrolean sericulture coincided with Grazioli's voyages to Japan, which took place regularly from 1864 until 1868. Worth mentioning is that the resources needed for his first expedition to the Far East were provided by the Salvadori firm, which supplied the necessary contacts with a banking house of international renown.[34] Thereafter, the Salvadori firm further supported Grazioli's expeditions. For instance, in 1868, they asked Frederick Huth & Co. of London to furnish the credit letters required for Grazioli's voyages in China and Japan, and anticipated the necessary funds.[35]

Amid a collective endeavour to cope with the crisis, several measures were taken from the late 1860s onward by the government and by local institutions and associations. Their purpose was both to fight the disease and to promote the rationalisation of silkworm raising. Besides the prizes and subsidies granted by the Ministry of Agriculture in Vienna, the Rovereto Chamber of Commerce also established a bacological station in order to produce cocoons from eggs selected by means of the cellular system, the ultimate objective being to free local sericulture from the need to import foreign eggs.[36] This initiative, far from representing an isolated attempt to counter the effects

---

32 Canella, 'Contributo', p. 11.
33 Federico, *An Economic History*, p. 38.
34 On Grazioli's voyages to Japan, see Canella, 'Contributo', pp. 19–20, and Zanier, *Semai*, pp. 338–41.
35 Since the Salvadori firm was unknown to the London bank, they indicated as reference providers the bankers Gebrüder Bethmann of Frankfurt and Paul von Stetten of Augsburg, with whom the firm was in regular correspondence. ASTn, AS, vol. 851, p. 77, Letter to Frederick Huth & Co. of London, 21 Feb. 1868.
36 Pisoni, *Il filo perduto*, pp. 137–44. In 1870, a third of the silkworm eggs were imported from Japan while two thirds were obtained through reproduction; whereas in 1877 the eggs were

of the disease, inspired similar endeavours by two local agrarian societies founded in that period.

By the early 1870s, thanks to an exhaustive search for healthy eggs and the efforts to develop a selection process, the local sericulture had overcome the critical juncture. Indeed, while in 1865 the output of cocoons was still at 40 per cent the level of 1854, in the following years there was a recovery, which reached a peak in 1871.[37] Japanese 'green' eggs replaced the traditional 'yellow' ones typical of the Italian regions, thereby sustaining the manufacture of silk, even though the substitution was not entirely problem-free. Indeed, besides being more expensive, the Japanese cocoons had a lower yield and quality. They consequently required greater attention from the reelers, and increased the cost of raw silk manufacture.[38]

This arguably promoted the spread of steam-reeling, which made it possible to obtain a better and more expensive silk, thereby partially offsetting the higher costs of inputs and production.[39] The statistics of the Rovereto Chamber of Commerce show that steam-reeling gained ground in the 1850s, and that it spread further in the following decade, although the mechanical movement of the reels was still restricted to a minority of plants. This took place amid a decline in the overall number of reeling mills paralleled by an increase in the average number of basins, which testifies to a gradual shift of the Tyrolean reeling industry from a high fragmentation of the operation among artisanal units and households to a more concentrated activity in larger plants (Table 14.1). Evidence from the Tyrolean case thus supports a contention already made for other regions in northern Italy: that the pebrine crisis promoted technological innovation as well as a restructuring of the reeling industry towards higher concentration.[40]

With regard to technical developments in the throwing industry, innovation was almost absent, though evidence is more scant. Valentino Salvadori himself, who was so ready to innovate reeling, does not seem to have introduced substantial changes in his throwing mills over the entire period considered, even if the plants were renovated to some extent. In 1854

---

almost entirely reproduced. ASTn, AS, vol. 679, p. 188, Letter to Henry Palluat & Testenoire of Lyon, 27 Apr. 1870; ASTn, AS, vol. 866, p. 97, Letter to Luigi Testa of Milan, 9 May 1877.

37   Andrea Leonardi, *L'economia di una regione alpina* (Trento, 1996), pp. 175–7.

38   Only the development of the cellular method allowed a shift back to traditional eggs in Italy, which occurred in the 1880s, when imports from Japan disappeared. See Federico, *An Economic History*, p. 89. In fact, a major purpose of the Tyrolean bacological stations was to promote a shift back to the yellow species; nonetheless, in 1877 the yellow eggs were still being cultivated only on experimental bases. ASTn, AS, vol. 866, p. 97, Letter to Luigi Testa of Milan, 9 May 1877.

39   Federico, *An Economic History*, p. 41.

40   See Tolaini, 'Una discontinuità', pp. 39–53.

Table 14.1. Reeling mills in Trentino (1850–99)

Year	Reeling mills	Of which steam-heated plants		Basins	Of which steam-heated basins		Workers employed
		No.	%		No.	%	
1850	245	38	15.5	5,304	2,170	40.9	
1860	214	50	23.4	5,348	2,693	50.4	
1870	185	69	37.3	5,352	3,295	61.6	
1875	162	67	41.4	4,614			6,757
1880	111	59	53.2	3,354	3,045	90.8	5,122
1885	50			2,593			3,932
1892	19			1,397			2,016
1899	16			1,076			1,500

Source: 1850–70: *La trattura*, p. 34 (as stated in the report, only reeling mills with at least 6 basins are included); 1875: *Relazione statistica 1875*, p. 56; 1880: *Relazione statistica 1880*, p. 141; 1885–99: Andrea Leonardi, *Depressione e 'risorgimento economico' del Trentino: 1866–1914* (Trento 1976), p. 49.

the throwing mill in Trento was restored and improved.[41] Two years later, Valentino Salvadori asked an artisan from Rovereto, Guglielmo Lange, for an estimate of the cost of renovating the throwing mill in Calliano, but he eventually decided to refrain from any intervention.[42] In 1858, urged by the silk manufacturer Palluat of Lyon to provide silk yarn with a higher degree of twist, Valentino decided to modernise his throwing mills. After gathering information from his correspondents in Milan, he was about to send an agent to agree the details for the construction of a modern throwing mill with some Milanese engineers, when rumours of political events that might damage the silk trade made him desist.[43] Thereafter, in 1864 Valentino Salvadori entrusted Lange with renovation of the silk mills in Calliano, which was concluded two years later.[44] However, this was evidently a fallback solution because the old wooden machines were retained.

The willingness to innovate was clearly influenced by expectations about the development of silk prices. To be stressed in this regard is that while

41 In 1853, the cost value of the reeling house amounted to 80,000 gulden, while the worth of the throwing mills was estimated at 20,000 gulden. The value of the improvements made in the following year amounted to 6,450 gulden. See the firm's ledger in ASTn, AS, vol. 40, pp. 96–7.
42 ASTn, AS, vol. 1028, p. 377, Letter to Guglielmo Lange of Rovereto, 6 Nov. 1856.
43 ASTn, AS, vol. 924, p. 21, Letter to Edoardo Martorelli of Milan, 18 Jan. 1859.
44 ASTn, AS, sc. 18, bb. 44, 92, Contract with Guglielmo Lange and final account, 1864–66.

Figure 14.1. Salvadori firm's shipments of silk (1855–83, kg)

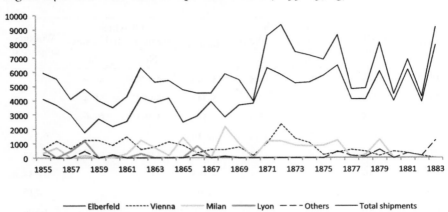

Source: Calculations on shipping data from ASTn, AS, vols 735, 1209.

pebrine contributed to boosting the price of silk to the extent that it reduced output, other events were responsible for a fall in demand, which had the opposite effect. Under these circumstances, a bad harvest might prove a blessing insofar as it acted as a counterweight and reversed the downward trend of prices. Thus, at the end of June 1859, on noting that the price of silk in Lyon and Milan had increased, the Salvadori attributed the causes to the shortage of silk, which, they argued, was almost more worrying than the war effects.[45] Similarly, in June 1866, the decline in silk prices was halted by the poor harvest, which was about half what had been expected.[46] It should be emphasised, however, that, in a period of low prices, the decline in sales was caused not only by a shortage of demand but also by the frequent decision by the manufacturers, who had been producing silk at relatively high costs, to refrain from selling and wait for a price upturn. One should take this into account when examining the trend of the Salvadori firm's shipments (Figure 14.1).

Exports of silk suffered a first severe fall simultaneously with the 1857 crisis. This was one of the first crises with a truly international scope, and it severely hit the USA, England, and the northern European countries, to the extent that a contemporary financial journalist wrote that 'the Crisis of 1857–58 … is admitted to have been the most severe that England, or any

45   ASTn, AS, vol. 924, p. 176, Letter to Giuseppe Grassi of Vienna, 25 June 1859.
46   ASTn, AS, vol. 704, p. 183, Letter to Giuseppe Grassi of Vienna, 23 June 1866.

Figure 14.2. Salvadori firm's profits and losses (1856–83, gulden)

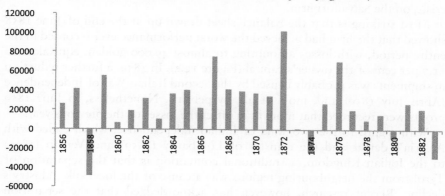

Source: Balance sheets of the Salvadori firm in ASTn, AS, vol. 112; sc. 86, b. 5.
Note: Years shown are those when the balance was struck; this took place at the end of June.

other nation, has ever encountered'.[47] A typical speculative crisis, it was essentially caused by an overexpansion of credit: 'an unwieldy edifice of borrowed capital was erected ready to topple down on the first shock given to that confidence which was, in fact, its sole foundation'.[48] Confidence was shaken first in the USA, while in the autumn of 1857 the shock reached England, and then spread to the continent. There was a credit crunch, a price fall, and a drop in demand on both the domestic and foreign markets, resulting in the stagnation of production and an increase in bankruptcies.[49] The export-oriented industries were the ones most severely damaged, such as the Rhenish silk industry, which suffered a prolonged reduction of output.[50] This was reflected in a sharp decline in the Salvadori firm's shipments to Elberfeld, which was partially offset in 1858 by unusually high exports of raw silk to Lyon, evidently driven by the total debacle of French sericulture.[51] It is interesting that, in such circumstances, the French crisis arising from the pebrine

47 D. Morier Evans, *The History of the Commercial Crisis, 1857–58, and the Stock Exchange Panic of 1859* (London, 1859), p. v.

48 Ibid., p. 33.

49 Hans Rosenberg, *Ascesa e prima crisi del capitalismo, 1848–1857* (Napoli, 1980), p. 187.

50 Ibid., pp. 188–9.

51 Echoes of the crisis are apparent in the correspondence of the Salvadori. In January 1858, in a letter sent to an English merchant house, they expressed the hope that the crisis, which had severely affected trade, would soon end, and that the price for silk was about to increase. ASTn, AS, vol. 1174, p. 2, Letter to Heath & Co. of London, 2 Jan. 1858.

epidemic helped mitigate the effects of another crisis, namely the financial crisis, on the Salvadori firm.

Most striking is that the balance sheet drawn up at the end of June 1858 showed that the firm had achieved the worst performance ever recorded in the entire period, with losses amounting to almost 49,000 gulden, equivalent to 11.7 per cent of the owner's capital (Figure 14.2). In 1859, a further reduction in shipments was probably caused by the Second Italian War of Independence (April–July 1859) and, most of all, by pebrine. Nonetheless, in June 1859 profits were recorded that more than offset the losses of the previous year.

With regard to the two wars of Italian independence, which ended with Austria's defeat and the transfer of Lombardy (1859) and Veneto (1866) to the Italian Kingdom, a traditional contention is that the separation of Tyrol from the neighbouring regions was a cause of the local silk industry's decline. Recent research, however, has acknowledged that the separation had more of a psychological impact than an economic one.[52] In fact, the Salvadori case shows that the changes in the southern borders of Austria had no long-lasting impact on shipments. Notwithstanding the separation from Lombardy, after a standstill in 1859, shipments to Milan were resumed, and they reached almost one fifth of the total in 1862. Above all, the Third War of Independence (June–August 1866), which overlapped with the financial crisis of 1866, did not have particularly negative repercussions on either the shipments or the profits of the Salvadori firm, which performed well in the late 1860s, with a substantial profit in 1867. In the following year, shipments increased sharply, being driven by exports to Milan, which were the highest ever recorded. This was due to the particularly poor cocoon harvest in Lombardy–Venetia and France, whereas it was less disastrous in Trentino, though below expectations.[53]

After a temporary decline in shipments in 1870 in conjunction with the Franco–Prussian War, which severely affected the silk trade,[54] exports rose steeply, especially to Germany and Austria, where an economic boom was under way. This period of dynamism and expansion – called the *Gründerzeit* or 'founders' period' and stimulated in Germany by the French war reparations and the unification process – witnessed the founding of dozens of new banks and hundreds of joint-stock companies, many of which were speculative in character.[55] Bank credit and industrial financing greatly increased, and several companies were quoted on the Vienna stock exchange. This effervescent

---

52   Leonardi, *L'economia*, p. 187.
53   ASTn, AS, vol. 851, p. 250, Letter to Giuseppe Grassi of Vienna, 8 June 1868.
54   See ASTn, AS, vol. 679, p. 414, Letter to the Brambilla brothers of Milan, 1 Oct. 1870.
55   For the Austrian case, see Herbert Matis, *Österreichs Wirtschaft 1848–1913. Konjunkturelle Dynamik und gesellschaftlicher Wandel im Zeitalter Kaiser Franz Josephs I.* (Berlin, 1972), pp. 198–203.

climate boosted the silk market, so that, in 1871, Valentino Salvadori turned to Lange for enlargement of the reeling mill, whose basins increased to 148.[56] The following year, the firm obtained the highest profits ever recorded.

The Panic of 1873 and the 'great deflation': towards the decline of the Tyrolean silk industry

The great euphoria that accompanied the economic boom of the early 1870s inflated a bubble, which burst with the crash of the Vienna Stock Exchange in May 1873 and caused several bankruptcies and liquidations. The echoes of the financial debacle reached the Austrian periphery, including Trentino, where in the weeks following the crash the local press reported several excerpts from journal articles published in Vienna. In fact, the Tyroleans perceived the crisis as a distant phenomenon, which would remain confined to the financial sphere without repercussions on productive activities and the local economy.[57] But things went differently. The Panic of 1873 was followed by the first structural crisis after the rise of industrial capitalism, 'a long-run depression which involved important alterations or innovations in the economic structure, and in part a decisive break with previous trends'.[58] An upward trend in physical production was paralleled by a steep downward trend of prices, which was closely related to technological improvements and the greater efficiency of plants. This inaugurated a deflationary period and had a long-lasting impact on the economies and the trade policies of European countries.

The crisis had severe repercussions on the Tyrolean silk industry. The fall in the price of silk led to a decline in profitability clearly evidenced by the Salvadori firm's accounts. The firm's shipments fell abruptly in 1873, while profits first disappeared in the season 1872/3, and then turned into losses in the balance sheet drawn up in June 1874. Months before the stock market crash of May, the Salvadori had already complained about the unease produced by bankruptcies in Milan and especially in London, while prices had already dropped sharply at the beginning of April.[59] Notwithstanding a temporary recovery in 1876, by 1883 the price of silk had fallen even below

---

56   It was Valentino's initial intention to add 15–20 basins to the reeling mill. ASTn, AS, vol. 679, p. 386, Letter to Guglielmo Lange of Rovereto, 6 Sept. 1870. The final number of basins is drawn from *La trattura*, p. 61.

57   Andrea Leonardi, 'Krach borsistico, depressione economica, esodo di massa, segnali di ripresa', *Studi Trentini di Scienze Storiche*, 80, I (2001), pp. 436–9.

58   Hans Rosenberg, 'Political and Social Consequences of the Great Depression of 1873–1896 in Central Europe', *The Economic History Review*, 13 (1943), p. 61.

59   ASTn, AS, vol. 704, p. 27, Letter to Vinciguerra & Bosma of Vienna, 17 Jan. 1873; p. 181, Letter to Luigi Testa of Milan, 2 Apr. 1873.

the 1874 level.[60] Hence, it is not surprising that the Salvadori firm's performance, amid heavy fluctuations of shipments, was very poor, with the sole exception of 1876. In fact, even if the smaller businesses equipped with obsolete technologies were the ones most deeply affected by the crisis, the manufacturers who had introduced some, albeit modest, innovations also saw their condition deteriorate. As pointed out by Andrea Leonardi, the local entrepreneurs proved unable to respond adequately to the crisis because they failed to introduce new industrial production methods, or they did so only to a limited extent.[61]

This may be inferred from a report compiled by the Rovereto Chamber of Commerce, and published on the occasion of the Paris International Exhibition of 1878, which furnishes an overall picture of the state of the silk-reeling industry with details on the types of technologies adopted. According to the report, in 1877 there were 191 reeling mills endowed with 5,902 basins. Nonetheless, only 101 reeling mills, endowed with 3,843 basins, were actually operating, while the rest were idle.[62] Three out of five of the reeling plants in operation had steam heating, though only one out of six used steam also for the movement of the reels. In other plants, the reels were driven by water power or animals; however, about 60 per cent of the reeling mills were still based on hand-reeling.[63] Other technologies were even rarer: in particular, one out of seven plants had introduced the reel-covering system, while only two reeling houses were equipped with brushing machines.[64]

The 1870s and 1880s witnessed a dramatic fall in the number of reeling firms, paralleled by a decline in the number of basins, though this latter was less than proportional because of the growing size of plants. The concentration process is shown by the average number of basins per reeling plant, which increased from 30 in 1880 to 51 in 1885, and reached 73 in 1892. In the 1890s, fewer than 20 reeling plants were in operation, which means that nine out of ten reeling mills had ceased operations in the previous two decades.

By contrast, in the 1880–1890s the output of cocoons in Tyrol was higher

---

60   See Federico, *An Economic History*, p. 209.

61   Leonardi, 'Krach borsistico', p. 447.

62   For details on the reeling mills in operation in 1877, see *La trattura*, pp. 48–67.

63   Ibid., pp. 38–40.

64   The brushing process removed the external layer of the yarns from the cocoons and found the beginning of the filament. In Italy the operation was usually performed by the reeler herself in the same basin. But this system, besides diminishing the worker's productivity, reduced the quality of the silk, and wasted fuel because brushing required much hotter water than reeling. These latter problems were solved by separating brushing from reeling and assigning the operation to a specialised worker who performed it in a separate basin, whereas productivity actually increased only after brushing was mechanised. See Federico, *An Economic History*, pp. 105–6. In 1877 only seven reeling mills in Trentino had separate brushing, and in two of them the operation was mechanised.

on average than in the 1870s.[65] This owed much to improvement in the selection of silkworm eggs, which was entrusted from the early 1880s onward to a new bacological institute established in Trento under the direction of the Landeskulturrat, a public agency created to promote local agriculture.[66] A growing number of eggs, however, were exported instead of being processed within the region. In the meantime, the quantity of cocoons processed on average by the Tyrolean reeling basins increased, which was to some extent made possible by a higher number of days worked per year;[67] but it was also the result of a productivity increase due to the extinction of the small fire-reeling mills. This notwithstanding, competing with the Italian and Japanese producers was still difficult.

Following the spread of pebrine in the Mediterranean countries and the opening of Japan to international trade, Asian silks had made large inroads into the Western markets, which were favoured by the opening of the Suez Canal in 1869. After the recovery of European sericulture, imports of raw silk from China and Japan exerted a downward pressure on prices. Moreover, although the Italian silks had traditionally obtained higher prices because of their better quality, they lost much of their advantage owing to the replacement of the yellow eggs with the lower-quality green ones. As a result, at the beginning of the 1880s the price gap was substantially lower than it had been a decade earlier.[68] In the following years, the new social provisions enforced by the Austrian government, which substantially increased labour costs, severely hampered the ability of the Tyrolean manufacturers to withstand the Italian competition.[69] Besides shortening the workday, the new regulations imposed special restrictions on the employment of women and children, introduced new hygiene standards and rules for accident prevention in the workplace, and stipulated compulsory health and accident insurance.[70] It is thus not surprising that the Tyrolean silk manufacturers became less competitive than the Italian ones, who did not bear a similar burden.

As had occurred in the reeling industry, at the beginning of the 1890s, nine

65 Pisoni, *Il filo perduto*, p. 234.

66 Ibid., p. 176.

67 The reeling mills operated 70 days on average in 1870, 90 days in 1875, and 100 in 1880. Data from *Rapporto statistico 1870*, p. 28; *Relazione statistica 1875*, p. 55; *Relazione statistica 1880*, p. 140. The prolongation of the reeling season was made possible, in its turn, by the spread of drying chambers, which ensured preservation of the cocoons for a longer period.

68 [Tambosi], 'Brevi considerazioni', pp. 3–7.

69 Unione dei filatori trentini e goriziani, *La filatura della seta in Austria dopo il 1850* (Trento, 1909).

70 Leonardi, 'Il setificio austriaco', I, pp. 385–8. To understand the impact on the silk manufacturers, suffice it to note that 87 per cent of the 6,000 workers employed in the Trentino reeling mills in 1877 were women, 10 per cent children, and only 3 per cent men. Data from *La trattura*, p. 43.

Table 14.2. Silk throwing in Trentino (1870–1900)

Year	Throwing mills	Workers employed	Thrown silk (kg)
1870	37	1,400	54,390
1875	33	1,600	55,400
1880	17	696	22,440
1885	11	564	21,670
1892	3		
1900	1		

Sources: 1870: Rapporto statistico 1870, pp. 29–30; 1875: Relazione statistica 1875, p. 57; 1880: Relazione statistica 1880, p. 142; 1885: Leonardi, 'Il setificio', pp. 396–7; 1892, 1900: Camera di commercio, pp. 78–9.

out of ten throwing mills had ceased to operate in Trentino (Table 14.2); but this time competition from China and Japan had no effect because the Asian manufacturers never succeeded in exporting thrown silk.[71] Undoubtedly, the Tyrolean producers – whose lack of entrepreneurial spirit induced them to adopt rent-seeking behaviour instead of investing in renovation of the throwing mills – paid the price of the technical backwardness of their plants compared with those of their Italian competitors and, from the early 1880s, of a higher cost of labour. While in Piedmont and Lombardy the silk firms had modernised their machinery, to the extent that in the 1870s the modern 'squared' and 'cylindrical' machines accounted for most of the equipment,[72] the Tyrolean manufacturers adhered to the old technology. In 1877, a contemporary observer, Ruggero Cobelli, stated that only very recently had a few owners opened their eyes and introduced some improvements in their throwing mills.[73] The Bettini brothers of Rovereto were among those who innovated. Indeed, in the early 1870s, the Salvadori firm commissioned the processing of raw silk into strafilati from the Domenico e Giovanni Bettini firm,[74] which owned one of the largest throwing mills.[75]

In the following years, the worsening prospects for the throwing industry

71   Federico, An Economic History, p. 41.
72   Ibid., p. 143.
73   Cobelli, 'L'industria serica', p. 10.
74   See ASTn, AS, vol. 1160, p. 152, Letter to Domenico and Giovanni Bettini of Rovereto, 2 May 1871.
75   It is not surprising that the Bettini throwing mill was the only one that remained in operation until the early twentieth century. See Giuseppe Chini, I filatoi di Rovereto, Sacco e Lizzana (Rovereto, 1912), p. 29.

further curbed investments. The import duties, which had protected Tyrolean thrown silk in the 1850s, and which had already been lowered in 1865, were completely removed in 1878.[76] Thereafter, pressures on the Tyrolean silk yarns further increased in 1888, when France imposed a prohibitive duty on imported Italian thrown silk, which consequently flooded the German and Austrian markets in search of alternative outlets.[77] At any rate, the throwing industry, whose location was not constrained by the availability of the raw material, as was instead the case of reeling, gradually shifted from silk-producing countries to silk-consuming countries as a consequence of trade barriers and productivity gaps. In the 1890s, Germany would emerge as a new competitor in the throwing industry.[78] Moreover, the throwing was made superfluous, albeit to a limited extent, by the innovation of weaving raw silk instead of tram or organzine, a novelty that emerged in the 1820s and spread in the second half of the century.[79]

At the end of the nineteenth century, while the reeling branch underwent severe retrenchment, the Tyrolean throwing industry suffered a debacle. Even the Salvadori firm, the oldest silk manufacturer in the region, ceased to operate. The reasons for the firm's liquidation, even if not clearly specified, can be inferred from the accounting books and from the family correspondence. Besides growing fluctuations in shipments and a decline in the average profitability paralleled by an increase in risk, the Salvadori family had to resolve a problem of intergenerational succession. Indeed, the designated successor as head of the firm was not at all inclined to become a merchant, while the worsening prospects of the Tyrolean silk industry made investment in public securities more attractive. The combined effect of these two circumstances spelled the end of the family business.

In the second half of the nineteenth century, all hopes for continuation of the family and the business rested on the eldest son of Valentino Sr, Valentino Jr (1851–1933). As was usual among the merchant families engaged in long-distance trade, Valentino spent a couple of years in Germany to serve his apprenticeship. However, it is evident from Valentino's correspondence with the family that he disliked the tasks assigned to him, and that he found it tedious to spend his time copying letters. After a carefree childhood, he

76   In the attempt to promote the manufacture of silk fabrics in the core industrial regions, the trade policy enacted by the Austrian government sacrificed the interests of the Tyrolean silk manufacturers, and made silk yarns the only textile merchandise exempt from protection. See Leonardi, 'Il setificio austriaco', I, pp. 374–9.

77   Leonardi, *Depressione e 'risorgimento economico' del Trentino: 1866–1914* (Trento, 1976), pp. 48–50.

78   Federico, *An Economic History*, pp. 41–2.

79   In the 1900s, the amount of raw silk that was directly woven did not reach one fifth of the total. Note that only good-to-excellent silk was used because it withstood the stress of weaving. Ibid., p. 55.

had been catapulted into a world of hard work and sacrifice, among people whom he did not know. Moreover, his temperament was not exactly that of a would-be merchant since he disliked company, preferring a solitary dinner in his room.[80] In the late 1860s, Valentino Sr had renovated some of the throwing mills with a view to his son's succession as head of the firm,[81] but contrary to his hopes, he failed to instil fondness for the family business in him. Furthermore, owing to his father's age and the precarious health of the firm's agent, Valentino Jr faced the prospect of taking full responsibility for the business within a few years, with limited time to arrange the transition of the firm's guidance.

The turning point came in 1883. In the balance struck in June, Valentino Sr's capital in the firm amounted to around 673,000 gulden. Investments in bonds, still limited to 15,000 gulden, grew rapidly thereafter; they exceeded 132,000 gulden in 1885 – the year of Valentino's death – and soared to over 334,000 gulden by June 1887.[82] In the same year, the reeling plant in Calliano was sold to the Antonio e Luigi Tambosi firm of Trento, the largest silk manufacturer in the region at the turn of the century.[83] As for the throwing mills, after being leased for a few years they were sold or allocated to different uses.[84]

Thus, the fate of the Salvadori firm resembled that of several silk manufacturers who, in the end, preferred to invest in safe assets. As pointed out in 1877 by Cobelli, there were multiple factors underlying the decline of the silk industry: the silkworm disease, the importing of Asian silk, the replacement of silk fabrics with less expensive woollen ones, and yet others. But the most important factor was that several families who had built their fortunes on the silk trade preferred to invest their capital – with great profit and small effort – in public securities, so that the silk industry, deprived of capital, was like a machine without an engine. A further factor mentioned by Cobelli was the slower pace of technical and scientific progress in small towns like Trento and Rovereto, in contrast with the dynamism of larger centres,[85] which indeed had witnessed more rapid improvement in the technology for silk manufacture.

The local entrepreneurs, faced by government policies that subjected them to growing competition, failed to modernise their equipment, and they adopted a defensive attitude by asking for more protection and the loosening of social provisions. First, because the request for increased tariff protection

80   ASTn, AS, sc. 36, b. 27, Letter from Giovanni a Prato to Valentino Jr, 11 Jan. 1870.
81   ASTn, AS, sc. 36, b. 27, Letter from Afra to her brother Valentino Jr, 11 May 1868.
82   See the firm's ledger in ASTn, AS, vol. 665, pp. 32, 60.
83   The reeling mill, which was valued at 80,000 gulden in 1853, and at 58,500 gulden in 1881, was eventually sold for 10,400 gulden. See the ledgers in ASTn, AS, vol. 40, p. 97; vol. 665, pp. 34–5.
84   See the ledger in ASTn, vol. 878, pp. 48, 50; and AS, sc. 18, b. 58, Sale contract, 15 Jan. 1894.
85   Cobelli, 'L'industria serica', p. 14.

was unaffordable, the Tyrolean silk manufacturers asked for subsidies to the reeling industry similar to those of the French incentive scheme. Secondly, they attempted to transfer the adjustment cost to the labour force by avoiding application of the social legislation. With regard to the duration of the workday, the silk manufacturers obtained a temporary derogation, and were allowed to prolong the workday by one hour, which was supposed to facilitate the transition from the traditional 14 hours to the 11 hours prescribed by law.[86] As for the monetary incentives, only in 1904 did the Tyrolean manufacturers succeed in obtaining from the Ministry of Trade a bonus, which was granted to those few reeling houses that met specific technical requirements. This intervention, however, was too modest and belated to make any difference, and it allowed the mere survival of the local reeling industry until the war.[87]

Conclusion

At the outset of the twentieth century, the Tyrolean region was still the most important area for cocoon production in Austria.[88] However, the bulk of cocoons (almost two thirds in the period 1905–07) were exported, mainly to Lombardy.[89] The last vestiges of the silk industry, for which Trentino had gained renown in the previous centuries, were a handful of reeling plants and one or two throwing mills.[90]

The decline of the Tyrolean silk industry cannot be explained without taking account of the many crises that punctuated the earlier decades and which differed in nature, duration, and impact. This study has sought to delve more deeply into the consequences of the crises by combining the existing literature with first-hand evidence on the operation of a major silk business. The examination of the pebrine crisis has cast light on two salient aspects. The first is the prompt reaction of landowners and silkworm raisers through a concerted effort supported by the Tyrolean government and by a merchant house as prominent as the Salvadori firm, which profited from the collaboration of enterprising and skilled operators like Grazioli. The second aspect relates to the dual effect of pebrine. On the one hand, the epidemic threatened

---

86 Leonardi, 'Il setificio austriaco', I, p. 388.
87 Ibid., II, pp. 96–126. This notwithstanding, the fact that a major company from Milan took over ownership of a Tyrolean reeling plant in 1907 signals that there still were opportunities for profitable investment.
88 With an average output of over 17,000 quintals of cocoons per year between 1905 and 1913, Tyrolean production amounted to more than four fifths of the overall Austrian output: Leonardi, L'economia, pp. 175–7.
89 Unione, La filatura, p. 15.
90 Leonardi, L'economia, p. 184.

the survival of the local silk industry; on the other, it helped counterbalance, to some extent, the fall in prices due to critical demand-side junctures such as wars and financial and commercial crises. The impact of the latter varied enormously, the most severe blow being dealt by the 1857 crisis, but their effect was short-lived. By contrast, pebrine had more structural consequences inasmuch as it induced innovations in reeling technologies aimed at offsetting ever-growing costs. Although the shift to the lower-quality Japanese eggs reduced the price differential with respect to Asian silks, microscope selection made it possible to hope for the reintroduction of the yellow eggs and the development of better-quality hybrid species.

The Panic of 1873, which put an end to the great euphoria of the early 1870s, marked a turning point in that it engendered an enduring fall in the price of silk. Moreover, Austria's trade policy and welfare provisions put the local silk manufacturers at a disadvantage with respect to foreign competitors, and thus contributed to changing their expectations for the worse. In this framework of lower profitability and higher risks, the local entrepreneurs, who could hardly hope for the resumption of earlier conditions, became less and less prone to invest and innovate, and even as old a merchant house as the Salvadori firm ceased to operate. Although at work in this last case were some specific factors which had to do with the transition to the sixth generation, it should be borne in mind that the silk firms were frequently family-owned; hence, all of them sooner or later had to address the issue of intergenerational succession.

With some reason, the decline of the Tyrolean silk industry can be blamed on the lack of entrepreneurial spirit among the individuals involved in the crisis. The merchant-manufacturers failed to invest in technological and organisational improvements that would have increased the competitiveness of local silk, although, taking the worsening prospects into account, the main shortcoming that can be attributed to them is rather their unwillingness and inability to risk their capital in new industrial branches. As stated by Giovanni a Prato in a letter to Valentino Salvadori Jr:

> our country greatly needs someone who has capital available, and who has the courage to invest it in industries other than the mere reeling of silk, the only industry of importance that exists in our country, from whence millions of raw materials leave though they could be processed to a large extent here.[91]

Unfortunately, the silk merchant-manufacturers, who were among those most endowed with capital in Tyrol, did not have such courage.

---

91   ASTn, AS, sc. 36, b. 27, Letter from Giovanni a Prato to Valentino Jr, 25 Nov. 1869; my translation. Giovanni a Prato (1812–83) was a charismatic figure and a careful observer of his times. Cousin to Valentino Jr's mother, he was an abbot, intellectual and journalist.

15

The Stabilising Effects of the Dingley Tariff and the Recovery from the 1890s Depression in the USA

PETER H. BENT[1]

Introduction

The causes of economic crises have increasingly become a focus of academic research.[2] Important research has also focused on how economies have broken out of periods of depression. Yet this vein of the literature remains underdeveloped. A case in point is the recovery from the economic depression in the USA following the panic of 1893.

The economic depression of the 1890s was 'one of the worst in American history', and 'Investment, commerce, prices, employment, and wages remained depressed for several years' after the 1893 panic.[3] During this period of crisis, 'Hunger, nakedness, fear, disaster, trouble were to be encountered everywhere.'[4] Academic research has emphasised that both domestic and international factors led to the 1893 financial panic, and that this turbulent time led to political and economic developments that shaped the urbanising

1   I thank the editors of this volume, Peter Howlett, Thilo Albers, Stefan Nikolic, Juan Montecino, Zoe Sherman, Mark Stelzner, and participants at the London School of Economics MSc in Economic History (Research) workshop (2012), the Centre for Economic and Business History workshop in Nottingham (2013), the 'Coping with Crises' conference in Durham (2013), the Summer School on History of Economic Thought, Economic Philosophy and History of Economics in Ankara (2013), the Eastern Economics Association annual conference in Boston (2014), and the Economic and Business History Society annual conference in Manchester (2014) for helpful comments. Errors are mine alone.
2   See, for example, C.M. Reinhart and K. Rogoff, *This Time is Different: Eight Centuries of Financial Folly* (Princeton, 2011); J.M. Lepler, *The Many Panics of 1837: People, Politics, and the Creation of a Transatlantic Financial Crisis* (New York, 2013).
3   D. Whitten, 'The Depression of 1893', *EH.Net Encyclopedia*. [online]. Available at: http://eh.net/encyclopedia/the-depression-of-1893/ [accessed on 1 May 2015].
4   C.H. Grosvenor, 'A Republican View of the Presidential Campaign', *North American Review*, 171 (1900), p. 42.

and industrialising US economy through the Progressive Era and beyond.[5] There has been, however, only one significant attempt at analysing how the US economy pulled out of this economic downturn.[6] Each of these accounts at least briefly discusses the 1897 Dingley Tariff Act and the impacts of its protectionist policies on the US economy. There is no consensus in the existing literature, however, as to how the Dingley Tariff affected the post-1897 recovery.

The Dingley Tariff Act of 1897 was strongly protectionist. The average tariff rate under this bill was 52 per cent.[7] Increased tariff rates were imposed on a range of goods, from castor oil to bleaching powder to fish bladders. More significant items included the 'reimposition of duties on wool and lumber, higher duties on sugar and a large number of manufactures, especially textiles'.[8] The tariff survived longer than any previous tariff in US history, remaining on the books for twelve years until the Payne–Aldrich Tariff Act of 1909 was enacted. This widespread turn towards protectionism was characteristic of Republican political goals during the late nineteenth century. Just several months after the higher tariff rates took effect in 1897, President McKinley supported the Dingley Tariff by suggesting that 'while its full effect has not yet been realised, what it already accomplished assures us of its timeliness'.[9]

The goal of this chapter is to assess the impact that protectionist policies can have during periods of economic crisis. The role that the Dingley Tariff played in promoting economic recovery from the 1890s depression in the USA is analysed as a historical case study towards this end. An in-depth analysis of the Dingley Tariff suggests that this protectionist policy did indeed support economic recovery by boosting investor confidence and stabilising the business environment. Increased tariff revenue and a move towards a balanced federal budget were important factors leading to renewed confidence in the state of the economy, thereby contributing to the recovery from the 1890s depression.

To assess the impacts of the Dingley Tariff on the US economy in the late nineteenth and early twentieth centuries, this chapter employs both qualitative and quantitative data. The historical context of the Dingley Tariff is an important part of this discussion, as it places the economic data within the specific political and social, as well as economic, conditions of the 1890s. The American wool industry of this time is presented as a case study. The wool

5   Whitten, 'The Depression of 1893'; C. Hoffmann, *The Depression of the Nineties: An Economic History* (Westport, 1990); D. Steeples and D.O. Whitten, *Democracy in Desperation: The Depression of 1893* (Westwood, 1998).
6   G.T. White, *The United States and the Problem of Recovery after 1893* (Tuscaloosa, 1982).
7   H.U. Faulkner, *Politics, Reform and Expansion* (New York, 1959).
8   White, *The United States and the Problem of Recovery*, p. 66.
9   Ibid., p. 91.

industry provides an example of a major industry with interests spanning East Coast manufacturing centres and Western agricultural regions. During the debates about the goals and effectiveness of the Dingley Tariff, raw wool and woollen products were at the 'storm center' and were a highly contentious issue.[10] Overall the tariff did indeed help the economy recover from the 1890s depression. The broader implication is that government policies aimed at stabilising expectations can encourage renewed economic growth during crises.

Background: historical context and political economy of the 1890s depression

In order to better appreciate the significance of the Dingley Tariff, it is useful to examine the historical context in which the tariff was enacted, as well as the debates about the importance of the Dingley Tariff in the existing literature. To that end, this section briefly outlines the unfolding of the 1890s depression, then discusses the political economy of the Dingley Tariff and looks at issues related to the Dingley Tariff in previous research.

The economic depression of the 1890s was triggered by the panic of 1893, and recovery did not set in until 1897. Only in 1907 did the US economy reach full capacity again.[11] The 1890s depression coincided with important developments in American economic history. Broadly, this was the period 'when the economy was rapidly taking on its modern industrial-manufacturing shape'.[12] This depression also came after the period of renewed growth that followed after the Long Depression of the 1870s.[13] During this increasingly globalised era, these types of economic phenomena were taking place on international scales.[14] Protectionist policies had international repercussions, though these policies were often implemented as a result of domestic political conditions.[15] In the USA, such policies could vacillate between election cycles. The Democratic Party, for example, enacted free trade policies in 1894. Then when the Republicans returned to power in 1897, they imposed the protectionist

---

10 C.W. Wright, 'Wool-Growing and the Tariff since 1890', *Quarterly Journal of Economics*, 19 (1905), p. 610.
11 Hoffmann, *Depression of the Nineties*.
12 Ibid., p. 4.
13 J.H. Davis, 'An Improved Annual Chronology of U.S. Business Cycles since the 1790s', *Journal of Economic History*, 66 (2006), pp. 103–21.
14 K.H. O'Rourke and J.G. Williamson, *Globalization and History: The Making of a Nineteenth-Century Atlantic Economy* (Cambridge, MA, 1999).
15 K.H. O'Rourke and A.M. Taylor, *Democracy and Protectionism*, NBER Working Paper 12250 (2006).

Dingley Tariff legislation, arguing that the Democrats' free trade policies had made the depression more severe.[16]

Other issues during the 1890s depression in the USA included widespread banking problems and business failures, along with persistently high unemployment rates and heated debates about the role of the government in responding to these problems. A significant feature of the US economy during the late nineteenth century was the lack of central bank to coordinate the government's responses to financial crises. Protectionism was one of the main policy options available to the federal government at this time.

The USA has imposed tariffs on imports since its earliest days as a nation. The first law enacted by the US Congress was a tariff bill. James Madison, the Representative of Virginia, introduced this bill in 1789.[17] The intentions were twofold: to raise revenues for the government and to protect domestic industries. These trends continued through the nineteenth and twentieth centuries. The first twenty Congresses passed twenty tariff acts, and about 90 per cent of the total federal income during this period came from duties raised through tariffs.[18] By 1890 tariff duties still accounted for 57 per cent of the federal government's revenues.[19] Only several years after the federal government began collecting income taxes in 1913 did tariff duties start to decline in significance as a source of government revenue.[20]

The mid-1890s was a time of instability in the USA, as described by contemporary observers:

> There was more idle labor than ever had been known before. There were more idle spindles, mills, factories and shops than had been known before. Foreign trade was falling off. Home markets had been destroyed. Confidence was to be found nowhere.[21]

These features of the economic and social history of the 1890s support the claims of scholars who identify the post-1893 depression as a particularly challenging time in American history.[22]

More technical contemporary analyses of the onset of the 1890s depression

---

16   White, *The United States and the Problem of Recovery.*
17   A.G. Peterson, 'Commerce of Virginia, 1789–1791', *The William and Mary Quarterly,* 10 (1930), pp. 302–9.
18   S. O'Halloran, *Politics, Process and American Trade Policy* (Ann Arbor, 1994).
19   US Department of Commerce, 'Federal Government Finances –Treasury Receipts, and Surplus or Deficit: 1789 to 1945, Series P 89–98', *Historical Statistics of the United States, 1789–1945: A Supplement to the Statistical Abstract of the United States, Part 1* (Washington, DC, 1949), p. 296.
20   Ibid., p. 296.
21   Grosvenor, 'A Republican View', p. 42.
22   Whitten, 'The Depression of 1893'.

focus on the role that financial institutions played in the Panic of 1893. For example, Stevens dated the beginning of the panic to the May 1893 crash in the market for industrial securities.[23] While this crash was not entirely unforeseen, there was a general uncertainty about economic fundamentals in the months leading up to the crash. Stevens described a 'manifest unease' among bankers as gold flowed out of the USA and the banks insisted upon increasingly conservative lending practices.[24] With a few years of hindsight, Noyes argued that leading up to the 1893 panic banks had been overextending themselves through widespread lending, based on the newly expanded role of using bank-deposit funds as a basis for credit.[25]

Recent studies of this period highlight the role that banks played in causing the 1893 panic. Carlson, for example, finds that liquidity problems were closely connected to bank failures at local levels during the 1893 panic.[26] On a national scale, Carlson's empirical analysis suggests that real economic shocks were the most important factor in explaining the propagation of the panic. Similarly, Dupont uses data from local bank reports to Kansas newspapers, and finds that bank runs were contagious as they affected both solvent and insolvent banks.[27] Overall this research demonstrates that during the 1893 panic banks served as gauges by which to assess general economic conditions, and banks were culprits themselves as they engaged in overly ambitious lending. As the panic of 1893 developed into a serious depression, the social and economic consequences of the panic became apparent as unemployment rates increased dramatically.

The 1893 panic and ensuing economic depression led to unemployment rates peaking at nearly 13 per cent in 1897.[28] Writing just after the panic, Closson discussed the widespread unemployment that resulted from the crisis.[29] While the estimates of the numbers of unemployed workers vary from city to city in Closson's data, some trends are clear. A sudden increase in unemployment occurred in the summer and fall of 1893, following the initial panic. This finding aligns closely with the more precise unemployment

---

23 A.C. Stevens, 'Analysis of the Phenomena of the Panic in the United States in 1893', *Quarterly Journal of Economics*, 8 (1894), pp. 117–48.

24 Ibid., p. 124.

25 A.D. Noyes, 'Banks and the Panic of 1893', *Political Science Quarterly*, 9 (1897), pp. 12–30.

26 M. Carlson, 'Causes of Bank Suspensions in the Panic of 1893', *Explorations in Economic History*, 42 (2005), pp. 56–80.

27 B. Dupont, 'Bank Runs, Information and Contagion in the Panic of 1893', *Explorations in Economic History*, 44 (2007), pp. 411–43.

28 C.D. Romer, 'Spurious Volatility in Historical Unemployment Data', *Journal of Political Economy*, 94 (1986), pp. 1–37.

29 C.C. Closson Jr, 'The Unemployed in American Cities', *Quarterly Journal of Economics*, 8 (1894), pp. 168–217. Closson presents contemporary unemployment data from a sample of cities across the USA, before there was a systematic nationwide method for collecting unemployment figures.

estimates calculated by Romer. During the past 120 years of US economic history only the 1930s saw more severe unemployment levels than the 1890s.[30]

Widespread unemployment during the 1890s crisis had significant social impacts. Rezneck surveys viewpoints from a variety of popular print sources written during the 1890s depression, and documents a surge in populist and socialist tendencies as people became dissatisfied with their economic circumstances.[31] Similarly, the 1890s depression influenced the development of what became 'Progressivism,' as people began to think that the government should take a more active role in directing the course of the economy.[32] The crisis of the 1890s, with its elevated unemployment levels, had significant political consequences.

The US government believed that it had a role in responding to this depression. Yet it has been argued that '[g]overnment responses to depression during the 1890s exhibited elements of complexity, confusion, and contradiction'.[33] In his study *The United States and the Problem of Recovery after 1893*, White focuses extensively on the measures offered by the government to alleviate the 1890s economic depression.[34] He begins by contrasting this depression with the previous American depression after the Panic of 1873. During the earlier panic, only very limited government action was taken to stem the economic downturn. In contrast, the government took a much more active role in the 1890s, as seen in the debates surrounding tariff legislation.

US Representative Nelson Dingley, Jr – 'Destitute of humor but soundly versed in finance' – presented a bill to the House of Representatives on 26 December 1895.[35] Dingley, a Republican from Maine, was the Chairman of the Ways and Means Committee. In the early years of the 1890s depression government actions mainly focused on addressing currency concerns. Yet by 1895 it was clear that addressing these monetary issues would not be enough to bring the economy out of depression. Further government action was needed to promote renewed economic growth. To this end Dingley introduced a bill that would increase government revenue, which had been declining during the preceding years of economic depression. The committee determined that the decline in government revenue had resulted in the 'creation and promotion of that serious distrust that has paralyzed business and dangerously shaken confidence'.[36]

---

30 Romer, 'Spurious Volatility', pp. 1–37.
31 S. Rezneck, 'Unemployment, Unrest, and Relief in the United States during the Depression of 1893–97', *Journal of Political Economy*, 61 (1953), pp. 324–45.
32 M. McGerr, *A Fierce Discontent: The Rise and Fall of the Progressive Movement in America, 1870–1920* (Oxford, 2005).
33 Whitten, 'The Depression of 1893'.
34 White, *The United States and the Problem of Recovery*.
35 Committee on Ways and Means, *Dingley, Nelson, Jr. (1832–1899)* [online]. Available at: http://waysandmeans.house.gov/legacy/portraits/1789-1898/dingley.htm [accessed on 1 May 2015].
36 White, *The United States and the Problem of Recovery*, p. 52.

The tariff issue then became a major feature of the 1896 presidential elections. Republicans actively pushed for further increases in tariffs with the goal of generating more revenue for the federal government and stabilising domestic business conditions.[37] As mentioned above, Republicans argued that the low Democratic tariff of 1894 was partially to blame for the ongoing economic depression, in that it interrupted thirty years of a high-tariff environment built by Republican policies.[38] For example, Senator Justin Morrill of Vermont suggested that new and higher tariffs would be 'something which the people would be likely to approve as looking toward a revival of the business interests of the country' as domestic manufacturers would be protected from foreign competition.[39] Following the same party line, Representative Dingley argued that Republicans 'shall reestablish that policy of protection to American industries which for thirty years gave the United States such prosperity and elevated the wages of the people of this country as was never known in the world'.[40] The Republicans won the election of 1896, McKinley became president, and the strongly protectionist Dingley Tariff was signed into law on 24 July 1897.

Political concerns were at the forefront of the push for and against tariffs during the 1890s. In his 1887 presidential message, Cleveland established the Democrats as being counter to the imposition of a protective tariff.[41] However, it was the Republicans who came to power next, and enacted the McKinley Tariff in 1890. The Democrats then returned to power and implemented the Wilson 'Free Trade' Act in 1894. Tariff reform became a central concern of government policy during the 1890s, from the implementation of the 'anxiously conservative' 1894 tariff to its being overturned 'with surprising quickness' when political power returned to the Republicans and they enacted the protectionist Dingley Tariff Act in 1897.[42]

Aggregate economic data

This section presents an analysis of aggregate economic data to get a sense of the broader economic trends that were operating in the USA during the 1890s. It is argued that the 1890s depression was a period of general economic instability and crippling uncertainty, which was characterised by relatively extreme fluctuations in economic activity. This was not simply a period of constant

37   Ibid.
38   Ibid.
39   Ibid., p. 54.
40   Ibid.
41   F. W. Taussig, *The Tariff History of the United States*, 8th edn (New York, 1964), pp. 321–2.
42   Ibid., p. 321.

economic decline. As seen in Figure 15.1, the GDP data, rough though it is, shows the economy crashing after the 1893 panic then briefly moving towards recovery in 1895 before declining again in 1896. Full-fledged recovery did not begin until 1897. This interpretation of the macroeconomic conditions of the 1890s is based on widely available data estimates, and it supports the argument of this chapter that the Dingley Tariff encouraged recovery from the 1890s depression by assuring the business community that American commercial interests would be afforded the benefits of strong and continued protection from foreign competition, and that uncertainty about tariff policy, and economic conditions more broadly, would end. Thus the significance of the Dingley Tariff is that it helped end the 1890s depression by stabilising expectations about future tariff rates, thereby encouraging economic activity. This was crucial during this period of crisis, as bank runs and unemployment heightened the sense that the economy was unstable. After this period of intense uncertainty and economic distress, the tariff helped stabilise the economy. Business owners, such as the woollen textile mill operators discussed in the next section, were hesitant to invest in expanded production under the uncertain free trade conditions imposed by the Democrats in the mid-1890s. After McKinley came to power, the Dingley Tariff assured manufacturers that they could expect protection from cheap imports, and promoted recovery by asserting an element of certainty in the face of the mid-1890s crisis.

Real GDP estimates offer a broad-based starting point for analysing the macroeconomic trends of the 1890s (Figure 15.1).[43] These estimates show the negative effects of the panic of 1893. From 1890 to 1892 real GDP increased by 9.5 per cent. Then came the 1893 panic, when real GDP fell 8.5 per cent through the trough year of 1894. The abortive recovery of 1895 saw real GDP increase, only to fall again in 1896. However, the GDP level in 1896 was still higher than in any previous year excluding 1895. Again, it is seen that the 1890s was not a period defined by constant economic decline, but rather was a time of uncertainty, which prevented investment and forestalled a take-off of economic growth. Sustained recovery only came in 1897, the year the Dingley Tariff legislation was passed. The trajectory of the real GDP estimates during the 1890s shows that the enactment of the Dingley Tariff coincided with a period of sustained economic growth beginning in 1897, after years of economic turmoil following the 1893 panic and the ensuing period of uncertainty.

Real GDP per capita estimates follow similar trends, and offer insight into the standard of living during the last decade of the nineteenth century (Figure 15.2). Real GDP per capita began declining from a peak in 1891, two years before the panic of 1893 sent real GDP falling sharply. This early

---

43 *Historical Statistics of the United States*, Millennium Edition (2012), Table C89–19: Gross Domestic Product: 1790–2002.

Figure 15.1. Real GDP, 1885–1905 (1996 millions of US dollars)

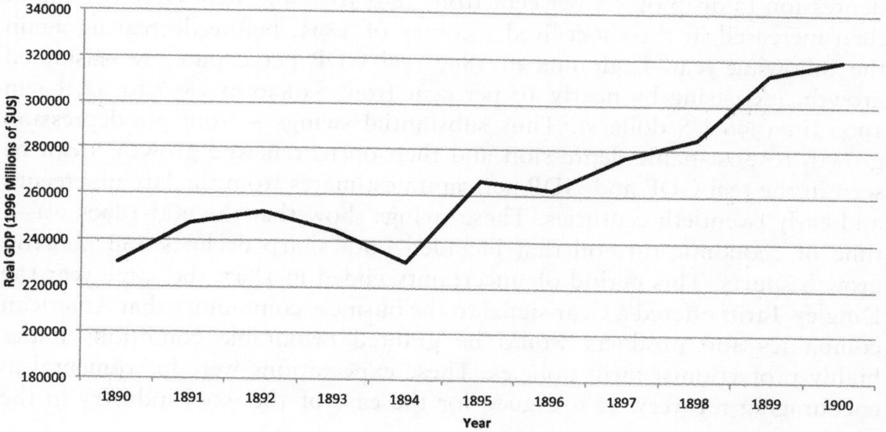

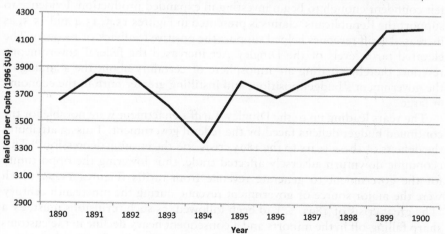

Source: Historical Statistics of the United States, Millennium Edition (2012), Series Ca9: Real Gross Domestic Product: 1790–2002.

Figure 15.2. Real GDP per capita, 1885–1905 (1996 millions of US dollars)

Source: Historical Statistics of the United States, Millennium Edition (2012), Series Ca11: Real per Capita Gross Domestic Product: 1790–2002.

decline, however, is less significant than the fall seen at the beginning of the depression (a drop of 5.5 per cent from 1892 to 1893). Real GDP per capita then increased in the short-lived recovery of 1895, before decreasing again the following year. Beginning in 1897 real GDP per capita saw sustained growth, increasing by nearly 10 per cent from $3,830 in 1897 to $4,204 in 1900 (in 1996 US dollars). Thus substantial swings – from pre-depression growth to post-panic depression and then on to renewed growth – can be seen in the real GDP and GDP per capita estimates from the late nineteenth and early twentieth centuries. These swings show that the mid-1890s was a time of economic turmoil that included both sharp declines and abortive growth spurts. This period of uncertainty ended in 1897, the same year the Dingley Tariff offered a clear signal to the business community that American companies and products would be granted favourable conditions under highly protectionist tariff policies. These expectations were instrumental in encouraging recovery, as is argued for the case of the wool industry in the next section.

The federal deficit is another metric useful for framing the historical macroeconomic context of the Dingley Tariff's impact on the US economy. When McKinley came to office in 1897, the federal government had been running a deficit for four years.[44] As quoted above, Republicans argued that balancing the budget would stabilise the economy and encourage faith in future economic growth, which would be realised as businesses and farmers felt confident enough to begin investing in expanded production. Evidence to support the Republicans' claims is presented in Figures 15.3, 15.4 and 15.5, as increased tariff revenues helped support the positive feedback of recovery. The elevated tariff levels of the Dingley Act increased the federal government's revenue, thereby creating an atmosphere of certainty about the standing of the government's budget position, and instilling greater faith in the economy at large.

The years leading up to the Dingley Tariff's enactment were notable for the continued budget deficits faced by the federal government. Taussig attributes the deficits of these years to the 1893 crisis and the ensuing depression.[45] This economic downturn adversely affected trade, thus lowering the opportunity for the government to generate revenue from tariffs (Figures 15.3), which were the major source of government revenue during the nineteenth century. 'The great crisis of 1893 ... had been followed, as such revulsions must, by a sharp falling-off in the imports and a consequent heavy decline in the customs revenue.'[46] Taussig also blames the low tariffs enshrined in the 1894 legislation

44   Taussig, *Tariff History of the United States.*
45   Ibid.
46   Ibid., p. 324.

Figure 15.3. Tariff revenue, 1890–1900 (current US dollars)

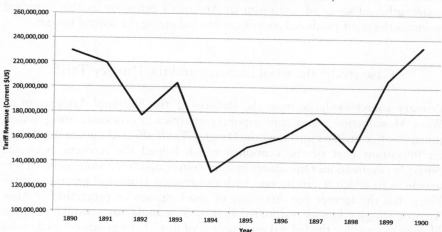

Source: US Department of Commerce, 'Federal Government Finances – Treasury Receipts, and Surplus or Deficit: 1789 to 1945, Series P 89–98', *Historical Statistics of the United States, 1789–1945: A Supplement to the Statistical Abstract of the United States, Part 1* (Washington, DC, 1949), p. 296.

for this decrease in customs revenue.[47] The data in Figure 15.3 align with Taussig's findings, in that there is a marked decrease in tariff revenue in 1894. Taussig describes the political dialogue of the late 1890s as focusing on 'the failure of the [free trade] act of 1894 to yield the revenue needed at the time'.[48] This same sentiment is evident in the arguments made by Dingley and his fellow Republicans in support of higher tariffs during the 1896 presidential election (as quoted above).

The years of government budget deficits during the 1890s depression created a sense of economic unease, as explicitly declared by the wool manufacturing business community, as discussed below. Within a couple of years, the Dingley Tariff saw the return to higher tariff revenues and an end to the government deficit, thus bringing about the economic stability that the bill's Republican proponents had hoped for. The Republicans applauded the success of the tariff in this regard at the 1900 convention: '... the revenues from the Dingley Bill marched steadily upwards, until soon our normal income exceeded our normal expenditure, and we passed from a condition of

47   Ibid.
48   Ibid., p. 325.

threatened insolvency to one of National Solvency'.[49] The tariff brought about a strengthened sense of optimism in America's economy as the increased revenues the tariff produced contributed to balancing the federal budget.

Case study: the wool industry and the Dingley Tariff

Primary source evidence from the *Bulletin of the National Association of Wool Manufacturers* and contemporary analyses in economic and political journals offer insights into how the Dingley Tariff affected the wool industry, an important part of the economy, which helped the recovery from the post-1893 depression. One contemporary source described wool as being 'the article as to which it can be said with the greatest truth and greatest plausibility that the farmer gets his share of the largesses of protection'.[50] Also, Senator Dingley himself estimated that wool manufactures would yield the highest revenue for the federal government of any of the goods covered under the 1897 Dingley Tariff Act (Figure 15.4). The wool industry allows for a more pointed analysis of how the protectionist measures of the Dingley Tariff restored investor confidence, and how it reassured the business community that the federal government was willing to commit to pro-business policies and take steps to actively stabilise the economy.

Earlier tariff bills had imposed duties on wool based on its quality. The Dingley Tariff took the more extreme step of imposing high tariffs on essentially all types of wool, including low-quality carpet wool that was not even produced in significant quantities in the USA at that time.[51] These increases in duties on raw wool and woollen product imports helped farmers and manufacturers. Farmers, as primary wool producers, gained under the protectionist policies imposed by the Dingley Tariff. Manufacturers were also granted the benefits of protection as duties were raised on finished woollen goods. Also, as discussed in detail below, manufacturers benefited by having the strong tariff legislation in place because it allowed them to plan for the future of their businesses while being certain about the level of protection they would be given. This was a significant and stabilising change brought

---

49   E.O. Wolcott, 'Address of the Temporary Chairman', *Official Proceedings of the Twelfth Republican National Convention, 1900* (Philadelphia, 1900), pp. 36–7.

50   Taussig, *Tariff History of the United States*, p. 280.

51   Wright, 'Wool-Growing and the Tariff since 1890', p. 616; The actual tariff rates imposed on individual classes on woollen items can be found on pp. 23–5 in *The Dingley Tariff. H.R. 379. Fifty-fifth Congress. An Act to provide revenue for the government and to encourage the industries of the United States. Comparison of the Dingley Tariff (July 1897) and Wilson Tariff (August 1894).* Available online at http://catalog.hathitrust.org/Record/100200513 [accessed on 20 February, 2015]. Examples of tariff rates include a 60 per cent *ad valorem* tax on ready-made woollen articles.

Figure 15.4. Estimated revenues from duties on imported items, by schedule (1897 US dollars)

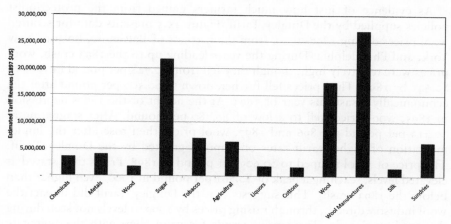

Source: 'Mr Dingley's Estimates', *The New York Times*, 16 March 1897.

Figure 15.5. Wool prices (US dollars per pound) in eastern US markets, 1890–1900

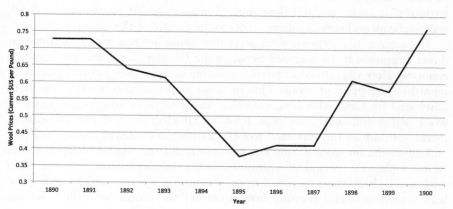

Source: NBER Macrohistory, 'U.S. Wholesale Prices of Wool, Eastern markets, Boston, Bureau of Labor Statistics 01/1890–12/1917', *NBER Macrohistory: IV. Prices. m04087a* (2008).

Note: All price data is in current dollars, from 1 January in each year. The Eastern markets the data comes from are Baltimore, Boston, New York and Philadelphia. The 'wool' specification includes data for wool, Ohio, fine fleece (X and XX grades), scoured.

about by the Dingley Tariff, in contrast to the uncertainty that paralysed businesses during the mid-1890s depression.

As evidence of just how much farmers gained from the protectionist policies supplied by the Dingley Tariff, Figure 15.5 presents data for scoured wool prices during 1890–1900, from the markets of Baltimore, Boston, New York, and Philadelphia. During the years leading up to the 1893 crash, wool prices were relatively high, though they fell from $0.728 per pound in 1890 to $0.641 by 1893. Then prices fell further, down to $0.500 per pound after the economically disastrous year of 1893. At the height of the 1890s depression in 1895, wool prices fell to a low of $0.380 per pound. After stagnating at $0.413 per pound in 1896 and 1897, wool prices then rose after the implementation of higher tariff rates on imports granted by the Dingley Tariff. The price of wool jumped to $0.609 per pound in 1898. Prices then stayed at elevated levels, reaching a peak of $0.761 per pound in 1900 (even higher than before the 1893 crash). This suggests that the Dingley Tariff did impact the wool industry directly, through raising prices by 1900 to levels not seen during the previous decade. These price trends for wool align with the aggregate economic trends analysed above.

Price increases directly benefited farmers, but manufacturers also pushed for the Dingley Tariff to be enacted. They argued that wool growers and manufacturers should work together to promote a stable tariff policy that would allow each group to benefit from relatively certain prices. Manufacturers argued that wool growers and manufacturers should 'act in harmony' in order to fulfil their mutual mission of 'of furnishing ... good, warm, cheap, and serviceable raiment, to the people of this country'.[52]

The aggregate economic data presented above are too broad to allow for direct causation to be ascribed between the Dingley Tariff and the growing economy after 1897. In contrast, it is possible to draw such a connection with regard to the price of wool. This increase in prices also fits the argument developed by Line, who suggested that sheep farmers anticipated a rise in wool prices following the 1896 presidential election and the subsequent increase in duties on imported wool.[53] Wright, in contrast, argued that the lack of tariffs on wool during the mid-1890s did not impact sheep farmers: 'states ended the period of combined industrial depression and free wool with more sheep than they had at the beginning – a fact which cannot but lead one to raise the question how necessary the protective tariff is for the

---

52   J.B. McPherson, 'Some Facts about Shoddy: Remarks Made at the Annual Convention of the National Wool Growers' Association, at Portland, Oregon, January 12, 1904', *Bulletin of the National Association of Wool Manufacturers*, 34 (Boston, 1904), p. 31.
53   R.C. Line, 'The Effect of Free Wool in the Northwest, 1893–96', *Quarterly Journal of Economics*, 26 (1912), pp. 528–30.

wool-growers of this section'.[54] Line turns Wright's argument around by suggesting that the 'free wool period was not only short, but expected to be short'.[55] Line supported his argument by citing the prices of sheep during the mid-1890s. For example, a ewe could sell for $3.50 in 1892, but was priced at only $2.00 in 1894, as the economy sank into depression.[56] Thus if farmers did indeed expect the Republicans to win the 1896 election and to thereafter impose higher tariff duties on wool in 1897 when McKinley was in power, then a rational sheep farmer would hold on to his flock until prices rose again under protectionist policies, rather than selling at a loss at 1894 prices. Thus expectations about a price recovery were an important aspect of the ways in which the Dingley Tariff impacted the wool industry during the last years of the nineteenth century.

The Dingley Tariff also affected the business decisions of wool manufacturers. The main primary source for information on the views of these mill owners is the *Bulletin of the National Association of Wool Manufacturers*. This *Bulletin* was published by the National Association of Wool Manufacturers, which represented the interests of prominent businessmen involved with producing woollen goods, mainly in the north-eastern USA. Wool manufacturers were mostly in favour of the protectionist policies of the Dingley Tariff bill, since it placed high duties on imported finished woollen products. The main focus of the manufacturers' advocating for the Dingley Tariff was their contention that 'Certainly no industry in this country has suffered more from unstable [tariff] conditions than that of wool and its manufacture.'[57] The manufacturers emphasised the impact of the Dingley Tariff as being a stabilising force in the economy. The pre-Dingley Tariff economy was harmed as businesses were held back due to uncertainty regarding future tariff conditions.

Weld analysed these trends through a case of the Arlington Mills in Lawrence, Massachusetts.[58] This mill produced woollen tops, which are the washed, combed, and sorted long wool fibres prepared for spinning into woollen products. The Arlington Mills were the first American mills to make these tops, and they began production in 1894. In his analysis of the success of the Arlington Mills top-making industry, Weld found that the mill owners were motivated by the success of their top production to expand output and construct a new mill entirely dedicated to combing wool for worsted spinners. These developments in the wool and worsted industries took place under the

---

54 Ibid., p. 528.
55 Ibid., p. 529.
56 Ibid.
57 McPherson, 'Some Facts about Shoddy', p. 30.
58 L.D.H. Weld, 'Specialization in the Woolen and Worsted Industry', *Quarterly Journal of Economics*, 27 (1912), pp. 67–94.

generally low tariff conditions set in place by the 1894 Wilson–Gorman Act. Weld argued that Arlington Mills was motivated to build the new mill for tops based on the presumption that it was 'very likely' that the 'next tariff revision would render the duty on tops prohibitive [for foreign competitors to export woollen goods to the USA] (as it had been previous to 1894)'.[59]

The case of the Arlington Mills supports the argument that the Dingley Tariff, and the subsequently higher prices and legislated protection for domestic industries, were anticipated by wool manufacturing businesses during the 1890s. This finding supports the similar case for wool producers, as described by Line.[60] This range of evidence suggests that both the growers and manufacturers of wool had the common interest of promoting price stability through tariff legislation, by discouraging foreign competition. Protectionist policies allowed both groups to be assured high and stable prices for their output. Thus the Dingley Tariff can be seen as having a stabilising influence on the American economy during the 1890s, by imposing elevated tariff rates in a way that met the expectations of a range of domestic business interests. The evidence shows that this was enough to induce an increase in economic activity, as expectations of high prices encouraged Western farmers to continue raising sheep and Eastern manufacturers to invest in expanded production facilities.

Conclusion

The panic of 1893 has been described as a 'watershed event in American history ..., [associated with] the creation of a new political balance, the continuing transformation of the country's economy, major changes in national policy, and far-reaching social and intellectual developments'.[61] Its causes and consequences have been thoroughly documented and analysed.[62] Yet the recovery from this depression is less studied. Past studies of the 1890s depression mention the Dingley Tariff and discuss the role that it may have played in promoting recovery from the 1890s depression. However, there is no consensus as to just how important the Dingley Tariff was in spurring the economy out of the depression.

It has been argued in this chapter that the Dingley Tariff played a significant role in helping the economy recover from the downturn, as it instilled confidence in the business community by generating revenue for the federal government

---

59   Ibid., p. 92.
60   Line, 'The Effect of Free Wool in the Northwest', pp. 528–30.
61   Whitten, 'The Depression of 1893'.
62   Hoffmann, *The Depression of the Nineties*; Steeples and Whitten, *Democracy in Desperation*.

and stabilising the economy. This in turn encouraged the business community to begin investing more readily, as they were able to feel more certain about future economic conditions in the country. Anticipated price recovery was an important aspect of this renewed confidence. With these changing conditions, the economy reversed its downward trend and began to grow again as farmers continued to raise sheep and manufacturers expanded production based on anticipated price increases. These trends are supported by the aggregate economic data estimates for the late nineteenth and early twentieth centuries, which show that the economy was unstable during the mid-1890s. This instability is a useful way to interpret the economic conditions of the mid-1890s, in that it emphasises how the economy was wracked with uncertainty during the depression. This analysis of the data suggests a role for the Dingley Tariff as being a stabilising factor that helped bring the economy out of the depression, as it erased significant elements of uncertainty by providing the government with increased revenue and by assuring American businesses that they would be afforded generous protection under new the tariff legislation:

> The passage of the Dingley Tariff in July, 1897, was reported in one journal to have 'been welcomed by people generally throughout the country' who were 'anxious for the removal of all influences making for the maintenance of … economic disturbance and against the return of that tranquility and confidence which are so necessary for the development of business'.[63]

This chapter has argued in greater depth and scope that this indeed was the case, and that these stabilising influences of the Dingley Tariff were the most important ways in which it promoted recovery from the post-1893 depression.

This chapter has therefore expanded upon themes suggested in other research. Steeples and Whitten, for example, clearly identify the Dingley Tariff as serving an important role in spurring economic growth in the late 1890s:

> The increased duties of the Dingley Tariff assured home markets to domestic entrepreneurs just as consumers became able to make purchases they had deferred during hard times. Merchandise imports remained low after recovery got under way, and expanding business made investment in protected industries extremely attractive.[64]

This aligns with the common textbook analysis of the effects of tariffs, where tariffs are helpful for protected industries in the short term, though the long-term impacts of protection are more difficult to sort out.[65] Given

---

63 Hoffmann, *The Depression of the Nineties*, p. 86.
64 Steeples and Whitten, *Democracy in Desperation*, p. 75.
65 R.J. Carbaugh, *International Economics*, 13th edn (Boston, MA, 2010), p. 124.

the political economy of the 1890s, when there was no central bank in the USA and the federal government had limited options for shaping economic activity, the Dingley Tariff offers an example of how protectionist policies can stabilise expectations and promote economic growth in these circumstances.

Still, the evidence in this chapter only tells part of the story of the recovery from the 1890s depression. Other factors, including the Klondike Gold Rush, also played a part in this recovery. And the wool industry, while an important part of the late-nineteenth-century US economy, was only one industry among many, and industries that relied more heavily on imported inputs, for example, could have been hurt by increased tariff rates. Further research can tie all these factors together in order to have a wider-ranging analysis of the US economy at the turn of the century.

Even given the particular focus of this chapter, broader conclusions can be drawn from this study. The main such finding is that government intervention can stabilise economies during crises. This has relevance today, with the continuing debate surrounding the role the government should play in the economy. In the late 1890s, government action in the form of newly imposed protectionist policies helped the business community feel confident enough about the state of the economy to begin expanding production. The stabilising role of strong government action was a key factor in promoting recovery from the 1890s depression. In general, however, protectionist policies themselves do not always guarantee recovery from economic crises. Henn and McDonald find, for example, that protectionist policies that have been implemented in reaction to the 2007–08 crisis have resulted in a decrease in global trade.[66] While there is a role for government action during crises, great care should be taken that the policies will promote recovery. Stabilising expectations about future economic conditions, to the degree possible, is a goal governments can pursue when designing policies to promote recovery from economic crises.

---

66   C. Henn and B. McDonald, 'Crisis Protectionism: The Observed Trade Impact', *IMF Economic Review*, 62 (2014), pp. 77–118.

Index

PEOPLE, MARKETS, GOODS:
ECONOMIES AND SOCIETIES IN HISTORY

ISSN: 2051-7467

Printed and bound by CPI Group (UK) Ltd, Croydon, CR0 4YY

13/04/2025

14656520-0005